CW00602936

# Administrative Receivership:
## *Law and Practice*

# Administrative Receivership:
## *Law and Practice*

*First Edition*

Louis G Doyle, LLB, LLM, *Solicitor*

**LAW & TAX**

© Pearson Professional Limited 1995
ISBN 0752 001523

*Published by*
FT Law & Tax
21–27 Lamb's Conduit Street
London WC1N 3NJ

A Division of Pearson Professional Limited

*Associated offices*
Australia, Belgium, Canada, Hong Kong, India, Japan, Luxembourg,
Singapore, Spain, USA

**First edition 1995**

All rights reserved. No part of this publication may be reproduced,
stored in a retrieval system, or transmitted, in any form or by any means,
electronic, mechanical, photocopying, recording or otherwise, without either
the prior written permission of the publishers or a licence permitting restricted copying
issued by the Copyright Licensing Agency Ltd, 90 Tottenham Court Road,
London W1P 9HE.

No responsibility for loss occasioned to any person acting or refraining from
action as a result of material in this publication can be accepted by the
authors or the publishers.

A CIP catalogue record for this book is available from the British Library.

Printed in Great Britain by Mackays of Chatham
Typeset by Intype (Input Typesetting Ltd)

*To Eleanor and Malachey
with love*

# Contents

# Preface

The aim of this book is to provide the practitioner with a basic guide to the law of administrative receivership together with an indication of the practice.

In a book of this length it is impossible to examine exhaustively the minutiae of the area and all of its aspects. The text cannot therefore hope to do more than provide a sense of orientation. However, where the position appears unclear I have attempted to provide solutions based on common sense and legitimate commercial expectation.

I wish to express my gratitude to a number of individuals by name. Those who remain anonymous must forgive me; my list of credits simply grew too long.

My thanks are due to my friend and colleague Jeremy Rowland for characteristic encouragement and the benefit of discussion on some of the more esoteric points raised in the text. Thanks are also due to Mike Saville of Grant Thornton and Willie Duncan of Pannell Kerr Forster who provided feedback on the text in one form or another.

I am indebted to Keith Hearn and Stephen Kirkbright at Ford and Warren solicitors, Leeds, for ongoing support.

Michelle Angus typed the bulk of the text and my own secretary Michelle Arnold pitched in as the deadline drew near. Each succeeded in deciphering my spider-like hieroglyphics and I am grateful to both for their robust support and sense of humour throughout.

Thanks are also due to my publishers FT Law and Tax, in particular Nick Bliss and Dean Gurden, for their co-operation and patience with an occasionally difficult author.

I took the perhaps lunatic step of writing the book whilst redrafting a PhD thesis on public issues of securities and in the course of working full time within a busy and developing practice. There have been a number of understanding casualties of my time constraints for whose forbearance I am deeply grateful.

Finally, I must make special mention of my son and daughter, Malachey and Eleanor. Each showed a healthy disinterest in the text and little enthusiasm for discussions on the subject. Nevertheless, their distracting playfulness threw sunlight on some of their Daddy's darker moments and made the task seem worthwhile.

The work, and of course the errors, are my own.

Louis G Doyle
Westgate Point
Leeds

Midsummer Day 1995

# Table of Cases

# Table of Statutes

# Other Legislation

# Table of Statutory Instruments

# Chapter One

# The Legal Nature of Administrative Receivership

## 1.1 Introduction

Receivership is a formal method of debt enforcement which can be traced back to Elizabethan times. Administrative receivership is a particular form of receivership and is an invention of the Insolvency Act 1986 (IA 1986—to which all subsequent references relate unless otherwise stated), although the concept behind it in law is far from being a new one.

Whilst the definition of an administrative receiver is provided for in s29(2), much of the law concerning the position has been and continues to be developed by the courts. Administrative receivership represents a true legal *maelström*. The actual appointment of an administrative receiver is not itself provided for by the legislation but by the specific terms of each debenture. Evaluating the validity of the appointment of the administrative receiver involves an amalgam of company law, property law and security law. The administrative receiver finds the ultimate source of his powers in IA 1986, yet these are subject to modification by the debenture pursuant to which the appointment was made. Whilst the qualification of the office-holder is stipulated by statute and regulation, as are various reporting and accounting duties, the office-holder finds himself subject to fiduciary duties, the extent and implications of which the courts continue to refine and develop. As administrative receiver, the office-holder may be subject to interplay with other office-holders, be they liquidators or supervisors of company voluntary arrangements, each of which has posed its own peculiar problems in the context of administrative receivership in recent years. Similarly, the effect of the appointment of the administrative receiver on the powers of the directors is not yet wholly clear and begs for judicial clarification as does the question of who may appoint an administrative receiver where competing claims exist.

In its truest sense, receivership—of which administrative receivership is merely a species—is not, in fact, an insolvency proceeding *per se*. Rather, it is a private-law remedy whereby an invariably secured creditor enforces its security against the charged assets of a company. The private-law nature of

1

receivership nevertheless remains subject to public policy considerations which govern, for example, the right of parties to contract out of provisions otherwise imposed by the legislation.

In practice, administrative receivership is closely connected with insolvency proceedings, particularly winding-up. This is because a very large proportion of administrative receiverships culminate in the company in administrative receivership being put into liquidation. The legislation also frequently refers to receivership as a process inalienable from insolvency. For example, s247 provides that 'insolvency' in relation to a company includes the appointment of an administrative receiver. Similarly, for the purposes of the Company Directors Disqualification Act 1986 s6, a company is deemed to become insolvent *inter alia* if an administrative receiver is appointed in relation to it, although in reality this need in fact never be the case. 'Insolvency proceedings' are also deemed by the Insolvency Rules 1986 (hereinafter referred to as IR) to mean any proceedings under the 1986 Act or the Rules themselves (IR r13.7).

Notwithstanding the technical status of administrative receivership as a method of debt enforcement, the procedure has become an established feature of the insolvency landscape. The reasons for this stem largely from the demanding standards imposed by the legislation which require professional oversight and management on the part of office-holders, predominantly in practice from and by those accountants who are qualified to act as licensed insolvency practitioners for the purpose of ss388 and 389 of IA 1986. In addition, the legislation imposes on the administrative receiver specific obligations to report to creditors of the company and to Companies House (ss47, 48 and 49) and to account to preferential creditors in priority to and out of assets subject to a floating charge (s40). The office-holder is deemed personally liable for certain contracts adopted by him, including contracts of employment (s44). He also incurs duties owed to the company which require him indirectly to consider the position and interests of other creditors and employees. Administrative receivership should not therefore be seen in isolation merely as a debt recovery mechanism.

## 1.2 The Historical Development of Receivership

Historically, a mortgagee, faced with a defaulting mortgagor, was able to apply to the court for an order appointing a receiver, as agent of the mortgagee, whose function was the collection of rents and profits accruing from the mortgaged property. This income was then applied in payment of mortgage interest. The mechanism was cumbersome, and led to the creation of contractual loan arrangements whereby a mortgagee was empowered to act as agent of the mortgagor in appointing a receiver as agent of the *mortgagor* without recourse to the court. This type of arrangement became so common-place that the power to appoint a receiver without court involvement was eventually implied by statute into mortgages created by deed subject to the contrary intention of the parties ( see now Law of Property Act 1925 s101). The practical advantage to the mortgagee of appointing a receiver as agent of the mortgagor without court involvement was that the mortgagee was not liable to account to the mortgagor as strictly as would have been the case if the mortgagee himself had taken possession or the receiver had been appointed as agent of the mortgagee himself. The appointment by the mort-gagee as agent of the mortgagor, together with the inherent advantages of such a course of action and the risks of taking possession, are clearly discus-sed in the dissenting judgment of Rigby LJ in *Gaskill v Gosling* [1896] 1 QB 669 at 691–3. This was subsequently approved by the House of Lords on appeal *sub nom Gosling v Gaskill* [1897] AC 575. The following extract from this classic judgment is worth recounting at length;

A mortgagor left in possession of the mortgaged property, whether real or personal, had a right to receive the income and apply it to his own use, without becoming liable to account to the mortgagee. If there was no receiver, the mortgagee could only make the income available for keeping down the interest on his security by entering into possession. This entry into possession by a mortgagee was always considered a strong assertion of his legal rights, since he did not come under any obligation to account to the mortgagor except in a suit for redemption. He was accordingly treated with exceptional severity in a suit for redemption and made to account, not only for what he actually re-ceived, but for what he might without wilful default have received. This was bad enough when there was only one mortgagee; but the position became much worse when the mortgagee was a second mortgagee, since the second mortgagee could at any moment be turned out by the first, and for the sake of such a precarious possession it could seldom be worthwhile for a second mortgagee to incur the liabilities of a mort-gagee in possession. Still greater were the risks and less desirable the possession when the mortgaged property consisted of or included, as it might do, property embarked in trade and subject to the vicissitudes of commercial business. It follows of course from the almost penal liabili-ties imposed upon a mortgagee in possession that courts of Equity were very slowly to decide that possession had been taken, and would not do so unless satisfied that the mortgagee in possession took the possession in his capacity of mortgagee without any reasonable ground for believ-ing himself to hold in any other capacity...The courts also favoured any means which would enable the mortgagee to obtain the advantages of possession without its drawbacks. Mortgagees began to insist upon the appointment by the mortgagor of a receiver to receive the income, keep down the interest on encumbrances, and hold the surplus, if any, for the mortgagor, and to stipulate often that the receiver should have extensive powers of management. Presently mortgagees stipulated that they themselves should in place of the mortgagor appoint the receiver to act as the mortgagor's agent. This made no difference in the receiver's position, and imposed no liability on the mortgagee appointing. Though it was the mortgagee who in fact appointed the receiver, yet in making the appointment the mortgagee acted, and it was the object of the parties that he should act, as agent for the mortgagor ... Of course the mortgagor cannot of his own will revoke the appointment of a receiver, or that appointment would be useless. For valuable consideration he has committed the management of his property to an attorney whose appointment he cannot interfere with. The appointment so made will stand good against himself and all persons claiming through him, except encumbrancers having priority to the mortgagee who appoints the receiver.

The power to appoint a receiver of income under a mortgage charge deed or debenture was previously contained in the Trustee Act 1860 (Lord Cranworth's Act) ss11–30. These provisions were repealed and developed in the Conveyancing Act 1881, ss19, 20 and 24, and are now embodied in the Law of Property Act 1925, ss101(1)(iii) and 102. This power is now subject to the contrary intention of the parties under s101(4) of the 1925 Act. This means that a Law of Property Act 1925 s101(1)(iii) appointment is one of a receiver (an 'LPA receiver') of income of mortgaged property, as opposed to an appointment over the mortgaged property itself in respect of which the receiver has no power of sale unless the statutory power is varied or extended by the mortgage deed pursuant to Law of Property Act 1925, s101(3). In the case of registered land, the power of sale cannot be exercised until the mortgagee has been registered as proprietor of the charge (*Lever Finance Ltd v Needleman's Trustees* [1956] Ch 357).

   The statutory grounds for appointment are invariably expanded extensively in the charge documentation notwithstanding the broad statutory power in s109(3) of the 1925 Act which permits the LPA receiver to demand and recover all of the income in respect of which he is appointed receiver. The LPA receiver may pursue this by an action (distress or otherwise) in the name of either the mortgagor or the mortgagee, to the full extent of the estate or interests which the mortgagor himself could dispose of. He may give effectual receipts and execute any powers which are delegated to him by the mortgagee. The decision in *Bayly v Went* (1884) 51 LT 764, for example, prevents distraint by the mortgagor following the appointment of the receiver even in the face of an allegation of negligence against the receiver by the mortgagor.

4

If the mortgage of or charge over the company's property is vested in the trustees of a trust deed securing an issue of debentures or debenture stock, then this statutory power of appointment falls to the trustees and not to the holder of the debenture or the debenture stock. This area of the appointing debenture-holder's security is one which has become particularly topical in view of the recent unreported decision of Vinelott J in *Meadrealm Ltd and Commercial Bank plc v Transcontinental Golf Construction Ltd* (29 November 1991, ChD). For a recent illustration of the practical deficiencies which may arise on the appointment of an LPA receiver see *Knight v Lawrence* [1991] BCC 411.

In the second half of the nineteenth century, with the advent and development of the floating charge as a form of security over the whole or substantially the whole of a company's undertaking and the accompanying expansion in commercial credit, it became established practice for the appointor of a receiver of income also to appoint a manager of the company's business. Invariably, and for convenience, these two office-holders were one and the same person. As Jessel MR put it in *Re Manchester and Milford Ryl Co* (1880) 14 ChD 645 at 653:

> A receiver is a term which was well known in the Court of Chancery, as meaning a person who receives rents or other income, paying ascertained outgoings, but who does not, if I may say so, manage the property in the sense of buying or selling or anything of the kind. We were most familiar with the distinction in the case of a partnership. If a receiver was appointed of partnership assets, the trade stopped immediately. He collected all the debts, sold the stock-in-trade and other assets, and then under the order of the Court the debts of the concern were liquidated and the balance divided. If it was desired to continue the trade at all, it was necessary to appoint a manager, or a receiver and manager as it was generally called. He could buy and sell and carry on trade.

In practice, it is difficult to draw a clear line between the tasks undertaken by an administrative receiver in his capacity as either receiver or a manager—since, by definition, he necessarily undertakes both functions—although the distinction is not problematic.

## 1.3 The Jurisdiction of the Court

In theory, the holder of a legal or equitable fixed charge or a floating charge (which, by its nature, must be either an equitable charge until crystallisation, whereupon it becomes a fixed equitable charge) may apply to the court for the appointment of a receiver or receiver and manager. This may be done either on an application in a creditor's action or on a specific originating summons issued for that purpose. Since the Judicature Acts 1873-75, the power to appoint a receiver has been available in all divisions of the High Court where it appears to be just and convenient to the court to do so. This is now provided for in the Supreme Court Act 1981, s37(1), replacing the Supreme Court of Judicature (Consolidation) Act 1925. Whilst it is possible for a receiver to be appointed in the Queen's Bench Division, usually by way of equitable execution, the application is usually made in the Chancery Division, where adequate provision is available for the making of necessary inquiries and the taking of relevant accounts (see RSC Ord 30 r1, Ord 88 r1, Ord 102). Equitable execution in this sense refers to the method by which a judgment creditor obtains payment of his debts where legal execution cannot recover the interest of the debtor, although the court will not appoint a receiver by way of equitable execution simply because it represents a more convenient method of obtaining execution (*Harris v Beauchamp Bros* [1984] 1 QB 801).

A receiver may be appointed by the Family Division of the High Court although such appointments will be exceptional (see the unprecedented decision in *S v S* (1973) *The Times*, 23 June). A receiver may also be appointed by the county court for the preservation of property within the scope of the causes of action inherent in the county court's jurisdiction either before or after the trial, although such appointments will in practice be very rare (see County Courts Act 1984 s38, CCR Ord 32). A receiver may also be appointed in the county court by way of equitable execution in the same circumstances as in the High Court for the purpose of enforcing any county court judgement. This extends to land, interests in land and personalty (County Courts Act 1984 s107).

A receiver may also be appointed by the House of Lords where a lower court has failed to do so, although such appointments will continue to be rare (see, for example, *Houlditch v Marquess of Donegal* [1834] 2 Cl & Fin 470). The same power is available to the Civil Division of the Court of Appeal although no such appointment appears ever to have been made (see *Hyde v Warden* (1876) 1 Ex D 309).

The appointment of a receiver by the court is considered only in passing in the remainder of this book. For a concise and authoritative exposition of the law and procedure relating to the remedies for enforcing security against a company's property with the assistance of the court—including orders for payment of the amount secured, orders for sale, orders for foreclosure and orders for the delivery of possessions of property—reference should be made to Pennington, *Corporate Insolvency Law*, 1st edn (1990) 413–27.

In practice, it is exceptionally rare for a receiver of what is referred to hereafter as a non-administrative receiver to be appointed by the court although the particular circumstances of the case may dictate this (see *Bank of Credit and Commerce International SA v BRS Kumar Bros Ltd* [1994] BCLC 211).

Receivers are invariably appointed   under the terms of a debenture (as opposed to pursuant to a court order) for a number of practical reasons. These are primarily the time and expense of obtaining an order, the fact that a court appointed receiver is under the direction of the court and is obliged to act impartially between the parties and the broad scope and powers which derive from well-drafted modern standard-form debentures.

Two possible circumstances in which an application to court for the appointment of a receiver may be anticipated are (a) where either the debenture documentation is found to be clearly defective for the purpose of making the appointment, or (b) where an unsecured creditor avails himself of the court's inherent jurisdiction to appoint a receiver. A recent example of the latter arose in *J H Rayner (Mincing Lane) Ltd v Department of Trade and Industry* [1990] 2 AC 418, which involved an application by an unsecured creditor to appoint a receiver to the International Tin Council. The House of Lords held that it was impossible to appoint a receiver over the assets of an international organisation, because its members were sovereign states, because it did not constitute a company for the purposes of the Companies Acts and because the English courts also had no jurisdiction over it as regards winding-up. See also *Re International Tin Council* [1989] Ch 309.

One practical implication of the fact that an administrative receiver will not be appointed by the court concerns the standards by which the office-holder will be judged in the discharge of his duties. Since the administrative receiver is appointed out of court, it follows that he will not be an officer of the court as would be the case with a court-appointed receiver (see *Ward v Shew* (1833) 9 Bing 608 and *Toronto-Dominion Bank v Fortin (No2)* (1978) 88 DLR (3d) 232). As such, the administrative receiver will not be bound by the duty to act honourably in accordance with the bankruptcy-law rule in *ex parte James* (1874) LR 9 Ch App 609. (The rule has also been held to extend to an office-holder who acts as an officer of the court in insolvency proceedings such as a liquidator or administrator (*Re Wyvern Developments Ltd* [1974] 1 WLR 1097)).

The facts of *ex parte James* involved an execution creditor who had paid over to the trustee-in-bankruptcy the proceeds of levying execution. This was done on the basis of a view of the existing law which was subsequently shown to be incorrect. As such, the trustee-in-bankruptcy was obliged to repay to the execution creditor the proceeds which had been handed over, despite the fact that he had been successful in recovering them from him in the first place (see also *Re Clark (a bankrupt)* [1975] 1 WLR 559, per Walton J). The scope of the rule is not easy to define although it has been stated as connoting an obligation not to employ 'dirty tricks' nor to behave in a shabby manner or contrary to the rules of natural justice (*Re John Bateson & Co Ltd* [1985] BCLC 259; *Re T H Knitwear (Wholesale) Ltd* [1986] STC 572). Certainly it is clear that the rule is not restricted to mistakes of law (*Re Bell*

(1908) 99 LT 939). However, the fact that the administrative receiver's duties will be governed by commercial standards of skill and care and related considerations probably covers such malpractices, particularly when one considers the high professional standards observed by the licenced insolvency practitioners taking appointments as office-holders under IA 1986. On the other hand, the administrative receiver will not be bound by the principles of the rule in *Ex parte James* in terms of acting so as to do the fullest equity to all parties; rather, he must act so as to maximise recovery on behalf of his appointor, even if this means appropriating assets in the face of litigation or disputes with other parties as to his right to do so, provided that, in so doing, he acts honestly and fairly throughout. This is stated on the basis that the administrative receiver's duties are owed primarily to his appointor as regards protecting and realising the assets subject to his appointment (*Gomba Holdings UK Ltd v Homan* [1986] 1 WLR 1301).

## 1.4 Jurisdiction of the Insolvency Act 1986

The statutory framework for receiverships is set out in IA 1986 ss28–49, which apply only to receivers and managers appointed under English law. Sections 42–9 relate specifically to administrative receivers and should be read in conjunction with ss28–41 which apply to receivers and managers generally, including administrative receivers. The new statutory framework is far from being a codified area and, together with the provisions in Part 3 of the IR 1986, forms a framework for the developing case-law.

Receivers in Scotland are subject to IA 1986 ss50–71, which are not examined in this book. Notably, however, s72 permits an English or Scottish receiver to act throughout Great Britain provided local law permits. The concept of the floating charge was only introduced in Scotland by the Companies (Floating Charges) (Scotland) Act 1961, and a mechanism resembling administrative receivership had no role in Scottish law until the advent of the Companies (Floating Charges and Receivers) (Scotland) Act 1972. Although Scots law operates on broadly the same lines as English law, there remain disparities between both which are beyond the scope of this book. A fixed security over land, for example, is only capable of creation in Scotland by a standard form of security as introduced by the Conveyancing and Feudal Reform (Scotland) Act 1970; this invalidates fixed charges over land created in any other form after that date. Further reference should therefore be made to ss462–6, which relate specifically to the floating charge in Scotland and the Receivers (Scotland) Regulations 1986 (SI 1986 No 1917). Analogous provisions relating to receivers and administrative receivers in Northern Ireland are contained in the Insolvency (Northern Ireland) Order 1989 (SI 1989 No 2405). Again, specific reference is not made to those provisions in this book.

8

The provisions of IA 1986 relating to administrative receivers now appear to extend to the appointment of an administrative receiver over English assets of a company notwithstanding the fact that the company is not registered as a limited company in the United Kingdom: see *Re International Bulk Commodities Ltd* [1992] BCC 463. That decision rested on the definition of a company contained in Companies Act 1985 s731(1) which applies 'unless the contrary intention appears', according to Companies Act 1985 s735(4). Mummery J held that 'the subject matter and manifest purpose of the relevant provisions where construed in the context of both the immediately relevant provisions and of the Act as a whole' constituted a sufficient contrary intention in that case. For the purposes of s29(2) of IA 1986, the term 'a company' would therefore appear to include a company which is not registered in England and Wales under the Companies Act 1985 where a debenture (which included a floating charge in the *International Bulk Commodities* case) creates requisite security over assets of the company which are actually located in England and Wales. (See Companies Act 1985 s735(1) as referred to in s388(4) for the meaning of a company registered in England and Wales.)

This decision clearly envisages an administrative receiver being appointed over a foreign company's assets. It has to be said that this is a curious conclusion, since the nature of administrative receivership is such that it relates to the company to which the office-holder is appointed, as opposed to the assets subject to the administrative receivership itself. Certainly in English law the Companies Act 1985 is restricted to companies registered in England and Wales, and the apparent imposition of the legislative regime providing for administrative receivership under English law on a company registered in an overseas jurisdiction poses potential problems in that the overseas company may display characteristics which render it incapable of compliance with the English domestic legislation. The position will be equally precarious where the overseas company has apparently created security over assets in England and Wales where no such power exists. The decision in the *International Bulk Commodities* case is also in conflict with the position under IA 1986 under which only companies registered under the Companies Act 1985 or earlier Acts and unregistered companies may be wound up (ss73, 221, 225). The fact that such a company does not have assets within the domestic jurisdiction does not affect the jurisdiction of the court to wind up the company, provided a sufficient connection with the jurisdiction exists and there is a reasonable possibility that the creditors will benefit from the winding-up (*International Westminster Bank plc v Okeanos Maritime Corp* [1987] 3 All ER 137).

The provisions of IA 1986 will not extend to a society registered under the Industrial and Provident Societies Act 1965. This narrow point arose in *Re Devon and Somerset Farmers Ltd* [1993] BCC 410, a test case in which Nigel Hague QC, sitting as a High Court judge, held that receivers appointed to enforce a floating charge granted by an industrial and provident society were not obliged to make good preferential claims as the society was not a 'company', being one registered in accordance with the Companies Act, for the purposes of s40 of the 1986 Act. Notably, the judge was also critical of the liberal interpretation of the term 'company' adopted in the *International Bulk Commodities* case. The reasoning in *Devon and Somerset Farmers* would suggest that a foreign company (ie one not registered in accordance with the Companies Acts) is not capable of being 'a company' for the purposes of s29(2) of IA 1986. On the basis of the observations set out above, it is suggested that this approach has much to commend it. However, in *Re Devon and Somerset Farmers* the judge chose to avoid the *International Bulk Commodities*' decision by distinguishing it and confining it to cases concerning powers of receivers over foreign companies. This still begs the question as to why it is that s29 is drafted in such imprecise terms if its scope is intended expressly to extend to foreign corporations.

Further reference on this area should be made to Moss (1993) 6 Insolvency Intelligence 19 which deals with administration orders and foreign companies, and Moss (1994) 7 Insolvency Intelligence 33 for an incisive discussion of the provisions.

## 1.5   The Administrative Receiver Defined

Chapter 8 of the Report of the Insolvency Law Review Committee, *Insolvency Law and Practice*, Cmnd 8558 (1982) (the Cork Committee Report) recommended that the law relating to receiverships should be amended and placed on a broadly statutory basis with the aim of improving the general effectiveness of receiverships and competence of receivers. This approach was in line with the Report's commendable aim of improving the rescue mechanism available for companies in financial difficulties. The Cork Committee Report's recommendations were largely enacted in Chapter IV of the Insolvency Act 1985, which first introduced what has been referred to as the unfortunate term 'administrative receiver'. These provisions, together with some provisions of the Companies Act 1985, are now consolidated in the Insolvency Act 1986.

The scheme of the Act is merely to define, in not altogether clear terms, the receiver or manager constituting an administrative receiver. No provisions specify the circumstances or method in which appointment may be effected; that is a matter for the debenture itself. However, once a receiver or manager fulfils the statutory definition in s29(2) he is vested with a considerable arsenal of statutory powers as set out in Sched 1, which are implied into the debenture pursuant to which he is appointed except to the extent that they are varied by the debenture itself. In addition, he may employ the power to apply to the court for directions, seek a disposal of prior-ranking charged property or avail himself of the extensive investigatory powers in ss234–6. Conversely, a number of statutory duties are imposed as is the requirement that the office-holder must be a person entitled to act for the purposes of ss389 and 390 on pain of criminal sanction.

Section 29(2) defines an administrative receiver as:

> (a) a receiver or manager of the whole (or substantially the whole) of a company's property appointed by or on behalf of the holders of any debentures of the company secured by a charge which, as created, was a floating charge, or by such a charge and one or more securities; or
>
> (b) a person who would be such a receiver or manager but for the appointment of some other person as the receiver of part of the company's property.

It is worth noting that the concept of administrative receivership is not a new one. The Companies Act 1948, s372, for example, recognised the position of a person appointed to be receiver and manager of the whole, or substantially the whole, of the property of a company registered in England without using the term 'administrative receiver'.

The terminology 'receiver or manager' employed in s29(2)(a) may appear curious. There is a simple reason for the word 'or' (as opposed to 'and') being employed. Since the offices of receiver or manager are diverse, a person holding both offices simultaneously will act either as receiver *or* manager depending on the various acts he carries out in his capacity as administrative receiver, although in practice the distinction between the two is frequently blurred.

Section 29(2)(b) is an interesting provision. Effectively, it means that an administrative receiver for the purposes of s29(2)(a) will not be prevented from acting as such by the prior appointment of a receiver of part of the company's property. This includes a receiver or manager, or receiver only, of part only of the company's property or of income arising from the property or from part of it by virtue of s29(1)(a). It follows that the appointment of a non-administrative receiver (as defined in s29(1)(a)) over a class of the company's assets, or specific assets of it, will not preclude the appointment of an administrative receiver; and he may then opt to employ s43 in seeking an order of the court to dispose of prior-charged property (ie property subject to either a prior-ranking fixed or, less commonly, floating charge). This is defined in s43(7) as property of which the administrative receiver is or would be receiver or manager but for the appointment of some other person as receiver of (that) part of the company's property.

It may appear that s43 is not a mechanism which needs to be employed in relation to charges ranking as subsidiary to the relevant charges pursuant to which the administrative receiver is appointed, since the office-holder and his advisers may consider that the administrative receiver can simply dispose of the charged assets subject to the subsidiary charge or charges, the interests-holders seemingly being overreached and thereby attaching to the proceeds of sale (if any). Whilst a number of commentators have suggested this to be the position as regards s43, it is respectfully submitted that that view is incorrect. The better view is that s43 relates also to charges which are subsidiary to those pursuant to which the administrative receiver is appointed. The reasoning behind this approach is that an administrative receiver himself is incapable of over-reaching subsidiary interest on a sale of property, for which see Chapter 8 at para 8.5.

One view of s29(2)(b) is that it does not apply if a receiver has already been appointed by another creditor in respect of the whole or substantially the whole of the company's property; that is, an administrative receiver appointed by another creditor who is secured by a floating charge over the company's property, whether ranking in priority or not. This is not a satisfactory conclusion since it discounts the possibility of an application to the court under s45 for the removal of an appointed administrative receiver by a prior-ranking debenture-holder on the basis that the nominee of the prior-ranking creditor would therefore, by definition, be incapable of definition as an administrative receiver. This does nothing to undermine the view, set out below at 1.11, that there cannot be two or more concurrent appointments of administrative receivers by the holders of different floating charges. In other words, whilst there may not be more than one concurrent appointment of an administrative receiver (or joint administrative receivers), there is nothing to prevent more than one individual from being eligible for appointment by suitably secured debenture-holders at any one time. In other words, it is submitted that all individuals potentially eligible for appointment as administrative receiver for the purpose of s29(2)(a) will qualify as such under s29(2)(b) where another administrative receiver has been appointed prior to this (ie 'but for the appointment of some other person who would be such a receiver or manager'). It is conceded that the use of the phrase 'receiver of part of the company's property' as opposed to 'receiver of the *whole* or part of the company's property' is unfortunate for the purposes of this analysis, although it does little to contradict it. In any case, on the basis of an appointment of a subsidiary chargee, and on the basis that contemporaneous appointments are conceptually impossible, it would be incumbent on the prior-ranking chargee to apply to the court for the removal of the subsidiary chargee's administrative receiver under s45(1).

Section 29(2)(b) requires the fulfilment of two conditions:

(a)   the appointment of a receiver (apparently by the court or otherwise) other than the administrative receiver himself over assets which, the question of priorities apart, are also potentially subject to one or more of the securities held by the appointor of the administrative receiver. The incumbent receiver might thus be appointed either by the court or pursuant to a fixed charge (or even a floating charge which extends only to a part of the company's property); and

(b) the property over which the incumbent receiver is appointed, must constitute property which would also be subject to the administrative receiver pursuant to the securities held by his appointor which must necessarily amount to the whole or substantially the whole of the company's property.

The wording of s29(2)(b) appears to suggest that it would be possible for a non-administrative receiver to be appointed and to remain in office, notwithstanding the appointment of an administrative receiver, where the property subject to the non-administrative receiver is of such low relative value as to render possible the administrative receiver's appointment one over substantially the whole (i.e the remaining portion of, as opposed to the whole) of the company's property.

## 1.6  The Security Requirement in s29

Section 29(2)(a) imposes an express requirement that in order for a debenture-holder to be entitled to appoint an administrative receiver, he must be secured 'by a charge which, as created, was a floating charge, or by such a charge and one or more other securities'. This requirement is not only fundamental to the right to appoint an administrative receiver, it also entitles an entitled debenture-holder to veto the appointment of an administrator by virtue of s9(3)(a) and the decision in *Re Croftbell Ltd* [1990] BCC 781.

The principal proviso to the security element of s29(2)(a) is that it must provide security over 'the whole (or substantially the whole) of a company's property'. It is not clear from the Act what might amount to 'substantially the whole' of the company's property (as defined in s436), and consequently it is not possible to say with any degree of precision to what extent the property of the company might be free of the debenture-holder's security so as to retain the right of the debenture-holder to appoint an administrative receiver. The most useful and accurate suggestion on this point is made by Lightman and Moss, *The Law of Receivers of Companies*, 2nd edn (Sweet & Maxwell 1994) para 1-05 at 3, in which the authors consider that the criteria of whether the subject of the receivership is substantially the whole of a company's property is primarily value to the company. As the authors put it, 'this would appear to be necessary if (for the purposes of the judgement to be made) like is to be compared with like'. It is respectfully submitted that the suggestion that the valuation formula is based on value *to the company* is misleading. This would suggest a formula based on valuations according to the company's own perception of its various asset values. This does not accord with practice, in which a secured creditor will usually wish to establish its own subjective valuation of the various assets constituting a company's property (usually on a written-down sale-valuation basis). Alternatively, a secured creditor will base its subjective valuation on the valuation attributed to an asset by an objective and expert valuer, such as a land agent. The better view, it is suggested, is that the valuation of the company's property for the purpose of s29(2)(a) is that which the debenture-holder attributes to the property subject to his security. Thus, in cases of doubt, it will be a matter for the debenture-holder to prove that the property subject to its security constitutes at least substantially the whole of the company's property at the time of appointment.

The requirement as to security subsisting over at least substantially the whole of the company's property would appear to be a single test, which need only be satisfied at the time of the administrative receiver's appointment. This conclusion avoids the loss of status of an administrative receiver subsequent to appointment where the debenture-holder (a) voluntarily releases property from the security held by it, or (b) where the administrative receiver disposes of secured property, thereby rendering his appointment as being over less than substantially the whole of the company's remaining property. This could otherwise occur if, for example, purchase monies or sale assets were never to be forthcoming or assets suffered a depreciation in value through, say, market collapse.

Where a debenture-holder releases property voluntarily from its security, it is clear that the release need only be unilateral on the part of the debenture-holder (*Re Scottish & Newcastle plc* [1993] BCC 634). In the case of sale of an asset an argument may also be made out that the debenture-holder's security subsists by virtue of its floating-charge security over the right of action in respect of the purchase monies or assets, pending their payment or the handing-over to which action might be attributed the value of those monies or assets.

The reference to a floating charge in s29(2)(a) is an interesting one, and accords with the definition of such a charge in s251. Section 29(2)(a) begs the question whether the floating charge must itself extend to the whole or substantially the whole of the company's property, although it is subject to any prior-ranking fixed charges which are (but need not necessarily be) comprised in the debenture pursuant to which the administrative receiver is appointed. It is clear from the decision in *Re Croftbell Ltd* [1990] BCC 781 that a so-called lightweight floating charge to which no assets are subject does not affect the operation of the charge for s29(2) purposes. This does little, however, to further the question of whether the floating charge itself must be of a 'global' nature in extending potentially to the whole of the company's undertaking and business (apart from the case in practice where a floating charge is frequently stated to attach to assets other than those specifically charged by way of fixed charge). Neither does *Croftbell* advance the debate as to whether the floating charge may secure only a single asset or class of assets which may well not exist at the time of the creation of the charge or, indeed, subsequently.

The better view, it is submitted, is that an administrative receiver must be appointed by a debenture-holder whose security comprises *inter alia*, but as a minimum requirement, a floating charge of the general or 'global' type extending to the entire undertaking and business of a company. This applies even where the security is framed as being subject to any other fixed (or floating) charge held over the property of the company by the debenture-holder, those 'supplemental' securities constituting 'one or more other securities' for the purposes of s29(2)(a). This view is supported by the fact that the concept of administrative receivership was conceived by the Cork Committee as being founded on the basis of a receiver and manager appointed pursuant to a floating charge (*Cork Committee Report*, Cmnd 8558, paras 495–520). It is this implicit assumption which underlies the service of a notice of a petition for an administration order by virtue of s9(2)(a) on any person who is or may be entitled to appoint an administrative receiver. A different conclusion as to the pre-requisite 'global' nature of a floating charge would also potentially entitle the holder of a floating charge over, say, one very limited class of assets, who also holds fixed-charge security over the other assets of the company, to block an administration order by virtue of s9(3)(a) irrespective of the relative priority of that security. That conclusion not only runs contrary to the legislative purpose of both the administration and administrative receivership regimes, but would also permit the creation of highly artificial security for such purposes.

The final part of the security element in s29(2)(a) which provides for security in the form of a floating charge 'and one or more other securities' also warrants some consideration. In practical terms, the provision permits the usual arrangement in standard-form bank debentures whereby security is created in the form of a series of fixed charges (eg over book debts, plant, machinery, leasehold/freehold property, etc) which is supported by a 'global' first floating charge. It should be noted, however, that there appears to be no reason why any of the 'other securities' needs actually be comprised in the debenture containing the floating charge pursuant to which the administrative receiver is appointed. It would also appear that the term 'other securities' may comprise not only other floating charges (as well as fixed charges) in favour of the debenture-holder but also other types of security defined in s248(2) as meaning 'any mortgage, charge, lien or other security'. This conclusion is not problematic provided that the debenture-holder is secured by the requisite 'global' floating charge for s29(2)(a) purposes.

The full extent of the security held by the debenture-holder in terms of supplemental fixed and floating charges and their value and relative priority is not rendered redundant by the existence of a floating charge in favour of a debenture-holder discussed above. These matters are relevant to the question of the relative priority of right of appointment of an administrative receiver although only security of the fixed or floating variety remains relevant. Other than where the contrary is expressly stated in the remainder of this book, the assumption in terms of security underlying any reference to s29 is that the debenture-holder must be secured by way of a 'global' floating charge and any other securities as discussed above in order to be eligible to appoint an administrative receiver.

## 1.7  Further Problems with s29

Section 29(2)(a) makes specific reference to an administrative receiver as being

> appointed by or on behalf of the holders of any debentures of the company secured by a charge which, as created, was a floating charge, or by such a charge and one or more other securities.

This definition is further qualified by a person who would be such a receiver and manager but for the appointment of some other person as the receiver of part of the company's property s29(2)(b).

The definition raises two questions. First, where a debenture-holder holds a floating charge which is complemented by a number of fixed charges over specific assets, as is common in standard-form debentures, is it possible for the debenture-holder to appoint a receiver pursuant to only one or more of the fixed charges who is not then deemed to be an administrative receiver notwithstanding the presence of a floating charge in the debenture-holder's 'package' of securities? Secondly, if such an appointment is possible, how is it best given legal effect? This second question is dealt with further in 1.7.4 and 1.7.5 below.

On the first question, one view is that the mere existence of a floating charge over the whole of a company's business and undertaking (irrespective of questions of priority) is sufficient to bring any receiver appointed by the charge-holder within the definition of an administrative receiver.

If a debenture-holder chooses specifically to appoint a receiver pursuant to a fixed charge without reference to the floating charge by which he is also secured, it would seem strange if the relative burdens of administrative receivership (in terms of cost, statutory obligations, duties and qualification) were to be imposed on the office-holder, and indirectly the debenture-holder, if that was not in fact what the debenture-holder either wished or intended. Indeed, in practice, this could be potentially hazardous and even illegal, since it is common for a chartered surveyor to be appointed as an LPA receiver over a fixed charge asset such as a single development property. Such individuals, whilst expert in their respective professional field, are rarely qualified as licenced insolvency practitioners for the purposes of IA 1986.

Policy grounds would also appear to preclude the imposition on an appropriately secured creditor of a constrained right of action in appointing a receiver where that constraint restricts the receiver's and manager's status exclusively and unconditionally to that of an administrative receiver. The logical extension of an argument which requires a receiver appointed by a floating-charge secured creditor to have the status of an administrative receiver, might give rise to further bizarre consequences which stem from the wording in s29(2). Nevertheless, and whilst not the preferred view, there remains a very valid argument that a debenture-holder falling within the security definition in s29(2) must be the appointor of an administrative receiver even if he appoints pursuant to a fixed charge only; this can be founded on the very plain wording employed in s29(2)(a).

### 1.7.1 Fixed and floating security

The definition in s29(2)(a) makes no reference to a requirement that the floating and any fixed securities constituting a debenture-holder's security must be comprised in a single debenture. Rather, s29(2) appears to require that the cumulative extent of the debenture-holder's security (again, without reference to question of priority) relates to the whole or substantially the whole of the company's property. This would enable a debenture-holder to appoint an administrative receiver where the debenture-holder holds a floating charge over the whole of a company's business and undertaking, plus a number of fixed charges over specific assets where each was evidenced in a separate debenture. The meaning of the term 'debenture' is relevant here since, whilst s29(2)(a) makes specific reference to 'the holders of any debentures of the company', it is not clear whether or not that term is qualified by the words 'secured by a charge'.

The term 'debenture' itself finds no precise definition in IA 1986 or elsewhere. Section 744 of the Companies Act 1985 however, does, contain a definition, although this is non-exhaustive and is framed in very broad terms as including 'debenture stock, bonds and other securities of a company whether constituting a charge on the assets of the company or not'. Thus, a debenture has been deemed to include a legal mortgage of freehold, and presumably leasehold, property (in *Knightsbridge Estates Trust Ltd v Byrne* [1940] AC 613).

The wording in s29(2)(a) is such that, irrespective of its qualification, the words 'secured by a charge' appear to refer only to 'a charge which, as created, was a floating charge'. That is, there appears to be no requirement that the latter reference in the provision to 'and one or more securities' necessitates that those securities should actually be secured on the company's property in relation to which any administrative receiver is appointed. However, this must be the preferable view of the provisions since the scheme of the Act does not operate to assist a debenture-holder in appointing an administrative receiver to recover unsecured debts.

The following basic example may be of illustrative use here. Y Ltd grants a fixed charge to its bank over a commercial property development in 1987 in consideration for a cash injection. In 1988, further cash is injected by the bank for expansion in return for a fixed charge over the company's own freehold property. A similar exercise is undertaken in 1989 when a purported fixed charge is taken over book debts, together with a series of secured income bonds by which the company undertakes to repay a new loan out of its profits which will constitute debentures (*Lemon v Austin Friars Investment Trust Ltd* [1926] Ch 1). In 1993 the company experiences financial difficulties and begins to suffer cash flow problems. As a consequence its bank agrees to advance further sums as evidenced by a committed facility letter and, in return, is granted a general floating charge over the company's business and undertaking. Following payments into and out of the company's bank account, the company defaults in early 1995 on repayment under the terms of the 1987 debenture, and the bank considers the appointment of a receiver and manager. One argument, which it is submitted is not the preferred one, is that the receiver must be an administrative receiver even if the appointment is made solely pursuant to the fixed charge comprised in the 1987 debenture, on the grounds that the floating charge created in 1993 brings the debenture-holder within the s29(2)(a) definition. In accordance with the manner in which the debenture-holder's security was taken, the most appropriate and commonsensical approach, it seems, is to permit the debenture-holder to appoint either a receiver (and manager) under the terms of 1987 fixed charge debenture (ie a non-administrative LPA receiver) or an administrative receiver, on the basis of the global security held over the company's property which is underpinned by the prerequisite 1993 floating charge for the purposes of s29(2)(a).

In practice, the bank may well not wish to appoint a receiver and manager over the whole of the company's assets for commercial reasons and, furthermore, may wish specifically to appoint an individual who is a specialist chartered surveyor as a receiver and manager to the commercial property development. Similarly, the bank may wish to appoint a receiver to the income arising from book debts and/or any of the outstanding series of secured income bonds granted to it by way of fixed charge in 1989 without, for obvious reasons, interfering substantially with the running of the company's business. Further, it is relevant to the argument supporting the right of choice in terms of appointment by the debenture-holder that the debenture-holder's right to benefit from a so-called lightweight floating charge, conferred specifically to veto the making of an administration order, and presumably, to afford the appointment of an administrative receiver, has been judicially recognised in *Re Croftbell* [1990] BCLC 844. The implications of this decision must be that, whilst the debenture-holder may benefit from the existence of such artificial security, it remains his prerogative to stop short of appointment of an administrative receiver, usually for commercial reasons. Certainly the intention of the company at the time of the execution of the debenture, and any knowledge of it as perceived by the debenture-holder, was rejected by Vinelott J in *Re Croftbell* in the following terms:

> I do not think that the answer to the question whether the holder of a debenture, which on its face creates a floating charge, has power to appoint an administrative receiver can turn on the intentions of the company when the debenture was executed or the knowledge by the debenture-holder of those intentions.

Indeed, it is submitted that an approach which denies the secured creditor the benefit of these two choices has little to recommend it.

### 1.7.2  Fixed-charge appointments

Notwithstanding the above, there remains a problem with the suggestion that a receiver appointed pursuant to a fixed charge by the holder of a floating charge over the whole or substantially the whole of the company's property will not, by definition, constitute an administrative receiver. This stems from a construction of the wording used in s29(2)(a). A reading of the provisions begs the question of whether the words 'secured by a charge which, as created, was a floating charge, or by such a charge and one or more other securities' qualify the words 'the whole (or substantially the whole) of a company's property' or, alternatively, whether they qualify the words, 'the holders of any debentures of the company'. Either way it remains both bizarre and even self-defeating, yet inescapable in relation to the example given above, that any receiver appointed by the bank, whether pursuant to a fixed or floating charge or both, must constitute an administrative receiver on a plain reading of these elements of the provision. As Marks and Emmett put it in their excellent article in [1994] JBL 1–7 at 4 as follows:

> whichever view is taken of the precise grounds of the subsection it should not matter whether the appointment takes place under the floating charge aspect of any security package or the fixed charge element thereof, provided the debenture-holder held a charge which at the time of the appointment was, when created, floating.

(The irony of this construction not being dissimilar to the overall approach of Vinelott J in the *Re Croftbell* decision should not be missed.)

This conclusion is not a happy one since it suggests that, in certain circumstances, a debenture-holder will simply be unable to appoint a fixed charge LPA receiver if, at the time of the appointment, he also holds a security constituting a 'global' floating charge over the property of the company. This will be the case even where the floating charge has crystallised prior to the appointment by virtue of the wording of s29(2)(a). The definition of a floating charge (ie 'as created') in s251 was introduced to prevent the use of crystallised floating charges to defeat the claims of preferential creditors under s40. Furthermore, the same conclusion may arguably be reached even where the floating charge held by the debenture-holder extends only to a restricted or even non-existent class of assets which, together with the cumulative security of any other fixed charges held by the debenture-holder, constitute the whole or substantially the whole of the company's property (on the basis of the *Croftbell* decision). The better view, it is submitted, is that an administrative receiver may only be appointed pursuant to a 'global' floating charge as discussed in 1.6 above.

In truth, the uncertainty in the provisions owes much to poor draftsmanship, since a strict application of s29(2) might bring about conclusions which, at one extreme, are both non-commercial and even prejudicial to the debenture-holder, and, at the other extreme, are so perverse as to be unjustifiable. Indeed, the provision would well appear to operate to impose all of the statutory obligations, powers and duties needlessly and bureaucratically on an appointee who, in reality, is nothing more than a fixed charge LPA and is intended as such by his appointor and, indeed and ironically enough, by the company itself. This is supported by the fact that the perceived purpose of s29(2) would be achieved equally well, and without the above problems, if the specific reference to the debenture-holder being secured by a floating charge in s29(2) was to be omitted; that is, if the property qualification in s29(2) simply required security to be held over the whole or substantially the whole of the company's property.

### 1.7.3 The *Meadrealm* security problem

Section 29(2) is, in practice, further undermined by the fact that a debenture-holder may arguably fall within its provisions notwithstanding the fact that one of his 'package' of securities is a floating charge over substantially less than the whole of a company's property, typically a floating charge over a class of assets such as book debts. Whilst the wording of s29(2) in its current form appears to envisage that the only type of floating charge held by a debenture-holder will be a floating charge which extends to the whole of the company's business and undertaking, there are grounds on which it may be argued why this may not be the case, although this view is not to be preferred as discussed in 1.6 above. Why, one might ask, has the draftsman not employed more explicit language and rendered the area free from doubt? Furthermore, the *Croftbell* decision (above) illustrates how the benefits of administrative receivership may be obtained in the most artificial of ways. Criticism of s29(2) is furthered again by the unreported decision of Vinelott J in *Mead-realm Ltd and First National Commercial Bank Plc v Transcontinental Golf Construction Ltd* (1991).

*Meadrealm* involved a claim for summary possession under RSC Ord 113. For unclear reasons the whole transcript of the decision appears to be unavailable. However, the relevant passage of Vinelott J's judgment runs as follows;

> First, it is said that the receiver was never validly appointed a receiver, because he is not qualified as an insolvency practitioner and cannot therefore be an administrative receiver, and that the terms of his appointment were wide enough to satisfy the definition of an administrative receiver. I think the short answer to that is that an administrative receiver is a receiver under a charge which as created was a floating charge and that the receiver was not appointed under the floating charge but only under the fixed charge.

This statement does much to advance the argument that, in relation to the example cited above, a receiver appointed pursuant to (as opposed to the less suitable term 'under') a fixed charge will be a fixed charge LPA receiver, notwithstanding a floating-charge security being held over the whole of a company's property by the appointing debenture-holder. However, the fact remains that this statement simply runs contrary to any sensible reading of the unsatisfactory wording in s29(2) as discussed earlier. Further, the issue was apparently not argued fully in *Meadrealm*. Moreover, the learned judge did not address the possibility of non-global floating charges for s29(2) purposes. The decision, therefore, should not be seen as binding, in the absence of further specific judicial clarification. Indeed, it is difficult to see how any judicial statutory interpretation of the provision could sensibly construe its wording in any other way than as set out above. Parliamentary intervention may therefore be required in the course of time if the unacceptable and far-reaching implications of s29(2) are realised when the points raised above come to be considered by the courts.

## 1.7.4 Evading the s29 definition

The above discussion throws up one further question, namely, is there any way in which the holder of floating- and fixed-charge securities over a company's property may circumvent the implications of s29(2) and appoint a fixed charge LPA receiver? The answer is that there are a number of possibilities, each with apparent flaws which should signal caution in all cases.

The first possible and perhaps the most effective solution to the s29(2) problem is that the debenture-holder may release his floating-charge security prior to the appointment of the receiver. This action would result in the debenture-holder no longer falling within s29(2)(a) as, at the time of the appointment, he would no longer be 'secured by a charge which, as created, was a floating charge...'. Any receiver appointed, therefore, would appear not to be capable of being an administrative receiver. The problem with this approach is that it may be argued that the debenture-holder has been secured by way of floating charge over the whole or substantially the whole of the company's assets and, as such, any receiver appointed would necessarily be an administrative receiver if the fixed security held by the debenture-holder at the time of the appointment extends to the whole or substantially the whole of the company's property, on the basis that there is no express requirement in s29(2) that the floating charge should be held by the debenture-holder at the actual time at which the appointment is effected.

A second possible solution to the s29(2) problem might simply be an appointment made pursuant to a fixed charge only, on the basis of the *Meadrealm* decision. For reasons explained above, however, an appointment of this type should be seen as being far from watertight in terms of avoiding the appointment of an administrative receiver.

One further alternative to the above solutions may be felt to be more appropriate in certain circumstances. It is clear from s29(2) that nothing precludes the appointment of a receiver or receiver and manager of part of the company's property contemporaneously with the appointment of an administrative receiver. In relation to the example given previously, this would permit the appointment of a specialist fixed-charge LPA receiver over a specifically charged fixed asset, such as a commercial property development, together with the appointment of an administrative receiver over the remainder of the company's business and undertaking which, together with the fixed asset, must necessarily constitute the whole or substantially the whole of the company's property (s29(2)(a), and see s29(2)(b) which effectively permits the administrative receiver's contemporaneous appointment).

Finally, the potentially oppressive effects of s29(2) may be avoided where the floating charge as created which is held by the debenture-holder does not extend to the whole or substantially the whole of the company's business and undertaking (irrespective of question of priority) but floats over, or indeed attaches to, a specific class of assets such as book debts or a freehold property. This is because, whilst a receiver and manager appointed under the global security held by the debenture-holder over the company's property will constitute an administrative receiver, this will not be the case if one receiver and manager is appointed pursuant to security or securities, say of the 'restricted' floating charge, and another receiver and manager is appointed on the basis of any other fixed charge(s), which also extend(s) to less than substantially the

whole of the company's property. Either receiver and manager will, by definition, be incapable of being classed as an administrative receiver, assuming
that, in either case, no receiver was appointed over what might be viewed by
the debenture-holder as the whole or substantially the whole of the company's
property. Indeed, it is arguable that the debenture-holder would be incapable
of appointing an administrative receiver in any case.

### 1.7.5  Quasi-administrative receivers?

Is it possible to bestow on a receiver appointed by a fixed-charge holder (ie a
non-administrative receiver) the statutory powers conferred on an administrative receiver by the 1986 legislation, together with the corresponding
responsibilities? On the basis of s29(2) the answer to this must be in the negative, in the absence of the appointing debenture-holder being secured by a
charge which, as created, was a floating charge, apparently at the time the
appointment is made. Furthermore, it is submitted that it would be impossible
for a debenture-holder secured solely by way of fixed charges, as created,
even those securing the whole or substantially the whole of the company's
property, to agree on a contractual basis with a debtor company for the
conferring of powers and obligations in precisely the way as are conferred
and imposed on an administrative receiver by the 1986 legislation. Whilst it
may be possible and, indeed, is common in practice for wide-ranging powers to
be conferred on a receiver by agreement between the parties, the same cannot
be said of the statutory powers and duties which impinge upon third parties
such as the power in s43 to dispose of property charged in favour of a prior-
ranking chargee or the restriction in s45 which limits the power of removal of
an administrative receiver to the court. In the former case, this is because the
power is conferred by statute as a matter of law in relation to other third party
creditors of the company and is beyond the scope of agreement between the
company and the debenture-holder; in the latter case such an agreement
will amount to an attempt by the company's board to fetter the powers of
its directors.

Finally, the acts of an individual as an administrative receiver are valid
notwithstanding any defect in his appointment, nomination or qualifications
by virtue of s232. Whilst this provision is clear, it is submitted that it will not
cure defects which arise where an individual is expressly appointed as a fixed-
charge LPA receiver but, by reason of s29(2)(a), is deemed to be an administrative receiver, because, as such, the LPA receiver cannot fairly be described
as carrying out acts 'as … administrative receiver' since that is not the basis
on which his appointment was made.

## 1.8  Can an Administrative Receiver be Court Appointed?

It is arguable from the definition in s29(2), which refers to an appointment 'by or on behalf of the holders of any debentures of the company', that a receiver who is appointed by the court is incapable of being an administrative receiver. This is a view concurred with in Stewart, *Administrative Receivers and Administrators* 1st edn (CCH 1987), 13. On the other hand, it is arguable that a receiver and manager appointed by the court on the application of a debenture-holder would be an administrative receiver on the basis that the appointment is made by the court 'on behalf of' the debenture-holder, assuming that the appointment is made over the whole or substantially the whole of the company's property. Against this is the argument that a court-appointed receiver is not actually appointed 'on behalf of' a debenture-holder or holders, a view supported by Picarda, *The Law Relating to Receivers, Managers and Administrators*, 2nd edn, (1990) 7. This view apparently runs contrary to the context in which the words 'on behalf of' the holder of debentures of the company, and its variations, are employed in various other pieces of legislation. These include IA 1986, s32, which re-enacts the Companies Act 1985 s491, and the Employment Protection (Consolidation) Act 1978, ss127(1)(c) and 106(5)(c) dealing with various situations in which a receiver is deemed to be insolvent; see Schumacher [1993] IL&P 43–5 for further analysis and comparisons in this regard.

One other view concerns the position within the legislation occupied by s29(2) of the IA 1986. The provision appears within a sub-chapter to Chapter III of the 1986 Act which is concerned with preliminary and general provisions. Those provisions do not apply to every receivership as do ss39–41, which are contained in a further sub-chapter; neither does s29 appear within the sub-chapter comprising ss33–8, which deals exclusively with receivers and managers appointed out of court. The issue is therefore fudged, since the draftsman has effectively located the provision in an apparent no-man's land between court and out-of-court appointments.

The better view, it is submitted, is that a court-appointed receiver and manager cannot amount to an administrative receiver notwithstanding the appointment by the court over the whole or substantially the whole of the company's property. This is because an application to the court for the appointment of a receiver and manager, if successful, will not bring about an appointment which can strictly speaking be regarded as being made 'on behalf of' the debenture-holder. Instead, the appointment will be made by the court itself on terms prescribed by the court. This is not to say that the reference in s29(2)(a) to an appointment 'on behalf of' the holders of any debentures of the company is otiose. The term would come in to play if, for example, a charge, being a floating charge together with any further fixed charge or charges over the whole or substantially the whole of the company's property, was to be vested in the trustees of a trust deed which secured an issue of debentures or debenture stock. In that case, the appointment of an administrative receiver would be made by the trustees of the trust deed 'on behalf of' the holders of the debentures of the company.

In practice, applications to the court by a debenture-holder for the appointment of a receiver and manager are and will continue to be rare, largely on account of the standard form of debenture widely employed in corporate finance transactions. Such applications might realistically only be envisaged (a) where a debenture is defectively drafted in that it does not prescribe specific events upon which an appointment may be made or (b) where the debenture itself is otherwise substantially defective in some material way, eg it is invalidly executed. On the other hand, a debenture-holder may perceive some advantage in the appointment by the court of a receiver and manager, as opposed to an administrative receiver appointed out of court. This could occur in particular where the administrative receiver risks non-recognition in a foreign jurisdiction in which significant assets may be located and where a court-appointed receiver is formally recognised as an officer of the court. The developing number of cross-border insolvencies suggests that decisions to opt for a court-appointed receiver in this way are likely to increase.

## 1.9 Administrative Receivers and Non-Administrative Receivers Compared

An examination of administrative receivership begs some distinction to be made between an administrative receiver and a non-administrative receiver. The term 'non-administrative receiver' in this section refers both to a receiver who is appointed as a receiver of income only, under the Law of Property Act 1925 s101 (ie as an LPA receiver), and to a receiver or receiver and manager of property appointed by the court. Technically, the term non-administrative receiver will also extend to a receiver or manager who would be an administrative receiver but for the prior appointment of another administrative receiver over the same charged property. However, for the purposes of this section, administrative receivers, whether appointed or merely eligible for appointment, are treated as synonymous. This is because it is not possible for two administrative receivers (other than joint administrative receivers) to be appointed of the whole or substantially the whole of a company's property on a contemporaneous basis; see para 1.11 below.

It is also possible for an individual farmer to create an agricultural charge for the purposes of raising finance under the Agricultural Credits Act 1928 s5, which provides specific definitions of both fixed and floating charges for the purposes of that legislation. Agricultural receivers are not considered further in this book, although it is submitted that such a receiver could never constitute an administrative receiver on the basis of the specific reference in s29(2) of the IA 1986 to an appointment in respect of 'a company's property'.

The significant differences between an administrative receiver and a non-administrative receiver may be summarised as follows:

(1)   Any person (other than the Official Receiver) acting as an insolvency practitioner in relation to a company by acting as an administrative receiver must be qualified as a licenced insolvency practitioner who is qualified to act as such at that time on pain of criminal sanction (ss388(1), (2), (4), (5), 389(1), 390(2)(a),(b),(4)). A non-administrative receiver need not be a licenced insolvency practitioner.

(2)   The appointment of an administrative receiver in practice invariably precludes the making of an administration order by the court. This is because the so-called moratorium provisions in s10(1), which become operative on an administration order being made, will not operate where there is an administrative receiver in office without the consent to the making of the administration order by the debenture-holder by or on whose behalf the administrative receiver was appointed (s10(3)(a),(b)). (The relationship between administrative receivership and other insolvency proceedings is considered further in Chapter 2 at para 2.5.)

(3)   As is usually also expressly stated to be the case in most well-drafted standard-form debentures, an administrative receiver is deemed to be the agent of the company unless and until the company goes into liquidation under s44(1)(a) and, as such, is entitled to an indemnity out of the assets of the company under s44(1)(c). An express statement to this effect also avoids an allegation (based on *Deves v Wood* [1911] 1 KB 806) to the effect that the statutorily implied powers considered in (7) below are the only powers in respect of which the implied agency in s44(1)(a) operates, to the exclusion of any further expressly stated powers. An LPA receiver is also deemed to be agent of the company until liquidation (Law of Property Act 1925 s109(2)). However, any other non-administrative receiver's agency relationship with the company will be governed by the agreement between the parties, the receiver being deemed to be the agent of the debenture-holder in the absence of contrary intention (*Deves v Wood* [1911] 1 KB 806). (The agency relationship of the administrative receiver with the company is considered further at para 1.10 below.)

(4)   The circumstances in which an administrative receiver may be appointed are not prescribed by legislation. In practice, the events in which the appointment may be made will invariably be set out expressly in the debenture, since these will also cater for the possible appointment of a non-administrative receiver. The types of events in

which the appointment of an administrative receiver may be envisaged are set out in Chapter 3 at para 3.3. In the very unlikely event that a debenture does not set out events on which an administrative receiver may be appointed it will be necessary, and will be both cumbersome and costly in terms of time and expense, for the debenture-holder to make an application to court for the appointment of a receiver and manager. No statutory provisions exist for the appointment of such a receiver and manager by the court, and the appointment appears to be made pursuant to the court's inherent jurisdiction (*Edwards v Standard Rolling Stock Syndicate* [1893] 1 Ch 574). Although not entirely clear, it is submitted that such a court-appointed receiver and manager will not amount to an administrative receiver for the reasons set out in para 1.8 above and will not, therefore, be subject to the statutory regime of the Act in relation to administrative receivers. This is notwithstanding the receiver and manager's appointment by the court over the whole or substantially the whole of the company's property. The power to appoint an LPA receiver, on the other hand, arises where monies secured by the mortgage have fallen due provided that the lender has become entitled to exercise its powers of sale (Law of Property Act 1925 ss101(iii), 109(1)). This entitlement is further subject to the rather elaborate provisos contained in the Law of Property Act 1925 s103. These provisions largely account for why the circumstances in which an LPA receiver may be appointed, as provided for by statute, are varied and extended in practice by the mortgage deed, as is permitted by the Law of Property Act 1925 s101(3). Typically, the mortgage deed will provide that monies secured by the mortgage (or debenture depending on the terminology employed) shall become due for the purposes of the Law of Property Act 1925 s101 upon service of a demand by the creditor, and that s103 of the 1925 Act shall have no application in relation to any of the charges contained in the mortgage or debenture.

(5) An administrative receiver is an office-holder for the purposes of the Act and, as such, may avail himself of the powers of management in respect of supplies of utilities (s233) and the provisions relating to the getting in of company property and the examination of company officers and other individuals under ss234–6, together with the orders which the court may make as set out in s237. These provisions are considered further in Chapter 8, which deals with the powers of the administrative receiver. A non-administrative receiver does not have recourse to these provisions and they may not be conferred by contract.

(6) An administrative receiver is under a duty both to require the submission to him of a statement of affairs of the company in the prescribed

form and to provide a report to all secured creditors (which is also made available to unsecured creditors) and to the Registrar of Companies within three months of his appointment, subject to extension by the court (ss47–8). The administrative receiver also has a duty to discharge obligations to any committee of creditors appointed (s49). No such obligations are imposed on non-administrative receivers other than the account reporting obligations which are now contained in s38.

(7)  The powers of an administrative receiver derive from Sched 1 to IA 1986 which, by virtue of s42(1), are conferred on the administrative receiver by implication from the terms of the debenture pursuant to which he is appointed, except to the extent that they are varied by the debenture itself. In practice, these powers are usually expressly set out in the debenture pursuant to which the administrative receiver is appointed. The powers of a non-administrative receiver, on the other hand, emanate directly from the terms of the debenture pursuant to which the receiver is appointed apart from those powers implied by statute. In the case of an LPA receiver, these implied powers are very restricted and are limited to the obtaining of income from the mortgaged property (which must then be applied in accordance with the Law of Property Act 1982 s109(8)) and the insuring of the mortgaged property at the direction of the mortgagee (s109(7) of the 1925 Act). In practice, there are potential and very considerable problems with the extension of an LPA receiver's powers where the property in respect of the income of which the receiver is appointed, is distinguishable from the property over which the mortgagee holds security. This is because the extended powers will confer on the receiver the power to manage, develop, sell and deal with etc the mortgaged property in respect of which he is theoretically not actually appointed as receiver. *Knight v Lawrence* [1991] BCC 411, for example, involved an LPA receiver who gave notification to the mortgagors of the property that he had been appointed as receiver of the mortgaged property when, in fact, he was appointed as merely a receiver of the rents and profits of the mortgaged property. When the receiver failed to serve rent review notices as provided for in the leases over the property subject to the receivership, he was held liable for breach of duty both to his appointor and to all persons having an interest in the property, including the mortgagor.

(8)  An administrative receiver may apply to the court under s43 of the IA 1986 for an order authorising the disposal of property which is subject to a prior ranking charge as if the property were not subject to the security. Potentially and practically, this power to overcome a senior chargee's interest is an extremely useful one to an administrative

receiver who is faced with an uncooperative prior-ranking charge holder. Section 43 also robs a prior-ranking chargee of the important rights of timing and conduct of the realisation of the prior-charged assets. As is submitted in Chapter 8 at para 8.5, s43 also applies to sale by an administrative receiver of property charged in favour of junior or subsidiary secured creditors. There is no statutory provision analogous to s43 which a non-administrative receiver may utilise.

(9) An administrative receiver may only be removed from office by order of the court ('but not otherwise'): s45(1). This represents a considerable strengthening of the administrative receiver's position as compared with the pre-Insolvency Act 1985 situation, where the power to remove a receiver was also available to the debenture-holder if the debenture so provided. The former position continues to prevail in relation to non-administrative receivers at common law. An administrative receiver may, of course, resign his office voluntary, and he is obliged to vacate office if he ceases to be qualified to act as an insolvency practitioner in relation to the company (ss45(1), (2), 388(1), 389(1)).

(10) The acts of an administrative receiver are valid notwithstanding any defect in his appointment, nomination or qualifications (s232). No such provision operates in relation to a non-administrative receiver. In the absence of any judicial authority on s232, the scope of the provision is unclear. It has been suggested that the wording of s232 is broad enough to cover any defect whatsoever, including the invalidity of the security under which the administrative receiver is appointed. It is submitted that this view is too liberal and that s232 will not extend to defects other than those relating to the form or procedure pursuant to which the appointment of the administrative receiver is made. Section 232 is considered in more detail in Chapter 5 at para 5.6.2.

## 1.10 The Administrative Receiver's Agency Relationship with the Company

It is convenient at this stage to examine the legal foundation of the relationship whereby the administrative receiver is deemed to be an agent of the principal company in administrative receivership until the subsequent termination of that relationship on the liquidation of the company (s44(1)(a)). This would also appear to be the case with an LPA receiver (*Gosling v Gaskill* [1897] Ch 575). This peculiar principal/agency relationship is particularly relevant to the common practice of purportedly excluding or limiting an administrative receiver's liability for breach of duty in the terms of the debenture.

The administrative receiver's powers are implied into the terms of the debenture pursuant to which the administrative receiver's appointment is made except to the extent to which they are varied or excluded by the debenture itself (s42(1)). *Prima facie* this raises a problem of privity, since it would appear that the administrative receiver is appointed by virtue of an instrument to which the company itself is not a party and is also charged with powers which are deemed to emanate from a debenture to which he himself is not party. This privity problem and its possible solutions has been the subject of some debate. Notable examples include Lightman and Moss, *The Law of Receivers of Companies*, 2nd edn (Sweet & Maxwell 1994), pp 54–66, Goode, *Principles of Corporate Insolvency Law*, 1st edn (Sweet & Maxwell/ CCLS 1990) at 93–8 and Milman (1981) 44 MLR 658 (which remains relevant to the post-1986 legislation).

### 1.10.1 Objects and powers of the companies

The objects clause of the company's memorandum of association sets out the purpose or purposes which the company is formed to achieve or the type of activities or business in which the company is to engage. The objects clause will also contain the powers which are incidental to the achievement of the company's objects. The House of Lords held in *Att-Gen v Great Eastern Railway Co* (1880) 5 App Cas 473 that a company is impliedly granted all powers necessary for it to achieve its stated objects. In achieving its objects and exercising the powers pursuant to the objects, the company acts through its directors. Most modern forms of articles of association, including Table A, art 70, confer on the board of the company all of the powers of the company other than those which the Companies Acts and the company's memorandum of association require to be exclusive to the company in general meeting. These include the removal of directors, the putting of the company into liquidation, the appointment of directors and the declaration (as opposed to recommendation) of dividends.

The objects clause of a trading company will invariably include express powers to borrow money and to give security for its loans. Commercial reality dictates this and thus the law responds by providing that, even when such express powers are not set out in the objects clause (as will be usual in practice), a trading company has an implied power to borrow money and to give security over any of its property for debts properly contracted by it (*Re Patent File Co ex parte Birmingham Banking Co* (1870) 6 Ch App 83; *Re International Life Assurance Society* (1870) LR 10 Eq 312; *General Auction Estate and Monetary Co v Smith* [1891] 3 Ch 432). This implied power will not, however, extend to creating a charge over uncalled capital although an express power to this effect is commonly included in modern standard form debentures (see *Re British Provident Life and Fire Assurance Society* (1864) 4

De GJ & Sm 407; *Re Colonial and General Gas Co Ltd* (1870) 23 LT 759. Certain agency problems may arise where the powers conferred by the debenture exceed those inherent in the company's objects clause. Notwithstanding this, any express or implied power may be exercised incidental to or conducive to the carrying on of any trade or business carried on by the company where the company's object is stated to be 'to carry on business as a general commercial company' (Companies Act 1985 s3A, as inserted by Companies Act 1989 s110(1)).

The objects and powers contained in the memorandum of association invariably enable the company to lend money, to give to the lender the required security over the company's assets and to execute a debenture to that effect. The administrative receiver's powers, on the other hand, acting as the company's agent if and until the company goes into liquidation by virtue of s44(1)(a), derive from the debenture itself (s42(1)). The board is usually empowered to delegate its powers in most modern forms of articles of association. Table A, art 71, for example, empowers the board to appoint any persons, whether directors or members of the company or not, to be the agents of the company for such period as the board thinks fit with authority to exercise any of the directors' powers during that time. (Significantly, the appointment need only be made by deed under the common seal of the company or be otherwise executed as a deed, if the attorney is empowered to execute deeds on behalf of the company as will usually be so in the case of an administrative receiver.)

### 1.10.2 The delegation of power by the board

Although the board executes a debenture pursuant to which an administrative receiver may be appointed, the directors effectively delegate their powers of management, other than residual powers which remain with them, to the administrative receiver in the event that the security created by the debenture is enforced. This delegation—which is a matter separate from the administrative receiver's agency relationship with the company—will be effected for the period of the administrative receivership. In practice, this will continue following the company going into formal liquidation.

A potential problem with the disparate sources of the directors' and administrative receiver's powers comes to light when one considers that the broad effect of the appointment of the administrative receiver is to divest the directors of the company of their powers of management during the period of the administrative receivership to the extent that they impede the proper conduct of it (*Re Emmadart Ltd* [1979] Ch 540, per Brightman J at 547; *Re Moss Steamship Co Ltd v Whitney* [1912] AC 254 per Atkinson LJ at 263. See also *Re Foster Clark Ltd's Indenture Trusts* [1966] 1 All ER 43, *Griffiths v Secretary of State for Social Services* [1973] 3 All ER 1184 and *Re Joshua Shaw & Sons Ltd* [1989] 5 BCC 188 and Chapter 8 at 8.11. This is for the simple reason that the powers implied by Sched 1 to IA 1986, as varied by the debenture, may exceed the scope of the objects and powers conferred by the company's memorandum of association from which, of course, the administrative receiver's powers do not emanate. Similarly, it would also be possible, in theory at least, for the terms of the debenture to operate so as to state the administrative receiver's powers as being more restricted than those conferred on the company's directors, although in practice such a debenture would be very unusual, not least on account of its clear detriment to the debenture-holder.

Professor R M Goode suggests in his book *Principles of Corporate Insolvency Law*, 1st edn (1990) at 95 that '... the express or implied provisions of the debenture may enable the receiver to perform acts which cannot be performed by the directors without the sanction of the memorandum or articles [of association] or a resolution of the company in general meeting'. It is respectfully submitted that this statement is accurate but is subject to one important qualification. That is, to the extent that the powers implied by Sched 1 do exceed the scope of the company's objects and powers as contained in its memorandum of association, and which are therefore *ultra vires* the company, the administrative receiver will not act as an agent of the company. This conclusion runs contrary to the express provision of s44(1)(a) since, by virtue of the very nature of the company's constitution, the company is in law incapable of such acts. It is a well-established tenet of the law of agency that an agent may not be charged with a power of which the principal is incapable. Accordingly, in no case can the authority of an agent exceed the power of a principal to act on his own behalf (*Shrewsbury and Birmingham Railway Co v North Western Railway Co* (1857) 6 HL Cas 113; *Montreal Assurance Co v McGillivray* (1859) 13 Moo PCC 87; *Ashbury Railway Carriage and Iron Co v Riche* (1875) LR 7 HL 653). For this reason, an administrative receiver cannot be empowered to do any act *as an agent for the company* which the company itself was not able to do under its memorandum of association *Lawson v Hosemaster Co Ltd* [1966] 1 WLR 1300.

### 1.10.3   The position of third parties

There are ramifications here for third parties which stem from the Companies Act 1989 and its virtual abolition of the *ultra vires* rule. In favour of third parties, the validity of an act done by a company (eg by an administrative receiver as agent of the company) may not be called into question on the ground of lack of capacity by reason of anything in the company's memorandum (Companies Act 1985 s35(1), as substituted by Companies Act 1989 s108(1)). Furthermore, where a third party deals in good faith with a company, the power of the directors to bind the company, or to authorise others to do so (eg the administrative receiver to whom powers are delegated on a contingent basis on his execution of the debenture) is deemed free from any limitation under the company's constitution (Companies Act 1985 s35A(1), as inserted by Companies Act 1989 s108(1)). The third party dealing with the company (the administrative receiver acting as agent of the company) need not enquire into whether the company's power is permitted by the memorandum or as to any limitation on the directors' powers (Companies Act 1985, s35B, as inserted by Companies Act 1989 s108(1)).

### 1.10.4  Personal liability of the administrative receiver

It follows that to the extent that the administrative receiver performs acts *ultra vires* the company, he will incur personal liability for loss arising as a result of this apparent breach of agency. The relevance of this should not be underestimated, since s44(3) would appear to preclude any right of indemnity from the company's assets for liability incurred in connection with such *ultra vires* acts, which by virtue of that provision includes 'liability on contracts entered into or adopted without authority'. This lack of indemnity does nothing to undermine the impact of the personal liability imposed by s44(1)(b) in respect of any contract entered into in the carrying out of the administrative receiver's function, irrespective apparently of whether the carrying out of his function is *intra vires* or *ultra vires* the company. However, this apparently exposed position should not be problematic for the administrative receiver in practice as it is usual for well-drafted modern standard-form debentures to contain an express provision affording the administrative receiver a full indemnity from the company in respect of his acts, defaults and any liabilities incurred by him on any contract or other matter, even where the administrative receiver is not acting as agent of the company.

For practical purposes, the risk of personal liability to the administrative receiver need not necessarily be of concern to the third party dealing with him. This is because s42(3) provides that a person dealing with an administrative receiver in good faith and for value is not concerned to inquire whether the administrative receiver is acting within his powers. This brings into the insolvency legislation a provision which mirrors Companies Act 1985 s35 (as amended) and the company law rule in *Royal British Bank v Turquand* (1855) 5 E & B 248 which provides that, where a person deals in good faith with the directors of a company or other representative body of the company which is exercising powers of management and director of the company and its business, that third party is not affected by or concerned with either defects in procedure within the company or any failure to fulfil conditions which are required by the company's articles or memorandum of association to be fulfilled before the act or transaction in question is effected. It is worth noting that, for the purposes of *ultra vires* transactions in company law, a person is not deemed to act in bad faith merely by reason of his knowing that an act is beyond the powers of the directors under the company's constitution (Companies Act 1985 s35A(2)(b)). This suggests a requirement for some further operative factor which might include the coercing of the board or any of its members by the third party to act *ultra vires* or proving that the board knew it was acting *ultra vires* at the time of the transaction. It is suggested that considerations analogous to these would apply to s42(3) of IA 1986.

### 1.10.5 Is divestment of management an abuse of power by directors?

The actions of the company's directors in executing a debenture which, at least on a contingent basis, operates to divest them of the broad powers of management, may not be challenged on the basis that the board is effectively acting to discharge itself from its management powers and responsibilities. At first sight, it may appear that this contingent divestment of power constitutes an exercise of the powers of the directors for an improper purpose or, alternatively, an abuse of power on the part of the directors. This would entitle the company to treat the transaction as void against the debenture-holder or any third party who was aware of the abuse or improper purpose, even if the third party had provided good consideration for it, as an exception to the rule in *Royal British Bank v Turquand* (1855) 5 E & B 248: see *Re W & M Roith Ltd* [1967] 1 All ER 427 and *Re David Payne & Co Ltd* [1904] 2 Ch 608. It is submitted that this view may be discounted for the following two reasons:

(1) In executing a debenture, the company's directors are not solely divesting themselves of their management powers (other than any residual powers which remain exercisable by them) on the happening of some future event. Rather, they are delegating those management powers—which may be returned to them on the successful completion of the administrative receivership—for the specific purpose of enabling the administrative receiver to protect, preserve or realise the assets subject to the debenture. This is borne out by s42(2)(b) which provides that, in the application of the powers in Schedule 1 to the administrative receiver, references to 'the property of the company' are deemed to be to property of which he is receiver or manager or would be but for the appointment of some other person as the receiver of part of the company's property. In other words, the administrative receiver does not assume the directors' powers of management in their broader sense as being conferred for the purpose of carrying on of the company's business; instead, they are assumed pursuant to the administrative receiver's primary function of protecting, preserving and realising the assets charged in favour of his appointor.

(2) The administrative receiver's powers do not arise as the principal consequence of the execution of the debenture by the company's board.

Instead, these arise as powers subsidiary to the debenture's main purpose. In other words, the principal consequence of the execution of a debenture is the granting of a security interest in favour of the debenture-holder over the company's charged assets. The administrative receiver's powers will only become exercisable in the event that the holder takes legitimate action to enforce that security. In the absence of such enforcement, the administrative receiver's powers will not, of course, become operative.

On the basis of the above two principal assumptions, it is submitted that the execution of a debenture by the board of a company will be unimpeachable apart from the case where the directors' actions are capable of being shown to be other than '...*bona fide* in what they consider—not what a court may consider—as in the interests of the company, and not for any collateral purpose' (*Re Smith & Fawcett Ltd* [1942] Ch 304, at 306 per Green MR; see also *Rolled Steel Products (Holdings) Ltd v British Steel Corp* [1986] Ch 246 per Slade LJ at 288 and *Re Lee Behrens & Co Ltd* [1932] Ch 46 per Eve J at 51). Perhaps the most obvious example of a breach of duty by the directors in this regard is the creation of a security interest (typically in favour of one of their number or a connected person) which may also be avoided under s238, 239 or 245 in the event that the company goes into liquidation or, less commonly, administration. The creation of a security which is subsequently avoided under s238, 239 or 245 may also give rise to an action by the liquidator or administrator in misfeasance proceedings for breach of duty against the directors of the company who authorised or ratified the transaction. It appears from the decision in *Re Washington Diamond Mining Co* [1893] 3 Ch 95 that the giving of any preference under s239 constitutes a breach of duty by the directors, irrespective of whether or not they benefit in any way in giving it. Presumably this would also apply in the case of a transaction-at-undervalue or vulnerable floating charge under ss238 and 245 respectively.

Finally, it should be noted that an exercise by the directors of their power in breach of their fiduciary duties which is nevertheless *intra vires* is not an action in excess of their powers. The actions of the directors will be voidable, therefore, only at the instance of the company, as opposed to being void *ab initio* (*Spackman v Evans* (1868) LR 3 HL 171 per Romilly LJ at 244; *Bamford v Bamford* [1970] Ch 212). The avoidance of such a transaction is subrogated to the liquidator or administrator on the making of a winding-up or administration order.

## 1.11   Can there be more than one Administrative Receiver in Office Simultaneously?

Other than in the case of joint appointments, the possibility of concurrent administrative receiver appointments has yet to be dealt with specifically by the courts. The area remains of significant practical importance for two principal reasons. First, it raises the question whether debenture-holders must engage in a race to effect an appointment where each holds the requisite security for s29(2) purposes. (That matter is considered further in Chapter 5 at 5.2, which considers priority rights of appointment.) Secondly, if there may only be one office-holder at any one time, then the question of appointment becomes of fundamental importance in terms of obtaining control of the management and realisation of the charged assets and, in particular, the use of s43 as considered further in Chapter 8 at 8.5. It is also fair to say that the appointee will not be unduly restrained in terms of the duties imposed on him to subsequent encumbrances (see *Downsview Nominees v First City Corp* [1993] AC 295 and Chapter 9 at 9.2).

The Act contains no provision regarding contemporaneous appointments, and the language of s29(2) does little to solve the problem other than by implication. In practical terms, however, concurrent appointments would give rise to significant difficulties and the almost insurmountable problems of how the courts might go about reconciling primary duties owed by two (or more) appointees to their appointors in dealing with the same assets. Apart from the perhaps exceptional case where appointees are prepared to operate harmoniously and exercise their powers consistently and with reference to each other, the real possibility is that contemporaneous appointments would bring about calamitous results for the company and its creditors, and most probably its secured creditors also. From a pragmatic view, therefore, the possibility of concurrent appointments has many disadvantages. Certainly it would do little to further the scheme of the Act and the special protection afforded to the secured creditor which falls within s29(2) in terms of its power to veto and avoid administration appointments, in limiting the jurisdiction for removal of the administrative receiver to the court and in view of the statutorily based powers conferred on the office-holder.

Practicalities apart, the wording in s29(2), as considered previously in this chapter, appears to suggest the viability of contemporaneous appointments. This is because s29(2) seems to require only an appointment which is effected by or on behalf of any eligible debenture-holder. The implication may be that one appointment precludes another in view of the nature of the s29 office, yet it is curious that the legislation does not spell this out. Indeed, s29(2)(b) might be read as permitting a second or subsequent appointment, although the use of the term 'receiver' as opposed to 'receiver or manager' might be seen as unusual in view of the wording in s29(2)(a). One might argue that an administrative receiver is appointed irrespective of whether appointed as receiver or manager, although this view misses the real point of the word 'or' (as opposed to 'and') in s29(2)(a), in that the terminology employed permits the appointee to act as either in the course of his office. In reality, the use of the term 'receiver' in s29(2)(b) envisages the prior appointment of a non-administrative receiver, which of itself will not affect the appointment of an administrative receiver by virtue of the provision. Nevertheless, there is nothing to prevent an administrative receiver being appointed as 'receiver' only. In practice such appointments are common and do nothing to undermine the s29(2)(a) definition.

One further possibility which exists in justifying the appointment of a second administrative receiver contemporaneously with a first, is that the second appointing debenture-holder may argue that it is secured over substantially the whole of the company's property following a previous appointment to the extent that its security extends to the principal debtor's equity of redemption. This suggestion is also made by Oditah (1991) JBL 49. Following an appointment by a first debenture-holder, both fixed and floating charges in favour of the debenture-holder will operate to assign the charged property in favour of the appointing debenture-holder. Nevertheless, the debt secured by those charges may in reality be small despite its being secured by extensive security. In such a scenario, as in all cases where the value of the security exceeds the debt due, the principal debtor enjoys the equity of redemption (which, in theory, comes into existence at the time the charges are created). Where the debt due to the first debenture-holder is small, the principal debtor's equity of redemption may be so significant as, in monetary value terms, to constitute substantially the whole of the company's property, thereby potentially bringing the second debenture-holder within the s29(2)(a) definition.

In certain circumstances, therefore, it may appear that a second debenture-holder will be able to effect the appointment of an administrative receiver. The problem with this lies in ascertaining whether the principal debtor's equity of redemption (as opposed to its equitable right to redeem) may be viewed as company property over which a debenture may give fixed or (as is more likely) floating charge security for s29(2) purposes. On the basis of a string of judicial decisions, dating as far back as that in *Pawlett v Attorney General* (1667) Hard 465 at 469, the equity of redemption may be viewed as amounting to an equitable interest in property. This suggests that it will fall within the scope of the s436 definition of property which extends to '. . . every description of property wherever situated and also obligations and every description of interest . . .' for the purposes of the IA 1986. The s436 description is wide although not all embracing; see, for example, *Re Rae* unreported, (1994) and see *Welsh Development Agency Ltd v Export Finance Co* [1992] BCC 270 (in the context of s234).

Furthermore, Nourse J in *Re G L Sanders Limited* [1986] BCLC 40 was of the opinion (at 44) that much clearer words would be required before assets subject to a floating charge could be held to include the equity of redemption. That view (which is supported by Marks and Emmett in their article at (1994) JBL 1 at 2) is, it is submitted, the correct one. So serious would be the implications of including the equity of redemption within the scope of company property for the purposes of s29(2) that the terms must be excluded for interpretation purposes, even though a literal construction appears to point to the contrary conclusion.

The better view must be that only one administrative receiver may be appointed at any one time. The practical uncertainty posed by the question of concurrent administrative receiverships could easily be alleviated by further guidance in the Act which is notable by its absence. Furthermore, if the 'one appointment only' conclusion fielded above is correct, this brings to the fore the very significant question of who may appoint an administrative receiver where two or more eligible debenture-holders wait in the wings. Again, the Act is silent on this point, which is considered further in Chapter 5 at para 5.2.

# Chapter Two

# The Commercial Nature of Administrative Receivership

## 2.1 Causes of Administrative Receivership

Lawyers, certainly as a general rule, are little concerned with the reasons why companies go into administrative receivership other than perhaps in the most cursory way. The domain of lawyers is usually the distribution of the assets of the failed company and disputes relating to those assets. Corporate failure is afforded equally sparse treatment by economists, other than perhaps in the compilation of empirical evidence as to the justification or otherwise of various economic theories. These theories invariably follow and reflect corporate failure. Financiers, and specifically accountants, are perhaps those most concerned in practice with the diagnostics of why corporate bodies should fail financially, yet they have little input in any real sense in the legal process embodied in insolvency law. This, it is suggested, is why English law fails to achieve its stated objectives in the insolvency field of rescue and rehabilitation. It is also why, as a general rule, once a company has become subject to one or other of the formal insolvency procedures prescribed by the legislation, its longterm survival as a corporate entity remains an exception to the norm. For a refreshing and incisive development of some of these views see Campbell and Underdown, *Corporate Insolvency In Practice*: *An Analytical Approach*; 1st edn (PCP 1991), pp 17–72.

It is difficult and in fact misleading to attempt to summarise the factors which most commonly give rise to administrative receivership. Whilst predictions may be made as to the probability of the future success of a company on the basis either of performance indicators or an analysis of the company's management and its strategic planning, this does little to advance accurate predictions as to why the company may ultimately fail. In reality, a combination of factors will inevitably accompany the financial demise of a company. In their book *Sharpbenders & The Secrets of Unleasing Corporate Potential* 1st edn (Basil Blackwell 1988) Gringer, Mayes and McKiernan identified a significant number of companies in a sample, all of which had suffered financial demise. The companies identified had all experienced adverse economic factors such as high cost structure, poor management, inadequate financial control and involvement in projects the relative financial size of which had brought down the company identified (usually through poor design, planning and control). See also Argenti, *Corporate Collapse*, (McGraw-Hill, 1976) for models of the three types of corporate enterprises most prone to failure and Slatter, *Corporate Recovery*, (Penguin, 1984) for an identification of the typical ways in which acquisition by a corporate body may bring about the financial demise of the acquirer.

Whilst the primary causes of corporate failure ultimately remain a matter of conjecture and particular circumstance, it has to be said that the serious published research works on the area do point to a pattern of indicators which appears to be symptomatic of business failure. Put very briefly, these main causes of failure may be summarised as:

- poor management (eg over-domineering executives and/or inadequately expert managers);
- inadequate control by management (eg poor planning and/or inadequate financial control);
- economic environmental changes (eg volatile interest rate increases— particularly relevant to highly geared companies—and/or product competition); and
- operational imbalances (eg over-expansion, high gearing and/or inadequate financial planning/ resources).

The recent record number of appointments of (administrative) receivers has come about during and following the most severe financial recession in the United Kingdom in decades, a period which also saw unprecedented variations in interest rates which ultimately culminated in the United Kingdom's exit from the ERM. Indeed, interest rate fluctuations should not be underestimated as a primary cause of administrative receivership. Following significant rises in 1990, for example, the number of receiverships in the second half of that year almost equalled the entire number of appointments made in the previous year. Administrative receivership is therefore of significant importance to corporate trends in the United Kingdom, indeed of increasing relevance in recent years when one considers that in the period 1970–74 the London clearing banks appointed on average approximately only 150 receivers per annum.

In legal terms, the right of a debenture-holder to appoint an administrative receiver will arise on the happening of any of the events set out in the debenture. The debenture-holder need not, of course, effect an appointment on the happening of an appointing event, although self-interest and at least short-term commercial views will usually give rise to an appointment being made. One alternative or addition to the inclusion of a list of appointing events is a provision in a debenture enabling the debenture-holder to effect an appointment simply by giving notice of it to the company. This type of provision in the debenture clearly operates very strongly in favour of the debenture-holder, who may therefore make the appointment without any default on the part of the company. The law offers considerable support to the debenture-holder in this regard, as it has been expressly held that a debenture-holder owes no duty of care to the company or its creditors in effecting an appointment of an administrative receiver. See *Re Potters Oil Ltd (No 2)* [1986] 1 WLR 201 at 206 and *Shamji v Johnson Matthey Bankers Ltd* [1986] BCLC 248 at 278 per Hoffman J.

Recently there has been considerable criticism of the lending institutions for engaging in the practice of appointing administrative receivers over the assets of apparently unsuspecting companies, usually following a report by an investigating accountant appointed by the lender for reasons not always commercially clear to (or even disputed by) the board of the company under investigation. The abuse of this process remains a matter for the institutions concerned, whose views have traditionally accorded with what they apparently consider to be enlightened self-interest. For practical and legal purposes, however, a check should always be made by an adviser in all cases to ensure that the right to appoint an administrative receiver has arisen in accordance with the specific terms of the debenture. If it has not, then the appointment may be challenged and injunctive relief sought on an *ex-parte* basis to restrain it.

## 2.2   The Investigating Accountant and the Investigation Report

Where a company experiences financial difficulties, these will usually become apparent first to the company's bankers who, in practice, are most commonly the party holding the requisite security over the assets of the company to effect the appointment of an administrative receiver. It is common in such circumstances for the bank, or less commonly another creditor, perhaps jointly with the bank, to appoint an investigating accountant to undertake a review of the company's business and overall financial position for any of a number of reasons. These might include a review of the valuation of the company's assets for the purpose of reviewing the banks security; indeed, it is common for standard-form bank debentures to include a covenant allowing the bank, or any person appointed by it in writing, full access to the company's charged property at all reasonable times (ie without notice) for survey, inspection or valuation purposes. Alternatively, the review may provide a starting point for negotiations with the company in reviewing its credit facilities. Most commonly, however, the review will ultimately take the form of a viability report, which will provide the bank with sufficient information to form a view as to whether or not an (administrative) receiver should be appointed. In practice, the effect of an investigating accountant's report in the form of a viability report is usually to confirm a view which is already actually held by the bank.

A bank will usually appoint an investigating accountant when, in broad terms, it detects financial problems within the company. These problems may be either perceived or real and, as such, may take the form of cash flow difficulties, persistent exceeding of agreed overdraft facilities, financial results which are adversely out of line with company projections, an insolvent or potentially insolvent balance sheet or even pleas for assistance from the company's board itself; see the comments in *Huxford v Stoy Hayward & Co* [1989] 5 BCC 421 for the responsibilities of the investigation.

There are two practical factors of which the company and its auditors should be aware on the appointment of an investigating accountant. The first is that in virtually all cases the investigating accountant will be appointed administrative receiver of the company subsequently, if an appointment is recommended as a conclusion of the accountant's investigation, assuming of course that the bank holds sufficient security to effect the appointment of an administrative receiver. Where such security is not held, the taking of it will usually be a recommendation of the investigating accountant and will commonly form part of any subsequent reappraisal of the company's facilities with the bank. The second practical factor which comes into play on the appointment of an investigating accountant is that the control of the company's account with a bank is usually moved to a national or regional centre dealing with insolvency and potential insolvency matters. In practice, this fact is not always communicated to the company as early as it might be. The company should not, therefore, anticipate as a matter of course a continuation of what may well have been hitherto an intimate and flexible banking relationship with its local bank branch.

### 2.2.1  Costs of the investigation

It is imperative that the company and its advisers ascertain at the earliest moment who will bear what may well be the considerable costs of the investigation. In practice, the costs an of investigation are invariably and ultimately borne by the company itself, although there is no good reason why a contractual arrangement should not be reached to the contrary, particularly (a) where the company is openly opposed to the investigation, or (b) where the bank perceives its own heavy reliance on the co-operation of the company in making the investigation worthwhile or useful. A note of caution should, however, be sounded for any company which is unreasonably hostile to an investigation in that a bank may simply rely on its security in appointing an administrative receiver if it sees the company's attitude as such as to impede any viable on-going bank/customer relationship.

Where the company itself is to meet the costs of the investigation, as is usual, the level of the fees involved should be clarified from the outset so far as is possible, as should also the scope and nature of the investigation. In practice, matters such as these are often ignored, or left vague or ill-defined. A check should also be made that a provision for payment of the costs and expenses of an investigation is actually provided for in the debenture in favour of the bank. In practice, such a provision is and would be rare. A company will virtually always prefer to make stage payments rather than lump sum payment where it is to bear the costs of an investigation, if only for obvious cash flow reasons. Accordingly, agreed dates and amounts of stage payments should be agreed with the bank, and express authority for the payments to be debited from the company's account given to the bank. Again, it is common for a bank simply to deduct the costs of an investigation from a company's current account without prior notice. This practice hardly represents best practice on the part of the bank. Discussions at an early stage between the bank, the company and its advisers might seek to avoid the financial distress and commercial bad feeling which such a course of action by the bank will inevitably bring.

## 2.2.2 Objectives of the investigation

The basis and objectives of the investigation instigated by the bank will usually be set out in a broadly standard-form letter of instruction to the investigating accountant from the bank. Indeed, the letter of instruction usually forms the basis of the contract between the bank and the investigating accountant. The bank's review may take the form of a full review of the whole of the company's operations and position (including, for example, past performance and forecasts). Alternatively, it may be a review concentrating on a particular aspect or aspects of the company's operation and/or position in relation to which the bank perceives it requires further up-to-date information on which to review its position and consider recommendations. Full reviews have tended to be less common in recent years, not least in view of the vastly reduced cost and time in drawing up focused reviews and the avoidance of a needlessly detailed analysis in the form of a bulky document which, for the most part, may well be irrelevant. The move towards focused reports does, however, require the bank to be more specific in terms of the instructions given to the investigating accountant and the areas of the company's operations and position to which he is to focus his attention. To some extent, this has also led to a move away from the standard-form letters of instruction on the part of the banks, although this is by no means the norm. Where an investigating accountant is of the view that a letter of instruction fails to anticipate a need to review a particular aspect of the company's business, then this should be communicated to the bank at the earliest possible time, preferably in writing. Anomalies which exist between the letter of instruction and any antecedent verbal discussions between the bank and the accountant should also be clarified at an early stage. In the final analysis, however, the onus rests on the bank to issue clear terms of engagement to the investigating accountant in its letter of instruction, and to ensure that these terms encompass all of those key aspects of the company's operations and position into which an investigation is required and in respect of which conclusions and recommendations are sought by the bank.

In some cases, particularly involving medium-sized and large companies or a group of companies, it may not be realistic for a bank to issue clear instructions in terms of the aspects on which an investigation should focus, without some initial investigation work being undertaken on a preliminary basis prior to a full review of the company's operations and financial position being undertaken. Therefore any initial investigatory work, and the basis and arrangement for its carrying out and discharge, should ideally be agreed between the company, the bank and the investigating accountant before any investigatory work is undertaken. After the initial investigation, an initial report may be made to the bank. Following this formal instructions are then usually issued to the investigating accountant, except where the bank perceives no benefit in undertaking a further investigation. Again, as in all cases, it is imperative that the accountant takes up with the bank, preferably in writing, any aspect of the investigation which he considers unclear or deficient in scope; otherwise he risks subsequent criticism where it transpires that the investigation failed to address some key aspect of the company's or group's activities. This is of particular relevance where the bank has agreed with the company to limit the scope of the investigation in return for a reduced fee and/or where the investigating accountant feels that his terms of engagement, as set out in the letter of instruction, do not offer sufficient scope for his conclusions and recommendations to meet the expectations which he believes the bank has of his investigation.

The conduct of the accountant's investigation will depend on the scope of the bank's instructions to the accountant. Two matters warrant consideration from the outset of the investigation. First, the level of co-operation which may be expected from and the general attitude of the company's board. Secondly and following from this, the question of whether the company's board will be provided with a copy of the investigating accountant's report.

### 2.2.3   The company's perspective

From the point of view of the company, the board members should bear in mind that it is likely that the investigating accountant will also be the administrative receiver subsequently appointed if the bank chooses to effect such an appointment following the completion of the investigation. The board should, therefore, be aware that a lack of co-operation on their part with the investigating accountant is unlikely to be anything other than prejudicial in terms of practical inconvenience and expense in the longer term. In short, the administrative receiver may avail himself of the statutory powers conferred in IA 1986 ss234–6 (as discussed in Chapter 8) although short term co-operation may avoid such steps being taken.

It is usual in practice for a company to be provided with a copy of the investigating accountant's report, or at least the bulk of it. The report is actually made for the benefit of the bank (and not for the company), although it is usually deemed appropriate to permit the company sight of the report and invite comments on it before reporting formally to the bank. In all cases, however, it is commonly considered appropriate, if not merely polite, to omit comments from the report provided to the company which relate specifically to the management of the company. It is also common for comments relating to the adequacy of the bank's security to be omitted from the report provided to the company, primarily because this may be a matter on which the bank subsequently wants to negotiate with the company, usually as a pre-condition of continuing or extended facilities.

The question of whether an investigating accountant chooses to incorporate the comments or views of the company's board largely depends on the approach which the accountant chooses to adopt. Some investigating accountants choose to report to their appointing bank wholly independently of the board and any views aired by it; others, on the other hand, will actively seek the input of the board. It is worth noting from the outset that a collaborative approach to the board, together with an indication that any feedback provided is likely to be communicated via the accountant's report to the bank, is more likely than not to elicit a positive and co-operative response from the board generally, usually once it has been established that the investigation itself is not an optional matter. In addition, as may be pointed out to the board (usually in the most diplomatic of terms), the co-operation of the board is likely to give an indication of the company's attitude to finding common ground in pursuing a positive and constructive way forward for the company in financial terms. On a note of caution, the investigating accountant should take care to ensure that comments and views aired by the company's board do, in fact, appear in the report to the bank where this has been stated to the board as being the case. This is of particular relevance where the bank requires an interim report, often on short notice, or where an indication is sought by the bank on an informal basis at an interim stage without notice. One other practical advantage to the investigating accountant seeking the input of the company's board is that both obvious and less obvious material and factual errors may be corrected, occasionally thereby avoiding evasive action on the part of the bank on the basis of mistakes of fact as they appear in the report.

### 2.2.4  Potential liability for the report

Finally, the reporting accountant should be mindful of those parties who may rely on the contents of his report. Recent decisions of the courts have suggested that it may be difficult for a third party to establish negligence against the auditors of a company for financial misstatements of fact, even, it would appear, if the auditors are specifically asked to prepare a special report for a third party for a particular purpose. See *Caparo Industries v Dickman* [1990] 2 WLR 358, *JEB Fasteners Ltd v Marks, Bloom & Co* [1983] 1 All ER 583, *Al Saudi Banque v Clarke Pixley* [1990] 2 WLR 344 and cf *Scott Group Ltd v McFarlane* [1978] 1 NZLR 553 (New Zealand Court of Appeal) and *Twomax Ltd v Dickson, McFarlane & Robinson* (1982) SC 113. However, these decisions do not safeguard against the possibility that a reporting accountant, in a situation very similar and analogous to that of an auditor, may be aware or ought to be aware that any third party to whom his report is provided will or may rely on the contents of the report. The report should therefore clearly state the basis and purpose for which it is made and that reliance should not be placed on its contents for any other purpose. The reporting accountant may also consider it prudent to request in advance from the bank a list of parties to whom the report will be provided and to consider writing to those parties stating that reliance should not be placed on the report.

## 2.3  The Function of Administrative Receivership

The primary function of the administrative receivership is best described as having a dual nature:

(a)  the realisation of the assets comprised in the security given for the loan or indebtedness of the company which created the security. This security may actually extend to assets other than those of the company itself, such as assets of a subsidiary company or those of other members of a group of companies by way of a so-called 'cross-collateralisation' agreement. This assumes, however, that the company creating the security has power and/or agreement to create such security over those assets;

(b)  the application of the net proceeds of realisation in discharging the secured loan or indebtedness of the company after meeting the costs, expenses and remuneration of the administrative receiver.

This dual function is of a primary nature. The exercise of the administrative receiver's powers (as implied into the debenture by Sched 1 to IA 1986, except to the extent that they are varied) will necessarily also involve the office-holder in subsidiary functions such as the insuring of the company's assets, management of the company's business, the negotiation of contracts, the dismissal of staff, initiation of legal actions and the like. The administrative receiver is not, therefore, engaged in agreeing claims of unsecured creditors or in mounting investigations into the company's affairs, although the office-holder wields considerable powers to do this, essentially for the purposes of discharging his primary function, under ss234–6 with orders being provided for by s237.

Duties are imposed on the office-holder in the conduct of the administrative receivership both by common law and statute. These duties are multi-faceted in that they are owed by the office-holder to (a) the appointing debenture-holder, (b) the company (as its agent until liquidation), (c) unsecured creditors (in terms of reporting obligations), (d) subsequent mortgagees and preferential creditors in discharging liabilities to them.

The primary and overriding duty of the administrative receiver, however, remains to the appointing debenture-holder throughout (*Gomba Holdings UK Ltd v Homan* [1986] 1 WLR 1301 at 1306, per Hoffman J). This accords with the fact that a mortgagee has an inherent right to give priority to his own interests, provided he acts in good faith, notwithstanding the conflict of interests which must inevitably arise on the appointment of a receiver (*Cuckmere Brick Co Ltd v Mutual Finance Ltd* [1971] Ch 949). This primary responsibility to protect the interests of the debenture-holder continues throughout the administrative receivership, despite the office-holder's agency relationship with the company which subsists until the onset of liquidation. It is also this relationship which distinguishes administrative receivership from administration, where the office-holder will act in the interests of the company and creditors generally.

The discharge of the administrative receiver's primary function inevitably affects the longer term viability of the company. If, during or following the administrative receivership, the company's assets are such that they are exceeded by the liabilities of the company, including those of a contingent or prospective nature, or the company is unable to pay its debts as they fall due, then the company is liable to be wound up by the court following the presentation of a petition by an eligible party on the ground that it is unable to pay its debts (ss122(f), 123(1),(2) and 124). Alternatively, the company may opt for voluntary liquidation under s98 or apply to the court for a winding-up order where, for example, the company's assets are such that no eligible person is willing to take on the office of liquidator. A voluntary winding-up is likely to be more effective in terms of time and expense and may also guard the directors against personal liability for wrongful trading to the extent that the immediate liquidation constitutes 'every step' in attempting to minimise losses to creditors (see s214(3)).

An application may, of course, have been made for a compulsory liquidation of the company by the administrative receiver himself or by the company. Alternatively the company may have opted for voluntary liquidation. It appears from the decision in *Re Television Parlour plc* [1988] 4 BCC 95 at 98 that the court will be prepared to accept a winding-up petition which is presented by the administrative receiver as the company's agent in its name, pursuant to the express powers to present or defend a winding-up petition conferred by Sched 1, para 21. (See also *Re Emmadart Ltd* [1979] Ch 540 which also applies to non-administrative receivers). Whilst no express provision permits an application for a winding-up order by an administrative receiver in his own right, an application by an administrator is envisaged by IR r4.7(7)(a).

Even if a company is rendered insolvent following the conduct of the administrative receivership, this does not necessitate the discontinuance of the company's business. This is because the administrative receiver, acting in his capacity as manager of the company's business, may be able to salvage all or part of the company's business or undertaking by way of a hive-down operation. Hiving-down involves the sale of the viable parts of the company's business as a going concern, usually to an (initially) wholly-owned subsidiary. This process is invariably undertaken without an assignment or discharge of outstanding debts and liabilities which remain with the company in administrative receivership. In practice, this will typically arise where a company is put into administrative receivership on account of, say, cash flow problems which gave rise to default on debenture-secured payments, notwithstanding the fact that the company retains a strong order book and significant customer goodwill.

A hive-down operation may be employed following a 'tactical' receivership, where the administrative receiver is appointed on the invitation of the company's board with a view to effecting a tactical restructuring or work-out of the company's operations; but it may also be an alternative to what is viewed as unavoidable liquidation. The same operation may also be an effective way of achieving a de-merger of operations, particularly where the only alternative appears to be litigation between antagonised board members. This may also avoid the costly and notoriously messy process, in both legal and commercial terms, of litigation under the Companies Act 1985, s459 or, as is less likely, under IA 1986, s122(1)(g) or one of the exceptions to the rule in *Foss v Harbottle* (1843) 2 Hare 461.

Theory apart, it is rare in practice for a company to emerge from administrative receivership with its assets and business wholly intact. Indeed, the contrary is the experience of recent practice in the United Kingdom. Despite the strictly legalistic approach to receivership as a method of debt enforcement, a receiver should been seen less as a doctor but more as an undertaker. However, the possibility of curative action should not be ignored. On the conclusion of a successful administrative receivership, the general powers of management of the company and its business (other than those of a residual nature or those which relate to assets outside of the administrative receivership which remain with the directors) are returned to the directors of the company following the suspension for that period (*Moss Steamship Ltd v Whinney* [1912] AC 254 at 263 per Lord Atkinson). Administrative receiverships which prove successful in this sense necessarily depend on a number of practical factors. These will usually include:

- the ongoing co-operation of the company's directors and employees;
- speedy action by the administrative receiver on the basis of a realistic, clear and well publicised strategy;
- the establishment and maintenance of confidence with suppliers, customers, employees and, perhaps most importantly, trade and institutional creditors;
- the co-operation of any prior ranking chargees or the tactical use of s43 proceedings;
- and close liaison and co-operation between the administrative receiver, his assistants and legal advisers.

## 2.4 The Impact of Administrative Receivership on the Company

In legal terms, the appointment of an administrative receiver will have an impact on the company somewhere between that of liquidation and administration. In the former case, the directors will be discharged from office, although they continue to retain their statutory duties, such as that to co-operate with the office-holder under s235. In an administration, the directors—in their capacity as fiduciaries as opposed to as executives of the company under any contract of service—are not discharged from office, although the continued exercise of their powers will be subject to agreement with the administrator, and this may be general or specific (see s14(4)). In administrative receivership, the directors remain in office but are effectively divested of their powers. The basis of this suspension of powers is contractual, in that the debenture pursuant to which the administrative receiver is appointed will vest wide powers in the office-holder which may enhance or, less commonly, restrict those powers implied into the contract by Sched 1 (s42(1)). These powers are, however, confined to the relevant charged assets which will, by definition, amount to the whole or substantially the whole of the company's property (ss42(2)(b) and 29(2)).

49

### 2.4.1 The position vis-à-vis the directors

In administrative receivership the directors will retain certain residual powers, and consequently duties and liabilities, which fall outside the scope of the administrative receiver's function in relation to the company. The residual function of the directors, however, is exactly that. There are a number of clear *dicta* to the effect that the commercial purpose of the power conferred on a debenture-holder to appoint a receiver and manager is to undertake the realisation and management of the company's property without interference from the board (*Gomba Holdings Ltd v Homan* [1986] 1 WLR 1301 at 1306 per Hoffman J; see also *Meigh v Wickenden* [1942] 2 KB 160 and *Macleod v Alexander Sutherland* 1977 SLT 44). In practical terms, therefore, the directors' residual powers should be seen as being very much of a subsidiary nature rather than co-existing with those of the administrative receiver. Perhaps the most important residual power of the directors is the power to deal with assets, including choses in action such as rights of action, which either fall outside the scope of the administrative receivership or which it is clear that the office-holder either wishes to ignore or does not wish to pursue (*Newhart Developments Ltd v Co-operative Commercial Bank* [1978] 2 All ER 896). Notably, the administrative receiver may be able to take steps to attack the proceeds of any judgment for the benefit of the debenture-holder by whom he is appointed (*ibid*, per Shaw LJ at 901).

The *Newhart* decision is authority for the premise that the company may bring an action against a debenture-holder for the improper exercise of his powers. The facts of the case concerned the plaintiff company and defendant bank, which were engaged in a property development as a joint venture. The bank provided finance for the project and took security over the company's assets. Subsequently when the project ran into financial difficulties the bank appointed a receiver over the company's assets. The board of the company took the view that the bank was in breach of its contract with the company in relation to the joint venture and, whilst not disputing the appointment of the receiver, issued a writ against the bank in the name of the company. The receiver sought to have the writ set aside on the basis that it was issued without his consent. The receiver was unsuccessful in setting aside the writ and the action by the company proceeded to trial. The Court of Appeal held that the appointment of a receiver did not prevent the board from exercising its powers provided that the acts of the directors in so doing did not threaten or jeopardise the assets subject to the receivership.

The decision in *Newhart* has recently been doubted in *Tudor Grange Holdings Ltd v Citibank NA* [1992] Ch 53 where Browne-Wilkinson V-C took the view that a more appropriate course of action would be an application for directions by either the administrative receiver or the debenture-holder, under s35. Notably, in the *Newhart* case the company was indemnified for any costs which it might incur in proceeding against the receiver, and it is this factor which, it is submitted, will be crucial in any future decisions on this area. Indeed, the absence of an indemnity for costs was the basis on which the *Newhart* decision was distinguished in the *Tudor Grange* case.

Some commentators have sought to justify the *Newhart* decision on the basis that a right of action against the debenture-holder may constitute an asset of the company which falls outside the scope of the administrative receivership and which, therefore, is subject to the residual powers of the directors. This is a difficult line to sustain when one considers that the debenture-holder's security must necessarily comprise at the very least a 'global' or general floating charge for the purposes of s29(2). It follows that the floating charge will catch a chose in action such a right of action if it is not actually caught by one or more of the fixed charges also comprising the debenture-holder's security as in the *Newhart* decision. On the other hand, this is not to say that the directors maintain an inalienable right of action against the appointing debenture-holder and/or the receiver in administrative receivership. It is submitted that the right of action will be subject to its not prejudicing the assets subject to the debenture-holder's security. In practice, this will necessitate an undertaking from the directors in respect of the costs of the action and any liability incurred by the company in the event of a hostile costs order being made. Such an undertaking was present in the *Newhart* case and was absent in the *Tudor Grange* case, where the directors' action was struck out. The maintaining of a right of action by the directors in this way will do nothing to undermine the recognised function of the administrative receivership if the secured assets are in no way prejudiced by the litigation. One side effect of this, however, may be that, where the debenture-holder itself is pursued successfully as a defendant by the directors on behalf of the company, the secured debt may be discharged in whole or in part by payment over by the debenture-holder itself to the company. In conclusion, the suggestion that the appointment of an administrative receiver divests the directors of any right of action without the consent of the administrative receiver is entirely rejected. To date, no authority exists to that effect and it is difficult to conceive how such a conclusion could be reached in any case.

In practice, it is imperative that the directors ascertain the administrative receiver's position as regards any specific tangible or intangible asset on pain of potential liability for trespass for wrongly interfering with it. To this extent, the *Newhart* decision is concurred with by the later decision in *Watts v Midland Bank* [1986] BCLC 15 which permitted an action against the receiver himself. *Watts* illustrates that the power to use the company's corporate name in litigation by the directors will preclude a derivative action by a minority shareholder against an administrative receiver (and see also *Shanks v Central Regional Council* 1988 SLT 212 which followed a number of Scottish *dicta* on this point). It remains clear from a number of Commonwealth authorities that action may be taken by the directors to challenge the administrative receiver's appointment. See *Hawkesbury Development Co Ltd v Landmark Finance Pty Ltd* [1969] 92 WN (NSW) 199, and *Paramount Acceptance Co Ltd v Souster* [1981] 2 NZLR 38 which permitted a challenge by the directors as to the validity of the debenture itself.

With the onset of administrative receivership, the directors still retain a power (or rather a duty) to maintain the company's statutory books, prepare annual accounts and file statutory returns. To this end they may require from the office-holder such papers, information and accounts as are necessary to enable them to make these returns, including the amount necessary for the discharge of the debenture (*Gomba Holdings UK Ltd v Homan* [1986] 1 WLR 1301). In *Gomba* Hoffman J was of the view that equity imposes on a receiver a duty to a company which is broader in scope than the statutory obligation imposed on him (at 1305–6, see also *Re Geneva Finance Ltd* [1990] 10 ACLC 688, a decision of the Australian High Court). The provision by the office-holder of information relating to unrealised assets may be of immense practical use where the directors propose to arrange new finance for the company which will apparently fall within their residual powers as directors (*Smiths Ltd v Middleton* [1979] 2 All ER 842).

Failure by the administrative receiver to furnish information reasonably requested of him will render him potentially liable in misfeasance proceedings under s212. Alternatively, the company may sue the administrative receiver for breach of duty on the basis of *Watts v Midland Bank plc* [1986] 1 BCLC 15. However, in the *Gomba Holdings* case, Hoffman J recognised that the board must be able to demonstrate a *bona fide* 'need to know' basis for requiring the information. (The request was refused in that case.) Whilst recognising the directors' right to detailed information where the company has an intention and ability to redeem its indebtedness, the learned judge went on to state:

> ...I think that the receiver's duty to provide such information must be subordinated to his primary duty not to do anything which may prejudice the interests of the debenture-holder.

In practice, this would avoid needless and usually costly asset valuation and investigation into the company's assets and trading position at the request of a frivolous or vexatious board.

It has also been held that the directors retain a residual power to oppose a winding-up petition (*Re Reprographic Exports (Euromat) Ltd* 1978 12 SJ 400). However, this power would now appear to be superfluous in view of the administrative receiver's implied power both to present and defend a winding-up petition (see Sched 1, para 21). It would appear that the directors may not oppose a petition where an administrative receiver pro-actively chooses not to defend the petition on the basis of the *Newhart* decision in that the right of action, as with any asset of the company caught by a floating charge and any number of fixed charges, does not fall outside of the scope of the administrative receivership. This point is considered further in Chapter 8 at para 8.11.

As well as the powers retained by the directors in an administrative receivership, there is imposed on them a statutory duty to co-operate with the office-holder under s235 and to comply with requirements made of them by the office-holder for the preparation of a statement of affairs under s47 subject to an express release from the obligation to do so (see IR r3.6). These matters are also considered further in Chapter 8 at paras 8.8 to 8.10.

### 2.4.2  The position vis-à-vis shareholders

The position of the shareholders of a company as such will remain largely unchanged with the onset of administrative receivership. Whilst the right of a shareholder to transfer his or her shares will be unaffected this will remain an unlikely possibility, since few individuals are likely to be willing to wish to purchase the shares of a company in administrative receivership. In theory there is no good reason why the company should not continue to operate normally in terms of its board recommending a dividend on shares which is then subsequently declared by the company in general meeting. In reality, however, this is very unlikely since the assets, being distributable profits, from which such a dividend may be paid will invariably be subject to the property of the company over which the administrative receiver is appointed and, therefore, any distribution will be subject to the approval of the office-holder. In the case of a listed company the shares of the company in administrative receivership must remain freely transferable. This is a condition for listing imposed as a continuing obligation on the company by the Stock Exchange's Listing Rules. However, it is usual that a listed company in administrative receivership will be suspended from listing, invariably at the request of its own directors, prior to or on the appointment of the administrative receiver.

It was held in *Watts v Midland Bank plc* [1986] 1 BCLC 15 that shareholders may not pursue a derivative action as against a receiver and/or debenture-holder where those (majority) shareholders were also the directors of the company or the company would be hopelessly insolvent.

### 2.4.3  The position vis-à-vis employees and subsisting non-employment contracts

As regards contracts of employment, the general rule is that the appointment of an administrative receiver has no effect on contracts *per se* (*Re Mack*

*Trucks (Britain) Ltd* [1967] 1 All ER 947; *Re Foster Clark's Indenture Trust* [1966] 1 All ER 43; *Deaway Trading Ltd v Calverly* [1973] 3 All ER 773). There are, however, three exceptions to this general rule. The first two arise where the administrative receiver either expressly dismisses an employee or, alternatively, closes down the company's business (*Griffiths v Secretary of State for Employment* [1973] 3 All ER 1184). The third exception, which stems from the *Griffiths* decision, is that the administrative receiver's appointment may of itself terminate a contract of employment which is inconsistent with it. Typically, this will extend to a contract of service held by a managing director in view of the broad powers of management assumed by the administrative receiver. It has been suggested the termination would appear to come about as a result of the repudiation of the contract by the company on the appointment of the receiver as its agent. However, it is suggested that this justification for the third exception is too far reaching and that each case will very much depend on its own circumstances. Liability for contracts of employment and methods of dealing with them are considered in Chapter 10 at para 10.6 and in Chapter 13 at para 13.9 respectively.

Administrative receivership is also likely to have a considerable undermining effect on the confidence of employees generally in terms of their own position with the company. If nothing else, the appointment of an administrative receiver signals very clearly and very publicly that all is not well financially with the company. Whether or not the board wishes to take steps to inform the workforce of their individual positions remains a matter for the company's management. However, the position in law is now that an administrative receiver is deemed to adopt contracts of employment 14 days after his appointment although it remains arguable that the liability imposed in this regard by the Insolvency Act 1994 may be contracted out by the administrative receiver. See Chapter 13 at para 13.9. The administrative receiver may choose to circulate details to employees of the company as regards their perceived ongoing position with the company. Of course, in practice, the office-holder may choose simply to implement widespread dismissals if only to avoid adoption of the contracts of employment.

As with contracts of employment, the general rule with other types of contract is that the appointment of an administrative receiver is of no significance *per se*. The reason for this is essentially one of privity. Subsisting contracts are made between the company and third parties. On the appointment of the administrative receiver as receiver and manager of the company's business there is no good reason in law why that contractual relationship between the company and a third party should end, since the main practical effect of the appointment is merely to displace the powers of the directors. The appointment of a receiver may, however, be provided for expressly by the contract (*Barclays Bank v Simms* [1980] 2 WLR 218). This is particularly the case in certain standard form building and engineering contracts.

Alternatively, the administrative receiver may choose to novate the contract thereby incurring personal liability on it. Indeed, this may be necessary if a contract terminates automatically on the appointment of an administrative receiver. Novation must, however, be express and will not be inferred merely by the administrative receiver carrying out the contract (*Parsons v Sovereign Bank of Canada* [1913] AC 160; *Nicoll v Cutts* [1985] BCLC 322). Non-employment contracts are considered further in Chapter 10 at para 10.5.

### 2.4.4 The position vis-à-vis creditors

The appointment of an administrative receiver will cause any floating charge over the company's assets to crystallise (*Re Panama, New Zealand and Australia Royal Mail Co* (1870) 5 Ch App 318). The appointment of a receiver is, in fact, the most common method of crystallising a floating charge. There is no good reason why the parties should not contract out of the appointment of a receiver as a crystallising event in respect of any floating charge held by a secured creditor although, in practice, this would be most unusual and would almost certainly only apply to the parties to that agreement. One technique employed in some modern standard-form debentures is to provide expressly for crystallisation only to occur on the service of an appropriate notice by the creditor to the company (so-called 'semi-automatic crystallisation'). Such a notice, in legal terms at least, would appear superfluous, however, in certain instances, eg on any other event stipulated in the charge document, on the winding-up of the company or on the appointment of a receiver, which provide for automatic crystallisation of the floating charge in any case.

The appointment of an administrative receiver will also prevent the making of an administration order in relation to the company. This point was considered earlier in the comparison between administrative and non-administrative receivers in Chapter 1. Following the appointment of an administrative receiver the presentation of a petition for an administration order will have no moratory effect on the company unless the person by whom or on whose behalf the administrative receiver was appointed consents to the administration order (s10(3)). In practice, it will be an exception to the general rule for a debenture-holder to acquiesce in the appointment of an administrator for reasons set out in the final section of this chapter (2.5 below), which compares the inter-relationship between administrative receivership, administration, and liquidation and company voluntary arrangements (CVAs).

Some early research produced data which seemingly represented administration as a very viable alternative to administrative receivership: see Homan, *A Survey of Administrations under the Insolvency Act 1986: The Result of Administration Orders made in 1987*, a report by Price Waterhouse for the Research Board of the Institute of Chartered Accountants in England and Wales (1989). The Homan Report suggested, at para 2.05, that out of the 129 administration orders made in 1987, holders of floating charges had refrained from appointing administrative receivers in some 40 per cent of cases. It should be remembered, however, that a large number of administration order petitions are never actually presented on account of the relative speed of the debenture-holder in appointing an administrative receiver or the widely-publicised unwillingness of the debenture-holder to even entertain a petition for an administration order. In reality, a debenture-holder will need very good commercial reasons, as well as a great degree of confidence, for effectively surrendering a significant element of the security offered by the debenture in favour of an administration order. Indeed, more recent research suggests that the widespread adoption of so-called 'lightweight floating charges' (ie a floating charge which prohibits the creation of charges ranking prior to or *pari passu* with its and the associated power to appoint an administrative receiver with all the office-holder's attendant statutory powers) are specifically taken as security for the specific avoidance of administration orders (see *Corporate Recovery: The Immediate Impact of the Administration Scheme, A Report by City University Department of Law*, April 1988 at 8). This finding, it is submitted, is somewhat closer to the reality of the relationship between administration and administrative receivership than is suggested above.

### 2.4.5 The position vis-à-vis the company's trading position

From a practical commercial perspective, the impact of administrative receivership is likely to be very significant. The appointment is a very public matter in the sense that every invoice, order for goods or business letter issued by or on behalf of the company of the administrative receiver (or liquidator of the company), being a document on which the company's name appears such as a delivery note, must contain a statement that an administrative receiver has been appointed (ie 'in administrative receivership' or 'administrative receiver appointed') on pain of criminal sanction for default (ss390 (1), (2), 430). It is difficult to generalise as to the effect on a company vis-à-vis its creditors and trade suppliers of an administrative receiver being appointed, since the reality very much depends on the circumstances in which the appointment is made. At one extreme, the appointment may be made at the request of the company as an efficient method of effecting a restructuring, hive-down or de-merger of the company's business activities. This should not be problematic if creditors and suppliers are appraised of the position, are agreeable and the operation is effected speedily. At the other extreme, the appointment may be forced on an unco-operative and protesting board or, worse still, a board which is wholly unsuspecting of the appointment until it is made. Appointments made in such circumstances are notorious for their alienating effect, not only on the board but also on employees, suppliers and customers, not to mention other creditors. In such cases it is not uncommon for statements to be made, particularly in the press, media and workplace, not altogether sympa-thetically, to the effect that 'the receivers have been called in'. The obvious danger with such a statement is the implication that the receivership has been opted for by the company at its own volition rather than, as is normally the case, the appointment being a matter in which the company has no say. Thus, it may be of considerable importance that the fact that the onset of the receivership does not emanate from the company directly is made widely known. This is particularly relevant to employees and unsecured creditors, to whom the receivership is likely to cause considerable concern and whose assistance will be vital for any rescue plan. How a suitable statement, if indeed any, in this regard is circulated is clearly a matter for individual approach. Nonetheless, the dangers of rumour and apparent acquiescence on the company's part should not be underestimated.

In practice, confidence usually will only be maintained in an administra-tive receivership if a realistic plan can be formulated and implemented for the continued trading of the company's business in a relatively short period of, literally, days or even weeks. Failure to achieve this, and to secure the neces-sary finance to underpin the plan, will inevitably lead to liquidation, not least because the office-holder will be loath to continue trading and incur further expense from the company's assets to the detriment of both preferential credi-tors and the floating-charge holder. Most appointments will inevitably fall between these two extremes. An exacting commercial view will have to be taken at an early stage if it is to remain viable so as to permit the company's business to trade for a sufficient period to enable either its sale as a going concern or even its recovery in whole, or more likely, part.

Other alternatives to administrative receivership do exist, although the first two of these may usually be discounted at an early stage. Company voluntary arrangements (CVAs) are generally felt to be unworkable on account of their troublesome nature in practice and their lack of any moratorium, unlike an interim order in an individual voluntary arrangement. Similarly, liquidation effectively discounts the prospect of any ongoing trading by a liquidator. Administration, on the other hand, is a seemingly attractive alternative for a business looking to survive as a going concern. It remains, however, mutually exclusive with administrative receivership and, as such, warrants careful consideration by both the company and the debenture-holder, either in conjunction or otherwise, at the earliest time.

## 2.5   The Relationship between Administrative Receivership and Other Insolvency Proceedings

### 2.5.1   Company voluntary arrangements

The IA 1986 introduced the company voluntary arrangement (CVA) (in ss1–7 and IR rr1.1–1.30) as a supposedly more effective method of reaching a compromise between a company and its creditors than either the scheme of liquidation and reconstruction under Companies Act 1985 s582, the scheme of compromise or arrangement under Companies Act 1985 ss424–7 or the rarely employed binding arrangement under Companies Act 1985 s601. The basic philosophy of the CVA envisages a binding arrangement between a company and its creditors on the basis of a relatively simple procedure. In practice, CVAs are less commonly utilised than had originally been contemplated, predominantly because they may only be made binding on those secured and preferential creditors who consent to them and because the legislation offers no moratorium during the period in which the proposed arrangement is being drawn up and considered. However, this may be achieved, albeit at greater cost in terms of the time and expense, by coupling the proposed CVA with an administration order. Indeed, an administration order may be sought specifically for that purpose, CVAs being commonly proposed by administrators (see s8(3)(b)).

Where no administration order is in effect, a debenture-holder may avoid the binding effect of a CVA as a secured creditor by withholding consent to it (s4(3)). Section 4(4) affords similar protection to preferential creditors both as regards their right to priority as provided in Sched 6 and their right to rank *pari passu* between themselves. The CVA, therefore, offers no protection to the company against the appointment of an administrative receiver. Likewise, there is no bar to an administrative receivership and CVA operating simultaneously, although this would assume, as is unlikely, that the debenture-holder had consented to the making of the CVA for the purposes of s4(3). Whilst this co-relationship makes for interesting theory, in practice a debenture-holder is more likely to withhold consent to a CVA, if only because of the prejudicial effect which the CVA will necessarily have in practical terms on any administrative receiver appointed.

A co-existing CVA and administrative receivership also poses problems as regards preferential creditors. This is because the preferential creditors for the purpose of the CVA will be determined by the 'relevant date' as defined in s387(2) for the purposes of s4(7), whereas the 'relevant date' in an administrative receivership will be determined by s387(4)(a) for the purposes of s40. On a strict reading of s40(2), however, it would appear that the two separate categories of preferential creditor will be unconnected, assuming that the company is not also in the course of being wound up. Finally, it is worth noting that an administrative receiver has no *locus standi* to propose a CVA (s1).

In *Re Leisure Studies Group Ltd* [1994] 2 BCLC 65 Harman J held that funds held by the supervisor at a CVA were not subject to a floating charge in a subsequent administrative receivership. (The debenture-holder was not entitled to vote on the proposed CVA as a secured creditor.) As agent of the company, the administrative receiver was not able to seek return of monies paid to the CVA supervisor for the benefit of the creditors. Although the CVA funds were held in an account by the CVA supervisor in his own name, these were not held on trust for the creditors bound by the terms of the CVA, which did not include the debenture-holder. The decision may well have been different in the case of a liquidation, since the court did not consider the question of whether the CVA survived the administrative receivership, the matter in issue being whether the CVA funds were held on trust for the CVA creditors only. (See also *Re Bradley-Hole, ex parte Knight* (1994) unreported, on the relationship between the IVA funds and a bankruptcy, and the comments in Frieze (1995) 8 Insolvency Intelligence 30–1.)

## 2.5.2 Administration orders

The appointment of an administrative receiver prevents the making of an administration order by the court in that this will require the consent of the debenture-holder by or on whose behalf the administrative receiver was appointed (s10(1),(3)(a)(b)). The consent of a debenture-holder to the making of an administration order is not common in practice, primarily because any administrative receiver of the company is required to vacate office on the making of an administration order under s11(1) or if his security is found liable to be invalidated under s9(3)(b). A non-administrative receiver, on the other hand, is not required automatically to vacate office although he must do so at the request of the administrator (s11(2)). This is not usually problematic since the enforcement of any security by the non-administrative receiver over the company's property would require the court's leave in any case under s11(3)(c) even, it would appear, if the receiver was a court-appointed receiver over all of the company's assets.

An administrative receiver may not be appointed during the period for which an administration order is in force (s11(3)(b)). Whilst a non-administrative receiver may be appointed during the course of an administration order, again he may not take steps to enforce his appointor's security without leave of and subject to any terms imposed by the court (s11(3)(c)). An attempt might conceivably be made by a debenture-holder to seek leave to appoint and enforce his security pursuant to a fixed charge contained in a debenture without recourse to his floating charge security. Depending on the attitude adopted by the court to such an application it is suggested that such an attempt to enforce will probably be flawed by the general bar in s11(3)(b), since any receiver appointed pursuant to such security may well be deemed, by virtue of the definition in s29(2), to amount to an administrative receiver on the basis that the definition therein is fulfilled. This line of argument should be read in conjunction with the suggestion that an appointment made pursuant to a fixed charge solely will not necessarily amount to appointment of an administrative receiver, notwithstanding the retention of floating charge security by the debenture-holder. On the other hand, a fixed-charge holder might seek leave to appoint a receiver and enforce his security if, for example, his secured asset was in jeopardy or the administrator himself was, say, guilty of undue delay in disposing of some significant asset such as land in a rapidly falling market. On s11(3)(c) generally reference should be made to the judgment of Peter Gibson J in *Re Meesan Investments Ltd* [1988] 4 BCC 788 and the guidelines set out by the Court of Appeal in the landmark decision in *Re Atlantic Computer Systems plc* [1990] BCC 859. On policy grounds alone it is submitted that the court is extremely unlikely to approve the appointment of a receiver and certainly not an administrative receiver during the course of an administration order, in all but perhaps the most very exceptional circumstances. One such case could arise where a fixed charge asset is in real jeopardy of diminution or depreciation in value without the prospect of intervention by the administrator (*Report of the Review Committee of Insolvency Law and Practice* (1982, Cmnd 8558, Chap 9). The same is not always true, of course, of other forms of security such as retention of title claims (see *Re Paramount Airways Ltd* [1990] BCC 130 and *Re Exchange Travel Agency* [1991] BCC 341).

There have been a number of recent cases in which the court has granted administration orders on the basis of an *ex parte* application. This is despite the fact that IR rr2.6 and 2.9 envisage notice of the application being served on the charge-holder. However, it has to be said that the decision in *Re Cavco Floors* [1990] BCC 559 (in which an order was actually made prior to the issue of a petition!), *Re Shearing & Loader Ltd* [1991] BCC 232 and *Re Chancery plc* [1991] BCC 171 have been exceptional, and the orders made have usually been justified by the need for haste in view of the dangers of trading while insolvent. In the *Re Chancery* case there was a very real danger of a banking institution being unable to meet its obligations, the application in that case having the approval of the Bank of England. Similar considerations applied in the administration order made in respect of Barings Bank in February 1995.

Harman J had previously criticised the practice of *ex parte* applications for administration orders in *Re Rowbotham Baxter* [1990] BCC 113 as 'an undesirable practice which should not continue'. Ironically, the same judge entertained the successful application in all three of the above *ex parte* applications. It should be noted, however, that the *Re Cavco* application had the consent of the debenture-holder, and the order made in the *Re Shearing* case was made on the basis of an undertaking to provide evidence exhibiting the consent of the debenture-holder to the order together with a statement that there was no intention to appoint an administrative receiver.

### 2.5.3 Liquidation

A company may also be in liquidation and in administrative receivership simultaneously. The impact of the winding-up is to terminate the administrative receiver's agency relationship with the company (s44(1)(a)). Notwithstanding this, the administrative receiver will retain any power of attorney conferred on him by the debenture as is usually comprised in the creditor's security 'package' (*Sowman v David Samuel Trust Ltd* [1978] 1 WLR 22). The most practical implication of this is that the administrative receiver will be able to execute deeds as the company's attorney even though he will be unable to use the company seal; see Chapter 8 at para 8.2. The effect of the termination of the administrative receiver's agency with the company is that the administrative receiver will no longer be afforded the statutory right of indemnity out of company assets in respect of his personal liability for contracts adopted by him (s44(1)(c)). However, the indemnity will continue to operate in relation to contracts entered into before the commencement of the winding-up (which may, of course, be sought by the administrative receiver himself) since these will have been entered into or adopted with authority for the purpose of s44(3). The significance of the continuation of the administrative receiver's *in rem* powers in a liquidation, as opposed to his purely personal powers, is considered further in Chapter 8 at para 8.3. The question of creditor priority, particularly preferential creditor priority, is also considered in a case of a contemporaneous liquidation and administrative receivership in Chapter 4 at para 4.2.

In reality, a winding-up will usually do little to impede the administrative receiver in the conduct of his function since, until he vacates office, there is little in practical terms for a liquidator to do. The liquidator may, however, require at any time the rendering by the administrative receiver of proper accounts of his receipts and payments, as well as the payment over to him of any surplus property payable to him on sanction of applying to the court for an enforcement order (s41(1)(2)). The administrative receiver is also obliged to furnish the liquidator with a s47 statement of affairs within time limits prescribed in s48(4). In practice, however, it is not uncommon for delays, sometimes very considerable delays, to arise in the drawing up of a statement of affairs. In reality, the administrative receiver may be prepared to pay over funds or release monies to the liquidator before the conclusion of the administrative receivership where it is obvious that these will not be subject to claims or actions by the administrative receiver. This will usually be done on the basis of an undertaking from the liquidator that he will return funds or assets to the administrative receiver at his request on, say, the emergence of undisclosed and subsisting claims or preferential claims. The undertaking will invariably and for obvious reasons be limited to the funds or assets transferred to the liquidator and remaining in his hands at the time of the request. It is also usual for the administrative receiver to require the liquidator to give notice to him of any proposed distribution of funds or assets to creditors. This type of arrangement serves to underline the mutual advantage to the two office-holders of reaching agreement at an early stage as to how they will discharge their functions whilst in office contemporaneously.

A liquidator may take the view that the administrative receiver's appointment is invalid on the basis of information coming into his hands. He may, therefore, choose to apply summarily to the court for the removal of the administrative receiver thereby cutting short the whole receivership process if he is not satisfied with the validity of the administrative receiver's appointment or the manner in which the administrative receiver is discharging his office. This summary application is clearly envisaged by IA 1986 s45(1) and IR r3.33 (as amended). Indeed, it is preferable for an application to be made by the liquidator at the earliest possible time to avoid any further erosion of company assets by the administrative receiver. Following, or more usually, concurrent with a successful application for the removal of an administrative receiver, the liquidator may proceed with an action against the administrative receiver for damages in trespass and/or conversion. Alternatively, it may be that the liquidator and administrative receiver are able to reach some compromise between themselves thereby avoiding the time and expense of an application to the court and the rather public process of obligatory removal from office. It may be the case, for example, that the administrative receiver is prepared to accept that grounds exist which at least call into the question the validity of his appointment albeit that those grounds do not come to light until some time into the administrative receivership, typically following some degree of investigation by the liquidator. (Whether or not the administrative receiver wishes to take a separate action for negligence against the solicitors who advised on the validity of his appointment in such circumstances of course remains a matter for the office-holder.) In those circumstances the administrative receiver may be willing to vacate office voluntarily although the office-holder and his appointor will usually wish to exact some price for agreeing to do so. This might include an agreement with the liquidator whereby the administrative receiver is entitled to retain or recover his expenses, costs and remuneration from assets purportedly subject to the administrative receivership. Whether or not any agreement covers such expenses, costs and remuneration relating only to the time at which the liquidator called into question the validity of the administrative receiver's appointment or goes beyond it remains largely a matter for the liquidator. In addition, the administrative receiver may require an undertaking from the liquidator that the liquidator discharge any preferential liability for which the administrative receiver may be or may become liable (s40(1),(2)).

In practice, it is less common that a post-liquidation receiver appointment is made than one pre-liquidation. The post-liquidation appointment of an administrative receiver is only likely to be of real use where the secured assets appear to be in jeopardy and warrant the appointment of a receiver and manager over them as opposed to their being left to the domain of the liquidator (see, eg *Re Foxhall & Gyle (Nurseries) Ltd* 1978 SLT 29). It is clear from the decision in *Re Potters Oil Ltd (No 2)* [1986] 1 WLR 201 at 206 that a debenture-holder is under no duty to refrain from effecting an appointment 'merely because to do so may cause loss to the company or its unsecured creditors'. The same judge, Hoffman J, delivered a similar judgment in *Shamji v Johnson Matthey Bankers Ltd* [1986] BCLC 248 at 278, where he suggested that an appointment might only be challenged on grounds of bad faith. Evidentially, this may pose an onerous hurdle for a liquidator or the company itself, or even a subsequent encumbrancer, wishing to oppose an administrative receiver's appointment.

The *Re Potters Oil* decision is also noteworthy in that it involved an unsuccessful (and rare) challenge by a liquidator under s36 in respect of the receiver's remuneration. Hoffman J was dismissive of the application and confirmed that s36 has no operation in relation to disbursements. The judge went on to make clear that s36 would only be employed by the court when the receiver's costs were clearly excessive and that the provision was not to be seen as a convenient device for the taxation of those costs. See also *Moodemore Pty Ltd v Waters* [1987] 5 ACLC 790, [1980-90] IJ 312.

## 2.6 Administrative Receivership or Administration?

The administrative receivership and administration regimes are mutually exclusive in the sense that an administrative receiver may not be appointed during the course of an administration order (s11(3)(b)). Conversely, the appointment of an administrative receiver will generally preclude the making of an administration order since this will require the consent of the debenture-holder by virtue of s10(1),(3)(a),(b) which, in practice, will rarely be forthcoming. Administrative receivership is a procedure instigated by a debenture-holder effectively as a method of debt recovery in self-interest (which, for practical purposes, will survive liquidation). Administration, on the one hand, is a mechanism the purpose of which is intended as a means *inter alia* of rehabilitating all or part of the company's undertaking as a going concern, or at least a means of bringing about a more advantageous realisation of the company's assets than would otherwise be achieved on a liquidation (s8(3)).

Administration, in terms of administration orders which have proved successful in practice, is also a regime which is heavily dependent on the company voluntary arrangement (CVA) procedure as introduced by Part I of IA 1986. This is because a CVA may be used in certain cases in respect of excluded assets and the sale price arising from the sale of the company and its assets where the company and the assets comprised in the sale are sold as a going concern. The CVA is, of course, subject to the consent of secured and preferential creditors and offers no moratorium pending the drawing up of the proposal, although these drawbacks may be overcome where creditors are convinced of the viability of the administration order itself. In particular, the administration/CVA has been particularly useful in the case of football clubs, the assets of which are not easily saleable.

## 2.6.1  Whose choice?

The choice between administrative receivership and administration for a company is really not a matter for the company, but is rather a decision for any debenture-holder entitled to appoint an administrative receiver. This is because s9(3) obliges the court to dismiss a petition for an administration order until it is satisfied either (a) that the person by whom or on whose behalf the administrative receiver was appointed has consented to the making of the order or, (b) that the security pursuant to which the administrative receiver was appointed is susceptible under ss238–43 and/or s245. Where more than one debenture-holder holds security entitling it to effect an appointment of an administrative receiver, each debenture-holder would appear entitled to notice of any application for an administration order. An administrative receiver may, of course, be appointed pending an application for an administration order, thereby bringing about the dismissal of the petition at the subsequent hearing (s10(2)(b) and note the cases referred to in para 2.5.2 above, concerning recent successful *ex parte* applications for administration orders.

It is also worth noting in relation to abridged periods of notice in relation to applications for administration orders that in *Re A Company No 00175 of 1987* [1987] 3 BCC 124, counsel for the company argued that the court was empowered to grant an adjournment of the application for an administration order where an administrative receiver was in office in order to enable the company to raise funds thereby discharging the appointing debenture's debt and thus bringing about a termination of the administrative receivership, with the result that the court would be able to grant an administration order free of the constraints of s9(3). Vinelott J, perhaps unfortunately, rejected this argument and held that the provision did not envisage such a discretion and that, as a consequence, the court was obliged to dismiss the application for the administration order where an administrative receiver was in office, on the assumption that the consent of the debenture-holder to the making of the order was not forthcoming.

### 2.6.2 The floating charge holder's veto

The stumbling-block to the vast majority of companies wishing to seek an administration order is the existence of security (which is not susceptible of invalidation) in favour of a secured creditor entitled to appoint an administrative receiver. Avoidance of this problem will almost invariably necessitate the non-existence of a floating charge over the company's assets which, in practice, is a matter of considerable irony since very few companies seeking an administration order will not have granted a floating charge over their assets to secure borrowing. One can only wonder at how realistic or credible the proposals made by the Cork Committee in Chapter 9 of their Report may be considered to be with the wisdom of hindsight, in that the administration provisions were supposedly drafted as a method of providing a method of financial rescue for ailing companies which had not granted floating charges over their assets. In reality, such a proposition is only viable and realistic in relation to those companies over which security has not been taken entitling a debenture-holder to appoint an administrative receiver. Despite this criticism it has to be said that a small number of highly publicised administration orders, predominantly involving football clubs, have been granted as an alternative to administrative receivership (and liquidation), primarily on account of the potentially adverse publicity facing any creditor appointing an administrative receiver as an alternative. A number of less well-publicised orders have also been granted in similar circumstances, albeit perhaps more surprisingly, in relation to commercial undertakings such as manufacturing, service industry and finance companies. Those orders have been brought about by the acquiescence of the debenture-holders of those companies for whom some or all of the factors considered in the following account have been significant considerations.

The underlying consideration which will be of primary importance to a debenture-holder in considering the giving of consent to an administration order is whether it will inhibit the company's ability to service the secured debt and its longer term ability to offer good security for the debt in terms of the maintenance of its assets. As regards the latter consideration, an administration order offers significant protection because of the automatic moratorium against both the making of a winding-up order and enforcement proceedings against the company, this being granted on the presentation of the petition pending the dismissal of it under s10(1) (see, eg, *Bristol Airport plc v Powdrill & Cors* [1990] Ch 744, and the Court of Appeal's guidelines on the court's decision to grant leave under s11(3) in *Re Atlantic Computer Systems plc* [1990] BCC 859). Whether the administration order serves the purpose of ensuring a company's ability to service a debenture-secured debt remains a matter of conjecture pending the making of the order itself. However, in view of the fact that the administration order itself will necessarily mean that the debenture-holder will be unable to enforce its debt, the debenture-holder will need to be satisfied that the proposed administration order is realistic in terms of proposals, projections and time, and that the position of the debenture-holder as a significant creditor of the company has been specifically considered. This latter matter is not merely a matter of posturing on the part of the company and its advisors. It is inevitable that the administration order will be the subject of a creditors' meeting. Prior to this, the company must court and ensure the co-operation of the debenture-holder(s) so far as is possible since other creditors are likely to be influenced heavily by the attitude adopted by what is likely to be the most significant of the company's creditors.

A debenture-holder is likely to be strongly influenced in deciding between administrative receivership and administration by the fact that administrative receivership is a speedier and cheaper method of recovery of the debenture-holder's debt. The appointment of an administrative receiver will also avoid the delay involved in the drawing up, application for and implementation of an administration petition and order and the accompanying uncertainty in the initial stages as to whether the court will be satisfied that an administration order should be made. These considerations may not, however, weigh so heavily in favour of administrative receivership where, say, the company's assets are not easily realisable or are unlikely to fetch a sale value on a forced sale basis which approximates to their written down book value or below. The same may also be true where the value of the company's assets are perceived as exceeding the level of the secured debt. By contrast, administration may be a more attractive option to the debenture-holder where the value of the company's assets are such that the debenture-holder would be likely to recover only a fraction of the sum secured by the debenture. This will be particularly relevant where, say, the company is actually or prospectively engaged in profitable contracts which will serve to enhance its balance sheet position.

### 2.6.3 Practical and commercial considerations

In some cases a pending administrative receivership or administration is likely to involve a disposition of the company's business or substantially the whole of its assets. Where this is so, an administrative receiver is far better placed than an administrator to effect an immediate sale of the whole or part of a company's business as an ongoing concern or substantially the whole of its assets. This is largely because an administrator will usually be reluctant to dispose of a business, or indeed any assets, without the sanction of the court pending a meeting of the company's creditors. Such a meeting must be convened within three months of the making of the administration order (s23(1)(b). It is suggested, however, that this reluctance is not well founded following the decision in *Re Charnley Davies Ltd* [1990] BCC 605. In that case Miller J held that an administrator may exercise his statutory powers in disposing of substantially the whole of the company's assets pending the s23 creditors' meeting. In practice, it is easy to understand an administrator's reluctance from his own position to effect such a sale. On the other hand, in *Re Consumer and Industrial Press (No 2)* [1988] 4 BCC 72 leave was refused by the court on an application to sell the title of a magazine which represented substantially the whole of a company's assets, which were subject to a fixed charge. See also *Re Smallman Construction Ltd* [1989] BCLC 420, *Re N S Distribution Ltd* [1990] BCLC 169 and *Re Charnley Davies Business Services Ltd* [1987] 3 BCC 408, in which Harman J discharged an administration order before a s23 creditors' meeting had been held as the meeting had nothing to discuss, the administrator having taken action of his own volition which effectively left no proposals that might have been discussed by the meeting.

An administrative receiver, unlike an administrator, is not constricted by any meeting of creditors in disposing of assets and, indeed, may do so immediately following his appointment. In discharging his function, an administrative receiver owes his duties primarily to his appointor (*Gomba Holdings UK Ltd v Homan* [1986] 1 WLR 130). Furthermore, the law expressly recognises that the administrative receiver is appointed to get in and realise the assets of the company for the benefit of the debenture-holder (*Airlines Airspares Ltd v Handley Page* [1970] Ch 193). The fact that an administrator acts in the interests of creditors generally and, as such, must take reasonable care to obtain the best price on the sale of an asset of the company's business as the circumstances permit, effectively means that an administration order may result in some delay before the administrator is able to effect a sale of a particular asset or the company's business. Delay may be avoided in particular circumstances if, for example, a willing buyer is found or presents itself at an early stage and is prepared to pay an objectively reasonable price for the assets or business.

Depending on the circumstances of the appointment, the existence of pre-appointment contracts and consequent liabilities may be of significant relevance in the distinction between administrative receivership and administration. There is some similarity in the relationship between an administrative receiver, an administrator and the company to which they are appointed in that an administrative receiver is deemed to be an agent of the company until liquidation whilst an administrator is deemed to act as agent of the company when exercising his powers (ss44(1)(a),(c), 14(5) and *Re Hartlebury Printers Ltd* [1992] BCC 428). However, whilst the administrative receiver owes his duties primarily to his appointor, the scope of the administrator's duties are wider than one which is owed merely to the company (*Astor Chemicals Ltd v*

*Synthetic Technology Ltd* [1990] BCC 97 at 106, per Vinelott J). Again, for this reason, an administrator will be less inclined to act in breach of pre-appointment contracts since it was judicially recognised in the *Astor Chemicals* case that administrators do not enjoy a prerogative in bringing about such a termination. It remains arguable, albeit not expressly judicially recognised, that such a right should exist.

In the case of an administrative receiver, the decision in *Airlines Airspares Ltd v Handley Page Ltd* [1970] Ch 93 suggests that the office-holder does not attract personal liability for work done in respect of pre-appointment contracts and does not owe specific duties to pre-appointment debtors of the company. An administrative receiver will therefore be less concerned with the operation of pre-appointment contracts than will an administrator. However, this relative freedom should be seen against the fact that the administrative receiver's appointment will not preclude the other contracting party from applying or an order for specific performance. This arose in *Telemetrix plc v Modern Engineers of Bristol (Holdings) plc* [1985] 1 BCC 99, 417 where joint receivers were joined in as parties to proceedings taken against the company.

Furthermore, a creditor whose debt was incurred prior to the appointment of the administrative receiver will be able to set off amounts owed by the creditor to the company prior to the appointment, as in *Biggerstaff v Rowatt's Wharf Ltd* [1896] 2 Ch 93. In that case the Court of Appeal rejected an argument by counsel for the debenture-holders that the floating charge held over the company's assets constituted an assignment to the debenture-holder, thereby negating any mutuality of the debts owed by and to the creditor and the company. As a consequence, set off of pre-contract debt was permissible. (Compare *N W Robbie & Co Ltd v Witney Warehouse Co Ltd* [1963] 3 All ER 613 where set-off was refused by the Court of Appeal due to a lack of mutuality of debts and see also *Parsons v Sovereign Bank of Canada* [1913] AC 160.)

There is also judicial statement, albeit *obiter*, to the effect that a receiver may be personally liable in tort for taking steps which effectively preclude the completion of a pre-appointment contract; see *Re Botibol (decd)* [1947] 1 All ER 26 at 28 per Evershed J, although that case concerned a court-appointed receiver who would not be an agent of the company, as would an administrative receiver until liquidation by virtue of s44(1). The case may, therefore, be distinguished on its facts in administrative receivership. For an informative discussion of the implications of trading by administrative receivers and administrators see also Moss and Segal (1994) 7 Insolvency Intelligence 49–51.

Perhaps the most important practical factor in determining between administrative receiver and administrator is the ability of either office-holder to secure the finance necessary to bring his term of office to a satisfactory conclusion. In practice, an administrator is likely to want to continue and maintain the trading operations of a company's business, in whole or part, for a longer period than an administrative receiver who will usually seek to secure a sale of the company's business in a relatively short time if a sale is considered viable from the outset. Basically, an administrative receiver is unlikely to wish to engage in the time, expense and risk of ongoing trading at the expense of asset realisation which could otherwise be applied in discharging the debts of his appointor, preferential creditors and, possibly, any prior ranking secured creditor. This explains why an administrative receiver will usually opt to close down a company's operations if a sale of its business cannot be secured within a short period following his appointment, usually days or even hours.

On the other hand, administrators have been known—particularly in recent highly publicised cases—to continue trading for significant periods. For these reasons, the level of finance sought by an administrator is likely to be significantly higher than that sought by an administrative receiver and may have to take account of trading throughout the duration of the administration order where survival of the business of the company is identified in its terms as the purpose of the order. The finance arranged by the office-holder will also have to take account of his own professional costs and those of his advisors which, in practice, tend to be higher in administrations than in administrative receiverships.

In the case of administrative receivership, the finance sought by an office-holder is invariably supplied by his appointor although there is no good legal reason why it should not be sought or provided from elsewhere. Whilst such finance arrangements are usually agreed on the basis of personal liability on the part of the office-holder this is not problematic, since s44(1)(b),(c) affords the administrative receiver an indemnity out of the assets of the company in respect of any contract entered into by him in any way out of his functions, except insofar as his contract otherwise provides, in respect of his personal liability. This statutory indemnity operates to secure the position of the appointor, since without it any repayment from floating charge assets would be the subject to prior claims by preferential creditors. Perhaps the only situation in which the statutory indemnity arrangement in s44 will not be satisfactory is where the extent of the company's assets is insufficient to cover the cumulative personal liabilities of the administrative receiver. In such a circumstance, the office-holder, for whom this situation poses most problems, would be well advised to seek a general indemnity from his appointor against all personal liability incurred by him in the discharge of his functions.

The arrangement of finance in an administration tends to be more vexed than in an administrative receivership. This is because it will usually involve reaching satisfactory arrangements with a potentially large number of creditors so as to render the company's balance sheet sufficiently viable to continue operations on a realistic basis. In addition, a possibly significant degree of core finance, invariably in the form of an agreed bank facility, will need to be arranged with the company's main creditor or creditors.

Four other factors will also be relevant to a varying degree depending on the circumstances in which the option between administrative receiver and administration arises.

(1)    An administrator may avail himself of the provisions enabling the avoidance of antecedent transactions, being transactions-at-under-value, preferences and void floating charge transactions under ss238, 239 and 245 respectively. These provisions do not operate in favour of an administrative receiver.

(2)    In view of the disparate purposes of administrative receivership and administration, the office-holder may be expected to maintain a closer liaison and relationship with the directors in the case of administration than in an administrative receivership. This may give rise to the appointment of an office-holder who is preferable to the directors of the company in administration as opposed to the choice of the appointing debenture-holder in an administrative receivership. This offers an effective bargaining tool to the debenture-holder, however, in considering whether to give consent to an administration order in the sense that the debenture-holder may insist on the appointment of an office-holder of his choice as a condition of his giving consent to the application for the administration order.

(3)    In an administration the effect of s15 should be considered. This obliges the administrator to discharge fixed-charge holders out of the proceeds of sale of relevant property, whereas the proceeds of sale of floating-charge assets need apparently not be distributed to either the holder of the floating charge or to those creditors who would rank as preferential creditors in the event of a liquidation or administrative receivership (s15(1),(2),(4) and *Re ARV Aviations Ltd* [1988] 4 BCC 708). This explains why administration is frequently followed by liquidation in practice, on its transpiring that no surplus remains from realisations for distribution to unsecured creditors.

(4)    An administrator, as a court-appointed office-holder, is likely to en-counter fewer problems in getting and realising overseas assets than a privately appointed administrative receiver where this is relevant.

## 2.6.4  Administration or liquidation?

The above considerations concerning the relative merits of administrative receivership and administration warrant a short mention of factors which might be relevant in considering whether administration or liquidation is the most appropriate insolvency procedure for a particular company. Administration, of course, envisages the continued survival of a corporate entity whereas liquidation is, quite simply, a formal procedure for bringing about the termination of the company's life. The starting point, therefore, is ascertaining whether or not the whole or part of the company's business is viable and may be salvaged, either to be sold off in a liquidation or administration or with a view to continuing operations without a sell-off in an administration. The conclusion that a business is viable, in either whole or part, raises the question of whether realistic arrangements may be made for the obtaining of the requisite finance. If so, this in turn raises the question of whether administrative receivership may be a more realistic and beneficial alternative for the debenture-holder. Where requisite finance cannot be raised, then liquidation invariably remains the only realistic alternative. In this regard it should be noted that a liquidator is unlikely to wish to continue the trading operations of a company for anything other than the shortest possible time, say in completing a specific and clearly profitable contract. Indeed, the powers of the liquidator are conferred by the legislation to permit the liquidator to carry on the business of the company only so far as may be necessary for its beneficial winding-up (see Sched 4, Part II, para 5).

In practice, administration is simply not a realistic option for smaller companies since the cost of the procedure is not usually justifiable in terms of the company's budget, cash-flow and operations. Even where administration is adopted as an alternative to liquidation or administrative receivership, the petition remains subject to the approval of the court which itself must be satisfied that an order would be likely to achieve one or more of the purposes set out in s8(3), usually the survival of the company and the whole or any part of its undertaking as a going concern or a more advantageous realisation of the assets than would be effected on a winding-up. In addition, the court must be satisfied that the company is or is likely to become unable to pay its debts within the meaning of s123 (s8(1)(b)). For the degree of likelihood required by s8(1)(b) see *Re Harris Simons Construction Ltd* [1989] 5 BCC 11 at 13 per Hoffman J. The practice of applying for an administration order which is then adjourned, typically for 28 days, merely for the purposes of obtaining a short term moratorium during which a CVA arrangement is put in place without pursuing the administration order application, is to be discouraged as an abuse of the process of the court.

In all circumstances where the company is suffering financial difficulties the directors should consider their potential liabilities, particularly for wrongful trading (see s214(3)). This necessitates the obtaining of independent legal advice at the earliest possible time, which will invariably amount to a justifiable expense.

## 2.7   Is a Workout an Alternative Solution?

It has to be said that the choice between administration and administrative receivership, and to some extent a CVA, is not an altogether satisfactory one. In effect, the choice is one for the debenture-holder since the company can do little to prevent the appointment of an administrative receiver. The latter may also block an administration order for which the company may make an application. In addition, the debenture-holder may simply choose not to be bound by any proposed CVA. One alternative is the possibility of a so-called workout, a term commonly used in referring to what is otherwise known as a rescue operation, standstill or turnaround. A workout is effectively a contractual operation which may be used by a company or a group of companies whereby an agreement is reached with its creditors in the hope that the agreement will enable the company or group to trade out of its difficulties.

In practice, there are a number of considerable drawbacks with workouts, all of which stem from the various legal provisions themselves. The first is that a debenture-holder may simply choose to appoint an administrative receiver who effectively displaces the powers of the directors, thereby rendering any workout arrangement impossible. The second drawback is that a workout has no statutory basis and, as such, offers no protection from creditors wishing to enforce their security, protection which would be available under an administration order. The third major drawback is that the mechanics of the operation will inevitably involve the giving of further security to existing or new creditors as consideration for continued support. With the potential for impending liquidation or even administration, such security is vulnerable to attack by a subsequently appointed liquidator under ss238, 239 and/or 245, which clearly renders the taking of security less attractive for creditors than it might be if some sort of statutory protection were to underpin the arrangement. From the point of view of the directors, the financial circumstances of the company which necessitate the possibility of a workout will raise question of potential liability for wrongful trading under s214 and, in extreme cases, fraudulent trading under s213. The practice to date has been that applications to the court under s214 have been accompanied by applications against the directors for breach of duty under s212 in misfeasance proceedings, usually on separate but related grounds, and this will also therefore be a further inevitable consideration.

The poverty of the legal provisions in offering any real basis for a workout-type arrangement is apparent from a number of flaws which exist in the current options available under the legislation and by way of the appointment of a receiver pursuant to a debenture. From the point of view of a debenture-holder, the appointment of an administrative receiver will bring with it the possibility of carrying on the company's business and an effective stay on the power of the directors, who nonetheless remain in office and are duty bound to co-operate with the office-holder by virtue of s235. On the other hand, the appointment of an administrative receiver will also usually necessitate a sale of company assets on a forced sale basis which will usually translate to a value well below book value. Furthermore, these assets may well be of significant practical importance to the company's business and, in practice, this accounts for why a large number of administrative receiverships culminate in liquidation. Whilst administration is often cited as an alternative to administrative receivership, in practice this is simply unrealistic in many cases, largely on account of costs and the reluctance of secured creditors to engage such arrangements.

Although the administration regime was heralded as a rescue mechanism for companies in financial trouble, the reality has been quite different. Since 1986 the highest number of administration orders made in any one year was in 1992 when 214 orders were made; furthermore, no data is available in relation to unsuccessful attempts to obtain administration orders. The regime has not, however, been wholly unsuccessful. Certain types of undertakings have been able to avail themselves of the process with some consistency. Other highly publicised administration orders serve to illustrate the viability of the regime in certain cases. In practice, however, such successes depend more on the co-operation of major creditors than anything else. Other factors also impede the viability of administration. One widely perceived condition for the making of an order is that the company must be insolvent within the meaning of s123 of the IA 1986. Technically, the company need not be insolvent as a condition for the making of an order since s8(1)(a) actually reads 'is or is likely to become unable to pay its debts'. Nevertheless, the insolvency-related connotations of an administration order are likely to have a detrimental effect on customer and supplier confidence and goodwill generally, as well as undermining the realisable value of assets which will invariably be disposed of on a forced sale basis. The fact that the powers of management of the company vest in the administrator on the making of the order—which may divest power from a highly skilled and specialised board and management team—does little to mitigate these factors. Furthermore, the administration order application will ordinarily require a report by an independent person (usually the proposed administrator!) to the effect that the appointment of an administrator is expedient for the purposes of IR r2.2.

Rule 2.2 reports tend to be bulky and are both expensive and time-consuming in terms of preparation. This further impairs the operation of the administration regime as a rescue mechanism. Rule 2.2 actually provides that a report 'may' be prepared which suggests that it may be dispensed with entirely. If this is the case an explanation should be included in the affidavit supporting the application as to why the report has been omitted. A Practice Note issued by the Vice-Chancellor on 17 January 1994, *Administration Order Applications: Content of Independent Reports* [1994] BCLC 347, urges practitioners to slim down rule 2.2 report which need not contain (often overly) detailed financial projections in the funding of the administration and which may not be needed in some straightforward cases. It remains to be seen how much practitioners will heed the Vice-Chancellor's words, particularly in view of the professional costs involved in obtaining the reports, and in the light of Harman J's comment in *Re Shearing and Londer Ltd* [1991] BCC 232 that a r2.2 report is 'an absolutely vital and essential document' without which the court 'would hardly proceed at all with administration petitions'.

In conclusion it should be noted that the relative failure of the administration regime in the United Kingdom is not unique. Similar mechanisms in other jurisdictions, such as in South Africa (judicial manager), Ireland (court examiner), Australia (official management), France (*suspension provisoire des poursuites*) and Singapore (judicial management) have also experienced only limited success rates in terms of corporate survival. Despite its greater flexibility, such as affording protection to companies which are still solvent but unlikely to remain so, and the continued vesting of management powers in the directors, the widely cited Chapter 11 of the US Bankruptcy Code has little, if anything, more to offer than other systems in terms of its success rate.

The other statutory alternatives to administration have even less to accommodate a company in financial difficulties. Schemes of arrangement or compromise between companies and creditors under the Companies Act 1985 s425 are uncommon in practice despite their potential use in altering creditors' rights, reconstruction and/or mergers. Section 425 arrangements involve a notoriously cumbersome court application and tend to be too slow in practice to be of any practical use. Similar practical drawbacks in the case of CVAs have been discussed previously at para 2.5.1.

It remains to be seen whether Parliament will ever put into motion the conception of a legal mechanism which seeks to put the protection so badly needed by a workout arrangement on a statutory basis. It is suggested that merely tinkering with the existing provisions will do little to improve matters, since it is the very nature of those provisions which are defective for reasons set out above. In response to the Insolvency Service's Consultation Document of October 1993 on CVAs and administration orders, the Law Society suggested to the DTI that a moratorium should be incorporated into CVA arrangements and that control of a company should be left in the hands of the directors subject to the supervision of an insolvency practitioner. Such suggestions are no doubt laudable, but such amendments would, it is suggested, do little more than paper over cracks. What is needed is some form of protection regime (a) which involves creditors, shareholders and directors from the outset, (b) which would also require the making of an order by the court, (c) which might be made on an *ex parte* application, at least on an interim basis, and (d) which would have retrospective effect in relation to the broad moratorium necessarily offered by any new and realistic regime.

# Chapter Three

# The Debenture Holder's Security: 1

## 3.1 Introduction

This and the following chapter are primarily concerned with the security interests pursuant to which an administrative receiver is appointed. This necessitates a consideration both of the nature of fixed and floating charges and common problems which arise in connection with both, particularly in relation to security taken over real and leasehold property, book debts and other species of property. The registration requirements applicable to charges are also considered. This will be relevant both to those taking security over a company's assets and those seeking to challenge either the validity of the administrative receiver's appointment or the extent of the company's assets which may be subject to the office-holder.

The definition of an administrative receiver in s29(2)(a) makes specific reference to the debenture-holder secured by '... such a [floating] charge or one or more other securities ...'. It is necessary, therefore, to say something of these areas at the outset, both as regards the practical use of each and the conceptual ideas standing behind each.

## 3.2 Fixed Charges

It is common for a standard form debenture to create fixed charges over specific company assets. These will usually include

- present freehold and leasehold property and all present and future estates or interests therein;
- plant, machinery, furniture, fixtures, fittings, equipment and the like;
- present and future goodwill and uncalled capital of the company;
- present and future stocks, shares and other securities (eg loan notes) belonging to the company;
- intellectual property rights, choses in action and claims both present and future belonging to the company; and
- present and future book and other debts.

For the avoidance of doubt, the lender may wish to specify that 'choses in action' includes conversion rights, shares and rights issues, warrants to subscribe, option warranties and the like. This series of fixed charges or some variation thereon is usually complemented by a general floating charge over all the present and future undertakings and assets of the company, although the charge may be framed to apply only to those assets not specifically subject to a fixed charge comprised in the debenture. There is actually a theoretical danger in this, in that the floating charge may potentially not be of a 'global' type as is submitted is required by s29(2) (see Chapter 1 at para 1.6).

The rules applicable to fixed charges are broadly those applicable to mortgage law. A fixed charge attaches to a specific asset from the moment of creation, thereby conferring immediate security over it. This process is delayed in the case of a future asset until such time as the asset comes into existence, provided that the property is suitably identified if it has yet to be created at the time of creation of the charge (*Re Yorkshire Woolcombers Association Ltd* [1903] 2 Ch 284 at 294; *Siebe Gorman & Co Ltd v Barclays Bank Ltd* [1979] 2 Lloyd's Rep 142; *Tailby v Official Receiver* (1888) 13 App Cas 523 at 533). The consequence of the fixed charge security is that the chargor may not dispose of the asset without the consent of the chargee. It follows that a purported fixed charge over all of the company's assets would render a company incapable of carrying on its business, since the ongoing consent of the charge holder would be required to deal with assets throughout (*Bickerstaff v Rowlatt's Wharf Ltd* [1896] 2 Ch 93). The fixed-charge holder's position is bolstered by the fact that a fixed charge remains effective even if the chargor purports to dispose of the asset, unless the chargee agrees to release it, any subsequent purchaser taking subject to the charge (*Re Ind Coope and Co Ltd* [1911] 2 Ch 233).

A fixed charge confers two further advantages on the chargee. First, the chargee maintains priority over any preferential creditors of the company (subject to any subordination agreement as discussed below, Chapter 4 at 4.2 and see *Re Lewis Merthyr Consolidated Collieries* [1929] 1 Ch 498). Secondly, in the case of fixed charges taken over chattels, the charge needs only to be registered at Companies House, the cumbersome Bills of Sale Acts 1878 and 1882 having no application in the case of companies.

Fixed charges are not without their problems. The courts have continued to tackle particular problems with purported fixed charges over book debts in what is suggested below to be a largely artificial way, and in a manner quite distinct from fixed charges taken over other species of property. Book debts nonetheless remain a potentially volatile form of security on account of their intangible nature and their potential susceptibility to counterclaims by creditors of the company. Freehold and leasehold property also pose a number of problems in this regard, as do fixed and floating charges over certain types and classes of other property, each being considered later. Other species of property may also, of course, pose problems in terms of ascertaining whether a charge over assets is fixed or floating. One recent example rose in *Re CCG International Enterprise Ltd* [1993] BCC 580 in which the company created a debenture that included a purported fixed charge over its premises. The terms of the debenture obliged the company to insure its premises and to apply any proceeds of the insurance policy in either reinstating the premises or in repaying the charge holder, at the option of the debenture-holder. Lindsay J held at first instance that the obligations both to insure the premises and to apply the proceeds of the insurance policy as directed by the charge holder gave rise to a fixed charge having been created over the insurance policy proceeds.

## 3.3  Floating Charges

There is no statutory or common law definition of what amounts to a floating charge. The approach of the courts in practice is to consider the peculiar characteristics of each charge or loan security before it in order to establish its legal nature. Perhaps the most useful and widely cited judicial test in this regard is that laid down by Romer LJ in *Re Yorkshire Woolcombers Association Ltd* [1903] 2 Ch 284 at 295 which attempts to identify the characteristics of a floating charge as opposed to laying down a universal definition of it as follows:

> ...I certainly think that if a charge has three characteristics that I am about to mention it is a floating charge. (1) If it is a charge on a class of assets of a company present and future; (2) if that class is one which, in the ordinary course of the business of the company, would be changing from time to time; and (3) if you find that by the charge it is contemplated that, until some future step is taken by or on behalf of those interested in the charge, the company may carry on its business in the usual way as far as concerns that particular class of assets I am dealing with.

Lord McNaughton's subsequent statement in *Illingworth v Houldsworth* [1904] AC 355 at 358 is equally indicative of the characteristics which may be attributed to a floating charge:

> A specific charge, I think, is one that without more fastens on ascertained and definite property or property capable of being ascertained and defined; a floating charge, on the other hand, is ambulatory and shifting in nature, hovering over and so to speak floating with the property which it is intended to affect, until some event or some act is done which causes it to settle and fasten on the charge within its reach and grasp.

The equitable nature of a floating charge by virtue of which it must rank subject to any legal or equitable fixed charge—subject to an operative 'negative pledge' clause—is outweighed by a number of practical advantages. These go some way to explaining the legal development of the floating charge as a form of corporate security in other common law jurisdictions such as Canada, New Zealand and Australia. First, a floating charge may constitute security over the entire property and undertaking of a company. Secondly, a floating charge may extend to present and future property as diverse as land, receivables and book debts, contracts, patents, goodwill, securities and uncalled capital. Further, unlike a fixed charge, no permission is required of the charge holder to dispose of the charged assets. The fourth advantage of a floating charge over the whole of a company's assets and undertaking is that the charge will automatically extend to the assets of the company notwithstanding any change in their form. For example, the proceeds of sale of stock in trade or the realised proceeds of a book debt will all fall subject to a floating charge over the whole of a company's property and undertaking, without the requirement for any further formalities or the execution of any supplemental documentation. A floating charge need not, of course, be taken over a company's entire property and undertaking, as was recognised recently in *Re Cimex Tissues Ltd* [1994] BCC 626 at 634. It may extend, for example, only to the stock-in-trade of a company from time to time or the company's book and/or other debts. The drawback with such a restricted charge is that once the assets subject to it are disposed of or realised by the company, their proceeds will not fall subject to the floating charge as they would in the case of a floating charge over the company's entire property and undertaking.

The distinction between fixed and floating charges has caused particular problems in relation to book debts. For example, in *Siebe Gorman & Co Ltd v Barclays Bank Ltd* [1979] 2 Lloyd's Rep 142 a charge over present and future book debts of a company was held to be a specific fixed charge over book debts where (a) the charge was stated to be a 'fixed charge', (b) the charge prohibited the company from assigning or dealing with the book debts (eg by factoring, assigning or selling), and (c) it required their realised proceeds to be paid into a bank account with the lender immediately on receipt by the company as agent of the lender (see also *Re Keenan Bros Ltd* [1986] BCLC 242 a decision of the Irish Supreme Court which followed the *Siebe Gorman* decision). On the other hand, a debenture which did not purport to control the company's dealings with sums standing to the credit of the company's account was held to be a floating charge in *Re Brightlife* [1987] Ch 200. The recent approach of the court has been to concentrate on whether the parties actually intended to create a fixed or floating charge. This is well evidenced by the Court of Appeal decision in *Re New Bullas Trading Ltd* [1994] BCC 36 which held that a charge created a fixed charge over book debts and a floating charge over book debt realisations, primarily on the basis of what the parties had intended to create in terms of the charge. The taking of security over book debts is consider further in Chapter 4 at para 4.3.

A floating charge would have little or no use as a means of taking security if it did not at some specific point actually attach to specific assets (if any) which are subject to it. This process of attachment is known as 'crystallisation', a term first employed (by counsel) in *Re Standard Manufacturing Co* [1891] 1 Ch 627. Prior to this attachment taking place, as Lord McNaughton put it in *Government Stocks and Other Security Investment Trust v Manila Railway Co* [1897] AC 81 at 86, '[the floating charge] remains dormant'. However, on crystallisation, the floating charge effectively metamorphoses into a fixed charge which, by definition, must be equitable in nature. This is not to say that a floating charge does not create immediate security on creation; it does. The proviso to this, however, is that the assets (if any) which are subject to the security are not ascertained until the time of crystallisation. This process is probably best understood with further recourse to judicial metaphor, of which perhaps the most notable appears in the judgment of Nourse J in *Re Woodroofes (Musical Instruments) Ltd* [1986] Ch 366 reviewing the authorities on crystallisation. The learned judge considered that, on crystallisation, 'that which kept the charge hovering has now been released and the force of gravity [has] caused it to settle and fasten on the subject of the charge within its reach and grasp'. The assets subject to the floating charge at the time of crystallisation will not, however, be the only assets subject to it since the charge may also extend to after acquired property if it is so drafted (*Business Computers Ltd v Anglo-African Leasing Ltd* [1977] 2 All ER 741). In practice, the floating charge will be framed in the following terms or some variation thereon:

> The company ... charges to the bank ... by way of floating charge all the undertaking and all the property assets and rights of the company present and future not subject to a fixed charge under this deed.

For the purposes of the IA 1986 the significance of crystallisation is largely undermined, to the extent that the floating charge takes on the form of a fixed equitable charge. This is because of s251 which defines a floating charge as a charge which, 'as created', was a floating charge. The practical effect of this is that a floating charge which crystallises prior to the appointment of a receiver will not operate to defeat the claims of preferential creditors. An example of this arose in *Re Brightlife Ltd* [1987] Ch 200 where a debenture-holder was effectively permitted by the court to serve a notice crystallising a charge specifically for that purpose. A similar point arose in *Re Woodroffe's (Musical Instruments) Ltd* [1986] Ch 366 where 'automatic crystallisation' on the cessation of a business was deemed to have the same effect. This point has now been affirmed in the case of liquidations in *Re Portbase Clothing Ltd* [1993] BCLC 796. (Further reference should also be made to Milman (1987)

79

8 Co Law 30). Earlier decisions under the old law such as *Re Griffin Hotel Co Ltd* [1941] Ch 129 and *Re Christionette International Ltd* [1982] 1 WLR 1245 therefore no longer appear to represent good law. The s251 definition also has some significance for the operation of subordination agreements, which are referred to in Chapter 4 at para 4.2.

The definition of a floating charge as it appears in s251 has seriously undermined the floating charge as a method of taking security since, irrespective of subsequent crystallisation, the approach is firmly 'once a floater, always a floater', assuming the charge has been created as a floating charge. Notwithstanding this, crystallisation retains important practical implications for three reasons:

(1)   Since the floating charge will have become fixed, the company will in theory be unable to continue its business operations without leave of the charge holder. In practice, however, it is common for business operations to continue in the absence of a physical bar. One solution to this might be the 'decrystallisation' of the fixed equitable charge, thereby causing it to 're-float'. In Scotland, the Companies Act 1985 s478(6) expressly provides for de-crystallisation although there is no analogous provision applicable to English companies. However, even the concept of a re-floated fixed equitable charge following crystallisation will be defeated to some extent by s251 since, notwithstanding crystallisation, the charge itself will remain a floating charge 'as created'. Whilst it has been suggested that there is no objection in principle to this concept, the matter remains one largely unexplored by the domestic courts.

(2)   The process will often provide the impetus for a winding-up petition to be presented if that has not caused the crystallisation itself.

(3)   Crystallisation also has implications for judgment creditors of the company. It has been held that judgment creditors who issue execution against the company's assets have no better title to them than the company, and the rights of those judgment creditors are, therefore, subject to the claims of the holders of a floating charge which has subsequently crystallised (*Davey & Co v Williamson & Sons Ltd* [1898] 2 QB 194 at 200 per Russell LCJ). However, the general conclusion in the literature is that this view goes too far (see Pennington, *Company Law*, 6th edn. (1990) at 457), Farrar, *Company Law* 3rd edn (1991) at 269), *Calnan* [1982] 10 NZLR 111). The real solution to the problem posed by crystallisation to judgment creditors is in ascertaining the stage to which the execution must proceed prior to crystallisation for the charge-holder to benefit from the execution. The short answer to this hinges on the method of enforcement adopted by the judgment creditor, executions being deemed to be completed at

varying times in each case. The position of judgment creditors in an administrative receivership is dealt with in Chapter 12.

It is also clear from *Griffiths v Yorkshire Bank* [1994] 1 WLR 1427 that a second floating charge (which crystallises on service of a notice) may take priority over an earlier floating charge which is not lost on the appointment ofreceivers under the first floating charge in the absence of contrary agreement to that effect.

In summary, a floating charge will crystallise in any of the following circumstances. Where more than one such event occurs the first gives rise to the crystallisation (*N W Robbie & Co Ltd v Witney Warehouse Co Ltd* [1963] 3 All ER 613).

### 3.3.1 Any event stipulated in the charge documentation

A standard form debenture will usually reserve to the secured creditor the unconditional right to serve a notice of crystallisation in writing on the company, thereby converting the floating charge into a fixed charge in relation to any of the property specified in the notice. The process is commonly known as 'semi-automatic' crystallisation.

In addition, a debenture will usually stipulate any number of events which will be deemed to give rise to crystallisation without notice. These events may include the company closing its bank account with the lending bank, the purported creation by the company of subsequent charges, the levying of execution against the company or the company's assets or liabilities falling below or exceeding specified levels. It now appears well settled that the parties may agree that any specified event may cause a floating charge to crystallise (*Permanent Houses (Holdings) Ltd* [1988] BCLC 563 at 567 per Hoffman J). Notwithstanding this, the mere power to appoint a receiver will not *per se* cause a floating charge to crystallise on the happening of a specified, relevant event giving rise to the power to appoint the receiver. Rather, crystallisation will only occur on the appointment of the receiver (*Government Stock and Other Securities Interest Co v Manila Railway Co* [1897] AC 81).

The whole question of so-called 'automatic' crystallisation has been the subject of considerable judicial debate. Despite the common usage of such provisions, which provide for crystallisation on any number of specific events or defaults by the company, some judicial uncertainty remains in both the domestic and Commonwealth courts. The main problem, which is largely a technical one, is that a floating charge may continue to float where the so-called 'automatic crystallisation' event does not, in fact, preclude the company from carrying on its business, for example by the issuing of a writ as in *Re Hubbard & Co Ltd* (1898) 68 LJ Ch 54. It may well be that the evidence shows that the company had continued to trade following the service of a notice of crystallisation. In practice, such a continuation of business in this way is not uncommon. Nonetheless, it is submitted that the better view on this point is that expressed *obiter* by Hoffman J in *Re Brightlife Ltd* [1986] 3 All ER 673, approving the decision of Speight J at first instance in the New Zealand case of *Re Manurewa Transport Ltd* [1971] NZLR 909. Speight J's view was that crystallisation may be brought about by the happening of a specified event without the need for further formality such as the service of a notice of crystallisation or the appointment of a receiver. This view is preferred, since to hold otherwise would be to offend the strict terms of the debenture as such between the parties. Furthermore, it is difficult to see the justification for a requirement for further formality where the parties have impliedly dispensed with the need for it between themselves in the terms of their agreement. The view expressed by Speight J relied on a number of English decisions on the point and on *Painting & Nottingham Ltd v Miller Hale and Winter* [1971] NZLR 164 (see also *Geoghegan v Greymouth – Point Elizabeth Railway and Coast Co Ltd* [1898] 16 NZLR 749 at 711 (a decision of the New Zealand Court of Appeal) and Pennington (1960) 23 MLR 630 which strongly supports this view).

It is worth noting here that in the *Brightlife* case Hoffman J expressly rejected both the arguments of counsel 'that public policy required restrictions upon what the parties could stipulate as crystallising events' and the view of Berger J in the Canadian case of *R in Right of British Columbia v Consolidated Copper Corporation Ltd* [1978] 5 WWR 652 where the concept of 'self-generating' crystallisation was rejected. As Hoffman J put it, 'I do not think it is open to the courts to restrict the contractual freedom of parties to a floating charge on such grounds'. Hoffman J's view, it is submitted, has much to commend it (see also *Robson v Smith* [1895] 2 Ch 118 and *Evans v Rival Granite Quarries Ltd* [1910] 2 KB 979 on the apparently non-viable concept of so-called 'partial' crystallisation).

In view of the apparent judicial uncertainty on the point, the debenture-holder's position is best protected, clearly in cases of doubt, by the service of a notice of crystallisation as is commonly provided for expressly by the charge itself. Where two or more events, including service of a notice of crystallisation, give rise to crystallisation, then it is submitted that crystallisation must take place on the happening of the first event in time, notwithstanding any subsequent crystallising event. Such a subsequent event will have no effect for crystallisation purposes unless possibly the crystallised floating charge is permitted to 're-float' in the interim in accordance with the terms of the debenture.

### 3.3.2 The appointment of a receiver

On the appointment of a receiver, a floating charge will crystallise at the time of appointment (*Re Panama, New Zealand and Australian Royal Mail Co* (1870) 5 Ch App 318; *Re Florence Land and Public Works Co* (1878) 10 ChD 530; *George Baker (Transport) Ltd v Enyon* [1974] 1 WLR 462). Where a receiver is appointed by the court, it is irrelevant to the crystallisation process that the receiver fails to give any security ordered within a time specified by the court (*Re Sims and Wood Ltd* [1916] WN 223).

The mere presentation of a writ or other preparatory steps relating to the appointment of a receiver will not operate to crystallise a floating charge (*Re Hubbard & Co Ltd* (1898) 68 LJ Ch 54; cf *Re Victoria Steamboats Ltd* [1897] 1 Ch 158 at 161 per Kekewich J). Further, the appointment of a receiver which is invalid will, it is submitted, cause a floating charge to crystallise since it is the appointment itself which is crucial to the charge's metamorphosis, as opposed to its validity. A contrary conclusion might also necessitate the obligatory decrystallisation of the charge on the appointment being successfully challenged.

The absence of a provision in a debenture which expressly contemplates the charge-holder being able to appoint a receiver does not undermine the creation of the charge as a floating charge (*Re Cimex Tissues Ltd* [1994] BCC 626 at 634–5). In addition, the absence of such a provision will not preclude an appointment since the debenture merely evidences the terms of the loan agreement which may well have actually contemplated an appointment being made in certain circumstances (see Chapter 5 at para 5.6).

### 3.3.3 The winding-up of the company

Winding-up remains relevant to the area of administrative receivership since the winding-up of the company in no way precludes the appointment of an administrative receiver contemporaneously (eg *Re Potters Oil Ltd (No2)* [1985] 1 BCC 99). It is long established that crystallisation will occur on the commencement of the winding-up of a company (ie on the passing of a resolution for winding-up in a voluntary winding-up or on presentation of a winding-up petition in a compulsory liquidation) (ss86 and 129 and see *Re Colonial Trusts Corporation, ex parte Bradshaw* (1879) 15 ChD 465; *Wheatley v Silkstone and Haigh Moor Coal Co* (1885) 29 ChD 715). However, in *Re Borax Co* [1901] 1 Ch 326 it was held by the Court of Appeal that a floating charge which was to crystallise into a fixed charge on an order or resolution for winding-up did not prevent the company from selling the whole of its undertaking. Accordingly, the charge was not deemed to crystallise on the sale itself prior to the commencement of the winding-up. This should call into question the terms of any debenture which effectively permits a company to dispose of its assets or undertaking without triggering any 'crystallisation' event in the particular debenture.

### 3.3.4   Cessation of trading by the company

The cessation of a company's business is frequently cited as giving rise to the crystallisation of a floating charge. Prior to *Re Woodroffes (Musical Instruments) Ltd* [1986] Ch 366 there was no express decision to this effect although there appear to be general assumptions made *obiter* in a number of decisions to this effect (for example, *Robson v Smith* [1895] 2 Ch 118; *Edward Nelson & Co v Faber & Co* [1903] 2 KB 367). In the *Woodroffe's* case, however, Nourse J made a statement expressly to the effect that 'crystallisation takes place on a cessation of a business... A cessation of business necessarily puts an end to the company's dealing with its assets'. Notwithstanding this clear statement, the decision in that case would appear to have been the same even if that approach had not been adopted by the court. Indeed, as Professor Pennington points out in *Company Law* 6th edn. (1990) at 448, despite suggestions in the literature to the effect that a floating charge crystallises automatically if a company ceases to carry on business, there are only two cases which appear to support this statement. In neither of those decisions was the matter so material as to resolve the question in issue whereby it may have been decided differently; see *Re Victoria Steamboats Ltd* [1897] 1 Ch 158 at 161 and *Edward Nelson & Co v Faber & Co* [1903] 2 KB 367 at 376-377. As such, it is suggested that the cessation of the company's business will do nothing more than provide a ground for the appointment of a receiver, which will only itself cause the floating charge to crystallise on being effected, notwithstanding the view widely expressed by various commentators to the contrary.

To a large extent, the effectiveness of an automatic crystallisation clause as a method of defeating claims of preferential creditors has been removed by the definition of a floating charge in s251. This states that a charge will be deemed a floating charge if it is such 'as created' notwithstanding its subsequent crystallisation into a fixed equitable charge. The problem posed by crystallisation to other creditors—who may be oblivious of it—would have been ameliorated by the implementation of the new Companies Act 1985 s410 (as inserted by Companies Act 1989 s100) which would have permitted the Secretary of State to make regulations requiring notice to be given to the Registrar of Companies of the occurrence of crystallising events (eg the appointment of a receiver or any event stipulated in the charge documentation) or any action taken to crystallise a charge (eg the service of a crystallisation notice). Notably, the consequences of failure to give such notice would have included treating the crystallisation as ineffective. Any proposed new legislation on the area is likely to incorporate such provisions and, indeed, would provide practical benefit in so doing.

## 3.4 Priority between Fixed and Floating Charges

The question of priority between fixed and floating charges is relevant to administrative receivership for two reasons. First, the collective security held by a debenture-holder is the significant factor in establishing a priority right to appoint an administrative receiver where more than one debenture-holder is in a position to make an appointment, the contemporaneous appointment of two or more administrative receivers being considered an impossibility in legal terms. Priority is also relevant to s43 which permits an application to the court by an administrative receiver for an order for the disposal of property which is subject to a prior-ranking charge. This will usually relate to a fixed charge. Section 43 is considered in more detail in Chapter 8 and is to be regarded, it is submitted, as having relevance to the disposal of property subject to both prior and subsequent encumbrancers.

The following text assumes that a charge is properly registered in accordance with the Companies Act 1985. In short, if the registration formalities are not complied with then, generally speaking, any priority afforded by the charge by law will be lost vis-à-vis third parties.

Neither the IA 1986 and the IR nor the Companies Act 1985 contain any specific rules as to priority between fixed and floating charges, other than the provisions in the IA 1986 relating to the relationship between preferential debts and assets subject to a floating charge. Indirectly, this impinges upon the priority of other charges where any operative subordination or subrogation agreement is in force. Section 40 provides that where a receiver (ie not necessarily an administrative receiver) is appointed pursuant to a floating charge, as defined by s251, then, assuming that the company is not at the time in the course of being wound up, the preferential debts of the company are to be paid out of the assets coming into the hands of the receiver in priority to any claims for principal or interest under the terms of the debenture (s40(1),(2); and see the virtually identical provision in Companies Act 1985 s196 as substituted by IA 1986 s439(1)). The definition of a floating charge in s251 avoids defeating the claims of creditors where the charge crystallises (ie into a fixed equitable charge) prior to the commencement of the receivership. *Re Woodroffes (Musical Instruments) Ltd* [1986] Ch 366, which involved the automatic crystallisation of a floating charge on cessation of a business, illustrates the effect of s251 well enough.

The effect of s40 is further mitigated by s11(5) which provides that, where an administrative receiver vacates office on the making of an administration order, he is not required on or after so doing to take any steps to comply with the duty imposed on him by s40 (s11(1)(b)). In such a case it appears that, on vacating office, any floating charge assets in the hands of the administrative receiver must be surrendered by him to the administrator. Substantially similar provisions to s40 are found in s175, which is concerned with payment of preferential debts on a winding-up. The inter-relationship of these two provisions has yet to be fully worked out by the courts.

It now appears from the decision in *Re Portbase Clothing Ltd* [1993] BCLC 796 that preferential claims which rank ordinarily in priority to a floating charge, where an authentic prior-ranking fixed charge is subordinated to the floating charge must also rank subject to it. Somewhat curiously from a practical point of view, liquidation expenses were also deemed in *Portbase* to be payable as a first claim of floating charge assets. For the operation of priority claims under fixed and floating charges, and how the parties may vary the regime and the consequences for preferential creditors, further reference should be made both to the *Portbase* decision and *Griffiths v Yorkshire Bank* [1994] 1 WLR 672, as referred to in Chapter 4 at para 4.2.

The starting-point on priorities is that fixed charges, whether legal or equitable, rank in priority to floating charges for payment out of assets over which they are realised, even where the legal or equitable fixed charge is created subsequent to the floating charge (*Wheatley v Silkstone and Haigh Moor Coal Co* (1885) 29 ChD 715). The basic reason for this is that, prior to crystallisation, the company will be free to deal with and dispose of the assets subject to the floating charge without the consent of the chargee. As between fixed charges, the basic rule at common law is that charges take priority in the order in which they are created, not from the date of their registration. It follows from this that a company will, generally speaking, be unable to grant a fixed charge in priority to a floating charge which has crystallised, since that charge will then constitute a fixed equitable charge, albeit that it may extend to after-acquired property as well as that subject to it at crystallisation; see *N W Robbie & Co Ltd v Witney Warehouse Co Ltd* [1963] 1 WLR 1324, but cf *Rother Iron Works Ltd v Canterbury Precision Engineers Ltd* [1974] QB 1 where set-off was permitted as between after-acquired property and a pre-crystallisation liability.

As between fixed charges the general rule is that a legal charge ranks in priority to a equitable charge, even if created subsequent to it, provided that the legal charge holder is a *bona fide* chargee without notice of the equitable charge. As between fixed equitable charges, and indeed equitable charges generally (which embraces floating charges which are necessarily of an equitable nature) the general rule is that charges rank in priority in chronological order of creation, fixed equitable charges prevailing over floating equitable charges (*Dearle v Hall* [1823-28] 3 Russ 1, as extended by Law of Property Act 1925 ss136 and 137 which provide that the priority of charges over choses in action (eg book debts and other debts), equitable interests in land

and capital (and security derivatives thereof) is governed by the order of whoever gives notice to the appropriate debtor or trustee as specified in the statutory provisions). These common law rules are modified by the company charge registration regime but, for present purposes, the following two points are relevant. First, an unregistered charge which is void under the Companies Act 1985 s399 loses its priority, and its holder therefore ranks as an unsecured creditor. Secondly, the registration of a charge under the Companies Act 1985, s395 gives deemed notice of the existence of the charge (*Wilson v Kelland* [1910] Ch 306) although priority remains determined by the date of creation of each charge.

As regards priority between floating charges over the whole of a company's business and undertaking, it is possible for a company to create a second floating charge which ranks before the first, but only if the debenture which secures the first charge expressly makes provision for such a prior ranking charge (*Re Automatic Bottlemakers Ltd* [1926] Ch 421). Without such express authority the creation of such a prior-ranking second floating charge is not possible, notwithstanding any provision in the first floating charge permitting the company to deal with its property as it thinks fit and to mortgage or sell it or any part of it (*Re Benjamin Cope & Sons Ltd* [1914] 1 Ch 800). At the same time it is clear from the *Re Automatic Bottlemakers Ltd* decision that the creation of a floating charge over the whole of a company's undertaking and business will not *per se* preclude the creation of a prior-ranking floating charge over a specific class of assets, such as book debts. However, and in the absence of clear judicial statement on this point, it is submitted that this approach could not be employed effectively as a method of circumventing the above rule in *Re Benjamin Cope* either by the creation of numerous floating charges over the whole or substantially the whole of the company's property or by the creation of a floating charge over a specific class of assets which constitutes the whole or substantially the whole of the company's property.

It is common in practice for a floating charge, or the debenture securing a floating charge, to contain a charge by which the company contractually undertakes not to create any fixed or floating charge which would rank in priority to or *pari passu* with the floating charge for repayment of the debt secured by it. The effect of a so-called 'negative pledge' clause operates in equity to prevent any subsequent chargee with knowledge of the clause from obtaining priority where the chargee or the company purports to do so (for a recent Scottish example, see *AIB Finance Ltd v Bank of Scotland* [1994] BCC 184). This in itself gives rise to a problem since it is not clear as to precisely what constitutes notice of the clause and its contents for present purposes. Certainly it has been held that a subsequent chargee will not be fixed with constructive notice of a negative pledge clause merely by virtue of knowledge of the debenture's existence or the fact that the debenture in which the clause is contained is registered at Companies House (which merely gives notice of the existence of the debenture to those persons dealing with the company); see *Siebe Gorman & Co Ltd v Barclays Bank Ltd* [1979] 2 Lloyd's Rep 142.

Furthermore, on being on notice of the existence of a debenture by virtue of its registration, any third party is under no obligation or duty to scrutinise the provisions of it. Indeed, the effect of the registration of a charge under the Companies Act 1985 is merely to give notice to the whole world of the existence of the charge (*Re Standard Rotary Machine Co Ltd* (1906) 95 LT 829; *Wilson v Kelland* [1910] 2 Ch 306). However, in practice, it is usual for the Registrar of Companies to register a negative pledge clause since these are usually included on Form 395 or 397 for registration purposes by chargees, notwithstanding the fact that it is not in fact one of the prescribed particulars required by Companies Act 1985 s395(1). It is arguable that a party conducting a company search which reveals a registered negative pledge clause should be fixed with actual notice of it, even though this may not actually be the case if the search is not perused in its entirety in detail. Nevertheless, even without a search of the company's register, it may be argued that a party will have inferred, as opposed to constructive, notice of a negative pledge clause in view of the common practice of including such clauses in floating charges as a matter of course; see Farrar (1976) 40 Conv (NS) 397. This argument is reinforced by the fact that the negative pledge clause would be revealed by an inspection of the charge in the company's own register of charges (which it is required to maintain and which any person may inspect at the registered office and take a copy of; Companies Act 1985 ss308 and 407). This suggestion would, however, run contrary to judicial opinion on the point, which is best put by Wright J in *G & T Earle Ltd v Hemson Rural District Council* (1928) 44 TLR 65 as follows;

> No doubt it is quite common for debentures to be subject to this limiting condition as to further charges, but that fact is not enough in itself to operate as constructive notice of the actual terms of any particular [debenture].

This decision was subsequently followed by the Supreme Court of the Republic of Ireland in *Welch v Bowmaker (Ireland) Lt*d [1980] IT 251. Thus, whilst the 'inferred knowledge' approach remains at least arguable, particularly as against sophisticated, corporate lenders, the perceived wisdom at the present time appears to be that it is not to be preferred.

The problems with notice of negative pledge clauses under the existing provisions of the Companies Act 1985 would have been alleviated to some extent by implementation of the 1989 Act's provisions. Whilst the 1989 Act had sought to abolish the doctrine of constructive notice generally by virtue of s711A(1), this should be seen in light of Companies Act 1985 s416(1) (as inserted by Companies Act 1989 s103) which provided that a person taking a charge over a company's property should be taken to have notice of any matter requiring registration and disclosed on the register at the time the charge was created. The practical effect of that provision would have been that, in relation to properly registered charges, a subsequent chargee would be deemed to be fixed with notice of both the existence of a registrable charge (as set out in Companies Act 1985, s396) and the prescribed particulars of it had they been duly registered. Unlike the current position in England and Wales, and as with the Scottish system, it is certain that the prescribed particulars which would have been laid down in regulations to be issued by the Secretary of State would have included negative pledge clauses (Companies Act 1985 s415(1),(2)(a) as inserted by Companies Act 1989 s103). Any proposed future legislation would be made all the more effective by the inclusion of such provisions.

Finally, a registered charge will take priority over an unregistered charge, the holder of the unregistered charge being demoted to the status of an unsecured creditor. This will be the case even where the registered charge holder acquires an interest in or over property subsequent to the unregistered charge holder, with notice by whatever means of the unregistered charge. This arose in *Re Monolithic Building Co* [1915] 1 Ch 643 where a company secured a loan to it by way of fixed charge over its land. The charge was not registered. Nine months later the company granted a floating charge over its business and undertaking in favour of one of its directors who had actually witnessed the execution of the previous charge over the property. The floating charge was registered and subsequently it was held that it took priority over and free of the fixed charge over the land. One way in which this situation may be avoided in practice would appear to be where the subsequent chargee contracts with the company and agrees in the terms of the charge or, indeed, elsewhere to take the charge subject to the unregistered charge. This might also be useful in relation to charges which are not registrable under the current provisions of the Companies Act 1985 s396 (but which will nonetheless require to be entered in the company's own register of charges under Companies Act 1985 s407). Presently, those include charges on certain choses in action (such as options to purchase) insurance policies, company shares and pledges of the company's property, none of which are listed as being registrable charges in Companies Act 1985 s396.

Virtually no consideration is afforded above to the question of priority as between legal and equitable security interests in their sense as security interests *per se*. The distinction between legal and equitable charges is most relevant in the situation in which a chargor deals with the property subject to the charge. However, as between charge-holders themselves, and as is most relevant to the question of priority right in appointing an administrative receiver, the system of registering company charges envisaged by the Companies Act 1985 does not rely on the form and legal nature of the legal or equitable interests as such to register for priority purposes. Rather, registration is a method of giving notice to a third party of a charge's existence which is adhered to strictly for priority purposes even, for example, if a person acquiring priority by registration does not act *bona fide* (*Midland Bank Trust Co Ltd v Green* [1981] AC 513). On the other hand, the rules discussed above are relevant as a pre-requisite as between charges which are registered properly in terms of priority.

## 3.5   Registration of Company Charges under the Companies Act 1985

The registration of the company charge(s) constituting the security of a debenture is fundamental to the quality of the security and its validity vis-à-vis the company and other creditors. Registration requires the delivery to the Registrar of Companies of prescribed particulars within 21 days of the creation of the charge, failing which the charge is void against (a) any subsequently appointed liquidator or administrator and (b) other creditors subject to any late registration as authorised by the court.

Sections 395 and 396 of the Companies Act 1985 provide for the registration of certain charges created by a company which is registered in England and Wales or a company incorporated outside England and Wales which has an established place of business in England and Wales (*Re Oriel Ltd* [1985] 1 BCC 99, 444). The position in Scotland is a separate subject which is not discussed in this book.

The Companies Act 1989 originally envisaged the insertion of new provisions into the Companies Act 1985 but the new provisions will not now be brought into force. A variety of reasons as to why the proposed provisions will remain unimplemented have been fielded, some official, some not. These include problems encountered in ensuring an efficient cross-flow of information between Companies House and the Land Registry, various technological problems encountered at Companies House and the perceived practical unworkability of the new provisions. These should be seen against the background of the difficulty posed by the lack in English law of a cohesive framework of charge registration in relation to real property generally. These difficulties have long been realised although various proposals have been largely ignored by Parliament. These include those made by the Crowther Committee in 1971, *Report of the Committee on Consumer Credit* (1971) Cmnd 4596 at Chap 5, and the final report of Professor Diamond in 1989, *A Review of Security Interests in Property*, which advocated a universal register of security interests in real property—including company charges—in the style of the US Uniform Commercial Code.

At the time of writing, the Department of Trade and Industry is reconsidering the question of reforms to the company charge registration system. It has become a sad fact of life of the legislative process in recent years in the field of commercial law that proposed legislative change in substantive areas has not adequately benefited from feedback from those practitioners and individuals who deal with the legislation on a day-to-day basis in practice on the ground. It is to be hoped that any newly proposed statutory changes in the field of company charge registration are not flawed in this way.

### 3.5.1  Registrable charges

Sections 395 and 396 apply to the following categories of charge (which term includes mortgages):

(a)  a charge for the purpose of securing any issue of debentures, which, would appear to include large scale issues of debentures, as in the case of the creation of debenture stock under a deed;

(b)  a charge on uncalled capital of a company;

(c)  a charge created or evidenced by an instrument which, if created by an individual, would require registration on a bill of sale (Bills of Sale Act 1878 s4). This category will not extend to a pledge or a genuine hire purchase transaction (*Wrightson v McArthur and Hutchison* [1921] 2 KB 807; cf *Dublin City Distillery v Doherty* [1916] AC 823 and *Stoneleigh Finance Ltd v Philips* [1965] 2 QB 537). It is arguable that certain retention of title or *Romalpa* clauses will and do require registration subject to certain criteria being satisfied. An example of this arose in *Re Bond Worth* [1980] Ch 228 where a clause in a contract, which provided that equitable and beneficial ownership of goods would remain with the seller until full payment was made, and that any conversion of the goods would create an equitable interest in the new goods in favour of the seller, amounted to a registrable charge for the purposes of Companies Act 1985 s395. The same would be true of security created for a loan which did not amount to a genuine hire purchase transaction (*Yorkshire Railway Wagon Co v Maclure* (1882) 21 ChD 309);

(d)  a charge on land (ie wherever situated, inter- or extra-territorially), or any interest in it, but not including a charge for any rent or other periodical sum issuing out of the land (note that registration may also be required under the Land Registration Act 1925);

(e)  a charge on book debts of the company (but note not 'other debts');

(f)  a floating charge on the company's undertaking or property;

(g)  a charge on calls made but not paid (*Bank of Australia v Abrahams* (1875) LR PC 265; see also here  *Re South Australian Barytes Ltd* [1977] 3 ACLR 52 for the technical distinction between uncalled share capital and uncalled share premiums);

(h)  a charge on a ship or aircraft, or any shares in a ship;

(i)   a charge on goodwill, on a patent or a licence under a patent, on a trademark or on a copyright or a licence under a copyright. This category would appear not to extend to registered designs.

### 3.5.2   Registration formalities

Within 21 days of the creation of a registrable charge, a written statement (on Form 395) providing the prescribed particulars of the charge together with the instrument creating the charge, must be filed with the Registrar of Companies (Companies Act 1985 s395). The date of creation of the charge is the date on which the charge is executed and therefore comes into existence, and not the date on which monies secured by it are advanced to the company or a third party (*Esberger & Son Ltd v Capital Counties Bank* (1913) 2 Ch 366). The same rule applies where monies are advanced prior to execution of the charge, the charge being incapable of registration before creation (*Re Colombian Fireproofing Co Ltd* [1910] 2 Ch 120).

Failure to register a charge within 21 days of its creation renders the charge void against a liquidator or administrator and other creditors. This does not, however, render the charge itself void. Rather, the charge remains valid as between the company and chargee (*Independent Automatic Sales v Knowles & Foster* [1962] 1 WLR 972; *Sanderson v Clark* [1913] TLR 579; *Re Ehrmann Bros Ltd* [1906] 2 Ch 677). Furthermore, the debt due as secured by the charge remains due albeit that the creditor will rank merely as an unsecured creditor on the liquidation of the company. These two apparently contradictory statements are reconciled to some extent by the fact that the money secured by a charge which subsequently becomes void becomes immediately repayable in full (Companies Act 1985 s395(2) and see *Wright v Horton* (1887) 12 App Cas 371). It is not clear whether the monies fall due to be repaid on the expiration of the 21-day period or on the appointment of a liquidator or administrator. The better view, it is submitted, is the former since this would avoid the chargee being prejudiced by having no immediate right of payment whilst remaining unsecured for the period between the expiration of the 21 days and the subsequent appointment of a liquidator or administrator. This does not, of course, preclude an application for late registration under Companies Act 1985 s404, as considered below, where the chargee wishes to establish its security (as opposed to seeking immediate repayment as due, which the company may well be unable to make).

The duty to register the particulars of every registrable charge created by a company, together with issues of debentures of a series requiring registration (on Form 397), falls on the company. It may, however, be effected by any person interested in the charge, most obviously the chargee (Companies Act 1985 s399(2)). In default, the company and every officer in default is liable to a fine and to a daily default fine for continued contravention (Companies Act

1985 s399(3)). Since the 1985 Act provides that registration may be effected by any person with an interest in the charge, it is common for a chargee, or its solicitors, to undertake to register the charge. Certainly this is the approach of banks and other financial institutions and serves to protect their own interests. Reference should be made on this point to *Trustees of PAF Foster v Crusts* [1986] BCLC 307 for the circumstances in which solicitors may be liable for negligence for failure to register a charge.

The main implication for a secured creditor arising on non-delivery of a charge to the Registrar within the 21-day period is that, to the extent that the charge confers any security over the company's property or undertaking, the charge is void against a liquidator or administrator and any creditor of the company.

### 3.5.3  Registration procedure and formalities

It is the duty of a company which is registered in England and Wales to deliver to the Registrar of Companies particulars of every registrable charge created by the company (including issues of a series of debentures) within 21 days of the creation of the charge (s399). These particulars are referred to as prescribed particulars, and are stated as being those particulars envisaged and contained in Form 395 by virtue of the Companies (Forms) Regulations 1985 (SI No 854 reg 4) (see Companies Act 1985 s744). These prescribed particulars are as follows:

(a)  the name of the company;
(b)  the date of creation of the charge;
(c)  a description of the instrument (if any) creating or evidencing the charge (eg a charge or a debenture);
(d)  the amount secured by the mortgage or charge;
(e)  the names and addresses of the mortgagees or persons entitled to the charge;
(f)  short particulars of the property mortgaged or charged;
(g)  particulars of any commission, allowance or discount.

Neither Form 395 nor Form 397 envisages the registration of a negative pledge clause as a prescribed particular. However, it is usual for such clauses to be included in the particulars submitted to the Registrar, usually in the space on the prescribed form for particulars of the property mortgaged or charged. Unless a negative pledge clause is stipulated as a prescribed particular, however, as was envisaged by the new Companies Act 1985 s415 (as was to be inserted by Companies Act 1989 s103), the position will remain that third parties, other perhaps than subsequent chargees, will not be fixed with constructive knowledge of the existence of any such charge which is registered or, indeed, any prescribed particulars which are duly registered.

(It should be noted that the general concept of constructive knowledge in this regard was to have been abolished by Companies Act 1985 s711A(1) as inserted by Companies Act 1989 s142 although this will no longer be the case pending newly-proposed legislation.)

Since the present prescribed particulars do not include negative pledge clauses, it would appear that only actual knowledge will be effective for such a clause to operate for present purposes. This would arise where, for example, a third party makes a search of the company's register which reveals the clause as registered. However, significant evidential problems exist in establishing fixed knowledge in this way although an argument might be raised that a subsequent chargee is fixed with inferred actual knowledge of the negative pledge clause, rather than constructive knowledge of it. This would be based on the premise that actual knowledge is inferred where the subsequent chargee has failed to inspect the register on the basis that negative pledge clauses are so common in modern commercial transactions (see Farrar (1976) 40 Conv (NS) 397 which remains relevant, and the earlier points raised in Farrar (1974) 38 Conv (NS) 315 which are probably now outdated). The inferred actual knowledge argument is obviously made more credible in the case of large, sophisticated institutional chargees who choose not to search the company's register as maintained by the Registrar; cf *G&T Earle Ltd v Hemsworth Rural District Council* (1928) 44 TLR at 65 per Wright J.

Section 397 of the Companies Act 1985 is applicable to the issue of a series of secured debentures where the holders rank *pari passu*. The prescribed particulars which must be delivered on Form 397 are as follows:

(a)  the total amount secured by the whole series;
(b)  the dates of the resolutions authorising the issue of the series of debentures and the date (if any) of the 'covering' deed by which the security is created or defined;
(c)  a description of the property charged;
(d)  the names of the trustees (if any) for the debenture-holders (ie of any 'covering' deed).

Form 397 should be used where an issue is made of secured debentures within a series, Form 397a being applicable to an issue of an entire series of secured debentures.

Whilst, in strict legal terms, there would appear to be no strict obligation for Forms 395 and 397 to be used to effect the registration of a charge, there are obvious dangers in failing to do so, not least the possible rejection by the Registrar of any non-standard documents submitted—which itself would run the risk of the charge not being registered within the statutory 21-day period. Furthermore, the Court of Appeal has made it clear in *R v Registrar of Companies, ex p Central Bank of India* [1986] 1 QB 1114, in relation to earlier but analogous legislation, that the chargee is ill-advised to submit particulars on non-standard documentation.

Following submission of the relevant form and the debenture to Companies House, the Registrar will check the terms of the registered particulars against the terms of the charge so as to ensure the accuracy of the particulars as submitted. If the particulars submitted appear defective or are otherwise incomplete or nonsensical, the Registrar will reject them and allow for amendment to be made. The danger for the chargee and his advisers here is that the statutory 21-day period for registration continues to run and, unless amended particulars can be returned within the period, any attempt at late registration will require an accompanying order under Companies Act 1985 s404. This will involve time, delay and expense and runs the risk that a subsequent chargee, who registers his interest properly, may acquire priority over the original chargee who registers outside the 21-day period. The implications of this are serious for the legal advisers to the chargee who undertake to deliver the particulars within the statutory period.

In practice, the Registrar will usually permit late registration of a company charge where the original particulars are defective only in some minor way. This might arise through typing or administrative error and may relate, for example, to a misstated company name or its number. Certainly late registration will not be permitted where the original particulars were defective in a substantial material way. Indeed, technically speaking, the Registrar would be at liberty to reject any late submission of particulars outside the 21-day period without an authorising court order, irrespective of the nature of the error or omission on the original particulars. For this reason, no reliance should be placed on the possibility that the Registrar will entertain late registration of any sort without a court order.

When the Registrar is satisfied that the particulars submitted to him are satisfactory they are entered by him on the company's register. The Registrar then issues a certificate of registration, which is deemed to be conclusive evidence that all of the particulars submitted comply with the requirements of the Companies Act 1985 even if, apparently, in fact they do not (Companies Act 1985 s401(2)). This approach favours the Registrar in the event of an administrative error on his part or that of his office and operates in substantively the same way as a defective certificate of incorporation which is deemed effective in the terms of any defects which appear in it. Consequently, the rights of the chargee under the terms of its debenture are not affected, irrespective of the defective particulars which may appear on a search of the company's register following registration. This arose in *Re C L Nye* [1971] 1 Ch 422 and *Re Eric Holmes (Property) Ltd* [1965] 1 Ch 1052 where incorrect dates of creation appeared on the particulars submitted to the Registrar. This approach was also adopted where there were mis-statements as to the full extent of the security comprised in a debenture (*National Provincial and*

*Union Bank of England v Charnley* [1924] 1 KB 431) and as to the amount secured by the charge (*Re Mechanisations Eaglescliffe Ltd* [1966] 1 Ch 20).

Although the registration of a charge is susceptible to judicial review, the Court of Appeal made it clear in *R v Registrar of Companies, ex p Central Bank of India* [1986] QB 1114 that the court will not be receptive to evidence which rebuts the particulars reflected in the certificate of registration in accordance with s401(2) of the 1985 Act.

### 3.5.4 Late registration: procedure and practice

The court is empowered to make an order under the Companies Act 1985, s404 to extend the registration period to a date specified in the order. In making an extension of time order, the court must be satisfied that the omission to register the charge within the 21-day statutory period was either accidental or due to inadvertence (eg arising out of genuine pressure of work) or some other sufficient case (such as ignorance of the law, as in *Re Jackson & Co Ltd* [1899] 1 Ch 348). In addition, the court must be satisfied that the omission to register is not of a nature which prejudices the position of creditors or shareholders of the company. Nonetheless the court is vested with a broad discretion to grant late registration if it considers it just and equitable to do so (*Re Braemar Investments Ltd* [1988] 4 BCC 366). The court may also grant interlocutory relief under the same rule if the statutory requirements are satisfied (*Re Chantry House Developments plc* [1990] BCC 646). However, the court is unlikely to be satisfied that late registration should be permitted without specific reference to genuine reasons for the failure to register and the circumstances in which these arose (*Kris Cruisers Ltd* [1948] 2 All ER 1105). On the obtaining of an order from the court for late registration of a charge, the prescribed particulars (on Form 395 or 397 as appropriate) together with the instrument creating the charge and an office copy of the court order are filed with the Registrar of Companies. The Registrar will then check the various documents submitted to him and, if satisfied as to their accuracy, will issue a certificate of registration.

One recent case illustrates a number of common practical problems encountered in relation to late registration of company charges. *Barclays Bank v Cyprus Popular Bank* [1993] BCC 404 involved a charge created over real property in January 1989, which was registered at the Land Registry in July 1989 but not registered with the Registrar of Companies. When the omission became apparent in October 1989, the chargee attempted to obtain a fresh charge over the assets of the chargor on a number of occasions, each time unsuccessfully. In October 1990, a third party obtained a charge over the real property of the chargor company. In December 1992, the original chargee obtained an order under the Companies Act 1985 s404 extending the time for registration, although this was conditional on the usual proviso that the charge took effect subject to any charge subsisting at the time of registration. The chargee appealed against the condition and the third party applied to prevent the charge being registered. The original chargee was refused an extension of time to register the charge created in January 1989. This was because the court had not been provided with the material enabling it to establish whether it would be just and equitable to grant relief in the circumstances. Furthermore, the original chargee's solicitor did not advance reasons explaining the failure to register the charge when created. In addition, the court could not be satisfied that the failure to register would not prejudice other creditors and, therefore, considered that it had no discretion to grant relief. Indeed, even if such a discretion had existed, the court held that it could not have been exercised due to the long delay in applying for relief and the fact that the original chargee had attempted to obtain a fresh charge over instead of applying for immediate relief under the Companies Act 1985 s404.

The *Popular Bank of Cyprus* case is not unique in terms of indicating the unwillingness of the court to grant extensions of time under the Companies Act 1985 s404 other than in circumstances where genuine and excusable reasons for the non-registration or non-delivery of the particulars can be established. These have included an ignorance of the requirements on the part of a director (*Re Jackson & Co Ltd* [1899] 1 Ch 348), delays caused by the Inland Revenue's Stamp Office and misunderstanding on the company's solicitors' part as to the registration provision (*Re Bootle Cold Storage and Ice Co Ltd* [1901] WN 54) and delays arising as a result of registration formalities being complied within a foreign jurisdiction (India) (*Re Tingri Tea Co Ltd* [1901] WN 165).

Perhaps the most useful recent *dictum* on this point is that of Hoffman J in *Re Braemar Investments Ltd* [1988] 4 BCC 366 which explained that the establishment of an omission to register on the ground of inadvertence is itself subject to the question of whether it would be just and equitable in the circumstances for the court to exercise its discretion in permitting late registration. The *Braemar Investments* case involved an order permitting late registration where a bank had instructed its solicitors to register the charge and, on discovering omission to register, had acted speedily in effecting registration itself (see also *Re MIG Trust Ltd* [1933] Ch 542 at 560 per Lord Hanworth MR.)

One particular factor of which the courts have always been mindful in granting an order for late registration of a charge is the imminence of liquidation of the company. The leading authority on this area is *Re Ashpurton Estates Ltd* [1983] 1 Ch 110 which involved a chargee who actively chose not to seek late registration, because the company was experiencing financial difficulties and an application to register the charge may have jeopardised the pending sale of a number of charged properties. Following the convening of a meeting to wind up the company, the chargee applied for an order for late registration which was refused, primarily on the grounds that a winding-up of the company was imminent. Two appeals on this point were unsuccessful, the second to the Court of Appeal being founded on the ground that the chargee had actively chosen not to seek late registration on becoming aware of non-registration and the legitimate entitlement of the court to consider the solvency of a company when granting an order for late registration and the protection of other creditors (see Farrar [1983] JBL 253 on this point, and see also *Re Resinoid & Mica Products Ltd* [1983] Ch 132, a 1967 decision which was approved of by the Court of Appeal in the *Ashpurton* case to the extent that it supported the court's refusal of late registration on the grounds of imminent winding-up).

### 3.5.5  Late registration in liquidation

Where a company is actually in liquidation at the time at which the application for late registration is made, there is arguably little point in obtaining an order since, as mentioned earlier, in its usual form the order will contain a proviso which effectively preserves the security rights of creditors over charged assets that were or are acquired prior to the effecting of the late registration. As such, the holder of the charge will gain nothing by late registration in relation to other secured creditors, since the order itself will do nothing to affect or alter the priority of creditors' rights in the liquidation. The late registration order might, however, be of use where it serves to establish the chargee's priority over unsecured creditors in the event that any dividend is likely to be paid out to that class of creditors in the liquidation. Where an order serves no useful purpose, the applicant chargee clearly runs the risk of incurring costs unnecessarily, as in *Re Abrahams & Sons Ltd* [1902] 1 Ch 695 where no useful purpose for the application could be established.

In the event of liquidation, late registration of a charge will only be granted in very special circumstances such as fraud as was suggested in *Re Ashpurton Estates Ltd*; see also *Re John Bateson & Co Ltd* [1985] BCLC 259 and *Re Barrow Borough Transport Ltd* [1989] 5 BCC 646 where leave was refused when an application for late registration was made in the course of an administration order which it was clear would be followed by liquidation.

Perhaps the only other circumstances in which late registration may be envisaged in the event of liquidation is where secured creditors, who would otherwise be affected by the order, acquiesce to it and no detriment arises on the making of the order to unsecured creditors. This scenario arose in *Re Arnold & Co Ltd* [1984] BCLC 535 where an application for late registration was made by Canada Permanent Trust at a time when the liquidation of the company was virtually inevitable. Harman J was, however, prepared to grant to late registration of the charge on the grounds that unsecured and preferential claims were unaffected by the late registration, the only real issue being as between the applicant and Lloyds Bank which had previously entered into a priority agreement with Canada Permanent Trust expressly consenting to a fixed charge (ie the unregistered charge) in favour of the applicant. In the circumstances Lloyds Bank raised no objection to the late registration on the basis that Canada Permanent Trust's equitable charge over the same property under the debenture had been properly registered. This factor had significant influence on Harman J in granting the late registration, although it should be noted that a proviso was included in the order protecting the legal interests of any creditor(s) acquired over the property subject to the unregistered charge between the date of acquisition and the date of late registration. For an unsuccessful application for late registration on similar circumstances and an unsuccessful attempt by counsel to justify late registration on the basis of the rule preventing unjust enrichment of an insolvent company under the rule in *ex parte James* (1874) LR 9 Ch 609, see *Re John Bateson & Co Ltd* [1985] BCLC 259 and the incisive comment in McCormack, *Registration of Company Charges* 1st edn (Sweet and Maxwell, 1994), at 124–5.

The unregistered chargee may, of course, seek an order which does not contain a proviso protecting prior registered rights in favour of other creditors. It is submitted, however, that in view of the difficulty faced by an applicant in obtaining an order permitting late registration where a company is in liquidation, the obtaining of an order effectively enabling the unregistered chargee to jump the queue of secured creditors will be difficult in the extreme except in the most exceptional circumstances. Indeed, such an order would appear to contravene the general policy underlying the IA 1986, which seeks to establish a framework for the orderly distribution of legitimate claims by creditors on a company's assets in liquidation. Furthermore, it is arguable that such an order would contravene the general rule on post-liquidation distribution as provided for in s127 which prevents post-compulsory liquidation distribution of company assets without sanction of the court.

Although the solvency of a company is not a prerequisite for the obtaining of an order permitting late registration of a charge under the Companies Act 1985 s404, the matter is of significant practical importance. This is because the court will only exceptionally make an order if the company is either insolvent, in the sense that its solvency cannot be established, or if the company is in formal liquidation. In *Re Ashpurton Estates Ltd* [1983] 1 Ch 110, for example, the Court of Appeal considered that very special circumstances would need to be established for authority to register a charge out of time, following a resolution to wind up a company having been passed, particularly where the chargee had been aware of the lack of registration for some months as in that case (and see also *Re John Bateson & Co Ltd* [1985] BCLC 259). However, in *Braemar Investments Ltd* [1988] 4 BCC 366 Hoffman J discounted an imminent liquidation as merely one relevant factor and, in considering the *Ashpurton Estates* case, continued:

> As a matter of strict law an application to extend time is not too late if the registration can be effected before the liquidation actually commences.

It is submitted that these two cases can be distinguished on their particular facts.

The registration of a charge on or following a liquidation may nonetheless be problematic since, in a winding-up by the court, any disposition of the company's property after the commencement of the winding-up is void subject to contrary order by the court (s127). This rule does not apply in a voluntary winding-up although the directors may not dispose of property after the date of the winding-up resolution by the company, subject to authorisation by the liquidator or a committee of creditors (s91(2)).

Perhaps the most commonsensical approach in the face of imminent liquidation where an application is made for an order authorising registration of a charge out of time, is that adopted by the Court of Appeal in *Exeter Trust Ltd v Screenways Ltd* [1991] BCC 447. In that case the court's order granted liberty to the liquidator to apply to the court within a specified time to discharge the order following the company going into liquidation by a specified date. (See also *Re L H Charles & Co Ltd* [1935] WN 15 for a similar approach.) This is common practice in such circumstances, as is the practice of the Registrar of Companies of delaying registration of the charge until after the specified date. It is also common practice for the court to insert a proviso into an order of the *Popular Bank of Cyprus* type as regards the actual authorised late registration of the charge in favour of third party creditors' rights (*Re MIG Trust Ltd* [1933] Ch 542; see also *Re Joplin Brewery Co Ltd* [1902] 1 Ch 79). The court is unlikely, however, to grant such a proviso in favour of third parties where their rights are acquired either fraudulently or on the basis of their knowledge of want of crystallisation of the charge for which late registration is subsequently sought (see, for example, *Re Fablehill Ltd* [1991] BCC 590).

### 3.5.6   Late registration by the administrative receiver

One question which remains unanswered judicially is whether a receiver, including an administrative receiver, who will invariably be appointed as agent of the company, should be subject to a charge which is registrable but actually unregistered. At first instance in *Clough Mill Ltd v Martin* [1984] 1 WLR 1067, O'Donoghue J had expressed that an unregistered charge was void against a receiver on the basis that the debenture-holder appointing the receiver amounted to a creditor against whom an unregistered charge is invalid by virtue of the Companies Act 1985 s395(1). Whilst the *Clough Mill* decision was subsequently reversed, this was on other grounds and O'Donoghue J's view remains. It is submitted that this view is the correct one. In the converse situation there appears to be good ground for doubting the argument that a receiver should be stopped from pleading the company's want of compliance with the registration requirements imposed by the Companies Act 1985 on behalf of the company. However, the position remains without judicial clarification. Notwithstanding the implied statutory agency relationship between the administrative receiver and the company, the reason for this doubt rests on the primary duty owed by the administrative receiver to his appointing debenture-holder. It would be wholly inequitable to prejudice a debenture-holder by prohibiting the administrative receiver from seeking to register a charge purely on the basis that it is strictly necessary that the company itself pleads its own default. This view is supported by the fact that an administrator—whose powers are synonymous with those of an administrative receiver under Sched 1 and the office of which was modelled on the receiver appointed under a floating charge—is entitled to pleaded non-registration without direct involvement of the company itself (cf *Independent Automatic Sales Ltd v Knowles and Foster* [1962] 1 WLR 974 per Buckley J).

## 3.6 The Company's Register of Charges

The Companies Act 1985 ss406 and 408 require respectively that a company keeps at its registered office a copy of every instrument creating a charge and that the register of charges is open to public inspection. The keeping of copies of charging instruments extends only to those charges requiring registration under the Companies Act 1985 as set out above.

The requirement that a register of charges must be maintained by the company extends to all charges (eg including those arising by operation of law such as certain classes of lien) and not simply those requiring registration under the existing legislation. The register itself need not be in any prescribed form but must contain an entry giving a short description of the property charged, the amount of the charge and the names of the persons entitled to the charge other than in the case of bearer securities. As with charging instruments, the register is open to inspection by members and existing creditors (but not prospective creditors) free of charge or by any other persons on payment of a prescribed fee.

Whilst a failure to register a charge in a company's own register of charges does not invalidate the charge in any way, any officer of the company who knowingly and wilfully permits such an omission is liable to a fine (Companies Act 1985 s407). The company's own register of charges potentially offers a safety mechanism for cross-checking the existence of charges as revealed by a search of the company's file as maintained by the Registrar of Companies. In practice, however, office-holders rarely avail themselves of this opportunity, largely on account of what is widely (but not altogether accurately) perceived as the unimpeachable nature of the results of enquiries made of Companies House.

*Chapter Four*

# The Debenture Holder's Security: 2

## 4.1 Introduction

This chapter deals with the taking of security over specific assets and considers some of the conceptual and practical problems which may arise in the course of and as a consequence of such transactions. Initially, the important question of the variation by creditors of the relative priority of their rights is addressed.

## 4.2 Varying Creditor Priority: Subordination, Subrogation and Related Problems

The priority rules considered in the previous chapter have a clear bearing on the willingness of certain creditors to commit themselves to financing a company where the security offered by the company is weak in terms of priority vis-à-vis other secured creditors.

In practice, a company and/or its creditors may be willing to agree to vary the normal priority rules whereby an ordinarily weak creditor, in terms of priority, is promoted to rank above or in lieu of another creditor or creditors ('subrogation') or where one creditor (the subordinated or junior creditor) agrees not to be paid until the other creditor (the senior creditor) is paid ('subordination'). On this area see generally Wood, *The Law of Subordinated Debt*, (Sweet and Maxwell, 1988). The company itself being party to such an agreement is highly relevant and is referred to below.

Subordination, and less commonly subrogation, will usually arise in circumstances where a new or existing creditor is prepared to introduce new funds into a business in return for security which is not subject to existing security. A subordination agreement will often arise in an insolvency workout and will usually take one of three forms. First, and most commonly, it will involve the complete subordination of one or more secured debts to a new debt. Alternatively, it may 'cap' or limit the priority of a first-ranking creditor to a stipulated amount. Thirdly, and less commonly, the agreement may restrict the security of the first-ranking creditor to one or more specified class or classes of assets.

In administrative receivership, creditor priority is particularly relevant for three principal purposes. First, where there are two or more secured creditors who may potentially appoint an administrative receiver, the cumulative priority of the creditors' security, it is submitted, will dictate which creditor has a prior-ranking entitlement to appoint an administrative receiver (see Chapter 5 at para 5.3). Secondly, the question of priority is of fundamental importance to the employment of s43 as a means of disposing of property by an administrative receiver which is subject to a prior-ranking charge. Thirdly, creditor priority is of particular significance to the question of priority as between fixed, floating and preferential creditors. Subordination agreements are potentially problematic in both receiverships and liquidations, particularly as between senior and subordinated creditors who are the holders of fixed and floating charges respectively. This is because, in the ordinary course of things, fixed charge holders will take priority over preferential creditors whereas floating charge holders will not. This point is borne out in the recent decision in *Re Portbase Clothing Ltd* [1993] BCLC 796.

*Portbase* concerned the question of whether preferential creditors had priority in a claim on book debts and other debts of the company, over another creditor who held a purported fixed charge over those assets in a winding-up. The creditors had executed a deed of priority as regards their interests in the winding-up of the company which effectively constituted a subordination agreement. Stemming from that problem was the question of whether the liquidator's costs and expenses of the winding-up were payable in priority to the claims of the preferential creditors.

On 21 June 1989 Portbase Clothing Ltd (the company in question) created a debenture containing fixed and floating charges over its assets in favour of Creditor 1, the company's bankers. On 18 April 1989 the company created a floating charge in favour of Creditor 2 (ie two of its directors). On 16 January 1991 the company purported to create a fixed and floating charge over its assets in favour of the directors' pension fund (Creditor 3). By a deed of priority, also executed on 16 January 1991, Creditor 3 was deemed to rank ahead of all charges in favour of Creditors 1 and 2. Creditors 1, 2 and 3 and (notably) the company were all party to the deed of priority. Subsequently the company went into voluntary insolvent liquidation with insufficient assets to discharge all preferential and secured creditors. Notably, the liquidation followed the crystallisation of the floating charge other than by appointment of a receiver. The company realised £97,848 in its liquidation and subsequent contemporaneous receivership. That amount did not take account of £39,500 payable to the Inland Revenue and Customs and Excise as preferential creditors. This meant that if liquidation expenses and preferential creditors were paid in priority to the claims of secured creditors there would be little, if any, surplus for remaining creditors. Conversely, if the liquidation expenses did not rank ahead of the claims of the trustees of the directors' pension scheme (Creditor 3) then there would be insufficient sums remaining to discharge the liquidator's expenses and, indeed, nothing for preferential creditors. Irrespective of the question of priority, no monies would be available to discharge the secured liability Creditor 1 or Creditor 2 under the debenture or the claim of unsecured creditors.

The case turned on two questions: (a) whether or not the claims of the preferential creditors, which were to be paid out of the book and other debts of the company, had priority over the claims of Creditor 3. (Interestingly, the question of whether the trustees' debenture created a fixed or floating charge over book debts was never argued, the floating charge nature of the security being conceded by Creditor 3 on the basis of *Re Brightlife* [1986] BCLC 418.); (b) and following from this, if the preferential creditors did have such priority, were the costs and expenses of the winding-up payable in priority to the claims of the preferential creditors? These questions centred on the interpretation of ss175(2)(b) and 115.

A substantially similar provision to s175(2)(b) in relation to receiverships—to which this judgment was also relevant—operates where a company is not in the course of being wound up. This requires that preferential debts are paid out of the assets coming into the hands of the receiver in priority to any claims for principal or interest in respect of a floating charge as contained in a debenture. This is by virtue of ss40 and 59 (applicable to Scotland) which effectively impose a positive obligation on every receiver appointed to enforce a floating charge to discharge preferential claims (*Inland Revenue Commissioners v Goldblatt* [1972] Ch 498; *Woods v Winskill* [1913] 2 Ch 303; *Westminster Corp v Haste* [1950] Ch 442).

The operation of this provision is highlighted by the decision in *Re Berkeley Applegate (Investment Consultants) Ltd (No2)* [1988] 4 BCC 279 in which it was held that a liquidator was entitled to recover his proper expenses and remuneration as a charge on floating charge assets, despite the fact that these did not constitute 'company's assets' (in that case) for the purposes of s115. This was notwithstanding the fact that the liquidator had done substantial work in relation to assets which, after investigation, turned out to be assets in which the company had no beneficial interest.

In *Portbase*, Chadwick J held further that the effect of the deed of priority was that Creditor 1 only became entitled to be paid out of the assets after payment of the debts secured by Creditor 3's floating charge. Section 175(2)(b), it followed, applied to the book debts and other debts. Preferential creditors would be paid out of those assets in priority to the floating charge and Creditor 1. Furthermore, assets which were subject to a charge which, as created, was a floating charge but which had crystallised prior to the commencement of the liquidation were still to be regarded as 'company's assets' within the meaning of s115. The expenses of the liquidation were therefore payable out of those assets. On the question of what constituted 'company's assets', Chadwick J specifically chose not to follow the decision in *Re Christionette International Ltd* [1982] 2 All ER 225 which had held that company assets included assets covered by a floating charge—in accordance with the decision in *Re Barleycorn Enterprises Ltd* [1970] Ch 465—unless the floating charge has crystallised before the commencement of the winding-up (ie for the purposes of the previously operative and analogous Companies Act 1948 s309). The approach adopted by Chadwick J reflects s251 which now extends the definition of a floating charge to a charge, which 'as created' was a floating charge notwithstanding the fact that it has crystallised before the commencement of the winding-up (see also here *Re Pearl Maintenance Services Ltd* (1995), unreported, 2 March). Chadwick J's approach confirms some speculation on the point as to the practical effect of s251. The learned judge's reasoning also displayed deference to the established legal principle that respective charge-holders should be at liberty to agree between themselves that the priorities of their respective charges should differ from what would ordinarily be implied by law (*Cheah Theam Swee v Equiticorp Finance Group Ltd* [1992] 1 AC 472).

Chadwick J held further that, as a matter of construction, the deed of priority between the parties to it had expressed that monies arising in the liquidation should be applied first in payment of the amount secured by Creditor 3's debenture. The practical effect of this was that Creditor 1's fixed and floating securities had effectively, by virtue of the agreement of the debenture-holder, become subject to Creditor 3's debenture. That is, Creditor 1's fixed charge over book debts and other debts became subordinate to the ordinarily subordinate floating charge in Creditor 3's debenture. The effect of this was that the deed of priority provided that Creditor 1 did not become entitled—under either its fixed or floating charge—to payment until the debts secured by Creditor 3's floating charge had been satisfied. The assets available to satisfy Creditor 3's debts were assets to which the provisions of s175(2)(b) were applicable. Preferential creditors, therefore, would be paid out of the assets comprising the book and other debts, in priority to the fixed and floating charges of Creditor 1. In short, the effect of the judgment was to treat the priority of the various creditors as follows:

(i)   preferential creditors (by virtue of s175(2)(b));
(ii)  Creditor 3's purported 'fixed' charge over book and other debts (which was conceded as a floating charge);
(iii) Creditor 3's floating charge;
(iv) Creditor 1's fixed charge (over book and other debts);
(v)  Creditor 1's floating charge;
(vi) Creditor 2's floating charge.

A substantially similar problem is suggested by Professor R M Goode in his collected lectures *Legal Problems of Credit and Security*, 2nd edn (1982) at 97–8 *et seq*. Chadwick J actually made reference to relevant elements of Professor Goode's hypothetical problem in which two creditors, A and B, agree to the treatment of their own debts *inter se* in an agreement to which, unlike *Portbase*, the company is not a party. In Professor Goode's problem, preferential creditors have priority over B (under statute) whereas they do not over A, a fixed charge holder, (again, under statute). A and B then execute an agreement whereby B has priority over A in the discharge of their debts. Professor Goode's solution to this circular question of priority on liquidation was to treat B's interest as subrogated to A's interest to the extent necessary to give effect to the parties' subordination agreement. That is, B would collect in priority to the preferential creditors such amount as was due to A as fixed chargee, or such part of that amount necessary to discharge B's claim, any balance being payable to A subject to the discharge of preferential creditors under s175(2)(b). Professor Goode's solution actually accords with the decision of Nourse J in *Re Woodroffes (Musical Instruments) Ltd* [1985] 2 All ER 908 at 912 although Chadwick J chose to refine the analysis. The learned judge held that in the *Portbase* case there could be no question of Creditor 1's fixed charge being subrogated 'clear' of preferential creditors to the interest of Creditor 3's purported fixed charge, on the basis that it had been conceded by Creditor 3 that the charge was, in fact, a floating charge.

The *Portbase* decision was distinguished in *Griffiths v Yorkshire Bank* [1994] 1 WLR 1427 where Morritt J recognised that the nature of a floating charge is such that proprietory rights which rank in priority to the rights of the floating charge debenture-holder may be granted in priority to it without the need for further formality. The case involved a company which had created two debentures consecutively, each containing fixed and floating charges. The second debenture contained a provision whereby the second debenture-holder could give notice converting its floating charge to a fixed charge (over all stock-in-trade and any book debts). The second debenture-holder subsequently demanded payment and gave notice converting its floating charge. Later on the same day the first debenture-holder demanded payment and appointed receivers. The receivers applied for directions as to the determination of the rights of the company's preferential creditors. Morritt J held that when the floating charge in the second debenture had crystallised on service of the notice, it took priority over the floating charge in the earlier debenture which was not lost on the subsequent crystallisation of the first debenture's floating charge (ie on the appointment of the receivers). In contrast to *Portbase*, this was held to be the case because there was no agreement between the parties to produce that effect. As a consequence, the second debenture-holder, as first and fixed chargee, was entitled to the stock and book debts and their proceeds of realisation. It was immaterial that the receivers appointed had realised the proceeds in that they were not entitled to do so. Consequently, the proceeds of the stock and book debts were applied in the order:

(a) First debenture-holder under its fixed charge;
(b) Second debenture-holder under its fixed charge;
(c) Preferential creditors;
(d) First debenture-holder under its floating charge;
(e) Second debenture-holder under its floating charge;
(f) Unsecured creditors.

In *Portbase* the fact that the floating charge had crystallised prior to or on liquidation did not mean that the crystallised charge ranked prior to preferential debts. This was because of the 'once a floater, always a floater' definition now contained in s251. The fact that the floating charge had crystallised (whether automatically, by conversion, service of a 'crystallising' notice or otherwise, such as on winding-up), still rendered the charge a floating charge following liquidation (ie at the 'relevant date' as prescribed by s387). As such, the crystallised floating charge remained subordinated to preferential creditors and, therefore, constituted 'company's assets' for the purposes of s115, from which all expenses properly incurred in the winding-up were payable in priority to all other claims. This approach reverses the law as it had previously stood. Decisions such as *Re Woodroffes (Musical Instruments) Ltd* [1985] 2 All ER 908, where the court gave effect in this regard to the concept of automatic crystallisation on the cessation of a business, and *Re Brightlife Ltd* [1986] 4 BCC 279, where the court permitted a debenture-holder to serve a notice crystallising a floating charge so as to defeat preferential claims in an impending liquidation, therefore no longer represent good law. The same is true of the decisions in *Re Griffin Hotel Co Ltd* [1941] Ch 129 and *Stein v Saywell* (1969) 121 CLR 529, a decision of the Australian High Court, both of which were referred to in *Portbase*.

*Portbase* amounts to a sound decision in strictly legal terms in view of what the parties, including the company, had freely agreed between themselves. Nevertheless the decision has a bizarre practical implication in that it appears to permit a liquidator to avail himself of floating charge assets subject to an administrative receiver irrespective of whether the administrative receiver is appointed prior to or following the liquidation. In effect, the decision in *Portbase* virtually abolishes the practical implication of the crystallisation of a floating charge and imports the s251 definition into the scope of the term 'company's assets'. With respect, that conclusion is misguided and would be much improved by a return to the approach in *Re Christionette International Ltd* [1982] 3 All ER 225. Nevertheless, it is worth noting that Chadwick J's reasoning and decision accord with two Australian cases, *Waters v Widdows* [1984] VR 503 and *Deputy Commissioner of Taxation v Horsburgh* [1984] VR 773, which held that, where a fixed chargee willingly subordinates himself to a floating chargee who is subject to preferential creditors, the fixed chargee has necessarily subordinated himself to the preferential creditors as well as to the floating chargee.

The point raised earlier concerning the relevance of the company being a party to the deed of priority is significant to the decision in *Portbase*. Were the company not to be a party to the deed, it would follow that the liquidator, (acting on behalf of the company) would have no contractual relationship with any of the creditors as regards the treatment of the application of assets other than in accordance with the application regime applied by IA 1986. As such, the liquidator would be required, indeed bound on pain of the institution of proceedings against him by creditors for breach of statutory duty, to distribute assets as required by IA 1986. This would almost certainly have been the case in the *Portbase* decision had the company not in fact been a party to the deed of priority. This would not, of course, detract from the right of those creditors who were subject to a deed, and in the absence of the company being contractually bound to it, to initiate proceedings *inter se* to bring about an equitable distribution of assets in accordance with the terms of any contractual agreement made between themselves. Such an action would be founded most appropriately on the equitable doctrine of restitution, on the basis that applied funds were held on constructive trust for the true beneficiary creditor. Such an approach accords with the decision in *Cheah Theam Swee v Equiticorp* [1992] 1 AC 472 which is good authority for the proposition that two successive mortgagees may contract as to the treatment of monies arising *inter se* on a mortgagee's sale without the prior consent of the mortgagor as to such a distribution, the mortgagor and the mortgagees having no contractual arrangement as regards the treatment of such proceeds as between the mortgagees themselves.

Subordination agreements clearly turn on their own particular provisions and are clearly not limited to liquidations. Particularly relevant is whether or not the company is privy to, and therefore bound by, any such agreement. Any creditor who agrees to subordinate his interest to that of another is better protected where the company is party to the subordination agreement. This is because the company is then bound by the agreement and may be precluded from distributing assets in accordance with statute, thereby leaving the creditors to sort out matters between themselves subsequently. The position is most acute where a fixed-charge holder—who would otherwise take free of preferential creditors—subordinates his interest to that of the significantly weaker floating-charge holder (ss40(1),(2) and 175(2)(b)). One possible solution to this in practice is to seek an alternative to the method of 'demoting' the fixed-charge holder to a priority position ranking 'behind' the floating-charge holder under the agreement. An alternative is to retain the fixed charge status and to subrogate the subordinate security interest to it, whereby that subordinate security interest holder receives monies *in rem* of the fixed-charge holder as such. However, in his book *The Law of Subordinated Debt* 1st edn (Sweet and Maxwell, 1988) at 84 Professor Philip Wood suggests that '[this] solution... is plainly better for the senior creditor. Whether subrogation could be achieved by contract is a matter for conjecture.'

The 'subrogate rather than subordinate' approach is clearly one requiring careful drafting, willing parties and a weather eye on the nature of charges 'as created'. It is nevertheless submitted that the viability of contractual subrogation need not be as conjectural as Professor Wood suggests. The prerequisites for contractual subrogation would appear to be the following:

- privity between the company and the respective charge holders in the form of, say, a deed of priority;
- the technical avoidance of a purported fixed charge (to which the floating-charge holder's interest is subrogated) being deemed a charge which is, in fact, a floating charge 'as created' for the purposes of s251; and
- the avoidance of the fixed charge being attacked as a preference under s239.

The validity of the floating-charge holder's subrogation to the fixed-charge holder's interest *in rem* would, it is considered, be less troublesome if the preferential creditors were also to be party to the deed of priority although, in practice, such an agreement is highly unlikely because of the preferential creditors' usual unwillingness to prejudice their own position.

Furthermore, neither will this commercial objective be validly achieved by the service of a notice of assignment of dividend by the fixed-charge holder on the liquidator under IR r11.11(1), which requires the payment of his dividend to the subrogated floating-charge holder in his stead. This is not least because, in practice, it is very unusual for a fixed-charge holder to surrender his security and prove for the full amount of his debt in the liquidation, as this will have the effect of the creditor being deemed to surrender his security. The creditor may, however, choose to value his security in his proof and prove for the balance of his debt or prove for any deficiency after realising his security, where he is not fully secured (IR rr4.75(1)(g), 4.88). The practical drawback which accounts for the ineffectiveness of a notice of assignment or dividend in the above scenario is that preferential creditors could attack such an arrangement both as a sham and as an attempt by the fixed-charge holder to transfer an *in rem* entitlement in the liquidation to a subordinate creditor by way of a non-*in rem* entitlement which, by its nature, must be subordinate to the entitlement of the preferential creditors. One obvious method by which an effective subrogation arrangement might be achieved is the taking of a fixed charge by the subordinate floating-charge holder over those assets over which the 'subrogating' fixed-charge holder already holds such a charge. The major drawbacks with such an arrangement are that it might be attacked subsequently by a liquidator as a preference under s239, as well as requiring the acquiescence of the company.

Notwithstanding the *Portbase* decision, there remains a further question which has yet escaped specific judicial attention. Suppose that an administrative receiver is appointed and discharges his functions contemporaneously with the liquidator of the company. What is the position of floating charge assets falling into the hands of the receiver, as regards the liquidator's entitlement to them in respect of his costs, expenses and remuneration? Specifically, does the liquidator have a right to these out of the floating charge assets in priority to the same claims by the administrative receiver? These are matters which are considered elsewhere, as are the related questions of the status of floating charge assets as 'company's assets' (following the decision of Ferris J in *Re ELS Ltd* [1994] All ER 833) and whether a subordination agreement requires registration under the Companies Act 1985 (see Doyle [1994] 10 IL&P at 134–42).

## 4.3 Fixed and Floating Charges over Book Debts

### 4.3.1 What are book debts?

A consideration of specific fixed and floating charges over book debts initially requires consideration of the term 'book debts' itself. Buckley LJ put the matter thus in *Independent Automatic Sales Ltd v Knowles & Foster* [1962] 1 WLR 975 at 983:

> If it can be said of a debt arising in the course of a business and due or growing due to the proprietor of that business that such a debt would or could in the ordinary course of such a business be entered in well-kept books relating to that business, that debt can properly be called a book debt whether it is in fact entered in the books of that business or not.

This approach is in keeping with Esher MR's description of book debts in the subsequently affirmed decision in *Official Receiver v Tailby* [1886] 18 QBD 25 as 'debt arising in a business...which ought to be entered in the company's books' (at 29). In *Robertson v Grigg* (1932) 47 CLR 257 Cravan Duffy CJ went further and made reference to 'debts owing to a business, of a kind entered in books of account of the business and in fact so entered' (at 266). This definition is qualified by the decision in *Re Welsh Irish Ferries Ltd* [1986] Ch 471 which refers to book debts which arise in the course of the normal business of the company (or other business undertaking). Thus, in *Tatung (UK) Ltd v Cralex Telesure Ltd* [1988] BCC 325, rental payments due from customers in respect of equipment to a company which let electrical goods on hire were held to be subject to a fixed charge over book debts where the payments had arisen in the normal course of the company's business.

The judicial approach to the meaning of book debts is not altogether satisfactory, since the definitions proffered appear to take no account of debts arising which are due to the company but which are extraordinary in the sense that they do not arise in the normal course of its business. The facts of *Paul Frank Ltd v Discount Bank (Overseas) Ltd* [1967] Ch 348 illustrate the point. In that case the company had obtained an insurance policy against non-payment of debts due from overseas customers from the Exports Creditors Guarantee Department (ECGD). In accordance with common practice, the company had borrowed money from the bank on the basis of debts due to it from overseas customers. Pursuant to this arrangement the company presented the ECGD with a letter of authority which authorised the ECGD to pay over to the bank monies which became due under the insurance policy in the event of default in payment by overseas customers. The question before the court was whether the insurance policy amounted to a book debt and whether, therefore, the letter of authority in favour of the bank amounted to a book debt. Pennycuick J held that it did not, primarily on the basis of expert evidence. This established that, in accordance with standard accounting practice, a credit insurance policy would not ordinarily be entered in the company's books as a book debt either prior to or subsequent to an admission of liability by the credit insurer, irrespective of the ascertainment of the amount then payable.

The *Paul Frank* decision was distinguished in *Re Brush Aggregrates Ltd* [1983] BCLC 320 which remains a questionable decision on the basis that the charge in question was held to catch contract monies when they became due, despite the fact that expert evidence showed that they would only be entered in the company's books if payment was actually received.

In practice, it is common for debentures and charge documentation to include reference not simply to 'book debts' but 'book debts and other debts' or some variation thereon. The term 'book and other debts', for example, was employed in *Re Brightlife Ltd* [1987] Ch 200 although for reasons considered below, the charge over book debts in that case was held to be a floating charge. Effectively, this represents an attempt to avoid some of the problems associated with the limited scope of the term 'book debts'. In isolation, however, the mere employment of broader terminology in a charge may do little to improve the position of a creditor subsequently acting in reliance on the charge in terms of its scope. In particular, regard should also be had to the nature of the business carried on by the company and the way in which the company deals with debts due to it.

For example, where a company commonly employs bills of exchange in the course of its business, it is clear that a book debt which arises from a contract between the company and a customer will continue to be treated as a book debt (in accordance with standard accounting practice) following the securing of the debt by the company by the issue to it of a bill of exchange. This is on the basis that a debt of that kind would be entered in a bills receivable account in the company's books (*Dawson v Isle* [1906] 1 Ch 633). Conversely, a bill of exchange, debenture, bond, loan note or derivative thereof which is issued to a company in consideration for a loan made by it will not ordinarily amount to a book debt, since the debt will not have arisen in the normal course of the company's business, except where the company's business includes the making of such loans. However, in practice, and for normal accounting purposes, investment companies do not usually regard either secured or unsecured debts as book debts where the debt is other than a short-term loan payable within a period of three months. Longer-term loans which are not entered in the company's books as book debts may, however, be caught by a broader debenture definition of the term 'book debts'. It appears that there is no authoritative judicial statement on this point.

Whilst the nature of the company's business is one factor in determining the scope of the term 'book debts', equally important is the terminology employed in the debenture itself in terms of the debts secured. This has implications from both the company's point of view and that of the debenture-holder as regards security. One common alternative to the term 'book debts' is 'book debts, howsoever arising'. Alternatively, and perhaps with a higher degree of certainty for the creditor, a debenture might provide for a fixed charge over 'book debts' together with a further fixed charge over 'all debts howsoever arising and due to the company other than book debts'. These drafting techniques do appear to catch all debts although the creation of two specific fixed charges over debts should seek to maintain, so far as possible, mutual exclusivity of the debts to which they relate for the avoidance of doubt (see further Linnane (1992) 11 Co Law 230).

### 4.3.2 Charges over credit balances

Conceptual and practical problems have arisen in relation to the concept of a charge being created over a book debt where the book debt is constituted by a credit balance on an account, invariably a bank account. In *Re Brightlife Ltd* [1987] Ch 200 Hoffman J held that a credit balance in excess of £19,000 on a bank account did not fall within the scope of the term 'book and other debts' on the basis that a credit balance, in the parlance of a commercial business-man, would not amount to a debt. This accords with previous *dicta* on the point, such as the New Zealand decision in *Watson v Parapara Coal Co* [1915] 17 GLR 791, where it was ruled that cash held at a bank did not amount to a book debt. The position was put in more robust terms in *Re Charge Card Services Ltd* [1987] 1 Ch 150 where Millett J held that it is conceptually impossible for a company to charge a credit balance on an account, commonly known as a 'charge back', which is held with a bank in favour of the bank. In the words of the learned judge, 'a charge in favour of a debtor of his own indebtedness to the chargor is conceptually impossible'. *The Charge Card Services* decision was the subject of considerable and very legitimate criticism, notably see Wood (1987) 8 Co Law 262. The position was clarified by the Registrar of Companies, who indicated that charges over the bank balance of a company in favour of the bank which are presented for registration should be registered notwithstanding the accepted view that such charges are not registrable in technical terms (see (1987) 137 NLJ 548 and (1988) 9 Co Law 107). This ran contrary to a previous decision by the Registrar of Companies to the effect that charges over a company's credit balance in favour of a bank would no longer be accepted for registration (see the notice of the Registrar of Companies dated 13 March 1985). The notice had been issued in anticipation of the decision of Hoffman J in *Re Brightlife Ltd* [1987] Ch 200 which held that a charge over a credit balance on a company's bank account did not amount to a book debt. The *Brightlife* decision accords with certain Commonwealth dicta on the point, such as the *Watson v Parapara Coal Co* decision.

Law and practice on the meaning of book debts requires consolidation to promote certainty and to promote consistency in judicial decisions on the area. It is unhelpful that neither the Companies Act 1985 nor the amendments which were envisaged by the Companies Act 1989 provide for whether a purported fixed charge over a credit balance on a bank account in favour of the bank is conceptually possible. Creditors will take little solace in the fact that a credit balance will certainly be caught by the security offered by a floating charge. Any future legislation in this area represents a clear opportunity for the matter to be clarified.

### 4.3.3   Conceptual difficulties

A charge over book debts has obvious commercial appeal for a creditor. Nonetheless, recent experience reveals the area as a troublesome one, largely on account of the problems associated with the nature of fixed and floating charges. (For a useful commentary see Moss (1995) 8 Insolvency Intelligence at 25–8.) Two phenomena present real problems in practice. First is the continued judicial acceptance of the wholly artificial concept of a fixed charge in equity over future book debts. The Cork Committee, it should be remembered, had actually recommended a statutory reversal of the decision in *Siebe Gorman & Co Ltd v Barclays Bank Ltd* [1979] 2 Lloyd's Rep 142 (see Cmnd 8558 at para 1586). The proposal was never implemented, largely on account of perhaps understandable pressure from the banks. Certainly in law the *Siebe Gorman* decision should not be seen as unimpeachable, the concept of fixed charges over future book debts having met also with some Commonwealth opposition (see *Royal Bank of Canada v Madill* (1981) 120 DLR (3d) 17 and *Hart v Barnes* (1983) 7 ACLR 310.

The second problematic phenomenon in the area is the recent attitude of the courts in acceding to the apparent intention of the parties to a debenture, as stated by them, in deciding whether or not a charge is of the fixed or floating variety. The most obvious recent example of this is the doubtful decision of the Court of Appeal in *Re New Bullas Trading* [1994] BCC 36 in which Nourse L J, delivering the leading judgment, stated:

> [T]he question depends on the intention of the parties, to be ascertained from the terms of the debenture; legal impossibility apart, that there are no considerations of public policy which prevent them from making whatever contract they chose; that it were possible for them to create a fixed equitable charge over future as well as present further debts; that their declared intention was to create such a charge; but that that intention was nevertheless defeated if the other provisions of the debenture were inconsistent with it.

Whilst the decision in *Re New Bullas* turns on its own facts, it is not a general pronouncement of law on fixed and floating charges over book debts, it is respectfully submitted that the substance of the Court of Appeal's decision owes more to policy considerations than to legal analysis. Indeed, as Knox J had put it in his first instance decision in the *Re New Bullas* case—which it is submitted had a far sturdier legal basis to it than that of the Court of Appeal—'if the transaction is a cow and has cloven hooves, the parties cannot turn it into a horse by using equine terminology or by saying that it is a horse...' It is probably the case that *Re New Bullas* will be distinguished on its own facts for the purposes of most future cases on the area. The approach of the Court of Appeal nonetheless remains an unhelpful one.

The area of fixed and floating charges over book debts has produced a plethora of literature. For recent and analytical examples see Moss supra and Capper [1995] Insolvency Lawyer (February 1995) at 2–8.

The two leading cases on fixed and floating charges over book debts are *Siebe Gorman & Co Ltd v Barclays Bank Ltd* [1979] 2 Lloyd's Rep 142 and *Re Brightlife Ltd* [1987] Ch 200. *Siebe Gorman* involved a first fixed charge in favour of the bank over present and future book debts of the company. The debenture also contained an express covenant which precluded the company from charging or assigning (eg factoring) the book debts or their proceeds, which had to be paid into a specific account held with the bank. The company was also required by the covenant to execute a legal assignment of the book debts and other debts if required to do so by the bank. Slade J held that the effect of the covenant was not such as to oblige the bank to allow the company to draw monies when owed money under the debenture. This permitted the bank to assert a lien under the charge over the proceeds of book debt realisations which were paid into the specified account with the bank even, rather curiously it seems, if the account was in credit. It followed from these prohibitions that the terms of the charge did not contemplate that, until the bank had taken steps to enforce it, the company would be able to carry on its business in the ordinary way as regards dealing with its charged book debts. This third characteristic of Romer LJ's test as set out in the *Re Yorkshire Woolcombers'* case [1903] 2 Ch 281 at 295 was thus not fulfilled and, therefore, the charge was construed as fixed (see also *Evans, Coleman & Evans Ltd v R A Nelson Construction Ltd* (1958) 16 DLR (2d) 123 upon which the decision relies).

The *Brightlife* case involved a substantially similar purported fixed charge on present and future book debts. However, unlike *Siebe Gorman*, the charge contained no covenant prohibiting the company from charging or assigning the book debt and book debt realisations, the company therefore being free to deal with the book debt realisations as it wished. In holding the charge to be a floating charge Hoffman J considered that '... once in the account [the proceeds] would be outside the charge over debts and at the free disposal of the company ... a right to deal in this way ... is a badge of a floating charge'. Hoffman J also considered that the decision of Slade J in the *Siebe Gorman* case was of no assistance to the creditor in the present case. In short, the crucial difference between the *Siebe Gorman* and *Brightlife* cases was that the charge in the former case constrained the debtor company in terms of its right to deal with the charged debts, whereas in the latter case it did not.

### 4.3.4   *Re New Bullas Trading*

*Re New Bullas Trading* [1994] BCC 36 involved a debenture in favour of corporate financiers 3i (which, it should be noted, is not a clearing bank). The debenture purported to create a fixed charge over present and future book debts, and required the company to pay all book debts realisations into a current account or, if required, a separately designated account with Lloyds Bank. The debenture also required the company to deal with book debt realisations standing to the credit of the account in accordance with any directions given by 3i. Furthermore, in the absence of directions from 3i, book debt realisations which were paid into the account were expressly released from the fixed charge and were to stand subject to the floating charge also created by the debenture. The debenture expressly provided that the release of sums from the fixed charge paid into the specified account did not affect the continued operation of the fixed charge in relation to unrealised book debts. No directions were given by 3i. The administrative receiver of the company applied to the court under s35 for directions as to whether the debenture created a fixed or floating charge in favour of 3i. At first instance Knox J held the security in favour of 3i as a whole to be a floating charge, on the basis that the company was able to realise its book debts in the ordinary course of business and pay them into the specified bank account. The company was then at liberty to deal with the proceeds as it wished, in the absence of directions from 3i. As such, the charge had all of the characteristics of a floating charge identified by Romer J in *Re Yorkshire Woolcombers Association* [1903] 2 Ch 284 at 295. Although Knox J accepted that the parties had employed the plainest terms in the charge documentation in purporting to create a fixed charge, he considered that the court was at liberty to subject the charge to an analysis of its true nature irrespective of what the parties might have intended. This accorded with the submission by counsel for the Inland Revenue (who represented all preferential creditors of the company) that once the charge had been identified as having those characteristics in Romer J's test, it was inescapable that the charge was a floating charge. This was despite an unsuccessful argument by counsel for 3i that an implied licence to deal with an asset was not inherently inconsistent with a fixed charge being taken over it, based on the decision in *Evans v Rival Granite Quarries Ltd* [1910] 2 KB 979.

An appeal was granted on the question of whether the law permitted an agreement whereby the parties intended to create a fixed charge over uncollected book debts and a floating charge over book debt realisations on their being paid into the specified account. Unfortunately, Knox J's first instance decision was reversed. The Court of Appeal accepted the assertion by counsel for 3i that there is no legal bar to an arrangement, as envisaged by 3i's debenture, whereby a distinction is drawn between book debts prior to and following realisation in terms of the operation of fixed and floating charges respectively. On this basis, Nourse LJ considered that '...[u]nless there is some authority or principle of law which prevented [the parties] from agreeing what they have agreed, their agreement must prevail'. The grounds on which the case had been decided by Knox J at first instance did not therefore arise. With respect, it is submitted that the approach of the Court of Appeal is not satisfactory in this respect although the decision is obviously of considerable comfort to financial institutions, not least because of problems previously associated with the creation of fixed charges over book debts in favour of financial institutions such as 3i which were not themselves clearing banks. Not only does the decision avoid any real deliberation on the applicability of the relevant authorities, it also gives credibility to the idea that the parties to an agreement may create a charge of a specific nature simply by referring it as such irrespective of its true legal substance. For this reason, and on the peculiar facts of the case, it must be anticipated that the decision will be heavily distinguished. Of some note here is the later decision of Carnworth J in *Re Pearl Maintenance Services Ltd* (1995), unreported, 2 March, that cases governing fixed charges over book debts which pre-date the *New Bullas Trading* decision remain unimpaired by it.

### 4.3.5 'Charge as labelled'?

The *Re New Bullas* decision apart, there is considerable danger in the parties to an agreement—particularly one purporting to create a fixed charge over book debts or, indeed, any asset—proceeding on a 'charge-as-labelled' basis. This does not, of course, prevent the parties from creating that which they intend to in terms of a charge over book debts. As Slade J put the matter in *Siebe Gorman & Co Ltd v Barclays Bank Ltd* [1979] 2 Lloyd's Rep 142 at 159, 'I see no reason why the court should not give effect to the intention of the parties'. Slade J's comment did, however, follow an analysis of the charge in the present case and a conclusion that:

> In my judgement . . . it is perfectly possible in law for a mortgagor . . . to grant to a mortgagee a charge on future book debts in a form which creates in equity a specific charge on the proceeds of such debts . . . and consequently prevents the mortgagor from disposing of an unencumbered title to the subject matter of such charge without the mortgagee's consent, even before the mortgagee has taken steps to enforce its security.

(See also *Kelly v McMahon Ltd* [1980] IR 347.) In other words, whatever the parties label a charge must reflect its underlying legal nature. Conversely, as regards the three characteristics of a floating charge identified in Romer LJ's decision in the *Re Yorkshire Woolcombers* case (*above*), the learned judge considered that '. . . if a charge has all three characteristics that I am about to mention it is a floating charge'. The Court of Appeal's decision in the *Re New Bullas* case takes some reconciling with that statement.

The classification of a charge over book debts as fixed or floating is not always an easy task in practice. The case law does, however, provide some useful guidelines, the *Siebe Gorman* and *Brightlife* cases constituting the most useful starting points. *Siebe Gorman* has been followed by the Irish Supreme Court in *Re Keenan Bros Ltd* [1986] BCLC 242, again on the basis of what the parties had intended to create between themselves. The debenture in that case contained a charge in favour of a clearing bank which required the company to pay the proceeds of all book debts into a specified account with the bank and 'not without the prior consent of the bank in writing to make any withdrawals or direct any payment from the said account'. The charge was held to be fixed, *Re Keenan Bros* being followed subsequently in *Re Masser Ltd* (1987) 5 ILT 43.

The validity of a fixed charge over book debts is further established by the somewhat artificial decision in *William Gaskell Group Ltd v Highley* [1993] BCC 200. In that case it was held that a fixed charge over book debts remained fixed notwithstanding assignment of the debenture to a third party. Notably, the assignee of the debts was not a bank whereas the assignor was a clearing bank. The decision of Morritt J was made on the basis that the debenture provided expressly that withdrawals could only be made from the company's bank account with the consent of the debenture-holder once payments in had been made. The decision holds that the restriction continued to subsist even though the assignee did not hold the account as had the assignor. This view, it is submitted, is difficult to justify although it would appear to receive support from the Court of Appeal's decision in *Re Bullas Trading Ltd* (1993) BCC 251. The case also begs (but failed to consider) whether a fixed charge is capable of transformation to a floating charge in view of s251.

In *Barclays Bank Plc v Willowbrook International Ltd* [1987] 1 FTLR 386 the Court of Appeal accepted a charge and covenant of the *Siebe Gorman* type as constituting a fixed charge. Harman J adopted a similar interpretation of a charge in *Re Permanent Houses (Holdings) Ltd* [1989] 5 BCC 151 although it was held that the fixed charge could not extend to book debt realisations which constitute a credit balance on the company's bank account; the latter was, therefore, subject to the accompanying floating charge contained in the bank's debenture. Conversely, and in accordance with the subsequent decision in *Re Brightlife Ltd* [1987] Ch 200, the High Court of Northern Ireland distinguished the *Siebe Gorman* decision in *Re Armargh Shoes Ltd* [1984] BCLC 405 on the basis that the charge over book debts contained no covenant precluding the company from dealing with the book debts or book debt realisations. (See also *Re Lakeglen Construction Ltd (In Liquidation)* [1980] IT 347 on the same point.)

### 4.3.6 Non-clearing creditor accounts and missapplied funds

One particular problem concerning purported fixed charges over book debts and book debt realisations concerns creditors who are not themselves clearing banks which operate specified accounts into which book debt realisations must be paid in accordance with the terms of the charge. This was not a problem in the *Siebe Gorman* case since the creditor was a clearing bank and, as such, was able quite legitimately to draw upon the account held by the company with it at any time at which monies were due under the debenture. On the other hand, where the creditor is a non-banking institution this right will not be operative, even if purported as being so. The simple reason for this is that the account will be maintained in the name of the company and, as such, will remain a matter between the company and the bank subject to the contractual and non-contractual rights, such as set-off, between them. That is, the company may enter into a charge as a contractual agreement with a non-clearing bank creditor which purports to prevent the company from dealing with book debts (eg by factoring) or with their realisations without the consent of the creditor. This agreement will, however, be merely contractual in that the company will retain the capacity to deal with book debt realisations which, typically, will be held in a specified account with a clearing bank in accordance with the terms of the charge. Furthermore, the non-clearing bank creditor will have no form of redress as regards appropriating or otherwise dealing with any sums held by the company with the bank where, say, sums are due to it under the terms of the debenture as in *Siebe Gorman*. It is submitted that such a charge will not amount to a fixed charge since the charge will not effectively preclude the company from dealing with book debt realisations held in the account—or indeed, those not paid into it—without the consent of the non- clearing bank creditor (see *Re Brightlife Ltd* [1987] Ch 200 at 208–9 per Hoffmann J). This observation would not apply to a purported fixed charge taken over unrealised book debts since the agreement would remain a matter between the company and the non-clearing bank creditor, and it would be unaffected by the fact that the specified account was not held and operated as between company and creditor.

Perhaps the best possible solution for non-clearing bank creditors in relation to the problem of privity identified above would be an arrangement whereby the specified account with a clearing bank was held on trust for the non-clearing bank creditor. However, even this solution is problematic; it is far from clear whether a trust arrangement of this type would confer rights on the non-clearing bank creditor which would correspond to those enjoyed by a clearing bank regarding the lien in its favour in respect of sums held in an account with it. Indeed, such a conclusion, it is submitted, remains doubtful.

One final problem area which remains is the question of the legal ownership of book debt realisations and the status of funds misapplied by a company in contravention of any restrictions imposed by a debenture. The starting point is to ascertain whether, in fact, the debenture creates a purported fixed charge over book debts and their proceeds, or whether a purported fixed charge over unrealised book debts is created with a specific charge (fixed or floating) being created over realisations. This latter scenario is now specifically envisaged by the Court of Appeal's decision in *Re New Bullas Trading* [1994] BCC 36. In relation to a floating charge, of course, a company may carry on its business in the ordinary way as regards the class of assets charged, and it may therefore dispose of the assets in full or part before the holder of the charge takes steps to enforce it (ie on crystallisation but see the definition in s251).

In the absence of a specific fixed or floating charge over book debt realisations it can be argued, on equitable principles, that the proceeds of book debt realisations are held by the company on trust for the creditor. Nevertheless this suggestion was rejected by Walsh J in *Re Keenan Bros* [1986] BCLC 242 which held that sums held in a credit balance on a special realisation account with a bank are not subject to the bank's fixed charge over book debts. This approach has been the subject of some criticism although in practice this point will not usually cause difficulty. Since it is standard practice for debentures to contain an express fixed or floating charge over book debts, although an obvious problem arises if the matter is disputed by preferential creditors.

Where a company misapplies the proceeds of book debt realisations by paying over the proceeds into another bank account or by acquiring property with the proceeds, then the equitable doctrine of tracing will apply. This permits the creditor to 'follow' the misapplied monies or, in the case of the purchase of property, 'elect either to take the property purchased, or to hold it as a security for the amount of trust money laid out in the purchase' (*Re Hallett's Estate* (1880) 13 ChD 696 at 709 per Jessel MR). Where monies are simply paid over into another bank account in contravention of the terms of the debenture it has been held by the Court of Appeal in *Barclays Bank plc v Willowbrook International Ltd* [1987] 1 FTLR 386 that the monies are held in the account by the company, together with the bank to whom the monies are incorrectly paid over, on trust for the chargee bank. It follows that any transaction involving the disposal of those trust assets by the chargor company will be susceptible to being set aside at the instance of the chargee bank on an action under the constructive trust, even if the chargee actually itself benefits from the subsequent transaction as in the *Willowbrook* case. In the case of the misapplication of book debt realisations an action may also lie against the payee of the monies.

Whilst the *Willowbrook* case recognised the payee bank as a constructive trustee of the book debt realisation for the chargee bank, it was held in the *Siebe Gorman* case (*above*) that the payee was not liable in an action for the tort of inducing a breach of contract, because the payee bank would not have constructive notice of the company's obligations to pay over the book debt realisations to the chargee bank. In practice, the position would presumably be difficult if actual notice of the prohibition could be proved. Whilst constructive notice was intended to be abolished by Companies Act 1985 s711A(1) (as was to be implemented by Companies Act 1989 s142) this provision will not now be brought into force. However, it has been suggested that knowledge of the prohibition on dealing with book debt realisations may be deemed as inferred by a payee bank, if it would have been discovered by the making of such enquiries and inspections as it ought reasonably to have made. It is submitted that there is good reason for doubting this suggestion.

Prior to the realisation of a book debt, legal title to it, as a chose in action, remains subject to the legal ownership of the company. The debt is, however, held subject to the chargee bank's equitable interest in it and its proceeds. Assuming the charge over the book debt for the property to be registered, it follows that any assignee of the book debt will obtain legal title to the debt notwithstanding any contractual prohibition on assignment etc, but will continue to hold the right to the debt on constructive trust for the chargee bank. As such, on realisation, the chargee bank will thus retain a right to the proceeds of the debt under the constructive trust which operates for its benefit.

## 4.4   Fixed and Floating Charges over Freehold and Leasehold Property

Charges on land (which for the purposes of this section is taken to mean charges on freehold or leasehold property) are registrable under the present provisions of the Companies Act 1985 (and those which were envisaged by the Companies Act 1989). The types of charge on land which require registration extend to any charge on land wherever situated (ie including land situated overseas) or any interest in land, but not including a charge for any rent or other periodical sum issuing out of the land (Companies Act 1985 s396(1) (a)). The provisions as they relate to rent or any periodical sum issuing out of the land will typically relate to rent or rent charges arising out of the land (although rent charges may no longer be created by grants made on or after 22 August 1977; Rent Charges Act 1977 ss2 and 18). However, a charge or mortgage created by a company over a lease or reversion or rent charge will be registrable as a charge on land. Nevertheless, in practice the terms of each specific debenture should be construed to ensure the creditor is afforded an interest in a tenancy or lease (see *Cunliffe Engineering Ltd v English Industrial Estates* [1994] BCC 972 where a bank could not take advantage of Law of Distress Amendment Act 1908 s1 on having an interest in a tenancy on premises by virtue of its debenture).

The types of charge which must be registered will extend to both legal or equitable charges or mortgages over any interest the company has in land, including any such charge or mortgage to which land or an interest in land acquired by the company is subject (*Property Discount Corporation Ltd v Lyon Group Ltd* [1981] 1 WLR 300). A charge will be also registrable irrespective of whether the charge or mortgage is created expressly or arises on a deposit of title deeds (*Re Wallis & Simmonds (Builders) Ltd* [1974] 1 All ER 561).

The company charges regime excludes charges which arise by operation of law. In land, perhaps the most obvious example is a lien which arises in favour of a vendor where a corporate purchaser fails to pay over the agreed purchase price for an interest in land. Whilst this type of charge is not registrable, a charge created over land by a purchaser company in favour of a vendor to secure the balance of an agreed purchase price will be registrable as a charge on land (*Capital Finance Co Ltd v Stokes* [1969] 1 Ch 26). The exclusion would not appear to apply to a mortgage created by deposit of title deeds since the mortgage will remain of a contractual nature and, as such, will not arise by operation of law. Nevertheless, it is no longer possible to create a charge merely by deposit of title deeds (*United Bank of Kuwait v Sahib* [1994] *The Times*, 24 June).

As well as registration with the Registrar of Companies, further formalities are necessary where a company creates a charge over land. In the case of registered land, all specific charges created over a company's property must be registered at the Land Registry pusuant to the Land Registry Act 1925. Specific charges created by a company after 1 January 1970 over unregistered land also require registration under the Land Charges Act 1972, which replaced the Land Charges Act 1925. Land Registry registration is not, however, necessary in the case of either specific charges created over unregistered land prior to 1970 or floating charges. In both cases, registration under the Companies Act 1985 (and earlier legislation) is sufficient registration, which takes effect also under Land Charges Act 1972 s3(7) (see *Re Molton Finance Ltd* [1968] Ch 325 and *Property Discount Corporation Ltd v Lyon Group Ltd* [1981] 1 WLR 300). In the case of floating charges, this derogation effectively saves administration, time and expense at the Land Registry, since a floating charge would appear to be registrable *per se* in any case as a general equitable charge which affects the land for the purposes of the Land Charges Act 1972 s2(1), (4)(iii). Nevertheless, a floating charge over registered land is only capable of protection by a notice or caution against dealings. A notice will be dependent on production by the company of the land certificate, a caution against dealing being entered in the register in the absence of production (Land Charges Act 1972 s3(7), (8)). Notably, the *Property Discount* case concerned the registration with the Registrar of Companies of a charge on an equitable interest which was held to take effect for the purposes of Land Charges Act 1972 s3(7) notwithstanding the fact that the charge was actually registered against the company creating the charge over the equitable interest and not the estate owner itself.

The following basic rules apply to registration of charges with the Land Registry. First, the registration of the security interest amounts to actual notice of the interest registered (Law of Property Act 1925 ss198, 199). Secondly, non-registration of the interest generally renders the interest void against purchasers for value of the land itself or any interest in it subject to certain statutory exceptions provided for in the 1925 Act. These exceptions apart, the date of creation of a charge (ie the date on which it is executed as opposed to an advance being made) by a company will prevail in determining the respective priority of a charge, assuming that it is registered in accordance with the provisions of the Companies Act 1985.

There are a number of other matters requiring consideration in relation to charges created by a company over land. First, unlike charges taken over book debts and other property, it is not possible to create a fixed legal charge over after-acquired property, since the creation of the legal charge depends on the legal estate in the land being vested in the company. As with a floating charge it is nonetheless possible to create a fixed equitable charge over after-acquired property. It should be noted here that heritable property in Scotland is only capable of being charged by way of fixed charge as prescribed by Scottish law. This will not usually be achieved by the execution of a standard form debenture in accordance with English law and should be dealt with, if appropriate, as a matter separate from the debenture itself. There is, however, no bar to land in Scotland being subject to a floating charge over the property of a company registered in England and Wales.

One further problem in this area is defining the scope of what amounts to land, fixtures and chattels for the purposes of a particular transaction. In practice, it is common for a standard form debenture to contain purported fixed charges over all freehold and leasehold property of a company, plant, machinery and the like. The definition of 'land' is contained in Law of Property Act 1925 s205(1)(ix) and extends to earth, minerals, buildings and fixtures. Of these items, fixtures are perhaps the most potentially troublesome for practical purposes. Whilst any asset which is not subject to a specific fixed charge may well fall subject to a floating charge, a chargee will usually wish to ensure that those assets intended to be subject to a fixed charge are, in fact, subject to it. This necessitates an understanding of those assets which will constitute fixtures and which, therefore, constitute part of any land over which a fixed charge is taken and, conversely, those which do not.

There is no satisfactory definition of the term 'fixtures' which puts beyond doubt the question of whether or not an asset situated on or even affixed to land constitutes a fixture. Land law throws up a number of novel examples such as *Berkley v Poulett* (1976) 242 EG 39, in which it was held that a statue weighing approximately half a ton was not to be regarded as part of land since the statue was not fixed to the land in any way. The requirement for some substantive degree of annexation is highlighted by *Hulme v Brigham* [1943] KB 152 in which two printing machines weighing respectively nine and twelve tons were each held not to constitute fixtures despite the fact that they were attached to motors which were themselves fixed to a factory floor. This was on the basis that the affixing of the machines to the motors was necessary to stabilise the latter; furthermore, the degree of physical annexation of the machines to the land was slight. One of the most useful of the older cases on this area is *Buckland v Butterfield* (1820) 2 Brad & Bing 54 which held that a conservatory attached to a house by way of eight nine-inch cantilevers constituted a part of the land. This case is good authority for the general proposition that anything fixed to a building (which amounts to land for the purpose of the definition in Law of Property Act 1925 s205(1)(ix)) will itself constitute a part of the land. This is to be contrasted with items which are merely placed on land notwithstanding the fact that certain items so placed may be deemed to constitute an integral part of the land and, therefore, part of it (see, for example, *D'Eyncourt v Gregory* (1866) LR 3 Eq 382).

In practice, certain items of plant and machinery are potentially problematic in terms of whether they constitute fixtures for the purposes of a fixed charge or are merely subject to what, in effect, will be a residual floating charge. The facts of *Reynolds v Ashby & Son* [1904] AC 466 provide a not untypical example. The case involved a number of machines which were secured with nuts and bolts to concrete beds which had been laid specifically for the installation of the machines on the ground floor of a factory. It was possible to show, however, that the machines were capable of removal from the factory floor without causing damage to it by the mere unscrewing of the nuts and bolts. The House of Lords held that the machines amounted to fixtures and, therefore, passed with a mortgage over the factory. Lindley LJ provided the following useful guidelines in such cases:

> In dealing with [all the cases on fixtures] attention must be paid not only to the nature of the thing and to the mode of attachment, but to the circumstances under which it was attached, the purpose to be served, and last but not least to the position of the rival claimants to the things in dispute.

This statement is as specific an authority as has been made judicially on this area. As Birkett J put it in *Hulme v Brigham* [1943] KB 152 at 155, '...the cases show that each case must be considered as decided on its own circumstances...' see also *Holland v Hodgson* (1872) LR 7 CP 328 per Blackburn LJ which makes reference to the intention of the parties on whether a specific asset should continue to be regarded as a chattel or a fixture.

The points raised above suggest that the taking of fixed charges over land may be a troublesome matter if assumptions are made that any asset affixed to or resting on the land form part of it. It is convenient to deal with practical solutions to these problems in the conclusion to the next section.

## 4.5  Fixed and Floating Charges over Other Property

As considered previously in Chapter 3, the Companies Act 1985 s396 contains a list of charges which are subject to the registration regime currently in force in relation to company charges. Pledges and liens are specifically excluded from the regime, as are charges permitting the charge-holder to take possession either of the goods themselves or a document of title to them (eg documents of title for the purpose of the Sale of Goods Act 1979, consignment notes and air waybills). The charges listed in s396 do not, of course, comprise the entire spectrum of charges which may be created by a company, merely those which require registration. Examples of those charges not requiring registration include those arising by operation of law such as an unpaid vendor's lien or a solicitor's lien, liens on sub-freights, charges over company's shares, deposits of negotiable instruments to secure book debts and charges over insurance policies. Insurance policies may, however, be incorporated in any definition of book debts which may be contained in future legislation on the area (see *Paul & Frank Ltd v Discount Bank (Overseas) Ltd* [1967] Ch 348. Similarly, an escrow arrangement whereby an account is opened by two parties, and the money held therein is held for only one of them, does not constitute a registrable charge (*Lovell Construction v Independent Construction (in liquidation)* [1994] 1 BCLC 31).

For the purposes of this section, the principal assets over which a chargee may seek to take a charge as envisaged by both the present and revised (but unimplemented) provisions of the Companies Act 1985 will include:

- a charge on goods or any interest in goods;
- a charge on goodwill;
- a charge on intellectual property;
- a charge on uncalled share capital of the company (or calls made on it which remain unpaid);
- a charge security on issue of debentures; and/or
- a floating charge over the whole or a part of the company's property.

For these purposes the term 'goods' means any tangible moveable property other than money (s396(2)). In all cases, the term 'property' includes future property and for these purposes it is irrelevant where the property subject to the charge is situated (Companies Act 1985 s395(2),(3)).

### 4.5.1  Retention of title clauses

Perhaps the most troublesome of the above categories of charge in practice is a reservation or retention of title or *Romalpa* clause for the purposes of what may or may not constitute a charge on goods or any interest in goods. (The same category might also catch other matters such as genuine hire purchase or conditional sale agreements.) The area of reservation of title is a difficult one—'a maze if not a minefield' as Staughton J put it—and reference should be made to standard and up-to-date works on the subject. It is appropriate to say something on the area here, although reference should be made to the standard works and Chapter 12 at para 12.6 as well as recent literature which covers unreported decisions and Commonwealth decisions in the area (see eg Sealy (1995) 8 Insolvency Intelligence 17–20).

The decision in *Aluminium Industries Vaassen BV v Romalpa Aluminium Ltd* [1976] 1 WLR 676 has given rise to the widespread use of reservation of title clauses in practice, the basic concept being that title in goods is retained by the seller until certain conditions are fulfilled, invariably payment in full for specific goods or 'all goods' supplied. In practice, retention of title clauses manifest themselves in increasingly sophisticated guises. Commonly, for example, these seek to establish rights in favour of the seller in proceeds of sale of retained goods or over new products manufactured with the 'retained' goods supplied. The increased sophistication of these types of clause has led to the judicial conclusion that certain types of clause will amount to registrable charges. For example, in *Re Bond Worth* [1980] Ch 228 a company supplied yarn to a manufacturer who incorporated it in the manufacture of carpets. The reservation of title clause in the contract for sale provided that equitable and beneficial ownership of the yarn remained in the seller until the

126

goods were paid for in full; alternatively, the seller obtained an equitable interest in either the proceeds of any resale of the goods or any new product into which the yarn was converted. Slade J held that the reservation of title clause amounted to a floating equitable charge in favour of the seller as security for either the purchase price or his proceeds of the re-sale of the yarn or any product into which the yard was converted or incorporated. That charge was therefore registrable and, in the *Bond Worth* case, was void for non-registration.

It is significant that in *Bond Worth*, Slade J distinguished the *Romalpa* decision itself since there full legal ownership was retained by the Dutch sellers until payment was received, no charge having been created. In the *Bond Worth* case it appeared that legal ownership had actually passed to the purchasers, the retention of title clause merely making reference to equitable ownership. A similar conclusion was reached by the Court of Appeal in *Borden (UK) Ltd v Scottish Timber Products Ltd* [1981] Ch 25 which involved a clause purporting to retain title to resin until paid for in full, where the seller knew that the goods would be mixed with other goods in the manufacture of chipboard before the resin was paid for in full. This amounted to more than a mere bailment of the goods, the clause constituting security for the purchase price of the resin. As such, the clause was registrable as a charge. The validity of reservation of title clauses in processes involving the mixing of 'retained' goods has been fraught with difficulties peculiar to it (see, for example, *Re Peachdart Ltd* (1983) 1 BCC 98; *Clough Mill Ltd v Merlin* [1985] 1 WLR 111).

It is difficult to draw specific conclusions as to the types of reservation of title clause which will constitute registrable charges and those which will not. The principal danger for a seller is the incorporation of a reservation of title clause in a contract for the sale of goods which remains unregistered whereas, in law, the clause actually constitutes a registrable charge. What the cases do suggest in terms of avoiding the inadvertent creation of a registrable charge is that a charge—as opposed to the mere bailment of goods—is more likely to arise where the seller of the goods attempts to assert some legal or equitable claim to the proceeds of re-sale goods or any goods into which the 'retained' goods are mixed or incorporated. In other words, a mere retention of title clause should reserve full legal and equitable ownership of the goods to the seller until some specified condition is fulfilled, invariably payment in full for the goods being made. Similarly, the clause should not be framed in terms which suggest the conferment of legal or equitable ownership on the purchaser. Thus, in *Specialist Plant Services Ltd v Braithwaite Ltd* [1987] 3 BCC 119 the Court of Appeal held that a charge was void against a debenture-holder for want of registration. In that case a purported reservation of title clause provided that if materials supplied under a contract for repairs became constituent parts of another article, the seller obtained ownership of those other articles as a surety for outstanding monies owed by the purchaser.

As a matter of practice, a charge should be phrased as clearly as possible to achieve its purpose. An administrative receiver (or liquidator) or his advisers should construe closely the wording of any purported reservation of title clause as regards any assets subject to the administrative receivership. This is particularly the case in view of the fact that, as Goff LJ put it in the *Clough Mill* case (*above*), each case will depend on the wording of the particular contract involved and the commercial situation in which each dispute arises.

Retention of the title claims are dealt with further in Chapter 12 at para 12.6.

### 4.5.2 Ships and aircraft

Charges on ships (or a share therein) and aircraft are currently comprised in the list of registrable charges in Companies Act 1985, s396. Legal mortgages over ships must also comply with the provisions of the Merchant Shipping Act 1894 and must be registered at the port of registry of the ship (*Cunard Steamship Co v Hopwood* [1908] 2 Ch 564). These formalities do not apply to equitable mortgages taken over ships. In addition, it has been held that, since there is neither provision in the 1894 Act which affects a common law mortgage of an unregistered ship nor any formality requirement at common law for the creation of a chattel mortgage over a ship, a mortgage over a ship may amount to mortgage at common law if referred to as such by the parties notwithstanding non-registration under the 1894 Act, ships being exempt from registration under the Bills of Sale Act 1878 (*British Credit Trust Limited v Owners of Ship 'Shizelle'* (1992) (unreported)).

As regards mortgages of aircraft there is provision under the Civil Aviation Act 1982 for both the creation and maintenance of a Register of Aircraft Mortgages by the Civil Aviation Authority and the registration of such mortgages with the Registrar of Companies (Mortgaging of Aircraft Order 1972 (SI No 1268, Ord 16(2))). In view of the formalities peculiar to charges over ships and aircraft it is both advisable and usual in practice for such charges to be comprised in separate mortgage documentation. This is not problematic for the purposes of administrative receivership, since any charge will be relevant for the purposes of s29(2) provided the charge holder is also the holder of a relevant floating charge over the company's property.

### 4.5.3 Tangible moveable property

Particular problems commonly arise in practice in relation to purported fixed charges taken over specific or fixed assets of a company such as plant, machinery, computer equipment, stock-in-trade and the like. Indeed, the entire property of certain companies may comprise only one specific asset.

The particular question which needs to be addressed here is whether or not a purportedly fixed charge is actually, in law, a fixed charge. The distinction between a fixed and a floating charge is not always easily made, since the latter is not subject to a precise definition and, judicially at least, relies on the implication of metaphor in ascertaining and establishing its existence. Two points should be noted initially on this point. First, if a charge is not a fixed charge then it may safely be concluded that it is a floating charge. Secondly, a floating charge may be created over any type or class of asset or property, irrespective of whether that asset, class of assets or property displays the characteristics associated with a floating charge. On the other hand, it follows that, by definition, it would be conceptually impossible to create a fixed charge over an asset, class of assets or property which displays those floating charge characteristics.

As was mentioned in the previous section dealing with charges over book debts (see para 4.3 *above*), the better view is that the parties to a charge cannot create a fixed or floating charge merely by reference to it as such (see, for example, the preferable first instance decision in *Re New Bullas Trading* (1993) BCC 251 per Knox J and more generally, *Street v Mountford* [1985] AC 809 which involved a purported mere licence agreement that in fact amounted to a tenancy). This point was also identified by S J Burton QC, sitting as a deputy High Court judge, in *Re Cimex Tissues Ltd* [1994] BCC 626 in that the real test is whether there are other provisions in the charge which are inconsistent with a fixed charge (see also the view of the Court of Appeal in *Welsh Development Agency v Export Finance Co Ltd* [1992] BCC 270 on this 'inconsistency' test). Consequently, a purported fixed and specific mortgage and charge over the entire undertaking of a company was held to be a floating charge by the Australian High Court in *R in Right of British Columbia v Federal Business Development Bank* [1988] 1 WWR 1, where the charge also permitted the company to sell items subject to the charge in the ordinary course of business subject to the bank's right to halt sales. Indeed, the concept of a fixed charge over a company's entire business and undertaking amounts to something of a contradiction, since the company cannot dispose of or transfer assets subject to the charge without the consent of the charge holder. This makes for enormous practical inconvenience (perhaps except in the case of single asset companies) and constitutes the main reason for the development of the floating charge as a security device which enables a company to continue its business without constant recourse to the charge holder in disposing of or dealing with its assets (*Re Panama, New Zealand and Australian Royal Mail Co* (1870) LR 5 Ch App 318). The test of whether or not a particular charge constitutes a fixed or floating charge therefore very much hinges on the characteristics of the assets charged and the company's ability to deal with them under the terms of the charge itself.

The problem of ascertaining the true nature of a purported fixed charge over specific, fixed assets is made more acute where those assets do not comprise the entire or substantially the whole of the assets owned by the company. As with purported fixed charges taken over book debts, the danger for secured lenders in this respect is that the particular purported charge is, in law, construed as a floating charge (see, for example, *Re Brightlife Ltd* [1987] Ch 200). Purported fixed charges over specific assets present a dichotomy between the benefits in terms of the priority and relative control sought and potentially enjoyed by the chargee on the one hand, and on the other, the inconsistency inherent in the purported nature of the charge in terms of the chargor having to apparently seek the permission of the chargee in dealing with or disposing of any of the charged property. This inconsistency has long been judicially recognised. As Lindley LJ put it in *Bickerstaff v Rowlatt's Wharf Ltd* [1896] 2 Ch 93 at 101:

> It would be impossible for companies to get credit or carry on business at all if arrangements between them and their creditors could not be made without the assent of the debenture-holder.

This is not, however, to say that a fixed charge over the entire assets of a company is either conceptually or practically impossible; rather, the matter is simply one of circumstance of the particular fact of each case (see, for example, *Re Croftbell Ltd* [1990] BCLC 925 where a so-called lightweight floating charge was held to be valid and effective).

The first-instance decision in *Re S E Tunbridge Ltd* [1994] BCC 563 highlights some of the practical problems faced by creditors in taking purportedly fixed-charge security over tangible moveable property. The company carried on a car repair and sale business and created a debenture in favour of one of its directors which contained a purported fixed charge over all other chattels and book debts. A fixed charge by way of legal mortgage was also taken over freehold property and a floating charge taken over cars and spare parts. The charge over all other chattels and book debts became an issue between the debenture-holder and the subsequently appointed administrators of the company. The debenture specifically provided that the fixed charge assets could not be disposed of or otherwise attacked without the written consent of the debenture-holder, although the company was free to deal with floating charge assets in the ordinary course of business. In applying Romer LJ's three floating charge characteristics, the court held that it was unrealistic to assume that the class and nature of assets charged by way of the purported fixed charges were such that they would not be charged, removed or otherwise disposed of from time to time. All three of the floating charge characteristics were identifiable and, as such, the charge was in reality a floating charge. This was held to be the case notwithstanding the fact that the company was not a manufacturing company and despite the fact that the parties apparently intended to create a fixed charge. The question of a fixed charge also being taken over the book debt element of the company's assets was not ignored; the court held that the fixed charge was also a floating charge on its construction (see also *Re Cimex Tissues Ltd* [1994] BCC 626.) Charges over leasing agreements have caused particular problems in this field, for which see the Court of Appeal decision in *Re Atlantic Computers Systems plc* [1992] 2 WLR 307 (which it is respectfully submitted is incorrect), *Re Offshore Ventilation Ltd* [1989] 5 BCC 160, and *Royal Trust Bank v National Westminster Bank* [1995] BCC 128, where the judgment of Parker J suggests in practical terms that in taking security by way of purported fixed charge over equipment leases, a chargee should schedule the equipment subject to the charge and exercise very tight control over dealings with the equipment and its proceeds (see also *Re Atlantic Medical Ltd* [1992] 3 BCC 653).

In reality, the sticking-point in the 'floating charge characteristic' test will usually be the third element of Romer LJ's test. That is, does the charge contemplate that, until some future step is taken by or on behalf of those interested in the charge (eg the service of a crystallisation notice on the happening of any specific 'automatic crystallisation' event), the company may carry on its business in the ordinary way as far as concerns the particular assets or class of assets charged? If the answer to this question is in the affirmative then, irrespective of the parties' intentions, it follows that the charge is capable of construction as a floating charge (assuming that the other two characteristics of a floating charge are also present). Nevertheless, the existence of some restriction on a company's dealings with assets does not automatically mean that the charge is fixed, since restrictions are not necessarily inconsistent with a floating charge by its nature (see *Re Cimex Tissues Ltd* [1994] BCC 626 at 635, which refers specifically to book debts, see also *Royal Trust Bank v National Westminster Bank* [1995] BCC 128 where the restrictions did give rise to a fixed charge). The same test is substantively conveyed in the following terms in *Robson v Smith* [1895] 2 Ch 118 at 124 per (then) Romer J:

> ...a 'floating security'... allow[s] the company to deal with its assets in the ordinary course of business until the company is wound up or stops business, or a receiver is appointed at the instance of the debenture-holder... So long as the debenture remain a mere floating security, or, in other words, the licence to the company to carry on its business has not been terminated, the property of the company may be dealt with in the ordinary course of business as if the debentures had not been given.

*Robson v Smith* was followed subsequently by the Court of Appeal in *Evans v Rival Granite Quarries Ltd* [1910] 2 KB 979 where a debenture-holder who had merely demanded payment (without crystallisation of the floating charge) was held to take subject to a creditor who obtained a garnishee order nisi over the company's bank account.

Further reference should also be made here to Pennington [1960] 23 MLR

630 for a highly perceptive account of the so-called licence and more recent 'mortgage of future assets' theories underlying the approach of the courts to the operation of the floating charge.

### 4.5.4 Practical Measures

What steps may a creditor take to avoid the deleterious effects of a charge being construed as floating instead of fixed? As with book debts, it appears that a mere restriction on the disposal of assets without the consent of the debenture-holder is insufficient to create a fixed charge. As pointed out in relation to charges over book debts, such a restriction does not affect the company's capacity to dispose of charged assets which are subject to the consent of the debenture-holder. In practical terms, apart from labelling the charge specifically as fixed, perhaps the most effective method of creating a fixed charge is the scheduling of assets. Indeed, the decision in the *S E Tunbridge* case would almost certainly have been different had specific chattels been listed in a schedule to the debenture. Nevertheless, even this technique will only provide further evidence of what the parties actually intended at the time of the execution of the charge.

The use of schedules to a debenture is a combative attempt at side-stepping the *Re Yorkshire Woolcombers Association* definition of the characteristics of a floating charge and, in particular, its third element. Nevertheless, this approach remains flawed if the chargee simply engages in the practice of disposing of or dealing in the assets charged without the prerequisite consent of the charge-holder. This gives rise to a circular problem in that the taking of a purported fixed charge, even over scheduled assets, may beg the judicial question of whether such a fixed charge can reasonably be viewed in the circumstances as such, particularly in view of the assets charged and the way in which the charger deals with them, possibly to the knowledge of the chargee. The Irish Supreme Court has rejected the admissibility of the conduct of the parties subsequent to the execution of a charge in relation to book debts in *Re Keenan Bros Ltd* [1985] IR 401 and, in so doing, relied heavily on the decision in the House of Lords in *Whitworth Street Estates v Miller* [1970] AC 583. Despite a similar approach in *Re Armagh Shoes Ltd* [1982] NI 59 and *William Gaskell Group Ltd v Highley* [1993] BCC 200 it must be that the facts in some cases will estop the chargee from insisting on its purported fixed charge rights. One other problem with the practice of providing a schedule of fixed charge assets to a debenture, particularly chattels, is that the assets may simply depreciate and require significant repair or replacement. In reality, the consent of the charge-holder to replacement is rarely sought, particularly with the passage of time. Again, repeated replacement in this way may provide evidence of the existence of a floating charge. It remains a matter for individual lenders as to how checks are maintained on the status and position of purported fixed-charge assets.

One practice which is frequently encountered is that schedules to debentures are not completed, not least because such details are often overlooked as needless or inadvertently omitted as, after case care work, or, worse still, as irrelevant in view of delusions on the part of the advisers to the effect that the parties know between themselves as to what they have contracted for. The undermining of the relevance and commercial value of schedules in this way is potentially disastrous for a lender, not least because a chargor may subsequently seek to rely on the absence of any specific assets in the schedule as evidence of the fact that, in fact, the charge created was a floating charge over an asset or a class of assets.

The common practice in standard-form debentures is for separate fixed charges to be taken over specific assets and classes of assets. In practice, it is inadvisable to rely on such 'standard' fixed charges as a matter of course. Certain bank debentures for example—in standard form at least—make no provision for fixed charges over computer software, hardware and/or certain intellectual property rights. In negotiating security and preparing documentation, an inventory of the company's assets should be taken in order that a specific list of those assets which may be made subject to fixed charges can be prepared. A commercial decision should also be taken at an early stage as to the efficacy of taking a fixed charge over certain types of asset and class of assets, such as stock-in-trade in a manufacturing company.

It may also be prudent to verify the inventory of the company's assets against an up-to-date copy of the company's latest accounts, and specifically the balance sheet, where this is practicable. If appropriate, enquiries should be made of the company's board and/or management to clarify any uncertainties which exist as to the extent of assets of the company; this in itself may be a useful exercise in sounding out the level of co-operation forthcoming from any particular board or its members. As regards specific assets and classes of assets charged, it is of considerable practical importance to ensure that the scope of each asset and class is defined accurately and extensively. Freehold and leasehold property, for example, should be specifically listed in schedules to the debenture, as should each item and asset as appropriate within a specific class of any other asset such as plant, machinery, vehicles, chattels, intellectual property rights, securities, etc.

## Chapter Five

# The Appointment of the Administrative Receiver

## 5.1 Introduction

By way of introduction to the validity of the administrative receiver's appointment, this chapter concentrates on those practical matters which relate to the appointment itself, notably letters of advice on the appointment. Other related areas covered are the implications for the office-holder and the debenture-holder of liability for trespass and the remedial action which may be taken on or following a defective appointment, including a consideration of indemnities in favour of the appointee.

## 5.2 Who may Appoint an Administrative Receiver?

The possibility of contemporaneous appointments of administrative receivers (other than joint appointments) was considered in Chapter 1 at para 1.11. The question remains as to who may exercise the right of appointment where two or more secured creditors each hold security over the company's property entitling each to appoint an administrative receiver. Does the right to appoint depend on the relative speed of either party in appointing or, alternatively, is the right of an inherent proprietary nature stemming from the relative priority of each of the secured creditors' security? This problem is a vexed one for both the academic and practitioner in that its solution is not advanced by either the provisions of the Act or judicial authority on the point.

As considered previously in Chapter 1 at para 1.11, the presumption must be that only one administrative receiver is capable of holding office at any one time. If, then, there exists more than one debenture-holder whose security satisfies the s29(2) requirement, which of those parties is entitled to appoint an administrative receiver and, if all are, does the right to appoint fall simply to the quickest to act?

The short solution to the problem of priority appointment, it is suggested, rests on the validity and relative priority of the security held by each debenture-holder (see Chapter 3 at para 3.4). That is, it is the debenture-holder whose security collectively, in terms of both fixed and floating charges, confers priority over all other debenture-holders which retains priority in terms of its right to effect in appointment, each subsequent debenture-holder ranking in relative priority according to its security.

Where, however, one inferior-ranking debenture-holder has effected an appointment with greater alacrity than other prior-ranking creditors, the question arises as to how that appointment may be challenged. Initially, the suggestion that the effecting of a mere appointment of an administrative receiver by the prior-ranking debenture-holder will of itself displace the appointment of the inferior debenture-holder's appointee should be discounted. As concluded previously in Chapter 1, the better view of the definition in s29(2) is that it appears to entertain the notion of only one administrative receiver (or joint appointees) simultaneously. Moreover, s45(1) makes clear that an administrative receiver of a company may at any time be removed from office by order of the court, but not otherwise. In effect, it is submitted, once a valid appointment is effected by one debenture-holder, the appointee may only be removed by the court (other than by resignation or disqualification from office). Any contrary conclusion suggesting some sort of implied displacement would appear to run contrary to this express provision. It might also give rise to practical problems where two appointees, whose appointors are in dispute as to the relative priority confirmed by their security, seek to take control of and dispose of charged assets.

The conclusion above does not, of course, preclude appointments by prior-ranking debenture-holders. Indeed, there will be very sound commercial reasons for making such appointments in most cases, in terms of control of the management and realisation of the charged assets. Conversely, inferior-ranking debenture-holders will wish to question the commercial wisdom of effecting a susceptible appointment, particularly if the motive behind it is merely to put off or stay the realisation of assets by a prior-ranking debenture-holder (see *Downsview Nominees v First City Corp Ltd* [1993] AC 245 and Chapter 9 at para 9.2).

The relative priority right of appointment held by a debenture-holder turns on the quality of its security. Creditors may of course agree between themselves to vary that priority, and this will have a corresponding effect on their priority rights in terms of appointment (see Chapter 4 at para 4.2).

The creation of purported fixed charges which, in effect, amount to nothing more than floating charges will have a corresponding effect. Similarly, a debenture-holder may attempt to protect its position by the use of a 'negative pledge' clause in its debenture, purportedly precluding the company from creating security subsequently which ranks *pari passu* or in priority to its floating charge. The validity of such clauses is considered in Chapter 3 at para 3.4 although, in the absence of a negative pledge clause constituting a prescribed particular as had been envisaged by the Companies Act 1989, ss102 and 103, the view must be that registration of such clauses will not bind subsequent chargees other than those fixed with actual notice. This is so notwithstanding a technical argument fielded in some of the literature that sophisticated, institutional chargees may be fixed with constructive notice in any case. Clearly, in some cases, the right of priority as between certain debenture-holders will give rise to disputes, particularly in relation to valuations which might only be resolved by way of application for removal under s45 or directions under s35.

For a further discussion of this area see the robust and perceptive views expressed by Oditah [1991] JBL 49 and Marks and Emmet [1994] JBL 1.

## 5.3  The Validity of the Appointment

The administrative receiver, or more commonly the joint administrative receivers (who, for convenience, are referred to hereafter as 'the administrative receiver'), will usually wish to take independent legal advice to confirm the validity of his appointment. Indeed, failure to do so may amount to professional negligence. Independent legal advice should always be sought, therefore, irrespective of the apparent validity of the appointment or the size and established reputation of the appointor. The legal advisers, invariably solicitors, called upon to advise on the validity of the appointment should be mindful of their position as a potential third party or co-defendant to proceedings instituted against the administrative receiver should it transpire subsequently that the appointment was an invalid one and where the advice proffered had suggested otherwise. Those proceedings are most likely to be instituted by either the legal owner of, or third party having an interest in, assets which are dealt with or disposed of by the invalidly-appointed administrative receiver or, alternatively, a subsequently-appointed liquidator or administrator of the company. Such proceedings are likely to include an action for damages for trespass and/or conversion together with a declaration that the appointment was invalid. The action will also usually seek an order requiring the return to the company or a third party that property be returned to the relevant party together with the rendering of an account by the administrative receiver and costs. The consequences of and remedial action which might be taken in the event of an invalid appointment are considered *below* at para 5.6.

The validity of the administrative receiver's appointment will depend on the legal adviser being satisfied that a number of pre-conditions are satisfied. Commonly, in practice, these pre-conditions take the form of a standard checklist which the adviser often uses as a basic guide to the structure of his advice. The drawback with most checklists of this type is that they cannot be universal and, realistically, there can be scope for some degree of indifference in deciding whether or not what an adviser considers to be the 'major' areas of concern are satisfied. At the risk of sounding cynical, this indifference may become all the more acute over a protracted period where there appears to be no apparent comeback on advice given on a significant number of appointments where, ultimately, it has to be said that much was taken as read or for granted in advising on the validity of the appointment. It hardly needs stating that such an approach to the provision of advice is highly dangerous. Any doubts in the mind of an advisor on the validity of the appointment should be taken up immediately with colleagues, ideally at partner level, and should be the subject of a detailed file note. Where appropriate, counsel's opinion should be sought or an application made to the court for directions.

Since the acceptance of the appointment is subject to time constraints prescribed by IR r3.1 and s33, the fullest possible information should be provided to the prospective appointee client. This should clearly identify those matters which raise problems for the validity of the appointment, and should also identify the possible causes of action which might be pursued. These might include an acceptance of the appointment on the basis of one commercial view taken of the matter, the implementation of remedial measures or an outright rejection of the appointment. It is a matter of individual choice for the prospective appointee as to whether or not a doubtful appointment is accepted. However, if such an appointment is accepted, the office-holder should take as little action as possible, if any, in relation to the company's assets and the incurring of costs until his position is clarified. Conversely, any subsequently appointed liquidator—or indeed, any other creditor seeking to take security over the company's assets—would do well to investigate fully the appointment of any previously-appointed administrative receiver.

## 5.4 The Letter of Advice on the Appointment

The legal adviser's letter of advice on the validity of the administrative receiver's appointment is largely a question of style. Some advisers will opt for lengthy expositions of all the apparently relevant legal principles together with conclusions, whilst others prefer a balder statement of advice with few or no supporting reasons. In reality, most letters of advice fall somewhere between these extremities. There is no right or wrong approach to a letter of advice, other than to say that the advice should be given with a sufficient level of skill and care as one might reasonably expect of a professional adviser. The letter of advice should seek to make a clear statement, preferably in conclusion, as to whether or not the legal adviser considers the appointment to be a valid one, together with such supporting reasons as the legal adviser feels appropriate to include. Also clearly set out should be any provisos or conditions to the advice given which might relate, for example, to relevant documentation which is not to hand. One obvious example of this is the original board resolution of the company which authorised the execution of the debenture containing the floating charge and any supplemental fixed charges pursuant to which the administrative receiver is appointed. Thus, where the legal advisers do not have sight of the original board resolution, their advice on any valid appointment should necessarily be so framed as to be subject to and conditional on the appropriate resolution having been validly passed.

In preparing the letter of advice, legal advisers should, as a matter of good practice, request originals (or at least good quality copies) of all documentation available to the appointee at the time the advice is sought. Although a prospective appointee has no inherent right to access company books and documentation, these may be requested from the company by the appointee for further clarification of his position. Likewise, the appointee's legal advisers should actively request any documentation which they believe to be outstanding and of apparent significant relevance to the validity of the administrative receiver's appointment. Again, failure to do so may amount to professional negligence.

In practice, it is not uncommon for legal advice to be sought as regards the validity of an appointment some time—weeks or even months—after the appointment is purportedly made. This is a dangerous practice, not least because of the extent to which the potentially invalidly-appointed administrative receiver may have dealt with or disposed of the company's assets as a trespasser. For this reason, delays of any period between an appointment being made and advice being sought as to its validity should be avoided at all costs and so far as practicable if only, on a worst case scenario, as a damage limitation exercise. Good practice dictates that advice should be sought on an appointment within 24 hours of its being purported to be made, at the very latest. This is because an administrative receiver wishing to accept an appointment must do so before the end of the business day next following that day on which the instrument of appointment is received by him or on his behalf (eg at his usual place of business) (s33(1)(a)). The effect of the acceptance of an instrument of appointment—which in legal terms effectively constitutes an offer—is to treat the appointment as retrospectively being made at the time at which the instrument it appoints is received (s33(1)(b)). As a practical formality, where the appointment of an administrative receiver is accepted other than in writing (eg by telephone or impliedly by conduct) then the appointee must confirm his acceptance in writing to his appointer within seven days of the date of appointment (IR r3.1(2),(3)). This provision does not affect the acceptance of the appointment at the time it is actually accepted; rather, its effect is merely confirmatory although the consequence of non-compliance is not apparent from the provisions.

## 5.5  The Obtaining of Indemnities by the Administrative Receiver

Other than in relation to s34 which is considered below, this section is not concerned with statutory rights of indemnity in favour of the administrative receiver, such as that under s44(1)(c) in respect of personal liability on contracts entered into on behalf of the company or contracts of employment adopted by him, other than to the extent that he incurs personal liability under the Insolvency Act 1994 and the amendments made by that legislation. The question of indemnities is, however, relevant to the s34 statutory indemnity on the company going into liquidation, since it would appear from s44(3) that, in such a case, s44 does not limit the liability of the administrative receiver on contracts entered into or adopted without authority. This will be the case following the company going into liquidation, on account of the termination of the administrative receiver's deemed agency under s44(1)(a). Furthermore, s44(3) expressly provides that '[section 44] does not limit any right to indemnity which the administrative receiver would have apart from it'.

Other than where a contract excludes personal liability under s44(1)(b), the statutory indemnity from the assets of a company in s44(1)(c) in favour of the administrative receiver in respect of personal liability incurred in connection with contracts entered into or contracts of employment adopted by him, raises the question of when it may be justifiable to seek an indemnity from the administrative receiver's appointor. It may well, of course, be deemed commercially inappropriate by the prospective appointee to seek an indemnity in the normal course of each appointment in respect of which he is proposed by, say, a major clearing bank. However, a general indemnity from a creditor will usually be justifiable where some or all of the following factors apply:

(a)  where the general assets of the company are insufficient to 'feed' any s44(1)(c) indemnity in favour of the administrative receiver;

(b)  where the administrative receivership is likely to involve a substantial amount of work giving rise to personal liability;

(c)  where there is a potential risk of the administrative receiver's appointment being set aside as invalid, thereby rendering him personally liable as a trespasser to the company's assets.

The circumstances of the appointment will dictate whether the indemnity sought is in respect of a specific liability arising in the administrative receivership or in relation to any personal liability arising in the course of the administrative receivership generally. Other factors are likely to include (d) whether or not the appointment is the first of its kind from the particular appointor and (e) the nature of the appointor itself in terms of whether it is an individual, a clearing bank or, say, a fringe bank or finance house which is not a clearing bank. In practical terms, where the indemnity takes the form of an amount maintained in an agreed account, a check should be made on the balance of the account from time to time to verify its sufficiency in view of the work and possible liabilities being undertaken.

The obtaining of an indemnity by an appointee prior to or as a condition of accepting an appointment as an administrative receiver is further justified by the apparent scope of s34 in the absence of specific judicial statement on it. Section 34 provides that, where the appointment of an administrative receiver is discovered to be invalid, whether by virtue of the invalidity of a debenture or otherwise, the court may order the administrative receiver's appointor to indemnify the administrative receiver appointed against any liability which arises solely by reason of the invalidity of the appointment. Some cursory observations are possible on the provision. The reference to liability arising 'solely' by reason of the invalidity of an appointment suggests that the court will be unable to make an order in respect of liability arising by, say, the appointor having supplied the appointee with incorrect information as to the extent of the company's assets, or arising through the negligence of the appointor in making the appointment or of the appointee in discharging his functions. Instead, s34 appears to be limited to liability arising on appointments which are either invalid *ab initio* or which are subsequently avoided. This might arise, for example, either where the debenture pursuant to which the appointment is made is unregistered or where it, or its requisite security, is avoided subsequently, typically by a liquidator, as a transaction-at-under-value, a preference or under s245. Other possible grounds on which an appointment may be invalid or subsequently avoided are those envisaged in the appointment validity considerations set out in Chapters 6 and 7. These might include the creation of the debenture constituting illegal financial assistance for the purposes of Companies Act 1985 s151 or no valid demand being made for the repayment of sums due by the appointor where this is required expressly by the terms of the debenture.

Section 34 should provide considerable comfort to a prospective appointee and, indeed, his advisers. The matters arising out of the appointment validity considerations, as considered later, are clearly complex and potentially far-reaching. Indeed, in many cases it is possible that certain vitiating factors will or would not become apparent without a significant and very specific degree of inquiry going beyond what might be deemed reasonable in most cases. This begs some degree of statutory protection in favour of a prospective appointee, which s34 provides.

In conclusion, however, it is submitted that s34 is unlikely to operate in favour of an appointee who applies to the court for relief where the matters giving rise to the invalidity of the appointment should have been clear, or could have been established, either in view of information available at the time of the appointment or because of facts which could and should reasonably have been ascertained by the appointee or his advisers.

## 5.6 Remedial Action on or Following a Defective Appointment

Consideration of the factors relevant to a valid appointment, as discussed in the next two chapters, may lead to the conclusion that an appointment is, in fact, defective or potentially defective. The implications of a defective appointment will be more serious where the appointment has been accepted, depending on the extent to which the appointee has purported to discharge his function and deal with the assets of the company. In the face of a defective or potentially defective appointment, the following account seeks to suggest a non-exhaustive list of possible remedial actions which may be pursued with a view to either perfecting the appointment of the administrative receiver or providing an effective means of damage limitation for the office-holder and his appointor. A consideration of defective appointments and remedial action necessitates a note of professional caution; genuine concern over the validity of an appointment necessitates a proactive approach. Any legal adviser who is prepared to reach a conclusion as to the invalidity or questionable validity of an appointment and who is equally prepared to remain passive or inactive in the light of that conclusion runs a very dangerous risk of allegations against him of incompetence, negligence and/or fraud. This is not, of course, to say that a technical conclusion as to the possible invalidity of an appointment should lead to the appointee being advised to decline the appointment in all cases; rather, the appointee should be appraised of both the risks in the appointment and the adviser's reasons for believing these to exist. From the adviser's perspective, conclusions as to the validity of what might subsequently be deemed to be a contentious appointment should be the subject of both full disclosure to the appointee and formal record for internal file purposes. Ideally, such matters should be discussed by the office-holders' advisers at partner level.

Liability for trespass and conversion is not considered in any detail here and further reference should be made to the standard works and see also Doyle [1995] 11 IL&P5. It is convenient, however, to make a number of cursory and practical observations. Perhaps the most important of these is established by *Mace Builders v Lunn* [1987] Ch 191 in which it was held that sums repaid to a debenture-holder under a floating charge which is subsequently avoided in liquidation are not susceptible to repayment to the company. It is submitted that there is good reason for questioning the principle established by this rule, because it is the general body of creditors which suffers by its operation and, furthermore, a debenture-holder may be spurred into effecting an appointment if it fears for the subsequent avoidance of security which will be subject to statutory time limits (see ss238, 239 and 245). Indeed, the irony of the rule in *Mace Builders* is that it offends the very anti-avoidance provisions which are designed to protect creditors generally from transactions affording individual creditors an unfair advantage over others. Furthermore, the office-holder himself is liable as a trespasser only from the date of service of a writ on him, where the invalidity of his appointment comes about as a result of the invalidity of a guarantee secured by the charge pursuant to which he is appointed (*Ford & Carter v Midland Bank* (1979) 129 NLJ 543).

A claim for trespass against a receiver also requires as a general rule proof that the company has suffered some loss as a result of the trespass (*Re Goldburg (No2)* [1912] 1 KB 606). In practice, such loss may be difficult to prove and may not be sought as against the debenture-holder where the receiver is appointed as agent of the company, as is usual practice (*Re Simms* [1934] Ch 1). It may equally be the case that the company has benefited during the period during which the subsequently-invalidated receiver held office. The cases considered in Doyle [1995] 11 IL&P5 consider this point further, although it should be said here that the receiver would appear able in such cases to establish a claim for reasonable remuneration on the basis of a *quantum meruit* claim (see also *Official Custodian for Charities v Mackey (No2)* [1985] 1 WLR 1308 for an unsuccessful claim of damages in trespass against a receiver for profit made under a lease which was held to be estopped).

The areas of remedial action which may be considered for present purposes may be deal with conveniently under the following headings. It should be noted that these are not arranged in any particular order of importance.

### 5.6.1 Indemnities

The question of indemnities was dealt with above in para 5.5. The observation made therein as to the uncertainty of the scope of s34 and the obtaining of a general indemnity from the appointing debenture-holder is particularly relevant here. Whilst the obtaining of a general indemnity may be justifiable prior to or on the taking of an appointment, this is unlikely to be the case subsequent to the appointment being made. Indeed, an appointor is unlikely to agree to such an indemnity, notwithstanding the availability of s34, on the grounds that it should have been sought at the time of the appointment on the basis of appropriate and proper advice. Once again, this underlines the importance of advice being sought as to the validity of the appointment prior to it being accepted.

### 5.6.2 Section 232

Section 232 was mentioned previously in Chapter 1 in distinguishing between receivers of an administrative and non-administrative nature and in this paragraph in relation to defective appointments. The provision provides that the acts of an office-holder, including an administrative receiver, are valid notwithstanding defects in his appointment, nomination or qualifications. Section 232 specifies that the office-holder must be an individual; a corporate administrative receiver is disqualified from acting as an insolvency practitioner as well as being disqualified from appointment as a receiver of the property of a company, and being liable to a fine for acting as such (s390(1), (3). Indeed, it was held that the acts of a corporate receiver were void *ab initio* for the purposes of previous but analogous legislation (*Portman Building Society v Gallway* [1955] 1 WLR 96).

Section 232 will not extend to perfecting acts of an administrative receiver where there exists no power to appoint *ab initio*. On the other hand, s232 would appear to extend to an appointment of a person not qualified to act as an insolvency practitioner in relation to a company for the purposes of s388(1). This will be without prejudice to any criminal liability which the unqualified person may incur for so acting. Section 232 also appears to extend to an appointment which is not accepted in accordance with the procedure laid down in IR rr3.1 and 3.2. The reasoning behind this approach is based on the judicial approach to Companies Act 1985 s285 (formerly Companies Act 1929 s143) which contains a substantially similar provision to s232 in relation to the acts of a director or manager of a company. (This statutory validation provision is also repeated and extended by Table A, art 92.) For these purposes, in *Morris v Kanssen* [1946] AC 459, Simmonds LJ drew attention to what he referred to as:

> a vital distinction between (a) an appointment in which there is a defect or, in other words, a defective appointment and (b) no appointment at all. In the first case if it is implied that some act is done which purports to be an appointment but is by reasoning of some defect inadequate for the purpose; in the second case there is not a defect, there is no act at all ... [T]he section and the article, being designed as such to try to avoid questions being raised as to the validity of transactions where there has been a slip in the appointment of a director, cannot be utilised for the purposes of ignoring or overriding the substantial provisions relating to such appointment.

*Morris v Kanssen* [1946] AC 459 involved a false claim by a company director C that a third party had been appointed as a director, a false board minute to that effect having also been recorded. C and the false director then purported to appoint Morris as a director. Those three then claimed that s285 validated their actions. The House of Lords rejected the claim on the basis that there had been no valid appointment of C and Morris in any case.

It has been held that a person seeking to rely on similar validation provisions must have acted in good faith (*Channel Colliers Trust Ltd v Dover, St. Margaret's & Martin Mill Light Railway Co* [1914] 2 Ch 506 at 512 per Cozens-Hardy MR). Furthermore, the defect must not have been known of at the time of the appointment, although the validation provisions will continue to operate if the individuals involved at the time of the appointment were aware of the facts rendering the appointment invalid but failed to appreciate their invalidating effect (*British Asbestos Co Ltd v Boyd* [1903] 2 Ch 439). In this regard it should be noted that s232 is broader in scope than Companies Act 1985 s285 in that the latter provision is restricted only to curing defects which are discovered subsequent to the appointment of a director or manager of a company. In practice, it is submitted that most defects for the purposes of s232 will only come to light after the administrative receiver's appointment in any case. By analogy with the company law provision, it appears that those directors or officers of a company who deal with an administrative receiver may also rely on the statutory validation of the office-holder's acts under s232 (*Dawson v African Consolidated Land Trading Co* [1898] 1 Ch 6).

Section 232 applies only to an individual which acts as an administrative receiver in relation to a company for the purposes of s388(1). A body corporate is not, in any case, qualified to act as an insolvency practitioner under s390(1) although, in practice, attempts at such appointments will be rare.

Section 232 offers some degree of comfort to office-holders, although the above observations suggest that the provision should not be relied on as a universal method of safeguarding against an appointment which is perceived as either invalid or potentially invalid, typically, at the instance of any subsequently appointed liquidator.

### 5.6.3  Section 35: Application to the court for directions

Section 35(1) permits an application to be made to the court for directions in relation to any particular matter arising in connection with the performance of the functions of a receiver or manager, including an administrative receiver. The application may be made to the court either by a receiver or manager of the property of the company appointed under powers contained in an appropriate instrument or, alternatively, by the persons by whom or on whose behalf the receiver or manager has been so appointed. However, it is submitted that an application should not be made by the administrative receiver himself in relation to matters concerning his appointment. This is because, where doubt exists as to the validity of the appointment, the administrative receiver would appear not to be, in clear terms at least, a receiver or manager 'so appointed' and would, therefore, appear to fall potentially beyond the scope of s35(1). Instead, the most appropriate party to make the application to court appears to be the appointing debenture-holder. Applications for directions under s35(1) by an administrative receiver are made by originating summons; see RSC Ord 102, r2.

On a s35(1) application, the court may give such directions, or may make such order declaring the rights of persons before the court or otherwise, as it thinks fit (s35(2)). In the absence of clear judicial authority, this provision appears to enable the court either to make an order declaring an appointment valid or invalid or even to give directions for such remedial action as it is necessary to render an appointment valid. In practice, s35 has been used, for example, in ascertaining the nature of charges taken over property, particularly book debts, and in clarifying anomalies relating to independent trustees appointed to company pension schemes; see Chapter 13 at para 13.11. Other uses might include a declaration that a debenture provision amounts to a sham in that the parties did not actually intend a particular provision to operate according to its terms at the time of the execution of the debenture (see *Snook v London and West Riding Investments Ltd* [1967] 2 QB 786 at 802).

An application under s35 is by originating summons with affidavit in support, and will normally be heard by the judge dealing with Companies' Court business, subject to local court practice. The costs of a s35(1) direction hearing application are ordinarily awarded against the unsuccessful party. However, the application may not always necessarily involve an 'unsuccessful party', such as when it is made on an *ex parte* basis to clarify, say, the validity of a purported appointment by a debenture-holder or the nature of a charge to which the company's property is subject. Thus, if the company's creditors generally have an interest in the outcome of the application then the court may, at its discretion, order costs to be paid out of the assets of the company comprised in the administrative receivership (see *Re Westdock Realisations* [1988] BCLC 354).

Section 35 is a useful facility and is commonly employed by both administrative and non-administrative receivers in seeking clarification on all aspects of receiverships. It is an appropriate and effective method of ascertaining any question which may arise as to the validity of an administrative receiver's appointment. Indeed, where a matter becomes contentious or proceedings are threatened over the validity of an administrative receiver's appointment, few options, if any, present themselves as equally effective methods of determining matters with equal authority. To this extent, the old law whereby a receiver should not apply to the court unless the circumstances were exceptional should no longer be seen as operative (see *Parker v Dunn* (1845) 8 Beav 497).

## 5.6.4 Rectification of the debenture document

Rectification is an equitable and discretionary remedy which may be granted by the court in appropriate cases. For a full analysis of the doctrine, reference should be made to the standard works such as Snell, *Principles of Equity* 29th edn at 626–36, Spry, *Equitable Remedies* (4th edn) at 593–606; see also Halsbury (4th edn) paras 682, 686 and 778.

Rectification permits the court to rectify the contents of a document on the basis that reliance by an applicant on a document in its original form would give rise to unconscionable risks or prejudice. This does not, however, permit the court to employ the doctrine in reformulating agreements; rather, the court may rectify a document in which an agreement is expressed or stated. As James V-C put it in *MacKenzie v Coulson* (1869) LR 8 Eq 368 at 375, 'Courts of equity do not rectify contracts; they may and do rectify instruments purporting to have been made in pursuance of the terms of the contract', see also *Shipley UDC v Bradford Corporation* [1936] Ch 375.

Essentially, rectification may be granted where it is based on a mistake of one or more of the parties to a document. In relation to administrative receivership, such a document might include either the debenture pursuant to which an appointment is purportedly made or the deed or instrument effecting the appointment. It would appear safe to assume that debentures will be subject to the doctrine of rectification, in view of the breadth of the class of documentation to which the doctrine has been judicially held to be amendable. These documents have included:

- conveyances (*Beaumont v Bramley* (1822) Turn & R 41, 37 ER 1009);
- deed polls (*Wright v Goff* (1856) 22 Beav 207, 52 ER 1087);
- settlements (*Rooke v Lord Kensington* (1856) 2 K&J, 753, 69 ER 986);
- life insurance policies (*Market Terminal Pty Ltd v Dominion Insurance Co of Australia* [1982] 1 NSW LR 105);
- bonds (*Hodgkinson v Wyatt* (1864) 9 Beav 566, 50 ER 462); and
- company registers (*Whitehouse v Carlton Hotel Pty Ltd* [1983] Qd R 336).

An instrument of appointment was expressly held to be the subject of the doctrine of rectification in *Daniel v Arkwright* (1864) 2 H&M 95, 71 ER 396.

The situations in which a mistake by one or more of the parties (ie the company granting the debenture, the debenture-holder and the office-holder) may manifest itself may be summarised as being within either of the following three categories:

(1) *Where all of the parties to a document are under a common mistake at the time of the execution of the document as to its provisions* (see *Joscelyne v Nissen* [1970] 2 QB 86 and the authorities discussed therein). This might arise, for example, where both parties to a debenture execute the debenture with a common intention as to its provisions which are not actually reflected in its terms. In a standard-form debenture this might extend to the inadvertent omission of a signifi-

cant or fundamental clause in the debenture as intended by the parties, or an inadvertent obliteration of a standard clause in the preparation of the debenture which precludes an appointment being made as envisaged by the parties at the time of execution. It would be unimaginable, for example, that the parties to a debenture did not intend that the debenture contained a power of appointment in the event of a specified default. This type of omission would provide grounds for an application for rectification of the debenture, provided the parties' intention could be proved in evidence. It should be noted that this type of defect may also be cured by the execution of a supplementary deed to the debenture or the re-execution of a new debenture as is considered below at para 5.6.5. The need for remedial measures of this type will also raise obvious questions about the quality of any independent advice proffered as to the provisions of the debenture at the time of its execution.

(2) *Where one party executes a document in the knowledge that another party has executed or will execute the debenture whilst mistaken as to the provisions contained in the document.* Whilst the general position in such a case is that rectification will usually be inappropriate (see *Riverlate Properties Ltd v Paul* [1975] Ch 133), the court will intervene where there exist circumstances which are such as to render unconscionable reliance on the document by the party intending reliance on its terms (*Thomas Bates and Son Ltd v Wyndham's (Lingerie) Ltd* [1981] 1 WLR 505 at 515 *per* Buckley LJ). Whilst Buckley LJ makes reference to 'sharp practice' as regards the availability of rectification in the case of unilateral mistakes, the learned judge goes on to state that 'the doctrine is one which depends more upon the equity of the position'. A view should therefore be taken as to whether either party to the debenture was or could have been aware of any defect in it and whether, in the circumstances, reliance on the mistake by the other party might be deemed inequitable. One obvious example of this would be where a company executes a debenture in favour of a bank under the mistaken belief that the debenture only permits the appointment of a receiver over its assets in specified, agreed circumstances whereas, in fact and to the actual knowledge of the bank, the debenture envisages and permits an appointment in further-reaching circumstances which operate to the detriment of the company. Notwithstanding the clear evidential problems posed by such circumstances, again, in the case of bank debentures and instruments of appointment, the availability of rectification as a remedy should be considered against the background of the formal record of any independent advice given as to the contents and/or effect of each particular document.

(3) *Where rectification appears appropriate to the court on the basis of breach of specific equitable duties, notably fiduciary duties.* Realistically, this ground is unlikely to arise in relation to a debenture, and if at all, in relation to an instrument of appointment, other than where it is executed on the basis of undue influence as exerted by one party, invariably by a secured creditor or its agent, over the other. In such a case it has been held that a deed may be rectified by the striking out of an inappropriate power in a deed (*Turner v Collins* (1871) LR 7 Ch 329. However, in the case of a debenture it is submitted that an allegation of undue influence will give rise to potential consequences which will be more far-reaching than the mere rectification of the debenture's provisions.

In conclusion, it should be remembered that rectification will be sought in few cases, largely on account of the evidential difficulties in seeking such relief. The remedy is, by its very nature, an equitable one and it is unlikely that the court will be prepared to grant relief where to do so would prejudice the rights of equity's darling, the *bona fide* third party purchaser for value without notice of the particular fact giving rise to the need for rectification. Delay is also likely to prejudice the obtaining of the remedy, although this will only be the case once grounds for the application to court become apparent. The court's approach is best illustrated by the decision in *J J Leonard Properties Pty Ltd v Leonard (WA) Pty Ltd* [1987] 5 ACLC 838 in which the court refused to rectify a debenture following the liquidation of the company, because to have done so would prejudice the rights of unsecured creditors whose interests vested in the assets of the company on the winding-up.

### 5.6.5  Re-execution of the debenture

Where questions are subsequently raised as to the validity of a debenture in terms of the appointment of an administrative receiver pursuant to it, one possible course of remedial action is the re-execution of the debenture itself. This may be undertaken, for example, to incorporate in the debenture documentation effective clauses which were either omitted or which appear incorrectly or incompletely in the original debenture.

A decision to re-execute a debenture, or the execution of a fresh debenture, should, however, be undertaken with a considerable degree of caution and with a weather eye on the company's financial and trading position. This is because a debenture executed in circumstances where the appointment of an administrative receiver is specifically sought is likely to be highly susceptible to attack subsequently as a transaction-at-undervalue, a preference and/or a transaction contravening s245.

Consideration of the re-execution or execution of a fresh debenture should also call into question the possibility of reconstructing the term of the present and apparently defective debenture as is now considered.

### 5.6.6 Construction/Reconstruction of the debenture on the basis of extrinsic evidence and examination of the company's directors

Where a debenture is found to be wholly or partially defective on its face for the purpose of appointing an administrative receiver, consideration should be given to the obtaining of extrinsic evidence and an examination of the company's directors in order to ascertain the circumstances in which the debenture was executed. A debenture document is, of course, necessarily only evidence of the terms contained in it, and is not *per se* necessarily an exhaustive account of the terms envisaged by the parties at the time of its execution. It is obviously highly unlikely, for example, that a company and a creditor would enter into a debenture which did not envisage the appointment of a receiver on the happening of any number of certain specified events. However, due to administrative inadvertence or professional incompetence in drafting, specific provisions facilitating such an appointment might conceivably be omitted from the debenture itself. Other permutations of the potential administrative shortcomings of debenture documentation are too numerous to mention, although the example given serves the purpose. Any administrative shortcomings apart, it remains that the terms of the debenture as envisaged and intended by the parties to it may not actually be reflected in the terms of the debenture itself. How then can evidence of the actual terms of the debenture be obtained?

Perhaps the best starting-point will be correspondence between the parties prior to execution. This will usually be standard-form documentation and may contain details or explanation of, say, the circumstances in which it is envisaged a receiver may be appointed by the prospective debenture-holder. Similarly, although perhaps less likely, the records of the company or the debenture-holder itself may contain agreed details of the relevant envisaged terms of the debenture. These records may take the form of formal board minutes (at which a nominee of the debenture-holder may well have been in attendance) or minutes of meetings between representatives of the company and the debenture-holder.

Finally, consideration should be given to a private examination of company directors for the purposes of ascertaining the relevant terms of the debenture in question. A private examination of the directors of a company by an administrative receiver is provided for by s236 which is considered more fully in Chapter 8. However, prior to engaging in formal examination proceedings, consideration should be given to the directors' apparent willingness to co-operate and provide on a voluntary basis, formal evidence, preferably in affidavit form, of the actual terms of the debenture pursuant to which the administrative receiver was appointed.

## 5.7  Joint and Several Appointments

It is common practice for two licensed insolvency practitioners to be appointed joint administrative receivers. This arrangement is usually perceived as advantageous, since either office-holder may act without recourse to the other. Furthermore, particularly where the administrative receivership is a large-scale one, workloads can be divided between the two office-holders. In advising on the appointment, however, a degree of caution is needed since the joint appointment of two (or more) administrative receivers does not necessarily authorise them to act both jointly and severally.

The clear danger with making an appointment on a joint and several basis where the appointment may not be made severally is that the appointment is potentially void. Similarly, a joint appointee, where no power to appoint jointly exists, runs the risk of liability for trespass. Sections 34 and 42(3) operate only to protect office-holders and third parties respectively in the face of liability, although it is far from clear that s42(3) will protect even *bona fide* third parties without notice of the defect in the appointment from the consequences of and liabilities arising from an invalid or void appointment.

It appears from the decisions in *Re Liverpool Household Stores* (1890) 59 LJ Ch 616 and *Guthrie v Armstrong* (1822) B & Ald 628 that express provision is required in a debenture as a condition for jointly appointed administrative receivers to act both jointly and severally. Indeed, both cases are commonly cited as authority for this proposition. The problem with these authorities is the particular factual circumstances to which they relate. The former case actually arose as a result of a charge of misfeasance by the Official Receiver, where a board resolution had purported to delegate all of the powers of the board of directors to a sub-committee of three directors. Similarly, the *Guthrie* decision appears to restrict itself to a confirmation that an exercise by one or named persons of a power of attorney is sufficient for execution purposes, where the power is given to a number of persons to execute certain policies as they consider jointly and severally to be proper on a joint and several basis. It is submitted, therefore, that either authority should not be regarded with a greater degree of authority than its facts permit.

To some extent, the problem with the question of whether an administrative receiver who has been appointed jointly has implied authority to act jointly and severally with his co-appointee has been alleviated by the more recent approach of the Commonwealth courts. It must be hoped that a similar approach will be adopted within the domestic jurisdiction in due course. In the absence of this, the Commonwealth decisions represent the most useful and constructive authorities on this area.

In *NEC Information Systems Australia Pty Limited v Lockhart* (1991) 101 ALR 95 the New South Wales Court of Appeal was not prepared to conclude that a debenture authorising a joint appointment, which did not envisage expressly the fact of the appointment both jointly and severally, did not thereby preclude the office-holders from acting on a several basis. The approach of the court was to consider the commercial purpose behind the making of joint appointments. This, it concluded, must be the need for convenience so as to facilitate an expeditious receivership. This clearly envisaged action being taken by one as opposed to both appointees in the course of the receivership. (A later decision of the High Court of Australia on appeal (1992) 108 ALR 561 in the same case did not affect the decision of the New South Wales court on this point.)

In the *NEC* case the debenture provided for the appointment of 'any person or persons' to be a receiver or a receiver and manager or 'receivers and managers' over charged property. The mortgagee appointed two persons who were referred to as acting 'jointly and severally' in the deed of appointment. The New South Wales Court of Appeal identified that the wording of the debenture would enable the appointment of any number of receivers and managers, but the question before it was whether the wording of the debenture envisaged the power on the part of appointees to act severally. The court's conclusion was that it did, primarily on the basis that the debenture clearly envisaged the appointment of more than one person as receiver and manager and the commercial purpose of such appointments was the facilitating of the expeditious conduct of the receivership itself. In other words, the court refused to accept that a joint appointment, as opposed to one which was joint and several (which strictly speaking the debenture did not provide for) could genuinely be construed as merely allowing for an appointment on a joint basis without its also being several. It is submitted that this view must be the correct one except where the contrary intention of the parties can be clearly demonstrated.

The decision in the *NEC* case follows the New Zealand Court of Appeal's decision in *DFC Commercial Services Limited v Samuel* [1990] 5 NZCLC 96–403. The debenture in that case contained a standard interpretation clause which imported a singular meaning into the plural references and vice versa. (This in fact reflects the implied effect of the Interpretation Act 1978 s6(c) in the United Kingdom, and of the IA 1986 s231.) In addition, in the definition section of the debenture the term 'receiver' was expressly stated to include references to 'a receiver and manager' or 'receivers and managers'. Whilst there was no express power in the debenture to appoint more than one receiver, other than where a single appointee was empowered to delegate with the consent of the debenture-holder all or any of his powers, the court was prepared to accept that the debenture envisaged a joint appointment of one or more receivers (and managers). This decision shows there is significant flexibility in the way in which the Commonwealth jurisdictions appear prepared to construe the language of a debenture where it at least anticipates the possibility of a joint appointment. Certainly in the *DFC Commercial Services* case this is apparent from the judgments of Somers J and Hardie-Boys J, both of whom identified the commercial and practical reasons for the implied power to appoint joint receivers on a joint and several basis notwithstanding the absence of express wording to that effect in the debenture. That flexibility would appear not to extend, however, to situations where the debenture expressly restricts the appointment of two or more receivers so as to preclude them from acting on a several basis but rather on a joint basis only. It is difficult to see in practice how such a restriction might benefit either the debenture-holder or, indeed, the appointees.

Both the *NEC* and *DFC Commercial Services* cases go further than the less helpful decisions in *Wrights Hardware Pty Ltd v Evans* [1988] 13 ACLR 631, a decision of the Supreme Court of Western Australia, and *Kerry Lowe Management Pty Ltd v Isherwood Sherlock* [1989] 15 ACLR 615, a decision of the New South Wales Supreme Court. The broad effect of those decisions was that joint and several authority could not be based solely on the inclusion in a debenture of an interpretation clause which connoted singular references as having plural meanings. Neither could such an interpretation be based on an express clause permitting the appointment of an additional receiver or receiver and manager such that the additional appointee would have full powers and authority to exercise all or any part of the powers conferred on the original appointee.

In the *Wrights Hardware* case Franklyn J adopted a strict and literal construction of the terms pursuant to which a receiver was appointed. Furthermore, and on the basis of *R J Ward Pty Limited v Sherlock*, (1988 unreported), a decision of the Federal Court of Australia, the joint appointment of receivers and managers did not confer a power to act severally unless the instrument of appointment either expressly or impliedly provided so. Neither was it possible for reliance to be placed on a 'for singular read plural' interpretation clause in the debenture in giving effect to the apparent joint and several authority of two or more receivers and managers, an express power being required on the basis of *Guthrie v Armstrong* (1822) B & Ald 628.

It must be said that the *Wrights Hardware* and *Kerry Lowe* decisions are disappointing when compared with the essentially commercial attitude adopted by the New Zealand and Australian courts in the *NEC* and *DFC Commercial Services* cases and certainly the approach in the latter cases is to be preferred. It should be noted, however, that in the *NEC* case the court distinguished the *Wrights Hardware* and *Kerry Lowe* decisions on the basis that the NEC debenture contained an express power to appoint one or more receivers and managers. The conclusion to which the above cases point appears to be that where a debenture expressly authorises the appointment of one or more administrative receivers, at least in the absence of an express provision to the contrary, there appears good reason to suppose that those administrative receivers will have an implied power to act jointly and severally. What is crucial here is that the debenture actually permits the appointment of one or more persons as receivers and managers. It should be noted that in the *Wrights Hardware* case the court identified, quite correctly it is submitted, that the power to appoint a receiver and manager must be distinguished from a power merely to appoint a receiver.

Although the Law of Property Act 1925 s61 effectively provides that a power to appoint one receiver and manager will enable an appointment to be made on the basis that it implies a singular meaning into plural references and vice versa other than where the contrary is expressed, as does the Interpretation Act 1978 s6(c), it is submitted that it is inadvisable to rely with any real confidence on such implied powers. The same would be true of any provision in a debenture which merely recited either or both of those statutory provisions. Equal caution should be exercised in reliance on s231(2) which provides, apparently in confirming s6(c) of the 1978 Act, that the appointment of an administrative receiver which relates to more than one person, or which has the effect that the office is to be held by more than one person, implies that any act required or authorised to be done by those persons is to be done by all or any one or more of the persons for the time being holding the office in question. The practical effect of this is to take singular references to an administrative receiver in a debenture or deed of appointment as referring to the plural. Again, sole reliance on this provision is inadvisable. In conclusion and in practice, doubt is clearly best avoided in this area by the terms of a debenture expressly providing for joint and several appointments which are then made on that basis, at least until clarification of this area is provided by the English courts.

For an enlightening discussion of the legislative history on this area and a further discussion of the above cases see the useful commentary in Marks and Wilson (1994) 7 Insolvency Intelligence 65–7. See also *Bass Breweries Ltd v Delaney* [1994] BCC 851 for a first instance decision in which a joint appointment of LPA receivers nominated by competing mortgagees with equal priority was effected.

# *Chapter Six*

# Appointment Validity Considerations: 1

## 6.1 Introduction

This chapter considers those principal areas on which attention should be focused in advising on the validity of the administrative receiver's appointment. Matters considered in the text which follow will not always be apparent to those offering advice on the appointment without further specific enquiries being made. Where doubt exists in the mind of the adviser, enquiry is invariably the best course of action. In reality, however, a detailed and rigorous investigation of every conceivable pitfall is simply not always practicable. One seemingly tempting solution to this is simply not to undertake investigations. However, appropriate enquiries made of any appointee, and the company itself via the appointee, will go some way to protecting an adviser against any subsequent liability arising in the wake of an invalid appointment, in the sense that advice was given on the basis of the fullest possible information.

As a matter of course, for example, a check should always be made as to any pending administration petition and a search made of the Companies Court's Central Compulsory Winding-up Registry.

The letter of advice on the validity of the appointment, depending on the style and format adopted, may seek to clarify the position on each of the matters considered below. Alternatively, the letter may deal simply with those which appear potentially problematic. These matters may also be of use to those who may wish to attack the validity of an appointment, most notably any subsequently appointed liquidator or administrator, or the directors of the company put into administrative receivership.

## 6.2 What is the Date on which the Debenture was Executed?

The date of execution of the debenture is relevant since the security comprised in the debenture pursuant to which the administrative receiver is appointed is liable to be set aside under one or more of the following headings—subject to applicable time limits—on the taking of successful proceedings by a liquidator or administrator.

### 6.2.1 Transaction-at-undervalue; s238

A company is deemed to enter into a transaction-at-undervalue with a person by virtue of s238(4) if it either makes a gift to that person or otherwise enters into a transaction with that person on terms that provide for the company to receive no consideration, or enters into a transaction with that person for a consideration the value of which is significantly less than the value, in money or money's worth, of the consideration provided by the company.

A number of points should be made in relation to the definition in s238(4) which are of use in assimilating the relevance of the provision in the context of a debenture.

First, although the term 'consideration' is not defined, it is probably best attributed its normal meaning for contract law purposes. It is therefore irrelevant that the consideration has no objective value, provided it has some intrinsic *quid pro quo* value to its recipient (*Currie v Misa* (1875) LR 10 Exch 153).

Secondly, as in contract law, past consideration will not amount to valid consideration and, therefore, will not be treated as consideration received by the purported recipient of it. One obvious example of this is the taking of security by an unsecured creditor for monies already advanced. However, to the extent that additional funds are provided for the security, these will amount to good consideration. This point is also relevant to the avoidance of a floating charge security under s245, which is considered at para 6.2.3. The crucial question for present purposes is whether the debenture has been executed in respect of an unsecured loan for which no new monies were advanced.

Thirdly, payment of an existing debt will be a transaction for full consideration in that the debt is extinguished; see *Taylor v Blakelock* (1886) 32 Ch D 560 (in which Bowen LJ equated a creditor receiving payment to a purchaser for value). Where payment of an existing debt is coupled with the giving of security over previously unsecured sums (ie in respect of which no new monies are advanced) it is submitted that the consideration will amount to past consideration and will, therefore, constitute invalid consideration.

Fourthly, the giving of security by a company—such as a debenture—in respect of an advance made to a third party may amount to a transaction-at-undervalue, since there is no value or benefit derived by the company granting the debenture of the advance made to the third party, in the absence of any arrangements between them in respect of those monies (eg typically a finance or trust agreement).

Section 238 poses particular problems in relation to the giving of guarantees by a company. The root of the problem is that a guarantee arrangement in

155

respect of a principal debtor involves the receipt of funds by the principal debtor—which may be of no intrinsic value to the guarantor company—in return for a liability on the part of the guarantor which is contingent in nature, since it will necessarily be conditional on the default of the principal debtor which may or may not actually arise. Despite the fact that monies are generally advanced by a creditor to a principal debtor under the terms of a guarantee agreement, it is suggested that this will still amount to good consideration for the guarantor company, because it is the executed consideration of the act or the executory consideration of the promise to act which is performed as the price of the giving of the guarantee by the guarantor (*Currie v Misa* (1875) LR 10 Exch 153). However, the real problem with this is the valuation in monetary terms of the benefit of the advance for the guarantor. Similar problems arise on the creation of security by a company over its assets, since the creation of security does not *per se* reduce the value of the company's assets. Whilst some commercial value may be attributed to a guarantee or the creation of security, particularly where the principal debtor and guarantor are members of the same group of companies and interact commercially as such, any specific valuation is likely to be impossible in real terms, albeit that valuation may be made for accounting purposes. Similar valuation problems exist in relation to the value of the guarantee to a creditor for s238 purposes. In the absence of judicial analysis of this problem, perhaps the best working guide to this is furnished by Professor R M Goode in *Principles of Corporate Insolvency*, 1st edn. (1990) at 150, which defines the value of the guarantee as:

> the amount (if any) for which, at the time of the guarantee, a prudent creditor with full knowledge of the debtor's affairs would make provision in his accounts for default, after taking into account what he could reasonably expect to recover from securities from the principal debtor and from co-surety in respect of their proportionate share of the suretyship liabilities... [Or], looked at from the viewpoint of the surety, it is the amount for which a prudent surety with full knowledge of the debtor's affairs would make provision in its accounts after allowing for the value of the securities taken from the principal debtor and contributions from co-sureties.

It remains to be seen, however, whether in practice a court would be prepared to accept such a specific valuation on the basis of appropriate supporting expert evidence, typically an independent accountant's report.

The question of the valuation of the benefit derived by a company for the giving of a guarantee by it is likely to be more vexed where the commercial relationship of the companies to the guarantee arrangement is not a close one. Benefit is more likely to be derived where a guarantee is given vertically 'downwards' (ie parent to subsidiary) within a group, with increasing problems becoming evident if the guarantee is given 'horizontally' (ie subsidiary to subsidiary) or 'vertically' upward (ie subsidiary to parent) within a group.

It is suggested that the real practical problem with guarantee arrangements lies with the liquidator, on whom the onus rests to prove what s238(4)(b) refers to as a 'significant' disparity between the benefit given and that derived by a guarantor company under a guarantee arrangement. In English law the decision in *Re M C Bacon* [1990] BCC 78 established the inability to quantify such benefits and burden in monetary terms, as a practical stumbling-block to a potential s238 action. The value attributable to a guarantee for the purposes of s238 has also recently been considered by the American courts for the purposes of analogous statutory principles to which very similar reasoning applies.

In *Commerce Bank of Kansas City v Achtenberg* [1994] CCH Bankr Dec 75, 631, two brothers jointly owned a company K, and jointly guaranteed a bank loan of US$7,000,000 to it. On the subsequent bankruptcy of both brothers their trustee applied to the court for a declaration that the guarantees were void as fraudulent transfers by the company for the purposes of the US Bankruptcy Code s584(a)(2), on the basis that both brothers had received 'reasonably equivalent value' in consideration for giving the guarantees. Having decided that the brothers had received no direct benefit as a consequence of giving the guarantees, the court then had to decide whether any indirect benefit had been conferred on them. Senior District Judge Sachs of the US District Court for the Western Division of Missouri noted that K had been insolvent at the time the brothers had guaranteed its bank loan and, as a consequence, held that the brothers could not have had conferred on them an indirect benefit which amounted to 'reasonably equivalent value' as consideration for the guarantees. The judge reached this decision notwithstanding the fact that the brothers had a very significant 'identity of interest' with the company in that they wholly owned it. It is worth noting that the earlier decision in *Branch v Federal Deposit Insurance Corp* (1993) 825 F Supp 384 was distinguished in the *Bank of Kansas* case, on the grounds that in the *Branch* case the wholly-owned subsidiary in respect of which guarantees had been given was solvent. In that case it had been held that an indirect benefit received from a loan to a wholly-owned company could amount to 'reasonably equivalent value' as consideration for guarantees. It remains to be seen whether the English courts will be prepared to entertain the notion of reasonably equivalent values or whether, as is submitted to be the better approach, a strictly adhered to 'finite values' approach will govern the operation of the provisions.

On an application by a liquidator where a company has entered into a transaction-at-undervalue, the court may make such order as it thinks fit for restoring the position to what it would have been if the company had not entered into that transaction (s238(3)). It is submitted that in the case of a debenture containing both fixed-charge and floating-charge elements, it is inconceivable in practice that either a floating or a fixed charge would be set aside by the court, without the very real possibility of the other charge also being set aside in the case of a debenture which fell within these provisions where the fixed and floating charges were created simultaneously. However, this need not necessarily be the case where the fixed and floating charges are created in separate debentures, the cumulative effect of which is to grant the requisite security in favour of the debenture, thereby entitling him to appoint an administrative receiver for the purposes of s29(2). The orders which the court might make as a remedy in relation to ss238 and 239 are set out in s241 and are stated to be without prejudice to any other remedy (s241(4)). These orders are considered at the end of the next section on preferences at para 6.2.2, below.

Despite the use of the word 'shall' as regards the making of an order for the purposes of s238(3) for the purposes of restoring the position between the parties, it appears that the court has an unfettered discretion which is equitable in its origin to make such order 'as it thinks fit' according to the wording of the same section. This view has recently been confirmed by Nicholls V-C in *Re Paramount Airways (in administration)* [1993] Ch 223 at 239, and is subject to academic support in Sealy and Milman, *Annotated Guide to the 1986 Insolvency Legislation*, 4th edn (1994) at 288) and Goode, *Principles of Corporate Insolvency Law*, 1st edn (1990) at 146 and 152.

The court will not make an order in respect of a transaction-at-undervalue if it is satisfied that both of two conditions are met.

(1) The company which entered into the transaction did so in good faith (ie the test is not a question of the *bona fides* of the transferee) and for the purposes of carrying on its business. See *Re Sarflax Ltd* [1979] Ch 592, which considered the meaning of the term 'carrying on a business' for the purposes of the Companies Act 1948 s332(1), it was held that the term extended to the collection of assets and the distribution in the closing-down of a business.

(2) At the time the company entered into the transaction there were reasonable grounds for believing that the transaction would benefit the company (s238(5)(a),(b)).

It is submitted that the second condition of this test will be onerously difficult to prove on a balance of probabilities without the fulfilment of the first condition. The second condition imposes an objective test, to be assessed by the court, in the light of the subjective views of the company (ie acting through its directors) even, it would appear, if the directors acted dishonestly. Those subjective views, for example in attempting to realise assets to ease cash flow problems, will clearly be best borne out by well-documented board minutes, particularly where the company entered into the transaction, which might extend to a debenture with one of the board's own members or a connected party, at a time when the company was in financial distress.

In the leading case of *Re M C Bacon* [1990] BCC 78 Millett J held that the creation of a security over a company's assets *per se* did not fall within the ambit of s238(4)(b) since it did not diminish or deplete the value of the company's assets. That is, a comparison must be made in monetary terms between the value obtained by the company and the value provided by it as consideration for the transaction. It was held that neither the loss by the company of its ability to apply the proceeds of the assets (other than in actual satisfaction of the debt) nor the consideration received by the company in return for it is capable of quantification in monetary terms. Similar reasoning has been applied by the Court of Appeal in relation to transactions defrauding creditors under s423 in *Menzies v National Bank of Kuwait* [1994] BCC 119. The analysis in *Re M C Bacon* [1990] BCC 78 may also have analogous implications in relation to the points made above regarding guarantees given by a company.

Apart from the more obvious examples of the giving of guarantees and security over assets as transactions-at-undervalue, other conceivable transactions which may be relevant to administrative receivership will include the giving of security by the company in return for other consideration. This might include the lease or hire of equipment with a rental value which is significantly less than the value of the security given or the acquisition of an asset by the company, or the provision of services to the company, the market value of which is significantly less than the value of the security given. Other examples might include the retention by the company of an asset with a market value significantly lower than the value of the security which is given in consideration for satisfaction of a claim against the company, or the exercise or grant of a right of set-off against a debt already owed by the company the value of which is significantly below the value of the security given. Again, the major problem in dealing with these types of transaction at any subsequent date is one of attributing specific valuations as to monetary value to the respective parties to the transaction.

One significant practical factor, which in practice will operate very much against the pursuit of transaction-avoidance litigation, particularly where the assets of the company are marginal, is the fact that a liquidator, and presumably an administrator, is not entitled to an order to recoup his losses out of a company's floating-charge assets as expenses of the liquidation where he has been ordered to pay costs on an unsuccessful claim under s238. This appears to be the case irrespective of the *bona fides* and reasonable grounds of the office-holder in pursuing the action (*Re M C Bacon Ltd* (No2) [1990] BCC 430, which included unsuccessful actions under ss239 and 214).

Finally, s238 (and presumably s239) has no extra-territorial effect, so that it is only available against a company registered in England or a foreign company carrying on business in England (*Re Paramount Airways Ltd* (*No* 2) [1991] BCC 559). However, the provision(s) may now be available against a foreign company with assets located in England and Wales on the basis of *Re Bulk International Commodities Ltd* (1992) BCC 463. Moreover, an order under s238 or 239 may be made against a person outside the jurisdiction on the basis of the decision in *Re Paramount Airways Ltd (in administration)* [1993] Ch 223, if the respondent has sufficient connection with the jurisdiction to render it equitable for the order to be made against him. In such a case, the court may order service to be effected within such time, on such person, at such place and in such manner as it thinks fit (IR r12.12(3)). Order 11 of the Rules of the Supreme Court and the corresponding County Court Rules are not relevant to the service of documents outside the jurisdiction in insolvency proceedings (IR r12.12(1)).

The time limits and types of order which may be made by the court in relation to s238 are equally relevant to s239 and are dealt with at the end of the following section.

### 6.2.2   Section 239 preferences

By virtue of s239(4) a company is deemed to give a preference to a person if:

(a)   that person is one of the company's creditors or a surety or guarantor for any of the company's debts or its liabilities; and

(b)   the company does anything or suffers anything to be done which (in either case) has the effect of putting that person into a position which, in the event of the company going into insolvent liquidation, will be better than the position he would have been in if that thing had not been done.

Clearly the creation of a debenture by a company may potentially constitute a preference even if created pursuant to a court order, since the giving of a preference is not affected by the fact that 'the thing done' by the company is pursuant to an order of the court (s239(6)).

The acid test of whether a transaction constitutes a preference is two-fold;

(1)   The recipient of the benefit of the transaction must be a creditor or surety or guarantor of the company.

(2)   That person must be put into a better position as a result of the transaction, ie on an immediate insolvent liquidation of the company following the transaction and not in view of any subsequent insolvent liquidation when further debts—especially preferential debts—may have arisen.

The practical implications of this two-fold test are thus also two-fold. First, if the beneficiary is not a creditor or surety or guarantor there can be no preference. Secondly, if the company is not insolvent following the transaction then it follows that the beneficiary's position cannot have been improved over what it would have otherwise been, since its debt or liability will be paid or met in full in any case, irrespective of the fact that the company subsequently becomes insolvent.

The two-fold test above permits an initial exclusion of certain transactions as potential preferences without further reference being made to the s239 statutory requirements. Where a transaction between the company and a third party is such that there is a contemporaneous or virtually contemporaneous transfer of value between the parties, as a consequence of which the other person is not put in a better position on an immediate insolvent liquidation thereafter, there can be no preference as defined in s239(4). Certain transactions, therefore, will not amount to preferences where the consideration provided by the company is the giving of security such as a debenture, provided that the value received by the company under the transaction is equal to the value of the security given. These include (a) a contemporaneous or subsequent advance of funds by a creditor or (b) the provision of some other new value such as (i) the provision of an overdraft facility or (ii) credit on a running account or (iii) a transfer of an asset or (iv) provision of services to the company. Such transactions may, however, be susceptible to avoidance under s245.

These exceptions to the general preference rules require some qualification. The exception to contemporaneous or subsequent advances of funds will only operate to the extent that any security given actually secures new funds advanced to the company. To the extent that the transaction does not (eg by securing an unsecured overdraft), the contractual arrangement effectively amounts to a reduction in the company's assets for the purposes of an immediate insolvent liquidation of the company; it will, therefore, potentially amount to a preference as a consequence. The question of what constitutes new value is returned to more fully below at para 6.2.3 below with regard to the avoidance of floating charges under s245. Furthermore, whilst a single transaction concerning the provision of goods or services is not inherently problematic, the position is not so clear where the parties transact on a regular course of dealings basis. For present purposes it is submitted that where security is given by the company so as to ensure the provision of further goods or services—particularly those fundamental to the company's business operations—there can be no question of a preference, since there will be no intention on the company's part to prefer the other party secured by the transaction.

The exceptions above apart, the court will not make an order under s239 until satisfied that in doing so the company was influenced 'in deciding to give it' by a desire to produce the effect set out in s239(4)(b) above. In considering the concept of a company being influenced by a desire to produce an effect Millett J, in *M C Bacon Ltd* [1990] BCC 78 at 87, held that a dominant intention as was previously required under the Bankruptcy Act 1914 s44(1) needs no longer to be established; nor is such a dominant intention sufficient to establish an intention. What is required in effect is nothing short of a desire on the part of the company to produce the effect in s239(4).

The establishment of desire for the purposes of s239 is an extremely onerous test, on the basis of Millett J's reasoning at least, in that it involves the objective inference by the court of intention on the part of the company. Consequently, a company may provide security to creditors, thereby improving their position on an immediate insolvent liquidation, without creating a preference under s239 where the security is given for ongoing financial support without the inherent desire to improve the creditor's position. Certainly this was the case in *Re M C Bacon,* where a charge created in favour of a bank was held not to be voidable as a preference as the only alternative for the company was the withdrawal of the bank's support and its own consequent liquidation.

Any party seeking to establish desire in the corporate sense is fixed with the further problem of establishing the requisite intention on the part of the board of the company. This may pose insurmountable evidential problems, particularly, for example, where minutes of the board's deliberations and decisions at the time the alleged preference was given show the influence of factors other than the desire to prefer the creditor concerned. Intention may well be easier to establish where the directors themselves stand to benefit personally as a consequence of the alleged preference transaction. The classic example of this is where a transfer of assets is made to a creditor, typically a bank, to reduce the liability of the directors under personal guarantees on an impending liquidation.

The onus in proving that a preference has been given to a creditor (ie in establishing the requisite elements of s239 outlined above) rests with the liquidator or administrator. The onus shifts, however, in that there is a rebuttable presumption that a preference has been given where it was given to a person connected with the company, other only by reason of that person being an employee (s239(6)).

The time limits relevant to ss238 and 239 are set out in s240, which provides that the provisions apply only to transactions taking place at a 'relevant time' as defined. Section 240 is largely self-explanatory, the 'relevant time' depending on whether a liquidator or administrator is able to show that the alleged transaction took place within two years or six months of the onset of insolvency (as defined both curiously and misleadingly in s240(3)) in the case of connected and unconnected persons respectively where a preference is attacked (s240(1)(a)). The relevant time period for a transaction-at-undervalue is two years in all cases (s240(1)(b)).

In all cases it will also have to be shown that, at the relevant time, the company was either unable to pay its debts or became so as a consequence of the transaction-at-undervalue or preference (s240(2) as defined in s123).

It follows that an alleged transaction-at-undervalue or preference may not be avoided subsequently if either the time limits prescribed are not met or the company cannot be shown to have been or become insolvent. However, it may be possible for such a transaction to be avoided as a transaction defrauding creditors as defined in s423. In terms of the company's alleged insolvency, the burden of proof ordinarily remains with the liquidator (or administrator), although it shifts to a 'connected' person (as defined in s435) where the company enters into a transaction-at-undervalue (but apparently not a preference) with such a person (s240(2)).

The types of order which the court may make for the purposes of ss238 and 239 are set out in s241(1) (as amended by the Insolvency (No 2) Act 1994). These orders are not exhaustive and include those orders which the court may make subject to the restriction on orders in s241(2). These restrictions broadly permit the joining in of a third party to proceedings and the protection of a *bona fide* third-party purchaser for value without notice of the 'relevant circumstances' prescribed in s241(3). Specifically, the orders in s241(1) are without prejudice to the court's general discretion to make such order as it thinks fit for restoring the position to what it would have been, in the event that the company had not given the transaction-at-undervalue or preference (ss238(3), 239(3)). Sections 238(3) and 239(3) apart, perhaps the most precarious order available to the court from the perspective of the debenture-holder and administrative receiver is the release or discharge (in whole or in part) of any security given by the company (see s241(1)(c)). Such an order would clearly prejudice the debenture-holder's security over the whole or substantially the whole of the company's assets. More seriously, it might render an office-holding administrative receiver's appointment invalid.

### 6.2.3 Section 245: avoidance of floating charges

Section 245 allows a liquidator or administrator to apply to the court for an order effectively avoiding a floating charge as defined in s251. This application for avoidance under the section is of critical importance to a debenture-holder and/or an appointed administrative receiver, as it potentially affects the validity of the appointment since a floating charge is an unconditional prerequisite for the purposes of the definition of an administrative receiver in s29(2).

Subject to the time limits set out in s245(3), a floating charge taken over a company's undertaking or property is invalid except to the extent of money paid or goods or services supplied to the company 'at the same time as, or after, the creation of the charge' as consideration for the creation of the charge (s245(2)(a)). This consideration will also include any discharge or reduction of any debt of the company or interest payable on that debt or in respect of money paid or goods or services supplied (s245(2)(b),(c)). It is unclear why the consideration in s245(2) is so specifically defined and why, as a consequence, at least on a literal statutory interpretation of the provision, consideration such as the transfer of interests in land, securities or other personal property other than 'money' or 'goods' should remain outside it. Indeed, such a literal construction of the provisions would appear to flaw its substantive purpose in some cases, particularly in view of the significantly expanded scope of the meaning of new value in s245 as compared with the previous legislation which extended to cash consideration only.

Section 245(a) makes reference to '...money paid, or goods or services supplied, *to the company...*' (emphasis added). Sub-subsections (b) and (c) of the provision are also framed in a way to infer the discharge or reduction of a debt or other benefit accruing to the company. It follows that where monies or other considerations within the scope of s245 are not made available to the company, then the provision will have no effect, such as where monies are paid to a third party by a creditor to reduce the debts of the company. This was held to be the case in *Re Fairway Magazines* [1992] BCC 924 where monies were paid direct into the company's bank current account, which had the consequential effect of reducing the directors' personal guarantee liabilities. This decision follows *Re Orleans Motor Co Ltd* [1911] 2 Ch 41, a decision under the analogous and formerly operative provision, although it should be noted that the company will not be deemed in such a case to have received any consideration in return for the creation of the floating charge (see also *Re Libertas Kommerz GmbH* 1978 SLT 222 which follows similar reasoning).

Any restrictions apparent in s245's scope should not detract from the following two important considerations which concern the validity of the floating charge. First, was *any* consideration (ie executed or executory) provided for the charge, irrespective of how insignificant in monetary terms? Secondly, at what time in relation to the creation of the charge was the consideration provided to the company? The first of these questions is itself relevant for two reasons. Initially it is the mere provision of consideration, however insignificant, which will *prima facie* validate the charge itself. Arising from this is the question of whether the floating charge may potentially be invalidated, which may affect the extent to which the charge-holder is secured over the whole or substantially the whole of the company's assets for the purpose of s29(2). It is clear from the wording of s245 that the floating charge must stand or fall as a result of attack under the provision; that is, there is no provision for partial invalidity of the security granted.

The second question; the time at which the consideration for the charge was provided here concerns. This point arose recently in *Re Shoe Lace Ltd* [1993] BCC 609. The question in that case was whether monies advanced by a creditor, sums of £300,000 (on 3 April 1990), £50,000 (in May), £75,000 (in June) and £11,500 (on 16 July 1990), were paid 'at the same time as' a floating charge contained in a debenture which was executed subsequently on 24 July 1990. (The question actually became relevant following a petition to wind-up the company and a winding-up order made on 4 September 1990 and 20 November 1990 respectively.) The unanimous decision of the Court of Appeal was that the advances had not been made at the same time as the creation of the charge. The decision emphasised that the requirements of s245 cannot be satisfied if advances preceded the creation of the charge by any time interval whatsoever other than one 'so short that it can be regarded as minimal and payment and execution can be regarded as contemporaneous' ([1993] BCC 609 at 620). A coffee break or similar *de minimis* period seems likely to constitute such a period as envisaged by the judgment.

For useful comment on apparent practical weaknesses in the new legislation see Pennington *Corporate Insolvency Law,* 1st edn (Butterworths, 1991) at 217.

The position where a creditor makes advances following the creation of a floating charge is not clarified by the *Shoe Lace* decision. Under the previously operative legislation contained in the Companies Act 1985 s617(1), which re-enacted Companies Act 1948 s322, a floating charge was effectively validated as security only for 'cash paid to the company at the time or subsequent to the creation of, and in consideration of, the charge'. The court's approach to this provision, as in *Re Yeovil Glove Co Ltd* [1965] Ch 148, a decision under the Companies Act 1984 s322, was to validate a floating charge for subsequent advances made as a result of the creation of the charge, if it could be shown that the parties intended that the advances were to be secured by the floating charge, even in the absence of specific contractual arrangements to that effect. It is suggested, however, that the approach adopted to s617 will not lend itself to s245 on the following grounds.

Section 245 is more narrowly framed than s617, in that it merely validates a floating charge to the extent of monies advanced specifically in consideration of the creation of the charge, as opposed to those made voluntarily, even in reliance on its existence as a security interest in favour of a creditor. On the other hand, there is no reason why s245 should not operate to validate security under a floating charge for advances made on a contractual basis subsequent to an advance made in consideration for the floating charge. This will be subject to the floating charge being described as security for advances subsequently made, as will usually be the case in practice. In legal terms, the consideration for the floating charge will be executed at the time of the creation of the charge to the extent that it includes both the initial advance and any advance (ie promise to pay which is exacted by the company at the time of the creation of the charge) which is to be made subsequently, notwithstanding the fact that the payment of the advance and, therefore, the enhanced amount secured by the floating charge, is postponed. This is to be contrasted with the situation where a floating charge is granted on an 'open-ended' basis where, at the time of creation, no specific consideration is either executed or promised. Thus, where a floating charge relates to 'all future monies paid to the company' (and possibly past consideration already paid to the company, which will not amount to valid consideration) it is suggested that the charge will be void under s245 if no consideration is either paid over 'at the time or subsequent to the creation of, and in consideration of, the charge' or is promised in specific terms in terms of quantum and time of payment at that time. Clearly evidence of such a promise may be given later by those who were party to the transaction, although this may meet with problems in terms of proving the matter on a balance of probabilities where the company is subsequently in liquidation or administration.

The warning signalled by the *Shoe Lace* decision is that those advising on the validity of an administrative receiver's appointment should investigate and ensure that any monies paid over as consideration for the floating charge comprising the debenture-holder's security were not received by the company at any time period significantly prior to (or, it is submitted, subsequent to) the execution of the debenture. Liquidators and administrators who may challenge the validity of the floating charge under s245 are well-advised to investigate this point with equal zeal.

Finally, s245(3) stipulates, in somewhat over-complex and confusing language, a number of definitions of what constitutes the 'relevant time' during which a floating charge is deemed invalid if created therein, subject to the aggregate of the exceptions in s245(2). Briefly, a floating charge may be invalidated retrospectively if created within two years of the onset of insolvency (as defined in s245(5) but which does not actually require inability to pay debts) in the case of a 'connected' person. The time period is 12 months in all other cases. Although it is not clear from the wording of the provision, it is suggested that a person will be deemed to be either 'connected' or 'unconnected' depending on their status at the time the transaction creating the floating charge takes place, notwithstanding any subsequent status of that person. This approach avoids an individual circumventing the disadvantages faced by a person not afforded the relative protection of s245(3)(a) and s245(4) simply by altering their status from connected to unconnected subsequent to the transaction. Similarly, an individual will not be prejudiced by becoming connected subsequent to the transaction for reasons totally unrelated to the transaction itself.

It is noteworthy that there is no requirement of insolvency where the floating charge is granted in favour of a connected person. This reflects the practical reality that a connected person may well be privy to inside information regarding the company's pending and potentially terminal financial state and may, as a consequence, take steps to secure himself over its assets at the costs of other creditors not privy to such information.

Where a charge is created in favour of a person unconnected with the company within 12 months of the onset of insolvency, and only then, the time will not be considered a 'relevant time' until the company is unable to pay its debts in that time (as defined in s123), or becomes so unable as a consequence of creating the charge (ss245(3)(b),245(4)). Three problems should be recognised here. First, the burden of establishing solvency would appear to fall on the chargee on the basis that it did so previously, and in somewhat clearer terms, under the Companies Act 1985 s617. Secondly, in practice it may be very difficult to prove on a balance of probabilities that, at any given time, a company is actually solvent on the basis of the alternative tests of ability to pay debts as defined in s123. Thirdly, a bank may be a connected person, and, therefore, may fall outside the scope of s245(4) if it constitutes a shadow director for the purposes of ss249(a),251 (see, for example, *Re A Company (No 005009 of 1987)* [1988] 4 BCC 424).

Finally, care should be taken to ensure that the granting of security to the debenture-holder does not amount to a transaction defrauding creditors under s423 or an extortionate credit transaction under s244. In practice, such cases will continue to be relatively uncommon, primarily on account of the onerous evidential problems encountered by plaintiffs.

## 6.3 Has the Floating Charge 'Hardened'?

The metaphysical notion of 'hardening' really raises the question of whether the company has received any money, goods, services or any other benefit as consideration (as limited and defined by s245(2)) for the floating charge. That is, has there been turnover on the company's account (viz a nominal floating charge account, in technical terms) with the creditor in whose favour the floating charge was granted since the time of creation of the charge? Section 245(2) makes clear that this consideration must have been derived by the company '... at the same time as, or after the creation of the charge ...', the charge being potentially void in default.

From the point of view of administrative receivership, the hardening of the floating charge is of paramount importance since, without it, the charge will be liable to avoidance by any subsequently-appointed liquidator or administrator. Such an attack is calamitous to an administrative-receiver since the floating-charge security pursuant to which he is appointed is the linchpin of his taking office, and its avoidance effectively renders his appointment invalid. Indeed, the court will not refuse a winding-up order if the petitioner maintains grounds on which a charge may be attacked (see, for example, *Re Airfast Services Pty Ltd* [1976] 2 ACLR 1). In addition, any delay in the making of a winding-up order will not affect the s245 provision in respect of which time is calculated from the actual presentation of the petition.

In practice, where a floating charge is created in favour of a bank, so-called hardening is best evidenced by a statement showing turnover on the company's account at some point subsequent to the creation of the charge, subject to the time constraints imposed by the *Shoe Lace* decision. Although the rationale behind s245 is to prevent the creation of a secured debt at a critical time in financial terms without a corresponding injection of monies, goods, securities etc by the creditor to the company, the approach of the courts on this point has served largely to circumvent this aim. For example, in *Re Yeovil Glove Co Ltd* [1965] Ch 148, a floating charge was created in favour of the company's bank to secure an existing overdraft on its current account of £65,000. Prior to a winding-up petition being presented some 353 days later, the company paid in £111,000 and withdrew £110,000 from the account. It was held that the payments in had discharged the £65,0000 liability existing at the creation of the charge and, therefore, at the date of the winding-up petition being presented, the existing £64,000 overdraft constituted new monies advanced by the bank to the company. This highly artificial approach followed substantially similar reasoning in *Re Matthew Ellis Ltd* [1933] 1 Ch 458, although in that case a floating charge was created in favour of a third party which injected funds which were to be used, in part, to discharge the company's indebtedness to an existing creditor. Both cases apply the ancient rule in *Clayton's case* (1816) 1 Mer 572 (see also *Mace Builders (Glasgow) Ltd v Lunn* [1987] Ch 191 and *Re G T Whyte & Co Ltd* [1983] BCLC 311 on this point).

The approach adopted by the courts is to examine whether the substance of the transaction involves the conferring of some benefit on the company (such as in the *Matthew Ellis* case where money was injected by a party wishing to save the ailing business) as opposed to the mere procuring of security for an otherwise unsecured debt. The relevance of *Clayton's* case to the area is that the provision of new money, goods, services etc after the date of creation of the floating charge will be treated as such, notwithstanding the presumption that payments into an overdrawn account by a company will, in accordance with both the usual operating terms of the account itself and the bank's common law right of set-off, be applied in the first instance against the company's indebtedness to the bank at the time of the creation of the charge.

One notable practical implication which arises from the above is that, in practice, it is not uncommon for one company to guarantee the debts of another company, typically another member of a group. The creditor of the principal debtor company may, as a condition of ongoing credit facilities, require a debenture containing fixed and floating charges to be executed in respect of assets of the guarantor company. It is unlikely in such a scenario that new monies, goods, services etc will be introduced to the guarantor in consideration for the floating charge at or subsequent to its creation. It follows that, without fresh consideration, the floating charge over the guarantor's assets will not harden and, therefore, will be highly susceptible to attack for invalidation. It should also be clear that, on this basis, turnover on the principal debtor's account or the provision of money, goods, services etc will have no effect in hardening the floating charge over the guarantor company's assets. Perhaps the best and most obvious solution to this problem—and possibly one most easily overlooked in practice—would be the payment over of nominal consideration (ie executed consideration as opposed to executory consideration in the form of a promise to pay) at the time of the creation of the charge.

## 6.4 Has the Debenture been Properly Registered?

The registration requirements for charges under the Companies Act 1985 were considered previously in Chapter 3 at para 3.5. The question of whether a debenture (ie the fixed and floating charges comprised in it) has been properly registered is wholly relevant to the validity of the administrative receiver's appointment since an unregistered debenture will be void against any subsequently appointed liquidator or administrator or, indeed, any other creditor. It will not, however, affect directly an appointment made pursuant to the security, unless the security is subsequently avoided, since the registration regime is designed to perfect the charges created in relation to third parties and will not affect the security between the company and the debenture-holder.

The primary concern of the debenture-holder will be that the charges comprising the debenture have been registered with the Registrar of Companies within 21 days of creation or within any extended period as permitted by court order under the Companies Act 1985 s404, no court order having been required under the proposed Companies Act 1989 Act amendments. Registration may be verified by way of a company search with Companies House, although it should be noted that no official search is possible and that a company search, therefore, offers no priority period. In any case, it is suggested that reliance on any company search should be no substitute for verifying the registration of charges with the actual certificate of registration.

The Companies Act 1985 s401 requires the following prescribed particulars to be registered:

(a) the property charged (short particulars);
(b) the amount secured;
(c) the name and address of the persons entitled to the charge;
(d) a description of the instrument (if any) creating or evidencing the charge; and
(e) the date of creation of the charge.

So-called negative pledge clauses are also commonly registered, notwithstanding these do not constitute registrable particulars for the purposes of the 1985 Act although they would have done under the 1989 Act.

The prescribed particulars are registered on Form 395 if the security is a single charge or on Form 397 in the case of a series of debentures.

The Registrar's certificate that a charge has been registered, including the amount of the debt secured by the charge, is conclusive evidence that the statutory requirements as to registration have been duly complied with (s401(2)). It should be noted, however, that the Registrar's certificate is merely conclusive that the prescribed particulars have been delivered in accordance with the statutory requirements and that the formalities as to registration have been duly complied with (s401(2)). The certificate will not, therefore, verify that the prescribed particulars are either correct or complete. For example, the parties may have agreed terms, say orally, which do not appear on the Form 395 (or 397 if appropriate) or on the charge itself; or the relevant form may include particulars which are included gratuitously, such as a 'negative pledge' claim which the Registrar of Companies is in the practice of registering, while having no obligation under the present legislation to do so.

It appears that the charge-holder's rights will be determined by the charge even if registered late (*Re C L Nye Ltd* [1970] 3 All ER 1061; cf *Re Eric Holmes (Property) Ltd* [1965] Ch 1052, set aside on other grounds) or described inaccurately (*Re Mechanisations (Eaglescliffe) Ltd* [1966] Ch 20; *National Provincial and Union Bank of England v Charnley* [1924] 1 KB 431). The position remains unclear, however, where the Registrar's certificate is obtained by fraud. Notwithstanding this, and the fact that the Registrar has no duty to ensure the accuracy of prescribed particulars, the following points should be verified as a matter of course:

(1)   Was the charge registered within 21 days of creation? If not, was late registration sanctioned by a court under the Companies Act 1985 s404?

(2)   If relevant, were the formalities for any late registration adhered to? In particular, was the order or late registration filed with the Registrar (without which in practice registration will be refused by the court) and did the order contain a proviso protecting any 'after-acquired' rights in favour of third party creditors? If so, do these have any relevant implications (such as affecting any priority right of appointment) in relation to the debenture-holder?

(3)   Do the registered particulars reflect those contained in the charge documentation itself?

(4)   Does the company number on the registered charge tally with that of the company in respect of which the administrative receiver is appointed? This question is particularly relevant in practice following a change or changes of name by the company.

It is also prudent to check the company's own register of charges, particularly in cases of doubt, to verify the details of the charge. Every limited company is required to keep at its registered office a register of charges and to enter in it all charges affecting its property (Companies Act 1985 s407). In practice, a check of the company's own register of charges is frequently overlooked or merely not undertaken as a matter of course on being deemed unnecessary.

In the case of land, a check should also be made to ensure that the appropriate registration formalities have been complied with irrespective of the registration of the charge granted by the company over its assets as registered with Companies House. Briefly, a charge over unregistered land, assuming it to be within the prescribed class of registrable charges which do not encompass floating charges, will require registration under the Land Charges Act 1972. The effect of failure to register the charge is that priority is lost by the charge holder *vis à vis* other charges appropriately registered against the land. In the case of registered land, specific charges require registration at the Land Registry pursuant to the Land Registration Act 1925.

## 6.5 Does a Search of the Company Register Reveal Subsisting Charges?

One problem which arises from time to time in practice is that a search of the company's file at Companies House reveals an apparently subsisting charge which ranks in priority to some or all of those securities pursuant to which the administrative receiver is or is to be appointed. Frequently, an apparently pre-existing charge of this type will appear to have been subsisting for some time. Indeed, a report of the apparent existence of such a charge will often be met with some degree of faint recollection of a long forgotten and apparently fully discharged secured debt and/or a mixture of incredulity and/or disbelief on the part of the company's board.

In the event that any charge revealed by a search of the company is actually valid and subsisting, then there is little that can be done, although care should be taken in the case of a floating charge containing a 'negative pledge' clause where charges have been granted subsequently that rank equally or in priority to it, such as a fixed charge. The existence of a prior-ranking charge will not necessarily preclude the appointment of an administrative receiver pursuant to subsidiary-ranking securities, although this may have a bearing on the question of any priority right to appoint (see Chapter 5 at para 5.2). Following appointment, s43 may also be of use in this regard in the face of an unco-operative prior-ranking mortgagee. Whether any or all of these matters are brought to the specific attention of the appointing debenture-holder or the administrative receiver by his legal advisers is a question of individual and professional approach; caution, however, dictates that they should be in all cases.

Where there is a suspicion that a charge as revealed on the Companies' Registry may not be subsisting, then checks should be made of both the company's directors, the company's own register of charges (as must be maintained by the company) and the apparent chargee. It is not uncommon for charges which have, in fact, been discharged years previously to remain on the register, usually because no Memorandum of Satisfaction was filed by the chargee and the company. Two possible approaches may be adopted to an apparent subsisting charge.

First, the apparent chargee in whose favour the charge apparently exists may be requested to forward to the company a completed Memorandum of Satisfaction in Form 403a, or Form 403b if part only of the property has been released from the charge or sold. The completed form may then be signed by or on behalf of the company and forwarded to the Registrar of Companies, who will then place a Memorandum of Satisfaction on the company's register of charges. The Registrar will then send a copy of the Memorandum, together with a note of the date of delivery, to both the company and the charge holder (Companies Act 1985 s403). The implementation of the new company charge regime as envisaged by the Companies Act 1989 would have done little to alter this area of law and practice, although, as with the present provisions, the delivery to the Registrar of a Memorandum of Satisfaction would have continued to remain optional. This method of discharge will not, however, be appropriate when the chargee simply refuses to accept that the charge should be released on the basis that, according to the company at least, the secured debt has been discharged. Creditors, particularly banks, will often adopt such a stance where their own internal records do not cover the period to which the charge relates, notwithstanding clear company records and board minutes to the effect that the debt has been extinguished. In this type of case, where the apparent charge-holder will not sign the memorandum of discharge, or the charge-holder cannot be traced, an application may be made to court authorising the delivery of the Memorandum of Satisfaction without the charge-holder's signature, if the court is satisfied that the debt secured by the charge has been discharged or otherwise satisfied (Companies Act 1985 s404). Following this, the Registrar is furnished with both the Memorandum of Satisfaction and a copy of the court's order which are filed on the company's register of charges. In practice, formal notice to a chargee of such proceedings will often spur co-operation, if only on the ground of costs implications, where it transpires that the secured debt has, in fact, been discharged.

A Memorandum of Satisfaction must also be filed with the Registrar of Companies following the avoidance of a pre-liquidation or pre-administration charge as a transaction-at-undervalue, preference or a voidable s245 floating charge or a s423 transaction. This would be relevant in the case where a liquidator has succeeded in setting aside the floating charge security and any fixed charge securities pursuant to which a contemporaneously appointed administrative receiver takes office.

The existence of a prior-ranking charge or a merely subsisting charge, be it fixed or floating, in favour of a creditor other than the appointing debenture-holder also raises questions of priority, not as to each secured creditor's right to appoint but as regards the order in which each creditor ranks in priority in making the appointment.

## 6.6  Has the Debenture been Properly Executed?

The execution of the debenture should be verified by referring, wherever possible, to the original debenture as opposed merely to a copy of it. An appointment of a receiver may also be effected following the assignment of a debenture once the assignment has been perfected. Here, the formalities for assignment should be checked.

In the case of a company, and for the purposes of English law, a company may enter into a contract as evidenced in writing 'under its common seal' (Companies Act 1985 s36(a)). Alternatively, the company's seal may be affixed by any person on behalf of the company who acts under its express or implied authority (Companies Act 1985 s36(b)). In practice, this refers to the company acting by resolution in general meeting or via its agents, such as its directors (*Ferguson v Wilson* (1866) 2 Ch App 77 at 89). For the position where the seal of a company is affixed by an officer of the company without authority, see *South London Greyhound Racecourses v Wake* [1931] 1 Ch 496. There is an additional requirement that the seal of the company should be affixed in the presence of and attested by 'its clerk, secretary or other permanent officer or his deputy, and a member of the board of directors, council or other governing body of the corporation' (Law of Property Act 1925 s74(1)). In practice, this will invariably refer to attestation by two directors or a director and company secretary.

In the relatively rare case of a deed executed before 1926, it is necessary to prove execution in accordance with the company's memorandum and articles of association, in the absence of any specific conditions (*Re Coper Thames Haven Dock and Railway Co* (1849) 3 Exch 841).

The authority for and procedure relevant to the affixing of the company's seal is usually provided for in the company's articles. Table A art 101 provides:

> The seal shall only be used by the authority of the directors or of a committee of directors authorised by the directors. The directors may determine who shall sign any instrument to which the seal is affixed and unless otherwise so determined it shall be signed by the director and by the secretary or by a second director.

Since 31 July 1990, a company need not have a common seal (Companies Act 1985 s36A(3) as inserted by the Companies Act 1989 s130(2) by virtue of the

Companies Act 1989 (Commencement (No 6) and Transitional and Saving Provisions) Order 1990 (SI No 1392)). The effect of this provision is that a document signed by a director and the secretary of a company, or by two directors, and expressed—in whatever form of words—to be executed by the company, has the same effect as if executed under the common seal of the company (Companies Act 1985 s36A(4)). Furthermore, a document executed by a company which makes it clear on its face that it is intended by those persons making it that it is to be a deed has effect, upon delivery, as a deed. Delivery, in the absence of contrary intention, is deemed to take place upon execution (Companies Act 1985 s36A(5)).

In practice, the signatures of those who either attest the seal of the company (which may, of course, be affixed post-31 July 1990) or who execute the debenture by their signatures on the company's behalf, may well be illegible. This causes no problems since there exists a statutory presumption that a document has been duly executed if it purports to be signed by the director and secretary of the company, or two directors, where it is clear on the face of the deed that it is intended by those persons for it to be a deed where a seal is affixed (Companies Act 1985 s36A(6)). A similar presumption exists in relation to deeds executed under a company's seal (Law of Property Act 1925 s74(1)). Both of these presumptions are stated as being conditional on the mortgagee acting in good faith as defined in both provisions (see Companies Act 1985 s36A and Law of Property Act 1925 s205(1)(xxi)).

Where a company has executed a debenture under seal it is important to verify that the seal used was the correct one. A company which has a common seal is required to have its name engraved on the seal in legible characters, on sanction of a penalty being invoked against the company and any persons authorising the use of the illegible seal (Companies Act 1985 s350). The apparently incorrect seal of the company may appear in the debenture for either or both of two common reasons. First, it may simply be that the incorrect seal, particularly in a group of companies, may have been used by the company. Secondly, the company may have changed its name since the seal was originally engraved. If this is the case it is vital to ensure that the new certificate(s) of incorporation issued by the Registrar of Companies following the change(s) of name bear the same registered number as the company which apparently executed the debenture. Further, a check should be made that the company in respect of which the administrative receiver's appointment is effected is, in fact, the company which executed the debenture.

Where there exists a minor irregularity as regards the sealing of the debenture, it is likely that s232 will operate to cure the defect. Section 232 is discussed further in Chapter 5 at para 5.6.2. This may even be the case where the wrong seal has been used but where there is clear evidence that this arose as a result of error and not intentionally, such as where the seal is, in fact, attested by two officers of the company intending to execute the debenture.

Where there is a patent defect with the seal which cannot be explained in such a way, then the secured creditor, its administrative receiver and those advising on the appointment and the administrative receivership generally should consider carefully their course of action.

Section 232 may be a superfluous consideration, however, in this regard to the extent that a debenture which is not sealed may continue to operate in equity; *Byblos Bank SAL v Al-Khudhairy* [1987] BCLC 232.

## 6.7 Was the Creation of the Debenture Commercially Justifiable?

The question of the commercial justifiability of the creation of a debenture stems from the exercise of the powers of the company by its directors, and the corresponding fiduciary duties owed by the directors as agents to the company as principal, in addition to the corresponding common law duty to exercise responsibility, skill and care in the management of the company's affairs. The legal rules on this area operate along very similar lines to those statutory provisions in s238 which permit the avoidance by a liquidator or administrator of a transaction-at-undervalue, in that they seek to protect against the company, acting through its directors, bestowing on a creditor the benefit of 'something for nothing' in terms of security other than on a *quid pro quo* basis. There is, however, one principal difference with s238 in that, unlike the statutory provision, a subsequent attack on an improper exercise by the directors of their powers is not subject to a time limit within which the action must be instituted. It is inappropriate to engage here in a full discussion of directors' duties generally and reference should be made to the standard texts, such as Pennington *Company Law*, 6th edn (1990) at 583-614 for a detailed exposition of the area.

It is well-established at common law and in equity that the directors of a company are under a duty both to act *bona fide* in what they consider subjectively to be in the interests of the company, and not to act for any collateral or self-serving purpose (*Re Smith and Fawcett Ltd* [1942] Ch 304; see also *Allen v Gold Reefs of West Africa Ltd* [1900] 1 Ch 656, from which the test originated). While a company is solvent its directors owe duties to the company itself and are not in a fiduciary relationship *vis à vis* shareholders individually (*Percival v Wright* [1902] 2 Ch 421). However, a duty may be owed to shareholders individually in certain circumstances, such as where the directors expressly undertake to act as agents of the shareholders (see, for example, *Allen v Hyatt* (1914) 30 TLR 444) or where the company is a target in a takeover bid (see *Heron International Ltd v Lord Grade* [1983] BCLC 244 and *Dawson International plc v Coats Patons plc* [1988] 4 BCC 305 (a decision of the Outer House of the Scottish Court of Session)).

For present purposes, the question remains as to whether, in executing a debenture, the directors have acted in a way which is in accordance with the duties owed by them and, therefore, whether the transaction is commercially justifiable. Perhaps the clearest test from a judicial perspective is the following analysis, given by Eve J in *Re Lee Behrens & Co Ltd* [1932] Ch 46 at 51. This was cited subsequently with considerable approval by Slade LJ in *Rolled Steel Products (Holdings) Ltd v British Steel Corp* [1986] Ch 246 at 288. The test runs thus:

> (i) Is the transaction reasonably incidental to the carrying on of the company's business? (ii) Is it a *bona fide* transaction? (iii) Is it done for the benefit and to promote the prosperity of the company?

This test should not be applied with the perceived wisdom of hindsight but as against the minds of the directors at the time they or their agents executed the debenture (*Re Smith & Fawcett Ltd* [1942] Ch 304 at 306). Before considering what factors may be relevant to the above test, it is worth considering who may take an action for an alleged breach of duty by the directors.

Since the duties of the directors are owed by them to the company, it follows that any breach of duty is actionable only by the company. This obvious conflict of interest between the company and the directors has given rise to a number of mechanisms whereby aggrieved shareholders may take proceedings *qua* members, namely (a) under the Companies Act 1985 s459 (as amended) for alleged unfairly prejudicial conduct, or (b) as is less common, in their capacity as (i) either members (a derivative action) or (ii) on behalf of the company itself (a representative action) or (iii) both (as is common practice in such an action) where it is possible to establish one of the exceptions to the rule in *Foss v Harbottle* (1843) 2 Hare 421. It has to be said that such an action by a shareholder is highly unlikely on the basis of the creation of a debenture as a breach of directors' duties, other than in the most obviously self-serving cases; see also here *Watts v Midland Bank Plc* [1986] BCLC 15.

Actions by creditors against the directors are equally unlikely, since a direct fiduciary relationship between directors and creditors is hardly well-established in law, except, perhaps, where the company is insolvent. In practice, creditors may be prepared to wait for a subsequent liquidation of the company. At that time their interests and the interests of the company become subrogated to a liquidator, who may then choose to pursue the directors of the company, usually for breach of duty in misfeasance proceedings under s212.

Again, this begs the question of what then amounts to non-justifiable action by the directors in executing a debenture, to the mind of the court. The short answer to this would appear to be any situation in which the powers pursuant to which the debenture is executed are exercised other than for a proper purpose.

The terms 'proper purpose', 'improper purpose' and 'collateral purpose' are widely used, often interchangeably, in the judicial examination of the area of directors' duties. It is suggested that, for present purposes, the difference in meaning will largely be one of a technical rather than substantive nature. The real question is whether there exists some other motive on the part of the directors in executing the debenture. Obvious collateral motives for such a course of action might include the case where a debenture is being granted in favour of a director or some other connected person, usually at some time closely proximate to the subsequent appointment of an administrative receiver and/or a liquidator. (The transaction might also be challenged by a subsequently appointed liquidator or administrator under s238, s239 or s245.) On the other hand, the granting of a debenture in this way might be justified if, say, the directors contend that the creation of the debenture and the inevitable appointment of an administrative receiver will be of greater benefit to the company than the presentation of a winding-up petition by some other, usually unsecured, creditor. Indeed, the creation of the debenture may be exacted by a significant creditor, usually a bank, as a condition of a continued credit facility, typically following a report by an investigating accountant appointed by the creditor.

The most useful area of company law from which analogies may be drawn in this area of commercial justifiability is the exercise of powers by directors to issue shares to defeat take-over bids or to dilute shareholdings, as opposed to the perceived proper purpose of issuing shares for raising capital. In *Mills v Mills* (1938) 60 CLR 150, a decision of the High Court of Australia, it was held that, where mixed motives are involved, regard should be had to the directors' dominant purpose (cf the majority decision in *Whitehouse v Carlton Hotel Pty Ltd* [1987] 11 ACLR 715, also a decision of the High Court of Australia).

The *Mills* case involved a board resolution which strengthened the voting rights of ordinary shareholders, but diminished the rights of preference shareholders in relation to particular assets on a subsequent winding-up. The board resolution was upheld by the court as valid, since the directors had acted honestly in what they perceived to be the best interests of the company. This contrasts with *Piercy v Mills & Co Ltd* [1920] 1 Ch 77, where it was held that it was improper for directors to use their powers to issue shares in order to deprive an existing majority of its voting control (see also *Punt v Symons & Co Ltd* [1903] 2 Ch 506). Similarly, in *Hogg v Cramphorn Ltd* [1967] Ch 254, it was held to be an improper exercise of directors' powers to issue shares with special voting rights to an employees' share scheme with the (subsequently successful) intention of defeating a take-over bid, even though the directors had acted in good faith. It should be noted, however, that the abuse of powers by the directors in that case was held to be capable of ratification by the company in general meeting. The above cases are difficult to reconcile with each other, particularly when one considers later conflicting Commonwealth authorities such as *Harlowe's Nominees Pty Ltd v Woodside (Lakes Entrance) Oil Co* (1968) 42 ALJR 123, where the High Court of Australia upheld as valid an exercise of powers by directors to defeat a take-over bid; and *Teck Corp Ltd v Millar* (1972) 33 DLR (3d) 288 in which Berger J rejected the decision in *Hogg v Cramphorn Ltd*, on the grounds that directors can only be said to have abused their powers if their purpose is not to serve the interests of the company.

In view of the rather confusing *dicta* on the area, perhaps the most useful and authoritative recent statement for practical purposes is that of Lord Wilberforce giving the opinion of the Privy Council in *Howard Smith Ltd v Ampol Petroleum Ltd* [1974] AC 821 at 835. (This has since been followed by the Court of Appeal in *Lee Panavision Ltd v Lee Lighting Ltd* [1991] BCC 620.) This statement, it is submitted, would have equal relevance to the exercise of the powers by directors in creating a debenture in favour of a creditor.

> ...it is necessary to start with a consideration of the power whose purpose is in question...Having ascertained, on a fair view, the nature of this power, and having defined as can best be done in the light of modern conditions those, or some, limits within which it may be exercised, it is then necessary for the court, if a particular exercise of it is challenged, to examine the substantial purpose for which it was exercised, and to reach a conclusion whether the purpose was proper or not. In doing so it will necessarily give credit to the *bona fide* opinion of the directors, if such is found to exist, and will respect their judgement as to matters of management. Having done this, the ultimate conclusion has to be as to the side of a fairly broad line on which the case falls.

The test is, therefore, to establish for what purpose the debenture was granted and, having ascertained this, to ascertain, or at least to take a view as to whether or not the exercise of the power to borrow to that end is commercially justifiable as a *bona fide* matter of management.

It does not follow that the creation of a debenture only a short period before the appointment of an administrative receiver is indicative of commercial non-justifiability. It is, nonetheless, a ground for suspicion. Well-documented and detailed minutes of the board's deliberations and a copy of the resolution pursuant to which the debenture was executed are the best evidence on which genuine *bona fide* grounds for the creation of the debenture may be founded. Similarly, where a debenture is granted as a condition of ongoing credit, typically in favour of a bank, correspondence to this effect should be checked together with bank statements and management accounts, in order to ascertain the degree to which the creation of the security can be deemed justifiable.

Where the directors are guilty of an abuse of their powers, the general rule is that the company, or any subsequently-appointed liquidator or administrator may, at its option, treat the transaction as void even if this prejudices a *bona fide* third party (*Re W & M Roith Ltd* [1967] 1 All ER 427; see also *The Cameron's Coalbrook Steam Coal and Swansea and Lougher Railway Co* (1854) 5 De G M & G 284). There are two exceptions to this rule:

(1) The *bona fide* third party may rely on the protection afforded by the 'indoor management' rule in *Royal British Bank v Turquand* (1855) 5 E&B 248, which provides that a person dealing in good faith with the board of a company or its representatives can presume that person or persons to be unaffected by defects of procedure within the company or by any failure of conditions prescribed in the company's memorandum or articles of association which are required to be fulfilled before the relevant transaction may be entered into.

(2) The company, or a liquidator or administrator, may only seek to set aside the transaction where it can be shown that the third party knew or was aware that the directors were abusing their powers or, alternatively, that it was the intention of the directors to achieve an improper or collateral purpose in entering into the transaction. In practice, such knowledge will usually be onerously difficult to impute.

Examples of the types of valuable consideration which might be provided by a third party creditor in return for the security created by a debenture would include the introduction of new monies to the company for it or a waiver of immediate payment of a due and payable debt (*Re David Payne & Co Ltd* [1907] 2 Ch 608 and *Rolled Steel Products (Holdings) Ltd v British Steel Corp* [1986] Ch 246). In the *Rolled Steel Products* case the Court of Appeal held a guarantee and debenture executed by one company to secure the debts of another to be unenforceable as the enforcing creditor company had actual knowledge of facts which showed that the giving of the guarantee and the debenture was an abuse of powers by the directors (see also the Australian decisions in *Northside Developments Pty Ltd v Registrar-General* [1990] ACSR 161 and *Seabird Corporation Ltd v Sherlock* [1990] 2 ACSR 111 where guarantees were successfully challenged).

In conclusion, any subsequently-appointed liquidator or administrator will be fixed with considerable difficulty in seeking to avoid a debenture on the basis of commercial non-justifiability where the members of the company, contemporaneously with the creation of the security, pass a resolution ratifying the acts of the directors notwithstanding any abuse of their powers. The effect of such a ratification, in the absence of fraud, is both to validate the transaction and to exonerate the directors from any liability arising from it (*Hogg v Cramphorn Ltd* [1967] Ch 254 and *Bamford v Bamford* [1970] Ch 212). A members' resolution, therefore, may be of considerable practical use to the company itself, the debenture-holder and the directors if passed at or subsequent to the execution of the debenture for obvious commercial reasons, and defending against an allegation of a voidable antecedent transaction in liquidation or administration. It should be noted, however, that ratification is not possible where a breach of duty by the directors amounts to fraud on the minority, for the purposes of the rule in *Foss v Harbottle* (1843) 2 Hare 421 (see *Clemens v Clemens* [1976] 2 All ER 268).

As a separate matter a check should also be made that there is no suggestion or evidence that the debenture pursuant to which the administrative receiver is appointed was given as a result of undue pressure on the part of the debenture-holder. In practice, this type of scenario is very unusual although it remains conceivable. The establishment of undue influence renders the debenture voidable and, as such, liable to be set aside. This would require proof of a special relationship of trust and confidence between the company and the debenture-holder giving rise to a fiduciary duty owed by the debenture-holder which was breached by the exertion of the undue influence (see, for example, *Lloyds Bank Ltd v Bundy* [1974] 3 All ER 757).

Finally, a check should be made to ensure that the creation of the debenture does not contravene the rules relating to loans made by companies, as provided for by Companies Act 1985, s330 (previously Companies Act 1980 s190). The Companies Act 1985 s330(2) contains a blanket prohibition on a company making a loan to, or entering into any guarantee or providing any security in connection with a loan made by any person to either its director or a director of its holding company. This prohibition is reinforced by two further provisions which prevent technical evasions of the general rule. First, no company may arrange for the assignment to it of rights or obligations which it could not enter into directly or in respect of which it could not assume such rights or obligations (Companies Act 1985 s330(6)). Secondly, no company may take part in an arrangement whereby a third party enters into a transaction which the company itself could not enter into, where the third party obtains some benefit from the company or some other company in the same group (Companies Act 1985 s330(7)). A check should be made to ensure that any apparently suspect transaction does not fall within one of the various exceptions to the general s330 prohibitions, contained in the Companies Act 1985 ss332–8. Of particular relevance here is the exception in the Companies Act 1985 s336, which permits inter-group loans to directors which are holding companies.

Where a loan contravenes the Companies Act 1985 s330 and does not fall within a specified exception, the transaction or other arrangement is voidable at the instance of the company making the loan (Companies Act 1985 s341). The right to avoid the transaction is lost, however, where restitution is no longer available, where the company has been indemnified for the loan or where a *bona fide* third party for value has acquired an interest in the loan proceeds without notice of the statutory contravention (Companies Act 1985 s341).

In the event of the transaction being avoided, the director or any connected person, together with any other director who authorised the transaction or arrangement, is liable to account to the company for any direct or indirect gain he has made from the transaction and any loss or damage incurred by the company as a result of it. The Companies Act 1985 s342 also provides for criminal sanctions against those directors who authorised or permitted the company to enter into the voidable transaction with knowledge or having reasonable cause to believe that a contravention of s330 was involved.

## 6.8 Did the Security Comprised in the Debenture Amount to Financial Assistance Contrary to the Companies Act 1985?

It is unlawful for a company or any of its subsidiaries to provide financial assistance directly or indirectly to any person for the acquisition of shares in itself (Companies Act 1985 s151). This general rule applies where the financial assistance is given before or at the same time as the acquisition of the shares takes place, or after the acquisition of the shares where the financial assistance is for the purpose of reducing or discharging a liability incurred in doing so. Breach of this provision is a criminal offence rendering the company (ie the legal person which the present provision is actually designed to protect!) and every officer in default liable to a fine. A transaction in breach of Companies Act 1985 s151 will also amount to a transaction which is *ultra vires* the company and, therefore, unenforceable.

On the creation of a debenture, s151 is most likely to be relevant where funds provided by the secured creditor in return for the debenture are then used to facilitate the purchase or purchases of shares by any third party. The financial assistance may be given by the company by way of (*inter alia*):

- a gift;
- a loan;
- the creation of security by the company (or a subsidiary) to finance a loan by the third party to finance the acquisitions of its shares; or
- the payment of the third party's legal or accounting costs in acquiring the shares in the company.

It should be noted that these examples are not definitive, since the term 'financial assistance' itself remains undefined, although Companies Act 1985 s152 sets out the various specific and general ways in which financial assistance may be given. These are by way of gift, guarantee, security or indemnity, loan or 'any other financial assistance given by a company the net assets of which are thereby reduced or which has no net assets'.

181

Sections 151 and 153 of the Companies Act 1985 also stipulate a number of specific exceptions to what would otherwise amount to financial assistance in contravention of the general rule against such transactions. These exceptions are:

- the payment of a dividend;
- the allotment of bonus shares;
- a reduction in share capital with court approval (ie under Companies Act 1985 s121); or
- the redemption or purchase by a company of its own shares.

One final and apparently broad exception in s151 is where the company's principal purpose in giving the financial assistance is neither the acquisition of its own shares nor the giving of the assistance for that purpose, but is rather an incidental part of some larger purpose. The proviso to this is that the assistance must be given in good faith (Companies Act 1985 s153(1)). It has to be said that the attractiveness of this final exception has been greatly diminished by the decision in *Brady v Brady* [1988] 2 All ER 617 in which the House of Lords held that the provision of financial assistance by a company to enable a de-merger of a group, following a management deadlock, was not part of some larger purpose. This was because in that case the acquisition of shares was the primary motive for the financial assistance, of which the commercial advantages of the de-merger were a subsidiary consequence. In reality, the rationale behind the decision is to avoid the creation of a broad, general exception to the rule in Companies Act 1985 s151. The position is perhaps put best by Lord Oliver (at 633):

> ... if the section is not, effectively, to be deprived of any useful application, [then] it is important to distinguish between a purpose and the reason why a purpose is formed. The ultimate reason for forming the purpose for financing the acquisition may, and in most cases probably will, be more important to those making the decision than the immediate transaction itself. But 'larger' is not the same thing as 'more important'; nor is 'reason' the same as 'purpose'.

Lord Oliver's statement means that in practice it is necessary to distinguish between motive and purpose. In *Brady* the 'larger purpose' exception was not applicable since the motive behind the giving of financial assistance was the division of the group, whereas the purpose of the transaction was to allow the acquisition of the company's shares.

There are also four other exceptions to Companies Act 1985 s151. These restrict the operation of the provisions in relation to (a) a scheme of arrangement or reconstruction pursuant to Companies Act 1985 s425; (b) Part 1 of the IA 1986 s110; (c) the provision of finance to employee share option schemes; or (d) the enabling of shares to be held by employees (Companies Act 1985 s153(4)).

In the event that doubt exists in any particular circumstance as to whether a transaction falls within one of the elaborate exceptions to the general rule in Companies Act 1985 s151, two tests should both be applied to the substance of the transaction.

(1) What is or was the purpose of the transaction? If the principal or dominant purpose was other than the giving of financial assistance by the company or any subsidiary for the purchase of the company shares, or if the financial assistance was part of or subsidiary to some larger purpose of the company, as was unsuccessfully argued by counsel for the company in the *Brady* case, then the substance of the transaction should not be problematic (Companies Act 1985 s153(1)(a); see also *Belmont Finance Corporation Ltd v William Furniture Ltd (No2)* [1980] 1 All ER 393).

(2) At the time of, and in approving the transaction, did the directors act in what they deem or deemed subjectively to be the interests of the company, and not some third party? Again, if the genuine response to this is in the affirmative then, subject to the first test above, the transaction should not cause problems provided sufficient evidence is available to prove the matter (Companies Act 1985 s153(1)(b)).

Of course, in practice the concepts of 'purpose' or 'good faith' in the absence of suitable definitions can be onerously difficult to establish. Similarly, these two tests necessitate the forming of a commercial view by those advising on the transaction. As always, such a view should be based on an appreciation of the full circumstances of the case and proper deliberations.

In view of the above exceptions to Companies Act 1985 s151, and particularly the decision in *Brady*, it is important to check that the security created by the debenture has not been granted in return for monies which are then used by the company, either directly or indirectly, to facilitate the acquisition of its shares. Similar considerations should be borne in mind where the financial assistance is given by a subsidiary in return for security over its assets. In particular, the company's operations and financial transactions immediately before and after the execution of the debenture, together with those of the recipients of any new funds introduced as consideration for the security, should be checked and a view taken as to whether the security was created in contravention of Companies Act 1985 s151. It is submitted on the basis of the authorities cited above that the result of the contravention of the financial assistance provisions is that the security will be unenforceable. It should also be noted that a foreign company is subject to s151 to the extent of a company incorporated in the UK giving assistance to an extra-territorial company, and therefore care should be taken when dealing with financial assistance by any overseas company or any overseas subsidiary. However, s151 does not apply to prohibit a non-UK company giving financial assistance to a UK company to purchase shares in its UK holding company (*Arab Bank plc v Mercantile Holdings Ltd* [1994] 2 WLR 307).

The creation of potentially unenforceable security in relation to administrative receivership commonly arises with management buy-outs where finance will most often be sought from a bank, typically in return for security in the form of a debenture secured over the company's assets. In *Victor Battery Co Ltd v Curry's Ltd* [1946] 1 All ER 519 it was held that a debenture remained unenforceable notwithstanding a contravention of the forerunner to Companies Act 1985 s151, where a purchaser of the company's shareholding effected the acquisition with bank funds. Following the share acquisition, a loan was taken out by the company and a debenture given in respect of it. Roxburgh J's decision in that case that the debenture remained unenforceable has had much doubt cast on it, particularly in *Selangor United Rubber Estates Ltd v Cradock (No 3)* [1968] 2 All ER 1073. The decision was, nonetheless, followed in *Curtis's Furnishing Stores Ltd v Freedman* [1966] 2 All ER 955. It is submitted that the better view is that a debenture will be void and, therefore, unenforceable if created in contravention of Companies Act 1985 s151. This is supported by the judgment of Fisher J in *Heald v O'Connor* [1971] 2 All ER 1105, which expressly rejected the decision in the *Victor Battery* case, a similar approach having been adopted in a number of Commonwealth jurisdictions.

The facts in the *Heald* case are far from untypical and are worth consideration. O purchased the shares of the company from H for £35,000, and virtually contemporaneously, H loaned £25,000 to the company. As consideration for the loan, the company created a floating charge in H's favour. O also agreed to personally guarantee the loan of £25,000 to H against default by the company. Following default in payment by the company H sought to enforce O's personal guarantee. O's defence to the claim was that the loan had in fact been made to him to enable him to complete the purchase of the shares, and as such, the floating charge amounted to the giving of financial assistance by the company. The court held that the company had given unlawful financial assistance by issuing the debenture, thereby rendering the debenture void. It also held O's personal guarantee to be void, on the grounds that it related to a void security purportedly given by the company. Reference should also be made to the analogous decision in *Ford & Carter Ltd v Midland Bank Ltd* (1979) 129 NLJ 543 where it was held that a receiver is not validly appointed where, although appointed under a valid debenture, there was a default in payment of sums due and payable under an invalid guarantee which was secured by the debenture. The guarantee had been given to a bank to cover debts of a group, but did not cover a company which joined the group subsequently—which would have required the execution of a fresh guarantee.

Clearly the particular scenarios in which questions concerning the enforceability of a debenture—and any related guarantees—may arise in connection with the giving of financial assistance are virtually limitless. Obvious examples would include a *Brady*-type scenario in which assets of the company are charged by way of a debenture, the loan raised by the company being utilised, albeit indirectly, in reducing or discharging a liability which is incurred in the acquisition of shares in the company by a third party. This might be the case even if, as in the *Brady* case itself, the transaction is purportedly justified on the basis that the giving of the financial assistance is an incidental part of some larger purpose of the company and is given in good faith (Companies Act 1985 s153(2)).

Alternatively, the validity of the debenture might be called into question where investors and/or prospective managers, including directors who are required to hold 'qualification' shares by the company's articles of association, are in receipt of funds to facilitate their buying into the company, where those funds are received by the company giving security over its own interests to a third party, such as a bank or other company, on their behalf. The potential vulnerability of such an arrangement only serves to illustrate the fact that the restriction in Companies Act 1985 s151 is not one which is restricted on grounds of privity.

Notwithstanding the above observations, the fact remains that Companies Act 1985, s153(2) is framed in sufficiently broad terms so as not to impede genuine and *bona fide* commercial transactions. The legal reality is that the *Brady* decision has done much to restrict that commercial facility. Further reference should be made here to the analysis in Sterling (1987) 8 Co Law 99 and the first instance decision in *Plaut v Steiner* [1988] 5 BCC 352, where the *Brady* decision was applied on similar facts although the company had become insolvent as a result of the financial assistance which, in the view of Morritt J, hardly suggested that the transaction was in the interests of the company.

The most important practical exception to the general prohibition on the giving of financial assistance, in addition to those exceptions mentioned above, is what is colloquially known as the 'whitewash' procedure. This procedure is available only to private companies. Furthermore, the exception may not be utilised by any subsidiary company, in a case where the acquisition of shares in question is or was an acquisition of shares in its holding company, if the company is also a subsidiary of a public company which is itself a subsidiary of that holding company, ie a corporate group which comprises a public company (Companies Act 1985 s155(4)).

The whitewash procedure is provided for by the Companies Act 1985 ss155–8. Essentially, the procedural requirements are as follows:

(1) A statutory declaration is made by all of the company's directors. This sets out; the nature of the financial assistance; the business of the company; and the identity of the person to be in receipt of the financial assistance (Companies Act 1985 s156(1)).

(2) The statutory declaration must state that the directors have formed the opinion, 'as regards the company's initial situation immediately following the date on which the assistance is proposed to be given', that there will be no ground on which the company could then be found to be unable to pay its debts (as defined in the IA 1986 s122) and that the company will be able to pay its debts as they fall due during the year immediately following that date (Companies Act 1985 s156(2)(b),(3)).

(3) Where it is intended to wind up the company within 12 months of the date on which the financial assistance is given, the directors' statutory declaration must state that the company will be able to pay its debts in full within 12 months of the commencement of the winding-up (Companies Act 1985 s156(2)(a)) (see here Sharma (1993) 137 SJ 318).

(4) The directors' statutory declaration must have affixed to it a report addressed to them by the company's auditors stating that, having enquired into the state of the company's affairs, there is nothing to render the directors' opinion unreasonable in all the circumstances (Companies Act 1985 s156(4)). Any director of the company who makes the statutory declaration without having reasonable grounds for the opinion expressed in it is liable to imprisonment or a fine or both (Companies Act 1985 s156(7)).

(5) A special resolution of the company in general meeting approving the financial assistance must be passed on or within one week of the date on which the directors made the statutory declaration (Companies Act 1985 s157(1)).

(6) At the meeting at which the special resolution is passed, the directors' statutory declaration, together with the annexed auditor's report, must be available for inspection by the members on pain of the special resolution being deemed ineffective, as may also be the case on an application to cancel the special resolution by the holders of not less than 10 per cent in nominal value of the company's issued share capital or any class of it (Companies Act 1985 s157(2)(a),(4)).

(7) The special resolution in (5) above is not necessary if the company giving the financial assistance is a wholly owned subsidiary (Companies Act 1985 s155(4)). However, where the financial assistance is to be given by a subsidiary, other than a wholly-owned subsidiary, for the acquisition of shares in a holding company, the holding company and any other company which is both the company's holding company and any non-wholly owned subsidiary of that other holding company

must approve the giving of the financial assistance by special resolution (Companies Act 1985 s155(5)).

(8) The statutory declaration, auditor's report and any special resolution must be delivered to the Registrar of Companies within 15 days of the special resolution being passed or, if no special resolution is required, within 15 days of the declaration being made (Companies Act 1985 s156(5)).

(9) Following the authorisation for the giving of financial assistance, the assistance itself must not be given within four weeks of the date of the special resolution (in which period an application may be made to the court to object to the transaction by an eligible member or members or class thereof) unless all members voted in favour of the resolution (Companies Act 1985 ss157(2), 158(2)). The financial assistance is not permitted to be made after the expiry of eight weeks from the date of the statutory declaration (or the earliest declaration where declarations are made by more than one company) (Companies Act 1985 s158(4)).

It should be noted that, provided the whitewash procedure is followed substantively, the validity of a debenture is unlikely to be challenged successfully solely because of very minor technical deficiencies, as was held by Mummery J in *Re S H & Co (Realisations) 1990 Ltd* [1993] BCC 60. The case concerned an application to court by the joint administrative receivers of the company for directions as to whether a debenture granted by the company was void because of a failure to comply with the prescribed whitewash procedure. The financial assistance had been given in the course of a management buy-out of the company in September 1989. The company providing the financial assistance, N Ltd, provided a loan to R Ltd, a company used as a vehicle for the buy-out transaction. R Ltd executed a guarantee and debenture in favour of N Ltd in return for the financial assistance. Although the statutory declaration completed by the directors of N Ltd made reference to the debenture in favour of the company, it did not contain a statement of the property charged, the nature of the charge granted (ie fixed and/or floating) or the fact that a guarantee had also been given by R Ltd in favour of N Ltd. Mummery J held that those omissions did not prevent the particulars contained in the statutory declaration from being reasonably and fairly described as particulars of the form and principal terms of the financial assistance. The financial assistance given by N Ltd was, therefore, valid and accordingly the validity of the debenture could not be called into question. The judgment, it is submitted, is correct, although it remains true that the omission of certain particulars from the statutory declaration may give rise to the contravention of the whitewash procedure where the omission(s) are of principal terms of the financial assistance itself. As such, the particular facts of each case should therefore be considered carefully.

Whether or not the whitewash procedure has been followed should be ascertainable from the documents which are filed pursuant to (8) in the procedure above. These will be revealed on a full search of the company's register at Companies House. In the event that the appropriate documents are not filed, or are filed incompletely, a corresponding check should be made of the company's own register and books, particularly the minutes of board and general meetings of shareholders.

As mentioned previously, a company acting in contravention of the general prohibitions in the Companies Act 1985 s151, subject to the permitted exceptions, commits a criminal offence and is liable to a fine. Every officer of the company (including directors, managers and company secretary: Companies Act 1985 s744) is also liable to imprisonment or a fine, or both (Companies Act 1985 s151(3)). Perhaps more precariously for the company itself is the fact that, if financial assistance was given by way of a loan which itself amounts to unlawful assistance, it follows that the company will be unable to recover the money under the contract for the loan since it will be unenforceable as illegal (see Companies Act 1985 ss151(2), 152(1)(iii)). However, it would appear that the company will retain an action against the directors of the company for breach of duty to the company where the unenforceable loan is made to the directors, who will be liable to the company as constructive trustees of its property (*Selangor Universal Rubber Estates Ltd v Cradock (No3)* [1968] 2 All ER 1073 at 1091–2; see also *Guinness plc v Saunders* [1990] 2 AC 663).

A breach of duty involving a misappropriation of the company's assets may not generally be ratified by the company in general meeting (*Cook v Deeks* [1916] 1 AC 554, PC (but cf the much-criticised decision in *Regal (Hastings) Ltd v Gulliver* [1942] 1 All ER 378; and see also Table A, art 85). It follows that the directors will be liable to an action for breach of duty in misfeasance proceedings instituted by a liquidator or administrator (or the Official Receiver, a creditor or contributory) in the course of a winding-up under s212(3). Such an action is not, however, available to an administrative receiver.

An action in misfeasance proceedings would appear to be available irrespective of whether or not the financial assistance has been given by the directors to a third party or any of their own number. Any damages arising in misfeasance proceedings will be caught by an appropriate charge which extends to future assets of the company (*Re Anglo-Austrian Printing & Publishing Union* [1895] 2 Ch 891; *Re Asiatic Electric Co Pty Ltd* [1970] 92 WN (NSW) 361). However, since any loan and security given in breach of Companies Act 1985 s151 will be unenforceable, it follows that any sums received will not be recoverable on behalf of the holder of the subsequently-unenforceable debenture which may contain fixed and/or floating charges over future assets. Instead, the damages will enure for the benefit of the creditors generally.

# *Chapter Seven*

# Appointment Validity Considerations: 2

## 7.1 Introduction

The matters dealt with in this chapter concern the creation of the security itself, the mechanics of the appointment and factors which concern the appointee in terms of qualifications, ethics and formalities. As in the previous chapter the matters considered here do not appear in any order of relative importance.

## 7.2 Does the Company have Power to Create the Debenture under its Articles and Memorandum of Association?

This requirement necessitates the checking of the following five specific points, dealt with in the following paragraphs.

### 7.2.1 Objects clause: to carry on the company's business

*Does the objects clause of the company enable it to carry on its business?* This question should not cause difficulties, since it is common for objects clauses to be framed in the broadest terms if only for historical reasons, to avoid contravening the *ultra vires* doctrine and the resulting personal liability of directors for acting outside of the company's objects. It should be noted here that a power, as contained in the objects clause, is not the same as an object. A power is something which may only be exercised for the fulfilment of an object. Any other exercise of the power, even if not strictly *ultra vires*, will amount to an abuse of power by the director (*Rolled Steel Products (Holdings) Ltd v British Steel Corporation* [1986] Ch 246). Nevertheless, the nature of the business carried on by the company at the time the debenture was executed should be ascertained and checked against the scope of the objects clause of the company, to ensure that it falls within it. Failure to satisfy this point, although unlikely in practice, may render the creation of the debenture void *ab initio*, which will have an equivalent effect on the appointment itself.

189

### 7.2.2  Objects clause: raising money by borrowing

*Does the objects clause enable the company to raise money through borrowing?* In practice, it will be very unusual for a company not to have an express power provided in its objects clause to raise money through borrowing. Even where no such express power exists in the company's objects clause, the courts have historically implied such a power in the case of a trading company (see, for example, *General Auction Estate and Monetary Co v Smith* [1891] 3 Ch 432).

As a general rule a check should be made of the company's memorandum and articles of association to ascertain whether or not the power to borrow, as exercised by the directors, is subject to a limitation in terms of either borrowing levels or the maximum amount for which the directors may grant security over the assets of the company. The latter limitation is more common in practice then the former. In the absence of such fetters on their powers, the directors will have unlimited power to borrow pursuant to their general powers of management. These are conferred by Table A, art 70 in the case of most private limited companies (and see also Table A, art 79 under the Companies Act 1948).

Whilst Table A, art 70 envisages that the exercise of the directors' powers is subject to any express directions given by a special resolution of the company in general meeting, it is clear from the same provision that this will not invalidate (and it is submitted is not capable of invalidating) any act previously performed by the directors in contravention.

The powers of the directors of a listed public limited company are generally more restricted than those of a private limited company, because it is a condition for the obtaining and maintenance of a listing of the company's securities on the Official List of the London Stock Exchange that the company's articles of association stipulate a maximum borrowing level (usually expressed as a multiple of capital and reserves) without prior authorisation by the company in general meeting by way of special resolution. The Listing Rules are statutory in nature as delegated legislation made pursuant to the Financial Services Act 1986, s142(6). No such fetter in terms of borrowing levels operates in relation to the powers of the directors of an unlisted public company, subject to limitations imposed by the company's memorandum and articles of association although an excessive loan may conceivably amount to a breach of duty.

It is a well-established tenet of company law that the directors of a company are under a duty not to act illegally or *ultra vires* the company without the sanction of the company in general meeting where this is expressly required, such as in the case of a proposed act which would otherwise be beyond the scope of the directors' powers (see *Selangor United Rubber Estates Ltd v Cradock (No3)* [1968] 1 WLR 1555). To the extent that the company suffers any loss as a result of a breach, which need not be negligent, the delinquent directors will be personally liable to the company (*Re Sharpe* [1892] 1 Ch 154; see also *Cullerne v London and Suburban General Permanent Building Society* (1890) 25 QBD 485).

### 7.2.3  Objects clause: charging assets to secure borrowings

*Does the objects clause of the company enable the company to charge its assets to secure borrowings raised by it?* It is usual in practice for a company's objects clause to include a specific power for the company to charge its assets in support of borrowings raised by it. Again, in the absence of such a provision, it has long been held by the courts that a trading company has an implied power to give security over its property in respect of debts properly contracted by it (*Re Patent File Co, ex parte, Birmingham Banking Co* (1870) 6 Ch App 83; see also *Re International Life Assurance Society, Gibbs and West's case* (1870) LR 10 Eq 312).

An investigation should be made into the company's memorandum and articles to establish whether any limitation is imposed on the limit of the value to which security in respect of borrowings may be given. The observations made in the previous section in relation to directors' potential personal liabilities on exceeding their powers are equally applicable here.

### 7.2.4  Objects clause: giving guarantees and charging company assets

*Where the appointment of an administrative receiver is to be made in respect of a guarantee liability, does the objects clause of the guarantor company confer a power on it to give guarantees and to charge its assets to secure the company's guarantee obligations?* This question is of relevance where an appointment is to be made in relation to a company where the company's liability has been incurred wholly or partially in respect of guarantee liability entered into by it. In the case of cross-guarantees between member companies of a corporate group, a check should be made for practical purposes at an early stage regarding an appointment which is to be made to a member of a group, as to whether or not there is a prospect of that company's liability being discharged by another group member.

The company's objects clause should also be checked for a specific power on the part of the guarantor company to give guarantees and to charge its assets in support of them. The authorities cited previously in this section will not imply a power or powers to this effect, since the giving of a guarantee by a company will not relate to borrowing in respect of its own property. The same is also true of the charging of the company's assets in support of its guarantee obligations. Furthermore, the judicial approach and authorities on this are unhelpful for those seeking to imply such powers. The courts have certainly not been prepared to imply a power unless there has been some reasonable connection between the company's objects and the power it seeks to exercise, provided also that it can be shown that the company will benefit, albeit indirectly, from the exercise of the power (*Evans v Brunner Mond & Co* [1921] 1 Ch 359; *Hutton v West Cork Railway Co* (1883) 23 ChD 654). Moreover, a power has been held not to be implied where a company sought to guarantee the share capital of another company which it had been instrumental in forming (*Colman v Eastern Counties Railway Co* (1846) 10 Beav 1). Similarly, and analogously, the close proximity relationship between a subsidiary company and its holding company was not recognised in *Ridge Securities v IDC* [1964] 1 WLR 479, where the subsidiary was held to have acted *ultra vires* in borrowing from its holding company merely to enable it to pay over a large proportion of its profits to the holding company in lieu of interest on the loan. Whilst it may be that judicial opinion would be to imply a power which permitted a company to give a guarantee and charge its assets in support of its obligations, the present position serves to emphasise the importance, if only for the purposes of certainty, of such express powers being set out in the company's objects clause.

On ascertaining that a company has an express or implied power to give a guarantee, it should also be checked that no limitations exist as to the class of persons in respect of whom such guarantees may be given and, if there are any, that the principal debtor for whose benefit the guarantee is given falls within this class.

On ascertaining that an express or implied power exists so as to permit the company to charge its assets in support of its guarantee obligations, a check should also be made that the power to do this is not restricted to certain assets or assets up to a specific value. Similarly, a power which merely enables the company to give security in respect of its own borrowing will not suffice where the monies advanced in consideration, in whole or in part, for the guarantee are advanced to the principal debtor, since this will not amount to 'own borrowing' on the part of the guarantor. Of course, where the guarantor in relation to which the proposed appointment is to be made is both a principal debtor and a guarantor simultaneously, the invalidity of any security given in support of guaranteed liabilities will pale into insignificance, since the appointment will be made purely on the basis of the company's default as a principal debtor in most cases. The point should, however, be clarified as a matter of course.

As discussed in Chapter 6 at paras 6.2.1 and 6.2.2, it is theoretically possible that a guarantee may be avoided by either a liquidator or administrator as a transaction-at-undervalue and/or as a preference under s238 and/or 239 respectively. A check should, therefore, be made of the date on which the guarantee was executed, together with a check that the guarantee is properly executed on the face of it. For reasons also discussed in Chapter 6, it should be noted that significant practical problems are likely to arise in relation to applications for the setting aside by the court of a guarantee as a transaction-at-undervalue or as a preference.

Finally, in view of the fact that a company's objects may have been amended since the date of execution of the debenture, and the fact that the objects clause itself may appear in a format which varies from that adopted previously, checks should be made as against the company's own record of its objects clause both at the time the debenture was executed and that registered with Companies House at that time. This information may be verified by way of a company search.

## 7.2.5 Effect of the Companies Act 1985 s35

*Are any constitutional defects cured by Companies Act 1985, s35 (as amended)?* The provisions of the Companies Act 1989 in relation to the area of *ultra vires* generally came into force with effect from 4 February 1991. These provisions virtually abolished the doctrine of *ultra vires* in relation to third parties. Internally, however, the doctrine is retained, thereby enabling a shareholder to obtain an injunction against the company for a proposed *ultra vires* act. Such injunctions are rare in practice, for the simple reason that most shareholders usually only become aware of *ultra vires* acts by a company after their perpetration.

Section 35A(1) of the Companies Act 1985 (as amended) provides:

> in favour of a person dealing with a company in good faith, the power of the board of directors to bind the company, or authorise other to do so, shall be deemed to be free of any limitation under the company's constitution.

It is clear that a lender taking security by way of a debenture will be deemed to be 'a person dealing with' the company for the purposes of this provision. Whether the lender deals 'in good faith' is a circumstantial matter. Section 35A(2)(b) of the amended 1985 Act stipulates that a person is not to be regarded as acting in bad faith merely by virtue of knowing that an act is beyond the scope of the directors' actions under the company's memorandum or articles of association. To lose the protection of the presumption of good faith, therefore, a third party would appear to have to be shown either to have coerced an *ultra vires* act on the part of the company knowing it to be such or, alternatively, to have acquiesced to the *ultra vires* act in the knowledge that the directors were aware of the *ultra vires* nature of their actions. Section 35A(2)(b) therefore offers considerable protection to institutional lenders which operate via branches or regional outlets, since the entering into of a loan which is *ultra vires* by one branch or outlet would appear protected on the basis of the s35(2)(b) presumption, even if any limitation in the company's memorandum or articles of association is unknown to another branch or outlet. This protection would appear to be lost, however, where a company search is carried out by the branch or outlet authorising the loan on the basis of actual knowledge, as is considered below.

Section 35A of the Companies Act 1985 does not offer absolute protection to a *bona fide* third party. This is because it operates only in relation to 'any limitation under the company's constitution'. The provision will, therefore, have no operation in relation to an *illegal* act by the directors, such as the obtaining of a loan to give illegal financial assistance for the preference of shares in the company contrary to the Companies Act 1985 s151. Nor does it apply where there is a limitation which is imposed on the financial level of transactions by the directors on themselves or on any of their members or committee (ie by way of a board resolution, as opposed to emanating as a restriction from the company's memorandum or articles of association). Such a restriction might include a limitation on the amount of borrowing which may be entered into by a finance director or a finance committee, or the level of borrowing secured annually by the board or any sub-committee without further board authorisation.

For the avoidance of doubt it is suggested that the following checks should be made as regards the dealings between the lender and the company in making the loan to the company and the giving of security for it:

(1) A full company search of the company's register at Companies House will reveal *inter alia* the company's memorandum and articles of association and its directors at the time the debenture was or is executed.

(2) It should be checked that the directors of the company who authorise the transaction have been properly appointed, s35A(1) making reference to 'the power of the board of directors to bind the company'. Reliance should not therefore be placed on the fact that an individual may constitute a shadow director or a *de facto* director or a director *de son tort* who acts as a director without being validly appointed as such (see *Re Canadian Land Reclaiming and Colonising Co, Corenbury and Dixon's Case* (1880) 14 ChD 660). A similar approach should apply to an individual who is not named as a director, despite the apparent scope of the definition of the term 'director' in Companies Act 1985 s741 which may, for example, extend to senior managers or executives.

(3) A company search will also reveal whether an administrator, administrative receiver or liquidator has been appointed which will impede the powers of the directors.

Companies Act 1985 s35A provides that a person is not deemed to have constructive knowledge of the memorandum or articles of association of a company or any other documents filed with the Registrar of Companies which relate to a company's capacity to enter into a particular transaction, even apparently, and again somewhat curiously, if the individual has actually read them. This is reinforced by Companies Act 1985 s711A(1), which provides:

> A person shall not be taken to have notice of any matter because of its being disclosed in any document kept by the Registrar of Companies (and being available for inspection) or made available by the company for inspection (eg at the company's registered office).

It may be tempting, even apparently advisable, therefore, to refrain from a company search to avoid being fixed with any otherwise inoperable constructive knowledge of any matters revealed by the search of the register. In practice, this is an unattractive option for two reasons. First, a positive decision not to carry out a company search suggests that a lender or his legal adviser is prepared to ignore, quite literally, any matter in the company's constitution which restricts its right to borrow or to charge its assets. This wilful ignorance is arguably overcome on the basis of what such a lender might reasonably be deemed to have knowledge of by implication as discussed below. Secondly, notwithstanding the effective abolition of constructive notice in Companies Act s711A(1), the provision is qualified by s711A(2) which provides:

> [s711A(1)] does not affect the question whether a person is affected by notice of any matter by reason of a failure to make such inquiries as ought reasonably to be made.

It is submitted that in a commercial transaction involving a loan to a company and the securing of its assets, it is reasonable to expect a lender, particularly a sophisticated institutional lender, to make reasonable inquiries, on a proactive basis, into the contents of a company's memorandum and articles of association and any other matters which may restrict its powers to transact in the manner proposed. This view is taken notwithstanding Companies Act 1985 s35B (as amended), which specifically provides that a party to a transaction (ie which does not include gifts) with a company is not bound to inquire as to any limitations on the power of the board to bind the company or authorise others, such as a board committee, to do so.

A company search is also recommended to ascertain whether the company's articles of association require any specific formalities to be observed in the execution of documents such as a debenture. Again, whilst it is far from clear from the wording of the provision, it may be that s35A(1) is not sufficiently broad to protect against defects in procedural formalities, because such formalities do not fall within 'the power of the board of directors to bind the company'.

A check should also be made on the board resolutions by which the company resolves to execute and/or executes the debenture or authorises an individual or individuals to do so. It should be noted for these purposes that a company is obliged to minute the proceedings of all board meetings in books maintained for that purpose, on pain of a fine for default and continued default (Companies Act 1985 s382(1),(5)). The minutes of a board meeting, if purported to be signed by the chairman of the meeting, or by the chairman of the next succeeding meeting, are deemed to be evidence of the proceedings. Further, until the contrary is proved, the board meeting and its proceedings will be deemed duly held and convened, and all appointments of directors deemed valid where the proceedings of the meetings are minuted in accordance with s382(1) of the 1985 Act (Companies Act 1985 s382(2),(4)).

Despite the provisions in the Companies Act 1985 s382 it remains a prudent move to obtain copies of the board resolutions, or at least certified copies of the resolutions, which purport to effect the execution of the debenture. These resolutions should be checked specifically to ensure that the resolution(s) have in fact been executed in accordance with the company's memorandum and articles of association and that the relevant board meeting is properly constituted in relation to matters such as quorum, notice and those purporting to vote as directors. This caution is not only good practice, but also guards against potential dangers and liabilities which may be posed by the Companies Act 1985 s322A.

Section 322A of the Companies Act 1985 constitutes the major exception to the protection ordinarily afforded to third parties dealing with the company by virtue of Companies Act 1985 s35A. The provision provides that, where one or more of the parties to the transaction is a director of the company or its holding company or is otherwise connected with the company (as defined in Companies Act 1985 s346), and the board of directors exceeds any limitation on its powers under the company's constitution, then the transaction is voidable at the instance of the company, unless it was previously authorised or is subsequently ratified by ordinary resolution of the company on general meeting (s322A(5)). The provision also lists the intervention of third party rights as a circumstance in which restitution will no longer be possible. The rationale behind the rule is simply an assumption that those persons listed above should be aware of any such limitation in the company's constitution and ensure compliance with it. Section 322A of the 1985 Act is particularly relevant to the giving of a guarantee or guarantees by a company, thereby creating liability which is secured by the debenture pursuant to which the administrative receiver is to be appointed. This is because, as is common in practice, a company within a group may give cross-guarantees in respect of other group company liabilities where those liabilities are secured by debenture. The companies comprising the group will also have substantially common boards. In such a case it would appear that the protection afforded by Companies Act 1985 s35A will not operate in favour of a group company dealing with a guarantor group company, on account of the provision in Companies Act 1985 s322A. Of course, this will only be relevant where, on the basis that the principal debtor company is linked to the company in connection with the guarantee transaction, the guarantor company's board is restricted by a limitation in its memorandum and articles of association in relation to the giving of the guarantee or the execution of the debenture. Any contract entered into by one company where there are common board members to both companies will also require formalities to be complied with in relation to the notification of interest in contracts under Companies Act 1985 s317 and the possibility of a substantial property transaction for the purposes of the Companies Act 1985 s320. Compliance with the company's articles of association will also be necessary (see Table A, arts 84, 94–6).

When the board of a company is constrained in effecting a transaction on account of the scope of its objects clause, one simple solution is to amend the objects clause by special resolution of the company in general meeting (Companies Act 1985 s4). In practice, many lenders will insist on such a change being made prior to any loan transaction being effected where relevant. Even where this is not required, s35A of the 1985 Act (as amended) would still appear to offer considerable protection to a third party dealing with the company in all but the most extreme circumstances (see Companies Act 1985, ss35A(2)(b), 322A). Even in a s322A 'exception' scenario, any defect may be cured by a retrospectively-operative ratification by the company in general meeting (Companies Act 1985 s322(5)).

Finally, it should be noted that the provisions considered above which are inserted into the Companies Act 1985 by the Companies Act 1989 have no retrospective effect. They operate only in relation to debentures and transactions executed on or after 4 February 1991. The considerable protection afforded by the new legislation has no bearing on securities executed prior to that date and reference should be made to the unamended provision of the Companies Act 1985 in such cases.

## 7.3 Has the Power to Appoint an Administrative Receiver Become Exercisable under the Terms of the Debenture?

The starting-point on this question is to investigate whether the debenture contains a contractual power to appoint an administrative receiver. The debenture will usually make reference simply to 'a receiver', commonly in a definition schedule. This arises because the terms of the debenture will necessarily seek to provide alternatively for the appointment of either an administrative receiver or a non-administrative receiver such as an LPA receiver. There is no standard format in the way on which such a power will be drawn. Some debentures are framed in terms of the power to appoint being exercisable on the debenture becoming enforceable, with specific reference to a list of stipulated events giving rise to enforceability. Others will simply contain an unconditional power whereby, for instance, 'the bank may under hand...or by deed appoint or remove a Receiver or Receiver of the Property...'.

Whilst an unconditional power is less common in practice, it offers greater flexibility to the secured lender in terms of enforcement, and is quite unobjectionable in law. Certain debentures will contain a more restrictive power to appoint such as:

> ...At any time after any of the monies hereby secured before payable or if requested by the Company or upon the presentation of a petition for administration of the Company the Bank may appoint [a receiver or receiver and manager].

Again, this approach is not problematic. Equally common is the debenture which stipulates a list of grounds which give rise either to the right of the debenture-holder to appoint a receiver or which provides a right to demand payment which will in turn give rise to the right to appoint a receiver if the demand remains unsatisfied within a stipulated time. It is essential to ascertain whether a debenture specifically gives rise to a right to appoint or simply a right to demand payment, since an appointment which is made on the basis of a mere 'stand alone' right to demand payment will clearly be invalid. The events which are typically cited as giving rise to either a right to appoint or to demand payment depending on the terms of the specific debenture, are as follows:

(1)  *The company fails to make payment on a due date of either principal and/or interest which may be due under either the debenture or any supplemental deed or document*: This is self-explanatory. However, where payment has been made other than in the currency in which the debenture is denominated, a check should be made as to whether this is provided for in the debenture. If it is not, the view may be that the company has defaulted on its obligations.

(2)  *The company fails to meet a demand for payment (ie made in the prescribed manner) of either principal and/or interest:* The debenture itself will invariably prescribe the method by which such a demand is to be effected and a check should be made that this procedure has been complied with (see also para 7.4 *below*).

(3)  *Any distress, execution, sequestration or other process of enforcement is being threatened (eg a demand for payment), levied against, enforced upon or sued out against all or any of the property subject to the debenture or any supplemental deed or document*: Frequently, this ground will be extended to include not only the company but also any company or individual who is a guarantor or surety for the repayment of all or any of the liabilities or monies secured by the debenture.

Again, a check should be made in each particular case to ensure the ground has actually arisen as specifically envisaged by the debenture.

(4) *The property of the company secured by the debenture is in jeopardy (otherwise than in (3) above)*: This ground is usually stated as one which depends on the subjective opinion of the debenture-holder. The 'jeopardy' ground is broad and should not be viewed merely within the context of the cessation of trading by the company. Briefly a company's assets may be viewed as being 'in jeopardy' where the debenture-holder is at real risk of being unable to realise its security, on account of the company's assets being liable to dissipation or seizure on execution by a third party. For example, the court was prepared to appoint a receiver on the basis that the debenture-holder's security was in jeopardy in *Re London Pressed Hinge Co* [1905] 1 Ch 576 where a creditor had served a demand on the company, obtained judgment and was in a position to proceed with execution. This was despite the fact that no express term of the debenture itself had actually been breached by the company thereby giving a right to appoint a receiver. Conversely, the court was not prepared to accept the jeopardy ground in *Re New York Taxicab Co* [1913] 1 Ch 1 in similar circumstances where there was no indication that any creditor was attempting to enforce against any of the assets secured by the debenture-holder security; see also *Hubbuck v Helms* (1887) 56 LJ Ch 536 (jeopardy acknowledged) and cf *Re Borax Co, Foster v Boran Co* [1899] 2 Ch 130 (no jeopardy) on very similar facts involving threats by the company to dispose of the whole of the company's undertaking and one of several businesses respectively.

Jeopardy is, in practice, the most common ground on which a debenture-holder will have recourse to the court for an appointment in the absence of an appropriately drawn ground in the debenture. In cases of this type the company is usually insolvent and may well have fallen into arrears on repayment of interest and/or principal under the terms of the debenture. This may itself constitute the debenture-holder's security being in jeopardy pending a petition for a winding-up and imminent liquidation, as in *Re Victoria Steamboats Ltd* [1897] 1 Ch 158 (see also *Re A Company (No 00175 of 1987)* [1987] 3 BCC 124). Alternatively, the default giving rise to alleged jeopardy may itself give rise to an event stipulated in the debenture which provides specifically for the appointment of a receiver.

(5) *The company (or any guarantor or surety of it in respect of liabilities, monies or secured by the debenture) is unable to pay its debts as defined in s123 or certifies that it is unable to pay its debts as and when they fall due*: For the purposes of the 'cash-flow' tests in s123 (1)(e), contingent and prospective liabilities of the company are not

taken into account, whereas, in the case of the 'commercial' or 'balance sheet' test in s123(2), actual contingent and prospective liabilities are set against 'the value of the company's assets' in deciding whether or not the company is unable to pay its debts (ie to the satisfaction of the court). For an incisive view of practical problems arising with asset and liability valuation in this regard see Goode, *Principles of Corporate Insolvency Law* 1st edn (Sweet & Maxwell 1990, at 40–4). It is clear for the purposes of both of the above 'insolvency' tests that neither test includes contingent assets (*Byblos Bank v Al Khudhairy* [1986] 2 BCC 99).

(6)  *The company or a guarantor or surety fails to comply with any of the covenants, conditions or provisions contained in the debenture or any supplemental deed or document*: This ground clearly hinges on the particular provisions of each individual debenture. Obvious examples of these types of provision would include:

   (i)   the company creating or permitting to arise any mortgage, charge or lien (ie including a lien arising by operation of law such as unpaid vendor's lien) on the charged property subject to the debenture without the consent of the debenture-holder;

   (ii)  a disposition by the company of any of its undertaking or property subject to a floating charge (but not subject to a fixed charge) other than in the ordinary course of business (eg the raising of an asset or chattel mortgage, which may itself contravene any negative pledge contained in the floating charge);

   (iii) a failure by the company from time to time to deposit with the debenture-holder all insurance policies (or usually copies, if agreed) deeds and documents of title relating to the company and property; or

   (iv)  the payment of the proceeds of book debts into a bank account other than that held with or specified by the debenture-holder (ie whether or not held with the debenture-holder such as in the case of a non-clearing bank).

(7)  *Any warranty given by the company, guarantor, surety or director to the debenture-holder turns out to be materially untrue*: This is a broad ground which guards against patent and latent defects in information given to the debenture-holder by any person referred to in the debenture even, it would appear, where the mis-statement is negligent or wholly innocent. Provisions of this kind are usually drafted so as to render silence capable of amounting to a misrepresentation in the disclosure of material statements of facts (see, for example, *With v O'Flanagan* [1936] 1 All ER 727.

(8)  *The property or chattels mortgaged by the debenture or any part thereof is compulsorily acquired by or by order of any local or other*

*authority (such as a government department or agency) and, as a result, the business of the company or a guarantor is seriously affected:* This ground very closely resembles the 'jeopardy' ground referred to in (4) *above* and caters for contingencies such as compulsory purchase orders being made against the property of the company.

(9) *A proposal is made to the company or a guarantor or its creditors for a company voluntary arrangement ('CVA') pursuant to the IA 1986 s1*: Other than where a company is subject to an administration order, the directors of a company may make a CVA proposal to the company and its creditors (s1(1)). Alternatively, an administrator or liquidator may make the proposal as office-holders (s1(3)). The right to make a formal demand for repayment or to appoint a receiver on this basis is an added protection to the debenture-holder, since a CVA is not capable of affecting the rights of a secured creditor without his consent (s4(3)). There is no technical bar to a CVA and an administrative receivership operating contemporaneously, although this may give rise to practical problems in dealing with assets (see, for example, *Rex Leisure Studies Group Ltd* [1994] 2 BCLC 65, where CVA assets were held not to be subject to a floating charge and Chapter 2 at para 2.5.1).

(10) *A meeting of the company or a guarantor or a surety is convened for the purposes of considering a resolution for the winding-up of the company or a guarantor or a surety or, alternatively, an application being made to court for an order for the winding-up of the company or a guarantor or surety*: This ground will require merely the formal consideration by the company of a resolution to wind-up ie including one contemplated as being passed voluntarily even if the resolution is not subsequently carried or even voted on. The practical implication of this ground generally for the debenture-holder is that the administrative receiver's appointment should be effected prior to the making of a winding-up order or the appointment of a provisional liquidator. This is because, after that time, no action or proceedings may be proceeded with or commenced against the company or its property, such as the appointment of a receiver, without the consent of the court and subject to any terms it might impose (s130(2)). However, in practice it is rare for a receiver's appointment to be refused, since the balance of convenience will usually favour the appointment, even if it means loss to the company or its unsecured creditors (*Re Potters Oil Ltd (No2)* [1986] 1 WLR 201 at 206 per Hoffman J; see also *Henry Pound & Sons Ltd v Hutchins* (1889) 2 ChD 402 and *Re Exchange Securities & Commodities Ltd* [1983] BCLC 186).

(11) *A meeting of the company or guarantor or a surety is convened for the purpose of considering a resolution for an application to be made*

*for the making of an administration order in respect of the company or a guarantor or a surety of it or, alternatively, an application is made to the court for an administration order in respect of the company or a guarantor or a surety of it*: Again, this ground requires only the convening of a meeting to consider a resolution for the company to apply for an administration order, even, it would appear, if the resolution is never carried or even voted on. A debenture-holder who may appoint an administrative receiver must be notified of a petition for an administration order by virtue of s9(2)(a) and IR r2.6(2)(a). This will not, of course, apply where the petition is presented in respect of a guarantor or a surety, although there is no reason why a term should not be included in the debenture expressly requiring the company to give notice to the debenture-holder of such a petition. The giving of notice will, however, be of a contractual, and not a statutory nature, which has an effect on the remedies available for breach of the term by the company. As an alternative, the debenture-holder may choose to check for the making of an administration order in respect of a guarantor or a surety of the company, albeit considerably later than the relevant resolution or application, by reference to the statutory advertisement of the order in the London Gazette pursuant to IR r2.10(2).

(12) *The company ceasing to trade*: As mentioned previously in Chapter 3 at para 3.3.4, the cessation of a company's business is frequently cited as an event which causes a floating charge to crystallise. The point was also made that this position is not perhaps as clear as some commentators might suggest, since there appears not to be a single authority which supports this view. This apparent ambiguity is avoided where a debenture expressly stipulates the cessation of the company's business as a ground for demanding repayment or appointing a receiver. Cases cited in Chapter 3 provide authority for the crystallisation of a floating charge on the actual appointment of a receiver itself being made, as opposed to the mere cessation of the company's business.

In all cases it is clear that the onus will be on the debenture-holder to prove that an event has arisen which permits the appointment of a receiver or the making of a demand for payment (*Kasofsky v Kregers* [1937] 4 All ER 374). Where the debenture documentation baldly provides for an appointment to be made unconditionally then no such proof will be required, since this is what the parties themselves have agreed. Furthermore, no duty is owed by the debenture-holder in making an appointment provided that it is made in good faith (*Shamji v Johnson Matthey Bankers Ltd* [1991] 3 BCLC 36). It must be assumed that the *Shamji* decision survives that in *Downsview v First City Corp Ltd* [1993] 2 AC 295 (for which see Chapter 9 at para 9.1) to the extent that a debenture-holder remains under a duty to the company to act in good faith in exercising the power of appointment, such as to appoint a duly qualified and experienced individual. Where the above grounds other than (2) *above* are stated as giving rise to a power to demand repayment by the debenture-holder, regard should also be had to the actual mechanics of the demand.

## 7.4 Has any Demand for Repayment been Validly Made?

The making of a valid demand for repayment, if envisaged by the debenture is of crucial practical importance in that an invalid appointment may not be perfected by the making of a subsequent valid demand (*Cripps v Wickenden* [1973] 1 WLR 944). However, a company may be estopped from challenging an invalid appointment and may well be unable to prove any loss arising as a consequence in any case. IA 1986 does not provide in any way for either the period which must elapse before the making of a demand for repayment by a debenture-holder or the effect of a defective demand. These matters are provided for by case law, although there are marked differences between the decisions of the English courts and those of the Commonwealth jurisdictions which are often also cited as authorities in the literature dealing with the area. Initially, it is appropriate to consider whether the right of the debenture-holder to demand repayment has actually arisen. Where no such right has arisen, an appointment made on the basis of it may be challenged by way of an injunction, and/or a payment being made to the debenture-holder or into court of sums admitted by the debtor. A claim of set-off will not *per se* avoid the right to appoint (*Ashley Guarantee Ltd v Zacaria* [1993] 1 WLR 62, CA). Nevertheless, the company's acquiescence to an invalid appointment may estop it from objecting even, it appears, if the company did not know of the invalidating factors (*Shamji v Johnson Matthey Bank Ltd* [1993] 2 BCLC 36).

### 7.4.1 Repayment on demand clauses

In the case of a bank, the lender's right to demand repayment will hinge on whether the loan to the company is by way of a fixed-term loan agreement, a repayment loan account (frequently in the form of a revolving credit facility) or an overdraft.

In the case of a fixed-term loan agreement, the terms of the loan, including a loan repayment schedule, will be set out in the standard-form loan documentation. This will normally also stipulate the events which amount to default by the company (such as failure to make payment of principal and/or interest on a due date) and which entitle the bank to demand immediate repayment of principal, interest, costs etc as a consequence of default. Initially, therefore, a check should be made of the loan documentation to ensure that an event constituting default has actually arisen at the time at which the demand for repayment is made. Since term loan agreements are usually intended by their nature to subsist over a fixed period, usually months or years, with the prospect of further negotiated lending, it is not the case that the loan is usually intended or even expressly stated as being repayable on demand. However, in practice this is commonly circumvented by the inclusion of a covenant in the standard fixed-term loan agreement which confers on the lender the right to repayment. This is invariably stated as arising on any breach on the part of the borrower of any covenant contained in the agreement. Indeed, some lenders will include a clause in the loan documentation to the effect that the entire loan under the agreement will be repayable on demand if in the view of the lender the circumstances appear to warrant the demand. Whilst a clause of this type may appear to very much strengthen the position of the lender, there is no specific authority on the validity of such a clause. Validity, it is submitted, may be very questionable indeed where the loan is clearly made on the basis of a previous facility letter which itself makes no provision for repayment of all monies on demand, and which is supplemented subsequently by formal loan documentation which itself does include such a condition. This would seem to be the case on basic principles of contract law, and the fact that subsequently and unilaterally introduced terms which appear in the loan documentation (which is in practice not agreed but which, at least, seeks to evidence the basis of the parties' agreement) may not purport to vary the terms of an original agreement which has come about on the basis of the bank's original facility letter (see generally the leading 'battle-of-the forms' decision in *Butler Machine Tool Co v Ex-Cell-O Corp* [1979] 1 All ER 965).

The mechanics of the agreement apart, equity might also operate against the operation of a 'repayment on demand' clause which provides for a purely subjective view on the part of the bank, if the view taken by the bank in making the demand is so unreasonable as to be perverse or unconscionable. The position is not so clear where a fixed-term loan agreement is entered into by the parties on the basis of the 'agreed' terms of a previous fixed-term loan which was supported by documentation containing a clause authorising the lender to demand repayment unconditionally or where it saw fit. The position is equally unclear where the lender engages in the practice of converting the borrower's 'hard-core' overdraft borrowing into a fixed-term loan where the overdraft has existed or exceeded a prescribed limit for an originally agreed period of time. In such a case, careful regard should be had to the specific terms of the loan facility under which the demand for repayment is made, since the ascertainment of those terms will necessarily dictate whether any right to demand repayment has actually arisen. Certainly, it would be arguable in certain cases that the nature of the loan agreement militates against a demand for immediate repayment being made, as in *Titford Property Co Ltd v*

*Cannon Street Acceptances Ltd* (1975) unreported, 22 May, which involved a fixed-term loan facility over a 12-month period.

### 7.4.2 Revolving credit and overdrafts

As an alternative to a fixed-term loan, the company's borrowing may be by way of a revolving credit facility and/or an overdraft facility. Essentially, a revolving credit agreement, which is neither statutorily nor judicially defined, involves the borrower agreeing to make periodic payments into a specific account in return for a borrowing facility from the lender up to a fixed limit. This is usually calculated as a multiple of the regular payment by the borrower. As a line of credit, a revolving credit facility is not dissimilar to an overdraft facility on a current account, although it offers greater security to the borrower in terms of agreed fixed receipts. An overdraft facility, on the other hand, may come into being by express agreement or impliedly, such as an overdraft which arises on a current account on a regular basis and in respect of which a bank lender is prepared to honour cheques (see *Brooks & Co v Blackburn Branch and Building Society* (1884) 9 App Cas 857 at 864 per Blackburn LJ; *Ritchie v Clydesdale Bank* (1886) 13 R 866, a decision of the Scottish Court of Session).

A revolving credit facility or an overdraft facility may be repayable on demand. Whether or not this is the case will again depend on ascertaining the precise contractual arrangements between the lender and borrower. In the absence of any agreed terms it has been held in relation to overdrafts that an overdrawn balance is repayable on demand or if ordinary commercial judgement dictates that it is essential for a demand to be made (*Barnes v Williams & Glyn's Bank* [1981] Com LR 205 at 205 per Gibson J; *Titford Property Co v Cannon Street Acceptances Ltd* (1975), unreported, per Goff J). Presumably, this assumption would also apply to the analogous revolving credit facility, as there appears to be no good reason why the arrangements should be distinguished, whereas the terms of a fixed-term loan facility may give rise to different considerations depending on the circumstances and the contemplation of the parties at the time the loan agreement was entered into. It is common, nevertheless, for banks to state expressly that a facility is repayable on demand or, equally commonly, to make reference to 'usual banking terms' or similar wording. In this latter case, consideration should be given to whether such a statement is irrelevant as a purported contractual term in that it is vague or meaningless or where no such term has been previously agreed either separately or by contract (see for example *Nicolene v Simmonds* [1953] 1 All ER 822 and more generally *Scamell v Ouston* [1941] AC 251). It must also be noted that indebtedness will not automatically be repayable on demand by its very nature. The court will have regard to the terms of the loan agreement and may consider any terms implied so as to give the agreement business efficacy in the absence of express agreement (see generally, *The Moorcock* (1889) 60 LT 654). Thus, it may be that immediate payment is not anticipated in a re-financing package or in the course of a workout arrangement. In *Williams & Glyn's Bank v Barnes* [1981] Com LR 205, for example, Gibson J considered that the company should be afforded up to one month for investigating the method and means of repaying a loan, in the absence of an express term.

The only realistic way in which the terms of the loan agreement between the lender and borrower may be ascertained is by reference to the documents purporting to set out the terms. One problem here is that standard banking practice is to set out in, say, a facility letter that an overdraft facility is available for a stated period of, say, six months after which the facility will then be subject to review. Facility letters will, however, also often contain a standard phrase or paragraph saying that the overdraft is repayable on demand. These two statements by the lender do not sit happily together. Further, the picture may be made more unclear by formal and ongoing reviews of the facility where, for example, the borrower exceeds the agreed limit persistently and the lender agrees to extend the limit of the facility pending the next review date. Often, the extended facility letter will not make reference to the overdraft being repayable on demand or, alternatively, it will do so whilst, ironically enough, at the same time stating the next review date. There is no simple formula for solving this contractual problem, but it remains of fundamental importance in terms of the validity of the demand for repayment. Therefore all correspondence, loan documentation, interview and meeting records and notes should be scrutinised to ascertain whether the document containing any 'repayable on demand' clause actually evidences the substance of the agreement between lender and borrower. Certainly, it is submitted, it will be difficult to sustain the validity of such a term where it is merely contained in unsolicited correspondence from the lender following the commencement of lending on a facility basis, although the term may be argued to be validly agreed and incorporated by the lender on the basis of the borrower's apparent acquiescence to the statement. Nevertheless, in contractual terms, silence is not capable of amounting to acceptance (*Felthouse v Bindley* (1862) 11 CBNS 869) unless the parties have agreed to such an arrangement.

### 7.4.3  Service of the demand

Most standard-form debentures will provide for the manner in which service of a demand for repayment must be effected (*Elwich Bay Shipping Co v Royal Bank of Scotland* (1982) SLT 62). There is no express requirement that a demand is stated as such and the matter is regarded as one of substance over form judicially; see *BCCI v Blattner* (unreported, 20 November 1986). In practice, a demand should be marked clearly as such to avoid uncertainty. Where a debenture does not stipulate the address at which a demand for repayment should be served then the document evidencing demand may be served by leaving it at or sending it by post to the registered office of the company (Companies Act 1985 s725(1)). In *Bank of Baroda v Panessar* [1987] Ch 335, Walton J suggested that service may also be effected at the company's principal place of business if different from its registered office. This view, it is submitted, is sound in that it operates in favour of the *bona fide* lender on a default by the debtor which may seek to avoid a demand by changing registered offices or by adopting an obscure location for it.

Whilst a demand is usually required to be in writing by a debenture, standard terms will also accompany a demand in facsimile or telex form. Faxed documents are also valid as a method of service under RSC Ord 65 r5(1).

### 7.4.4 The demand-appointment delay

One practical problem which arises commonly in this area is the question of the period of time which must elapse between the service of the demand and the subsequent appointment by the lender. Where a fixed-term loan is repayable on a specified date, the debenture-holder is not permitted to make payment before that date—even, it appears, where the security is in jeopardy—and the time for repayment will fall at midnight where the time is expressly agreed (see *Cryne v Barclays Bank plc* [1987] BCLC 548). The Commonwealth authorities on this area are generally less restrictive than those of the English courts. On the basis of Walton J's decision in the *Bank of Baroda* case (above), the position under English law is that a company is afforded an adequate period of time after the service of the demand as is necessary for the company to implement the mechanics of payment, with the admittedly rather unhelpful proviso that this will depend on the relevant circumstances of each case. Relevant circumstances will no doubt include the time of day at which the demand for repayment is served. If service is made outside the normal business hours, presumably the time period will not commence until normal banking hours resume thereby permitting the company access to its funds (if any). In the case of service of a demand at an overseas location it would also appear necessary to make adjustments to take account of business and banking hours where time differences exist. Watson J's so-called 'mechanics of payment' test was based on the instantaneous nature of electronic communication and fund transfer and expressly recognised that 'the time required [between the service of a demand and the appointment] is exceptionally short'. This approach accords with the previous decision in *Cripps (Pharmaceutical) Ltd v Wichenden* [1973] WLR 949, the time elapsing between service of the demand and the appointment of a receiver in both cases being approximately one hour. In practice, that time period is commonly adopted as the delay period between a demand being made and an appointment of a receiver being effected although the debenture-holder, and certainly most institutional lenders, will gain a good degree of comfort by confirming informally in advance that the company does not object to the appointment being made in this manner.

It is clear on the basis of the 'mechanics of payment' approach that a company is not afforded time in which to seek to arrange finance for repayment purposes. This represents a significantly more restrictive approach than that adopted by the Commonwealth courts, particularly those in Australia, which impose a 'reasonable opportunity' or reasonable notice test. Effectively, this affords a company some time in which to seek to raise funds (see *Banbury Foods Pty Ltd v National Bank of Australasia Ltd* (1984) 51 ALR 509, ANZ *Banking Group v Gibson* [1981] 2 NZLR 513, *Ronald Elwyn Lister v Dunlop Canada Ltd* (1982) 135 DLR (3d) 1 and *Whonnock Industries Ltd v National Bank of Canada* (1987) 42 DLR 1 where the period of reasonable notice hinges on all facts including risk to the creditor and the debtor's ability to raise funds). In English law it is also appears clear from the *Cripps* case that the period of time between demand and appointment of a receiver is irrelevant if the company was obviously incapable of meeting the demand. In practice, this will not be unusual.

It is also common for a demand for repayment to be served together with the instrument of appointment of a receiver. The demand will not be undermined by its being accompanied by an offer to accept a reduced amount or instalment payments as in *NRG Vision v Churchfield Leasing* [1988] BCLC 624 although the appointee is clearly in jeopardy if the company accepts the offer, even without any apparent prospect of meeting it. Unless it is the case that the company is clearly unable to meet any demand for payment made of it, the validity of such an appointment is obviously questionable since the company may be capable of discharging the demand made of it in full. This practice should, therefore, be used guardedly, particularly in view of the short period—seemingly one hour or thereabouts under English Law—which must elapse before a receiver may be appointed validly following a demand for payment (see *Ronald Elwyn Lister Ltd v Dunlop Canada Ltd* (1982) 135 DLR (3d) 1 for a telling example). Even when an appointment is made without a period of time elapsing for the mechanics of payment to be implemented by the company, the *Bank of Baroda* case (above) is also good authority for the principle that the company is estopped subsequently from objecting to the appointment where it acquiesces to it. The point here is that any objection to the appointment, such as where there is no lapse of time before the appointment is effected or where the instrument of appointment is served simultaneously with the demand, should be made immediately. An objection will not, however, *per se* succeed in terminating a receivership, since it appears that pending a full hearing a receiver should remain in office on a balance of convenience test (*Re Toynar Ltd (in receivership)* [1988] 4 BCC 6).

## 7.4.5 The amount demanded

One other practical problem which arises in relation to a demand for repayment relates to the amount demanded as set out in the demand. The courts have developed a number of rules on this point, a substantially similar approach being adopted by both the English and Commonwealth courts in this regard. A demand for an amount less than the full amount due will be sufficient for the appointment of a receiver (*Stubbs v Slater* [1901] 1 Ch 632; *NRG Vision Ltd v Churchfield Leasing Ltd* [1988] BCC 56 in which the question of an excessive demand was left open). Whilst there is no authority as to the validity of a demand where the amount demanded exceeds that due, it would appear that the demand may still be valid, if at least part of that amount demanded is due (*Fox v Jolly* [1916] 1 AC 1). The proviso to this is that any excess amount demanded must not be significantly more than that due. Assuming that the demand of an excessive amount by the debenture-holder does not prejudice the company—which will usually be unable to pay the amount actually due in any case—an analogy may be drawn with mortgage law under which the making of an excessive demand by a mortgagee does not discharge the duty of the mortgagor to tender the amount actually due at that time (see Goode, *Principles of Corporate Insolvency Law* 1st edn (1990) at 88), citing *Campbell v Commercial Banking Co of Sydney* (1879) 40 LT 137 and *Clyde Properties Ltd v Tasker* [1970] NZLR 754 as authorities for this proposition; see also *Cityland Property Holdings Ltd v Dabrah* [1968] Ch 166). The position may be different, however, where a mortgagee indicates a willingness to accept an amount less than that actually due at the time of an excessive demand. In *Re A Company* [1985] BCLC 37 and *Cryne v Barclays Bank plc* [1987] BCLC 548 demands of amounts in excess of that due were held to be invalid. This would seem to reduce excessive demands to the same invalid status of demands where no amount is actually due (as in *Jaffe v Premier Motors Ltd* [1970] NZLR 146). Nevertheless, the *Re A Company* and *Cryne* cases do appear to be justified on the basis that the excessive demands by both lenders were materially more than sums due to them thereby entitling the company to reject the demands. It would follow that, after an excessive demand, if the company tenders the amount actually due and payable at that time then any subsequent appointment of a receiver will be invalid on the basis that no default has, in fact, arisen. The cases appear to suggest a distinction be drawn between those in which a material overstatement of the amount due is made (thereby rendering the demand invalid) and those in which the overstatement is either technically incorrect so as not to be material (see here the comments of Walton J in the *Bank of Baroda* case). It is submitted here that an excessive demand will not automatically invalidate a demand for repayment other than where the demand is materially excessive and, in the circumstances of the case, the company is able to meet a demand for the amount actually due. In such a case it would follow that a fresh demand will be necessary. When the company is unable to pay the due debt in any case there would appear to be little purpose in invalidating even a materially excessive demand.

In practice, the potential problem inherent in demanding a specific amount may be avoided by the service of a demand requiring payment of 'all monies due', in the absence of contrary provision in the debenture, where the debenture itself secures 'all monies due' or some similar, variable amount. This was held expressly to be the case in the *Bank of Baroda* case (above) which followed the decision of the High Court of Australia in *Banbury Foods Pty Ltd v National Bank of Australasia* (1984) 51 ALR 609. In the *Bank of Baroda* case Walton J explained this approach as follows:

> I cannot see any reason why the creditor should not do precisely what he is, by the terms of his security, entitled to do, that is to say to demand repayment of all moneys secured by the [mortgage]...it would seem stupid that the creditor could put in, without imperilling the validity of the notice, an entirely wrong sum, and that is much more likely to give rise to confusion and difficulty than is the form of the notice adopted in ...the present case.

In practice, therefore, an 'all monies due' demand would appear to be the most effective method of framing a demand as a matter of course so as to avoid potential invalidity problems, assuming no contrary provision exists in the debenture. One alternative to an 'all monies due' clause is a term in the debenture whereby the parties agree that a written statement by the creditor of amounts due will be conclusive although such statements are capable of dispute in the absence of good faith; see *ANZ Banking Group (NZ) Ltd v Gibson* [1981] 2 NZLR 513.

### 7.4.6  Appointments at the invitation of the company

Frequently, a debenture, particularly of the standard form variety, contains a provision permitting the appointment of a receiver on the company inviting the creditor, usually a bank, to do so. Where an invitation is made on the basis of such an express provision it should be supported by a written resolution of the board to that effect. There is, of course, no obligation on the creditor to appoint a receiver, since the debenture's provisions will invariably be phrased so as to afford the creditor an option in appointing or not. A lender may refrain from an appointment if it perceives the invitation by the company as a means of effecting a convenient break-up of the business, say, after in-fighting between members of the board. The lender may consider a more appropriate course of action in such a case to be a shareholder's action, as under Companies Act 1985 s459 (as amended), or the removal, negotiated or otherwise, of certain board members. The lender will, of course, wish to guard against the possibly significant loss of goodwill and the effects of bad publicity which will inevitably arise during periods of corporate 'in-fighting' (which in the case of s459 litigation may be protracted) and choose to appoint a receiver, if only to protect its position and guard against any consequential damage to assets, particularly goodwill. Conversely, the creditor may refrain from effecting an appointment where it wishes to see the company continuing its operations in conjunction with key board members and in view of the very prejudicial effect which administrative receivership is likely to have on customer relations and goodwill, except perhaps then where these can be salvaged with the co-operation of certain board members.

An anomaly exists in the case of a 'company invited' appointment where the debenture does not actually envisage the company inviting the appointment of a receiver. One argument is that the subsequent appointment is invalid, although it would appear that the receiver will not be a trespasser in such circumstances as he will clearly be dealing with and disposing of charged assets at the invitation of the company. To avoid this uncertainty it is useful (and, indeed, a common safeguard) to combine any appointment at the invitation of the company, which may well not be envisaged by the terms of the debenture, with a formal demand for payment of sums due under the debenture or a notice of appointment, depending on the specific terms of the debenture. It is advisable that the reasons for this course of action are pointed out and, if necessary, explained to the board of the company, possibly with a recommendation that they seek independent legal advice, so as to avoid any unnecessary misunderstanding. These considerations will, of course, be irrelevant where the debenture-holder is entitled under the terms of the debenture to appoint a receiver merely by service of a notice to that effect on the company. In reality, many institutional lenders prefer to be seen as responding to an invitation to appoint as opposed to apparently initiating the appointment.

Where the terms of a debenture do not contemplate the appointment of a receiver without formal demand for monies being made, there is no legal reason why the directors should not waive the demand requirement on basic contractual principles which permit the parties to the debenture to agree to vary its terms. Whilst this may facilitate a speedier appointment thereby enabling assets to be more easily preserved, the practical matters identified above may outweigh the advantages of doing so.

### 7.4.7 Guarantors

Separate consideration should be given to the question of service of a demand for repayment on a guarantor where, as is common, the debenture secures liabilities of the guarantor as well as the principal debtor's liabilities. A guarantee will usually be framed in terms which render the guarantor liable for all moneys, obligations and liabilities, actual or contingent, owing or incurred on any specific account (invariably including a current account) together with interest, commission, costs, charges and expenses incurred by the creditor in relation to the guarantee. It should always be checked as a matter of course to ascertain whether the guarantee is stated as being limited or capped to a maximum liability and whether this amounts to 'bottom line' or 'top slice' borrowing. Similarly, it should be clarified whether the guarantor's liability under the guarantee is primary or secondary and, if primary (ie jointly with the company in respect of whom the guarantee is given on an indemnity basis) whether any specific formalities are required before the guarantee is enforceable.

Equally, a check should be made as to whether or not the liability arising under the guarantee is payable 'on demand'. Again, if this is the case the formalities for the making of a valid demand for repayment should be checked. The formalities required for the giving of a valid guarantee should also be checked to ensure that the guarantee is legally operative. Briefly, these formalities may be summarised as follows:

(1) The terms of the guarantee must be accepted (by either creditor or guarantor depending on the specific mechanisms of transaction) in accordance with a valid offer which must not have been revoked prior to acceptance (see *Hyde v Wrench* (1840) 3 Beav 334; *Henthorn v Fraser* [1892] 2 Ch 27).

(2) The parties must intend that the contract create legal relations between them. Whilst an invitation to create legal relations is ordinarily implied into contracts of a commercial nature (see, for example, *Edwards v Skyways Ltd* [1964] 1 WLR 349 at 355), this will not normally be the case on the giving of a 'comfort letter' which should be distinguished from a guarantee as discussed further below at para 7.4.8.

(3) The promise to guarantee the liability of the principal debtor must be made by the guarantor either by deed (ie where new funds are not introduced in return for the guarantee which will operate in relation to present or future indebtedness) or, alternatively, it must be supported by valid consideration. In legal terms, the consideration provided by the guarantor is the making of the advance in return for the guarantee. It is irrelevant that the guarantor is not the recipient of the funds, since the price of the promise given by the guarantor to honour the debts of the principal debtor is that funds are provided to the principal debtor. Where funds are not provided at the time the guarantee is executed, the promise to guarantee the liabilities of the principal debtor will be supported adequately by executory consideration in the form of the giving of a promise by the creditor to advance monies. In practice, however, creditors prefer not to commit themselves to such promises of future advances. Where funds are not advanced in return for the giving of the guarantee, therefore, investigations should be made to establish the consideration provided for the guarantee, except where the guarantee is executed by deed.

In relation to guarantees, the question remains as to whether a valid demand for repayment may be made against the guarantor where a demand has not been made of the principal debtor. Ultimately, this will depend on the terms in which the guarantee is framed. Where the guarantor's liability is stated as being payable 'on demand' then it would follow that no demand need be made of the principal debtor before the demand is made of the guarantor; this assumes that the guarantee liability is not of a primary nature, in which case demand should also be made of the primary liability guarantor (ie as indemnifier). However, where this is not expressly stated to be the case, regard should be had to the specific provisions of the guarantee defining when liability under it becomes operative. It may well be the case, for instance, that a formal demand cannot be made of the (secondary liability) guarantor without a formal demand being made initially of the principal debtor. In such a case, an appointment on the basis of a demand made solely of the guarantor will be potentially invalid. Consideration should therefore be given at an early stage to the serving of separate demands on the guarantor and the principal debtor simultaneously, subject to the operation of Walton J's 'mechanics of payment' test as discussed above.

The observations made in the previous paragraph will not apply where a debenture and/or any supporting guarantee contains a clause simply permitting an appointment to be made by notice, since this will reflect the terms in which the parties have agreed to the appointment without the need for further formality other than those relating to service of the demand and the mode of appointment.

### 7.4.8 Guarantees, indemnities and letters of comfort

A distinction should be drawn at this stage between a guarantee, an indemnity and a letter of comfort. An indemnity is in effect a contractual arrangement which imposes a principal liability on the indemnifier in the event of a stipulated loss arising. A guarantee, on the other hand, imposes a secondary liability on the guarantor in the event of a default by the principal debtor. The distinction was accurately drawn by Holdroyd Pearce LJ in *Yeoman Credit v Latter* [1961] 1 WLR 828 at 831 as follows:

> An indemnity is a contract by one party to keep the other harmless against loss, but a contract of guarantee is a contract to answer for the debt, default or miscarriage of another who is primarily liable to the promisee.

Whilst guarantees and indemnities are both mechanisms which seek to ensure that the creditor has recourse to a third party directly or indirectly on default by the principal debtor, the distinction between the two is important for present purposes. The liability arising under a guarantee will be unenforceable where the liability between the principal debtor and the creditor is unenforceable (see *Lloyds and Scottish Trust Ltd v Britten* (1982) 44 P & CR 249 where a mortgagor attempted unsuccessfully to enforce personal guarantees against two directors who had given personal guarantees in respect of a company's indebtedness when the debtor validly foreclosed on the mortgage on the basis of a court order and disposed of the charged property for less than the debt secured by the mortgage). Conversely, a receiver will be invalidly appointed where his appointment is effected on the basis of default in payment of guarantee liabilities where the guarantee itself is invalid and the debenture secures the guarantee liability (*Ford & Carter Ltd v Midland Bank Ltd* [1979] 129 NLJ 543 where, notably, the appointing debenture-holder was liable in trespass as a joint tortfeasor).

A letter of comfort, as opposed to a guarantee, is an assurance which is given to a creditor by a third party (eg a holding company) in respect of a company (eg a subsidiary) evidencing the third party's willingness to support the company in financial terms as an ongoing business. Commonly assurances of this kind are given by parent companies in support of subsidiaries, although they are not without their legal problems (see *Chemco Leasing SpA v Rediffusion plc* (1985) unreported, 19 July, per Staughton J). Letters of comfort, on the other hand, are a continental idea which are also widely used in most advanced commercial jurisdictions (eg German *Patronatserklargungen*). The advantage of comfort facilities is that they offer an alternative to a guarantee which may infringe guarantee limits as imposed by a (guarantor) company's articles or memorandum of association or a lending bank restriction and which, as such, effectively avoid the entry of a contingent liability on the company's balance sheet. Largely on account of the vague terms in which they are commonly phrased and their use as informal commercial credit devices, letters of comfort have been held to be legally unenforceable, although there is no reason in legal terms why they should not be framed in specific terms so as to be binding in law and not in honour only (see *Kleinwort Benson Ltd v Malaysia Mining Corporation Berhard* [1988] 1 All ER 714 in which the Court of Appeal held that a letter of comfort ordinarily imposed no more than a moral obligation; and more generally *Jones v Vernons Pools Ltd* [1938] 2 All ER 626).

If a letter of comfort is expressly stated as or is intended to create legal relations, there is no good reason why a debenture should not secure liabilities incurred by it although such an arrangement would perhaps be unusual. Again, a check should be made of the circumstances in which a letter of comfort was given to ensure that it is not expressly required by the terms of the debenture or the letter of comfort that a demand for repayment be made of the principal debtor before recourse may be had to the provider of the letter of comfort assuming, of course, that the letter of comfort is construed as imposing binding legal obligations.

## 7.5  Are the Assets of the Company Sufficient to Cover the Costs, Expenses and Remuneration of the Administrative Receiver?

There is a clear risk to a prospective office-holder, in terms of recouping both disbursements and remuneration, of taking an appointment where the assets subject to the charge(s) pursuant to which he is appointed appear to be of insufficient realisable value (ie a value which is most realistically and commercially viewed on a forced sale basis) to cover the total costs of the administrative receivership.

The administrative receiver's costs, expenses and remuneration will be met from different sources depending on the extent to which the charged assets comprised in the administrative receivership constitute fixed or floating charge assets. In the case of fixed assets, the administrative receiver's costs of sale, disbursements and remuneration will be met in that order, and so far as they relate to fixed-charge assets in the case of disbursements and remuneration, following the discharge of prior-ranking fixed charges. This will be subject to any contrary agreement with the fixed-charge holder, and in priority to any fixed charge pursuant to which the office-holder was appointed and any subsequent fixed charges. Preferential creditors at the date of appointment may only seek payment for preferred debts from the administrative receiver out of any surplus arising from floating charge assets, and not from any fixed charged asset surplus arising (*Re GL Sanders Ltd* [1986] 1 WLR 215).

In the case of floating charge assets, the administrative receiver's costs and expenses, disbursements and remuneration are met in priority to the claims of preferential creditors. As regards assets subject to a floating charge, an administrative receiver must pay preferential debts (as defined in s386 and Sched 6) out of the assets coming into his hands in priority to any claim for interest or principal under the floating charge (s40(2)). This is a positive obligation, and failure to account to preferential creditors in accordance with s40(2) will render the office-holder personally liable in tort for breach of statutory duty (*Inland Revenue Commissioners v Goldblatt* [1972] Ch 498; *Westminster Corporation v Haste* [1950] Ch 442). Nevertheless, an administrative receiver has a statutory right to recoup payments made to preferential creditors out of assets subject to a floating charge from assets of the company available for unsecured creditors generally (s40(3)). Whilst this may appear to shift the burden of meeting preferential debts onto the company's unsecured creditors, it should be checked that there are, in fact, assets available for this purpose where it appears likely that preferential debts will have to be discharged from floating-charge assets.

Prior to appointment it will also be necessary to investigate whether the company is in or is likely to go into liquidation. Liquidation will not only have the effect of terminating the administrative receiver's agency relationship with the company by virtue of s44(1)(a), but would also appear to have the effect of giving rise to a fresh set of preferential creditors for the purposes of s175. That provision is analogous to s40 but operates in liquidations. In practice this new set of 'liquidation preferential creditors' is likely to be insubstantial, primarily on account of the fact that preferential creditors no longer include assessed tax liability. These implications are, however, overshadowed by the vexed question of whether the costs and expenses of a liquidation have priority over preferential creditors under s175 where a floating charge and fixed charge are both deemed subject to preferential claims, following a contractual agreement giving the floating charge priority over the fixed charge. Certainly this was held to be the case by Chadwick J in *Re Portbase Clothing Ltd* [1993] BCC 96 where the liquidation preceded the administrative receivership but followed the crystallisation of the floating charge by other means. It appears from the judgment that this approach prevails irrespective of whether the administrative receiver is appointed prior to the liquidation (see further Doyle [1994] 10 IL&P 5 at 134–42).

Where a company appears to have substantial assets prior to the accepting of an appointment, it should be checked that these assets do, in fact, relate to charged assets which would be subject to the administrative receivership. It may be, for example, that a single fixed asset is subject to a prior-ranking single fixed charge in favour of a creditor other than that proposing the appointment. Without that single asset, the company's assets may be seriously depleted, and this should be a major consideration as regards the conduct of the proposed administrative receivership. Of course, the existence of a prior-ranking fixed charge will not preclude the appointment of an administrative receiver if the appointment is secured by a floating charge over the whole of the company's business and undertaking, even where a receiver and manager has been appointed as receiver of the fixed-charge asset (s29(2)(b)). The same fixed charge may also give rise to an application to court by the administrative receiver for an order authorising the sale of the relevant prior-ranking charged property under s43(1). Where the court orders a disposal of relevant property as defined in s43(7), the net proceeds of sale will not enure for the benefit of the administrative receivership and must be paid over to discharge the prior-ranking security or securities to the extent that they remain outstanding (s43(3),(4)).

Finally, prior to accepting an appointment as administrative receiver, the proposed appointee should ensure that what appear to be company assets are, in fact, such and, as such, are subject to the charge(s) held by the appointing creditor. Obvious examples of assets which will usually not constitute company assets are those held on trust for the company by a third party, such as a company pension scheme assets and goods supplied to the company under a valid reservation of title clause (*Carreras Rothmans Ltd v Freeman Matthews Treasure Ltd* [1985] 1 All ER 155 and *Re Kayford* [1975] 1 WLR 279).

## 7.6 Is the Appointee Qualified to Act as an Administrative Receiver?

IA 1986 implemented two major recommendations of the *Cork Committee Report* (in Chaps 15–17). These were that (a) all insolvency practitioners should be professionally qualified to recognised minimum standards and (b) each should be subject to a compulsory bonding requirement, in view of widespread and much-publicised abuses by unrecognised and fraudulent office-holders.

The introduction of these high professional standards has devolved much of the day-to-day responsibility for the conduct of insolvency proceedings on to those qualified to act as insolvency practitioners. This has to some extent reduced the responsibility for matters previously entrusted to the office of the Official Receiver. These changes reflect the very onerous responsibilities and expectations of those prospectively taking office as administrative receivers, or as a liquidator, provisional liquidator, administrator or a supervisor of a voluntary arrangement, but not as to anything done by the Official Receiver (s388(1), (4), (5)). These requirements do not apply to LPA receivers.

Section 388(1) provides that a person acts 'as an insolvency practitioner in relation to a company' by acting *inter alia* as an administrative receiver. IA 1986 does not prohibit an unqualified person from carrying on the business of an insolvency practitioner, such as conducting administrative day-to-day matters relating to an administrative receivership under the supervision of the qualified office-holder. This is in line with standard practice where a manager or team of managers, who are usually not qualified to act as insolvency practitioners although they are fully or partly professionally qualified, will undertake the day-to-day work of an administrative receiver, under the control and responsibility of a person so qualified to act, typically a principal or partner within a firm of accountants. Ultimately, the acid test depends on the specific tasks performed and responsibility undertaken by each individual member of the administrative receiver's team of support staff. The way in which the Act approaches this is to say that a person acts as an insolvency practitioner in relation to a company by 'acting' as an administrative receiver and, as such, a person is not qualified to act as an insolvency practitioner at any time unless at that time he is authorised to act by virtue of membership of a recognised professional body under s391 (eg ACCA, ICAEW, ICAS, ICSA, IPA or The Law Society) or is so authorised under s393 by a competent authority (ie the Secretary of State; ss393(1), 390(2)). In cases of doubt, therefore, one must ask if any particular individual has 'acted' as administrative receiver as well as considering steps to alleviate any doubt in the particular circumstances.

A person who acts as an insolvency practitioner in relation to a company, other than the Official Receiver, at any time where he is not qualified to do so is liable to imprisonment or a fine, or to both (ss389(1),(2), 430 and Sched 10).

A person is not qualified to act as insolvency practitioner if at that time:

(a)  he is either an undischarged bankrupt; or

(b)  sequestration of his estate has been awarded and he has not been discharged; or

(c)  he is subject to a disqualification order (seemingly conditional or not) under the Company Directors' Disqualification Act 1986; or

(d)  he is a patient under the Mental Health Act 1983.

A corporate body is not qualified to act as an insolvency practitioner (s390(1)). This bar on corporate receivers also extends to acting as a non-administrative receiver, such as LPA receivers, on pain of criminal sanctions by virtue of s30. This curious provision in relation to LPA receiverships is not problematic, since the purported appointment of a corporate receiver of any kind will be very rare. The bar, it is submitted, would also extend to any company employed by an administrative receiver as a vehicle for the discharge of his duties and functions, say, in an attempt to avoid personal liabilities arising.

The common practice in relation to LPA receiverships is to appoint an individual who is a qualified chartered surveyor as an LPA receiver over an asset such as a business (eg a nursing home or hotel), a building or tower block or some other substantial property such as a ship. These appointments are invariably made pursuant to fixed-charge securities. There is no requirement that such a non-administrative receiver should be a qualified insolvency practitioner and in practice few are, although it is not uncommon for some licenced insolvency practitioners to take such appointments from time to time in their work.

In cases of a defective appointment, s232 provides that the acts of an administrative receiver are valid notwithstanding any defect in its appointment, nomination or qualification. Section 232 does not extend to appointments of non-administrative receivers, although it has in any case been held that an appointment of a corporate receiver in breach of s30 is totally ineffective *ab initio* (*Portman Building Society v Gallway* [1955] WLR 96). It is submitted that s232 will not cure all defects in terms of appointment, nomination or qualifications of an administrative receiver as discussed in Chapter 5 at para 5.6.2.

Special care should be taken by advisers on appointments of non-administrative receivers who are appointed specifically pursuant to one or more fixed charges held by a debenture-holder or a floating charge or a combination of both in cases where the cumulative 'package' of securities held comprises security over less than substantially the whole of the company's property so as to qualify the receiver as an administrative receiver as defined in s29(2), provided that the security pursuant to which the receiver is appointed comprises the prerequisite floating charge. That is, as is suggested in Chapter 1 at paras 1.5–1.7, the debenture-holder retains the prerogative to refrain from appointing an administrative receiver even if the cumulative security held would permit such an appointment. For instance, a debenture-holder might opt to appoint an LPA receiver over a specific fixed asset on the basis of, say, the receiver's intimate knowledge of the asset and the business carried on with it. Alternatively, the appointment may be made to avoid the greater expense of an administrative receivership where the greater flexibility of an administrative receiver is not perceived as necessary for the purposes of the particular receivership in hand. The 'balance' of the debenture-holder's security may still permit the appointment of an administrative receiver subject to the extent of it for the purposes of s29(2)(b). Depending on the extent of the debenture-holder's security, and in particular the floating charge element of it, the residue of the cumulative security held by the debenture-holder may amount to less than substantially the whole of the company's property. In that case the receiver appointed pursuant to the security will, by definition, be incapable of being an administrative receiver.

Where an appointment is made pursuant to any security or package of securities which includes a floating charge extending to the whole business and undertaking of the company, it follows that, again by definition, the receiver appointed must be an administrative receiver for the purposes of s29(2). This is so even where a non-administrative receiver has already been appointed pursuant to any number of fixed-charge assets which may extend to the whole or substantially the whole of the company's property. In reality, this depends on whether any 'global' floating charge is stated in the debenture as extending to the whole of a company's business and undertaking or merely their portion which is not subject to a fixed charge in favour of the debenture-holder. For the purposes of flexibility, the former arrangement is preferable. Clearly, in all cases, care should be taken to ascertain in advance whether or not any particular receivership is of an administrative nature or not in view of the above and the potential criminal sanctions involved.

In the case of a joint appointment, as is common practice, and which may in theory comprise an unlimited number of persons, the appointment or nomination must declare whether any act done or authorised under any enactment to be done by the appointors is to be done 'by all or any one or more of the persons' for the time being holding the office (s231(2)). This has two important implications. First, all or any one or more of the jointly-appointed administrative receivers must be appropriately qualified, as set out above, to act as such in relation to the company. This is because s230(2) expressly provides that when an administrative receiver of a company is appointed, he must be a person who is so qualified. Whilst s231(1) imports a plural meaning into references in the singular in that particular provision, no such reference exists in relation to s230. Nevertheless, each appointee in the case of a joint appointment is, as such, appointed as an administrative receiver. Furthermore, the Interpretation Act 1978 s6(c) will import a plural meaning into any singular reference in the statute in any case. Secondly, and following from this, an appointor seeking to make a joint appointment should not permit an unqualified person, such as a qualified chartered surveyor who is not a qualified insolvency practitioner, to take up a joint appointment as an administrative receiver, on pain of criminal sanction.

The acceptance formalities applicable to the appointment are considered further in Chapter 11. A number of points arising in relation to joint and several appointments are considered in Chapter 5 at para 5.7.


## 7.7   Does the Appointee Possess Adequate Professional Expertise ?

Practically speaking, an adviser on the validity of an appointment will wish to consider carefully the commercial and professional expediency of raising the matter of professional expertise of an appointee who is also qualified to act as insolvency practitioner with requisite qualifications pursuant to s390. A licenced insolvency practitioner is, by virtue of his position, a highly qualified individual and, as such, is expressly permitted by the legislation to act as an office-holder (s388). This is not, however, to say that all insolvency practitioners are infallible and appropriate for all possible appointments, or that formal qualification is a substitute for practical experience. Indeed, in certain circumstances, it may be that the nature of the appointment and the particular identity, age, experience and specialisation of the appointee is such that it is only appropriate that the matter should be raised by appointee's adviser.

Two background factors warrant consideration here. First, any appointee will usually have the technical and administrative support of colleagues and support staff. This is subject, of course, to the proviso that any such person is neither appointed as administrative receiver nor is or will be entitled to act as such if not so qualified. Secondly, the adviser on the validity of the appointment is not usually (but may be) approached by a debenture-holder to suggest eligible appointee(s) to an office. Instead, usually the adviser's services are employed by the prospective office-holder *inter alia* to advise on the legal validity of the appointment and the conduct of the administrative receivership, as opposed to the commercial wisdom of the office-holder's appointment. This statement will not have a universal application and such advice may be sought in certain cases. Whether or not the adviser wishes in any particular circumstance to raise the question of the appointee is a matter for himself and his partners, although the matter clearly remains a sensitive one.

## 7.8 Does the Appointment Contravene Ethical Considerations?

The Department of Trade and Industry, together with each of the professional bodies of which a licenced insolvency practitioner may be a member, issues ethical guidelines which may give rise to a proposed appointee refusing an appointment, invariably on the grounds of a conflict of interest. The guidelines place heavy emphasis on the importance of ethical considerations relating to professional independence and conflicts of interests in relation to the acceptance of appointments. These epitomise the self-regulation of this area and call for a high degree of pro-active, subjective professional judgement.

An appointment should not be accepted *inter alia* where an insolvency practitioner or a practice associate (being a fellow partner, consultant or senior employee) has undertaken a previous professional appointment or work assignment involving administrative receivership following audit or liquidation (compulsory or creditors' voluntary) work itself following an administrative receivership where the work has arisen within a three-year period on a separate basis. These instances are not exhaustive, however, and the DTI guidelines go on to provide:

> It cannot be too strongly emphasised that [the matters discussed above] are not exhaustive of the cases in which a conflict of interest may arise. Any circumstances where the practitioner's interests may, or may seem to, conflict with the interests of those to whom he owes duties must be the subject of consideration by the practitioner as to whether he can act.

It should be noted that the test is not wholly subjective in this regard; the DTI Guidelines expressly provide that, with regard to the acceptance of appointments with a potential conflict of interest, 'the view of a reasonably informed third party conversant with insolvency law and practice ... should be considered'.

One situation in which the acceptance of an appointment will require special care is where the proposed appointee (or individuals connected with him) is a shareholder in the company to which the appointment relates. This is because the proposed administrative receiver may be privy in the conduct of his work to information on the basis of which he may benefit personally, either by selling his shares to avoid a loss or by retaining them with a view to making a profit on sale. This scenario would also give rise to potential financial liability on the part of the office-holder for insider dealing in certain public company securities. This potential conflict is actually less likely to arise in the case of a company listed on the Official List of the London Stock Exchange, as it is normal for a listing to be suspended, usually in advance of an appointment, at the request of the company, where a listed company goes into receivership or appears likely to do so.

221

One of the most common situations in which ethical considerations will arise is where a proposed appointee (or his firm) has undertaken an investigation of the company at the request of a creditor immediately prior to the appointment. The appointment of the investigating individual will not *per se* constitute a breach of professional ethics provided that, at the time of the investigation, the company was aware that the creditor instigating the investigation was the client of the individual (or his firm) undertaking the investigation, and that the individual's primary duty of care in conducting his investigation was owed to the creditor. Further reference should be made here to Chapter 2 at para 2.2.

It appears that there is no objection in principle on professional grounds to an individual taking more than one appointment as administrative receiver over member companies of a group. This will be the case even where the interests of those companies may conflict to some extent by, say, the existence of cross-group guarantees, the liabilities of which are secured by the debentures pursuant to which the various administrative receiver appointments are made, provided that, on balance of convenience, the advantages of having a single appointee or co-appointee can be shown to outweigh the disadvantages carried by conflict of interest problems within the group (*Re Arrows Ltd (No2)* [1992] BCC 121).

The DTI Guidance Notes for persons authorised by Accounting Professional Bodies to act as insolvency practitioner go on to provide (at para 10) that where a firm or a partner or persons at that time have, or during the previous three years have had, a continuing professional relationship with a company, no partner or employee of the practice should accept an appointment as an administrative or non-administrative receiver (or as a supervisor of a voluntary arrangement or administrator) of that company. For these purposes, a 'continuing professional relationship' is deemed to commence at the date of a practice appointed by a client, at the date of the issue of letters of engagement or at the commencement of work, whichever is earliest. Furthermore, in relation to practice mergers, transfers of parties and employees, the Guidelines also provide that where a partner or an employee of a practice has, in any former practice, undertaken work upon the affairs of a company in a capacity which is incompatible with an insolvency assignment of his new practice, he should not personally work or be employed on that assignment, save in the case of an employee of such junior status that his duties in the former practice did not involve the exercise of any professional judgement or discretion.

As stated previously, in all cases, a potentially unethical appointment should be fully deliberated and a full note of these deliberations made. Ideally, these deliberations should be undertaken with other members of the appointee's firm at partner level and, where appropriate, clarification should be sought from the relevant professional body. Where an appointment is felt to be unethical this will not render the appointment invalid *per se*. However, an unethical appointment brings with it the possible allegation of and sanctions for professional misconduct. Inevitably, this will also usually bring with it unwelcome publicity and professional criticism. It hardly needs stating that this particular brand of notoriety is best avoided at virtually any cost.

## 7.9 Have the Relevant Notification and Acceptance Formalities on Appointment been carried out?

The procedural formalities on and following appointment are considered in Chapter 11, to which reference should be made.

## Chapter Eight

# The Powers of the
# Administrative Receiver

## 8.1 Introduction

This chapter is concerned with the powers exercisable by an office-holder in
the course of an administrative receivership. It deals with those powers which
are conferred by statute, as well as dealing with the effect which the provisions of a debenture may have in modifying the statutorily implied powers.
For the purposes of this chapter and the remaining chapters of this book, it is
assumed that the administrative receiver and his legal advisers are satisfied
that he fulfils the s29 definition as such and has been validly appointed and
that the necessary acceptance formalities, as dealt with in Chapter 11, have
been complied with.

The administrative receiver's powers derive both directly and indirectly
from statute, and are encroached upon by the various duties (as developed by
the courts, and dealt with in the next chapter). Unlike a liquidator, an administrative receiver has no power to appoint a special manager, to disclaim onerous property or leasehold property or to make over assets to employees (see
ss166, 178, 179, 187). Similarly, unlike a liquidator or administrator, an
administrative receiver has no power to attack antecedent transactions under
ss238, 239 and 245 or to seek a variation or the setting-aside of a transaction
as an extortionate credit transaction under s244.

## 8.2 The Statutory Powers

The powers of an administrative receiver are far-reaching. The Cork Committee recommended that the powers should be put on a statutory footing to
avoid lengthy repetition of the powers in the body of debenture documents
generally. This was for the very practical reason that any person dealing with
an administrative receiver would not then have to make specific reference to
the debenture pursuant to which the administrative receiver was appointed in
order to check whether a particular power had been conferred on the office-

holder. This view was taken notwithstanding the provisions which would operate in favour of a third party in any case (see s42(3) and Companies Act 1985 s35 (as amended) and the rule in *Turquand's case* (1856) 6 E&B 327). The administrative receiver's powers had been put on a statutory footing in Scotland for some time previous to this by virtue of the Companies (Floating Charges and Receivers) (Scotland) Act 1972 s15 and had been seen to operate satisfactorily in that jurisdiction.

It is incorrect to state that the powers of an administrative receiver, as conferred by Sched 1 to the Act, derive directly from statute. Rather, the powers of the administrative receiver, as conferred by the debenture pursuant to which he is appointed, are deemed to include the very broad powers contained in Sched 1 to the Act, as set out below, except to the extent that they are inconsistent with any of the powers expressly conferred by the debenture. The statutory powers are therefore deemed to be implied into the debenture subject to contrary intention and, as such, may be viewed as being conferred on the administrative receiver by the directors of the company on a contingent basis (ie on the appointment being made) at the time the debenture is executed.

The 22 specific powers conferred in Sched 1 are very broad and are complemented by a 23rd general power 'to do all other things incidental to the exercise of the foregoing powers'. In practice, it is common for a debenture to set out a wide range of powers being conferred on the administrative receiver notwithstanding the implications of Sched 1. The reasons why such powers appear in standard-form debentures is that such documents must necessarily cater for the possibility that the receiver appointed under their terms is a non-administrative receiver, such as an LPA receiver, who will not enjoy the powers which are specifically conferred on every administrative receiver. The powers of an LPA receiver as provided for by statute are very limited, although the Law of Property Act 1925 s101 permits their exclusion in a debenture (which is common in practice). This is not problematic, since the scope of the powers commonly set out in standard-form debentures simply echo the powers implied by Sched 1, albeit in varying terminology. As a matter of course, however, a check should be made of the powers set out in the debenture since these will operate to vary, modify or limit the powers in Sched 1 to the extent that they are inconsistent with those powers by virtue of s42(1). In practice, substantive variations, modifications and limitations are rare. Alternatively, the powers set out in the debenture may actually extend the Sched 1 powers although it is difficult to see how the powers may usefully be extended, at least in the vast majority of cases, other than as suggested below.

The powers conferred on the administrative receiver as contained in Sched 1 are as follows:

(1) Power to take possession of, collect and get in the property of the company and, for these purposes, to take such proceedings as may be seen to him expedient.

(2) Power to sell or otherwise dispose of the property of the company by public auction or private auction or private contract or, in Scotland, to sell, feu, hire out or otherwise dispose of the property of the company by public roup or private bargain. The term 'otherwise dispose of property' would appear to permit the administrative receiver to exchange property of the company for any form of property and not only cash which apparently limits the scope of the term 'sell'; see *Re Westminster Property Group plc* [1985] 1 WLR 676 (a liquidation case).

The onset of liquidation will not affect the power of the administrative receiver to convey property in the name of the company notwithstanding the loss of the administrative receiver's deemed agency for the company. A prohibition would otherwise be imposed by s127, which precludes any disposition of the property of a company after the commencement of winding-up and which is applicable, for example, in the case of ss239 and 245. The reason for this is that the relevant disposition of the assets subject to the administrative receiver is deemed to be 'backdated' to the assignment in favour of the debenture-holder, which takes place on the crystallisation of the floating charge pursuant to which the administrative receiver is appointed (*Sowman v David Samuel Trust Ltd* [1978] 1 WLR 22).

(3) Power to raise or borrow money and grant security therefor over the property of the company. This would not appear to permit the creation of security which ranks in priority to that held by the appointing debenture-holder.

(4) Power to appoint a solicitor or accountant or other professionally qualified person to assist him in the performance of his functions.

This power enables the administrative receiver to appoint advisers to his office and to facilitate the delegation of specific tasks to third parties, such as debt collectors and land agents. It will also enable the administrative receiver to appoint an independent trustee, as required by the regulations made for the purposes of the Pension Schemes Act 1993. The power to appoint solicitors, accountants and other professionally qualified individuals is complemented by para 13, which enables payment to be made for those services. The reference to 'other professionally qualified person' would permit direct access to counsel and the employment of the services of other specialists such as valuers etc.

(5) Power to bring or defend any action or other legal proceedings in the name and on behalf of the company.

This power entitles the administrative receiver to protect company assets and to pursue any right of action belonging to the company in relation to a charged property, such as obtaining vacant possession or recovery of debts due to the company.

The onset of liquidation will not affect the power of the administrative receiver to enforce *in rem* rights (eg the benefit of contracts existing at the date of the winding-up) which may be pursued by the administrative receiver in the name of the company. This arose in *Gough's Garages Ltd v Pugsley* [1930] 1 KB 615 in which a receiver was entitled to pursue a right to apply for a new lease under the Landlord and Tenant Act 1927 s5 in the name of the company irrespective of its liquidation; see also *Hargreaves v Action 2000* [1993] BCLC 1111 (and at first instance per Fox-Andrews J).

In certain cases the courts may be prepared to permit the directors (or contributories of the company by way of derivative action) to commence or continue proceedings in the name of the company; see para 8.11 and also *Rottenberg v Monjack* [1992] BCC 688. The question of costs in litigation is dealt with in Chapter 13 at para 13.5.

(6) Power to refer to arbitration any question affecting the company.

(7) Power to effect and maintain insurances in respect of the business and property of the company.

(8) Power to use the company's seal.

Some doubt had existed previously as to whether a receiver may validly use the company's seal. This uncertainty stemmed from the fact that the power was invariably vested in the board of directors or their nominated agents by the company's articles of association. Doubt on the point is now obviated in the case of an administrative receiver by the operation of Sched 1. This is because the statutorily implied powers are conferred for the preservation, protection and realisation of the company's assets (s42(2)(b)) which the board may validly delegate to the administrative receiver, albeit on a contingent basis, by executing the debenture pursuant to which the office-holder is appointed.

(9) Power to do all acts and to execute in the name and on behalf of the company any deed, receipt or other document.

(10) Power to draw, accept, make or endorse any bill of exchange or promissory note in the name and on behalf of the company.

(11) Power to appoint any agent to do any business which he is unable to do himself or which can more conveniently be done by an agent, and power to employ and dismiss employees.

The actual appointment of the administrative receiver may of itself bring about the termination of an employee's contract of employment; see Chapter 2 at para 2.4.3.

(12) Power to do all such things (including the carrying out of works) as may be necessary for the realisation of the property of the company.

This would enable the office-holder to complete unfinished contracts.

(13) Power to make any payment which is necessary or incidental to the performance of his functions.

It is arguable that the power is not sufficiently broad to cover payment in respect of pre-receivership debts, although such payments may be permitted under the previous paragraph where payment is a pre-condition, for example, of continued supplies by a creditor.

(14) Power to carry on the business of the company.

(15) Power to establish subsidiaries of the company.

(16) Power to transfer to subsidiaries of the company the whole or any part of the business and property of the company.

This and the preceding power enable the administrative receiver to hive down the business of the company or any part of it together with the property of the company. Hiving down is considered more fully in Chapter 13 at para 13.6.

(17) Power to grant or accept a surrender of a lease or tenancy of any of the property of the company, and to take a lease or tenancy of any property required or convenient for the business of the company;

(18) Power to make any arrangement or compromise on behalf of the company.

(19) Power to call up any uncalled capital of the company.

As with the power to use the company's seal, doubt was cast previously on the ability of a receiver to call up uncalled capital of the company, on the basis that the power must be expressly conferred on the receiver by the articles of association as is rare, the power normally being conferred on the directors or their agent. Again, these doubts will no longer be relevant to an administrative receiver, assuming that the power is not removed by the debenture itself, since the power will be validly delegated by the directors, which will usually be permitted by the company's articles of association, in favour of the administrative receiver by the board executing the debenture in favour of the debenture-holder. This point again assumes that uncalled capital falls within the assets which constitute the debenture-holder's security. This will usually be the case in most standard-form debentures.

This power also puts beyond question the previously disputed matter of whether a receiver may call up uncalled capital of the company. This had been problematic since there are no statutory provisions which alter the normal position under a company's articles of association whereby the only persons entitled to get in the company's uncalled capital are the directors of the company. It would now follow on the basis of the wording in s42(2)(b) and Sched 1 that, on the creation of a debenture entitling the debenture-holder to appoint an administrative receiver, this power is effectively delegated on a contingent basis to the administrative receiver. Although not altogether clear, it is submitted that the onset of liquidation will not affect the administrative receiver's power to call up uncalled capital, assuming that this is subject to the security held by the debenture-holder (cf *Fowler v Broad's Patent Nightlight Co* [1893] 1 Ch 724).

(20) Power to rank and claim in the bankruptcy, insolvency, sequestration or liquidation of any person indebted to the company and to receive dividends, and to accede to trust deeds for the creditors of any such person.

The term 'person' employed in this provision will extend to both individual and corporate persons.

This power enables the administrative receiver to enter into formal insolvency proceedings and compromise arrangements on behalf of the company. As with the commencement of legal proceedings, it must be assumed that the power envisages action by the administrative receiver in the name of the company, since any debt claimed by him will enure for the benefit of the company itself. The power would extend to those in operation under either domestic or extra-territorial jurisdiction in the absence of contrary provision. Notably, the power would not appear to extend to participation in informal arrangements and work out arrangements. This is not problematic, however, since the power in para 18 *above* would probably cover such matters.

(21) Power to present or defend a petition for the winding-up of the company.

The express power conferred by Sched 1, para 21 to present a petition for the winding-up of a company operates to confirm the decision of Brightman J in *Re Emmadart Ltd* [1979] 1 All ER 599 which held that a receiver has power to present a winding-up petition in the name of the company as a power incidental to his power to take steps to preserve the property constituting the security of the debenture-holder. The decision in *Re Emmadart Ltd* is good authority for the contention that the petition may be presented by the administrative receiver as the agent of the company in the company's name. A petition presented by an administrative receiver to wind up the company may be made in the name of the administrative receiver although, possibly as a result of a drafting error, no express mention is made of the administrative receiver (or an administrator) in s124(1) which provides for the application. It is also noteworthy that IR r4.7(7)(a) makes reference to a petition presented by an administrator although again the rules themselves contain no mention of an administrative receiver. This too may well amount to a drafting oversight.

The cumulative effect of two recent decisions is that the courts will usually override objections to the winding-up by unsecured creditors, provided that the administrative receivers are able to show that by seeking a winding-up they are acting in the interests of unsecured creditors of the company as a whole.

In *Re Leigh Estates (UK) Ltd* [1994] BCC 292, Richard Sykes QC, sitting as a Deputy High Court Judge, refused to grant a winding-up petition presented by a rating authority in respect of unpaid rates of some £71,000. This was on the basis of evidence presented by the administrative receiver and its appointing bank which indicated that there would be financial disadvantages to the receivership, secured creditors and any unsecured creditors (in the remote case of a dividend being payable) if a winding-up order was to be made. Notably, the judge considered that the view of the company itself was one to which weight would not normally be attached in exercising the discretion as to whether a winding-up order should be made. No similar consideration was applied to other companies in the group, as these were indebted to the same syndicate of banks on whose behalf the administrative receiver acted and therefore could be treated as synonymous for the purposes of the petition. The judge made it clear that the court must weigh up the relative position of those for and against the winding-up petition. In the event that secured creditors would suffer a shortfall on their security, they should be treated as unsecured creditors for that balance. The motive for seeking the winding-up order should also be scrutinised and, in particular, the effect on the debt or security held by secured creditors generally.

*Re Anvil Estates Ltd* (1993), unreported, involved the issue of a petition by administrative receivers that was opposed by the company, which disputed the validity of the appointment. As a consequence, the appointing bank debenture-holder was substituted as petitioning creditor. This was opposed by the shareholders of the company, primarily on the ground that neither the administrative receivers nor their appointer was entitled to petition until the amount that would be recovered in the receivership had been ascertained. The court, in rejecting an argument by counsel for the shareholders based on *Re Exmouth Docks* [1873] Comm 181 to the effect that the petition should be adjourned until all assets had been realised, held that that decision was limited to its own special facts. Somewhat unfortunately, the judge felt unable to rely on the decision in the *Leigh Estates* case (*above*), since only an uncertified copy of the judgment was available at that time. Nevertheless, the judge did approve the submission by the banks in the *Leigh Estates* case to the effect that if the court is satisfied that there will be a shortfall on the claims of secured creditors then it should treat them as unsecured creditors to the extent of their shortfall. It is also unfortunate that the judge did not rule specifically on the proposition raised by counsel for the bank: that a secured creditor is entitled to petition for winding-up irrespective of any shortfall it may suffer. It is submitted that the better view is that it may not and, in accordance with both the *Leigh Estate* and *Anvil Estates* cases, should be treated as an unsecured creditor for the balance of any shortfall. Whilst the *Anvil Estates* case actually considered the right of a secured creditor to petition for winding-up, as was opposed by the receiver, the implication of both decisions, in effect, is that the court should weigh up the effect of the winding-up petition on both secured and unsecured creditors as it perceives them, and the motive behind it.

A number of practical points arise when an administrative receiver considers opposing or presenting a winding-up petition. First, where a petition is opposed there is likely to be at least one adjournment of the matter, since the winding-up petition will be heard in the first instance by a district judge who has no inherent jurisdiction to decide an opposed petition. The matter is then adjourned to the judge (see *Practice Direction* [1986] 1 WLR 1428). Secondly, an administrative receiver should be mindful of the fact that he may be ordered to pay the costs of the successful petition personally (ie not as an expense of the administrative receivership) where he unsuccessfully opposes a winding-up petition (see Supreme Court Act 1981 s51). In reality, an administrative receiver is unlikely in most cases to find that his decision to present a winding-up petition is challenged. Nevertheless, he will commonly wish to comfort unsecured creditors by providing confirmation of the time at which he intends or proposes to put the company into liquidation. In practice, the court will give very significant weight to the unsecured creditors; see *Re ABC Coupler and Engineering Co* [1961] 1 WLR 243. The application will usually be made on the basis that the company is insolvent for the purposes of ss122 and 123. Perhaps the best evidence with which the court can be presented in these circumstances is the statement of affairs drawn up for the purposes of s47 by the administrative receiver. This will contain a formal statement of his assessment of the company's assets and liabilities, which will reflect formal statements made to him by the company's directors.

Finally, a receiver may wish to consider negotiating a dismissal of the winding-up petition on terms such as in consideration of an undertaking to restructure the company and then present a winding-up petition. The personal risks posed by undertakings, however, render such a course of action unattractive for the receiver.

(22)   Power to change the situation of the company's registered office.

This power was inserted on the recommendation of the Cork Committee to enable the administrative receiver to relocate the company's registered office to an area of lower rents and rates.

(23)   Power to do all other things incidental to the exercise of the foregoing powers.

This general power relates only to the doing of those things specifically provided for in the preceding 22 paragraphs. Matters falling outside the scope of these specific and general powers will require specific authorisation in the terms of the debenture itself or, alternatively, express authorisation by the company itself; see, for example, *Simpson Curtis Pension Trustee Ltd v Readson Ltd* (1994) unreported.

Notwithstanding the broad scope of the powers implied by Sched 1 and the apparent relative safety provided by a sweeping-up 'general purpose' clause, it is also advisable to include four further express provisions into any debenture pursuant to which an administrative receiver is appointed. In practice, some, but not all, standard-form debentures as employed by many financial institutions contain some or all of these. The first of these is an extension of the scope of the general power in Sched 1, para 23 by the inclusion of a further general power empowering the receiver to do all other things incidental to or appropriate or necessary for the preservation, improvement, disposal or realisation of the assets, business or property of the company and any asset, business or property in which the company may have an interest. It is arguable, however, that a reference in such an extension to any property in which the company may have an interest probably goes too far to be correct on technical grounds. This is because the administrative receiver's appointment will only be effective for the purposes of s29 in relation to property of which the company is beneficial owner by virtue of the definition of property in s436; as such, it will not include property in which the company may have an equitable interest or property that is subject to an effective retention of title clause; cf s15(2) as applicable to administrators.

The second express provision to be considered in extending Sched 1 is an express power to pursue and complete any development work which the receiver considers it appropriate to undertake. Such a power does not sit squarely with any of the express powers in Sched 1 and this may therefore fall outside the scope of a power to do all other things incidental to the exercise of these powers. A power to undertake development work is of clear practical use where a particular asset is of little or negligible value in an uncompleted state but is likely to attract significant value on completion. In practice, a secured lender will usually consider, and is well advised to consider, taking separate security over such an asset in the terms of either a separate fixed charge or a fixed and floating charge debenture.

The third provision which should also be considered is a further express power to lease out assets of the company which, in practice, may be the only viable way of dealing with a particular and unusual asset.

Fourthly, consideration should be given to a debenture containing an express declaration that the receiver is appointed as agent of the company, notwithstanding the deemed agency implied until the onset of liquidation by virtue of s44(1)(a). The drawback with this statutory provision is that it may be argued that its scope does not extend to any power, such as the three further points suggested above, which do not appear in or are not implied by Sched 1 but which are expressly conferred on the receiver by the debenture itself. This argument, it is submitted, is a tenuous one. However, a debenture-holder will be well advised to guard against the possibility of such litigation, which would necessarily be founded on the rule in *Deyes v Wood* [1911] 1 KB 806.

In providing for extra powers to those implied by Sched 1 it is imperative that these are provided for in the debenture itself as applicable to both administrative and non-administrative receivers (or receivers and managers generally) since any receiver or manager appointed may of course not constitute an administrative receiver. The same consideration explains the provision of the Sched 1 powers in the debenture itself.

## 8.3 The Distinction Between the Administrative Receiver's *in rem* and Purely Personal Powers

There is an obvious temptation at a practical level to shy away from analysis of the legal nature of the administrative receiver's powers. This may be because the powers appear to be universal and such as to enable the office-holder to do virtually anything in the course of his office. This view is, however, rather one-dimensional, in that the legal nature of the administrative receiver's powers falls into two classes which, at times, overlap. The first class, the *in rem* powers, are those which are conferred on the administrative receiver for the purposes of the enforcement of the debenture-holder's security and which are exercised in right of the debenture-holder. These *in rem* powers will therefore include any power conferred for the getting in, maintenance of and realisation of the assets comprising the debenture-holder's security. The second class of the administrative receiver's powers, his purely personal or agency powers, comprise all other powers conferred on the debenture-holder which, broadly speaking, will relate to the carrying on of the company's business and notably the entering into of new contracts on behalf of the company as its agent.

Whilst the distinction between and exercise of *in rem* powers and personal powers is of purely academic relevance during the course of the administrative receivership, it becomes of paramount importance when the company goes into liquidation as defined in s247(2). This is because on a winding-up, the deemed agency of the administrative receiver for the company is terminated by virtue of s44(1)(a). As a consequence, the administrative receiver's purely personal powers will terminate other than to the extent that they are capable of being viewed as exercised for the enforcement of the debenture-holder's security. The administrative receiver's *in rem* powers, on the other hand, remain unaffected by winding-up. Essentially, this is because the commencement of the winding-up will do nothing to alter the fact that the company's interest in the charged assets remains in the equity of redemption of those assets which are subject to the administrative receiver who is appointed *inter alia* and primarily to protect, preserve and realise those assets as well as exercising his purely personal powers to manage and carry on the company's business and matters incidental thereto, those powers terminating on the commencement of the liquidation. The distinction between *in rem* and personal powers will be of relevance from the outset in the relatively uncommon scenario in which the administrative receiver is appointed following the commencement of the winding-up.

As a consequence of the termination of the administrative receiver's agency by virtue of s44(1)(a) and, as such, his purely personal powers, the administrative receiver will become personally liable on any contract entered into on the basis of the exercise of such powers and in respect of which no statutory indemnity from the company's assets will operate under s44(1)(c), other than with the authority or ratification of the liquidator. It follows that, after the commencement of winding-up, a clause inserted into a contract by an administrative receiver which purports to exclude personal liability will have no effect other than if it is authorised expressly or ratified by the liquidator. On the other hand, winding-up will not affect the administrative receiver's *in rem* powers, which will continue to be exercised for the benefit of the debenture-holder. As a consequence it remains of no significance whether the powers are exercised in the name of the company or in the name of the debenture-holder as chargee (*Sowman v David Samuel Trust Ltd* [1978] 1 All ER 616).

The *in rem* powers of an administrative receiver would appear to include both his power to realise company assets and to convey them, on the basis of the decisions in *Barrows v Chief Land Registrar* (1977) *The Times*, 20 October and the *Sowman* case (above), which both confirm the ability of a receiver to convey a legal estate following the commencement of winding-up. In practice, it will not always be clear whether the exercise of a particular power constitutes the exercise of an *in rem* power or of a personal power. In cases of doubt, therefore, an approach should be made to the liquidator with a view to his authorising the transaction, most effectively, by his joining into it.

The commencement of winding-up will also not affect any power of attorney conferred by the company in favour of either the administrative receiver and/or the debenture-holder. In practice, the former is more common than the latter. The power of attorney will be most useful in relation to disposal of the company's property. A power of attorney which is given to secure a proprietary interest or the performance of some obligation is not affected by winding-up provided the donee of the power is not aware of its revocation or discharge (Power of Attorney Act 1971 s4(1)(ii)). Furthermore, and provided the donee of the power is not aware that it has been discharged, a power of attorney may be agreed as being conferred on both the administrative receiver and the debenture-holder where it is only expressly conferred on the latter, but not vice versa. This is because the Power of Attorney Act 1971 s4(2) provides that a power of attorney given for the purposes as described in relation to s4(1)(ii) above may be given to the person entitled to the interest or obligation (ie the debenture-holder) and persons deeming title to that interest under him (ie the administrative receiver). As such, the administrative receiver will be able to exercise the power of attorney, which may include affixing the company's seal, for the purposes of realising and disposing of the company's property irrespective of winding-up.

## 8.4  Power to Apply to the Court for Directions: s35

Section 35(1) permits an application to be made to the court for directions in relation to any matter arising in connection with the performance of the functions of the receiver or manager, of which an administrative receiver is a species (s29(2)). Although the application may be made to the court either by a receiver or manager of the property of the company appointed under powers contained in an appropriate instrument, or by the persons by whom or on whose behalf the receiver or manager has been so appointed, it is submitted that an application should not be made by the administrative receiver himself where any aspect of his appointment is in question. This is because, where doubt exists as to the validity of the appointment, the administrative receiver would not appear to be, in clear terms at least, a receiver or manager 'so appointed' and, therefore, would appear to fall potentially beyond the scope of s35(1). Instead, the application would appear to be made most appropriately to the court by the appointing debenture-holder. The contrary view, of course, is that the office-holder is 'so appointed' albeit potentially invalidly.

On a s35(1) application, the court may give such directions, or may make such order declaring the rights of persons before the court or otherwise, as it thinks fit (s35(2)). In the absence of clear judicial authority, this provision would appear to enable the court either to make an order declaring an appointment valid (or invalid) or even to give directions for such remedial action as necessary to render an appointment valid.

In practice, s35 is an extremely useful device and may be utilised by an administrative receiver as a definitive method of problem-solving, particularly where an issue is contested by two or more interested parties and on which the formal legal advice provided to the office-holder by his solicitors, and possibly counsel, reveals that the issue is not one on which a clear answer may be given. One notable example of such disputes in recent years is the actual status of purportedly fixed and/or floating charges over book debts, the outcome of which clearly affected preferred creditors who take subject to fixed charges but in priority to floating charges.

An application under s35 is made by originating summons with affidavit in support, and will normally be heard by the judge dealing with Companies' Court business, subject to local court practice (see RSC Ord 102 r2). The costs of a s35(1) direction hearing application are usually awarded against the unsuccessful party, in accordance with normal practice. However, an application may not always necessarily involve an 'unsuccessful party', such as when it is made to clarify, say, the validity of a purported appointment by a debenture-holder. Thus, if the company's creditors generally have an interest in the outcome of the application then the court may, at its discretion, order costs to be paid out of the assets of the company which are subject to the administrative receivership (see *Re Westdock Realisations* [1988] BCLC 354).

## 8.5   Power to Dispose of Charged Property: s43

Section 43(1) provides that where, on an application by the administrative receiver, the court is satisfied that the disposal (with or without other assets) of any relevant property which is subject to a security would be likely to promote a more advantageous realisation of the company's assets than would otherwise be effected, the court may authorise the administrative receiver to dispose of the property as if it were not subject to the charge. This power is not available to non-administrative receivers. It will be impossible to confer a power equivalent to s43 on a non-administrative receiver except perhaps by way of a multi-party agreement to that effect which, in practice, would almost certainly be unworkable.

For the purposes of s43, 'relevant property' refers to that property of which the administrative receiver is or, but for the appointment of some other person as the receiver of part of the company's property, would be receiver or manager (s43(7)). It is clear from this provision that s43 will only extend to property which is beneficially owned by the company and not, for example, goods subject to an effective retention of title clause or trust assets.

Section 43(1) does not apply to security which is held by or on whose behalf the administrative receiver is appointed or in relation to any security to which a security so held has priority (s43(2)). The former exception extends, for example, to any member of the syndicate of banks where the appointment is effected by a lead bank on behalf of members of the syndicate. In the latter case it remains unclear as to whether s43(1) applies only to charges which rank subsidiary to the security pursuant to which the administrative receiver is appointed in terms of priority, notwithstanding the apparent clear wording of the provision. It is submitted that the better view is that s43 does in fact apply to subsidiary charges, for the simple reason that a conveyance which is executed either by the company at the direction of the administrative receiver, or by the administrative receiver himself as agent of the company, will not of itself operate to overreach any subordinate security interest since, in effect, the conveyance will be as if entered into by the company as principal in either case. As such, this is capable of overreaching neither the interests of the appointing debenture-holder nor any securities which rank subsidiary to it.

In effect, the only way in which subordinate security interests may be effectively dealt with in practice by an administrative receiver is for him to obtain from the holders of all subsidiary interests appropriate vacating receipts, which would usually be subject to undertakings as to handing over on completion to the purchaser or transferee of the property. The obtaining of such discharges and/or undertakings from subsidiary chargees is also likely to avoid delay at the Land Registry, because the Land Registry will require formal indication of the various discharges before amending the register to give effect to the transaction itself.

Since s43 appears merely to enable an administrative receiver to apply to the court for the purposes of effecting a sale of property which is subject to a prior charge, it is submitted that this may operate equally in the case of subsidiary charges as an alternative to the administrative receiver obtaining discharges from any subsidiary chargees. Clearly this will have an application where those chargees are either impossible to trace or uncooperative. The principal drawback with this view is that the wording of s43(1) and (2) appears expressly to exclude subsidiary charges from the scope of the provisions. In reality, it is submitted that the provisions must have effect in relation to subsidiary charges, since the presumption that the administrative receiver may dispose of property free of those subsidiary interests without the requirement for further formality is misguided.

There are two conditions which apply to the making of an order under s43. First, the net proceeds of the disposal of the charged relevant property must be applied towards discharging the sums secured by the security (s43(3)(a)). Where those net proceeds are less than the court deems to be the net amount which would have been realised on an open market sale of the property by a willing vendor, then any sums constituting the shortfall must be applied in making good that deficiency (s43(3)(b)). In other words, the deficiency will be made up from assets subject to the appointing debenture-holder's security which rank in priority to the debenture-holder and other creditors, including preferential creditors, unless of course, the prior-ranking securities are floating charge security 'as created' for the purposes of s251.

It is unclear whether the court has power to vary what it considers to be a 'willing vendor' and 'open market' value after that is fixed by the court initially. This would be relevant in an unstable market, and might operate to the considerable benefit of a prior-ranking security-holder if the price fixed was rendered unrealistic subsequently in a rapidly falling market. The same would also be true if it transpired that the evidence upon which the court based its judgment in exercising its discretion was shown subsequently to be defective. For these reasons it would seem inequitable to stipulate that the court may not amend its initial valuation. That variation may be effected, it seems, on the application of the administrative receiver himself, in the absence of any contrary provision in s43.

The second condition applicable to an order under s43 is an extension of the first, and deals with the situation where two or more securities rank in priority to the debenture-holder's security. Essentially, s43(4) requires that the net proceeds of the disposal, together with any deficiency which must be made up by the administrative receiver, must be applied towards discharging the sum secured by those securities in order of their respective priorities.

A s43 order is sought by way of an originating application to the court which is followed by an *inter partes* hearing. The procedure for this is set out in IR r3.31 and s43(5) and (6). These provide that the administrative receiver is responsible for giving notice of any s43 order to holders of prior-ranking security or securities although, in practice, service of the order itself will suffice for these purposes (IR r3.31(3)). A copy of any order must also be delivered by the administrative receiver to the Registrar of Companies within 14 days of the date of the order (s43(5)).

For further discussion on this area, including the applicability of s43 to the prior-ranking securities and the question of contracting out of the provisions, see Oditah [1991] JBL 49 and Goode, *Principles of Corporate Insolvency Law* 1990.

## 8.6 Power to Require Continued Supplies of Gas, Water, Electricity etc: s233

Section 233 permits an administrative receiver, amongst other office-holders set out in s233(1)(a)–(e), to request the 'giving of' essential public utility supplies from a relevant supplier, without first being required to discharge outstanding arrears incurred by the company to the supplier prior to the date of his appointment (s233(2)). This request may be made in respect of utility services supplied after the date on which the administrative receiver was appointed or the first of his predecessors was appointed (s233(4)(b)). Section 233 has no applicability to non-administrative receivers.

Section 233 actually implements a recommendation of the Cork Committee (at para 1462). It prevents public suppliers of utility services from taking advantage of their monopolistic position and holding the company to ransom in respect of outstanding pre-appointment arrears on pain of a discontinuation in the supply of services which are invariably vital to the continuation of the company's business. The full force of such commercial blackmail is highlighted in cases such as *Wellworth Cash and Carry (North Shields) Ltd v North Eastern Electricity Board* [1986] 2 BCC 99, 265 in which the court upheld a threat by North Eastern Electricity to discontinue utility supplies to a company in liquidation, which would have had the effect of destroying large stocks of frozen food. The threat was upheld despite the liquidator's agreement to make payment for supplies following his appointment but not to honour outstanding pre-appointment arrears. Section 233 prevents a utility supplier from seeking to recoup pre-appointment liabilities from an administrative receiver by either direct or indirect means. This would prevent indirect recoupment by a supplier which, for example, insisted on installing metering equipment calibrated in such a way as to regulate the units of supply of post-appointment supplies in terms of cost so as to cover the outstanding pre-appointment liabilities.

Section 233 is not all pervasive. Following a request by an office-holder for the giving of any of the supplies defined in s233(3), the supplier may make it a condition of giving the supply that the administrative receiver agrees to personally guarantee the payment of any charges of the continued supply (s233(2)(a)). However, the supplier may not take any steps to make it a condition of the continued supply that any outstanding charges in respect of pre-appointment supplies are paid (s233(2)(b)). The provision only offers protection, therefore, to the office-holder in respect of pre-appointment supplies, and will not afford any protection for supplies made after the appointment but before any request is made by the office-holder. To the extent that there are pre-appointment liabilities to suppliers within the scope of s233(3), as will be common in practice, they will rank as unsecured creditors of the company. In practice, it is imperative that a request for continued supply is made by the office-holder at the earliest possible time, as a matter of course, if only to avoid unnecessary disconnection and re-connection charges and the inevitable disruption and consequent expense and inconvenience which these are likely to bring about.

Section 233 has effect only in respect of public utility suppliers which operate under a legal obligation to provide their supply services. The provision, therefore, has no operation to private utility suppliers, although the following supplies, as defined, extend s233 to newly-privatised utility suppliers. Specifically, the supplies to which s233 applies are:

(a)   a public supply of gas (by the former British Gas Corporation or within the meaning of the Gas Act 1986);

(b)   a public supply of electricity (within the meaning of Part I of the Electricity Act 1989);

(c)   a supply of water (by a water undertaker, or in Scotland, a water authority as within the meaning of the Water (Scotland) Act 1980); and

(d)   a supply of telecommunication services by a public telecommunications operator (within the meaning of the Telecommunications Act 1984 other than to the extent that telecommunication services do not include local delivery services within the meaning of Part II of the Broadcasting Act 1990) (s233(3),(5)).

## 8.7   Power to Get In the Company's Property: s234

IA 1986 ss234–6 confers powers on an administrative receiver to get in the property of the company and to inquire into the company's dealings, with attendant court enforcement powers under s237, as well as imposing a duty on those broadly engaged in the management of the company, including its officers, to co-operate with the office-holder. These powers are now also available to administrative receivers as well as administrators, whereas prior to the 1986 Act they had been available only to liquidators. This, and the following two sections, consider those powers.

Section 234(2) confers a very broad power on the court to order that any person who has in his possession or control 'any property, books, papers or records to which the company *appears to be entitled*' (emphasis added) must 'pay, deliver, convey, surrender or transfer the property, books, papers or records' to the administrative receiver forthwith or within any period as the court may direct. This latter discretion exists so as, for example, to enable the person to whom the order is delivered to recover or assimilate the goods or records where they have since been disposed of or are not immediately easily recoverable. It is common in practice for an order to require the delivery up of property within seven days of the order.

An order under s234 is sought by way of an originating application which is issued with copies for service, upon which the relevant court will fix a date for the hearing. Following the service of the application on the respondent(s) affidavit evidence should be prepared, filed and served if this does not accompany the application itself. On the hearing of an application the (district) judge may grant or dismiss the application immediately, or he may give directions for the serving and filing of further affidavit evidence. Alternatively, he may refer the matter to a judge under IR r7.6(3). Following the determination of the matter the order is drawn up by the court.

One curious omission from s234 and the IR 1986 is any sanction for contravention of any order made under the provision. Notably, s234 is not expressly mentioned in IR r7.20, which provides specifically for orders enforcing compliance with the Act and the Rules. Whilst this may be taken to be an inadvertent omission by the parliamentary draftsman, it is assumed that such a matter might be dealt with as a matter of contempt by the court making the order under its own inherent jurisdiction, in the same way as applies under IR r7.20.

Section 234(3) and (4) have great practical relevance in affording the administrative receiver considerable protection where, as is common, the office-holder seizes or disposes of property which is not actually property of the company but in respect of which, at the time of the seizure or disposal, the office-holder has reasonable grounds for believing he is entitled to exercise the power of seizure or disposal (ie as empowered by the debenture, which may amend or vary the implied powers of Sched 1 of which see paras 1 and 2) (s234(3)). The provision applies whether or not the office-holder exercises his powers of seizure and/or disposal in pursuance of a court order (s234(3)(b)). The protection offered to the administrative receiver who seizes or disposes of property to which the company appears to be entitled but which is not prop-erty of the company, is that the office-holder is not liable to any person in respect of any loss or damage which results from the seizure or disposal, save to the extent that the loss or damage is caused by the negligence of the office-holder (s234(4)(a); and see s234(2)). Furthermore, in such a circumstance the administrative receiver is granted a statutory lien on the seized property or its proceeds of sale in respect of any expenses incurred in connection with the seizure or disposal (s234(4)(b)).

Section 234 will have obvious application to goods such as those on loan to or leased by or on hire purchase to the company or which are subject to an effective retention of title clause and also to those goods which are owned by, say, a company officer and which are not subject to formalised rental or hire payments. Following the appointment of an administrative receiver notifica-tion should be sent, initially by fax and subsequently by post or in person, to the office-holder at both his practice address and the address of the company, notifying the office-holder of the claim on the relevant assets and the grounds for it. The notification should clearly identify the goods to which title is claimed and should enclose copies of supporting documents such as standard terms of sale in which any retention of title clause is incorporated, delivery notes, sales invoices, etc. For the purposes of s234, notification to the office-holder of any claim on assets is important because s234(3) and (4) apply in favour of the administrative receiver only to the extent that the office-holder has 'reasonable grounds' for believing that he is entitled to seize or dispose of property.

The degree to which the reasonable grounds of the administrative receiver may be challenged for present purposes will hinge largely on the detail and accuracy of supporting documentation, and the speed with which the party alleging ownership of any property is able to bring this to the attention of the office-holder. These practical steps serve to put the administrative receiver on notice of the third party's claims on the goods, and will usually guard against the goods being disposed of or used in the company's business. If that occurs the goods may become amalgamated with other goods and therefore rendered unidentifiable. These steps should also be taken independent of any standard operational procedures implemented by the administrative receiver. These commonly involve the issuing of standard-form retention of title question-naires for completion by the apparent owner of the relevant goods or his adviser. In return for such a completed questionnaire, the office-holder will usually be prepared to enter into an undertaking for payment for the goods which are subsequently viewed as being subject to a valid claim by the third party. Such an undertaking should be insisted upon in any case as a matter of course. Nevertheless, these procedures involve some degree of delay, in which the administrative receiver will enjoy the protection of s234(3) and (4).

Subject to what is said in the next paragraphs, the practical effect of s234(4)(a) is to protect the administrative receiver from an action in conver-sion for disposing of goods which did not belong to the company, but which appeared to be goods which the office-holder had reasonable grounds for believing he was entitled to dispose of. It follows that any proceeds of sale will be held by the administrative receiver on a constructive or resulting trust for the true owner of the goods. However, in relation to these proceeds of sale, the administrative receiver benefits from the statutory lien over them created by s234(4)(b). The provision also operates without detriment to the deben-ture-hoider, since the goods disposed of by the administrative receiver could not be subject to any charge over the company's property if they had never in fact belonged to the company.

The protection offered by s234(4)(a) will apparently be lost where any loss or damage resulting from the seizure or disposal of goods which are not the property of the company, 'is caused by the office-holder's own negligence'. Such negligence might manifest itself in a failure to record or retain notifica-tion of a third party's proprietary claim to goods, such as in one of the circum-stances suggested above, or, alternatively, in the form of an error or inaccu-racy in authorising the incorrect disposal of specific assets. It is interesting that the provision refers specifically to the 'office-holder's own negligence', and does not appear to extend to negligence of any person other than the office-holder himself. This is of some importance, since it is common for much of the day-to-day administration work of an administrative receiver to be undertaken by managers and junior staff under the general oversight of the administrative receiver or joint office-holders. It is submitted that the most sensible approach to this apparent anomaly would be to treat an act of negligence by any person acting on behalf of the office-holder as an act of negligence on the part of the office-holder himself, on the basis that the negligence has been apparently authorised by the acquiescence of the office-holder in the act or omission of an individual perpetrating the negligent act or omission itself.

One further matter which remains unclear in relation to s234 is the construction of the term 'in respect of any loss or damage resulting from the seizure or sale' in s234(4)(a). One interpretation of this phrase would restrict the protection offered to the office-holder to loss or damage arising *per se*, as opposed to liability for interference with the goods themselves, other than on the basis of negligence. This should be distinguished from an action for conversion arising from wrongful seizure or disposal of goods belonging to a third party (see, for example, *Edwards v Bendall* (1953) 103 LJ 351, an analogous case on its facts which concerned a liquidation). Instead, the third party might seek to recover his assets or the proceeds of sale from the administrative receiver on the basis of the office-holder's wrongful interference *per se* with the goods, as opposed to any loss or damage resulting from the seizure or disposal of the goods. This point remains unclear, although it may be that the court will construe the scope of the present wording to include *any* loss arising as a result of seizure and/or disposal of a third party's goods other than on the basis of negligence.

It now appears that the court dealing with the hearing, and to which an application is made for an order under s234(2), may also appropriately deal with questions of disputed ownership of goods, although such a matter may be referred to a judge for a full hearing or for directions under IR r7.6(3). Alternatively, the matter may be adjourned for the filing and service of fuller evidence. The question of disputed ownership may arise since s234(2) refers to property 'to which the company appears to be entitled' and, coupled with the extensive procedures laid down in Part 7 of the IR, the court may save considerable time in deciding such matters in conjunction with a s234 application by an office-holder (see the comments of Warner J in *Re London Iron & Steel Co Ltd* [1990] BCC 159).

Finally, an administrative receiver does not enjoy the same rights as a liquidator and administrator under s246 to take possession of any property of the company which is subject to a lien over any of the books, papers or other records of the company, subject to specific exceptions, in favour of a third party, to the extent that the enforcement of the lien would deny the office-holder possession of any books, papers or other records of the company (s246(2), (3)). It is curious that s246 does not operate in favour of an administrative receiver in view of its usefulness in facilitating the insolvency procedures to which it applies, although administrative receivership may be distinguished from these as being essentially a private law remedy as opposed to a mechanism for the benefit of creditors generally. The non-applicability of s246 to administrative receivers does not, however, affect the right of the administrative receiver to inspect documents subject to the third party's lien under s236, such as in *Re Aveling Barford Ltd* [1988] 3 All ER 109, where administrative receivers were successful in obtaining an order for the production of documents over which solicitors unpaid by the company had obtained a lien.

## 8.8 Power to Require Co-operation from Officers, Employees etc: s235

Section 235 imposes a positive duty on a specified class of persons prescribed in s235(3) to co-operate with an office-holder. Office-holders for these purposes includes an administrative receiver although, notably, it does not include the supervisor of a voluntary arrangement (s235(1)). In particular, the specific class of persons to whom s235 applies must give to the administrative receiver such information concerning the company and its promotion, formation, business, dealings, affairs or property as the office-holder may reasonably require following the date on which the administrative receiver is appointed or, if he is appointed in succession to another administrative receiver, following the date on which the first of the predecessors was appointed (s235(2), (4)(b)).

### 8.8.1 Persons liable

The administrative receiver may also require attendance on him by any member of the specified class of persons at such time as the office-holder may reasonably require. No court order is required to invoke the powers of the office-holder in this regard. Section 235 is a very useful device in the sense that it enables an office-holder to elicit information on a voluntary basis from a broad class of persons in a relatively informal manner. However, where a person required to provide information or attend on the office-holder in accordance with s235 refuses to do so, the office-holder may choose to apply to the court either for such enforcement order as the court thinks fit under IR r7.20 or, alternatively, for an order summoning a person to appear before it for a private examination into the company's dealings under s236 as is considered in the next section (see para 8.9). One notable difference between s235 and s236 in this regard is that information provided under s236 must be given on oath whereas information disclosed under s235 need not be. The specified classes of person amenable to s235 comprise the following:

(a) *Those who are or have at any time been officers of the company*. The term 'officer' finds no definition in IA 1986, other than a reference in s251 to the definition in Companies Act 1985, s744. This provides a meaning which 'includes a director, manager or secretary'. Section 251 itself defines a director as including any person occupying the position of director, by whatever name they are called. Whilst the term 'officer' may be envisaged as giving rise to problems in terms of its scope, it is submitted that the matter need not be problematic on a purposive approach to the interpretation of the term. The rationale behind the apparent wide drafting of s235(3) appears to be to catch those individuals who had acted in some fiduciary capacity in relation to the company. This approach underlines the holding of the auditors of the company to be officers of the company (on which see *Re London and General Bank* [1895] 2 Ch 166, *R v Shacter* [1960] 2 QB 252 and *Re Thomas & Son Ltd* [1968] Ch 455). Therefore, it is submitted that a person will fall within the class of 'officer' of the company if they have at any time been engaged in the management of the company's business. This will include, for example, senior managers of the company, shadow directors (by virtue of s251 and Companies Act 1985 s744), or those who have at some time been engaged in the supervision of the board (see *Re A Company No 00996 of 1979* [1980] Ch 138 at 144 per Shaw LJ). This would thus extend to consultants and contractors employed by the company for whose services the company contracts, although such individuals may also fall within class (c) below.

(b) *Those who have taken part in the formation of the company at any time within one year prior to the appointment of the administrative receiver or the first of his predecessors*. This class would conceivably extend to the founders of the company as well as to the company solicitors or its bank, who have been held not to amount to officers of the company for the purposes of class (a) above (in *Re Great Western Forest of Dean's Coal Consumers' Co* (1886) 31 Ch 496 and *Re National Bank* (1870) LR 10 Eq 298 respectively).

(c) *Those who are in the employment of the company, or have been in its employment, including employment under a contract for services within the one year period prior to the appointment of the administrative receiver or the first of his predecessors*. This category includes both employees and others who render services to the company, effectively as independent contractors, under a contract for services. Thus, this provision covers accountants, solicitors, non-executive directors, consultants, agents and the like who provide services to the company and who, in practice, may have an integral role in the management of the company or a sector of its operations at a high level but who would

245

otherwise fall outside of the ambit of any other sub-class in s235(3). The liability of any person to co-operate with the office-holder under this specific class is subject to the proviso that that person must, in the opinion of the office-holder, be capable of giving the information which he requires (s235(3)(c)). It is noteworthy that no mention is made in this provision of a requirement of any degree of objective reasonableness on the part of the office-holder in forming subjective opinion on the capability of an individual to provide information sought by the office-holder. However, it may be that such a reasonableness requirement would be imposed by the court in any case.

*Prima facie*, this subsection would appear to enable an administrative receiver to require information from an entire class of employees, subject to the one-year time limit imposed by s235(3)(c) on a 'blanket basis' by, say, the distribution of standard-form questionnaires to staff. An office-holder would be well advised to inform employees of the fact that they may be in possession of information required by him and, perhaps more importantly, that a person who without reasonable excuse fails to comply with the obligation to co-operate with the office-holder under s235 is liable to a fine and, after continued contravention, a daily default fine by virtue of s235(5). An office-holder who seeks information from this class, or indeed any class, of person liable under s235(3) should ensure that the questions raised by him are clearly set out, and that those to whom interrogatories are put are afforded sufficient time to enter responses so as to fall within the scope of s235(2)(a) which enables an office-holder to seek from the specified class of person 'such information... as the office-holder may... reasonably require'.

(d) *Those who are, or have within the one-year period prior to the date of the appointment of the administrative receiver or the first of his predecessors, been officers of or in the employment of (including employment under a contract for services of) another company which is or was within the one-year period, an officer of the company in administrative receivership.* This class of persons effectively mirrors the previous class in (c) above, and extends it to those employed by any corporate officer of the company to which the administrative receiver is appointed. For the meaning of the term 'officer' reference should be made to the comments made in relation to sub-class (a) above.

(e) *In the case of a company being wound up by the court, any person who has acted as administrator, administrative receiver or liquidator of the company.* This sub-class would enable an administrative receiver in office during a liquidation to require information from an administrator, previous administrative receiver or the liquidator of the company where the company is being wound up by the court on one of the grounds in s122. It would appear that this provision operates without the imposition of any time limits where, for example, the company had previously emerged from administration or administrative receivership. It would also appear that a liquidator who is appointed by the court contemporaneously with an administrative receiver being in office will fall within the scope of the provisions of this sub-class once he has acted as such, since he would then appear to be a liquidator who 'has acted as... liquidator of the company'. Interestingly, this sub-class has no application to a supervisor of a voluntary arrangement or to non-administrative receivers such as LPA receivers. It is doubtful whether a supervisor of a voluntary arrangement is an officer of the company and a receiver and manager of a company has been held expressly held not to be an officer of it (*Re B Johnson & Co (Builders) Ltd* [1955] Ch 634). Furthermore, it is difficult to envisage how these two classes of person might fall within the scope of any of the other sub-classes in s235(3). If the omission of a supervisor of a voluntary arrangement and a non-administrative receiver from the scope of s235 was intentional, then it is a curious one, not least because such individuals will usually be amenable to formal examination under s236(2)(b) as persons whom the court may consider capable of giving information concerning the business, dealings, affairs or property of the company. Again, in practice, this may be of assistance to a subsequently-appointed administrative receiver.

## 8.8.2 Provision of information

Section 235 is concerned specifically with the provision of information as opposed to the giving up or delivery of goods or property of the company, as is dealt with by s234. The supplying of this information may take place in either of two ways envisaged by s235(2): that is, either a person may be required to give such information as the office-holder may reasonably require or, alternatively, a person must attend on the office-holder at such time as he may reasonably require (s235(2)). In practice a number of factors will determine whether an office-holder requires information to be provided to him in writing or by way of attendance. The former will usually suffice where the information is sought from a large number of persons, such as a workforce, or where the person to whom interrogations are directed is not suspected of having more than cursory or merely confirmatory information in their possession. An initial examination by way of informal attendance on an office-holder might be considered appropriate where the office-holder wishes to gauge the reaction of an individual to specific interrogations without that person having written notice of the matters to be raised with him, although an individual may choose to raise the argument, and refuse to attend on an office-holder as a consequence, that attendance may not be reasonably required by the office-holder if he refuses to disclose at least the broad nature of the matters which he wishes to raise with the individual summoned. It is submitted, however, that the words 'may reasonably require', as they appear in s235(2)(b), do not refer to the information sought by an office-holder but rather to the time and notice period applicable to an information examination. Attendance without previous written interrogatories may also be deemed appropriate and may reasonably be required by an office-holder where he believes that the person from whom he requires information is likely to abscond or leave the jurisdiction in the foreseeable future. Alternatively, the office-holder may be of the view that the matters which he wishes to raise are of such a nature and detail as to be most appropriately dealt with in person. Indeed, in the case of a person who is considered likely to abscond from the jurisdiction, private examination under s236 may be considered more appropriate, even as an initial investigation, than an informal inquiry under s235.

In the case of information which the office-holder requires without attendance on him, the term 'may reasonably require' suggests that the information must be such as to have some relevance to the investigation of the office-holder, as opposed to all possible information which a person liable under s235(3) may have in his possession or be able to produce (eg former records). The onus would appear to be on the office-holder to establish why he is being reasonable in requiring the information sought. As regards attendance on the office-holder, the term 'may reasonably require' will impose some degree of reasonableness as to the time of and notice given prior to any meeting with the office-holder, and will also probably require the possibility of rearranged times if those proposed are inconvenient or impracticable. Again, the onus appears to be on the office-holder in this regard. However, the reasonableness requirement does not appear to be framed in terms requiring the office-holder to show that the attendance of a specific person may be reasonably required by virtue of the wording in s235(2)(b) and it would appear, therefore, that a person may not refuse to attend on an office-holder solely on the ground that their attendance may not be reasonably required because they contend that they are not in possession of relevant information.

There is, of course, nothing in s235 which prevents an office-holder from requiring information from the same person on more than one occasion, irrespective of whether the requests relate to the same matter or not. A person may also be required to attend on an office-holder on more than one occasion. Similarly, nothing in the wording of the provision prevents the office-holder from requiring attendance on him by a person from whom information has already been requested under s235(2)(a). Indeed, such attendance is commonly required if the office-holder requires further and better particulars of information provided in writing which the office-holder considers is more appropriately sought by way of detailed, oral explanation.

Although no court order is required for an office-holder to invoke s235 and require compliance with its provisions, the office-holder may apply to the court for such order as it thinks fit for the enforcement of obligations imposed by the provision (IR r7.20(1)(c),(2)(d)). Such an order is without prejudice to any fine which may be imposed by the court for non-compliance with s235 under s235(5). Where an order for compliance is obtained under IR r7.20 the court may also order that all costs of and incidental to the application shall be borne by the person against whom the order is made, presumably (although this is not clear) on a full indemnity basis (IR r7.20(3)). Again, an office-holder would do well to bring this matter to the attention of any person who may be required to provide information or attend on the office-holder in accordance with s235.

## 8.9  Power to Inquire Into the Company's Dealings: s236

Section 236 permits an administrative receiver to apply to the court for an order to summon any of the persons specified within s236(2) to appear before it for the purposes of a private examination. The benefit of the order, however, is only enjoyed by the office-holder who obtains it, and is rendered inoperative on his vacating office (*Re Kingscroft Insurance Co Ltd* [1994] BCC 343 (subject to appeal)). That case held that administrators under a Companies Act 1985 s425 scheme of arrangement (which falls outside the scope of s236) are not entitled to the benefit of a s236 order obtained by them as previously-appointed provisional liquidators. An administrative receiver, unlike a liquidator, may not apply to the court for a public examination under s133, although the administrative receiver himself may be the subject of such an application (s133(1)).

### 8.9.1  Scope and application

Section 236 represents a significant improvement to the armoury of office-holders generally, in the sense that the previous private examination provisions restricted to windings-up by virtue of Companies Act 1985 s561 and its predecessor, Companies Act 1948 s268. As a consequence of this limitation, considerable use was made previously of *Anton Piller* orders and *Mareva* injunctions, whereby the court required the delivery up of documents or ordered a freeze on the company's assets respectively. The major practical drawback with such orders is that an applicant is usually required, at least on an *ex parte* application, as would be usual in such cases, to give security for costs, together with a cross-undertaking providing an indemnity in damages for loss suffered by the respondent if at the subsequent on notice hearing it should transpire that the original order should not be sustained. The risks inherent in the giving of such security and undertaking were and are only made all the more acute by the fact that any office-holder will frequently not have sufficient company assets available to make such an application possible or viable. This is not to say, however, that s236 may not be an expensive and time-consuming course of action to pursue. In reality, and in view of the significant litigation surrounding the provision in recent years, it is frequently so.

An order for a private examination under s236, which is conducted by the office-holder or his legal representatives, may be made by the court if, broadly speaking, the purpose of the application is an inquiry into the company's dealings and/or an investigation into the whereabouts of property of the company and/or the establishment of whether or not the person summoned before the court is indebted to the company.

Section 236 has very considerable practical use in obtaining information from recalcitrant company directors and other persons specified in s236(2). In practice, office-holders may find that those individuals subject to s235 are prepared to co-operate without the need for formal court involvement in accordance with the duty imposed by s235. Indeed, an application for an order under s236 is unlikely to succeed if the applicant is unable to show that an initial attempt has been made to obtain information from the person to whom the application relates. It was held in *Re Adlands Motor Holding Ltd* [1990] BCLC 68 that the court is unlikely to make an order for a private examination under s236 where there is either no evidence which indicates *prima facie* that a substantial case exists which warrants investigation or, alternatively, where there is no real possibility of a recovery of company assets being made for the benefit of creditors.

In reality, an office-holder will usually place greater reliance on information elicited under s235 than under s236 where there is some degree of suspicion of fraud in the company's records. This is because the information obtained on the enforcement of the s235 duty is often likely to be forthcoming more quickly from a respondent, who may be unco-operative or unhelpful in the face of more protracted and formalistic s236 dealings. Indeed, in the recent House of Lords decision in *Re Arrows Ltd (No 4)* [1994] BCC 641, Lord Browne-Wilkinson made specific reference to the service of the public interest in ensuring a free flow of informally obtained information under s235 between office-holders and the criminal prosecution authorities, which was of much greater importance under s235 than in relation to s236 transcripts.

The class of persons to whom s236(2) is potentially applicable extends to:

(a)   any officer of the company;

(b)   any person known or suspected to have in his possession any property of the company or supposed to be indebted to the company;

(c) any person whom the court thinks capable of giving information concerning the promotion, formation, business, dealings, affairs or property of the company.

Whilst this list is briefer than the class of persons subject to s235(2), the scope of the provision is far broader than that of s235 in view of the court's discretion under s236(2)(c), which is an unfettered and general one. The exercise of this discretion by the court, however, has evolved within what are now well-established parameters.

## 8.9.2 Procedure

The procedure for a private examination is set out in IR 1986 Chap 9. These provide for the form and content of the application, the examination procedure, the record of the examination and the award of costs. The reference in IR r9.1(1)(a) to the Rules in Part 9 as they relate to applications under s236 as regards '(inquiry into a company's dealings when it is, or is alleged to be, insolvent)' is misleading. This is because s236 is specifically stated as being applicable in the same way as s234, which operates *inter alia* in relation to an administrative receiver. There is of course no requirement that a company should be insolvent or alleged to be insolvent when it is in administrative receivership although, in practice, that is not uncommon. There is also no bar to a private examination being sought where the company is contemporaneously in administrative receivership and liquidation.

The application itself may be made on an *ex parte* basis, although it must be made in writing and supported by a brief statement of the grounds on which it is made (IR r9.2(1),(4)). Recently, however, Vinelott J indicated that *ex parte* applications should only be pursued if good cause can be shown as to the appropriateness of the cause of action in view of the time and costs which may be saved in clarifying the scope of the order on an on notice application (*Re Maxwell Communications Corporation plc* [1994] BCC 741).

It appears that the statement supporting the application need not be sworn and, as such, a simple memorandum of the facts alleged will apparently suffice, contrary to the pre-1986 position where a sworn supporting affidavit was expressly required in a winding-up. It had also previously been a long-established rule that the supporting statement was confidential (*Re Gold Co* (1879) 12 ChD 77 and *Re Aveling Barford Ltd* [1988] 1 WLR 360). However, there is no provision in IA 1986 or in the IR which substantiates any legal basis for this confidentiality. More recently, the courts have been prepared to permit disclosure of the statement where the application is opposed, where the court is satisfied that non-disclosure would render the court unable to deal with the application to set aside on a fair or equitable basis (see the Court of Appeal decision in *Re British & Commonwealth Holdings plc*

*(Nos 1 and 2)* [1992] Ch 342, subsequently approved at [1993] AC 426, HL). Whilst the onus will be on the respondent to show reason why disclosure should be made of the statement on an application to the court, it is submitted that the onus will shift onto the applicant where the application is challenged and the application to set aside appears to be made on grounds of some substance. The respondent must be sufficiently identified in the application (as opposed to reference to, say, a class of persons) as must the purpose or purposes of the application (IR r9.2(2), (3)). Although the application may be made on an *ex parte* basis, a respondent may not be ordered to appear before the court at a time and place specified (in accordance with IR r13.6) less than 14 days from the date of the order being made (IR r9.3(2)).

The order itself must be served personally on the respondent unless the court orders otherwise, if for example there are good grounds for believing that a respondent will attempt to avoid service of the order on him, in which case substituted service may be permitted by the court.

### 8.9.3  Extra-territorial effect

In *Re Seagul Manufacturing Co Ltd (in liquidation)* [1991] BCC 550, and in contrast to the position on s133 which deals with public examinations, Mummery J held that s236 does not have extra-territorial effect, a view affirmed by the Court of Appeal [1993] BCC 241. This should be contrasted with the more recent decision in *Re Joint Liquidators of First Tokyo Index Trust Ltd* [1994] BCC 410, a decision of the Scottish Court of Session, in which the court accepted that an order under s236 could be made against a respondent who was resident in New York. This was conditional, however, on the jurisdiction falling within the scope of a 'relevant country or territory' for the purposes of s426 and the Co-operation of Insolvency Courts (Designation of Relevant Countries and Territories) Order 1986 (SI No 2123). It should also be noted that in *Re Oriental Credit Ltd* [1987] 3 BCC 564 it was held that the court has the power to restrain an individual from leaving the jurisdiction pending a private examination under s236.

### 8.9.4  Practical implications

Any other person who may have applied to the court for an order for an examination under s236 may also attend the examination ordered, although this is subject to the leave of the court and the assent of the applicant (IR r9.4(2)). That person may also put questions to the respondent, again subject to leave of the court and with the co-operation of the applicant, although the questions must be put by the applicant, who may be represented by a solicitor or counsel (IR r9.4(1)). The court may, however, authorise a person other than the applicant, such as a creditor, to examine the applicant where there are two separate office-holders and where IR r9.4(2) applies (*Re Maxwell Communications Corporation plc* [1994] BCC 741).

As an alternative to summoning a person before the court, an application may be made requiring a person to submit an affidavit to the court or to produce such books, papers or other records as are ordered (IR r9.2(3)(c),(d)). In both cases, the application to the court for the order must specify either those matters on which the respondent is required to answer questions or the specific items to be produced to the court (IR r9.2(3)(c),(d)). In the case of an affidavit, the court's order must specify those matters to be dealt with in the affidavit and the time in which these must be produced to the court (IR r9.3(3)(a),(b)). In the case of production of books, papers etc, the time and manner of compliance must be specified in the order (IR r9.3(4)). An application for the production of affidavit evidence or books and records etc will not prejudice the office-holder's right to apply for a further order under s236 for, say, interrogatories, of which particulars must be given by the applicant of the matters in respect of which answers are sought. Alternatively, an application may be made for an appearance before the court.

There is an obvious need for an applicant to be clear, specific and succinct about particulars of the matters in respect of which answers are required for the purposes of affidavits or interrogatories under IR r9.2(3)(b) and (c). This is because any subsequent order made by the court is likely to be framed in terms of the particulars contained in the application itself. Any such order which is not specific enough for the purposes of IR r9.3(3) is unlikely to meet with approval from the courts if its terms are too general in scope, as in *Re Aveling Barford Ltd* [1988] 1 WLR 360. This will, at the least, cause unnecessary and costly delay for the applicant. Accordingly, requests for 'full particulars of full dealings' and the like in the application are usually best avoided. Somewhat curiously, IR r9.3(3) does not appear to require the same degree of specific disclosure from the respondent of the matters to be dealt with as responses to interrogatories as is required in the case of affidavits. Nevertheless, it is suggested that broad references to full disclosure of all matters on the part of a respondent in relation to interrogatories are best avoided so as to fulfil the 'specific notice' requirement applicable by virtue of r9.3(3), although on its face it only appears to apply to matters raised by way of affidavit evidence.

Rule 9.4(6) of the IR provides that record of the examination as the court thinks proper must be made in writing, and shall be read over to or by the respondent and signed by him at a venue fixed by the court. In practice, the court may be prepared to permit an interview to be tape-recorded and for support staff to be present for the purposes of taking a shorthand record of the s236 interview. As a matter of courtesy and practice, prior permission should be sought of the judge or district judge for such arrangements to be made, as well as advance notice being provided to the interviewee and his solicitor or counsel as appropriate. Rule 9.4(6) does not literally impose a requirement that the record of the examination should be read over to the respondent interviewee immediately following the conclusion of the examination. Therefore, at the discretion of the court, an order or direction may be made by the court whereby a transcript of the examination is sent to the respondent at a specified address for signature within a specified time, together with arrangements in the event of a dispute, the order typically providing for the matter to be referred back to the court in such a case. A judge or district judge in the High Court or county court may in writing nominate one or more persons to be official shorthand writers to the court, and may at any time in the course of insolvency proceedings appoint a shorthand writer to take down the evidence of a person examined under s236 (IR r7.16(1),(2) using IR Forms 7.3 and 7.4 respectively).

## 8.10   Section 236: Practical Applications

Section 236 has produced a plethora of case law since 1986, a body of law which is not only complex but also inconsistent. What has resulted is a somewhat incoherent set of rules which hardly provide for a uniform approach on the part of insolvency practitioners and, perhaps more importantly in the public interest, poses some problems for the prosecuting authority in the form of the Serious Fraud Office ('the SFO'). Broadly speaking, the case law on s236 is largely concerned with three areas which will now be considered in turn. First, the question of any possible privilege in favour of a respondent against any self-incrimination in any subsequent criminal proceedings; secondly, the position of third parties in the face of the investigations by an office-holder; and thirdly, the balancing act performed by the courts in protecting the public interest by ensuring proper investigation of the affairs of failed companies whilst protecting the respondent from any oppression in the face of a s236 examination.

### 8.10.1   The privilege against self-incrimination

The question of the privilege against self-incrimination has been raised and rejected, primarily on public interest grounds, in a number of recent cases involving company officers and former company officers. In *Bishopsgate Investment Management v Maxwell* [1993] Ch 1 the Court of Appeal held that there is no so-called 'right of silence' where answers might incriminate a respondent, the implication of s236 being that statute has effectively overridden and abrogated any privilege against self-incrimination. This decision expressly approved the earlier decision of Vinelott J in *Re Jeffrey S Levitt Ltd* [1992] Ch 457 which denied the benefit of the privilege against self-incrimination in the face of criminal proceedings. The *Levitt* decision had unhesitatingly overruled the unreported decision in *Barlow Clowes Gilt Managers Ltd v Mitchell* (1990) where Ferris J held that a respondent was unable to claim the defence of privilege against self-incrimination. (In *Re A Farr Ltd* [1992] BCC 151 Ferris J later chose not to follow his own decision in the *Mitchell* case.)

The Court of Appeal's decision in *Bishopsgate* led to an appeal by the Director of the Serious Fraud Office against the first instance decision of Hoffmann J in *Re Arrows Ltd* [1992] Ch 545, where the court had made an order for a s236 examination of the respondent subject to an express proviso that a transcript of the examination should not be disclosed by the liquidators to the SFO. Hoffman J had included this proviso in the original order in light of the considerable uncertainty of the position over self-incrimination, the idea being that the respondent would be more likely to make full disclosure in response to questions put to him with the protection which the proviso afforded. Although the SFO's appeal was allowed by consent, the appellant's subsequent application to have the original order for the s236 examination set aside was rejected by the court in *Re Arrows Ltd (No 2)* [1992] BCLC 1176, and was actually upheld subsequently by the Court of Appeal in June 1992 in an unreported decision. The Court of Appeal had also refused to allow an appeal by the respondent in the *Levitt* case, a further appeal being dropped subsequently.

It was the rejection of the application to set aside the original s236 examination in *Re Arrows Ltd (No 2)* which subsequently led to an application being made to the court for directions, following a request by the SFO for transcripts of the s236 examination. This is turn gave rise to the *Re Arrows Ltd (No4)* litigation (reported at [1994] BCC 641).

Whilst leave to appeal to the House of Lords was refused in *Bishopsgate,* it should be noted that the Court of Appeal's decision in that case has received approval from the House of Lords subsequently in *Re Arrows Ltd (No4),* in which Lord Browne-Wilkinson confirmed that 'a person examined under s236 can be compelled to give self-incriminating answers which are admissible against him in criminal proceedings'. The *Bishopsgate* decision, and the view of the House of Lords in *Re Arrows Ltd (No 4)* accord with the earlier first instance decision in *Levitt,* in which it was held that a respondent has no right to silence in a s236 examination, even where charges have been put in criminal proceedings. This approach also supports the views of Ferris J in *Re Wallace Smith Trust Co Ltd* [1992] BCC 707 to the effect that a pending investigation by the investigating authorities does not affect the statutory duty of a respondent to co-operate with an office-holder. Again, this decision reflects the approach of the courts in attempting to facilitate the rights of office-holders under s236 without unduly hindering criminal proceedings which may be seen as being broadly in the public interest, even though they

255

are prosecuted by a separate body. The *Levitt* decision is also itself consistent with the decision in *R v Director of the Serious Fraud Office ex p Smith* [1993] AC 1 which was decided under the Criminal Justice Act 1987 s2(3).

### 8.10.2   Third parties and office-holder investigations

The disclosure of information by third parties to the office-holder who pursues his powers of investigation under ss234–6 has also been the subject of some scrutiny by the courts. *Re Cloverbay Ltd (No 2)* [1991] Ch 90 concerned the question of whether an administrator could pursue inquiries against two employees of BCCI in a private oral examination which was to be conducted on oath where the employees may have been in possession of information relating to fraud in which BCCI was implicated. Specifically, the administrators wanted an explanation as to why certain markings appeared on cheques in relation to an alleged fraud by the bank and, on a particular issue, the knowledge of the employees, so as to ascertain whether BCCI knowingly took part in fraud and could thus be fixed as a constructive trustee of the monies involved.

Although at first instance Harman J had been persuaded to grant an order to the administrators permitting an examination of the former bank's books, the learned judge was not prepared to require the attendance of the employees at the interview, on the basis that the administrator did not strictly need the information in order to decide whether or not to sue BCCI. In other words, the administrators were attempting to improve their position by trying to obtain information in the private examination; this was oppressive in that the company itself would have been unable to acquire the information.

The Court of Appeal subsequently confirmed this view, although on different grounds. The Vice-Chancellor identified four factors which the court should consider in exercising discretion in making s236 orders. He held that Harman J's 'need to know' test was unworkable and would lead to endless arguments. (It is notable in this regard that Harman J had failed to allow the administrators to testify as to their state of mind.) As to when the discretion should be exercised, it was necessary for the court to consider the needs of the administrators on the one hand and the oppression of the third party employees on the other. The court was mindful of the fact that the office-holders had previously received information on previous transactions from the original applicant for the administration order, which amounted to as much information as the company would have had itself if solvent. To require the employees of the bank (who were considered as having no fiduciary duties to it) to make statements to the office-holder, where the employees themselves were suspected of fraud or dishonesty, was oppressive. Furthermore, the company could not be expected to build a case against itself where the office-holders were already in possession of sufficient information, and certainly as much as would have been possessed by the company itself if solvent, on which to decide whether or not to sue the company.

The question of disclosure by third parties received further analysis in *Re British and Commonwealth Holdings plc (Nos 1 and 2)* [1992] 3 WLR 853. This involved an attempt by administrators to obtain documents from accountants who had audited a company, Atlantic Computers, which was subsequently taken over by the company in administration. Notably, in the Court of Appeal, Ralph Gibson LJ was of the opinion that Browne-Wilkinson V-C had not intended in *Cloverbay (No 2)* to lay down a fixed rule whereby information obtained under s236 was limited to that necessary for the reconstruction of knowledge once held by the company or capable in legal terms of being so held. This was also the view of the House of Lords, who rejected a submission by the accountants that the production of documents by them was burdensome and oppressive in that it would carry with it a risk of negligence. In the leading judgment by Lord Slynn, the complexity of the case in hand and the large sums involved were specifically noted. However, it was reasonable for the administrators to require access to the documents sought, which included a working capital analysis, audit files and various documents relating to the takeover bid, for the purposes of verifying their accuracy. This outweighed any inconvenience, burden or oppression suffered by the accountants. What is also clear from the judgment is that the discretion of the court is not confined under s236 to reconstructing the state of the company's knowledge.

The decision of the House of Lords should not be seen as all-embracing. The House of Lords was particularly mindful of the exceptional nature of the case in terms of its complexity and the size of the sums involved. Similarly, whilst the discretion in s236 is an unfettered one, it is not ordinarily one to be exercised in excess of merely reconstructing the knowledge of the failed company. Whether or not the facts of the case can be seen as exceptional therefore is of considerable importance.

### 8.10.3  Public interest v proper investigation

The question of when the courts will permit the facilitation of a full and proper investigation into the dealings of a company to be overridden by the need to serve the public interest by ensuring a free flow of information between office-holders and the SFO is equally vexed (*Re Arrows Ltd (No 4)* [1993] Ch 453 at 476F–G). In this sense the term 'information' extends beyond mere transcripts of interviews conducted under s236 and includes all information, whether or not in documentary form, which an office-holder has required from a respondent in the discharge of his duties, following the House of Lords' decision in *Re British & Commonwealth Holdings plc (No 2)* [1992] BCC 977.

The starting point here is the first instance decision in *Re Barlow Clowes Gilt Managers Ltd* [1991] BCC 608. The case involved an application to court, by the liquidator of the company which was supported by the SFO, for directions as to whether they should make disclosure of the transcripts of confidential interviews conducted on the liquidator's behalf to other persons who were defendants in criminal proceedings and who had themselves requested the transcript from the office-holders. Millett J ordered that no disclosure should be made, subject to any order which may have been made by the Crown Court in the pending criminal proceedings (as was made: see *R v Clowes* [1992] 3 All ER 440). In other words, the use of transcripts obtained under s236 was limited to the beneficial winding-up of the company, subject to any order of the criminal courts. In reaching his decision, Millett J took account of the fact that a proper liquidation of the company would be put in jeopardy if the transcripts were to be made available to the defendants in criminal proceedings, as well as of the danger of undermining the undertaking of confidentiality which had been provided by the liquidators to the defendants. In addition, the learned judge was influenced by the submission of an expert witness to the effect that the prompt co-operation of directors is of vital importance in tracing and securing company assets, and that this might be threatened as an ongoing practice if it was generally held that transcripts relating to such matters could be made available to third parties with impunity. In short, the danger was that any respondent could simply refuse to co-operate voluntarily with office-holders as had been the case in *Barlow Clowes,* as a consequence of which an office-holder would be obliged to apply to the court for a s236 order, which would inevitably be opposed on grounds of oppression. The approach of Millett J in *Barlow Clowes* was unfortunately rejected by both the Court of Appeal and the House of Lords in the *Re Arrows Ltd (No 4)* decision (see Trace, *The Receivers, Administrators and Liquidators Quarterly* (1994) 1 at 13 for a useful and reasoned summary of the problems posed by the Court of Appeal's decision which largely remain following the Lords' judgment).

The decision of the House of Lords in *Re Arrows Ltd (No 4)* [1994] BCC 641 confirms that of the Court of Appeal, to the effect that the court has no discretion in relation to the disclosure of information by an office-holder following a request to him from the Director of the SFO to deliver up transcripts of examinations conducted under ss235 and 236 pursuant to the Criminal Justice Act 1987 s2(3). It follows from this that an office-holder will be bound to deliver up such transcripts, irrespective of any representation made to an interviewee as to whom the transcripts would be disclosed, and without any recourse to the court for an order protecting either his own position or that of an interviewee. It is equally clear from the House of Lords' decision that the admissibility of and prejudice caused by the admission of the transcripts in any criminal proceedings will be a matter for the trial judge and not the judge in the Companies Court.

The effect of the House of Lords' decision is somewhat disconcerting for the insolvency practitioner. On the one hand, he will wish to obtain the fullest possible information as to the company's position and assets as ss235 and 236 specifically enable him to do. On the other hand, he should not, apparently, make any representations to interviewees as to whom the transcripts of any interviews conducted under those provisions may be released. The position of the interviewee is equally precarious. He is obliged to co-operate with an office-holder under s235 and, indeed, has no right to remain silent (on the basis of the decision in *Re Jeffrey S Levitt Ltd* [1992] Ch 457 and the Court of Appeal's decision in *Bishopsgate Investment Management Ltd v Maxwell* [1993] Ch 1). In reality, the recalcitrant director may prefer to remain silent and face the consequences rather than impart what he knew or believed to be the position, for fear of its disclosure, even in the face of a s236 order being made against him. It hardly needs stating that the interviewee should seek professional and independent legal advice at the earliest possible time.

In practice, however, the most significant problem posed by the decision in *Re Arrows Ltd (No 4)* is the likely effect that respondents will be less inclined to co-operate on a voluntary basis with requests for information under s235, office-holders more commonly having to invoke s236 with its attendant costs and delay. In turn, a respondent may oppose the admissibility of any transcript evidence obtained on the basis of the s236 order in any criminal proceedings which subsequently ensue, on the grounds of oppression. This state of affairs, it is submitted, has little to commend it other than in cases of very substantial fraud. Certainly there is good practical reason to doubt the view aired by Dillon J in the Court of Appeal to the effect that office-holders will be faced with reducing levels of difficulty once the force of the legislation and the recent decisions surrounding it comes to be more widely appreciated.

It is respectfully submitted that by far the better view on this area is that contained in the judgment of Vinelott J in *Re Arrows Ltd (No 4)* at first instance, where a director and majority shareholder of a company argued that it would be oppressive to permit an interview of him by liquidators of the company where he had actually been charged with a criminal offence. This decision held that the disclosure of transcripts of statements made by the director under s236 should not be made to the Director of the SFO unless the SFO gave undertakings not to rely on the statements directly in evidence against the director in criminal proceedings which had already been commenced. The effect of this was that the Director of the SFO could not gain an unfair advantage in obtaining the transcripts, in that they could not be directed in evidence against the director unless the circumstances set out in the Criminal Justice Act 1987 s2(8)(a) and (b) could be made out.

That provision provides that a statement by a person may only be used in evidence against him either (a) on a prosecution under s14 of the 1987 Act for making a statement which was false or materially misleading and made knowingly or recklessly or (b) on a prosecution for some other offence when, in giving evidence, the defendant made a statement inconsistent with a previous statement for which privilege was claimed. The approach of Vinelott J in this regard accommodates the free flow of information between office-holders and the investigating authorities, without offering an unfair advantage for the latter, and thereby protects the position of both office-holders and interviewees. This is not only a state of affairs well within the jurisdiction of the court, it is also one which offers some degree of certainty and which may be seen to operate fairly.

The present unsatisfactory position surrounding the release of transcripts to the SFO largely stems from the legislation affecting the area. First, it appears that the civil court has no jurisdiction to determine whether evidence which is admissible in criminal proceedings by virtue of s433 (which provides that any statement made under the Act or the IR may be used in evidence against the person making it (or any person who concurred in its making)) can be used at any criminal trial (*Rank Film Distributors Ltd v Video Information Centre* [1982] AC 380). Thus in *R v Kansal* [1992] BCC 615 the Court of Appeal held that the statements of a bankrupt made in a public examination could be used against him in a theft prosecution notwithstanding the restrictions imposed by the Theft Act 1968 s31. It is arguable, however, that s433 is actually concerned with admissibility as opposed to whether or not the transcripts put in evidence should actually be made available in the first place. Furthermore, the Criminal Justice Act 1987 contains no provisions analogous to those in the Theft Act 1968 whereby statements made in civil proceedings are deemed inadmissible in criminal proceedings under the 1968 Act, although the *Kansal* decision might override this point. Nevertheless, the Court of Appeal had been mindful of this point in the *Re Arrows Ltd (No 4)* decision, Dillon LJ accepting no basis for imposing the restrictions contained in the Criminal Justice Act 1987 s2(8) on the SFO in using the s236 transcripts in evidence. Again, it is submitted that the preferable view, (rejected by the Court of Appeal and the House of Lords) is that of Vinelott J at first instance, which held that the Director of the SFO should not be permitted to obtain an advantage which he would not himself have enjoyed had he conducted an investigation of the s236 respondent under the Criminal Justice Act 1987 s2(2).

The decision in *Re Arrows Ltd (No 4)* holds that the Companies Court is unable in any circumstances to place restrictions on the use by the investigating authorities of evidence without the civil court's consent. This is a matter of very considerable importance in view of the apparent lack of control left to the court over its own officers under IA 1986 (which will not extend, of course, to administrative receivers) and the significance of the respondent's right of silence, or lack of it, in the absence of any discretion on the part of the civil court. Certainly the present authorities do not appear to focus sufficient attention on the qualifications which the legislation imposes on the rule that a civil court enjoys no discretion in the release of transcripts. These are apparent from IR r9.5(2) and 9.5(4), and appear to require that the court consent to disclosure and give directions to its officers as to the custody, disclosure and inspection of documents respectively (see *Re Mirror Group (Holdings) Ltd* [1993] BCLC 538, which involved directions given to administrators and which relied on *Re Atlantic Computer Systems plc (No 1)* [1991] BCLC 606).

Finally, it is very arguable that the court itself is a proper addressee of a notice served by the Director of the SFO under the Criminal Justice Act 1987 s2(3) (see Trace *op cit* and Gregory, *Company Law News*, 1993, 27 July). This view would effectively arm the court with a discretion as to any use to which s236 transcripts may be put (*Re Great Kruger Gold Mining Co ex p Barnard* [1982] 3 Ch 307 at 313–4). This accords with the previous law, under which the court enjoyed a discretion to exercise control over its own office-holders in the conduct of examinations (see, for example, *Re Scharrer* (1888) 4 TLR 627).

### 8.10.4 Practical conclusions

In conclusion, then, what guidelines, if any, may assist the office-holder in the exercise of his cumulative powers under ss234–6? The first of these would be to exhaust the practical remedies available under ss234 and 235 before embarking on a s236 application. Secondly, in seeking a s236 order the office-holder is obliged to disclose all material facts as to why the order is sought (cf *Re John T Rhodes (No 2)* [1987] BCC 588 which involved an unsuccessful attempt to commit a director for contempt). Thirdly, the office-holder should be clear and objective both in terms of the interrogatories which he intends to put to the respondent and his reasons for pursuing each line of enquiry. Fourthly, the office-holder should be cautious as to any assurances he makes to a respondent about which parties any transcripts may be disclosed to subsequently. Any assurance or comfort should be in writing, or at least confirmed in writing, and should state that it is subject to any order of the court made under the Criminal Justice Act 1987 s2 or by way of subpoena in a criminal trial.

## 8.11  The Residual Status of Directors in Administrative Receivership

The broad effect of administrative receivership on a company is that the directors remain in office, but are divested of their powers of management of the company and its assets to the extent that those powers are assumed and capable of exercise by the administrative receiver. The source of those powers was considered above at para 8.2. The position of the directors is perhaps best put by Lord Atkinson in *Moss Steamship Co Ltd v Whinney* [1912] AC 254 at 263 as follows:

> [The] appointment of a receiver and manager over the assets and business of a company does not dissolve or alienate the company, any more than the taking of possession by the mortgagee of the fee of land let to tenants alienates the mortgagor. Both continue to exist; but it entirely supersedes the company in all the conduct of its business, deprives it of all power to enter into contracts in relation to that business, or to sell, pledge, or otherwise dispose of the property put into the possession, or under the control of the receiver and manager. Its powers in these respects are entirely in abeyance.

This statement is of particular note in that it does not discount the powers of the directors as being wholly in suspension during receivership. Instead, certain powers of the directors are stultified whilst others are apparently capable of exercise. *Moss Steamship Co* was cited with approval in *Newhart Developments Ltd v Co-operative Commercial Bank Ltd* [1978] 2 All ER 896, which itself was notable in that counsel for the unsuccessful defendant argued boldly to the contrary albeit without any apparent authority and support. The *Moss Steamship Co* case was significantly absent from the argument in *Tudor Grange Holdings v Citibank* [1991] 3 WLR 750, in which *Newhart* was distinguished. *Moss* and *Newhart* were cited with approval in *Gomba Holdings v Homas* [1986] 1 WLR 1301 and in *Paramount Acceptance Co v Souster* [1981] 2 NZLR 38, a decision of the New Zealand Court of Appeal.

It seems clear that the directors of a company in administrative receivership will have power to deal with assets which are not subject to the security interests of the appointing debenture-holder. However, in practice, these assets will either be non-existent or of negligible value in view of the definition in s29(2). Technically, property which is not subject to the debenture-holder's interest might include assets held on trust by the company for third parties, or property released from the debenture-holder's security either prior to or during the conduct of the administrative receivership. Whilst the debenture-holder will be mindful of falling outside the s29(2) definition, it may consider it commercially expedient to release from its secured assets rights of action against it or its office-holder, although these will not usually undermine the requisite security for s29(2) purposes. Certainly it has to be said that it is very difficult to justify the argument that a right of action against a debenture-holder ordinarily falls outside the scope of a debenture-holder's security, and certainly the scope of a general floating charge in favour of that debenture-holder. Although this view is courted in Gower, *Principles of Modern Company Law*, 5th ed, Sweet and Maxwell (1992) at 436 n196) it is unclear on what basis it is made and it is respectfully submitted that it is incorrect.

One asset or class of assets in relation to which the directors may seek to exercise their powers are those which are ignored or remain unexploited by the administrative receiver. This view runs contrary to that of Hoffmann J in the *Gomba Holdings* case, where the learned judge considered that the board retains no powers over assets in the possession or control of the receiver during the currency of the receivership. The better view, it is submitted, is that of Shaw LJ in *Newhart*, to the effect that the directors may deal with any assets subject to the possession or control of the receiver subject also to an express licence from the receiver to deal with the assets. Any such licence should take the form of a clear written statement from the receiver that he has neither any intention nor any need or wish to deal with assets (which should be specifically identified) and that, as office-holder, he has no objection to the board dealing with those assets. The directors should be fully aware, however, that an administrative receiver may seek to claim any benefit which arises from the exploitation of a secured asset by them for the benefit of the debenture-holder, even where this exploitation comes about as a result of efforts on the part of the directors themselves. That view was aired concisely by Shaw LJ in *Newhart* where the learned judge considered that, not only might the directors be at liberty to exploit a particular asset, they may in fact be under a duty to do so. Thus:

> The receiver is entitled to ignore claims of anybody outside the debenture-holders. Not so the company; not so, therefore, the directors of the company. If there is an asset which appears to be of value, although the directors cannot deal with it in the sense of disposing of it, they are under a duty to exploit it so as to bring it to a realisation which may be fruitful for all concerned. If such an action [as was started in this case] comes to trial and there is a judgment in favour of the plaintiffs [ie the directors] then, if debenture-holders are still not fully satisfied, the receiver can take steps to attack the proceeds of the judgment for the benefit of the debenture-holders.

One troublesome aspect of the residual rights of the directors in administrative receivership relates to rights of action as against the administrative receiver and/or the appointing debenture-holder. Certainly, the better view, it is submitted, is that such rights of action will fall subject to a general floating charge in favour of the debenture-holder, and certainly to a valid fixed charge which extends to 'property [of the company] whatsoever and wheresoever both present and future' (as in *Newhart Developments Ltd v Co-operative Commercial Bank Ltd* [1978] 2 All ER 896). Nevertheless, the real question in issue appears not to be whether a right of action is subject to any particular security interest but, rather, whether that right of action is exercisable by the company with or without the interference or consent of the administrative receiver. Indeed, the availability of such an action was the central point in the *Newhart* and *Tudor Grange* decisions.

*Newhart* involved an action by the directors of a company against a bank (following the appointment of a receiver by it) for alleged breach of contract in relation to a joint venture. The receiver successfully applied to have the writ action set aside. The decision was subsequently reversed by the Court of Appeal, rejecting the first instance decision of Chapman J that it is inherent in the power of a receiver alone to bring an action on the company's behalf, and that the company itself cannot bring an action without the consent of the receiver. The Court of Appeal was very much influenced, in reinstating the company's writ action, by the fact that the company would not have to fund the costs of the action or to meet the costs of an unsuccessful action, because the directors had provided a full indemnity in favour of the company against any liability which it might incur as to costs. Such an indemnity was notable by its absence in *Tudor Grange* and this was one basis upon which the *Newhart* case was distinguished in that case (see [1991] 2 WLR 750 at 759). It should be noted, however, that it is not altogether clear that *Tudor Grange* would have been decided differently had an indemnity been subsisting or been given subsequently by the directors. Given the possibility of such an indemnity Browne-Wilkinson V-C had considered that '... if the case is otherwise appropriate to go on, I would not strike out *on this ground alone*, but wait to see whether this [indemnity] was available and the terms offered at that stage' (emphasis added).

In *Newhart* Shaw LJ went on to examine the rather curious scenario where the action by the directors is directed against the debenture-holder itself. Such an action would not only pose a clear conflict for the office-holder, but also raises the question of whether the fruits of such an action would only result in a circular transfer of assets from the debenture-holder to the debenture-holder via the company and the receiver and manager and the security held over its assets by the debenture-holder. The practical effect of that circular transfer, as counsel for the debenture-holder in the *Newhart* case had apparently overlooked, would be that the debt secured by the debenture would either be reduced or wholly discharged on account of the debenture-holder's consequential liability to the company. In addition, a debenture-holder may suffer in such an action by the depletion of company assets as a result of any costs order made although, as Shaw LJ put it, that position would be entirely different where the company's directors were prepared to undertake to meet the costs of the proceedings, as in the *Newhart* case. According to the learned judge:

> There is no prejudice or detriment whatever to the debenture-holders *qua* debenture-holders in as much as the corpus of assets available to satisfy them is not going to be diminished or affected in any way at all.

In reality, that diminution would be avoided by an appropriately-worded indemnity.

In conclusion, as regards litigation involving the company, receiver and debenture-holder, it is suggested that the approach of the Court of Appeal in *Newhart* is the correct one. In that case the court expressly rejected the argument by counsel for the defendant bank that the effect of the appointment of a receiver is to paralyse the powers of the company and the directors in dealing with properties subject to the appointment other than as provided for by the charge. In discounting the view to this effect of counsel (which relied on a passage in *Kerr on Receivers*, 14th edn, (1972) at 301, Shaw LJ stated:

> I see no principle of law or expediency which precluded the directors of a company … from seeking to enforce the claim [against the debenture-holder], however ill-founded it may be, provided only, of course, that nothing in the course of the proceedings which they institute is going in any way to threaten the interests of the debenture-holders.

In other words it would appear that an indemnity must be given by the directors themselves as a precondition of exercising any power which might fall to the receiver in the first place. That indemnity should extend to both the costs of pursuing the action and any hostile costs order made subsequently, including, for example, an order for security for costs to be given. This embodies the distinction between the facts of *Newhart* and *Tudor Grange*, as was recognised recently by Keane J in *Lascombe Ltd v United Dominions Trust* [1994] ILRM 227, a decision of the Irish High Court. Keane J found support for *Newhart* where an indemnity for proposed proceedings was available, the view of the court being that a residual role may be necessary for the directors depending on the circumstances of the case. The practical effect of *Lascombe*, therefore, is to reconcile *Newhart* with *Tudor Grange* on the basis of the indemnity proviso. In any case, whilst a company may not ordinarily interfere with a receiver in the proper exercise of his powers, it remains the case that a right of action is maintained against the office-holder for the improper discharge of his duties (*Watts v Midland Bank* [1986] BCLC 15).

265

# Chapter Nine

# The Duties of the Administrative Receiver

## 9.1 Introduction

The administrative receiver is subject to both fiduciary duties and statutory duties in the discharge of his functions. Some initial points should be made about the source and nature of the duties themselves.

Considerable difficulties have arisen judicially in attempting to define the scope of the common law and equitable duties owed by receivers generally. The administrative receiver is a fiduciary (*Nugent v Nugent* [1908] 1 Ch 546). However, this is of little assistance, since the duties of fiduciaries vary depending on the type of fiduciary position they occupy. Similarly, the fact that the receiver is ordinarily an agent of the company is also of little assistance since the agency relationship is a peculiar one in that the primary duty imposed on it is to realise the assets of the company in the interests of the debenture-holder. Furthermore, the powers of management and control conferred on the receiver in relation to the business of the company and its undertaking are themselves subject to that duty (*Gomba Holdings Ltd v Homan* [1986] 1 WLR 1301 at 1305 per Hoffmann J).

The unusual agency relationship with the company and the receiver's relationship with his appointor has been dealt with by the courts by the imposition in equity of duties which are owed, depending on the circumstances and broadly speaking, to those individuals and classes of individual who have either a direct interest in the actions and realisations of the receiver or who have an indirect interest in the equity of redemption. In certain instances the burden of these duties has been extended to the debenture-holder itself as mortgagee of the company's property. Thus, as well as the duty which is owed to the company itself by the statutory agency relationship created by s44(1)(a), fiduciary duties and a duty of reasonable skill and care are owed by the receiver to the debenture-holder (*Gomba Holdings*). Similar duties are owed to subsequent mortgagees (*Parker Tweedale v Dunbar Bank plc* [1991] Ch 12) and to guarantors of the debt secured by the debenture (*Standard Chartered Bank Ltd v Walker* [1982] 3 All ER 938). Conversely, the duties have been recognised not to extend to company officers (other than to the extent that they constitute also guarantors of the secured debt), members and unsecured creditors of the company in receivership. The rationale behind specifically excluding unsecured creditors from the scope of the receiver's duties is that their claims on the company are protected indirectly by the company's claim against the receiver for breach of duty to it (see *Lathia v Dronsfield Bros* [1987] BCLC 321). In a liquidation, of course, this right of action is assumed by the liquidator, who may pursue the breach by way of misfeasance proceedings under s212 on behalf of the unsecured creditors collectively. This type of action, however, is available against administrative receivers only and not against any other form of receiver (*Re B Johnson & Co (Builders) Ltd* [1955] Ch 634).

The nature of the duties owed by the receiver will also vary according to the legal justification for them. As such, the courts have been willing to allow a receiver a considerable degree of authority in the running of a company's business, for example, by permitting the receiver the right to sell the business on a *bona fide* basis without waiting for a rise in the market, as in *Cuckmere Brick Co Ltd v Mutual Finance Ltd* [1971] Ch 949 (although this is subject to the proviso that he takes reasonable care in obtaining a fair market value for the assets at the date of sale). Similarly, the court will not impose liability on a receiver who waits for a rise in the market pending which the value of the debenture-holder's security falls (*China and South Sea Bank Ltd v Tan Soon Gin* [1990] 1 AC 536). These duties have a consequential effect on the duty imposed in favour of guarantors of the secured debt, who will enjoy a release from the whole or part of their liability on the receiver taking reasonable care in the realisation of the secured assets. As has been pointed out, a correct analysis of this so-called duty of care by the receiver and his appointor to a guarantor or surety reveals it in effect as a condition of his right to enforce the guarantee, whilst the converse rights of the guarantor or surety are more accurately identified as immunities from the consequences of the negligence of the receiver or his appointor; see R M Goode, *Legal Problems of Credit and Security* 2nd edn (1988) at 192.

Attempts have been made in cases such as *Standard Chartered Bank* (above) and *American Express v Hurley* [1985] 3 All ER 564 to equate the various duties owed by the receiver to that established by the common law in negligence in *Donoghue v Stevenson* [1932] AC 562 and as developed subsequently. The effect of this is simply to confuse further an already complicated area and the inference has been discounted, notably by the Privy Council in *Downsview Nominees Ltd v First City Corp* [1993] 2 AC 295 at 315. The rationale behind this rejection is that the duties owed by an administrative receiver in realising the secured assets of a company are governed by equity, as is clear from the decision of the Privy Council in the *China and South Sea*

*Bank* case (*above*), the imposition of a common law nexus of pre-conditions as in negligence having no sensible part to play in such duties.

For example, in *Standard Chartered Bank v Walker* [1982] 1 WLR 1410 at 1415, in the Court of Appeal, Denning MR expounded the view that in realising charged property a mortgagee is under a duty to himself, the mortgagor and any guarantor of the mortgagor, a duty which the learned judge considered to be 'only a general duty of care to your neighbour' (at 1415). A similar view was expressed subsequently by Mann J in *American Express International Banking Corp v Hurley* [1985] 3 All ER 564 and by the Court of Appeal of Hong Kong in the *China and South Sea Bank* case. However, in that case the Privy Council was disparaging of this approach and, as a consequence, doubt must now attach to the credibility of any approach to duties in this area which is based on negligence principles. As Templeman LJ put it in the *China and South Sea Bank* case [1989] 3 All ER 839 at 841:

> The Court of Appeal [of Hong Kong] sought to find an authority in the tort of negligence but the tort of negligence has not yet subsumed all torts and does not supplant the principles of equity or contradict contractual promises or complement the remedy of judicial review or supplement contractual rights.

This view echoes similar warnings given by the House of Lords in extending the concept of negligence liability to encompass all manner of common law, equitable and statutory rights and duties, as has been expressed recently in *CBS Songs Ltd v Amstrad Consumer Electronics plc* [1988] AC 1013, *Caparo Industries plc v Dickman* [1990] BCC 164 and *Murphy v Brentwood District Council* [1991] 1 AC 398. This view finds further support in *Parker Tweedale v Dunbar Bank plc* [1990] 2 All ER 577. In that case, in the Court of Appeal, counsel for a spouse on behalf of whom the mortgagor held the charged property on trust, argued that the duty of the mortgagee bank extended to a beneficiary under a trust to which the mortgagor was trustee. This argument was founded on the basis of Lord Denning's neighbour principle as set out in the *Standard Chartered Bank* case. The Court of Appeal again rejected this view in uncompromising terms. The court considered that it is unnecessary for the duties owed by a mortgagee to a mortgagor and the surety to be expressed in terms of the tort of negligence if such a duty exists.

The effect of this statement should not, however, be seen as discounting the possibility of a relationship between mortgagee and surety or guarantor. Rather, it restricts the terms and language in which that relationship is framed. Indeed, Nourse LJ was prepared to entertain the idea put forward by counsel for the bank that a beneficiary under a trust would have an action against the mortgagee by way of a derivative action if the trustee had unreasonably refused to sue on behalf of that trust or had committed some other breach of his duties, such as by consenting to an improvident sale. The proviso to this was that the beneficiary would in such a scenario be enforcing a right in the name of the trust and on behalf of the trustee, and not some right which arose out of some duty owed to him as beneficiary by the mortgagee. This view finds some support in the comments of Templeman LJ in *Hayim v Citibank NA* [1987] AC 730 at 748, a decision of the Privy Council.

As mentioned previously, the administrative receiver also has a variety of duties imposed on him by statute. These include a duty to file accounts and to present a report to creditors by virtue of ss38 and 48, as well as a duty to account to preferential creditors (*Westminster City Council v Treby* [1936] 2 All ER 21). Those statutory duties are considered following a more specific examination of the non-statutory duties to which the office-holder is subject.

## 9.2 Duty to the Debenture-holder and to the Company

Whilst this section considers the duties owed by the administrative receiver to the debenture-holder, a number of the points raised about the nature of the duties are relevant to other parties who are considered in the following sections. The approach taken in the text is to consider initially the position in relation to the appointing debenture-holder and to the company, the implications for relevant third parties being referred to and developed where appropriate in the subsequent sections.

Generally, the administrative receiver is under an express duty to provide full information to the debenture-holder in relation to the administrative receivership and its conduct (*Gomba Holdings Ltd v Minories Finance* [1987] 3 BCC 643 at 644–5). This reflects the fact that the legislation imposes no direct formal reporting requirements on the administrative receiver as regards the debenture-holder. In practice, full information is usually rendered on a regular interim report basis and also in response to specific enquiries by the debenture-holder.

The agency relationship vis-à-vis a company and the administrative receiver is invariably provided for as standard form in well-drawn modern debentures. This has now been overtaken by s44(1)(a) which implies such a relationship until such time as the company goes into liquidation. Notwithstanding this, the courts have now well established that the administrative receiver owes his primary duty to his appointing debenture-holder. A number of the cases considered below address the question of duties from the position of a mortgagee in possession as opposed to that of a receiver and manager, such as an administrative receiver, who is appointed by and who effects a sale primarily in the interests of the debenture-holder. This distinction is not problematic since the net effect of either scenario is effectively the same, although it brings with it the possibility that both debenture-holder and administrative receiver may be liable for breaches by the latter.

This area also raises the question of why the receiver should be treated in a manner more onerous than any other agent of the mortgagor. The answer lies in the unique agency relationship between the administrative receiver and the company which subsists concurrently with the primary duty owed by the administrative receiver to his appointing debenture-holder.

### 9.2.1  The debenture-holder's duty in effecting the appointment

A mortgagee owes no duty to a mortgagor in effecting the appointment of a receiver who realises and enforces its security, even if this can be shown not to be in the best interests of the mortgagor company, except possibly where the appointment is made in bad faith. As Oliver LJ put it in *Shamji v Johnson Matthey Bankers Ltd* [1991] BCLC 36, in adopting a passage of Hoffman LJ at first instance in the same case:

> The appointment of a receiver seems to me to involve an inherent conflict of interest... It seems to me that a decision by the mortgagee to exercise the power cannot be challenged except perhaps on grounds of bad faith. There is no room for the implication of a term that the mortgagee shall be under a duty to the mortgagor to consider all relevant matters before exercising the power. If no such qualification can be read into the security documents, I do not think that a wider duty can exist in tort.

In *Re B Johnson & Co (Builders) Ltd* [1955] Ch 634 at 661–2 Jenkins LJ explained the rationale behind the duty as owed to the debenture-holder thus:

> The company gets [a] loan on terms that the lender shall be entitled, for the purposes of making their security effective, to appoint a receiver with powers of sale and of management pending sale, and with full discretion as to the exercise and mode of exercising those powers. The primary duty of the receiver is to the debenture-holders and not to the company. He is receiver and manager of the property of the company for the debenture-holders, not manager for the company... [and] the whole purpose of... [the] appointment would obviously be stultified if the company could claim that a receiver and manager owes it any duty comparable to the duty owed to a company by its own directors and managers.

These words met with approval in the judgment of Templeman LJ in the Privy Council's decision in *Downsview Nominees v First City Corp Ltd* [1993] BCC 46 (at 54), and also echo similar views expressed in *Cuckmere Brick Co Ltd v Mutual Finance Ltd* [1971] Ch 949 (at 965 per Salmon LJ) and by Hoffmann J in *Gomba Holdings v Homan* [1986] 3 All ER 94 (at 97) and in *Re Potters Oil (No 2)* [1986] 1 WLR 201 (at 206) (see also *Nash v Eads* (1880) 25 Sol Jo 95 per Jessel MR).

What limits then may be placed on the administrative receiver in discharging his primary function and his duty to the debenture-holder as regards the effect upon other third parties such as the company and any sureties, guarantors and subsequent encumbrances? This question is most relevant to the sale of charged property by the office-holder, to the extent that it creates a shortfall on the debt secured by the debenture and which, as a consequence, must be borne by one or more of the third parties, depending on the contractual arrangements in place. The courts have attempted to formulate rules which take account of the need on the part of the debenture-holder to realise security with relative speed, whilst at the same time guarding against the risks posed to the company and third parties by an improper or unconsidered sale or a sale to a connected party, as well as the hazards posed by volatile and rapidly rising or falling markets.

## 9.2.2 Sale of charged assets

The decision of the Court of Appeal in *Cuckmere Brick Co Ltd v Mutual Finance Ltd* [1971] Ch 949 was acknowledged in the *Downsview* decision as good authority for the proposition that if a mortgagee (or, by analogy, an administrative receiver appointed by a debenture-holder) decides to sell, he must take reasonable care to obtain a proper price. *Cuckmere* goes no further, however, as an authority and, as Templeman LJ pointed out in *Downsview*, no general duty to use reasonable care in dealing with the assets is imposed on the administrative receiver on the basis of the views above as expressed by Jenkins LJ in *Re B Johnson & Co (Builders) Ltd* [1955] Ch 634 at 661–2. This is a remarkable departure from the position recognised in the previous authorities. It discounts wholly the existence of a duty to take reasonable care when exercising powers under a debenture, other than a requirement that the administrative receiver (or mortgagor) should act in good faith. The rationale behind this approach appears to be that the duties imposed by equity on an administrative receiver would be wholly unnecessary if such a general duty in negligence was to be imposed on the office-holder such as to require him to take reasonable care in the exercise of his powers and in dealing with the assets. The position following *Downsview* is referred to again below, although it should be noted that, whilst strictly speaking the decision of the Privy Council is not binding on the courts of England and Wales, its decision remains of persuasive authority; as such, the *Downsview* decision represents a significant departure from the position as it had and continues to stand. A similar view to that aired in *Downsview* has been taken by the New Zealand High Court in *Moritzson Properties Ltd v McLachlan* [1994] 3 NZLR 250 where the receiver's duties in effecting a sale of assets was limited to acting in good faith and not recklessly.

The view expressed in the *Cuckmere* case is encapsulated in the following words of Salmon LJ, which serve as a useful starting point in considering matters affecting the conduct of the sale of charged assets:

> It is well settled that a mortgagee is not a trustee of the power of sale for the mortgagor. Once the power has accrued, the mortgagee is entitled to exercise it for his own purposes whenever he chooses to do so. It matters not that the moment may be unpropititious and that by waiting a higher price could be obtained. He has the right to realise his security by turning it into money when he likes. Nor ... is there anything to prevent a mortgagee from accepting the best bid he can get at an auction, even though the auction is badly attended and the bidding exceptionally low. Provided none of these adverse factors is due to any fault of the mortgagee he can do as he likes.

How then does an administrative receiver take reasonable care to obtain a proper price on the sale of charged property? Depending on the circumstances, the simplest answer appears to be in ensuring the sale particulars for the property are full and accurate, that the sale is properly advertised and that specialist and independent advice is sought as to the price which may reasonably be expected on the sale, albeit on a forced basis.

The *Cuckmere* case involved a sale of land by a mortgagee who failed to ensure that the sale particulars stated that the land benefited from planning permission for flats to be built on it. As a consequence, the mortgagee was held liable to the mortgagor for loss arising as a consequence of the negligence. In the same way, a sale was held to have been conducted negligently in *American Express International Banking Corp v Hurley* [1985] 3 All ER 564 where specialist music and technical lighting equipment was not independently valued and was not advertised for sale in the appropriate trade publications. A similar conclusion was reached in *Predeth v Castle Phillips Finance Co Ltd* [1986] 2 EGLR 144 where a mortgagee sold charged property on an apparently forced sale basis without first exposing it to a ready market for a proper period of time. On the other hand, negligence was not established in *Parker Tweedale v Dunbar Bank plc* [1990] 2 All ER 575 where mortgaged assets were sold by private agreement on the basis of what the *bona fide* mortgagee had honestly believed to be the best possible price for them in the circumstances. This was despite arguments by counsel for the mortgagor that a better price would have been obtained at an auction (which the court considered conjectural), the fact that other private purchasers had been prepared to pay more than the actual selling price (which was apparently unknown to the mortgagee at that time) and the fact that the purchaser of the assets had resold them within seven days for £700,000 having purchased them for £575,000. Whilst the facts of the case and the allegations made by the mortgagor clearly gave rise to questions being raised about the actions of the mortgagee, the court was not satisfied on the evidence before it that the mortgagee had acted either *mala fide* or negligently.

From the administrative receiver's point of view, the practical implications of the above cases are that he must take all steps to ensure that the best possible price may be obtained in the circumstances. Whether this necessarily requires independent valuations and advertisement of the sale to be undertaken necessarily depends on the nature of the particular charged assets, the volatility or readiness of a market for them, the price offered by any ready and willing buyer and the difference (if any) in price which it is anticipated may be obtained on an open market sale. These considerations necessarily involve something of a balancing act. This need not, however, be a problem, since relevant authorities make it clear that the question to be asked is not really whether the best possible price has been obtained for the assets, but rather whether, in the circumstances, a better price might be obtained by the taking of reasonable steps. As Denning MR put it in *Standard Chartered Bank Ltd v Walker* [1982] 1 WLR 1410 at 1416, 'the duty is one to use reasonable care to obtain the best possible price'. The question of the parties to whom this duty extends is considered in the next section of this chapter.

One of the problems which remains in this area is that the *Standard Chartered Bank* and *American Express* decisions cited above articulate the nature of the duty owed by a mortgagee (and thus again by analogy the administrative receiver) in the language of the common law duty in negligence. As stated previously, doubt has been cast on this approach in decisions such as that of the Court of Appeal in *Parker Tweedale v Dunbar Bank plc* [1990] 2 All ER 577 and most recently by the Privy Council in *Downsview Nominees Ltd v First City Corp Ltd* [1993] BCC 46. The *Downsview* decision is itself somewhat peculiar in that it discounts the question of a duty being owed by a mortgagee to a mortgagor or subsequently encumbrancers to exercise reasonable care in the discharge of his powers, although it recognises an equitable duty to act *bona fide*. The position thus remains in flux and requires judicial clarification, particularly in view of the lack of any discussion of the apparently relevant authorities, save for a passing reference to the *Cuckmere* case in the *Downsview* decision, the effect of which largely serves to insulate the administrative receiver from third party claims except in the most extreme cases. This approach follows the recent and rather unfortunate development in the law of tort which, rather than discounting the existence of a duty as in *Downsview*, has rather recognised the existence of a duty but placed certain classes of defendant, particularly accountants, beyond its scope (see, for example, *Caparo Industries plc v Dickman* [1990] BCC 164 and *Murphy v Brentwood District Council* [1991] AC 398).

One circumstance in which the duty owed by the administrative receiver becomes critical is where the charged assets are falling in value. This arose in *China and South Sea Bank Ltd v Tan* [1990] 1 AC 356 in which a guarantor for a mortgagor's debt pursued an action against the mortgagee for breach of duty in failing to exercise a power of sale at a time when the security held by it still had value. In rejecting this argument (the further implications of which are considered further below) the Privy Council made it clear that the mortgagee was under no obligation to effect a sale and certainly not one in favour of a guarantor. As Templeman LJ put it [1989] 3 All ER 839 at 842:

> If the creditor chose to exercise his power of sale over the mortgage security he must sell for the current market value but the creditor must decide in his own interest if and when he should sell...The creditor was not under a duty to exercise his power of sale over the mortgaged securities at all.

It is clear that this view will also be relevant as regards potential liability to the company itself. The position is best explained by reference to the words of Lindley LJ in *Farrar v Farrars Ltd* (1888) 40 ChD 395 at 411 from which it remains clear that the administrative receiver will be exonerated from liability in the absence of bad faith, for present purposes, which might be regarded as a breach of his duty to obtain a proper or reasonable price for the charged assets in the circumstances:

> ...if in the exercise of his power [to realise his security and to find a purchaser if he can, the mortgagee] acts *bona fide* and takes reasonable precautions to obtain a proper price, the mortgagor has no redress, even though more might have been obtained for the property if the sale had been postponed.

It is also clear from the decision in *Bank of Cyprus (London) Ltd v Gill* [1980] 2 Lloyd's Rep 51 that a mortgagee may effect a prompt sale, and need not delay in what may be the fruitless hope of obtaining a better price at a later date. The rationale behind this rule is to offer some relative degree of protection to a *bona fide* mortgagee who, after all, is not a trustee for the mortgagor of his power of sale (*Kennedy v De Trafford* [1897] AC 180). Nonetheless, it is suggested that the position will be different where it is clear that a higher price will be obtained following delay, say where a prospective purchaser makes it clear that he is only able to complete a purchase on a stipulated date on funds becoming available to him, particularly where the delay is relatively short and the price which may be obtained is significantly higher. It is not accepted, however, that any delay need not be undertaken other perhaps than where the subsequent sale is certain or virtually certain, since this might impose on the administrative receiver a never-ending cycle of possible contracts which never proceed to completion (see also *Tse Kwong Lam v Wong Chit Sen* [1983] 3 All ER 54 at 59 per Templeman LJ, which supports this view).

One method by which an administrative receiver may seek to obtain a proper price for charged assets is sale by auction. There is, of course, no requirement for such a method of sale to be employed as a matter of course prior to a sale by private treaty (*Davey v Durrant* (1857) 7 De G&J 535 at 553, 560). On a sale of charged assets by way of auction the case law indicates that certain steps will be necessary if the administrative receiver is to be able to show that he has taken reasonable steps to obtain a proper price for the assets. In *Tse Kwong Lam v Wong Chit Sen* [1983] 3 All ER 54, it was held that it is not sufficient for a mortgagee merely to accept the highest bid at an auction in a sale in which he himself was interested. This decision was one clearly affected by the conflict of interest posed by the mortgagee's interest in the sale. However, the court's view would seem equally applicable to a sale by an administrative receiver where no such conflict exists. In the *Tse Kwong Lam* case the Privy Council considered that the onus rested on the mortgagee to establish that he had acted *bona fide* and had taken reasonable steps to protect the interests of the borrower in obtaining the best price reasonably obtainable at the time of the sale (see also *ANZ Banking Group Ltd v Bangadelly Pastoral Co Ltd* (1978) 52 ALJR 529). Such reasonable steps would necessarily involve the taking of appropriate independent professional advice as to the appropriateness of an auction as a method of sale of the particular asset, the steps necessary or reasonable to make the auction a success (eg as to advertising, venue, approaching appropriate auctioneers etc) and the amount of any reserve price stipulated. The taking of reasonable steps may also include, for example, the selection by the mortgagee or administrative receiver of a competent valuer who is to be paid for by the mortgagor in accordance with the terms of the debenture and on whose valuation the mortgagee or administrative receiver knows the mortgagor will rely (*Smith v Bush* [1990] 1 AC 831 at 865).

Even the taking of such steps, however, will not necessarily safeguard the position of the administrative receiver since, as Templeman LJ put it in *Tse Kwong Lam v Wong Chit Sen* [1983] 3 All ER 54 at 60:

> On behalf of the mortgagee it was submitted that all the reasonable steps were taken where the mortgagee, with adequate advertisement, sold the property at a properly conducted auction to the highest bidder. The submission assumes that such an auction must produce the best price reasonably obtainable or, as Salmon LJ expressed the text, the true market value. *But the price obtained at any particular auction may be less than the price obtainable by private treaty and may depend on the steps taken to encourage bidders to attend* [emphasis added].

The implication therefore is that care should be exercised, and certainly specialist advice sought as to whether an auction is the most appropriate method of sale of particular assets. If it is considered to be appropriate, then advertisements should be posted and circulated to interested parties, particularly where the market in the assets is a specialist one, as in *American Express International Banking Corp v Hurley* [1985] 3 All ER 564. Indeed, in that case Mann J considered that a failure to take specialist advice from a person involved in the industry manifested a failure to take reasonable care on a sale by the mortgagee. Moreover, as Templeman LJ had stated previously in the *Tse Kwong Lam* case cited above, in seeking to establish in all respects that he acted fairly to the borrower and used his best endeavours to obtain the best price reasonably obtainable for the mortgaged property, the mortgagee (or administrative receiver) should bear in mind that a sale by auction does not necessarily prove the validity of a transaction.

The price which must be obtained on a sale of charged assets, has been described as 'the true market value at the date of sale' by Salmon LJ in *Cuckmere Brick Co Ltd v Mutual Finance Ltd* [1971] 2 All ER 633, 'a proper price' by Isaacs J in *Pendlebury v Colonial Mutual Life Assurance Society Ltd* (1912) 13 CLR 676 and by Lindley LJ in *Farrar v Farrars Ltd* (1888) 40 ChD 395, 'the current market value' by Templeman LJ in *China and South Sea Bank Ltd v Tan* [1989] 3 All ER 839 and 'the best price reasonably obtainable' by Templeman LJ in the *Tse Kwong Lam* case. This question was also considered by Millett J in *Re Charnley Davies Ltd (No 2)* [1990] BCLC 760 in connection with a sale by an administrator. The learned judge distinguished the positions of mortgagee and administrator on the basis that the former may effect a sale in order to give priority to his own interests, whether or not this is calculated to obtain the best price, whereas the administrator is obliged to take reasonable care to obtain the best price that the circumstances permit since he has no inherent interest of his own to which he may give priority. In other words, the mortgagee or administrative receiver is obliged to take reasonable care to obtain the true value of the property at the moment he chooses to sell it, whereas the administrator is under a duty to take reasonable care to obtain the best price that the circumstances, as the administrator perceives them to be, will permit.

In relation to the above, it is suggested that the onus of establishing the *bona fide* element and the taking of reasonable steps on the part of the mortgagee (or administrative receiver) in effecting a sale will shift to the mortgagor seeking to set aside the sale, where the sale had not been made to a party with an interest in the transaction. An example is the *Tse Kwong Lam* case, where the mortgagee held a beneficial interest in the shares of the purchasing company together with his wife and children, was a director of it and was solely responsible for its financing. This brings to the fore the question of conflict on a sale by a mortgagee or administrative receiver.

### 9.2.3   Sale of assets to an interested party

There is no general bar to an administrative receiver disposing of charged assets to a party which has an interest in the transaction. However, such an arrangement raises the standards of behaviour which become expected of the administrative receiver in effecting the sale. This should be contrasted with a sale by one party to itself in which the position is slightly altered as considered in the next paragraph. The position is best described by reference to the words of Lindley LJ in *Farrar v Farrars Ltd* (1888) 40 ChD 395 at 409 which involved a sale by a mortgagee to a company in which he was a member. The position was put thus (italics added):

> A sale by a person to a corporation of which he is a member is not, either in form or in substance, a sale by a person to himself... There is no authority for saying that such a sale is not warranted by an ordinary power of sale, and in our opinion, such a sale is warranted by such a power, and does not fall within the rule to which we have at present referred (*as is considered below*). But although this is true, it is obvious that a sale by a person to an incorporated company of which he is a member may be invalid upon various grounds, although it may not be reached by the rule which prevents this man from selling to himself or to a trustee for himself. Such a sale may, for example, be fraudulent and at an undervalue or it may be made under circumstances which throw upon the purchasing company the burden of proving the validity of the transaction, and the company may be unable to prove it.

The learned judge went on to give effect to the fact that every mortgage confers upon a mortgagee the right to realise his security and to find a purchaser if he is able to. As such, and in accordance with the judgments cited above, the mortgagor will have no redress where the mortgagee acts *bona fide* in exercising that power and takes reasonable precautions to obtain a price, even where a higher price might have been obtained on a proposed sale.

Where an administrative receiver proposes to effect a sale to a party in which either he or his appointing debenture-holder has an interest he will remain bound by the duty, as discussed above, to take reasonable care to obtain the best price reasonably obtainable at the time of sale. Furthermore, full disclosure of the interest in the sale should be made prior to its being entered into and appropriate independent advice sought as to the contractual arrangements themselves, particularly where the sale price, or the arrangements for payment, are likely to give rise to questions by the company, any guarantor or any subsequent encumbrancer of the company's assets. The position was settled thus by Templeman LJ in *Tse Kwong Lam v Wong Chit Sen* [1983] 3 All ER 54 at 59:

> ...there is no hard and fast rule that a mortgagee may not sell to a company in which he is interested. The mortgagee and the company seeking to uphold the transaction must show that the sale was in good faith and that the mortgagee took reasonable precautions to obtain the best price reasonably obtainable at that time. The mortgagee is not however bound to postpone the sale in the hope of obtaining a better price

> or to adopt a piecemeal method of sale which could only be carried out
> over a substantial period or at some risk of loss . . . .

In *Farrar v Farrars Ltd* (1888) 40 ChD 395, CA Lindley LJ considered that a
sale by a mortgagee to a company of which the mortgagee was a member did
not constitute a sale by a person to himself. This is significant, since the position on a sale by a mortgagee is wholly different where it is made to himself
in that the transaction is not deemed in law to constitute a true sale and, as
such, may be set aside or declared void (*Williams v Wellingborough BC*
[1975] 1 WLR 1327; *Downes v Grazebrook* (1871) 3 Mer 200). This is the
case whether or not the sale is effected by the mortgagee in possession or an
agent of it. This would appear to apply also to an administrative receiver who
exercises the power of sale implied by Sched 1 to IA 1986, and as invariably
conferred by a standard-form debenture in the interests of the appointing
debenture-holder, notwithstanding the implied agency relationship as between
the administrative receiver and the company by virtue of s44(1)(a). The
approach is really one of substance over form as set out by Lindley LJ in the
*Farrar* case:

> It is perfectly well settled that a mortgagee with a power of sale cannot
> sell to himself either alone or with others, nor to a trustee for him-
> self . . . ; nor to anyone employed by him to conduct the sale . . . A sale by
> a person to himself is no sale at all, and a power of sale does not author-
> ise the donee of the power to take the property subject to it at a price
> fixed by himself, even though such price be the full value of the prop-
> erty. Such a transaction is not an exercise of the power, and the imposi-
> tion of a trustee, although it gets over the difficulty so far as form is
> concerned, does not affect the substance of the transaction.

Extreme caution should therefore be adopted in relation to any sale by an
administrative receiver to a third party which acts on behalf of or in pursuance
of the interests of the debenture-holder at the risk of an application to set
aside the transaction.

Where an administrative receiver enters into a purchase on his own account,
he will be liable to the common law rule applicable to non-administrative
receivers whereby he must account for any profit made by him through the
purchase or any other dealing in the property (*Nugent v Nugent* [1908] 1
Ch 546). The administrative receiver will also require the consent of the court to
his purchasing any assets over which he is appointed irrespective of whether
the sale is to be made to him directly or to a trustee for him (*Alven v Bond*
(1841) Fl&K 196). This will apply even where the sale is effected by a mortgagee who sells the property free of the receivership (*Nugent v Nugent* [1908]
1 Ch 546). The rationale behind these rules is that a receiver, including an
administrative receiver, is a fiduciary and, as such, may not profit personally

from his position and the discharge of his function. In the case of an administrative receiver, the most appropriate method of obtaining the court's consent to a sale to the administrative receiver himself will be by way of an application to the court for directions under s35.

Where a debenture-holder is dissatisfied with the conduct of an administrative receiver, a removal of the office-holder may only be effected by the court (s45(1)). The rationale behind this rule appears to be to protect the administrative receiver in considering the interests of other parties to whom he may also owe duties in this exercise of his powers. These third parties are considered further below at paras 9.3 and 9.4.

### 9.2.4 Exclusion of liability

An administrative receiver may seek to protect himself in reliance on an exemption clause which seeks to exclude liability on his part for breach of duty. Such clauses commonly appear in standard-form debentures although their effect should not be seen as automatic. Assuming that an administrative receiver may be required to exercise reasonable care in the exercise of his powers, it has been held by the Court of Appeal in *Bishop v Bonham* [1988] BCLC 656 that a clause which sought to exclude liability on the part of a mortgagee '... for any loss howsoever arising in connection with any such sale' did not exclude liability for negligence where the debenture authorised a power of sale to be exercisable by the mortgagee 'in such manner and upon such terms ... as you may think fit'. The approach taken by the court was that this did not exclude liability for a loss arising as a result of failure to take care to obtain a proper price, even though that clause would apparently cover a non-negligent sale at undervalue which gave rise to loss (although it is unclear as to how such a sale would give rise to liability). It should be noted however that Slade LJ was of the opinion in *Bishop v Bonham* [1988] BCLC 656 at 665 that it might be possible, with an appropriately drafted clause, to exclude liability arising as a result of a breach of a mortgagee's duty to take reasonable care. However, any such a clause would be subject to a reasonableness test and would only be operative in relation to a party to the debenture contract (Unfair Contract Terms Act 1977 ss2(2) and 11(1)). Whilst the administrative receiver's agency relationship with the company might conceivably bring him within the scope of being a party to the contract, the better view is that it is actually the company which is party to the contract, and thus subject to the exclusion clause, where the office-holder acts as agent of the company. Conversely, the administrative receiver will act on a personal basis where he acts outside the scope of his authority, or acts on a personal basis by express agreement or where his agency relationship with the company has been terminated. It should also be noted that the 1977 Act has no application to the purported exclusion of liability in relation to the creation, transfer or termination of contracts in land (Unfair Contract Terms Act 1977 s1(2) and Sched 1, para 1).

Whilst the administrative receiver may be held liable to compensate the debenture-holder for breach of his duty in conducting a sale of the company's assets, this will only actually be of relevance to the debenture-holder in practice if the sale of all assets subject to its security creates a shortfall on the debt due to it. Even then, and notwithstanding any operative exemption clause in the debenture, it may also be argued that the debenture-holder has actually consented to the breach by virtue of the doctrine of *volenti non fit injuria*, although this defence will depend on the administrative receiver being able to establish that the debenture-holder had actual knowledge of the disposition or act giving rise to the alleged breach of duty on his part. In reality, an action is more likely to be forthcoming against an administrative receiver from a subsequent encumbrancer, the company itself or any guarantor where the administrative receiver fails to obtain what might be described loosely as a reasonable price in the circumstances of each particular case.

## 9.3   Duty to Subsequent Mortgagees and Encumbrancers

Mortgage law has traditionally recognised the existence of a duty owed by a mortgagee to a subsequent encumbrancer of charged property. From the point of view of the administrative receiver, the duties owed to subsequent encumbrancers of the charged property were considered most recently by the Privy Council in *Downsview v First City Corp Ltd* [1993] BCC 46. This case involved an appeal from the Court of Appeal of New Zealand on the question of the duties which a first debenture-holder and a receiver and manager appointed by a first debenture-holder owed to a second debenture-holder.

### 9.3.1   *Downsview*

The facts in *Downsview* may be summarised as follows. G, a company, carried on a motor dealership and issued two debentures to Creditor 1 and Creditor 2, the debenture to Creditor 1 securing the sum of NZ$ 230,000 in priority to the second debenture. Following financial difficulties and default, Creditor 2 appointed joint receivers and managers who removed the principal shareholder and manager of G's business from office on the basis of the provisional view of the receiver and manager, who were both chartered accountants experienced in receiverships, that a sale of the assets of the company would be necessary. P then approached R who controlled Downsview, the appellant company. Subsequently, Creditor 1 assigned its debenture to Downsview, which then appointed R receiver and manager pursuant to the first debenture. As a result, Creditor 2 agreed to withdraw temporarily its receiver and manager. R proceeded to reinstate P to manage the company's business and announced his intention to trade the company out of its difficulties. As a consequence, Creditor 2 offered to buy out the debenture held by Downsview or, alternatively, to sell its debenture to Downsview. The company continued to trade at a loss and incorporated a new subsidiary to receive the proceeds of sale of vehicles. Eventually, Creditor 2 obtained a court order for the first debenture, as held by Downsview, to be transferred to it on stipulated terms, and for R to cease acting as receiver and manager and to transfer the company's assets to receivers and managers appointed by Creditor 2, who then conducted what is referred to here as a second receivership of the company.

The plaintiffs, Creditor 2 and a second party to which Creditor 2 had subsequently also assigned its debenture, alleged that R and Downsview had acted, or omitted to act, in breach of its duties to them. Their duties were claimed to be: (a) to exercise their powers to proper purpose; (b) to act honestly and in good faith; (c) to exercise reasonable care, skill and diligence; (d) to discharge the first debenture immediately on being in a position to do so; and (e) to pay over to Creditor 2 the surplus assets of the company after satisfaction of the first debenture.

These duties were alleged to have been breached, in summary: by the acquisition by Downsview of the first debenture and the carrying on of the receivership pursuant to it for the improper purpose of preventing the plaintiffs from enforcing their security; by the conduct of the receivership in a reckless or negligent manner; and by the failure to accept the plaintiffs' offer to discharge the first debenture and to assign it to the plaintiffs.

At first instance Gault J held that R and Downsview had exercised their powers under the first debenture for their own improper purposes, in breach of duties owed to Creditor 2. As such, the plaintiffs were entitled to damages on the basis of the difference between the loss that would have occurred had the original receivership been allowed to proceed unimpeded, and the loss incurred as it emerged following the second receivership by the original receivers. Downsview and R appealed (asserting over 30 grounds for doing so). The New Zealand Court of Appeal considered that, on an application of negligence principles, a receiver and manager who elects to carry on the business of a company and trade it out of receivership owe a duty of care to subsequent debenture-holders to take reasonable care in dealing with the assets of the company. As such, R was in breach of his duty to Creditor 2 although Downsview was not. As a consequence, R appealed against the decision to which Creditor 2 (and its assignee) cross-appealed against R and Downsview for the reinstatement of the orders made at first instance by Gault J.

The Privy Council dismissed the appeal by R and allowed the cross-appeal (although an original order made by Gault J—equal to a five-year director disqualification order in the UK—made against R was not restored on grounds of a lack of jurisdiction).

### 9.3.2   The effect of *Downsview*

The *Downsview* decision may be sub-divided into the following four constituent parts.

First, the conclusion that no duty was owed by R and Downsview to Creditor 2, since Creditor 2 was merely a debenture-holder and not a mortgagee was rejected. A mortgagee owes a duty to a subsequent encumbrancer and to the mortgagor to use his powers for the sole purpose of securing repayment of monies owing under his mortgage and a duty to act in good faith. Templeman LJ suggested that it may well be that a mortgagee who appoints a receiver and manager may be guilty of bad faith if he knows that the receiver and manager intends to exercise his powers for the purposes of frustrating the activities of the second mortgagee or for some other improper purpose, or if he fails to revoke the appointment when the mortgagee knows the receiver and manager to be abusing his powers. On the facts, however, this question did not arise in *Downsview*. Specific equitable duties are also imposed on him in the exercise of his powers to go into possession and to realise the charged property. Exactly the same rules apply to a receiver and manager appointed by the mortgagee. However, there is no general duty to use reasonable care in dealing with the assets of the company. The express discounting by the Privy Council of the existence of a duty in negligence should not be under-estimated. The upshot of it, as in *Downsview*, is that liability to a second mortgagee must be based on a breach of the fiduciary and equitable duties identified previously. In most cases these will rest on establishing an improper exercise of powers or bad faith. Whilst the Privy Council was prepared to restore the order made at first instance, it did not do so on the basis of Gault J's contention that liability rested on a breach of duty in negligence, Downsview's position apparently being 'merely a specific example of the duty a mortgagee has to charge-holders to exercise his powers with reasonable care'. The New Zealand Court of Appeal had adopted a similar approach in that, whilst considering R to be in breach of his duty, it considered that Downsview had committed no such breach. Again, this approach was rejected by the Privy Council. The reasoning behind this is conveyed in the following passage by Templeman LJ:

> The general duty of care said to be owed by a mortgagee to subsequent encumbrancers and the mortgagor in negligence is inconsistent with the right of the mortgagee and the duties which the courts applying equitable principles have imposed on the mortgagee. If a mortgagee enters into possession he is liable to account for rent on the basis of wilful default; he must keep mortgage premises in repair; he is liable for waste. Those duties were imposed to ensure that a mortgagee is diligent in discharging his mortgage and returning the property to the mortgagor. If a mortgagee exercises the power of

sale in good faith for the purpose of protecting his security, he is not liable to the mortgagor even though he might have obtained a higher price and even though the terms might be regarded as disadvantageous to the mortgagor.

Apart from the injustice and confusion arising from the imposition of negligence principles on the defined equitable duties, the court also considered that the implication of a duty in negligence on a receiver and manager may expose the office-holder to undue risk:

> A receiver and manager liable in negligence will be tempted to sell assets as speedily as possible for the purpose of repaying the mortgage debt, a decision which, whether negligent or not, does not expose him to a suit for damages but may be disadvantageous to the company. A receiver who is brave enough to manage will run the risk of being sued if the financial position of the company deteriorates, whether the deterioration may be due to imperfect knowledge or bad advice or insufficient time or other circumstances. There will always be expert witnesses ready to testify with the benefit of hindsight that they would have acted differently and fared better.

The second element of the *Downsview* decision recognised the practical matter that a dissatisfied company could raise money to pay off the debenture-holder. However, in the event that a receiver and manager opted to continue to manage the company's business in good faith and for the purposes of preserving and realising the assets for the benefit of his debenture-holder, he would attract no further and greater liability. The court also established, on the facts in *Downsview*, that the dissatisfied second debenture-holder could have required the assignment of the first debenture to it under the terms of the first debenture, which would have further undermined the argument that the first debenture-holder had acted properly and in good faith. The court disparaged the contrary argument that Downsview were actually entitled to refuse such an offer to assign, on the basis of invalidity of the debenture provisions for want of registration.

Thirdly, a receiver and manager breaches his duties if he abuses his powers by exercising them other than for the specific purposes of enabling the charged assets to be preserved and realised for the benefit of the debenture-holder. The court did not consider that these duties required a receiver and manager to adopt any particular course of action, by selling the whole or part of the mortgaged property or by carrying on the business of the company or by exercising any other powers or discretions vested in him. However, on the evidence in *Downsview*, the court was satisfied that R had not accepted office and exercised his powers for proper purposes by enforcing the security conferred by the first debenture. Instead, R simply held office for the purposes of preventing the enforcement by the second debenture-holder of its security.

This third element of the *Downsview* decision rested on the court's recognition of the fact that a receiver and manager is under a duty to take reasonable care to obtain a proper price on the sale of charged assets, in accordance with the duty imposed on a mortgagee by virtue of *Cuckmere Brick Co Ltd v Mutual Finance Ltd* [1971] Ch 949. However, that duty apart, the general duty of a receiver and manager appointed by a debenture-holder, as defined by Jenkins LJ and in *Re B Johnson & Co (Builders) Ltd* [1955] Ch 634 at 661–2, imposes no general duty of care in dealing with the assets of the company. Again, the effect of this is to insulate from liability an administrative receiver who acts *bona fide* in exercising his powers to preserve and realise the charged assets in favour of the debenture-holder.

The fourth and final element of the *Downsview* decision related to the specific facts of the case but is relevant in that it identifies the grounds upon which the liability in *Downsview* arose. The court considered there to be overwhelming evidence that the manner in which R had conducted the receivership revealed an improper purpose. Indeed, the court considered that the receivership had been carried on in bad faith verging on fraud. The Privy Council concurred with Gault J's opinion that R had accepted the appointment as receiver and manager for the purposes of disrupting a receivership under the second debenture and preventing its enforcement. Liability on the part of Downsview, on the other hand, arose from its breach of duty in failing to transfer the assigned first debenture to Creditor 2 on being requested to do so in accordance with the terms of the first debenture.

The quantum of liability in *Downsview* is also worth considering since it would appear likely to be relevant to the judicial approach in future. The Privy Council concerned itself with the analysis of Gault J at first instance, which encapsulated the damages payable by R and Downsview as being the difference between the loss that would have been incurred had the first receivership by Creditor 2's receiver and manager been allowed to proceed unimpeded, and the loss actually incurred as it emerged following the second receivership by those two receivers and managers; see further [1993] BCC 46 at 58 per Lord Templeman.

As an afterword it is worth noting that in New Zealand the duty of a receiver and manager to protect the principal's interest by taking reasonable care in the exercise of the powers has been placed on a statutory basis by virtue of the New Zealand Receiverships Act 1993 s18. Interestingly, the Act also imposes a secondary duty in favour of unsecured creditors (cf *Lathia v Dronsfield Bros* [1987] BCLC 321), although it remains to be seen how this duty is worked out in practice by the courts.

The *Downsview* decision must be viewed as being generous to receivers in that it shelters them from the rigours of potential negligence liability, a trend adopted by the English courts of late. Whilst the decision is difficult to reconcile with the previous authorities, which equate the receiver and mortgagee's duties with those raised in negligence as discussed in the previous sections, it is submitted that the move away from that approach is to be favoured and that the adoption by the domestic courts of the Privy Council's approach would be of significant practical use. The area risks unnecessary convolution if the negligence principles—which are convenient but simply not appropriate to the area—continue to pollute the equitable duties which best reflect the relationship of the receiver and the various interested parties which constitute the unique scenario that is receivership.

From the point of view of the adviser to the administrative receiver, care should be taken where a subsequent encumbrancer retains an interest in the charged assets, particularly where that party expresses dissatisfaction with the conduct of the receivership by the receiver and manager(s) in office. Whilst *Downsview* was specifically concerned with a second encumbrancer only, there is no reason to limit the decision to second encumbrancers to the exclusion of subsequent chargees. *Downsview* suggests that the acid tests are whether or not the receiver and manager is acting *bona fide* in the course of his office, and whether the conduct of the receivership is undertaken in such a way as to protect and realise the charged assets in the interests of the debenture-holder. In the event that this test cannot be confirmed positively, a potential risk of liability must exist. Similarly, questions should be asked as to the notice given by the debenture-holder in effecting the appointment. Whilst the previously cited authorities, such as *Gomba Holdings* and *Re Potters Oil (No 2)*, made it clear that no duty is owed by the debenture-holder to the company in effecting an appointment, *Downsview* suggests the contrary, in favour of a subsequent encumbrancer of the charged assets who could obviously and alternatively appoint its own receiver and manager.

*Downsview* also underlines the importance of perusing the specific terms of each debenture for provisions enabling a subsequent encumbrancer to require a transfer or assignment of a prior-ranking interest or charge on request or demand. Failure to comply with such a provision will clearly give rise to liability on the part of the current debenture-holder. The relevance and use of s43 should also not be under-estimated in this regard for obtaining court approval for the disposition of prior-ranking charged property.

## 9.4 Duty to Discharge Preferential Debts

The duty to discharge preferential debts, as imposed by s40, is expressed as a duty rather than as a liability since the obligation is a positive one (*Inland Revenue Commissioners v Goldblatt* [1972] Ch 498). The duty falls on any receiver appointed to enforce a floating charge, although it will not now extend to industrial and provident societies following *Re Devon and Somerset Farmers Ltd* [1994] Ch 57.

The term preferential debts relates to both corporate and individual debtors, as provided for by s386 and the preferential debts listed in Sched 6 to IA 1986. These refer to:

(a)   debts due to the Inland Revenue over the preceding 12 months, VAT due to Customs and Excise over the preceding six-month period;

(b)   certain claims for social security contributions over the preceding 12 months;

(c)   contributions due by the company to occupational pension schemes and State pension scheme premiums under the Pension Schemes Act 1993;

(d)   certain employee entitlements due in the preceding four months (subject to a maximum limit currently prescribed as £800 by the Insolvency Proceedings (Monetary Limits) Order 1986 (SI No 1996); and

(e)   certain levies due on coal and steel production.

The date from which liability is computed is the date of appointment of the receiver (s378(4)(a)). Other than as stipulated by Sched 6, Crown debts no longer rank as preferential debts. The same is also true of unpaid rates, as was previously the case under the Companies Act 1948 ss94 and 319.

Where a company is not in the course of being wound up, its preferential debts must be discharged out of the assets coming into the hands of the administrative receiver in priority to any claim by the debenture-holder in respect of principal or interest (s40(2)). This provision refers only to any claim by the debenture-holder under its floating charge and not a fixed charge, although the crystallisation of a floating charge will no longer affect its status as such (s251, cf *Re Brightlife Ltd* [1986] 3 All ER 673). The administrative receiver is not, of course, only liable for those preferential claims of which he has notice. On s40 in practice see Anderson (1994) 15 Co Law 195.

The claims of a debenture-holder under a fixed charge, other than a crystallised floating charge, will not be subject to s40(2). This is clear from the decisions in *Re Lewis Merthyr Consolidated Collieries Ltd* [1929] 1 Ch 498, even if the debenture-holder holds both fixed and floating charges, and *Re G L Saunders Ltd* [1986] 1 WLR 215, which held that the claims of preferential creditors must fail in respect of any surplus remaining on assets and realisations following the discharge of a debenture-holder's claim in full from fixed charge assets under the Law of Property Act 1925 s105 (see also *Re Griffin Hotel Co Ltd* [1941] Ch 129). The status of a secured creditor is unaffected by his contemporaneous status as a preferential creditor (*Re William Hall (Contractors) Ltd* [1967] 1 WLR 948).

Preferential debts are subject to the administrative receiver's expenses and remuneration and the costs of realisation (*Re Glyncorrwg Colliery Co Ltd* [1926] 1 Ch 951). It is of significant practical importance, therefore, that an accurate and true allocation is made by the administrative receiver of the extent to which the expenses of the receivership are to be met as between fixed and floating charges, since the greater the degree to which these are to be borne by any floating charge assets, the less the amount available for discharging preferential debts. Similar considerations concern the advice sought and decisions taken as to the true nature of any purported fixed or floating charge taken over assets.

Payments made by the administrative receiver in respect of preferential debts may be recouped out of the assets of the company available for payment of general creditors. The definition in s29(2), however, dictates that those free assets will be minimal in practice, since the administrative receiver must be appointed over at least substantially the whole of the company's property. Nevertheless, s40(3) ultimately shifts the burden of the discharge of preferential debts onto unsecured creditors (*Re Mannesman Tube Co Ltd* [1901] 2 Ch 93 and *Re Christionette International Ltd* [1982] 1 WLR 1245). This would include monies recovered by a contemporaneously appointed liquidator under the transaction avoidance provision in ss238 and 239. For example, in *Re Yagerphone* [1932] Ch 392 monies recovered in respect of a fraudulent preference were held not to be caught by a floating charge. Nevertheless, that decision has been the subject of widespread criticism and it is submitted that the better view is that a floating charge extending to future assets should catch such recoveries as in the case of misfeasance proceedings (and arguably wrongful trading) recoveries (see *Re Anglo-Austrian Printing & Publishing Union* [1895] 2 Ch 891, *Re Asiatic Electric Co Pty Ltd* (1970) 92 WN (NSW) 361 and also Milman (1979) Conv 138 and Oditah (1990) LMCLQ 205).

Where the assets available to the administrative receiver are insufficient to discharge in full the claims of preferential creditors, these abate proportionally in the same way as unsecured creditors in a winding-up. However, where the company is also being wound up, the liquidator may apply to the court under the rarely employed s156 for an order conferring priority on the liquidator's costs, charges and expenses so that they are paid out of company assets in such priority as the court thinks fit (see *Re Barleycorn Enterprises Ltd* [1970] Ch 465).

It is convenient at this point to deal with potential liabilities of the administrative receiver in respect of preferential debts. It is well established that the misapplication by an administrative receiver of an asset or realisation in contravention of a preferential claim renders him personally liable to preferential creditors (*Woods v Winskill* [1913] 2 Ch 303; *Inland Revenue Commissioners v Goldblatt* [1972] 1 Ch 498). The claim may be made in either tort or for breach of statutory duty for the resulting loss, which will inevitably amount to the extent of the misapplication together with interest (*Westminster Corporation v Haste* [1950] Ch 442).

A misapplication need not arise strictly by payment over to a non-entitled creditor in terms of the priority of claims in the administrative receivership. The application of floating charge assets in, say, the continuance of the company's business, as in the *Westminster Corporation* case, would amount equally to a misapplication giving rise to liability on the part of the office-holder, since the positive obligation to discharge arises at the time of his appointment (ss40(2), 387(4)). However, when an administrative receiver misapplies assets or realisations on the basis of a misrepresentation by the debenture-holder or its agent of which he is unaware, then the debenture-holder is liable to indemnify the administrative receiver for any liability arising (*Westminster City Council v Treby* [1936] 2 All ER 21). Similarly, the debenture-holder will be liable to preferential creditors as a constructive trustee where he receives payment from the administrative receiver with notice of the misapplication (*IRC v Goldblatt* [1972] 1 Ch 498). Alternatively, the debenture-holder may be liable for wrongfully procuring and/or being a party to the misapplication with notice of it. It is difficult to see why the administrative receiver should be made personally liable for a misapplication in this way, even where the debenture-holder is not fixed with notice of the preferential claim, since the effect of this would be to unjustifiably enhance the position of the debenture-holder. Notwithstanding these liabilities, it would also appear that the company itself retains a right of action against the debenture-holder where monies are misappliedly paid over to the debenture-holder to the detriment of preferential creditors, the action being pursued by the liquidator in a winding-up (see *Westminster Corp v Chapman* [1916] 1 Ch 161).

An administrative receiver who vacates office under s11(1)(b) on the making of an administration order is not required on or after vacating office to take any steps for the purpose of complying with s40 (s11(5)). That provision ensures that the administrator is not troubled with another office-holder dealing with company assets on a continuing basis, in that these should be surrendered by the administrative receiver to the administrator with immediate effect on the order being made, irrespective of any outstanding preferential claims in respect of which he is thereby exonerated from liability.

The position where a company goes into liquidation whilst in administrative receivership is more difficult than in administration, in that the administrative receiver is not relieved from his obligation to discharge preferential claims (see *Re Eisc Teo Ltd* [1991] IRLM 760). The operation of s40(2) is limited to situations where the company is not 'in the course of being wound up', in which case the preferential debts arise from the date of the appointment of the administrative receiver by virtue of s387(4). However, s175, which provides for preferential debts in a winding-up, does not contain any provision which displaces the operation of s40. The effect of s175 therefore appears to be that a liquidation which follows an administrative receivership will give rise to a new set of preferential debts which, in a winding-up, must be paid in priority to all other debts (see s175(1)). However these new liabilities will invariably be relatively small or non-existent, not least because of the discontinued status of assessed taxes as preferential debts.

Finally, s40 will continue to operate both where the administrative receivership precedes a liquidation and vice-versa (see *Re Portbase (Clothing) Ltd* [1993] Ch 388 at 396). The decision is also authority (albeit questionable) for the contention that the expenses of a winding-up will rank in priority to both preferential claims and the claim of a creditor under a floating charge in an administrative receivership (see also *Re Barleycorn Enterprises Ltd* [1970] Ch 465 and ss107, 115 and 251).

## 9.5 Duty to Investigate the Conduct of Directors

By virtue of the Company Directors Disqualification Act 1986 s7(3)(c) an administrative receiver is one of the office-holders under an express duty to make a report to the Secretary of State if the conduct mentioned in s6(1) of that Act is present in relation to a person who is or has been a director of the company in administrative receivership. The conditions in the Company Directors Disqualification Act 1986 s6(1) are that the person is or has been a director or a director of a company which has at any time become insolvent (whether when he was a director or subsequently) and, furthermore, that his conduct as a director of that company (either taken alone or taken together with his conduct as a director of any other company or companies) makes him unfit to be concerned in the management of a company. In practice, ss234 and 236 will also be of significant use in obtaining information from company officers for the purposes of reaching a view for the purposes of these provisions.

Somewhat artificially, a company is deemed by the Company Directors Disqualification Act 1986 s6(2)(c) to become 'insolvent' at the time an administrative receiver (but no other species of receiver) is appointed. The same provision provides that a person's conduct as a director includes conduct in relation to any matter connected with or arising out of the insolvency of that company.

Section 6(1) applies equally to shadow directors, by virtue of the Company Directors Disqualification Act 1986, ss6(3) and 22(4). In addition, it is not subject to territorial restrictions. It has been held that a director of a foreign company which is being wound up in England and Wales may be subject to a disqualification order (*Re Eurostem Maritime Ltd* 1987 PCC 190). Presumably this would apply to a foreign company in administrative receivership within the domestic jurisdiction. The *Eurostem* case also held that the conduct of a director of a company registered in England and Wales in relation to a foreign company may be considered for the purposes of the Company Directors Disqualification Act 1986 s6(1).

The administrative receiver's report is made on statutory Forms D6, 6A and 6B as appropriate. The report is a detailed one and requires the disclosure of the following information:

(a)   a list of all persons who appear to be directors or shadow directors during the report period. This is supplemented by other descriptive information such as the date of incorporation;

(b)   the number of and claims of creditors, under four group headings: (i) trade and expense creditors; (ii) dispositions and pre-payments; (iii) connected companies with which the company has had dealings; and (iv) other creditors. Strangely, and somewhat perversely in view of the court's approach to hallmarks of unfitness, no disclosure appears to be required on the form in relation to Crown debts (see, for example, *Re Sevenoaks Stationers Ltd* [1991] Ch 164, *Re Austinsuite Ltd* [1992] BCLC 1047 and *Re GSAR Realisations Ltd* [1993] BCLC 419.

(c)   the extent to which a director has availed himself of company assets at the expense of third parties in the three-year period preceding the administrative receivership. The court has shown that such matters will clearly affect the period for which a disqualification order is made effective (see, for example, *Re Cargo Agency Ltd* [1992] BCLC 686 and cf *Re Synthetic Technology Ltd* [1993] BCLC 549);

(d)   those directors whose conduct in relation to the company in administrative receivership, or taken together with his conduct as a director of any other company, makes him unfit to be concerned directly or indirectly in the management of a company. In making this decision the office-holder should ensure that he has solid, reliable and certainly well-documented grounds for indicating those directors whom he considered to be within the ambit of the Company Directors Disqualification Act 1986 s6(1). A number of recent cases have brought to light allegations made by defendants that certain office-holders have been more spiteful than reasonable in making their decision in this regard. These are troubling and serious allegations, and they should be borne in mind by all office-holders as a potential hazard in any proceedings instituted subsequently by the Secretary of State.

The factors for which an office-holder should be watchful in general are not capable of specific definition. Schedule 1 to the Company Directors Disqualification Act 1986 comprises two parts, both of which will be relevant to an application for disqualification of a director of a company which has gone into administrative receivership. The office-holder should therefore have regard to those factors. More specifically, the office-holder should address himself to failures to keep proper records (as opposed to failures to make proper records for which see *Re New Generation Engineers Ltd* [1993] BCLC 435), breaches of s216 and willingness or otherwise on the part of the directors to co-operate with him.

The full procedure on reporting obligations, and the procedure for disqualification order applications, is contained in the Insolvent Companies (Reports on Conduct of Directors) (No 2) Rules 1986 (SI No 2134). The application may be by summons in the High Court or by originating application in the county court, but may be made by the Secretary of State only or the Official Receiver acting at his discretion (Company Directors Disqualification Act 1986 s7(1)). The appropriate court is provided for by s2(2) of the same Act.

The reality of director disqualification is less happy than its theory. The whole reporting process is regarded by many office-holders as a thankless task which produces results well below those predicted at the inception of the new legislation, or those which might be regarded as the reasonable expectations of those who fall victim to corporate failure or worse. Certainly recent DTI statistics bear out these misgivings.

## 9.6  Duty to Maintain and Render Accounts

The general rule on maintenance of accounts is that an administrative receiver is required to maintain the same records of the progress of the administrative receivership as a licenced insolvency practitioner is required to maintain in respect of an insolvent estate administered by him (Insolvency Practitioners Regulations 1990 (SI No 439)). On the other hand, the administrative receiver is not expressly required to maintain the same level of detailed accounts as are required of a liquidator in a compulsory winding-up or a creditors' voluntary liquidation (Insolvency Practitioners Regulations 1986 (SI No 439) and s192(1), IR r4.233(1) and (3) respectively). Non-administrative receivers (but not administrative receivers) are required to submit accounts to the Registrar of Companies as prescribed in s38.

In practice, the administrative receiver will keep and maintain detailed accounts of receipts and payments for two principal reasons. First, the maintenance of such accounts will be a relevant factor for consideration by the Secretary of State in ascertaining whether the administrative receiver is a fit and proper person to act as an insolvency practitioner, and whether or not his authorisation to act as such should be renewed (see s393(2)–(4), and Insolvency Practitioners Regulations 1990 (SI No 439) (as amended), reg 4). Secondly, IR r3.32 specifically requires the administrative receiver to render accounts to the Registrar of Companies and various other parties from time to time; by virtue of IR r3.32(4) this does not affect the administrative receiver's common law duty to account, which requires him to render true accounts to the company in administrative receivership as his principal (*Smiths Ltd v Middleton* [1979] 3 All ER 842).

The administrative receiver is under a duty to send to the Registrar of Companies, the company, his appointor and each member of any creditors' committee an account of his receipts and payments as administrative receiver in statutory Form 3.6 (IR r3.32(1)). These must be sent within two months after the end of the 12 months from the date of his appointment, and every subsequent 12-month period, and within two months after his ceasing to act as administrative receiver (IR r3.32(1)). In either case, the two-month period may be extended, on the administrative receiver's application to court, by virtue of IR r3.32(2), such as where the requisite accounts are subject to a dispute or challenge. Failure to comply with this requirement renders the administrative receiver liable to a fine and, for continued default, a daily default fine (see IR Sched 5).

The abstract of accounts contained in Form 3.6 must contain details of receipts and payments during the 12-month period to which the account relates or, where the administrative receiver has ceased to act, during the period from the end of the most recent 12-month accounting period until the time at which the administrative receiver ceased to act (IR r3.32(3)). Where appropriate, the abstract should also indicate the total amounts of the administrative receiver's receipts and payments since his appointment, as brought forward from the immediately previous 12-month period (IR r3.32(3)). Notably, no provision exists requiring an audit of the administrative receiver's accounts or his abstract of receipts and payments.

The administrative receiver is under a duty in equity to provide information to the company in administrative receivership. The leading *dictum* on this point is that of Hoffman J in *Gomba Holdings Ltd v Homan* [1986] 1 WLR 1301 at 1305–7. The statements made there make it clear that the administrative receiver's duty is qualified by the proviso that disclosure must not be to the detriment of the interests of his appointing debenture-holder. Furthermore, the company requiring information from the administrative receiver is fixed with the burden of establishing a *bona fide* need for the information, most obviously an indication of the amount required to discharge in full the secured debt and the costs and expenses of the administrative receiver or, alternatively, an indication of those charged company assets which remain undisposed of or at least subject to contract as entered into by the administrative receiver. In the former case, the disclosure of the information, if challenged by the administrative receiver as a vexatious or frivolous request requiring unnecessary inquiry and work on his part, may well be subject to the company being able to show the availability of sufficient funds to it to clear the outstanding second debt, costs and expenses. In practice, this will rarely be the case although again the administrative receiver will usually not wish to engage in unnecessary litigation or threatened proceedings with the company if the information requested is to hand and its disclosure does not prejudice the interests of the debenture-holder.

On the conclusion of the administrative receivership the ownership of the books, records, papers, receipts and associated documentation falls to either the administrative receiver, the debenture-holder or the company (*Gomba Holdings UK Ltd v Minories Finance Ltd* [1989] 1 All ER 261). This depends on whether the books, records, and papers came into existence to enable the office-holder to discharge his functions or to obtain advice or information to that end, or whether the documents exist so as to keep the debenture-holder informed about the progress of the administrative receivership, or whether they exist for the purposes of the management of the company and the realisation, disposal and application of its assets respectively. In practice, the distinction between these categories is easily blurred and calls for express agreement between the parties at an early stage in case of doubt, particularly where it appears that the company may continue to trade on in whole or part following the conclusion of the administrative receivership.

## 9.7 Statutory Duties Relating to Environmental Regulation

Recent years have seen a significant expansion in the statutory controls over companies in relation to environmental protection. These controls commonly impose personal liability, sometimes criminal, on company directors. Whilst the administrative receiver is not to be seen as a species of company director, it is clear that office-holders generally face the risks of personal liability to the extent that they are responsible for the day-to-day running of a company's business. Examples of this include the Environmental Protection Act 1990 s157(1), and the Water Resources Act 1991 s85(1) which makes reference to liability being incurred by 'persons' who commit or allow the commission of certain specific acts for the purposes of that Act (see also Edwards [1991] 7 IL&P 62 which examines the potential liability of the insolvency practitioner here).

This area is one of particular concern to the office-holder, since the various provisions are largely untried in the courts and tend to be framed in a way conferring liability on classes of persons responsible generally, which may well extend to the administrative receiver as a person responsible for the day-to-day running of the company's business. Examples of the new 'user' liability provisions include the Water Resources Act 1991 s161 (liability to the National Rivers Authority for clean-up expenses in respect of polluting substances in controlled waters) and the Environmental Protection Act 1990 s81 (liability to the Waste Regulation Authority for costs incurred in avoiding harm caused to health by condition of land).

A book of this kind cannot seek to cover in detail the whole gamut of potential environmental liabilities facing the administrative receiver. In cases of doubt, if not in all cases, it will be necessary to seek professional and specialist advice at the earliest possible time, and preferably immediately on appointment. A prospective appointee may, for example wish, to raise the question of advice on possible environmental liabilities at the same time as seeking advice on the validity of his appointment.

Criminal liabilities imposed by certain pieces of legislation do not arise conditional on environmental pollution actually occurring, but rather on the contravention of various regulatory controls. Certainly the courts have been prepared to give effect to this approach in the imposition of fines.

One other troubling aspect of the area is that it appears that criminal liability incurred by the administrative receiver—or, indeed, any office-holder—is beyond general indemnity from the company's assets. This is because of the general bar imposed by the courts on public policy grounds against permitting one party to indemnify another for criminal liability. The same point is true of insurance cover. It remains a matter for conjecture as to the extent to which insurers will be prepared to fund the legal action costs of an office-holder faced with personal environmental liability, although in practice such cover is usually expressly excluded from relevant insurance policies. This should, of course, be checked by the office-holder as a matter of course.

Although the statutory controls on environmental protection may appear to be somewhat diverse, the area is undergoing a period of gradual consolidation. Principally, the integral pollution control system is due to be implemented by April 1996. The legal mechanism for this is provided for in Part I of the Environmental Protection Act 1990 under the oversight and responsibility of Her Majesty's Inspectorate of Pollution. This aims to reduce or obviate the incidence of air, water and soil pollution by requiring prescribed operators—generally heavy industrial processors—to obtain authorisation which is itself conditional on operating and training compliance requirements. Those businesses which do not fall within the scope of the new control system are not necessarily exempt from control, in that they are likely to require separate authorisations for air and water pollution and must also comply with the new waste management licensing system; this obliges them to maintain records of waste disposal and to use only bodies authorised by virtue of Environmental Protection Act 1990 s34.

The value and protection offered by the obtaining of appropriate advice by the office-holder at the earliest possible time is clear. An administrative receiver should also consider carefully any potential liabilities for which he is responsible as a shadow director of any other company. Certainly it appears that contravention of the relevant control provision by the company itself prior to the office-holder's appointment will offer no defence against liability. It hardly needs stating either that liability for environmental pollution—which is likely to be significant and may extend to clean-up costs in the absence of any supporting fund in the UK—is likely to bring with it considerable bad publicity. In view of current social and political attitudes, this may well be highly-publicised because of the profile afforded to environmental matters generally in recent years. The lot of the office-holder is certainly not a hopeless one, however, particularly where the company in administrative receivership has operated its own environmental management system on a voluntary basis of a kind advocated, for example, by the British Standards Institute Specification for Environmental Management Systems (BS 7750).

The administrative receiver should at the outset of taking office consider a full environmental audit or an informal and possibly preliminary environmental investigation if the circumstances suggest this to be appropriate. Whilst the latter investigation will be cheaper and quicker than the former, it may also bring to light other problems, such as air emission and water discharge, which are not at first apparent. These matters may well affect the saleability of the charged assets and/or give rise to liability on the administrative receiver (who may well have to consider resignation) and/or his appointor. For this reason, the appointing debenture-holder should be amenable to funding the costs of the relevant audit or investigation, a matter to be concluded at the earliest possible time. Indeed, it is worth noting that in Canada the approach of the courts has been to permit the office-holder to give effect to environmental considerations to the detriment of the return made to secured and unsecured creditors. Whether the domestic courts will adopt such an approach is conjectural.

It is impossible to be exhaustive in terms of the checks which an office-holder should carry out in checking for potential environmental liability. The types of enquiries which should be considered may well involve the following:

(1) Does the company emit substances to air and, if so, do these require the consent of Her Majesty's Inspectorate of Pollution?

(2) Do effluents discharged by the company into drains and sewers benefit from the express consent of the relevant local water and sewerage company for the purposes of the Water Industry Act 1991?

(3) Do discharges which are made directly into waterways benefit from the consent of the National Rivers Authority for the purposes of the Environmental Protection Act 1990 or any special regulations relating to hazardous waste?

(4) Does the company use and store hazardous substances and, if so, does it have permission to do so?

(5) Is the company potentially liable for statutory nuisance in respect of, for example, noise, smell or waste deposits, in particular for the purpose of Environmental Protection Act 1990 s79?

(6) Does the company have all necessary consents for the purpose of the Town and County Planning Act 1990, the Planning (Hazardous Substances) Act 1990 and the Planning and Compensation Act 1990 or any other relevant or amending statute? Are any conditions imposed by the relevant district or borough county council being complied with?

(7) Has any property of the company been subject to a use which would bring the land within the meaning of contaminated land for the purposes of the Environmental Protection Act 1990? Could this have affected adjacent land?

(8) Does the company operate any voluntary environmental management system and, if so, why?

(9) Do the company's records and correspondence reveal any matters revealing potential environmental liability or related problems?

In relation to contaminated land, it should be noted that the Government is currently conducting a wide-ranging review which reconsiders the scope of the registration of land which may be contaminated, as had been envisaged would be maintained by district and borough councils for the purposes of the Environmental Protection Act 1990 s143.

The administrative receiver should be particularly aware of his environmental obligations in view of the duty imposed on him to obtain the best reasonable price in the circumstances on the sale of charged assets. Assets are less likely to be saleable, or at least their prospective sale value will be reduced, where they contravene environmental regulations or give rise to environmental liability. Steps may be put in place to remedy such a state of affairs. These should only be put in place on the basis of proper and appropriate advice, assuming time and costs to be reasonable. Certainly, a wilfully ignorant view on the basis of a self-enlightened so-called commercial view should be avoided at all costs.

For a fuller and helpful digest of the problems facing the insolvency practitioner in this area, see Philips [1992] 8 IL&P 3, 86–8; 4, 117–9; 5, 153–5.

## 9.8 Statutory Duties Relating to Employee Protection

The administrative receiver assumes certain duties under the Health and Safety at Work Act 1974 and under the Factories Act 1961 (see, for example, *Meigh v Wickenden* [1942] 2 KB 160).

The Factories Act 1961 imposes obligations on an employer as regards the safety, health and welfare of employees. The Act only applies to factories as defined in the Factories Act 1961 s175(1). This provision has, however, been given a wide interpretation and may include shops and sites. Broadly, the 1961 Act provides for general health provisions (in relation to matters such as cleanliness, temperature and ventilation), safety provisions (such as the fencing of machinery and maintenance of equipment) and various miscellaneous provisions and defences.

Primarily, responsibility for the observance of the Factories Act falls on the occupier of the factory. Clearly this may extend to the administrative receiver. The Act carries criminal sanctions and is enforced by the Factories Inspectorate, a statutory body which also enjoys powers under the Health and Safety at Work Act 1974, such as the power to issue important notices. In addition, an occupier of the factory may face a civil action for damages by an injured employee.

The Health and Safety at Work Act 1974 (as amended by the Consumer Protection Act 1987) applies in addition to the Factories Act 1961, and is designed to provide for a reasonable degree of safety at all places of employment. Unlike the 1961 Act, the 1974 Act extends to the general public and independent contractors, although it does not extend to domestic employees. The 1974 Act imposes duties specifically on an employer (by virtue of ss2, 3 and 9) and on persons who have control of any work processes (by virtue of ss4 and 5). It should be noted that ss6 and 7 also impose duties on manufacturers and installers and on employees. Clearly an administrative receiver, and certainly one who adopts contracts of employment, will fall within the ambit of the Act which provides for specific criminal offences in s33. Broadly speaking, enforcement of the 1974 Act and delegated legislation in the form of regulations is the responsibility of local authorities, who may appoint health and safety inspectors under ss19 and 20 of the 1974 Act. These inspectors may issue important notices and prohibition notices against which a right of appeal exists to an Industrial Tribunal within 21 days (Health and Safety at Work Act 1974 ss21 and 24).

The Regulations and Codes of Practice relating to safety representations and safety committees took effect from 1 October 1978. These bodies have authority to investigate hazards and complaints, inspect work places and to demand certain information from an employer relating to the health, safety and welfare of employees. Again an administrative receiver may clearly be liable on such matters. The administrative receiver should also be aware of his duty to notify accidents and dangerous occurrences to the Health and Safety Executive pursuant to the Notification of Accidents and Dangerous Occurrences Regulations 1980 (SI No 1794).

Finally, it should be understood that the area of health and safety legislation is in a state of flux. In due course it is intended that it will be replaced by regulation and various codes of practice. These are to be issued under the authority of the Secretary of State although any regulations, as a form of delegated legislation, will be legally enforceable. Regulations are likely to be supplemented by codes of practice, contravention of which may give rise to evidence of contravention of the regulations themselves. The office-holder should therefore make himself aware via his advisers of the relevant legislation and codes of practice applicable to him at the time of and during the currency of his appointment.

## 9.9  Duties of the Debenture-holder

The courts have made it clear that they will not burden a debenture-holder with a duty of any sort in the making of an appointment where that is provided for in the debenture (see, for example, *Shamji v Johnson Matthey Bankers Ltd* [1986] BCLC 278 and *Re Potters Oil Ltd (No 2)* [1986] 1 WLR 201). It is worth quoting here from the judgment of Hoffmann J in the former case (at 283–4) in rejecting as perverse an argument by counsel for the company, that a decision by the bank holding a debenture to exercise a valid power to appoint an administrative receiver was vulnerable, in the absence of an express term, to be set side by the court on the basis that the appointment was against the interests of the borrower company:

> In the absence of good faith, the bank could not owe the mortgagors or guarantors a duty of care in deciding whether to exercise that right. It might owe some duty in the way in which the right was exercised (eg it might owe a duty to take reasonable care not to appoint an incompetent) *but not as to whether it was exercised or not.* Counsel for [the company] relied on *Cuckmere Brick Co Ltd v Mutual Finance Ltd, Standard Chartered Bank v Walker* and *Tse Kwong Lam v Wong Chit Sen.* These cases demonstrated that a mortgagee or receiver exercising a power to sell mortgaged property owes a duty to the mortgagor or guarantor to take reasonable care to obtain the fair value. It is important however to observe that in this matter there can be no real conflict of interest between mortgagor and mortgagee...' [emphasis added]

In other words, and as the learned judge had put the matter previously in his judgment, as with the mortgagee's power of sale, the debenture-holder may exercise any valid power of appointment without regard to the company or any guarantor of its obligations. The proviso to this, as is clear from the *Johnson Matthey Bankers* case (above) and the judgment of Salmon LJ in *Cuckmere Brick Co Ltd v Mutual Finance Ltd* [1971] 1 Ch 949 at 965, is that the debenture-holder must act in good faith in effecting the appointment. One ground on which it is submitted that this *bona fide* requirement may be challenged in practice is a situation where a creditor, typically a bank, insists on taking of further security to secure indebtedness, thus bringing it potentially within the scope of s29(2), on the basis of representations by the creditor that the security is taken purely for ongoing security purposes and not for the purpose of the appointment of an administrative receiver which, in fact, transpires immediately or very shortly after the execution of the supplementary security documents. A debenture-holder may also be challenged in making an appointment by an application by the company for injunctive relief when the proposal is made in contravention of an express stipulation in a debenture such as a notice requirement before appointment is made. It must be said that the courts have shown a willingness to err in favour of the debenture-holder in the face of a challenge by the company in certain circumstances. The decision in *Bank of Baroda v Panessar* [1986] BCLC 505 recognised the validity of an 'all monies due' demand, for example, although this would appear subject to any contrary provision in a facility letter by virtue of *Cryne v Barclays Bank plc* [1987] BCLC 548. Furthermore, the courts have allowed appointments to stand on the basis of a second valid 'appointing event' where the appointment is actually invalidly and purportedly made on the basis of a prior event (see, for example *Bank of Baroda v Panessar* [1987] Ch 355 where the debtor was estopped from challenging an appointment after dealing with the appointee as validly appointed). Similarly, an appointment which is made or an incorrectly stated ground will be valid if a ground actually existed at the time of the appointment (*Byblos Bank SAL v Al-Khudhairy* [1987] BCLC 232). These allowances on the part of the court would appear to operate only in the absence of bad faith and, as such, recognise the general principle of mortgage law whereby a mortgagee may treat a debtor's interest as subordinate to his own.

The courts have also made it clear that a debenture-holder need not consider the commercial interests of the company or its unsecured creditors in making an appointment. Thus, the debenture-holder need not be concerned at the prior appointment of a liquidator (*Re Potters Oil Ltd (No 2)* [1986] 1 WLR 201 at 206 per Hoffmann J. As the learned judge put it (at 204):

> The debenture-holder is under no duty to refrain from exercising his rights merely because doing so may cause loss to the company or its unsecured creditors. He owes a duty of care to the company but this duty is qualified by being subordinated to the protection of his own interests.

These statements reflect the view of Jessel MR in *Nash v Eads* (1880) 25 Sol Jo 95 in holding that a mortgagee was not precluded from exercising a power of sale on the grounds of not being in urgent need of funds or even spite against the mortgagor, although this latter ground may now be susceptible to challenge on the basis of a lack of good faith as considered above.

The decision of the Privy Council in *Downsview Nominees Ltd v First City Corp Ltd* [1993] BCC 46 raises the question of the debenture-holder's liability to subsequent mortgagees and encumbrancers of the company's property. It is certainly clear from the judgment that any such duty is equitable and is not to be framed in terms of the tort of negligence. Whilst the Privy Council denied the existence of a general duty in relation to trading, the court did consider that a receiver, and by implication a debenture-holder, who conducted a receivership otherwise than for the principal purpose of recouping the secured debt, was guilty of a breach of duty if, as in *Downsview*, the motive in bringing about the appointment is other than the protection and realisation of the charged assets, such as blocking the appointment of a receiver by a subsequent mortgagee.

The suggestion by Hoffman J in the *Johnson Matthey Bankers* case (referred to above) to the effect that the debenture-holder probably owes a duty to take reasonable care not to appoint an incompetent, warrants further consideration. An administrative receiver must, by definition, be a licenced insolvency practitioner qualified to act as an administrative receiver in relation to the company (ss230(2), 300). As such, there will be a very strong presumption that such a duty has been discharged by the debenture-holder in making such an appointment, even, it would appear, if the office-holder in fact transpires to be incompetent, although this will be increasingly difficult to sustain as the administrative receivership progresses. Certainly the duty will be breached by the appointment of an unqualified person or a corporate receiver which, by virtue of s30, will be void *ab initio*. It must also be assumed that the statement of Hoffmann J in the *Johnson Matthey Bankers* case survives the decision of the Privy Council in *Downsview* as discussed previously in para 9.3.

# Chapter Ten

# Liabilities of the Administrative Receiver

## 10.1 Introduction

The liabilities of the administrative receiver considered in this chapter are not extensive in the sense that a number of them have already been dealt with in the previous chapter on consideration of the relevant and corresponding duties. The liabilities which are considered here to some extent stand alone and arise in the course of the administrative receivership, largely in relation to and in consequence of the exercise of powers of the administrative receiver as discussed in Chapter 8.

## 10.2 The Administrative Receiver as Company Director?

The directors of a company face a number of potential personal liabilities on the pending and subsequent insolvency of the company, notably in terms of fraudulent and/or wrongful trading, misfeasance and director disqualification. The question must be raised as to whether or not an administrative receiver is susceptible to those liabilities by construing his position as akin to a company director. The short answer to this, it is suggested, is in the negative, certainly as regards the company itself in administrative receivership.

The law recognises three classes of directors which are treated in a like manner; namely, a *de jure* director, a *de facto* director (or a director *de son tort*) and a shadow director. The first is a director who is validly appointed, including a person occupying the position of a director, by whatever name called (Companies Act 1985 s741). A *de facto* director, on the other hand, is either not appointed as a director or who is invalidly appointed as such (*Re Canadian Land Reclaiming and Colonising Co* (1880) 14 ChD 660). Nevertheless, the Companies Act 1985 s285 provides that the acts of a director are valid notwithstanding any defect in his appointment or qualification, including a void resolution to appoint the director under s292(2) of the 1985 Act. The object of this provision, as Farwell J put it in *British Asbestos Co Ltd v*

*Boyd* [1903] 2 Ch 439 at 444–5 is '...to make the honest acts of *de facto* directors as good as the honest acts of *de jure* directors'. Finally, a shadow director is statutorily defined in IA 1986 s251 as a person in accordance with whose directions or instructions the directors are accustomed to act. The same definition appears in the Companies Act 1985 s741(1) and the Company Directors Disqualification Act 1986 s22(5); see *Re Hydrodan (Corby) Ltd* [1994] BCC 161 for a detailed discussion of the concept in the context of wrongful trading.

In view of the management function assumed by the administrative receiver on his appointment, it is tempting to view his position as analogous to that of company director. That view is reinforced by the administrative receiver's deemed agency relationship by virtue of s44(1)(a), until such time as the company goes into liquidation. This approach is, however, misleading. The authorities cited in the previous chapter illustrate the well-established principle that the administrative receiver owes his primary duty to his appointing debenture-holder, and not to the company as is the case with company directors (see *Percival v Wright* [1902] 2 Ch 421 and *West Mercia Safetywear Ltd v Dodd* [1988] BCLC 250, where the Court of Appeal held that the director of an insolvent company must also have regard to the interests of its creditors). However, the position of the administrative receiver is not in assuming the position of a company director, which by way of argument would necessarily be as a *de facto* director. Rather, the office-holder is there to realise and manage assets of the company for the benefit of the debenture-holder, which is facilitated by a suspension of the powers of the company's directors as discussed in Chapter 8 at para 8.11, and subject to the duties discussed in Chapter 9. This is analogous with the case of an administrator, who in a similar manner could not be deemed to assume the office of director on account of the fact that he functions for the benefit of creditors generally and not the company or its members (see s14(1) and *Astor Chemical Ltd v Synthetic Technology Ltd* [1990] BCC 97 at 105 for a useful comparison of the administrator and the administrative receiver for these purposes). This accords with the view of Jenkins LJ in *Re B Johnson & Co (Builders) Ltd* [1955] Ch 634 at 662, which established that the whole purpose of the appointment of a receiver would be obviated if the company was able to claim duties owed to it by the office-holder in the same way as a director.

The consequence of discounting the administrative receiver as a director of the company in administrative receivership is that he will not be subject to any of the statutory and non-statutory duties to which company directors are otherwise subject. Thus, he will not be liable to the common law duty of care or the equitable or fiduciary duties in relation to exercise of powers, regard for the interests of creditors in certain circumstances and the rules against profiting and conflicts of interest and duty. Similarly, no duty will arise in relation to declarations of interest, substantive property transactions or director loans (see Companies Act 1985 ss317, 320, 330). Equally importantly in the context of administrative receivership, the administrative receiver will have no liability to have regard in the discharge of his function for the interests of the company's employees (see Companies Act 1985 s309).

It may be possible to argue that an administrative receiver is a shadow director of a company other than that in administrative receivership. This would of course not be possible in the case of the company in administrative receivership, since the powers of the company's directors are largely displaced on the appointment being effected, thereby rendering them incapable in any case of acting in accordance with the instructions or directions of the administrative receiver for the purposes of managing the company. Shadow directorship may, however, arise in the case of other group members, particularly subsidiaries, or debtor companies.

## 10.3 Liability for Wrongful and Fraudulent Trading

Since an administrative receiver is not capable of being construed as a director, he will not be susceptible to an action for wrongful trading under s214 by any liquidator to the company in administrative receivership. Wrongful trading may only be pursued against the directors of a company. As a shadow director of another company, however, the administrative receiver may be liable as a party to a wrongful trading action. In practice, this might be most likely to arise in relation to subsidiaries of the company in administrative receivership, including a newly-formed subsidiary following a 'hive-down' operation.

On the other hand, the administrative receiver will be liable to an action for fraudulent trading under s213 in the subsequent liquidation of either the company in administrative receivership or any other company of which he is a shadow director (*Re Leyland Daf Ltd* (1994) *The Times*, 11 August). This is because s213 is available to a liquidator against any person who was knowingly a party to the carrying on of any business of the company with intent to defraud creditors of any person, or for any fraudulent purposes. Thus, the administrative receiver may be liable for any period during which he carried on the business of the company as its agent. Fraudulent trading is also a criminal offence under the Companies Act 1985 s458, and carries with it also director disqualification provisions as with wrongful trading (see Company Directors Disqualification Act 1986 ss4 and 10).

## 10.4 Liability in Misfeasance Proceedings

In the course of a winding-up an application may be made to the court by the Official Receiver, the liquidator, any creditor or, with the leave of the court, a contributory, for the purposes of seeking a summary remedy in misfeasance proceedings (s212). The action may be pursued against *inter alia* an administrative receiver (but no other species of receiver or receiver and manager) on the basis of the misapplication, retention of or accountability for any money or other property of the company or, most notably in the case of an administrative receiver, 'any misfeasance or breach of any fiduciary or other duty in relation to the company' (s212(1)).

The liability which the administrative receiver may incur under s212 for breach of duty 'in relation to the company' is best understood by reference to Chapter 9 which dealt with the nature of such duties. The most relevant of these is the duty to exercise powers in good faith and to take reasonable care to obtain a proper price on the sale of charged assets (*Downsview Nominees Ltd v First City Corp* [1993] BCC 46). In practice, however, the duties owed by the administrative receiver will probably only give rise to litigation in the clearest and most extreme cases.

Section 212 creates no new right of action and will only be operative in pursuing a breach of duty. In the words of John Weeks QC, sitting as a High Court judge in *Re DKG Contractors Ltd* [1990] BCC 903 (an action also involving claims under ss214 and 239), '[s212] is procedural only and provides no remedy where there has not been a breach of duty'. Thus, s212 may not be utilised for repayment of a debt or in seeking a rescission order in respect of a contract to which the company is party, as had been the case under the earlier legislation (see *Re Etic Ltd* [1928] Ch 861 and *Re Centrifugal Butter Co Ltd* [1913] 1 Ch 188 respectively).

A modification is made in s212(2) in relation to a liquidator or administrator. These office-holders may be proceeded against for any misfeasance or breach of any fiduciary or other duty only in connection with the carrying out of their respective functions as liquidator or administrator of the company. This provision no doubt operates only as against a liquidator or administrator, since those office-holders discharge their functions in the interests of creditors generally. The administrative receiver, on the other hand, has a duty to his appointing debenture-holder and, as was recognised at common law in relation to a non-administrative receiver and manager in *Re B Johnson & Co (Builders) Ltd* [1955] Ch 634, owes no corresponding duty to manage the business for the benefit of the company or to preserve its goodwill. The decision in the *Downsview* case, though, suggests that an administrative receiver owes an equitable duty of good faith to the company in the exercise of his powers. Conceivably, therefore, an administrative receiver may be amenable to an action for misfeasance under s212 albeit outside the ambit of s212(2).

## 10.5  Subsisting Contracts (Other than Employment Contracts)

Generally, the appointment of an administrative receiver has no effect on subsisting contracts (which in this section does not include employment
contracts) other than where this is provided for in the contract itself. It is common, for example, in finance agreements or in subcontracting agreements, for
a contract to terminate automatically on the appointment of a receiver. The
receiver may, of course, pursue an action to obtain an injunction on behalf of
the company preventing repossession of goods under the contract, on the basis
that it is inequitable to do so. This arose in *Transag Haulage v Leyland DAF
Finance* [1994] BCC 356, a case involving heavy goods vehicles which had
been leased to the company prior to administrative receivership. In the
*Transag* case the company in receivership had kept up all payments on the
vehicles bailed to it on hire purchase. In the event of termination by the bailor
on the basis of an 'automatic' termination clause the receivers tendered a
cheque in full payment of sums remaining payable under the agreement. The
cheque was neither cashed nor returned. Knox J refused to permit termination
of the contracts by the bailor, on the grounds that equity precluded it in view
of the lack of any breach by the bailee and the fact that the bailor would have
profited by some £53,000 if termination were to be permitted on the basis of
previous rental payments which had been made by the company. This would
also have given rise to an unjustifiable loss to the company. Notwithstanding
this, the company was ordered to pay the bailor's costs, in keeping with the
practice in analogous landlord and tenant cases.

The fact that the appointment of an administrative receiver has so little
effect on subsisting contracts also largely explains why the administrative
receiver is not armed with the statutory power to disclaim onerous contracts,
unlike a liquidator under s178 (this power not being available either to administrators).

### 10.5.1  Personal liability of the administrative receiver

The administrative receiver assumes no personal liability for contracts subsisting at the time of his appointment. Furthermore, the fact of his appointment
and the discharge of obligations under the contract by him are not deemed to
imply novation on his part (*Nicoll v Cutts* [1985] BCLC 322, see also *Parsons v
Sovereign Bank of Canada* [1913] AC 160). The same is true if steps are taken
by an administrative receiver to bring about the continuance or completion of an
existing contract (*Re Newdigate Colliery Ltd* [1912] 1 Ch 469). Nevertheless,
the other contracting party enjoys a priority right for consideration payable to it
in respect of post-appointment goods or services as a proper expense of the
receivership, which will be payable in priority to the secured debt of the
appointing debenture-holder (*Re Glyncorrwg Colliery Co* [1926] Ch 951).

The administrative receiver may opt to assume personal liability on subsisting contracts, usually by way of novation or the giving of a guarantee or other undertakings. In practice, such arrangements will only be forthcoming from an administrative receiver where the other contracting party exacts it as a condition of the continued subsistence of the contract and where the contract itself is of fundamental importance for the company's business and cannot be replaced by an alternative supplier. In such circumstances the administrative receiver may rely on the statutory indemnity provided by s44(1)(c). In addition, the office-holder may also wish to seek a separate undertaking from the appointing debenture-holder where the liability to which he is exposed potentially exceeds the value of the charged assets.

### 10.5.2   Repudiation of contracts by the administrative receiver

It is now well-established that an administrative receiver may bring about repudiation by the company of a contract in its name or cause the company not to perform its part of the contract, without the office-holder incurring personal liability (*Airline Airspaces Ltd v Handley Page Ltd* [1970] Ch 193). However, liability will almost certainly be faced by the company in administrative receivership on the repudiation of a contract by it (*Re Newdigate Colliery Ltd* [1912] 1 Ch 468, see also *Telsen Electric Co Ltd v Eastwick & Sons* [1936] 3 All ER 266). In practice, actions of this type are rarely pursued as they are usually deemed worthless, although the entering of a judgment against the company may permit set-off by the other party in respect of sums owed by it to the company. The *Newdigate* case involved an application by a receiver to break a contract of the sale of goods by the company because the market price obtainable for the goods on delivery exceeded the contract price. The application was refused on the grounds that it would have prejudiced the goodwill of the company, this being part of the company's assets which would be consequently reduced in value (see also *Re Great Cobar Ltd* [1915] 1 Ch 682 where a similar application was granted because the consequent breach was not capable of diminishing the value of the company's goodwill).

*Airline Airspaces Ltd v Handley Page Ltd* [1970] Ch 193 involved a company, HP Ltd, over which a bank-appointed receiver was in office. The plaintiff was entitled to commission under a pre-receivership contract in respect of every aircraft of a particular type sold by HP Ltd. Following appointment, the receiver hived down a relevant part of HP Ltd's business to a subsidiary, and then pursued negotiations with a third party for the sale of shares in the subsidiary to it. The plaintiff sought an injunction restraining the sale of those shares, on the grounds that the sale would result in their losing their commission under the original contract with HP Ltd. Graham J held that the plaintiff was not entitled to the injunction because a receiver enjoyed a power to repudiate if the repudiation did not adversely affect the realisation of the company's assets or seriously affect the trading prospects of the company. This reflects the fact that the debenture-holder is entitled, by way of appointment of the administrative receiver, to deal with charged assets in any way it wishes subject to the various duties owed by the administrative receiver (*Kernohan Estates Ltd v Boyd* [1967] NI 27). In the case of contracts of the company, this is subject only to the proviso that the administrative receiver must act in such a way as he considers to be in the best interests of the business over which he is appointed (*Astor Chemicals Ltd v Synthetic Technology Ltd* [1990] BCC 97 at 105); that is, by acting in good faith and without incurring needless damage to the goodwill of the company. For the court to have held otherwise in the *Airline Airspaces* case would have opened the door for all manner of unsecured creditors seeking injunctive relief against a receiver, and indirectly against the appointing debenture-holder. The granting of such orders would undermine the priority status as a secured creditor held by the debenture-holder and the function of the administrative receiver appointed at its instance. Furthermore, the granting of injunctive relief might also potentially incur expenditure on the part of the receiver where specific performance is sought for a contract where the receiver proposes to or, indeed, causes the company to break a contract. This expenditure would necessarily impinge on the charged assets on which the debt of the debenture-holder is secured, which again would undermine the priority and secured status of the debenture-holder. This of course does nothing to prejudice the relative protection offered to other secured creditors by the doctrine of marshalling. Neither does it undermine any right of action by the other contracting parties in respect of proprietary rights acquired under the contract.

The reasoning in the *Airline Airspaces* decision was explained lucidly by Vinelott J in *Astor Chemicals Ltd v Synthetic Technology Ltd* [1990] BCC 97 at 105, an action for an injunction against a company in administration. The injunction was refused on the grounds that there was no analogy between a receiver and an administrator with regard to a debenture-holder's priority position over another unsecured party. Vinelott J observed that for the court to prevent a receiver getting in and realising the charged assets for the benefit of a debenture-holder would involve the preferring of the other party to the contract to other unsecured creditors and would in fact prefer that party to the appointing debenture-holder. Therefore, a receiver will be restrained from acting in breach of an obligation entered into by the company if the consequences of the breach would be to deprive the plaintiff of an equitable interest which ranks ahead of the debenture such (see, for example, *Freevale Ltd v Metrostore (Holdings) Ltd* [1984] Ch 199). Alternatively, injunctive relief might be granted where any other proprietary or contractual right binding on the debenture-holder who intervenes, as in *Telemetrix plc v Modern Engineers of Bristol (Holdings) plc* [1985] 1 BCC 99, 417. Vinelott J went on to make clear that certain limitations apply to a receiver's apparent freedom to disregard contractual obligations which are otherwise binding on the company. This freedom might be lost, for example, where doubt exists as to whether there will be a surplus of assets available to the company and other creditors after payment of the debt due to the debenture-holder where the breach would seriously damage the reputation of the company and impair its goodwill or, alternatively, where the charge does not cover all of the assets of the company and the ability of the company to trade with its other assets would be impaired by the breach. In the latter case of course the receiver appointed may well not amount to an administrative receiver (see s29(2)).

The *Airline Airspaces* case decision was distinguished in *Freevale Ltd v Metrostore Holdings Ltd* [1984] BCLC 72 where an order was granted requiring specific performance of a contract for the sale of land entered into by the company. The distinction which may be made between the two cases is that the latter related to the contract for which specific performance was sought, the plaintiff having already acquired an equitable interest in the property. Similar reasoning underpins the decision in *Telemetrix plc v Modern Engineering of Bristol (Holdings) plc* [1985] 1 BCC 99, 417 where Peter Gibson J granted an injunction prohibiting a receiver from assigning land options where they had already been assigned by the company in receivership to a third party. These decisions are in accordance with the earlier Australian decision of McPherson J in *Re Diesels Components Property Ltd* [1985] 9 ACLR 225 where a receiver withheld goods from a third party where the goods were subject to an equitable lien, notwithstanding the fact that the goods had not been received until after the appointment of the receiver where the third party had notice of the appointment. These decisions collectively reflect the fact that the administrative receiver would appear amenable to equitable remedies where the particular facts of a case require the intervention of the court to protect the plaintiff's legal or equitable proprietary rights (see also *Ash & Newman Ltd v Creative Design Research Ltd* [1991] BCLC 403). This view is supported to some extent by the decision in *CF de Mattos v Gibson* (1858) 4 De G and J 276 (and see *Swiss Bank Corporation v Lloyds Bank Ltd* [1979] 2 All ER 853 per Browne-Wilkinson J, affirmed [1981] 2 All ER 449, HL).

The distinction between the cases in which equitable relief will be available against an administrative receiver also appears to dictate whether the office-holder may also be liable in tort for a breach of the contract entered into by the company. The conclusion reached in *Lathia v Dronsfield Bros Ltd* [1987] BCLC 321 was that no such tortious liability could arise, since a receiver acts as agent of the company and, as such, is not liable for loss occasioned to the other contracting party (see also *Said v Butt* [1920] 3 KB 497). This decision runs contrary to that in *Telemetrix plc v Modern Engineering of Bristol (Holdings) plc* [1985] 1 BCC 99, 417 and it is unfortunate that the *Telemetrix* case was not cited in the *Lathia* case. *Telemetrix* involved receivers who threatened to ignore a pre-receivership agreement entered into by the company to assign the benefit of land options to the plaintiff. The court acknowledged that this threat by the receivers gave rise to possible tortious liability on their part which justified their being joined in as co-defendants, costs being awarded against the receivers. Although the *Lathia* and *Telemetrix* cases do not appear to sit happily together, they may be distinguished on their facts. The *Lathia* decision involved an action by an unsecured creditor in respect of a contract for the sale of goods, which did not involve the creation of any proprietary interest in favour of the plaintiff. On the other hand, the land options involved in *Telemetrix* did create such interests which were potentially prejudiced by the threatened action of the receivers. These decisions find further support in the decision of the Court of Appeal in *Amec Properties v Planning and Research Systems Ltd* [1992] 13 EG 109, where an argument by counsel for the company to the effect that injunctive relief in favour of another contracting party (whose interest amounted to nothing more than an unsecured claim for damages) was inequitable, was rejected by the court in the particular circumstances of the case. This area is clearly one which is far from settled, and judicial attention to it would be of considerable practical benefit.

The question remains of whether the administrative receiver incurs personal liability as a result of bringing about a repudiation or failure to perform a contract entered into by the company. In a situation where the appointing debenture-holder enjoys priority over all other interested parties, such as unsecured contracting parties and subsequent encumbrancers, as arose in the *Airline Airspaces* case, then it is clear that the administrative receiver will not be liable for the tort of inducing the wrongful breach of contract provided that he has acted *bona fide* and within the scope of his authority (*Lathia v Dronsfield Ltd* [1987] BCLC 321; see also *Welsh Development Agency v Export Finance Co* [1992] BCC 270, a decision of the Court of Appeal). This echoes the view of McPherson J in the *Re Diesels Components* case (above) to the extent that the 'right' to repudiate must not be exercised recklessly or dishonestly.

It is submitted that in the absence of clear authority to the contrary, the decision in the *Welsh Development Agency* case also offers immunity to the administrative receiver against personal liability where the debenture-holder does not enjoy priority over the other contracting party. This supposes that no injunction has been obtained or granted, as would otherwise appear available in such a case. The court will also take into account the question of whether the administrative receiver has acted in good faith and within the scope of his authority (see for example, *Edwin Hill & Partners v First National Finance Corp plc* [1989] BCLC 89). This immunity would, however, appear to be lost once the company goes into liquidation, since at that time the agency characteristic of the administrative receiver's position will cease. This will give rise to his acting as principal on his own account from that point onwards in bringing about the repudiation or breach of any contract originally entered into by the company (s44(1)(a)).

### 10.5.3 The consequences of liquidation

Until the company goes into liquidation, the administrative receiver is deemed to be the company's agent and as such is personally liable on any contract entered into by him in carrying out his functions (s44(1)(a), (b)). His personal liability is, however, offset by his being entitled to an indemnity in respect of that liability out of the assets of the company (s44(1)(c)). Where the assets of the company are or may be insufficient to feed that indemnity, the office-holder may seek a separate indemnity from the appointing debenture-holder, although the limited nature of the company's assets may raise questions as to the commercial wisdom of entering into the new contract in the first place. Alternatively, an administrative receiver may contract on terms which exclude his personal liability to the other party on the contract or which provide that he shall be personally liable only to the extent that the company's assets are sufficient for the fulfilment of the contract (see for example, *Re Ernest Hawkins & Co Ltd* (1915) 31 TLR 247).

Exclusion or limitation clauses of this kind will not be subject to the Unfair Contract Terms Act 1977, since although the administrative receiver contracts with personal liability on new contracts entered into on behalf of the company, he does not enter into them as a party to the contract *per se* but, rather, as agent of the company, which will itself be a party to the contract (cf *Bishop v Bonham* [1988] BCLC 656 at 665 per Slade LJ (possibility of mort-gagee excluding liability) and see Chapter 9 at para 9.2. One other practical implication of the total exclusion of personal liability on the part of the administrative receiver is that he will have no corresponding right to an indemnity out of the company's assets for liability which he would otherwise incur. As such, the other party to the contract will have no claim against either the administrative receiver or the company itself for liability arising under the contract, and nor will it be able to establish a claim on the company's assets by way of subrogating itself to the indemnity of the administrative receiver under s44(1)(c) since the administrative receiver himself will have no right to such an indemnity having no personal liability on the contract (*Re A Boynton Ltd* [1910] 1 Ch 519).

Where the agency of the administrative receiver terminates following the onset of liquidation, he will become personally liable on any subsequent contract made by him, since in such a situation he is neither the agent of the company nor of his appointing debenture-holder. Neither will the administrative receiver enjoy the benefit of a statutory indemnity from the company's assets in such a situation (see s44(1)(a), (c); *Gosling v Gaskell* [1897] AC 575). Indeed, the power to enter into a contract on behalf of the company, a purely personal power as opposed to an *in rem* power, will come to an end on the liquidation of the company (*Re Northern Garage Ltd* [1946] All ER 566). As such, the administrative receiver must contract with personal liability and, as a party to the contract, any exclusion clause purportedly relied on by him will be subject to the Unfair Contract Terms Act 1977.

Where an administrative receiver seeks to enter into a contract with an existing supplier, the supplier may (and very often will) wish to exact the discharge of existing indebtedness as a condition of a new contract. This is an arrangement for which the administrative receiver is afforded no protection, other than in the case of public service utilities which must supply the office-holder on request albeit that he may be required to give a personal guarantee for payment of future supplies (s233(2)). In practice, the administrative receiver will seek to contract on terms excluding the other party's right to set-off in respect of pre-receivership liabilities of the company. Set-off will not be available in respect of post-receivership liabilities, since the crystallisation of the floating charge pursuant to which the administrative receiver is appointed operates as an effective assignment of the assets subject to it, once the debtor is notified of the crystallisation. When the assignment takes place in the case of a fixed charge is not clear, although the better view is on actual notice being given to the debtor of the assignment, such as following the appointment of a receiver, as opposed to the mere execution of the charge itself. The major practical problem associated with an administrative receiver's establishing contractual arrangements with an existing supplier is that the supplier may seek to set off monies paid over by the administrative receiver against debts due to it for pre-receivership supplies. The position of the administrative receiver here is exacerbated further by the fact that although he may be prepared to discharge the pre-receivership debt, it is arguable that he has no power to pay over company assets in respect of it, although this may be justifiable where it is required as a pre-condition of future supplies. Of course, the administrative receiver may be prepared to give a guarantee on a personal basis in respect of the pre-receivership debt. This state of affairs necessitates the administrative receiver establishing a fresh contracting basis with any pre-receivership supplier, whereby the new arrangements are expressly made without prejudice to any pre-receivership debts which remain. It is advisable that the administrative receiver should place orders and pay over cash on express agreed terms without reliance on any established course of dealings. The supplier will, of course, be able to prove in any subsequent liquidation for any pre-receivership debts which remain, although in practice, it will often be that the supplier is simply not prepared to undertake further supplies without the discharge of the outstanding debt in full.

## 10.6  Subsisting Contracts of Employment

In practice the resolution of the status of employees' contracts of employment will be fundamental to the feasibility of continuing the business of a company with a view to its sale as a going concern. Of late the question of adoption of contracts by the administrative receiver has been a troubled one, culminating in the House of Lords' decision in *Re Paramount Airways Limited (No 3)* [1995] 2 WLR 312.

### 10.6.1  The effect of the appointment

The appointment of an administrative receiver *per se* does not affect contracts of employment (*Griffiths v Secretary of State for Social Services* [1974] 1 QB 48). The three exceptions to this rule as identified in the *Griffiths* case were, (a) the appointment of a receiver who subsequently sold the business of the company, or (b) the conclusion of new contractual agreements with employees by the administrative receiver, or (c) the implied termination of a contract of employment where its continued operation is inconsistent with the appointment of the administrative receiver. (This third scenario arose in the *Griffiths* case, although the dismissal argument failed in the case of the particular managing director involved on the facts.) The position of an administrative receiver contrasts with the appointment of a receiver by the court which will automatically terminate contracts of employment on the basis that the appointment effectively displaces the company as one of the parties to the contract (whereas the administrative receiver is merely an agent of the company) (*Reid v Explosives Co Ltd* (1886) 19 QBD 264).

In practice, the appointment of an administrative receiver will only serve to impliedly terminate contracts of employment of employees whose function is entirely displaced by or inconsistent with the role of the administrative receiver, who assumes overall responsibility of the management of the company's business. Typically, this exception was identified in the *Griffiths* case as extending to a full-time and active managing director. This implied termination may also apply to other directors depending on the extent of their own particular responsibility for the day-to-day management of the company's business. Legally, termination will amount to unilateral repudiatory breach of the relevant director's contract of employment, which will entitle the director as an employee to resign, claim constructive dismissal and subsequently bring a claim for wrongful dismissal, effectively for breach of contract. Where the company is insolvent the employee may apply to the Department of Employment for this sum to be paid out of the national insurance fund subject to prescribed limits (Employment Protection (Consolidation) Act 1978 s49(1)).

## 10.6.2 *Re Specialised Mouldings*

Following the decision of Harman J in *Re Withall and Conquest and Specialised Mouldings Ltd* (1987) unreported, it became standard practice for administrative receivers and administrators to issue employees with so-called *Specialised Mouldings* letters. These stated that each employee's contract with the company would continue as normal and was not adopted by the office-holder who would assume no personal liability for the employee's contract of employment. The decision had held, following an application by joint administrative receivers for directions under s35, that an administrative receiver could avoid adopting a contract of employment simply by stipulating expressly that he did not and would not adopt. The decision was justifiably the subject of considerable criticism, although it was timely and created an extremely useful device for insolvency practitioners seeking to avoid personal liability. In legal terms it did little to give effect to the previous unamended s44(2) of IA 1986. Indeed, the matter was put thus by Professor RM Goode in *Principles of Corporate Insolvency Law* Sweet & Maxwell 1st edn (1990) at 102:

> It is difficult to see how a receiver can claim not to have adopted a contract of employment if he allows the contract to remain in force and continues to make use of the employee's services. Such an interpretation drives a coach and horse through s44(2) and deprives it of any significant meaning.

It is equally surprising that the *Specialised Mouldings* decision, for which no transcript is available, provided for the mechanism it did for as long as it did—over eight years—before its parlous legal basis was judicially overturned. It is perhaps equally surprising that professionals were prepared to rely so heavily for so long on its dubious grounding.

## 10.6.3 *Re Paramount Airways (No 3)*

The *Paramount Airways* case arose following the issue of a more or less standard form *Specialised Mouldings* letter to all employees by the joint administrators of the company. This stated that the joint administrators acted at all times as agents of the company without personal liability for the purposes of s19 and that, furthermore, they did not nor would they adopt or assume personal liability in respect of contracts of employment. Some weeks later, so as to maintain the viability of the business as a going concern, the joint administrators offered additional 'loyalty' payments to certain staff to remain in the employment of the company. Subsequently, having been unable to sell the business as a going concern, all staff were dismissed. Two senior employees sought an order for relief under s27 as creditors of the company on the grounds that the company's affairs had been managed in a manner prejudicial

313

to their interests as creditors, it being argued that the administrators were truly liable to them as employees under contracts which had, in fact, been adopted by the administrators. The matter was appealed following the decision at first instance by Evans-Lombe J to the effect that, whilst a *Specialised Mouldings* letter would have been effective in receivership, it was inappropriate in administration where an alternative form of wording would be required.

The Court of Appeal held that the employees who had been retained by the administrators after the 14-day period, notwithstanding the *Specialised Mouldings* letter, were entitled to recover benefits and entitlements to which they would have been entitled under their original contracts of employment. In essence, the adoption of contracts of employment was a matter of fact. Dillon LJ expressly disapproved of the contention by counsel for the administrators that the adoption of a contract of employment necessitated some positive act by the office-holders. Dillon LJ utilised Professor Goode's interpretation of adoption which he said could not be avoided by a simple statement to that effect. He went on:

> [If the administrators] continue substantially after the 14 days to employ staff and pay [employees] in accordance with their contracts they will be held impliedly to have adopted those contracts of employment... if they want to use the existing staff they must... either adopt the existing contracts or negotiate new contracts. If they are going to negotiate new contracts this must not be a sham... the mere assertion by the administrator or receiver that he is not adopting the contracts is mere wind with no legal effect because adoption is a matter not merely of words but of fact.

Leggatt LJ was prepared to go even further than this and considered that adoption merely required the express or implied acceptance of a continuance of the relevant contract by the office-holder. This is very close to the view expressed by Lightman J in *Leyland DAF Ltd v Ferranti International plc* [1994] BCC 658 where (in referring to the learned judge's own co-authored work) the term 'adopted' was given the meaning 'treated as continuing in force'. Although the Court of Appeal's decision in the *Paramount Airways* case was concerned with administrators the decision holds good also for administrative receivers; indeed, Lightman J in the *Ferranti International* case (a case involving administrative receivers) expressly stated that no distinction can be drawn from the meaning of the word 'adopts' in ss44 and 19, thus confirming the view of the Court of Appeal in the *Paramount Airways* case.

### 10.6.4  Qualifying liabilities

Before considering the decision of the House of Lords in *Re Paramount Airways* (see below at para 10.7), it is worth considering the unprecedented legislative flurry which took place in the wake of the decision of the Court of Appeal. One month after the judgment was given, the Insolvency Bill was brought before the House of Commons on 21 March 1994 and received the Royal Assent three days later. Effectively, the provisions of the Insolvency Act 1994, which amends IA 1986, amount to a compromise. Whilst the new Act does not seek to deny the question of adoption by an office-holder, it attempts to minimise the liabilities arising therefrom by introducing the concept of 'qualifying liabilities' to which office-holders' personal liabilities will be limited. The rationale behind this is to avoid widespread lay-offs following the appointment of administrators or administrative receivers and to exclude the responsibility for accrued employee entitlements such as arrears of salary prior to adoption, unpaid pension contributions or contractual entitlements to be paid, wages in lieu of notice which do not amount to 'qualifying liabilities'. The 1994 Act—which applies only to contracts adopted on or after 15 March 1994—defines a qualifying liability as a liability to pay a sum by way of wages or salary or contribution to an occupational pension scheme which is in respect of services rendered wholly or partly after the adoption of the contract. For these purposes, wages or salary payable in respect of a period of holiday or absence through sickness or 'other good cause' is deemed automatically to be in respect of services rendered during the relevant period of holiday or absence, which therefore also amounts to a qualifying liability. It is curious that pension contributions of the same period do not appear to fall as a qualifying liability. However, contributions by employers to pension funds are commonly made in practice by way of a lump sum payment, and in practice, such payments are often actually obligatory on a contractual basis in making good any actuarial deficiency in the pension fund. It would seem that any such payment which arises following the adoption of the employee's contract after the statutory 14-day period may well amount to a qualifying liability.

The scope of qualifying liability as regards contractual bonuses also remains unclear. Such bonuses may well be very significant in the case of senior employees who are fundamental to the continuance of the company's business as a going concern. They are commonly performance-related and thus it would appear that an office-holder would be able to defeat a claim for these where the claim is not attributable to a specific period of time, as provided for in s44(2C) and (2D) of the amended 1986 Act. Finally, the scope of 'good cause' under the new provisions remains unclear. It is suggested that this term would catch absence through illness and temporary lay-off by an office-holder or a waiver by the office-holder of any period of required notice. A problem arises here where the employee's contract of employment does not provide for lay-off without pay. In such cases an office-holder may feel it preferable to simply dismiss an employee rather than make a later call on his services and render himself personally liable for the intervening period of inactivity as absence through 'good cause'.

Finally, the terms 'wages' and 'salary' find no definition in the 1994 Act, although 'wages' is defined in the Wages Act 1986 ss6 and 7 as any sum payable to a worker in connection with his employment. Consequently it must be assumed that the term wages will catch not only regular salary payments but also contractual bonuses, contractual contingency payments and any profit-related pay which is expressly provided for in the employee's contract. Although it is not clear whether damages for summary dismissal as a result of the employer's breach of the contract of employment falls within either 'wages' or 'salary', it is submitted that they will not, since such damages are not provided for in employment contracts. On the other hand, the concept of 'qualifying liability' would in this regard appear to extend to any termination payment which is expressly provided for in the contract. Finally, s44(2B) provides that where a qualifying liability is payable partly in respect of services rendered, and partly before and partly after the adoption of the contract, the liability shall be apportioned and will only cover the amount payable in respect of services rendered after adoption. (It is not altogether clear why that section and s19(8), which applies to administrators, differ in the way in which they are drafted, since the net effect appears to be the same.)

### 10.6.5  LPA receivers and pre-15 March liabilities

It is unclear why the new 1994 provisions do not also apply to LPA receivers although the reasons would appear to be more political than legal (see Hansard (240 HC Official Report (5th series), cols 49-50, and 553 HC Official Report (5th series), col 642)). The position may change as the Government has made it clear that it may reconsider the position if legislative intervention appears to be required. Nevertheless, the position of LPA receivers appointed pursuant to fixed charges over assets, such as hotels and nursing-homes, remains as precarious as it does for administrative receivers in respect of pre-15 March 1994 adoptions. The practical effect for employees is that LPA receivers may choose simply to dismiss employees prior to the expiration of the 14-day statutory period in order to avoid personal liabilities arising.

The 1994 Act makes no provision for contracts of employment adopted prior to 15 March 1994. In the case of an administrative receivership, the unamended s44 of IA 1986 will continue to make the office-holder personally liable on any contract of employment adopted by him. Unlike administrators, the liability of the administrative receiver in this regard is not limited to liabilities incurred during the period of his office and may extend to historical claims under the contract. Somewhat alarmingly, it would appear to follow that the administrative receiver could find himself personally liable for contractual redundancy scheme payments, together with any deficiencies arising on a contractual basis as regards the employer's contributions to any employee pension scheme, on the basis that such liabilities may arise 'on' the contract of employment. On the other hand, it is clear from the *Paramount Airways* decision that in relation to administrators under s19—which uses the word 'under' rather than 'on'—the contractual liabilities will not extend to unfair dismissal or redundancy claims, and the administrative receiver may therefore seek to argue that the same is applicable to his own particular species of office-holder. Indeed, it is submitted that this is the better view.

Liabilities incurred by the administrative receiver under the above provisions may be met by him from any property of the company which is in his custody or under his control, in priority to any security held by the person by whom he is appointed, by virtue of the statutory indemnity which operates under s44(1)(c). As discussed previously, this provision appears to extend to assets which are the subject of either fixed or floating charges, in contrast to s19(5) which applies in the case of administrations and provides that any contractual liability incurred by an administrator will be charged on floating-charge assets only. Where the assets of the company are insufficient to meet the claims on the administrative receiver, he will be personally liable for any shortfall, although he may be protected by any other contractual indemnity given in his favour by the appointing debenture-holder.

Although pre-15 March 1994 liabilities continue to pose significant problems for office-holders under contracts of employment before that date, those claims will continue to dissipate. Certainly it would appear that under the Limitation Act 1980, any claim relating to the period prior to 15 March 1988 will be statute-barred unless the office-holder has subsequently acknowledged the debt from a date from which the six-year statutory limitation period will then continue to run. At present it does not appear that the Government will have to put in motion its reserve proposals to intervene statutorily to guard against any significant liabilities which may arise as a result of the amending legislation not being backdated to 29 December 1986, as was suggested in some of the high-profile commentary following the Court of Appeal's decision in *Paramount Airways*.

### 10.6.6 Redundancy payments

The position also remains unclear as regards redundancy payments previously made by the Department of Employment from the statutory redundancy fund, those payments being made either via the office-holder's firm or to the employees directly. The Court of Appeal's decision in the *Paramount Airways* case suggested that those payments should not have been made. However, redundancy pay forms part of an employee's contractual rights and this will have been assumed by the office-holder on adoption. Whilst the Department of Employment may therefore seek to reclaim those monies from office-holders, it would appear unlikely to do so in the absence of an announcement by the Department of Employment to that effect, or on the basis of the argument that the Secretary of State is estopped from doing so because the payments out had been made out on a mistake of law. The entitlement of employees to claim against office-holders who remain liable for adoption of pre-15 March 1994 contracts apparently continues to subsist in respect of any amounts claimable as national insurance under any contractual arrangement in excess of the time and monetary limits operated by the Department of Employment under the Employment Protection (Consolidation) Act 1978. In the case of key and senior employees those contractual claims are often very significant, particularly in the case of fixed-term service contracts.

### 10.6.7  The consequences of liquidation

The effect of the termination of the administrative receiver's agency relationship with the company on the onset of liquidation does not appear to be envisaged by IA 1986 (as amended). Neither has the matter benefited from specific judicial attention. The effect of the termination of the administrative receiver's agency would be that he would then employ those employees whose contracts of employment he has adopted *as principal*. This begs the question as to whether his liability for the termination of those contracts differs as a result. Certainly it would appear that the administrative receiver would no longer benefit from the statutory indemnity out of the company's assets as provided for by s44(1)(c). In order to avoid personal liability for the entire claims of those employees dismissed by the administrative receiver on the contracts adopted by him, it would appear that the office-holder would have to argue that those contracts could still be classed as having been adopted within the meaning of s44(2), notwithstanding the termination of the administrative receiver's agency. It might be argued that such termination removed the limitations of qualifying liability which would otherwise be assumed by the administrative receiver. It is submitted that the better view is that this is not the case, and that the liability of the administrative receiver would be limited to those liabilities falling within the definition of 'qualifying liability' irrespective of the company's subsequent liquidation (see *Deaway Trading Ltd v Calverley* [1973] 3 All ER 776). This would also have the effect of protecting an administrative receiver from actions against him personally where the business is sold by him as a going concern, for the purposes of the Transfer of Undertaking Regulations 1981 (SI No 1794) where the company is contemporaneously in liquidation.

## 10.7  Adoption of Contracts of Employment

A contract of employment subsisting with the company is deemed adopted by an administrative receiver following the expiration of 14 days from his appointment, although the office-holder is not taken to have adopted a contract of employment by reason of anything done within the statutory 14-day period (s44). Following the *Re Specialised Mouldings Ltd* decision it became common practice for administrative receivers and administrators to avoid the consequences of adoption by simply issuing employees with a unilateral written notice to the effect as discussed in the previous section.

### 10.7.1  The effect of *Paramount*

The principal effect of the House of Lords' judgment in *Paramount Airways* is that *Specialised Mouldings* letters no longer enable an administrative receiver or an administrator to avoid the consequences of adopting a contract of employment following the expiration of the statutory 14-day period provided for in ss19 (administrations) and 44 (administrative receivership). Although unilateral attempts at contracting out of the consequences of adoption are no longer possible, it does not follow automatically that bilateral negotiations or the variation of a contract of employment are excluded. That matter is discussed further in Chapter 13 at para 13.7. Notably, the House of Lords' decision in *Paramount* makes clear that no distinction is to be made in this area between adoption of contracts of employment in administration and in administrative receivership (a view also shared by Lightman J in *Re Leyland DAF Ltd* [1994] BCC 166.

    The House of Lords held in *Paramount* that adoption of a contract of employment is a matter of fact and not of words. This went significantly further than the first instance view of Evans-Lombe J, who considered that it was necessary to show express or implied acceptance. In effect, the House of Lords, somewhat reluctantly, accepted that adoption occurs if an administrator or administrative receiver causes the company to continue the contract of employment for more than 14 days after his appointment. The Lords specifically rejected various alternative meanings of the term 'adopt' put forward by counsel such as a failure to disclaim, the meaning for the purposes of the Companies Act 1948 s323(4). The judgment of Lord Browne-Wilkinson, the only substantive judgment delivered with which the four other Law Lords concurred, went on to make it clear that a contract of employment with the company would only terminate if the company (ie acting by its administrator or an administrative receiver) gave notice terminating the contract of employment or, alternatively, if a company failed to pay wages as they fell due. It would follow from that latter view that the mere continuation of a contract of employment by the company does not necessarily lead to the conclusion that the contract had been adopted by the office-holder unless an employee is paid wages as they accrue (and assuming that the office-holder does not expressly terminate within the 14-day period). With respect, it is submitted that such a view is misguided. The failure by the company to pay wages as they fall due amounts to a breach of contract on the part of the company which may or may not give rise to repudiation on the part of the employee. To hold that this in some way undermines the adoption process would give rise to the suggestion, as the Court of Appeal had identified previously, that the contract of employment could be continued and an employee employed without the contract being adopted after the statutory 14-day period. It is respectfully submitted that this view has little to recommend it and cannot be correct for general purposes. In short, the better view is that either a contract is varied or terminated or, alternatively, it is adopted with no scope for a middle ground.

Rather more helpfully, Lord Browne-Wilkinson rejected a submission by counsel for the administrator that liabilities assumed by the office-holder were limited to those incurred in return for services actually rendered for the benefit of the administration.

The House of Lords also discounted any distinction between the terminology in ss19 and 44 whereby an administrator is liable 'under' a contract whereas an administrative receiver is liable 'on' any contract. The difference in terminology arises merely because an administrative receiver is personally liable for the consequences and liabilities arising on adoption, whereas in an administration those liabilities rank as what are effectively 'super-priority' claims on the company's assets.

### 10.7.2  Challenging pre-15 March 1994 adoptions

The *Paramount* decision appears only to be applicable to contracts of employment which were adopted in relation to the period 15 March 1988 to 14 March 1994 inclusive. Claims before that period will generally be statute-barred under the Limitation Act 1980. However, office-holders may seek to counter the consequences of adoption of pre-15 March 1994 contracts by a number of possible mitigating factors. These include insurance cover (which is only likely to be available in the case of large-scale claims) and the ongoing availability of statutory and non-statutory indemnities. Considerable practical problems are likely to be encountered, however, in enforcing those indemnities and insolvency practitioners may choose not to force the point against their appointors for obvious commercial reasons. It is also conceivable that an office-holder may maintain a right of set-off against employees claiming under a pre-15 March 1994 contract, any cross-claim being the subject of the normal rules on legal and equitable set-off, since IR r4.90 has no application in administration or administrative receivership other than where the company is in contemporaneous liquidation in the latter case; see *Hargreaves v Action 200 Ltd* [1993] BCLC 111.

Office holders may also attempt to attack claims made on contracts preceding the 1994 legislation on the basis that those claims are not perfected because there are administrative formalities outstanding in relation to the contractual claims on which they are based. This may arise, for example, in the case of claims under directors' service contracts, in respect of which the Companies Act 1985 imposes a number of prescriptive requirements, notably in terms of the requirement for an ordinary resolution by the shareholders of the company in general meeting authorising non-contractual termination payments and service contracts which are capable of subsisting for a period in excess of five years (Companies Act 1985 ss312 and 319). Additionally, or alternatively, an office-holder may consider challenging a claim on a service contract on the grounds that the terms of the service contract represent a breach of fiduciary duty to the company, on the part of the directors or a particular director because of disproportionately escalated remuneration terms which are brought into effect shortly before the administration or administrative receivership. Problems do, however, exist in this regard, in that actions founded on a breach of duty by the directors are only actionable by the company under one of the exceptions to the rule in *Foss v Harbottle* (1843) 2 Hare 421 and under the provisions of the Companies Act 1985 s459 (as amended). These courses of action do not lend themselves to the administrative receiver. In addition, an action in misfeasance proceedings is not available to an administrative receiver although it is available to a liquidator who may be prepared to pursue the action under s212.

### 10.7.3 Qualifying liabilities revisited

Following the Court of Appeal's decision in *Paramount* the Government took unprecedented steps in introducing new legislation to counteract the effects of the decision. (The legislation was not retrospective, and any further amending legislation which seeks to be may be questionable on constitutional grounds.) The approach adopted was to limit on a statutory basis the scope of liabilities assumed after the expiration of the 14-day period by office-holders who adopted contracts of employment. Those liabilities—known as 'qualifying liabilities' as considered in the previous section—are now provided for in s44 (as amended) as inserted by the Insolvency Act 1994 s2.

Broadly, a liability is a qualifying liability if it is a liability to pay a sum by way of wages or salary or contribution to an occupational pension scheme and it is payable in respect of services rendered wholly or partly after the adoption of a contract. Wages or salary payable in respect of a period of holiday or absence through sickness or 'other good cause' are treated automatically as services rendered during the period of holiday or absence and are therefore liable to payment. It is anomalous that this qualification does not apply equally to occupational pension contributions. The meaning of the terms 'wages' and 'salary' is not defined in the legislation. In keeping with other legislation notably the Wages Act 1986, it must be assumed that those terms will be given a broad interpretation and relate at least to sums payable to an employee in connection with his employment. Wages and salary are therefore likely to include contractual terms relating to bonuses or profit-related pay (which need not be conditional in the contract on net profit being made by the company), other contractual benefits (arguably even share options and the like) and termination payments such as so-called 'golden parachutes' which are commonly taxed as remuneration for the purposes of an individual contract of employment. Clearly a claim simply for damages for summary dismissal and breach of contract by the receiver (or administrator) will not be caught. It is submitted that an office-holder will have good grounds for challenging a so-called qualifying liability if it arises merely as a consequence of variations by individual employees' contracts of employment immediately prior to an administrative receiver being appointed (as would also apply in administration).

The reference to occupational pension scheme contributions in the 1994 legislation assumes the contributions to the pension scheme form part of any particular employee's contract of employment. In the event that those contributions do not form a contractual term, any claim for a short-fall in respect of contributions will rank as an unsecured and non-preferential claim. It should be noted here that an office-holder is under an express duty to give notice to the trustees of a pension scheme, as well as any eligible employees, of any charge in the basis of contributions to the scheme by the company (*Larsens' Executrix v Henderson* [1990] IRLR 512).

For a perceptive analysis of the Court of Appeal's decision in *Paramount* and the consequences thereof, much of which continues to apply following the Lords' decision, see Mudd (1994) 10 IL&P 2 at 38–41 and see also Mudd 11 IL&P 3 at 78–81 following the Lords' decision. Reference should also be made to Chapter 13 at 13.9 which deals with the possibility of avoiding liability under the 1994 legislation.

# Chapter Eleven

# Conduct of the Administrative Receivership: Procedural Formalities and Court Practice

## 11.1 Introduction

This chapter is concerned with the procedural matters which must be adhered to in the course of and following an administrative receivership. The area is of importance since whilst contravention of the procedural requirements does not give rise in itself to the invalidity of an appointment, it may bring with it civil liability in default, along with the inevitable questions of why such oversights arose.

The method by which an administrative receiver is appointed and the time from which his appointment is effective is not substantially dissimilar to that of a non-administrative receiver other than to the extent that IA 1986 and IR 1986 prescribe certain additional procedural requirements. The method of appointment referred to here should be contrasted with the right or power to appoint which is not provided for in the Act but which depends on the circumstances in which appointment is anticipated in the debenture, as discussed above in Chapter 3. In any case, it is usual for an appointment to be expressly required to be made in writing (see here *Windsor Refrigeration Co v Branch Nominees* [1961] Ch 375).

The form of the appointment of an administrative receiver does not affect the appointee's power to exercise the powers implied by Sched 1 to the Act, notably the power to use the company's seal and to execute deeds and other instruments in the name of and on behalf of the company, which are expressly conferred by Sched 1, paras 8 and 9. This contrasts with the position of the non-administrative receiver, who must be appointed in accordance with the terms of any particular debenture and whose power to exercise the aforementioned powers requires that appointment to be effected by deed, so as to permit an execution of a deed by them as agent of the company. That limitation would now appear to have been abolished, however, by virtue of Law of Property (Miscellaneous Provisions) Act 1989 s1(1)(c) (*Phoenix Properties Ltd v*

*Wimpole Street Nominees Ltd* [1992] BCLC 737, but cf *Sowman v David Samuel Trust* [1978] 1 WLR 22).

## 11.2  Acceptance Formalities

There is often some disparity between the theory and practice of seeking independent legal advice as to the validity of an appointment. This is in view of the tight time constraints imposed by s33(1)(a). The appointment of an administrative receiver (or non-administrative receiver) is deemed to be of no effect unless it is accepted by the appointee(s) before the end of the business day (as defined in IR r13.13(1)) next following that on which the instrument of appointment is received by him or on his behalf. In practice, it is not uncommon for advice to be sought on the validity of an appointment days or even weeks after an appointment is accepted or even acted upon. It is nevertheless imperative that independent legal advice is sought on the validity of each appointment at the earliest possible time. This may at least avoid potential liability for trespass and/or wrongful interference with assets of the company. There is also no good practical reason why, for time-saving purposes, an instrument of appointment should not be executed prior to any default or appointing event occurring, subject to acceptance by the appointee following the default or the happening of the appointing event (*Cripps (Pharmaceuticals) Ltd v Wickenden* [1973] 2 All ER 606).

The location of IR r3.1 in Part 3 of the Insolvency Rules is curious indeed, in that Part 3 deals specifically with administrative receivership whereas IR r3.1 applies to both administrative and non-administrative receivers (IR r0.3(2)).

Subject to an appointment being accepted in the manner prescribed by s33(1)(a) above, the acceptance is deemed confirmatory of the appointment, which itself is deemed to be made at the time at which the instrument of appointment was received (s33(1)(b)).

Whether a person is appointed solely or jointly, the appointee, if he accepts the appointment other than in writing (eg orally, by telephone or by conduct in acting), must confirm his acceptance in writing within seven days to the person appointing him (IR r3.1(1)). No form is prescribed for the confirmation or acceptance to be in writing in which case IR r3.1(2) has no application (IR r3.1(3)). An appointment which is accepted in writing must be effected using statutory Form 3.1, which provides for the insertion of the time and date of receipt of the instrument of appointment and the time and date of the acceptance itself as required by IR r3.1(5).

Although acceptance of the appointment may be in writing or otherwise confirmed in writing, it should be noted that failure to comply with these prescribed formalities does not invalidate the appointment, since there is nothing in the Act or the Rules to that effect. Since IR r3.1(2) clearly anticipates acceptance of appointment being made other than in writing, it is submitted that the act or conduct imputing acceptance, assuming that there is some such act or conduct, will suffice for acceptance purposes notwithstanding any failure to confirm the appointment in writing. This is so even where the debenture itself expressly requires the acceptance of the appointment to be made in writing, since the scheme of the Act and the Insolvency Rules overlay the terms of the debenture in the absence of some contrary provision in the debenture.

Where an appointment is made of two or more persons to act as joint administrative receivers, the joint appointment only takes effect when all appointees have each accepted the appointment in accordance with s33 as if each were a sole appointee (IR r3.1(1)). The same rule provides that in such a case the appointment is deemed to have been made at the time at which the instrument of appointment was received by or on behalf of all the appointees following compliance with s33. This rule is burdensome in the extreme. It is commonly avoided in well-drafted standard-form debentures by the inclusion of a provision authorising any person, including a joint appointee, to accept or confirm acceptance of the appointment on behalf of the joint appointees. This is reflected in IR r3.1(4) which provides for this type of acceptance.

It is common practice for a debenture-holder to appoint two joint administrative receivers, although the Act requires that the appointment should state whether any act or function may be discharged or carried out by all or any one or more of the appointees (s231(2)). Joint and several appointments are addressed more fully in Chapter 5 at para 5.7.

## 11.3  Notice Formalities

Section 39(1) provides that where an administrative receiver has been appointed, every invoice, order for goods or business document issued by or on behalf of the company or the administrative receiver or the liquidator of the company, being a document on or in which the company's name appears, shall contain a statement that an administrative receiver has been appointed. This usually takes the form of the company's name being following by the words '(in administrative receivership)' or less commonly, '(administrative receiver appointed)'. This provision notifies third parties dealing with the company of its status and complements the general requirement that a company's name appears on its correspondence (Companies Act 1985 s349). Section 39(1) apparently has effect immediately on the appointment of an administrative receiver. Furthermore, no requirement is stipulated as to how the statement should appear on company documents and it is therefore acceptable for the appropriate statement to be rubber-stamped, typed or apparently even handwritten on documents without the need for formal amended company stationery.

Although s39(1) appears to be a duty imposed primarily on the administrative receiver, s39(2) actually imposes a fine in default both on the company and any other officer or liquidator of the company who knowingly and wilfully authorises or permits a default (see *Gaumont British Distributors Ltd v Henry* [1939] 2 All ER 808 for the requisite mental element). A converse obligation is placed on a receiver and manager where a company is contemporaneously in liquidation by virtue of s188, again with criminal sanctions. The Act envisages that the administrative receiver and liquidator may be the same person (s46(3)).

On appointment, an administrative receiver is also under a new duty imposed by the Act requiring him forthwith to send to the company and publish in the prescribed manner a notice of his appointment and, within 28 days after his appointment (ie commencing on the date of the appointment: *Stewart v Chapman* [1951] 2 All ER 613), to send a notice to all creditors of the company so far as he is aware of their addresses unless the court otherwise directs (s46(1)). The court's direction to the contrary in such circumstances should be sought on a s35 application. Whilst such circumstances will be rare, this might involve a substituted advertisement where there are an inordinately large number of creditors, or the dispensing with the notice where the new addresses of creditors are unknown. The content of the notice of appointment is prescribed by IR r3.2 (as amended) which requires the inclusion of those prescribed matters set out in r3.2(a)–(g).

The administrative receiver must also advertise the fact of his appointment both in the London Gazette and (once) in such newspaper as he considers most appropriate for bringing the notice of appointment to the attention of the creditors of the company (IR r3.2(3) (as amended)). The advertisement must contain *inter alia* those matters set out in IR r3.2(2)(a)–(e). Most commonly, the newspaper in which the notice is placed is one local to the company's principal operations, although there is no reason why, despite the wording of IR r3.2(3), this should not be a national and/or local newspaper as appropriate.

The duty imposed by s46 does not apply to an administrative receiver who is appointed to act with an existing administrative receiver or one appointed to act in place of an administrative receiver dying or ceasing to act, save to the extent in the latter case that his predecessor has failed to comply with s46 obligations (s46(2)). Failure to comply with s46 renders the administrative receiver liable to fine and a default fine for continued contravention, subject to a defence of reasonable excuse for failure to comply with the provision (s46(4) for which see s430 and Sched 10).

The debenture-holder appointing the administrative receiver is required to give notice of the appointment (in statutory Form 405) to the Registrar of Companies within seven days of the appointment (Companies Act 1985 s405(1)). The fact of the appointment is then entered by the Registrar on the company's register of charges. Again, failure to comply with this provision carries with it criminal penalties in default.

Notably, the provision imposes no obligation on either the proposed appointee or the debenture-holder to give prior notice of the appointment to the company (*Byblos Bank SAL v Rushingdale Ltd* 1986 PCC 249; *Shamji v Johnson Matthey Bankers Ltd* [1991] BCLC 36).

## 11.4  The Statement of Affairs

The wide powers of the administrative receiver to manage the company's business and his duties to various parties are underpinned by a statutory power to require (by note in statutory Form 3.1B) the preparation and submission to him of a statement of affairs of the company in prescribed form (s47(1)).

It is misleading to refer to s47(1) as a power in favour of the administrative receiver, since the provision actually provides that, following appointment, the office-holder 'shall forthwith require some or all of the persons mentioned below [ie in s47(3)] to make out and submit to him' a statement of affairs. In short, the question for the administrative receiver is not as to whether a statement of affairs should be sought, but rather from whom to require it.

Although s47(3) sets out a broad class of persons from whom the administrative receiver may require the statement of affairs, in practice this obligation invariably falls on the company directors. Any person without reasonable excuse who fails to comply with any obligation imposed by s47 is liable to a fine and a continued daily default fine. This provision applies strictly, and notwithstanding the effective suspension of the powers of the directors as discussed in Chapter 8 at para 8.11.

The persons provided for in s47(3) who are subject to s47(1) are:

(a)  those who have been officers of the company (for which see Companies Act 1985 s744);

(b)  those who have taken part in the company's formation at any time within the 12-month period preceding the appointment;

(c)  those persons in the employ of the company, or who have been within the 12-month period preceding the appointment, and whom the administrative receiver considers capable of giving the information required; and

(d)  any person who is or has been within the 12-month period preceding the appointment an officer of or in the employment of a company which itself is, or was within the 12-month period, an officer of the company. For these purposes, the term 'employment' includes employment under a contract for services and will therefore extend to those who are, technically speaking, self-employed independent contractors.

The class of persons subject to s47(1) is very similar to the classes set out in s235(3) as discussed previously in Chapter 8 at para 8.8 to which further reference should be made.

Any person required to submit a statement of affairs by the administrative receiver must do so before the end of the 21-day period commencing with the day after that on which the prescribed notice of the requirement is given to them by the administrative receiver (s47(4)). However, the Act permits the administrative receiver to relax this requirement either of his own volition or at the request of a deponent, by either at any time releasing him from the obligation to submit a statement of affairs or by extending the statutory 21-day period by notice either in the prescribed notice itself or subsequently (s47(5); IR r3.6(1)). Where the administrative receiver has refused to exercise a power conferred by s47(5) the court may, if it thinks fit, exercise the power at its discretion on an application by a deponent (IR r3.6(2)). The court may also dismiss the application if in its opinion the deponent has not shown sufficient cause (IR r3.6(3)). This discretion may not be exercised until the applicant has had an opportunity to attend for an *ex parte* hearing of which he is given at least seven days' notice. If the application is not dismissed under IR r3.6(3), then the court must fix a venue for the *inter partes* hearing and give notice of it to the deponent who must, at least 14 days before the hearing, send to the receiver a notice stating the venue together with a copy of the application and any evidence which the deponent intends to adduce in support of it (IR r3.6(4)). The administrative receiver may appear and be heard at the *inter partes* application, irrespective of which he may also file a written report on matters which he considers ought to be drawn to the attention of the court (IR r3.6(5)). A copy of any such report filed with the court must also be sent by the administrative receiver to the deponent not later than five days before the hearing. On any application under IR r3.6 for a release from the duty to submit a statement of affairs, the costs of the deponents are payable by him in any event and, save as to where the court orders otherwise, no allowance being made towards the deponent's costs out of the assets under the administrative receiver's control (IR r3.6(7)). An obligation is imposed on the court to send sealed copies of any order made on the application to the deponent and to the administrative receiver (IR r3.6(6)). The notice requiring the statement of affairs must contain the following information, as prescribed by IR r3.3: the names and addresses of all others (if any) to whom the same notice has been sent; the time limit within which the statement of affairs must be delivered; the penalty for non-compliance as set out in s47(6); and the application in relation to the deponent, and to each of the other deponents, of s235.

The statement of affairs submitted by a deponent must be in statutory Form 3.2 with which, on request, the administrative receiver must furnish each deponent (although, in practice, no formal request is usually required)

(IR rr3.3(4), 3.4(1)). Section 47(2) provides that the statement must show: (a) particulars of the company's assets, debts and liabilities; (b) the names and addresses of its creditors; (c) the securities held by each such creditor; (d) the dates when those securities were given; and (e) such further information as may be prescribed by the administrative receiver.

The express requirements of s47(2) are expanded on by Form 3.2. Not only must the statement of affairs be in this form, but it must also contain all the particulars required by the form and must be verified by affidavit by the deponent using the same form (IR r3.4(1)). The additional information required by Form 3.2 extends to the setting out of particulars of the preferential creditors of the company and debts of the company secured by floating charges, a statement of the company's issued and called-up share capital and an estimate of the excess or deficiency of the company's assets to satisfy its preferential debts, its debts secured by floating charge and its creditors generally. The statement of affairs in Form 3.2 must be delivered by the deponent making the affidavit of verification, or by any one of them if more than one, together with a copy of the verified statement (IR r3.4(4)).

The provision by a deponent of a representation within the statement of affairs does not amount to a promise to pay on the part of the deponent. As such, a representation is ineffective as an acknowledgement of a debt for the purposes of the Jurisdiction Act 1980 s29 (*Re Overmark Smith Warden Ltd* [1982] 1 WLR 1195).

The administrative receiver may require from any of the classes of persons set out in s47(3) the submission of an affidavit of concurrence which states that he concurs with the statement of affairs submitted (IR r3.4(2)). The requirement by the administrative receiver for an affidavit of concurrence is effectively an alternative to requiring the submission of a statement of affairs and affidavit of verification from any of the persons prescribed by s47(3). The Insolvency Rules reflect each individual's perception and limited or specialised knowledge of the company's affairs, in that the affidavit of concurrence may be qualified in respect of matters which are dealt with in the statement of affairs where the maker of the affidavit is not in agreement with the deponent or, alternatively, where the maker of the affidavit considers the statement to be erroneous or misleading, or where he is without the requisite and direct knowledge necessary for concurring with it (IR r3.4(3)). Every affidavit of concurrence must be delivered to the administrative receiver by the person making it together with a copy which may then be retained, together with verified copies of the statement of affairs, as part of the records of the administrative receivership (IR r3.4(5), (6)).

In the face of an errant or unwilling deponent, the court may, on application by the administrative receiver, make such an order as it thinks necessary for the obligation falling on the deponent under s47 (IR rr7.20(1)(a), 7.20(2)(b)). Such an order may also provide that all the costs of and incidental to the application shall be borne by the person against whom the order is made (IR r7.20(3)).

The administrative receiver is obliged to make payment out of his receipts of any expenses incurred by the deponent in making the statement and affidavit of verification which the administrative receiver in his opinion considers reasonable (IR r3.7(1)). Curiously, there appears to be no provision in the rules for the payment of expenses in connection with an affidavit of concurrence. The administrative receiver's decision in this regard is subject to appeal to the court (IR r3.7(2)). Nonetheless, any dispute over the payment of expenses does nothing to relieve a deponent from any obligation as regards the preparation, verification and submission of the statement of affairs, or with respect to the provision of information to the administrative receiver (IR r3.7(3)).

## 11.5 The Report to Creditors

IA 1986 introduced new provisions which require the administrative receiver to report to both secured and unsecured creditors. Whilst the report to the latter may arguably only provide lip service to the idea of improving the position of unsecured creditors under the new legislation, the position of creditors generally is no doubt enhanced from the previous position where creditors had no statutory right to information from the receiver, who usually provided information on an *ad hoc* basis to his appointing debenture-holder only.

Within three months following his appointment (or such longer period as the court may allow) the administrative receiver is required to send a report to the following persons:

(a)  the Registrar of Companies;
(b)  any trustees for secured creditors of the company (ie including the trustees of any subsisting trust deed other than that pursuant to which the administrative receiver was appointed); and
(c)  so far as he is aware of their addresses, all such secured creditors.

by virtue of s48(1) and (5) the report must set out the following matters:

(a)  the events leading up to his appointment, so far as he is aware of them;
(b)  a summary of the statement of affairs made out and submitted to the administrative receiver under s47 and his comments (if any) on it (ie the statement of affairs itself is not sent out to the various parties);
(c)  the disposal or proposed disposal by him of any property of the company, and the carrying on or proposed carrying on by him of any business of the company;

(d)  the amounts of principal and interest payable to the debenture-holders by whom or on whose behalf (ie in the case of the appointment pursuant to a debenture stock trust deed) he was appointed and the amounts payable to preferential creditors;

(e)  the amount (if any) likely to be available for the payment of other creditors.

Subject to IR r3.5 as considered below, the copy of the report sent to the Registrar of Companies must have attached to it a copy of any statement of affairs submitted for the purposes together with any affidavits of concurrence (IR r3.8(3)). In the event that the statement of affairs or any affidavits of concurrence have not been submitted to the administrative receiver by the time his report is submitted to the Registrar of Companies, then these must be submitted as soon thereafter as they are received using statutory Form 3.3 (IR r3.8(4)).

Notwithstanding the broad nature of the matters requiring disclosure under the above heads, the administrative receiver is not required in any report to creditors to disclose any information which would seriously prejudice the carrying out by the administrative receiver of his functions (s48(6)).

Whilst it is not clear, it is submitted that the test of what constitutes seriously prejudicial disclosure for s48(6) purposes is a subjective one depending on the opinion of the administrative receiver subject to an objective reasonableness test. This view receives support from the decision of Hoffman J in *Gomba Holdings Ltd v Homan* [1986] 3 All ER 94 at 102, where the court permitted the receivers of the company to refuse to disclose details of future contracts to the company in receivership, on the basis of the affidavit evidence of one of the receivers to the effect that disclosure would not be in the interests of the appointing debenture-holder. In the view of Hoffman J, 'this is a view which on the evidence [the receiver] is reasonably entitled to hold'. Notably, the learned judge was impressed by the submission by counsel for the receiver that an order for disclosure would involve risk of loss to the debenture-holder, and the plaintiff companies were not in a position to provide any indemnity by way of cross-undertaking.

The administrative receiver is also afforded protection in terms of disclosure in the report sent to the Registrar of Companies pursuant to s48(1) which will be open to inspection (ie by way of a company search) to any member of the public (Companies Act 1985 s709(1)). This is by virtue of IR r3.5(1) under which the administrative receiver may apply to the court for an order of limited disclosure in the statement of affairs or a specified part of it. The order must be attached to the report submitted to the Registrar, together with copies of any affidavits of concurrence, pursuant to IR r3.8(3). The proviso to the court application is that the disclosure of the statement of affairs or a specified part of it would prejudice the conduct of the receivership (IR r3.5(1)). The court retains a discretion to order that the statement of affairs, or any specified part of it, shall not be open to inspection otherwise than with leave of the court (IR r3.5(2)). The court may also give directions as to the delivery of documents to the Registrar of Companies with the disclosure of relevant information to other persons, as is considered again below (IR r3.5(3)).

The rules in IR r3.5 should be contrasted with s48(6). The former provision permits the administrative receiver to apply to court for an order restricting disclosure of the contents of the statement of affairs, whereas the latter permits the administrative receiver to omit from his report (which by virtue of s48(5) must contain a summary of the statement of affairs) any information which in the opinion of the receiver would seriously prejudice the carrying out of his functions.

Within three months following his appointment, or such period as the court may allow, the administrative receiver is also required either to send a copy of his report to all unsecured creditors of the company (so far as he is aware of their addresses), or alternatively, to publish in the prescribed manner a notice which states an address to which unsecured creditors of the company should write for copies of the report to be sent to them free of charge (s48(2)). In the latter case, the notice must be published in the newspaper in which the receiver's appointment was originally published in accordance with IR r3.2(3) (IR r3.8(1)).

Unless the court otherwise directs, the administrative receiver must lay a copy of his report before a meeting of the company's unsecured creditors, summoned for the purposes of considering his report on not less than 14 days' notice (s48(2)). Section 48(3) provides that the court shall not give a direction for s48(2) purposes unless the report states the intention of the administrative receiver to apply for the direction, and either of the steps set out in s48(2)(a) and (b) (relating to the sending of a report to unsecured creditors of the publication of a notice in the prescribed manner, which must be published not less than 14 days before the hearing of the application) is fulfilled (s48(3)). Procedurally, if the administrative receiver proposes to apply to the court to dispense with the holding of the s48(2) meeting of unsecured creditors under s48(3), he must stipulate in his report to the creditors (ie under s48(2)(a)) or in the published notice (ie under s48(2)(b)) the venue fixed by the court for the hearing of the application (IR r3.8(2)). The court may therefore waive the requirement for the meeting of unsecured creditors, provided the s48(3) requirements are met. In practice, the administrative receiver will usually propose dispensing with the meeting of the unsecured creditors if no practical benefit is perceived as being served by holding the meeting, particularly if the assets of the company are minimal and would only be dissipated further, unjustifiably, by the holding of the s48(2) meeting.

One particular anomaly appears in IR r3.5(3). The provision permits the court, on the application of the administrative receiver, to give directions as to the delivery of documents to the Registrar of Companies and as to 'the disclosure of relevant information to other persons'. It is arguable that this permits the court to order that any information, be it in the administrative receiver's report or in the statement of affairs, must not be disclosed to any third party. (A summary of the statement of affairs must be comprised in any case in the report: s48(5).) It is arguable that IR r3.5(2) and (2) apply only to information which would otherwise be disclosed in the statement of affairs. The contrary argument may be that s48(6) expressly permits the administrative receiver to omit from his report any information which in his opinion would seriously prejudice the conduct of the receivership. However, IR r3.5(3) assumes that what it refers to 'relevant information' is, in fact, disclosed and is then the subject of the court's discretion. The better view, it is submitted, is that IR r3.5(3) is restricted only to information which would otherwise be disclosed in the statement of affairs.

The production of a report by the administrative receiver for s48(1) purposes is not affected by the fact that the company has gone or goes into liquidation (s48(4)). In that case, the administrative receiver must send a copy of his report to the liquidator within seven days of his compliance with s48(1) or, if later, the nomination or appointment of the liquidator. In practice, the administrative receiver will usually consider it inappropriate to send a copy of his report to a nominee where more than seven days is to elapse before the appointment is confirmed or otherwise (see ss98–100). Although the submission of a report in this way is expressly required by s48(4)(a) the administrative receiver will usually prefer to wait until the nomination is confirmed or an alternative appointment is resolved under s100(2) before submitting his report to the liquidator. On technical grounds, a delay of this kind constitutes a criminal default by the administrative receiver (see s48(8)). Where, as will be usual, the administrative receiver submits his report to the liquidator within the three-month or court-extended period stipulated in s48(2), he is relieved of his obligation to distribute his report to unsecured creditors or call a meeting of them in accordance with that provision.

The obligations imposed by s48 generally do not apply to an administrative receiver who is appointed to act with an existing administrative receiver or in place of an administrative receiver dying or ceasing to act, save to the extent that his predecessor has failed to comply fully with the obligations imposed by s48 (s48(7)). This rule operates in exactly the same way in relation to the obligation imposed by ss46 and 47 (s46(2)).

As with the preceding sections, contravention of s48 by an administrative receiver without reasonable excuse gives rise to criminal liability for a fine and continued daily default fine (s48(8) for which see s430 and Sched 10).

## 11.6   The Creditors' Meeting

The procedure for the convening and conduct of the creditors' meeting is set out in IR rr3.9–3.15. These rules are largely prescriptive and relate to matters of detail. It is curious that certain of these are not located within the body of the Act itself, in view of their importance.

The administrative receiver must have regard to the convenience of the persons intended to attend in fixing the venue of the creditors' meeting which, unless the court otherwise directs, must be summoned for commencement (but not necessary conclusion) between 10.00 am and 4.00 pm on a business day (IR r3.9(1) and (2); and see IR rr13.6 and 13.3(1) for the definition of 'venue' and 'business day'). At least 14 days' notice of the venue must be given to all creditors of the company who are identified in the statement of affairs or who are known to the administrative receiver and who had claims against the company at the time of his appointment (IR r3.9(3)). The notice summoning the meeting must be accompanied by a form of proxy in statutory Form 8.3 (IR r3.9(4)). In addition, the notice must include a statement to the effect that creditors whose claims are wholly secured are not entitled to attend or to be represented at the meeting. However, a secured creditor is entitled to vote in respect of the balance (if any) after deducting the value of his security, as calculated by himself (IR rr3.9(5) and 3.11(6)). Notice of the venue for the meeting must also be published in the newspaper in which the administrative receiver's appointment was originally advertised under IR r3.2(3), although no form is prescribed in this case, and both the notice to creditors and the newspaper advertisement must contain a statement setting out the effect of IR r3.11(1) which deals with voting rights (IR r3.9(6) and (7)).

The chairman of the creditors' meeting must be the administrative receiver or a person nominated by him in writing to act in his place (IR r3.10(1)). Any nominee must be either a person who is qualified to act as an insolvency practitioner in relation to the company or an employee of the receiver or his firm who is experienced in insolvency matters (IR r3.10(2)). In practice the absence of the administrative receiver or both (or more) joint administrative receivers from a creditors' meeting may have a very debilitating effect on the confidence and/or support of the unsecured creditors unless there are valid and clearly genuine reasons for the absence of the office-holder(s).

In order to vote at a meeting a creditor is required to give written details of its debt to the administrative receiver and lodge any proxy intended to be used by midday on the business day before the meeting (IR r3.11(1)). However, the chairman of the meeting enjoys a discretion to admit a creditor to vote if he is satisfied that the contravention of the preceding rule was due to circumstances beyond the creditor's control, such as a postal strike (IR r3.11(2)). The rule for calculating liquidation claims is contained in IR r3.11(4) whereby votes are calculated according to the amount of a creditor's debt as at the date of the administrative receiver's appointment, less any amounts paid in respect of that debt (and for no other purposes) after that debt. The position is more troublesome in the case of unliquidated amounts as provided for in IR r3.11(5); such claims will not give rise to a right to vote unless the chairman puts on the claim an estimated minimum value and admits the claim for voting purposes.

Rule 3.11(5) provides that a creditor shall not vote in respect of a debt for an unliquidated amount, or any debt whose value is not ascertained (eg in unliquidated damages), except where the chairman agrees to put upon the debt an estimated minimal value for the purposes of entitlement to vote and admits the claim for that purpose. Very similar wording appears in IR r1.17(3), which was considered in *Re Cranley Mansions Ltd* [1994] BCC 576 in relation to a meeting convened to consider a voluntary arrangement. The case concerned a creditor who lodged a claim for £900,000 which was given a nominal value of £1 by the chairman, thereby enabling the creditor to vote but with no effective power. Ferris J held that there was a material irregularity on the part of the chairman, although it could not be said that the claim should have been attributed some higher value. The learned judge made separate reference to the word 'agrees' in IR r1.17(3), as appears in IR r3.11(5), and held that, without some bilateral concurrence by both creditor and chairman as to the value substituted, the creditor could not be said to have agreed to the substituted value and was not therefore bound by the voluntary arrangement.

The *Cranley Mansions* decision should act as a warning to chairmen of creditors' meetings generally as to the valuation of similar types of claims. The practical point here is that, if real agreement cannot be reached with a creditor as to the minimum entitlement to vote, the chairman may be best advised to reject the claim entirely, as is permitted by IR r3.12(1) in relation to the whole or any part of any creditor's claim. Such an outright rejection is susceptible of an appeal to the court under IR r3.12(1), although it is submitted that this is preferable to both protracted and separate litigation as in the *Cranley Mansions* case or the admission of a claim which is marked as objected to by the chairman and subsequently appealed to the court by him under IR r3.12(3). Furthermore, where a creditor appeals to court against a decision of the chairman the creditor will usually have to bear the costs of doing so (IR r3.12(5)).

The quorum for a meeting of creditors is constituted by at least one creditor entitled to vote. This will include those persons present or represented by proxy by any person (including the chairman) and any corporate body which is represented under the Companies Act 1985 s375 (IR r12.4A(1)–(3)). However, a meeting must not commence until at least the expiry of 15 minutes after the time appointed for its commencement where the quorum present is satisfied by the attendance of the chairman alone or by one other person as well as the chairman and, in addition, the chairman is aware, by virtue of proofs and proxies received or otherwise, that one or more additional persons would, if attending, be entitled to vote (IR r12.4A(4)).

Notwithstanding the absence of a proper quorum, a meeting is deemed to have been duly summoned and held if it is not adjourned (IR r3.14(3)). This follows from the rule that a creditors' meeting must not be adjourned, even if no quorum is present, unless the chairman decides that it is desirable (IR r3.14(1)). If adjourned, the chairman is under an express duty to adjourn the meeting to such date, time and place as he thinks fit. The constraints in terms of convenience of venue and time of the meeting imposed by IR r3.9(1) and (2) continue to apply in an adjourned meeting (IR r3.14(1) and (2)).

Decisions of the meeting of creditors are taken by a simple majority (in value) of those present and voting in person or by proxy voting on a resolution (IR r3.15(1)). The chairman of the meeting must cause a record of the proceedings of the meeting to be made and kept as part of the records of the receivership (IR r3.15(2)). This record must include a list of the creditors who attended at the meeting personally or by proxy, together with the names and addresses of those individuals entitled to be members of any creditors' meeting which has been established (IR r3.15(3)).

## 11.7 The Creditors' Committee

Section 49(1) confers on the meeting of unsecured creditors summoned under s48(2) a power, if it thinks fit, to establish a creditors' committee which exercises the functions conferred on it by or under the Act. The function of the creditors' committee is to assist the administrative receiver in discharging what are specifically referred to as his functions (as opposed to duties) and to act in relation to him in such manner as may be agreed from time to time (IR r3.18(1)). In this regard, s49(2) empowers the committee, on the giving of not less than seven days' notice, to require the administrative receiver to attend before it at any reasonable time and to furnish it with such information relating to the carrying out by him of his functions as it may reasonably require. It appears that an administrative receiver may refuse to disclose information to the committee on the basis that it may not be reasonably required by the committee in substantially the same way as he may omit information from his report on the basis that it would seriously prejudice the carrying out of his functions for the purposes of s48(6). Where the creditors' committee requires the attendance of the office-holder under s49(2) it must give notice in writing to the administrative receiver, which must be signed by the majority of the members of the committee (or their representatives) at that time (IR r3.28(1)). Whilst the committee must stipulate the date, being a business day as defined in IR r3.13(1), on which the meeting is to take place, the time and place for the meeting must be determined by the administrative receiver following receipt of the notice (IR r3.28(2)). This represents an exception to the general rule in IR r3.18(2) whereby the office-holder fixes both the time and the place for the meeting, as does the rule whereby the committee members may elect one of their own members to be chairman of the meeting in place of the administrative receiver or his nominee, as otherwise provided for by IR r3.19 considered below (see IR r3.28(3)).

Notwithstanding s49(2) the functions of the creditors' committee in relation to the administrative receiver are unclear to the extent that they apparently require agreement with the office-holder from time to time by virtue of IR r3.18(1). This contrasts sharply with a liquidation committee in a creditors' voluntary winding-up, where certain of the liquidator's powers may only be exercised with sanction of the liquidation committee or the court (see s165(2)(b)).

It is clear that the decision to establish a creditors' committee must be made at the unsecured creditors' meeting itself or, presumably, any such adjourned meeting (IR r3.16(1)). The administrative receiver must issue a certificate of the committee's due constitution in statutory Form 3.4 but may not do so unless and until three of the persons who are to be members of the committee have agreed to act (IR r3.17(2A), (3)). IR r3.17(2) expressly provides that no person may act as a member of the committee unless and until he has agreed to do so, although agreement may be given by a proxy, or representative under the Companies Act 1985 s375 in the case of a corporate creditor, unless the proxy or authorisation itself contains a statement to the contrary (IR r3.17(2)). The rationale behind these provisions is to promote the establishment of a creditors' committee at the earliest possible time, which in practice is usually at the conclusion of the meeting of the company's unsecured creditors. There is limited scope for filling vacancies as provided for by IR r3.25, discussed below.

Technically, the creditors' committee does not come into being until the administrative receiver has issued a certificate of due constitution (IR r3.17(1)). Although it would follow that the committee may not act until duly constituted, any act of the committee is preserved by a provision common to various insolvency procedures whereby the acts of the committee are deemed valid notwithstanding any defect in the appointment, election or qualifications of any member of the committee or any committee member's representative or in the formalities of its establishment (IR r3.30A).

The committee must comprise at least three and not more than five creditors of the company (ie including those who are partly secured) elected at the meeting (IR r3.16(1), (2)). Any creditor whose claim has been rejected by the chairman for the purposes of his entitlement to vote is ineligible to vote (IR r3.16(2)). The position of corporate creditors is catered for by IR r3.16(3), which permits a body corporate to be a member of the creditors' committee subject to the proviso that it may only act as such through a representative duly appointed in accordance with IR r3.21.

The administrative receiver is charged with the duty of sending the certificate of the creditors' committee due constitution, and any amended certificate, to the Registrar of Companies using statutory Form 3.4 (IR r3.17(4)). Should there be any change in the membership of the committee following its first establishment, the change must also be reported to the Registrar in the same way using statutory Form 3.5. No time limit appears to operate in relation to either of these obligatory returns.

Whilst the administrative receiver determines the time and location of meetings of the creditors' committee, the first of these must be called not later than three months after the establishment of the committee (IR r3.18(2), (3)). Thereafter, the administrative receiver is obliged to call a meeting if requested to do so by a member of the committee or his representative within 21 days of the office-holder receiving the request (IR r3.18(3)(a)). Alternatively, the administrative receiver must call a meeting for a specified date if the creditors' committee has previously resolved that a meeting be held on that date (IR r3.18(3)(b)). There is, therefore, and in theory at least, no requirement that a subsequent meeting of the creditors' committee be convened following the obligatory first meeting, although in practice this would be unusual in view of the committee's functions. Seven days' notice of the venue (ie the time, date and place: IR r3.16) of a creditors' committee meeting must be given in writing by the administrative receiver to every member of the committee or its representative as designated for that purpose (IR r3.18(4)). The same rule avoids technical contraventions of this notice requirement, say by way of misdirected post or the impracticability of seven days' notice, by permitting the waiver of the notice requirement by or on behalf of any member. This may be signified either at or before the meeting itself.

The administrative receiver, or any person nominated by him in writing, must act as chairman of any meeting of the creditors' committee, other than where the committee members require the attendance of the office-holder before them pursuant to s49(2), whereupon they must elect any one of their number or any nominee to act as chairman in his place (IR rr3.19(1), 3.28(3)). In the former case, a nominated chairman must be either a person qualified to act as an insolvency practitioner in relation to the company or an employee of the administrative receiver or his firm who is experienced in insolvency matters (IR r3.19(2)). This rule mirrors the requirements for creditors' meetings contained in IR r3.10. A creditors' committee meeting is deemed quorate if due notice has been given to all members (although this may be waived by members as discussed above) and at least two members or their representatives are present (IR r3.20).

IR r3.21 permits creditors' committee members to appoint representatives to act on their behalf. However, no member may be represented by a body corporate or by a person who is either an undischarged bankrupt or subject to a composition or arrangement with his creditors (IR r3.21(4)). Further, a person may neither act simultaneously as representative of more than one committee member on the same committee nor act both as a member of the committee and as a representative of another member simultaneously (IR r3.21(5)). The rule does not prohibit a person acting as a representative on a contemporaneous basis on behalf of two persons on separate creditors' committees, even if those persons are actually also members of the same committee, provided the representation is not simultaneous and on the same committee.

A person who acts as representative for a committee member must hold a letter of authority entitling him to act. The letter may be either general or specific in scope and must be signed by or on behalf of the committee member. No form is prescribed for the letter of the authority and, unless a statement appears therein to the contrary, a proxy or authorisation for the purposes of the Companies Act 1985 s375 in relation to any creditors' meeting of the company must be treated as a letter of authority to act generally where it is signed by or on behalf of the committee member (IR r3.21(2)). For the avoidance of doubt, the chairman of the meeting of the creditors' committee may require a person claiming to act as representative of a committee member to produce his letter of authority and may exclude him from the meeting if it appears that the authority is deficient (IR r3.21(3)).

A member of the creditors' committee may resign by notice in writing delivered to the administrative receiver without further formality (IR r3.22).

Membership of the committee is terminated automatically if a member becomes bankrupt or compounds or arranges with his creditors (eg by way of voluntary arrangement) (IR r3.23(1)). Whilst the mere presentation of a bankruptcy petition will not terminate membership, any trustee-in-bankruptcy appointed in place of a committee member automatically replaces him as a member (IR r3.23(2)). Membership of the creditors' committee is also terminated automatically if a member is neither present nor represented at three consecutive meetings of the committee, although the committee itself may resolve at the third of those meetings not to apply this rule in which case, presumably, the same sanction will continue to operate subject to the member's attendance at the following committee meeting (IR r3.23(1)(b) and see IR r3.26 on voting rights here). Membership of the committee will also terminate automatically if it transpires that the member had never been a creditor of the company (IR r3.23(1)(c)).

Finally, a member of the committee may be removed by resolution at the creditors' meeting itself, on at least 14 days' notice being given of the intention to move the resolution. The procedure for passing such a resolution remains unclear, however, since neither the Act nor the IR envisage a meeting of creditors subject to the s48(2) meeting (which may itself be adjourned under IR r3.14). Neither do the rules permit the committee itself to remove an errant or irresponsible committee member other than by refusing to lift the automatic termination provision in IR r3.23(1)(b) on the particular member failing to attend three consecutive committee meetings. The creditors' control of its committee is of considerable practical importance, since the stewardship of the creditors' interests generally, which may be significant and numerous, are effectively subrogated to the committee on its being established. Presumably, therefore, notice of such a resolution must emanate from the administrative receiver, usually on the request of a creditor.

On a vacancy arising on the creditors' committee, the administrative receiver may appoint any creditor eligible under IR r3.16(2) to fill the vacancy, provided a majority of the other committee members agree (ie on a simple 'single vote' majority basis) to the appointment and the appointee consents to act (IR r3.25(3)). However, the vacancy need not be filled if the administrative receiver and a majority of the remaining committee members agree, subject to the total number of members not falling below three in accordance with IR r3.16(1) (IR r3.25(2)). It is curious that the rules appear to make no provision for the creditors themselves resolving to fill any vacancy, particularly in view of their power to remove a committee member under IR r3.24. In the absence of such an express power it must be assumed that no such power exists, notwithstanding its obvious desirability. In practice, the administrative receiver will usually be swayed by the views of the creditors in making an appointment under IR r3.25(3), although this is subject to the agreement of a majority of the remaining committee members.

Members of the creditors' committee may each cast one vote on each resolution, irrespective of their claims on the company, each resolution being passed when a majority of the members present or represented have voted in favour of it (IR r3.26(1)). Every resolution of the committee must be recorded either separately or as part of the minutes of the committee's meeting, each resolution being signed and kept as part of the records of the receivership (IR r3.26(3)).

IR r3.27 provides for some degree of procedural flexibility in allowing for resolutions of the committee to be passed by post. That is, the administrative receiver may seek to obtain the agreement of members of the creditors' committee to a resolution by sending a copy of the proposed resolution to every member or his representative designated for that purpose (IR r3.27(1)). No form is prescribed for a proposed resolution, although it must be set out in such a way that agreement or dissent from each of any separate resolutions may be indicated by the recipient of it on the copy sent to him (IR r3.27(2)). This rule avoids the distribution of separate documents in respect of each separate resolution proposed. The administrative receiver may not, however, seek to employ the postal resolution procedure as a means of avoiding meetings in dealing with sensitive or vexed issues, because any member of the committee may, within seven days of the date of the administrative receiver sending out the proposed resolution, require him to summon a meeting of the committee to consider the matters raised by the proposed resolution (IR r3.27(3)). Where no such requirement (or 'request' as it is somewhat confusedly referred to) is raised the proposed resolution is deemed to have been passed by the committee if and when the administrative receiver is notified in writing by a majority of the members that they concur with it (IR r3.27(4)). Copies of any resolution passed by post, together with a note of how the committee's concurrence was obtained, must be kept with the records of the receivership (as opposed to automatically comprising part of it) (IR r3.27(5)). There is no requirement that a copy of any resolution must be signed by the administrative receiver.

The administrative receiver is obliged to defray any reasonable travelling expenses directly incurred by members of the creditors' committee or their representatives in relation to their attendance at the committee's meeting, or otherwise on the committee's business (presumably with the committee's authority) as an expense of the receivership (IR r3.29(1)). These expenses are met out of the assets of the company, although they are not payable in respect of any meeting of the committee held within three months of a previous meeting other than where the meeting is summoned at the instance of the administrative receiver (IR r3.29(2)).

Membership of the creditors' committee does not of itself prevent a person from dealing with the company whilst in administrative receivership, subject to the proviso that any transaction in the course of such dealings must be entered into in good faith and for value (IR r3.30(1); cf IR r4.170 in the case of a liquidation committee which requires court or committee sanction). This rule gives legal effect to the common practical situation where suppliers, who usually represent significant creditors of the company, contract with the administrative receiver following appointment on behalf of the company on an ongoing basis, usually where an attempt is proposed to sell the company's business as a going concern or where completion of a specific contract is contemplated. On the other hand, on an application by any person interested, the court may set aside any transaction which appears to contravene this rule and may also give such consequential directions as it thinks fit to compensate the company for any loss which it may have incurred in consequence of the transaction (IR r3.30(2)). The rules do not stipulate who amounts to an interested person for these purposes, although the term would logically apply to creditors and shareholders of the company, the former being more likely in practical terms to be made aware of any impropriety. The court wields a wide discretion in remedying any wrong done to the company including, it must be assumed, a power to make the administrative receiver personally liable for any loss suffered by the company.

## 11.8   Vacation of Office by the Administrative Receiver

An administrative receiver must vacate office on removal by the court by resignation, on death, on ceasing to be qualified to act as such or on the formal completion of the administrative receivership (s45(1), (2), IR r3.34).

An administrative receiver may only be removed by order of the court and not otherwise (s45(1)). The office-holder is thus sheltered from undue pressure on the part of his appointor in view of the other (albeit subsidiary) interests to which he is subject. This approach also reflects the professional status of the office-holder and the high standards of performance expected of him in view of his position as an office-holder for the purposes of the Act. It follows from s45(1) that the former practice whereby a debenture-holder was able to remove a receiver of his own volition, will no longer operate. This will be the case even if the power to remove is expressly conferred in the debenture, since such a provision will be deemed void. Only administrative receivers as defined are free from such removal. A non-administrative receiver may still be removed by his appointor, usually a debenture-holder or, less commonly, the trustees of a debenture stock trust deed (see, for example, *Re Chic Ltd* [1905] 2 Ch 345). Nevertheless, an application to court may be necessary to remove such a non-administrative receiver if there is no power to remove the receiver and manager at will in the debenture (see, for example, *Re Slogger Automatic Feeder Co Ltd* [1915] 1 Ch 478).

There are three main scenarios in which an application to the court to remove an administrative receiver under s45(1) may be envisaged.

First, an application for removal may be made where the appointing debenture-holder is dissatisfied with the manner in which the administrative receivership is being conducted. Whilst no authority exists on the point at present, it is submitted that the courts will be to adopt an approach similar to the removal of a liquidator by the court in a voluntary liquidation under s108, where cause must be shown by the applicant. The case law on this point bears out that the behaviour complained of must be serious, such as acting in bad faith or improperly or non-independently (see, for example, *Re Charterland Goldfields Ltd* (1909) 26 TLR 132; *Re Rubber and Produce Investment Trust* [1915] 1 Ch 382). In practice, and in view of the fact that an administrative receiver is not an officer of the court, it may be that the court adopts a far less stringent approach than in liquidations. Notwithstanding this, cases where an administrative receiver actively refuses to vacate office are likely to be exceptional.

Secondly, an application for removal may be made where another party holding such requisite security as to enable it to appoint an administrative receiver for the purposes of s29(2) asserts a priority right of appointment. Where another party has already exercised its right of appointment, s45(1) makes clear that another administrative receiver may not take office merely by the party asserting its priority right in effecting an appointment and thereby allegedly displacing the subsisting office-holder from office, since removal may only be given effect by the court (see Chapter 5 at para 5.2).

Thirdly, the general creditors of the company may seek to petition the court for the removal of an administrative receiver where the company goes into liquidation, irrespective of whether the administrative receiver is appointed prior to or following the liquidation, on the grounds that the appointment is needless in that the liquidator will necessarily have to meet the appointing debenture-holder's claim on the assets of the company in any case. It is submitted that the court is unlikely to entertain such applications, notwithstanding its willingness to remove one liquidator and replace it with another in an insolvent liquidation on the basis that the latter office-holder was less costly (see *Re Corbenstoke (No 2)* [1989] 5 BCC 767). As mentioned previously, the courts have traditionally recognised and protected the contractual rights of appointment enjoyed by debenture-holders and have refrained from imposing any duty of care on the debenture-holder in effecting an appointment (*Shamji v Johnson Matthey Bankers Ltd* [1986] BCLC 278; *Re Potters Oil Ltd (No 2)* [1986] 1 WLR 201). This reflects the court's deference to the doctrine of freedom of contract and the rights of secured parties to benefit from their position over unsecured creditors, who themselves contract freely with the company in the real or constructive knowledge of secured claims on it.

Surprisingly, neither the Act nor the IR lay down any procedure resembling IR r4.143 for the removal of a liquidator in a members' voluntary liquidation. It must be assumed, however, that the practice adopted will resemble IR r4.143 in the form of an initial hearing for directions, at which the incumbent administrative receiver may submit that no case can be made out for the application on the basis of which it should be dismissed. Alternatively, the applicant may be given the opportunity to attend before the court on an *ex parte* basis to show cause, following which notification is given to the administrative receiver of the application and its hearing date together with any evidence on which the applicant intends to rely in support of it. Actual practice in this regard will ultimately hinge on local practice in the appropriate Companies' Court.

An administrative receiver may resign from office by giving notice of his resignation in the prescribed manner (s45(1)). IR r3.33(1) requires that prior to resigning his office the administrative receiver must give at least seven days' notice of his intention to do so to the following persons: the person by whom he was appointed; the company or, if it is in liquidation at that time, the liquidator; and the members of any creditors' committee which has been established. The notice, which need not be in any prescribed form, must specify the date on which the administrative receiver intends his resignation to take effect (IR r3.33(2)). It should be noted that no notice requirements operate for the purposes of IR r3.33(3). In such a case, s11(4) provides that the remuneration and any expenses properly incurred by the administrative receiver, and any indemnity to which he is entitled out of the assets of the company, shall be charged on and paid out of any property of the company which was subject to the administrative receivership at that time, in priority to any security held by the person on whose behalf the administrative receiver was appointed. Whilst this rule affords the administrative receiver a priority right over claims of his appointor out of the company's assets in respect of remuneration, expenses and indemnity benefits, the proviso to it is that the office-holder may not receive actual payment of his claim or take steps to enforce it without either the consent of the administrator or with leave of the court (s11(3)(c)). It should be noted that the resignation of an administrative receiver will not *per se* undermine the right of the appointing debenture-holder to continue with the process of the administrative receivership. The office-holder himself who resigns is effectively a figurehead who may be re-placed independent of the debenture-holder's rights to effect an appointment.

The appointment of an administrative receiver to act with an existing administrative receiver or to act in place of an administrative receiver who has died or otherwise ceased to act (ie by resignation, disqualification or, presumably, removal) will not trigger the notice of appointment and statement of affairs formalities discussed previously in relation to ss46 and 47, except to the extent that the vacating or deceased office-holder has failed to comply fully with those requirements.

In the event of an administrative receiver dying whilst in office, the obliga-tion falls on his appointor by virtue of IR r3.34 to give notice of his death forthwith on becoming aware of it to: the Registrar of Companies; the com-pany, or if it is in liquidation at that time, the liquidator; and to the members of any creditors' committee established at that time. The notice should be in statutory Form 3.7. No time limits are imposed other than the 'forthwith' requirement on the appointor becoming aware of the death. Again, the death of an administrative receiver will entitle the appointor to replace the deceased office-holder without prejudice to his right of appointment and the conduct of the administrative receivership itself.

An administrative receiver must vacate office if he ceased to be qualified to act as an insolvency practitioner in relation to the company as defined in s388(1), such as where authorisation is revoked by a recognised professional body or the Secretary of State (s45(2)). A person does not therefore automati-cally vacate office on ceasing to be qualified, but must vacate office immedi-ately (ie other than by resignation) on pain of liability to imprisonment or a fine or both by virtue of s389(1) (for which see s430 and Sched 10).

In all cases, other than where vacation of office arises on death, an outgo-ing administrative receiver must within 14 days of his vacation of office send a notice to that effect, for which there is no prescribed form, to the Registrar of Companies. Sanction for failure is liability to a fine where a reasonable excuse for failure cannot be shown (s45(4), (5) (as amended by Companies Act 1989 Scheds 16 and 24)). Since the Companies Act 1989, s405(2) also requires a notice to be given to the Registrar of the administrative receiver's vacation of office, the rules permit the notice to the Registrar to be given by way of an indorsement on the return for s405(2) purposes (IR r3.35(2)).

Other than in the cases dealt with above where the administrative receiver resigns or dies in office, namely as to where the administrative receiver vacates office on completion of the receivership, or as a consequence of his failing to be qualified as an insolvency practitioner, he must forthwith give notice of his vacation of office to the company or, if it is in liquidation at that time, the liquidator and to the members of any creditors' committee (IR r3.35(1)).

Finally, in a manner analogous to s11(4) as discussed above, where at any time an administrative receiver vacates office, his remuneration and any expenses properly incurred by him together with any indemnity to which he is entitled out of the assets of the company (eg under s44(1)(c)) shall be charged on and paid out of any property of the company which is in his custody or under his control at that time, in priority to any security held by the person by or on whose behalf the administrative receiver was appointed (s45(3)).

# Chapter Twelve

# Assets and Liabilities

## 12.1 Judgment Creditors

The position of judgment creditors in a receivership warrants special consideration if only because the law is so fragmented in this area. The rules developed by the courts are far from clear, and much practical benefit would derive from a clear statutory set of rules as are operative in a liquidation by virtue of ss183 and 184. The vagueness of the rules stems from the relative uncertainty of the courts in ascertaining the stage to which any particular enforcement procedure must be pursued before a floating charge is deemed to crystallise as a consequence. It is clear that this point or stage varies depending on the method of enforcement pursued by the judgment creditor. The position is further confused by the view that enforcement itself may give rise to cessation of the company's business, which itself may cause crystallisation of a floating charge, either of itself or on account of the company's ceasing to be a going concern. This confusion may, of course, be avoided by expressly stipulating in the debenture that such an event gives to crystallisation.

The problem in this area is to ascertain the stage at which the judgment creditor may rest easy in the knowledge that any receiver appointed pursuant to a floating charge may not interfere with the enforcement, in terms of either the goods against which enforcement was levied or their proceeds of sale (see, for example, *Robson v Smith* [1895] 2 Ch 118). The general view of the case is that enforcement must be completed before the intervention of the receiver appointed may be discounted (see, for example, *Taunton v Sheriff of Warwickshire* [1895] 2 Ch 319). However, this conclusion stems from case law which predominantly (and usually very considerably) pre-dates the 1986 legislation and which may not give full effect to modern commercial and judicial attitudes to the floating charge and the security created by it (see, for example, the discussions in RM Goode, *Legal Problems of Credit and Security*, 2nd edn (1988) at 47 *et seq* and in *Fire Nymph Products Ltd v The Heating Centre Pty Ltd* [1992] 7 ACSR 365).

The various methods of enforcement open to a judgment creditor—writ of *fieri facias*, garnishee order, charging order and the appointment of a

receiver—are considered here separately. Notably, save in the case of a charging order, none of these methods of enforcement as such creates a charge over
the company's assets. In what follows here, no consideration is afforded to
injunctions restraining the removal of a company's assets from the jurisdiction or sequestration orders. These are orders made against the company and
not against its assets and, as such, these two forms of enforcement do not
*per se* affect the right of a floating-charge holder *vis-à-vis* the assets subject to
the charge, even where the injunction or sequestration order precedes the
crystallisation of the floating charge. This was held to be the case in *Cretanor
Maritime Co Ltd v Irish Marine Management Ltd* [1978] 3 All ER 164 where
the Court of Appeal upheld a *Mareva* injunction over a vessel, thus restraining its removal from the jurisdiction prior to the crystallisation of a floating
charge.

   In the *Cretanor* case, the drawback for the owner of the vessel who
obtained the injunction over the assets of the company to guard its position
pending a claim by it against the company, was that the injunction itself did
not establish any right over the assets of the company; rather, the order merely
restrained the removal of the asset pending subsequent enforcement by the
creditor. As such, the appointment of a receiver and the consequent crystallisation of the floating charge created a fixed equitable charge over the assets in
favour of the debenture-holder, to which any later attempt at enforcement by
the creditor would have to be subject. Notably, the Court of Appeal was
prepared to add the debenture-holder as a party to the summons taken out by
the receiver without a fresh application to the court having to be made since
the application to release the asset from the injunction fell to be made by the
debenture-holder itself and not the receiver as agent of the company. For this
reason, and so as to avoid unnecessary delay and expense, it would appear
advisable to join the debenture-holder as a party to any action challenging
injunctive relief granted over the company's assets, so as to guard against
the receiver being deemed an agent of the company by the court and thus ineligible or inappropriate as a party to an action mounting such a challenge.

### 12.1.1  *Fieri facias*

A writ of *fieri facias* requires the sheriff to seize goods of the company and to
sell them in satisfaction of the unsatisfied judgment debt. Whilst there is no
requirement that the sheriff takes actual physical possession of the goods, this
is usual practice for sale purposes. However, even where possession is taken,
no sale may be effected once the floating charge over the company's assets
has crystallised (*Re Standard Manufacturing Co* [1891] 1 Ch 627). This
would appear to require actual completion of the sale as opposed to mere
exchange of contracts or mere pre-contractual negotiations (see *Re Opera Ltd*
[1891] 3 Ch 260). However, where a sale is effected by the sheriff prior to

crystallisation, the sheriff may retain the proceeds of sale for the benefit of the judgment debtor following crystallisation (*Re Opera Ltd* [1891] 3 Ch 260).

Since the judgment debtor will usually wish to avoid the sale of what may be a significant company asset, payment in whole or part will often be made following seizure of the goods. Once such payment is made, it appears that those monies may be retained following crystallisation of the floating charge (see *Robinson v Burnell's Vienna Bakery Co* [1904] 2 KB 624 (part payment) and *Heaton and Dugard Ltd v Cutting Bros Ltd* [1925] 1 KB 655 (full payment)). These decisions suggest that money may be retained even if those sums are still in the hands of the sheriff on crystallisation notwithstanding the contract and the questionable decision in *Taunton v Sheriff of Warwickshire* [1895] 2 Ch 319. It would follow that a judgment debtor may retain monies paid over to a third party either directly or to the sheriff for his benefit, whether or not such payment is made prior to or following crystallisation.

The above cases actually rest on a determination of whether enforcement is deemed to be completed in any particular circumstance. In the case of the sale of seized goods, enforcement may be deemed to take place either on completion of the sale or on the payment over of the sale proceeds to the sheriff or possibly the judgment creditor. In *The Law of Receivers of Companies*, Sweet & Maxwell, 2nd edn (1994 at 17–07) Lightman and Moss suggest that sale proceeds should be attributed the same status as goods to which the receiver may stake a claim upon crystallisation. In other words, the judgment creditor will acquire legal title to the money free of the debenture-holder's equity where the sale proceeds are actually paid over to the judgment creditor prior to or without notice of crystallisation. It is respectfully submitted that this conclusion goes too far and over-emphasises the relevance of the proceeds of sale being in the hands of the sheriff or the judgment creditor. Should the real question not be whether or not the payment over precedes the crystallisation of the charge, and not whether the proceeds themselves are held by the sheriff or the judgment creditor? Certainly the court has and exercises a discretion to this end in relation to an analogous provision in ss183 and 184 (see, for example, *Re Grosvenor Metal Co* [1950] Ch 63 per Vaisey J).

### 12.1.2  Garnishee orders

A garnishee order attacks a judgment debtor of the company and requires the debtor against whom the judgment debt is enforced to make payment over to the judgment creditor. The order is made absolute following an *inter partes* hearing which itself follows a preliminary *nisi* order that may be sought on an *ex parte* basis. The court's discretion in granting the order is absolute and, as with charging orders, the court will not make an order so as to give the judgment creditor an unfair advantage over other creditors of the debtor company

(RSC Ord 49 r1 and see *Rainbow v Moorgate Properties Ltd* [1975] 2 All ER 821 per Buckley LJ).

The general position with garnishee orders in receivership is that a judgment debtor may retain the realised proceeds of the attached debt only if the garnishee order has been made absolute, as was held in *Cairney v Back* [1906] 2 KB 746. It appears from that decision that it is irrelevant whether or not payment has already been made of the attached debt of the judgment creditor. *Norton v Yates* [1906] 1 KB 112 fits into this overall view in holding that a receiver may claim priority over a judgment debtor where the proceeds of the attached debt have not been paid over following the making of a garnishee order *nisi*.

The case law relating to garnishee orders in this area is troubled with the effect which a floating charge is perceived to have on enforcement rights before and on crystallisation. Whilst an order *nisi* does not constitute a charge *per se* on the assets of the company, the effect of the order being served on the company ordinarily will not be to preclude the company from carrying on its ordinary course of business. As such, the garnishee order *nisi* will not cause a floating charge to crystallise automatically on that ground, although crystallisation may of course occur on the fulfilment of any other grounds envisaged in the debenture. As such, notwithstanding the fact that the floating charge creates a security interest which is postponed to specific present and future assets, the mere existence of the floating charge offers no advantage in terms of priority to the debenture-holder as against the judgment creditor enforcing by way of garnishee order, since the company continues to carry on its ordinary course of business as it is impliedly licenced to do by the holder of the floating charge (see the third element of Romer LJ's classic definition in *Re Yorkshire Woolcombers Association Ltd* [1903] 2 Ch 284 at 295, *Norton v Yates* [1906] 1 KB 112 at 124 and the analysis of the floating charge in Farrar [1980] 1 Co Law 83).

Broadly, the approach of the courts is to give effect to the priority of a crystallised floating charge over a judgment creditor's claims, except where the garnishee order has been pressed to its ultimate conclusion, on the basis that, until that stage, the judgment creditor has no better claim to the attached proceeds of the garnishee order than the uncrystallised floating-charge holder has to the assets of the company. This concurs with the policy of the courts in dealing with enforcement by way of writ of *fieri facias*, where the process must be complete in order for a judgment creditor to obtain priority to the proceeds of sale of assets seized. This view is evidenced by the Court of Appeal in *Evans v Rival Granite* [1910] 2 KB 979 which followed *Robson v Smith* [1895] 2 Ch 118 where Romer J rejected the claim of a floating-charge holder to attached garnishee order proceeds paid over prior to the crystallisation of the floating charge.

Where a receiver or debenture-holder wishes to challenge a judgment debtor's right to the proceeds of a debt attached by way of a garnishee order, it may do so by injunction. Alternatively, an administrative receiver may apply to the court for an order under s234. Clearly the debt or its proceeds are not capable of seizure as intangibles for the purposes of s234(3). Neither may the judgment creditor defend its position by claiming the order constitutes an assignment to it of the judgment creditor's rights in the attached debt proceeds, since it is clear that it does not (see *Re Combined Weighing and Advertising Machine Co* (1889) 43 ChD 99).

## 12.1.3   Charging orders

A judgment creditor may seek to enforce a judgment debt by way of a charging order. The order is sought on an *ex parte* basis, at which the court may grant a charging order *nisi* following which an *inter partes* hearing determines whether or not the order should be made absolute (Charging Orders Act 1979, ss1 and 2, RSC Ords 50 and 88). A charging order may be sought against freehold or leasehold land of the company, shares and debt securities held by the company in other companies and certain funds held by the court on account for the creditors of the company. Unlike a writ of *fieri facias* and a garnishee order, the purpose of a charging order is to obtain security for the payment of a judgment debt, as opposed to the immediate payment of it, although there is no bar to seeking an immediate order for sale.

The order absolute takes effect as if the company had created a charge in writing over the property and assets comprised in the order as at the date of the order *nisi* (see Charging Orders Act 1979, s6). That is, the charge is created by the order absolute, the effect of which is to backdate the effect of the charge to those assets comprised in the order *nisi*. Following this the company will be precluded from dealing with the assets in any case after service on it of the order *nisi*. As such, an order absolute which is obtained prior to the crystallisation of a floating charge will take in priority to the floating-charge security in a manner analogous to writs of *fieri facias* and garnishee orders; cf *Re Overseas Engineering (GB) Ltd* [1962] 3 All ER 12 (which appears capable of being distinguished on its facts).

Charging orders themselves tend to cause few problems in practice, since most orders are made against property which will usually be subject to an existing fixed charge in favour of the debenture-holder. Consequently any question of priority will not usually be in issue. As with garnishee orders, the mere existence of an uncrystallised floating charge over an asset will not of itself preclude a charging order being made in relation to that asset, although a receiver and/or debenture-holder will be entitled to notice of an order absolute hearing, and may oppose the making of an order on the ground that the floating charge has crystallised. This assumes that the applicant has notice of the crystallisation of the floating charge which, in practice, may not necessarily be the case, no provision currently being in force requiring registration of a notice of crystallisation with the Registrar of Companies.

### 12.1.4 Appointment of receiver

A judgment creditor may also seek to enforce his judgment by applying to court for the appointment of a receiver by way of equitable execution (RSC, Ord 51). As with the aforementioned methods of enforcement, a judgment creditor who succeeds in appointing a receiver over the company's assets by way of equitable execution prior to the crystallisation of the floating charge will take in priority to the floating charge and its holder. Conversely, crystallisation of a floating charge, which will usually extend to the whole of a company's property, will shelter that property from the scope of a court-appointed receiver.

The problem posed here as to priority over the appointor of a receiver pursuant to a floating charge may be reduced to a question of which creditor is able to appoint its receiver first. In practice, this problem is largely obviated by the fact that the entering of a judgment against a company or the levying of execution will usually constitute grounds on which a debenture, and certainly a well-drafted standard-form debenture, will envisage the appointment of a receiver without court involvement. Such an appointment can clearly be made more quickly out of court than an appointment by the court by way of equitable execution. It may also be that the appointment of a receiver by the court constitutes a ground of jeopardy, on the basis of which a floating charge may be deemed to crystallise without the need for the appointment of a receiver by the debenture-holder, although the point appears not to have been considered specifically in the reported cases.

## 12.2 Taxation

Where an administrative receiver is appointed and continues the trade of the company's business, any trading profits or capital gains arising will be subject to corporation tax in the normal way and in the same way as if the company itself was carrying on the business and no administrative receiver had been appointed (Income and Corporation Taxes Act 1988 ss6(1), 12(1)–(3)). That is, the appointment of an administrative receiver, unlike the appointment of a liquidator, does not bring about a new accounting period for corporation tax purposes. As such, trading profits and capital gains made by the administrative receiver in the course of his office may be set off against trading and capital losses standing at the time of his appointment.

Corporation tax, including unabsorbed trading profits and capital gains accruing to the administrative receiver in the course of his office, may be assessed against the administrative receiver personally (*IRC v Thompson* [1936] 2 All ER 651). However, this tax liability represents an expense of the administrative receiver and, as such, the office-holder is entitled to a indemnity out of the company's assets for any tax liability arising. Furthermore, the administrative receiver may only be made liable to the Inland Revenue to the extent that assets of the company are available to meet the liability arising. Exactly the same principle applies in the case of VAT liability incurred to Customs and Excise for goods or services supplied by the company's business although, in the case of VAT, the administrative receiver is not personally liable for the tax (*Re John Willment (Ashford) Ltd* [1979] 2 All ER 615 applied in *Sargent v Commissioners of Customs and Excise* (1995) *The Times,* 23 February (LPA receiver obliged to account for VAT on rent arising from charged properties)).

Previously, VAT bad debt relief had only been available in liquidation by virtue of the Value Added Tax Act 1983 s22(3). Section 32 of the Finance Act 1985 amended the provision and extended the relief to administrative receivers (and administrators). The practical effect of this is that an unsecured creditor who has made a supply of goods or services to the company which is chargeable to VAT need no longer wait until the company goes into liquidation before being able to reclaim the VAT bad debt element of the amount due to him. However, no bad debt relief will be available to a supplier who maintains his claim to the goods supplied under a retention of title claim, although this position will change upon title being established in favour of the company. The extension of VAT bad debt relief to administrative receivers also has had a benefit for the company, since an unsecured creditor who has supplied goods or services chargeable to VAT to the company is likely to be less inclined to present a winding-up petition against the company. This is because he may reclaim the VAT element of the bad debt element of his claim immediately, assuming that the administrative receiver has formed the opinion that no surplus assets will be available for distribution to unsecured creditors. Nonetheless, no technical bar exists to such a petition being presented.

The administrative receiver is now under a duty to issue an appropriately headed certificate of insolvency which states the name of the company, its registered number, the name of the administrative receiver, the date of his appointment and the date on which the certificate was issued (IR r3.36). The certificate must be issued forthwith by the administrative receiver but only upon his forming the opinion that there will be no surplus assets available for distribution to unsecured creditors of the company. The certificate is retained with the company's accounting records in accordance with the Companies Act 1985 s222. In addition, it is the obligation of the administrative receiver to bring the existence of IR r3.38 to the attention of the directors on the completion of the administrative receivership (IR r3.38(a), (b)).

The administrative receiver is obliged to give notice of the certificate (the s222(3) certificate) within three months of his appointment or within two months of its issue, whichever is the later, to all unsecured creditors of the company of whose addresses he is aware and who have, to his knowledge, made supplies to the company which are chargeable to VAT at any time prior to his appointment (IR r3.37(1)). This obligation is ongoing in that notice must be given subsequently to any creditor of whose addresses and supplies to the company he becomes aware (IR r3.37(2)). There is, however, no obligation on the office-holder to supply creditors with a copy of the certificate itself (IR r3.37(3)).

## 12.3 Rates

Section 109(8) of the Law of Property Act 1925 provides that a receiver is under an express duty to pay rates. In practice this provision is invariably excluded in standard-form debentures, and in any case has been held to amount to nothing more than an implied term in the debenture, subject to variation or exclusion. As such, a rating authority has no means of enforcing the provision, as it does not amount to a statutory duty but rather an implied but excludable obligation (see *Liverpool Corporation v Hope* [1938] 1 All ER 492; cf *Re Kentish Homes Ltd* [1993] BCC 212).

The question of whether or not an administrative receiver or his appointing debenture-holder is liable for rates depends on whether the premises are occupied or, in the case of vacant premises, who is deemed to be the owner of them. In either case it is established that the appointment of a receiver does not alter the occupation status of premises for rating purposes (see, for example, *Peat Marwick v Consumers Gas Co* (1981) 113 DLR (3d) 754).

In the case of occupied premises, liability for rates ordinarily falls on the occupiers of the premises, occupation being a question of fact independent of legal title or other interests in the property. Occupation is not statutorily defined. It depends on there being exclusive control and physical occupation by the occupier, who must not be a casual or occasional occupier and who must also derive some value or benefit from being in occupation (see 39 Halsbury (4th edn) para 15). Whilst an administrative receiver may appear to fall within the meaning of occupier of the property, it is the company itself which is deemed to remain in occupation for rating purposes following the appointment, on the basis that the administrative receiver is merely the agent of the company (*Ratford v North Avon District Council* [1986] 3 All ER 193). This view contrasts with the comments of Ungoed-Thomas J in *Taggs Island Casino Hotel Ltd v Richmond upon Thames Borough Council* [1967] RA 78 although it is respectfully submitted that those comments must now be viewed as doubtful. It should also be noted that for rating purposes it is not generally thought possible for two occupiers to co-exist, a point relevant to contemporaneous liquidation (*Ratford v North Avon District Council* [1986] 3 All ER 193 at 207; see also *Re Briant Colour Printing Co Ltd* [1977] 1 WLR 942 at 952–3).

Where premises are vacant, the rule is that the person entitled to possession of the property is liable for rates (Local Government Finance Act 1988 ss 45 and 65). Certain vacant property is exempt from rates by virtue of the Non-Domestic Rating (Unoccupied Property) Regulations 1989 (SI No 2261). The properties which enjoy the exemption from rating liability fall within the following categories:

(a) property which cannot be occupied by law such as dangerous premises;
(b) listed buildings;
(c) certain factories and warehouses within the definition of 'qualifying industrial property;
(d) property with a rateable value of less than £1,000;
(e) property in the course of construction;
(f) property held by a liquidator in his capacity as liquidator; and
(g) property the owner of which is subject to a winding-up order or is being wound up voluntarily under Insolvency Act 1986 s98.

No definition of the term 'owner' is provided by the legislation. However, it is submitted that the better view is that the legal owner of the property, whether in possession or not, will ordinarily be liable for rates until such time as the administrative receiver is appointed, whereupon he may assume the liability in the same way as a mortgagee taking actual possession of the property.

Since the 1989 Regulations provide that a property is exempt for rating purposes where it is unoccupied and subject to a liquidator in his capacity as such or an owner which is being wound-up, it is necessary to consider the position of the administrative receiver *vis-à-vis* both occupied and unoccupied property prior to liquidation. In the case of property which is occupied, the liquidator will assume and continue to be liable for rates on the property. On the other hand, a liquidator may be able to show that a receiver should bear liability for rates where he has taken physical possession of the premises, although this should be considered against the two leading decisions, *Ratford v Northavon District Council* [1987] QB 357 and *Bannister v London Borough of Islington* (1972) LGR 239 which are considered below.

Prior to liquidation, the *Ratford* case remains good authority for the proposition that an administrative receiver is not liable for rates following appointment where the company remains in occupation of its premises. In that case Northavon District Council were unsuccessful in establishing that the receivers had either actually taken over possession of the company's premises in place of the company or, alternatively, that the receivers had acted beyond their agency by not taking possession of the property, on the grounds that the terms of the debenture did not actually oblige them to take possession. This vitiated the onus of proof which rested with the receivers in establishing that they had not taken up occupation of the premises for rating purposes. A very similar approach has been adopted in the recent Scottish decision in *McKillop v Watters* (1994) *The Times*, 14 April where a receiver acting as agent of a company (which had not gone into liquidation) was also held not to be liable for rates.

Prior to liquidation, in the case of unoccupied property the better view is that an administrative receiver will not incur liability for rates merely by virtue of his appointment, provided he does not enter into possession of the premises. That is, if the property remains unoccupied, liability for rates will fall on the owner of the property, which may well be the company in administrative receivership itself. There is a danger, however, that the administrative receiver will incur liability if he takes possession of the unoccupied premises in the course of collecting in and realising the charged assets of the company. This view is supported by the decision in the *Bannister* case, where the rating authority successfully argued that a receiver who took possession of the charged property and paid rates on it was the person entitled to possession of the property and therefore incurred personal liability for the rates. This was despite the fact that the receiver acted as agent of the company throughout, a point not raised in argument by counsel for the receiver. It has to be said also that the *Bannister* decision relies heavily on a number of earlier decisions cited by counsel which do not consider fully the question of a receiver's agency relationship with the company prior to the onset of liquidation and, to that extent, some doubt must remain as to the soundness of the decision.

The *Ratford* and *Bannister* decisions remain difficult to reconcile, the latter also being somewhat doubtful in its reasoning. It is equally unhelpful that no attempt was made in *Ratford* to either overrule or distinguish *Bannister*. Certainly it would appear that the receiver in the *Bannister* case would almost certainly have avoided liability had he not gone into actual occupation of the property in seeking to realise the charged assets. Even so, in going into possession it remains true that, prior to liquidation at least, the receiver acts as agent of the company and as such it is difficult to see why the position should be different from the *Ratford* position in the case of occupied premises, since one must assume that the receiver has no better right than the company to physical occupation of the premises. Furthermore, in *Bannister*, as in *Ratford*, the receiver was not obliged under the terms of the debenture to take physical possession of the property of his own volition.

In practical terms, the anomalies posed by *Bannister* and the possibility of doubt being cast on the *Ratford* decision may be avoided by the inclusion of appropriate provisions in the debenture. These should expressly provide that the administrative receiver is only obliged to take possession of charged property subject to rating liability, be it occupied or unoccupied, on express, and preferably written, notice being given to him by the debenture-holder. The administrative receiver may also wish to seek a separate indemnity from the debenture-holder in respect of personal liability arising, to the extent that this potentially exceeds the charged assets available to feed the statutory indemnity under s45(3).

## 12.4 Distraint

Where rates remain outstanding, there is nothing to preclude the rating authority from distraining against all assets belonging to the company for the unpaid rates. However, for practical purposes, this right to distrain against the assets of the company depends on whether the remedy can be sought prior to the administrative receivership or, more specifically, the crystallisation of a floating charge over the company's assets. In *Re ELS Ltd, Ramsbottom v Luton Borough Council* (1994) unreported, Ferris J held that the crystallisation of a floating charge perfected the assignment of the floating charge assets to the debenture-holder. As a consequence of this it followed that those goods could no longer be regarded as goods of the company and thus could not be distrained against by the rating authority. This decision is helpful to the extent that it does not follow the otherwise binding decision of the Court of Appeal in *Re Marriage Neave & Co* [1895] 2 Ch 663 which was distinguished. That case had held that the appointment of a receiver did not exempt a company from an obligation to pay arrears of rates, since there is no change in the occupier of the premises where the receiver is appointed as agent of the company; as such, the receiver is bound to discharge any arrears. The *ELS* decision is in line with that of the Court of Appeal in *Re Roundwood Colliery* [1897] 1 Ch 373, which held that floating charge assets are assigned to the debenture-holder on crystallisation and cannot be distrained against by a landlord (see also *Gyton v Palmour* [1945] KB 426). *Re Roundwood Colliery* [1897] 1 Ch 373 was expressly followed at first instance in the New Zealand courts by Jeffries J in *Metropolitan Life & Essere Print Ltd* [1990] NZCLC 66, 773, as affirmed by the New Zealand Court of Appeal [1991] 3 NZLR 170 although without making reference to the *Re Roundwood Colliery* decision.

Certain matters regarding distraint for rates remain unhappily settled. For example the *Re Marriage Neave* case does not appear to have considered the question of crystallisation of the floating charge, but addresses itself to the actual appointment of a receiver. Similarly, *Re Roundwood Colliery* does not make reference to *Re Marriage Neave*, although it was referred to by counsel in argument. Equally curious is the fact that Lindley and Lopes LJJ sat in both *Re Roundwood Colliery* and *Re Marriage Neave* without a clear connection being made between them. In addition, both Lindley and Lopes LJJ sat in

*Re Marriage Neave* and *Biggerstaff v Rowatt's Wharf Ltd* [1896] 2 Ch 93 without the *Biggerstaff* decision being cited in the *Marriage Neave* case. The *Biggerstaff* decision had held that a debtor of the company in receivership was not precluded from setting off a cross-claim against it notwithstanding notice of the crystallisation of a floating charge which covered the debt due to the company (see Fenton (1994) 7 Insolvency Intelligence 18–19).

For present purposes, it is submitted that the decision of Ferris J in the *ELS* case is to be preferred and represents the present position, whereby a rating authority is prohibited from distraining for rates following the crystallisation of a floating charge against goods covered by that charge. This is not least because a rating authority now enjoys a right of action to recover rates other than by distraint, by virtue of the Non-Domestic Rating (Collection and Enforcement) (Local Lists) Regulations 1989 (SI No 1058), reg 20. Generally, however, there are conceptual problems with Ferris J's decision which, whilst strengthening the position of the floating-charge holder generally and particularly in a liquidation, do not sit happily with the apparent right of a liquidator to avail himself of floating-charge assets in recovering his costs, expenses and remuneration as now provided for in *Re Portbase Clothing Ltd* [1993] BCLC 796. Finally, a creditor will not benefit from Law of Distress Amendment Act 1908 s4 where the company permits a creditor to remain in possession of goods thereby remaining reputed owner of them *(Cunliffe Engineering Ltd v English Industrial Estates* [1994] BCC 972).

## 12.5 Set-off

The rules applicable in administrative receivership as to set-off are the normal rules of legal and equitable set-off. Set-off only operates within those limits. Any other unliquidated and unconnected cross-claim amounts to a counterclaim.

### 12.5.1 Set-off or counterclaim?

The distinction between a counterclaim and set-off is important, because only a cross-claim which amounts to a set-off will entitle a defendant leave to defend as of right on an application to court for summary judgment. In the case of any other cross-claim, the court retains a discretion to stay execution of the plaintiff's judgment pending trial of the cross-claim (see *Modern Engineering (Bristol) Ltd v Gilbert-Ash (Northern) Ltd* [1974] AC 689 at 717, per Diplock LJ). Similarly, in the case of a winding-up petition the presentation and advertisement of the petition should be restrained if a company maintains a set-off claim (*Re McDonald's Restaurants* [1994] BCLC 306). Cross-claims other than set-off claims do not present a ground for restraining the petition, although the court will consider the matter at the subsequent winding-up hearing (for example, *Estee*

*Lauder v Valencienne* (1986) unreported). A claim of set-off may also prevent the invoking of certain contractual remedies such as forfeiture of a lease for non-payment of rent, there no longer being a bar to setting-off rent due under a lease for breaches of the lease (*British Anzani (Felixstowe) Ltd v International Marine Management (UK) Ltd* [1980] QB 637).

In administrative receivership, it is particularly relevant to check that no right of set-off is available to the company in respect of the amount alleged due by the secured creditor prior to the making of the appointment. Certain debentures do make provision for this by stipulating that the debenture-holder may issue a certificate of indebtedness, which is deemed by the parties to be conclusive evidence of the amount due. In the absence of such a provision, particular care should be taken, as the company may attempt to claim that no appointment may be made. Nevertheless, such a defence may be counteracted if an 'all monies due' demand is made (where of course it is envisaged by the debenture); in that case it may be established that at least certain monies are due under the terms of the debenture.

Legal set-off is subject to the requirement that the defendant must have a monetary cross-claim against a monetary claim by the plaintiff, where the defendant's cross-claim arose before the action by the plaintiff commenced (*Edmunds v Lloyds Italico* [1986] 1 WLR 492). In addition, the plaintiff's cross-claim must be for a debt or liquidated demand accrued due. Both the demand and cross-claimed set-off between the parties must be ascertained with certainty at the time of pleading (*BICC plc v Burndy Corp* [1985] Ch 232 at 247). This rule is both ancient and well-established. It will not suffice that a cross-claim can only be ascertained following litigation or arbitration, as in *Hargreaves v Action 2000 Ltd* [1993] BCLC 1111 where the Court of Appeal required that the debts should be 'readily and without difficulty ascertained'. Legal set-off is not therefore available against a claim for damages, nor where a claim under a guarantee cannot be quantified at the time set-off is sought (*Hargreaves v Action 2000 Ltd* [1993] BCLC 1111). Conversely, in legal set-off there is no requirement for a demand and cross-claim to be connected in any way, although the debts between the parties must be mutual in that each party must be beneficially entitled to claim and each party personally liable on the debt. This requirement of mutuality does not mean that the debt should be connected or unconnected. Mutuality will not exist, for example, if one party's claim is held on trust for a third party and not beneficially (*N W Robbie & Co Ltd v Witney Warehouses Co Ltd* [1963] 1 WLR 1324; *Axel Johnson v Mineral Group* [1992] 1 WLR 270).

### 12.5.2 Equitable set-off

Equitable set-off is available in respect of unliquidated claims by both the plaintiff and the defendant (*Hargreaves v Action 200 Ltd* [1993] BCLC 1111).

Nevertheless, there is no reason why a defendant should not be able to set off in equity against a liquidated claim of the plaintiff. Indeed, to conclude otherwise would necessarily be perverse (see the comments in *The Raven* [1908] 2 Lloyd's LR 266 at 271 per Parker J). Unlike legal set-off, however, both the claim and cross-claim must be connected for equitable set-off purposes. That is, the claim of the defendant must be

> 'so closely connected with [the plaintiff's] demand that it would be manifestly unjust to allow [the plaintiff] to enforce payment without taking into account the cross-claim' (*Federal Commerce and Navigation Ltd v Molena Alpha Inc* [1978] QB 927 at 975, per Denning MR).

This underlines the approach of equity, which is to permit a cross-claim where it would be otherwise inequitable to permit the enforcement of the claim without regard to it (see for example, *Insituform (Ireland) Ltd v Insituform Group Ltd* (1992) unreported). Again, as with legal set-off, there is a requirement that the claim and cross-claim must be mutual in the sense that they are held beneficially by each party for their own use.

Mutuality in both legal and equitable set-off will be lost where a party is not able to show that it beneficially 'owns' its particular claim. It follows from this that a joint debt is not available for set-off against a several debt (*Re Pennington and Owen* [1925] Ch 825). However, it also follows that a company in administrative receivership is not able to claim set-off following the crystallisation of a general floating charge over its assets, since that crystallisation amounts to an assignment of the assets subject to the charge in favour of the debenture-holder at the date of notice of the assignment being given to a debtor (*Edward Nelson v Faber* [1903] 2 KB 367 at 375). That is, the assignment of the floating charge assets in favour of the debenture-holder is perfected on the giving of notice of the appointment to the debtor of the company, at which point the rights between the debenture-holder and the debtor are determined (*Re Cushla* [1979] 3 All ER 415). Again, a debtor is entitled to set off against the administrative receiver any sums to which he has set-off rights against the company prior to and as at the date of notice of the assignment.

## 12.5.3 Assignment of assets

Particular problems arise in relation to determining what constitutes notice of assignment where assets are charged by way of fixed as opposed to floating charges. The better view is that an assignment of a fixed-charge asset takes place and is perfected to the date of the charge between the company and the debenture-holder. This is particularly relevant in the case of book debts and other debts charged by way of fixed charge. The problem here is the question of what constitutes notice of the assignment to the debtor, since this will determine the point at which rights of set-off are determined as between debenture-holder and debtor. It is submitted that a notice of assignment of an asset by way of fixed charge will only be perfected where a debtor receives nothing short of express notice of the assignment. Thus, it is submitted that it would not suffice that a debtor might be deemed to have notice of a fixed charge merely by way of its registration at Companies House, since this would operate unfairly to the advantage of the company and to the clear detriment of the debtor. Perhaps the only situation in which this might realistically be anticipated is where the debtor has made a search of Companies House and had been fixed with actual notice of the assignment by way of fixed charge of the book debts on perusal of the charge itself (as opposed to merely being aware of its existence). In practice, that scenario poses obvious evidential problems.

In administrative receivership it would follow that set-off is available in relation to connected claims arising out of the same transaction or series of transactions, or where a debt arises following a receiver's acceptance or performance of contract which was actually entered into by the company before the date of the receivership (*Handley Page Ltd v Customs & Excise* [1972] Lloyd's Rep 459; *Biggerstaff v Rowatt's Wharf* [1892] 2 Ch 93; *Rother Iron Works Ltd v Canterbury Precision Engineers* [1974] QB 1). On the other hand, set-off will not be available where debts are acquired by a debtor from a third party after the commencement of the receivership, or where debts accrue following notice of assignment of the charged assets (*N W Robbie & Co v Witney Warehouse Co Ltd* [1963] WLR 1324).

### 12.5.4 Mortgagee or company's agent?

The position of a debenture-holder is clearly far more favourable where an administrative receiver effectively acts as mortgagee on behalf of the debenture-holder, in the sense that the debenture-holder will only be subject to equities existing at the date of the notice of assignment (*Astor Chemicals Ltd v Synthetic Technology Ltd* [1990] BCC 97 at 105). On the other hand, the administrative receiver will be bound by any set-off which would otherwise bind the company, where he acts as agent of the company. The position is best reconciled by the comment of Lightman and Moss in *The Law of Receivers of Companies*, (Sweet & Maxwell 2nd edn (1994) at 16–09) where the authors state that in practice, to save costs the parties permit the receiver suing in the name of the company to claim the more protected position of an assignee, without requiring the debenture-holder to be joined as a party to the action (*Business Computers Ltd v Anglo African Leasing Co Ltd* [1977] 1 WLR 578).

Perhaps the best recent example of the shortcomings of set-off in administrative receivership arose in *Hargreaves v Action 2000 Ltd* [1993] BCLC 1111. In that case A Ltd contracted to construct filling stations for Petrofina. A Ltd sub-contracted the work to H Ltd, separate contracts being established and administered separately. H Ltd then went into administrative receivership and contemporaneously into liquidation, the effect of liquidation being to terminate the administrative receiver's agency relationship with the company but without prejudice to his right to realise assets to the benefit of the debenture-holder. The administrative receiver of H Ltd sought summary judgment for £58,000 owed to it by A Ltd, which was admitted by the company. A Ltd sought to exercise a right of set-off for amounts due under the contracts and separate claims for defective workmanship. Andrews-Fox J refused equitable set-off on the basis that the claims under the separate contracts were not connected and that the expectation of the parties had been that claims under each contract would be dealt with separately. In the same way, legal set-off was also refused on the grounds that at the time of the set-off it was not possible to quantify the claims of defective workmanship, since these were subject to quantification by a quantity surveyor and/or by arbitration. Subsequently, the Court of Appeal affirmed the first instance decision and rejected an argument by counsel for A Ltd that the claims for defective workmanship could have been quantified which raised a triable issue as to whether they could be ascertained on the basis of which unconditional leave to defend should have been granted.

The Court of Appeal conceded that the conditions prevailing for legal and equitable set-off are and remain narrow notwithstanding the unfortunate consequences in the case before it. Although the point was not raised in the case, it should be noted that there does not appear to be any good reason why the liquidator should not have been able to claim set-off under IR r4.90 in the *Hargreaves* case, the rules on set-off in insolvency being more of an accounting exercise and less concerned with the requirements of legal and equitable set-off as discussed above.

## 12.6  Retention of Title ('ROT') Claims

ROT clauses are perhaps the most common method by which a seller will attempt to preserve rights over goods sold (and/or their proceeds of sale) in addition to an action for outstanding sums due in respect of payment. Mention was made of the clauses earlier at paras 3.5.1 and 4.5.1.

In practice, ROT clauses appear in a variety of guises of varying sophistication. In reality, however, these often do not confer the practical benefit their terms appear to afford the party relying on them. The principal reason for this is that all too often the purchaser, struggling to fend off financial demise, will deal with the goods or their proceeds of sale in contravention of the arrangement anticipated by the ROT clause leaving the seller with no obvious redress other than to revert to a claim for the price of the goods or to attempt to recourse to the goods themselves in a usually costly and uncertain tracing action.

The landmark decision of the Court of Appeal in *Aluminium Industrie Vaasen BV v Romalpa Aluminium Ltd* [1976] 1 WLR 676 involved a successful claim by a seller under a clause requiring payment of all sums due from the buyer before title passed (an 'all-monies clause'). This was coupled with a requirement that the goods were stored separately by the buyer for identification purposes. The Court of Appeal held that the seller retained a tracing claim to the proceeds of (re)sale even in the absence of a request in the ROT clause that such proceeds should be kept separately (say, in a deposit account). This result is surprising and hinges on the assumption by the receiver that the buyer company had a fiduciary relationship with the seller and bailee of the goods as a result of the clause's operation. Indeed, it is submitted that the *Romalpa* decision is incorrect, the better conclusion being that in *Specialist Plant Services v Braithwaite* [1987] 3 BCC 119 where an opposite view was drawn on a very similarly worded clause (albeit with no explanation). It should also be understood that certain translation problems are apparent from the case as is the peculiar use by the Dutch suppliers of certain English legal concepts. In reality, the *Romalpa* decision has now been distinguished so extensively that its applicability is really an exception to the norm. In particular, the fiduciary relationship established by the case has been questioned in *Borden (UK) Ltd v Scottish Timber* [1981] Ch 25 per Templeman LJ in referring to comments of Roskill LJ in the *Romalpa* case which themselves appear to restrict the scope of the decision. Similar doubt has been cast by the decisions in *Re Peachdart Ltd* [1984] 1 Ch 131, *Clough Mill v Martin* [1985] 1 WLR 111, CA (which strongly supports the basic proposition of a simple clause of the Romapla case) and, in cases where proceeds of sub-sale clauses have been employed, by the decisions in *E Pfeiffer Weinkellerei-Weineinkauf Gmbh & Co v Arbuthnot Factors Ltd* [1987] 3 BCC 608, *Tatung (UK) Ltd v Galex Telesure Ltd* [1989] 5 BCLC 325 and *Compaq Computers Ltd v Abercorn Group Ltd* [1991] BCC 484 (see also *Re Weldtech Equipment Ltd* [1991] BCC 16).

## 12.6.1 Types of clause

Essentially, ROT clauses are of two types: namely, simple and complex. Simple clauses merely retain legal ownership of goods to the seller until payment is made notwithstanding possession by the buyer (see, for example, *Hendy Lennox (Industrial Engineers) Ltd v Grahame Puttick Ltd* [1984] 2 All ER 152). Simple clauses are commonly reinforced by an 'all-monies' provision whereby the title to all goods supplied does not pass until all indebtedness of the buyer has been discharged under all contracts between the parties. The House of Lords recently gave approval to variations of the simple clause of this kind in *Armour v Thyssen Edehlstahlwerke AG* [1991] BCLC 28 (see also *Accurist Watches v King* [1990] FSR 80 where branded goods were held subject to a simple clause).

One practical implication of the retention of legal ownership by the seller is that the assets will not fall subject to the crystallisation of a floating charge. Nor can the retention of title clause be subject to registration requirements as a security interest since it does not relate to company assets over which security is taken.

Simple clauses of the type identified above are limited in their scope in that their effect may be defeated where goods are no longer capable of identification or have been sold on. It is common, therefore, to encounter clauses which seek to extend the proprietary rights of the seller although, again, on the whole the attitude of the courts has tended against such claims. It is in this way that simple clauses must be distinguished from complex clauses which do effect transfer of legal ownership to the buyer on purchase but which reserve equitable or beneficial ownership to the seller. Complex clauses attempt to create a trustee/beneficiary relationship between buyer and seller, to the extent that the buyer retains legal title to the goods albeit on trust for the seller (see, for example, *Re Bond Worth Ltd* [1980] Ch 228 where the clause retained only equitable and beneficial title to the seller). In reality, clauses of the trustee/beneficiary type are largely unsuccessful in that they fail to effect in law the relationship which is practically anticipated by their provisions.

The usual attempts at extending the seller's rights involve either or both of two possible variations to the simple clause. First, the buyer is expressly licenced to sell on the goods subject to a claim by the original seller to the proceeds of the sub-sale. Secondly, the buyer is expressly licensed to deal with the goods in working on, treating or incorporating them into other goods subject to the seller's ownership of the new goods or product (see, for example, *Re Peachdart Ltd* [1983] Ch 131 where the seller asserted both such claims and failed on both heads and see the similar reasoning of the Court of Appeal in *Specialist Plant Services Ltd v Braithwaite Ltd* [1987] BCLC 1). In the *Specialist Plant* case a repairer who supplied spare parts made a perhaps inadvisable attempt to claim the ownership of an entire piece of machinery where the parts were incorporated into it on the basis that the machinery constituted surety for the repair bill under the clause. Perhaps not surprisingly, the Court of Appeal found that the clause was in effect a charge over the machinery which was wanting for non-registration.

The use of an ROT clause to create a trustee/beneficiary relationship is of particular benefit to a seller where the buyer goes into liquidation since proceeds of a sub-sale or processed 'new' goods are held on trust for the original seller and thus beyond the scope of the liquidator who may not deal with trust assets held for third parties. In practice, however, it is common for sale proceeds to be dealt with by the liquidator where he remains unsatisfied at the evidence supporting the clause and its incorporation. Furthermore, attempts at creating such a trust relationship by contract have been largely unsuccessful other than in the *Romalpa* case itself. Nevertheless, it remains standard practice for a complex clause to be complemented by a simple clause which offers some comfort to sellers in that the invalidity of the complex clause (say, through non-registration of a charge) will not of itself invalidate the simple clause; see *Clough Mill Ltd v Martin* [1984] 3 All ER 982. This comfort is limited, however, in that the goods may well have been disposed of or treated or incorporated by the buyer thereby defeating the simple clause's provisions in any case.

### 12.6.2  Trust or charge?

The approach adopted by the courts in considering 'complex' ROT claims has tended towards establishing a chargor/chargee relationship between the parties as opposed to the creation of a trust. Basically, this is because the courts construe the seller's strategy as protecting its position by securing its debt by way of charge as opposed to 'separating' it by operation of a trust. As considered previously in Chapter 3 at para 3.5.1, a registrable charge is generally void on grounds of non-registration if not registered within the 21-day period provided for in the Companies Act 1985 ss395 and 396 (or in accordance with the Bills of Sale Acts 1878 and 1882 in the case of an individual buyer). In reality, ROT clauses are infrequently registered as charges since that is not usually what the parties—and certainly the seller—will usually have intended (see *Re Bond Worth* [1980] Ch 228 where a clause retaining an equitable interest failed for non-registration and the similar reasoning in *Stroud Architectural Systems v John Laing Construction* [1994] BCC 18).

The courts' reasoning in reaching its broad 'charge not trust' conclusion is largely policy based and may be difficult to circumvent by even very detailed and careful drafting although this should not be discounted. The courts have been equally unimpressed by attempts to create a 'sale-and-purchase-back' contract as opposed to a trust (see, for example, *Curtain Dream plc v Churchill Merchandising Ltd* [1990] BCC 341). One particular problem with the notion of assumed ownership on the part of the unpaid supplier of goods, for instance, is that a seller's assumed ownership of processed or treated goods may confer a benefit the monetary value of which potentially far outweighs the contract price due. In addition, difficult problems of identification arise where more than one original seller asserts rights to processed or treated goods (see *Re Goldcorp Exchange Ltd* [1994] 2 All ER 806, *Mercer v Craven Grain Storage Ltd* (unreported, 17 March 1994), *Re Sapylton Fletcher Ltd* [1994] 1 WLR 1181 and the excellent analysis in Sealy (1995) 8 Insolvency Intelligence 17–20).

A purported trustee/beneficiary relationship may also be further undermined by the terms of the sale contract other than those contained in an ROT clause. This will invariably provide for a period of trade credit pending due payment and will by implication permit the seller to deal with the goods supplied to it at its absolute discretion and for its own benefit. Indeed, any attempt to impose constraints on such dealings will be both commercially unattractive and almost certainly unenforceable in practical terms. The freedom thus enjoyed by a buyer does not square with the duties strictly imposed by a trust whereby a trustee (ie purportedly the buyer) holds and deals with trust assets for the benefit of the beneficiary (ie purportedly the seller) who must be clearly identifiable. The arrangements anticipated by most ROT clauses of the complex type smack rather of attempts by a seller to protect its debt by way of security interest as opposed to by way of trust—even if the intention is not for such an arrangement—which must be protected by the registration of a charge as discussed previously. This conclusion is supported by the fact that the buyer's liability may be discharged at any time by the payment of the purchase price, as in the case of a charge, whereas under a trust the beneficiary's interest remains vested in the trust assets themselves (see *Re Bond Worth Ltd* [1980] Ch 228).

In all cases a pragmatic view should be taken as to whether an ROT clause may be construed as creating a trustee/beneficiary relationship. In the event that the view is taken that a charge is created, that interest will only be validly maintained and protected by registration of an appropriate charge within the 21-day statutory period. In practice, ROT clauses are rarely protected by way of registration as a matter of course.

### 12.6.3 Is the ROT clause incorporated?

Any ROT clause will be ineffective *ab initio* if it is not incorporated into the contract for sale. Incorporation is strictly a matter of contract law although, briefly, a clause may be incorporated by either of the following methods. First, by express agreement (eg signature of the document containing the clause, even if not read; *L'estrange v Graucob* [1934] 2 KB 394); secondly, by putting the other party on notice of the clause prior to the contract (ie by taking reasonably sufficient steps to bring the clause to the notice of the other party; see, for example, the unsuccessful challenge in *John Shaw and Co Ltd v DBG Woodcroft Ltd* [1985] BCLC 54 per Boreham J) or, thirdly, on the basis of a regular course of dealings (see, for example, *Circle Freight International Ltd v Medeast* [1988] 2 Lloyd's Rep 427).

Incorporation, therefore, remains a question of particular fact to each case, particular problems being caused by conflicting terms and the so-called 'battle of the forms' in purported offer and acceptance and attempts by the parties to enforce their own terms on the other (see *Butler Machine Tool Co v Ex-cell-o Corp* [1979] 1 WLR 401 and *Sauter Automation Ltd v Goodman Mechanical Services Ltd* [1986] 2 FTLR 239 for an unsuccessful attempt to argue that a seller's clause was incorporated into a subcontract which failed through non-incorporation and inconsistency with the main contract).

### 12.6.4  Practical steps in administrative receivership

From the administrative receiver's perspective the resolution of ROT claims against the company is of significant practical relevance since a supplier may refuse to supply further goods until pre-receivership debts incurred under a retention of title clause are discharged in full. This has obvious ramifications where a sale of the company's business is anticipated or planned, particularly where no alternative supplier can be located. In addition, the Court of Appeal has held that the withholding of supplies pending settlement of pre-receivership debts does not amount to an abuse of a dominant position for the purpose of art 86 of the EEC Treaty (*Leyland DAF Ltd v Automotive Products plc* [1993] BCC 385). For this reason an office-holder may deem it necessary to discharge the supplier's claim without recourse to the usual ROT dispute resolution method outlined below. Whilst care should be taken in such circumstances it may be that in many cases the company suffers no loss—and, indeed, may well avoid it—by the taking of such action. Nevertheless, the office-holder may face liability subsequently in conversion for wrongful disposal of the goods.

The usual practice on the appointment of an administrative receiver is that suppliers are issued with standard form documentation detailing their claims. These should be completed speedily and returned to the address stipulated by the office-holder. Delays and problems commonly arise for sellers who are unable to provide sufficient supporting documentation to support their claims. In reality, a significant number of ROT claims fail for this reason.

On becoming aware of an appointment, a seller should request standard form documentation directly if this is not supplied immediately. Any faxed correspondence should be supported by posted copies and addresses and numbers for communication verified.

Documents supporting the ROT claim should not as a general rule exceed those requested. However, supplementary information may be supplied where this assists in the identification of the goods supplied and the terms of the contract entered into. These might include quotations, telephone notes, delivery notes, invoices and copy accounts. Documentation should also be clearly identified. Uncoordinated bundles of unrelated documents may serve only to antagonise and may be rejected or ignored by the administrative receiver or his legal advisers if sense cannot be made of them.

The reality of ROT claims is that a commercial standard is expected of both buyers and sellers in stating and dealing with claims. The decision in *Re Sabre International Ltd* [1991] BCLC 470 makes clear that office-holders are under no obligation to make provision for a seller's inexperience in dealing

366

with an ROT claim. Professional advice is therefore likely to be of considerable benefit.

Where an inspection of goods at the buyer's premises can be agreed, this should be undertaken without prejudice to the seller's claim, the object of the inspection being to establish proof of ownership on the part of the seller. Sellers commonly employ independent parties to assist in such inspection such as stocktakers. In all cases, the procedure for the inspection, including methods such as photography, labelling and the taking of an inventory, should be agreed with the office-holder in advance and confirmed in writing.

### 12.6.5  Use, ownership and disposal of ROT assets

The administrative receiver is empowered to seize and dispose of property of the company under s234 together with certain protections in the event that property is not actually company property but is believed to be such on reasonable grounds at the time of the seizure or disposal (s234(3) and (4)). It may be possible to obtain an injunction against an office-holder on an *ex parte* basis where seizure or disposal is threatened. Alternatively, pending resolution of any ROT claim, the office-holder may agree to hold sale proceeds in a separately designated account.

In practice, the office-holder may well wish to use the assets subject to an ROT clause dispute pending resolution of it. This is particularly relevant where it is proposed to dispose of the company's business as a going concern. The usual solution to this is the giving of a personal undertaking by the office-holder to pay to the supplier the value of the goods used or disposed of in the receivership in the event that the supplier establishes good title to the goods. (The administrative receiver will of course benefit from an indemnity from the company's assets in respect of liability under the undertaking (s44(1)(c)).) In theory, a supplier may attempt to obtain injunctive relief to prevent the use or disposal of assets in this way pending resolution of the dispute. In granting an injunction the court will consider the balance of convenience test set out by the House of Lords in *American Cyanamid Co v Ethicon Limited* [1975] AC 396 (*Lipe Limited v Leyland DAF Limited* [1993] BCC 385). However, the view of the Court of Appeal in the *Lipe* case is that in the majority of cases the giving of an undertaking of the usual type by the receiver will prevent injunctive relief.

Finally, it should be noted that the court now appears able to settle matters of disputed ownership in the course of a s234 hearing following the decision of Warner J in *Re London Iron & Steel Co Ltd* [1990] BCC 159. This is a welcome development and will save unnecessary expense in resolving claims involving ROT matters. Nevertheless, the court has no jurisdiction to settle matters of disputed ownership where that question falls to a foreign court. Where a receiver and debenture-holder are bound by a retention of title agreement they are also bound by an exclusive jurisdiction clause to the agreement which will depend on the law applicable to each agreement (*Re Leyland DAF Ltd* [1994] BCC 166).

## Chapter Thirteen

# Specific Transactions and Miscellaneous Problems

## 13.1 Sale of Company Property

Unlike an LPA receiver, an administrative receiver enjoys a statutory power of sale of property of the company of which the company is beneficial owner. The power is implied by Sched 1 to the Act, which contains a power, in para 2, 'to sell or otherwise dispose of the property of the company by public auction or private contract'. A purchaser from an administrative receiver will wish to ensure that the administrative receiver has been properly appointed. Whilst extensive investigation into the validity of the office-holder's appointment will usually be inappropriate and impracticable, a purchaser would be well-advised to ensure that the administrative receiver has been appointed and has accepted office in accordance with the formalities discussed in Chapter 11. In particular, it is suggested that a purchaser should not rely merely on the protection of either s232 or s33 by opting not to investigate the circumstances in which the administrative receiver's appointment was effected and accepted, in view of the uncertain scope of some provisions. Nevertheless, there is nothing in either section to suggest that actual notice of any defect in an appointment will operate to the disadvantage of a purchaser. Further, a purchaser from an administrative receiver may take some solace from s42(3), which provides that a person dealing with the administrative receiver in good faith and for value is not concerned to inquire whether the office-holder is acting within his powers. In effect, this offers substantially similar protection to that afforded by the Companies Act 1985 s35 (as amended) and the rule in *Turquand's* case (1856) 6 E&B 327 (see *Inverness District Council v Highland Universal Fabricators* 1986 SLT 566).

An administrative receiver may sell company property in either of two ways. First, the sale may be by the administrative receiver acting in the name of the company or by the administrative receiver acting under a power of attorney conferred on the office-holder by the debenture to act on behalf of the company. Alternatively, the administrative receiver may sell under a power of attorney granted under the terms of the debenture in favour of the debenture-holder, the sale being entered into by the administrative receiver by or on behalf of the debenture-holder. In practice, it is more common for a power of attorney to be granted in favour of a receiver than a debenture-holder. One alternative to a sale by the administrative receiver is a sale by the debenture-holder as mortgagee under the Law of Property Act 1925 ss101–7. The practical advantage of a sale by the debenture-holder as mortgagee is that the sale will operate to overreach any security interests which are s ubordinated to the debenture-holder's security. A purchaser from the mortgagee will therefore take the property subject to any prior-ranking security interest but free from the rights of the vendor mortgagee and any subsequent mortgagee (Law of Property Act 1925 s104(1); see also Land Registration Act 1925 s34(4)). As suggested in Chapter 8 at para 8.5, a sale by an administrative receiver will not operate to overreach either the interests of the debenture-holder or the holder of any subordinate security interest.

## 13.2 Sale of the Company's Business

A sale by the administrative receiver of the company's business assumes that the office-holder is validly appointed and that the security pursuant to which the office-holder is appointed covers the assets to be sold.

### 13.2.1 The purchase price

There is no standard format in which an offer to purchase and subsequent sale of a company's business should be structured. The nature of the business may be such that only one purchaser, such as a rival competing business in the immediate vicinity, can be found for the business. On the other hand, the administrative receiver may be inundated with offers for a business which is perceived as lucrative and potentially highly profitable. The practical implications here are that the level of demand for the business clearly affects the sale price and any arrangements for its payment, as well as any warranties and indemnities which the administrative receiver may be prepared to give. This will also have a bearing on the duty of the administrative receiver to obtain a reasonable price for the assets on sale, as discussed in Chapter 9 at para 9.2.

There is no requirement that the purchase price for a business should be paid over immediately on completion. In practice, however, an office-holder is invariably more likely to prefer such an arrangement as opposed to a deferred payment arrangement which may or may not include an initial deposit being paid by the purchaser. Where no other purchaser can be found, deferred payments may be necessary if the purchaser is simply unable to raise the purchase monies in full in time for completion or, alternatively, if it is intended to fund the purchase with profits arising from the business itself. In the latter case there is no reason why the administrative receiver should not seek a charge over the business in favour of the vendor company and its assets. Ideally, these should also be supported by personal guarantees from the directors of the purchaser if a limited company. However, in virtually all cases the purchasers will seek an immediate transfer of title to the business and its assets on completion irrespective of the payment arrangements.

### 13.2.2 The sale agreement

Preparation of the business or asset sale agreement is usually undertaken by the administrative receiver's solicitors. It is fair to say that that agreement will usually not be subject to negotiation in significant terms, and certainly as regards price and payment arrangements, in that those matters will usually have been settled prior to the contract being drafted. The purchaser and its solicitors should peruse the contract carefully, since it is common for sale agreements to be drawn up on a standard-form basis which may well include onerous terms as a matter of course, say in respect of risk and transfer of title, and may also be lacking warranties and indemnities which the purchaser may have understood to have been agreed or at least implied following pre-contractual negotiations. As mentioned below, however, the terms of a business or asset sale agreement are usually non-negotiable on a sale by an office-holder save in exceptional cases.

In reality, the terms of the sale agreement, and particularly the price, will depend upon the speed with which it is perceived the administrative receiver wishes to dispose of the business and the existence of competing and realistic offers for it. Clearly the former will be of diminished importance if the administrative receiver is able to continue the business's activities, at least on a break-even basis for any period of time.

The price and payment arrangements on the sale apart, one significant factor which remains is the allocation of the purchase price in accounting terms between the various assets comprised in the sale. The administrative receiver will usually wish to allocate as much of the price as possible to fixed charge assets, particularly where there exists a significant liability to preferential creditors, so as to avoid the preferential creditors satisfying themselves from floating charge assets (see s40 and *Re Portbase Clothing Ltd* [1993] BCC 96). As such, the purchaser may have difficulties in insisting on a contrary arrangement where it would be preferable to it to pay over an enhanced amount for floating charge assets of a fixed nature, such as plant, machinery and other tangible property, usually for tax purposes, on a subsequent disposition by the purchaser.

### 13.2.3 Warranties and indemnities

It is standard practice for the administrative receiver to give no warranties and indemnities in a contract for the sale of a business. This may be justified on the basis that the administrative receiver is not usually in a position to have investigated the company's business sufficiently so as to satisfy himself about the provision of warranties; furthermore, the giving of warranties potentially gives rise to litigation at some future time, which would be highly unattractive to the office-holder. The absence of warranties and indemnities should not been viewed as overly burdensome, however, in that as a consequence the purchaser of the business and its assets will usually acquire them for a price significantly lower than what would otherwise be an open market sale value.

The absence of warranties and indemnities from the sale agreement is commonly reinforced with an express statement that no reliance is or has been placed by the purchaser on any acts, omissions or statements made by the administrative receiver, the company itself as vendor and/or the agents or employees of either. This type of clause provides considerable comfort to the administrative receiver for continuing liability purposes and also guards against the possibility of silence amounting to a misrepresentation where any relevant party has failed to notify the purchaser of a change in any material circumstances which are reflected in the terms of the sale contract itself. It also guards against liability should the terms of the contract itself be materially affected by any matter which is not expressly disclosed in the sale contract itself and in relation to which the vendor company, the administrative receiver or its agents or employees remains silent (see *With v O'Flanagan* [1936] Ch 575 and *R v Kyslant* [1932]).

### 13.2.4 Pre-sale enquiries

Depending on the circumstances of the sale, it may be that a purchaser is simply unwilling to proceed without certain warranties and/or indemnities being given. Whether or not these will actually be forthcoming depends upon any market in prospective purchasers for the business. Nonetheless, the absence of warranties and undertakings may be mitigated by a certain degree of self-help on the part of the purchaser. This may take the form of specific enquiries made by him and relevant third parties and might typically include the matters discussed below:

(1) The identity of the bailors of any equipment on hire purchase (or some variety thereof such as a deferred discount purchase scheme) which is stated as being subject to the contract for sale should be ascertained. The consent of the administrative receiver should be obtained for these to be contacted for the purposes of agreeing transfer of the assets to the purchaser who will effectively amount to a new bailee of the

goods. The bailor may opt either to continue the existing hire purchase agreement in which case the sale price should reflect any payments already made by the vendor company or, alternatively, it may wish to enter into new agreements with the purchaser itself. Clearly, from the administrative receiver's perspective, the latter arrangement is preferable.

(2) Where the sale contract includes leasehold premises, the identity of the lessor should be ascertained and that party contacted with a view to the grant of a licence to assign to the purchaser. In practice, and particularly in a depressed property market, this does not usually cause problems. A check should also be made with the lessor as to whether any action for distraint on goods at the leased premises is pending in respect of outstanding rent or service charges (in respect of which distraint is apparently available).

(3) A specific enquiry should be made of the vendor to check whether the carrying-on of its business or the use of any specific assets requires a recognised licence or permit to be obtained. If so, the relevant licensing authority should be contacted with the view to obtaining such a licence or permit or, alternatively, for the purposes of ascertaining whether or not a transfer of any existing licence or permit is possible.

(4) Existing employment contracts and other contracts should be checked, preferably with sight of them being given to the purchaser. In the case of contracts other than employment contracts, the extent of any liability under the contract should also be ascertained as should be the willingness of the other contracting party to novate the contract in favour of the purchaser. In the case of employment contracts, potential liabilities assumed by operation of the Transfer of Undertakings (Protection of Employment) Regulations 1981 (SI No 1794) should be ascertained together with any other employment contract liabilities which are not assumed under the regulations.

(5) So far as is possible, checks should be made to ascertain the existence and extent of prior-ranking security over any assets subject to the sale contract although the existence of such security will not *per se* affect the status of the office-holder as administrative receiver (s29(2)(b)). As a matter of course relevant searches should be made at the Land Registry, the Central Land Charges Department, Companies House and any other relevant property register such as those relating to intellectual property and patent rights.

(6) Certain intangible property rights which are subject to the sale contract may be further subject to the consent of a third party. Typically, these will relate to intellectual property rights, such as computer software, and book debts. In either case a check should be made to ensure that the consent of the relevant party, such as a software house or

bank, is obtained so as to avoid an objection being raised to the transfer or assignment at a later date.

### 13.2.5  Exclusion of liability

Any clause in the sale contract which seeks to exclude liability in the absence of warranties will be subject to the provisions of the Unfair Contract Terms Act 1977. The reasonableness of any such exclusion clause will necessarily depend on the circumstances of the case, although it is now common practice for an express statement to accompany any exclusion clause which provides that the exclusion is deemed by the parties to be fair and reasonable in the circumstances. Such a clause will commonly recite the insolvency of the vendor and the necessarily limited knowledge on the part of the administrative receiver of a business as relevant factors for these purposes, together with the fact that the purchaser is being expressly given an opportunity to inspect and make enquiries about the assets comprised in the sale and the trading records of the business. For most purposes, it is submitted that an exclusion clause in these circumstances will be deemed reasonable; certainly there is no reported litigation on the point to the contrary although the point remains arguable.

### 13.2.6  Specific assets

Certain assets comprised in the sale of a business by an administrative receiver will require special attention depending on the circumstances in each particular case. A number of points are worth making here. Prior to effecting a sale of any property the administrative receiver should ensure that the property to be disposed of is subject to the security pursuant to which he is appointed. This is particularly problematic in the case of goods which are purportedly subject to a reservation of title clause considered in Chapter 12 at para 12.6. The obvious problem posed to the office-holder is that in dealing with such assets he risks personal liability for damages for trespass to the goods, as well as personal liability for wrongful interference under the Torts (Interference with Goods) Act 1977.

Where the administrative receiver and the supplier of the goods are willing to proceed on the basis that the goods are actually used in the course of the business itself, it may be acceptable to the supplier for the administrative receiver to undertake to indemnify him for any of the goods subject to the reservation of title clause which are actually used subsequently by the administrative receiver in the course of the company's business. The administrative receiver should not proceed to dispose of assets subject to a purported reservation of title clause where doubt exists as to whether title vests in the company or in the supplier. On the other hand, the supplier of the goods may be happy to permit the administrative receiver to dispose of the assets to which title is reserved in a sale of the business on the basis that he is then more likely to see payment made for the goods supplied by him. The administrative receiver may also seek to rely on the Sale of Goods Act 1979 s25(1) whereby a purchaser of the assets subject to the reservation of title clause will be deemed to obtain good title to them provided that he does not have notice of the fact that the goods are actually subject to a reservation of title claim. This protection will clearly not be available where the purchaser of the company's business requires verification of title as vested in the vendor company which the vendor is unable to satisfy. Finally, caution should be exercised by the office-holder in the sale of a business which comprises reservation of title assets to the extent that the consideration attributable to those assets at least matches that claim by the supplier of the goods. In the event that it does not, the administrative receiver would be well-advised to obtain an indemnity from the purchaser of the business to cover any shortfall between the consideration paid over and the amount claimed by the supplier of the goods.

One further common problem encountered in business sale agreements in administrative receivership is the occupation of the company's premises by the purchaser for the purposes of running the company's business, in circumstances where the purchaser does not wish either to purchase the freehold of the property or to pay a market rent for it. This problem is more acute where a prospective purchaser makes it clear that he is not prepared to take on liabilities in respect of the business premises themselves and will only consider those in relation to the company's business, where that purchaser is the only ready buyer in the market. Effectively, the administrative receiver has two options in these circumstances. First, he may grant a licence to the purchaser to occupy the property on a short-term basis, which affords him time to give notice to quit on an agreed basis or to require vacation of the premises on a pre-arranged date. Alternatively, and preferably, the purchaser may be prepared to take on occupation of the business premises on a short-term tenancy in respect of which the protection provisions contained in the Landlord and Tenant Act 1954 ss24 to 28 are excluded following an application to and sanction by the court. Whilst a licence arrangement may be easier in terms of administration and the time taken to arrange and execute, the 'excluded 1954 Act' method of occupation is far preferable to an administrative receiver, because vacation is effectively guaranteed to the extent that any claim to security of tenure by the purchaser is effectively excluded with the consent of the court. This protection is not guaranteed in the case of a licence arrangement which the purchaser may attempt to argue constitutes a lease and which may give rise to potentially protracted disputes as to the purchaser's right to occupy the premises on an ongoing basis (*Street v Mountford* [1985] AC 809). This not only prejudices the sale value of the premises themselves, it also poses potential and very considerable liabilities in terms of costs and time commitments.

Specific arrangements should also be made on the sale of the business in respect of the administrative receiver's retention of a right to gain access to the company's premises and its records. This is particularly relevant in relation to the company's trading, tax and employee records. An oversight in resolving the question of access expressly in the business sale agreement may give rise to considerable problems and disputes between the administrative receiver and the purchaser/occupier of the company's business and premises. Again, these may be protracted and costly in terms of time and expense.

### 13.2.7 Book debts

Perhaps the most important asset in relation to which specific arrangements should be made clearly in a business sale agreement is book debts. The administrative receiver will naturally wish to dispose of these assets provided that the consideration paid for them equates to their book value or does not represent a significant reduction in the amount which it is anticipated will be realised in due course. There may well, however, be exceptional circumstances in which the administrative receiver wishes to exclude the book debts from the sale assets. Typically, this may be either where the purchaser is simply unwilling to take the book debts on, where the administrative receiver has already put in place debt collection procedures for collection which are at an advanced stage or where the administrative receiver does not wish the purchaser to pursue debtors who are also suppliers to any other part of the company's business which is not subject to the sale and on whom the retained business is reliant for supply contracts. In practice, it is equally common for the purchaser of a business to agree to collect book debts and hold them on trust for the administrative receiver pending payment of the book debt realisations into an account nominated by the office-holder. The business sale agreement will usually stipulate expressly that the purchaser of the business waives any rights over the book debt realisations by way of lien or set-off.

It is also common for the administrative receiver to retain a right to take over the book debt collection exercise for the benefit of the company in administrative receivership in his absolute discretion, such as where he remains dissatisfied with the debt collection exercise undertaken by the purchaser in view of the perceived quality of the book debts. In all cases, the purchase price of the business will usually be variable to take account of book debt collections to the extent that the purchaser is entitled to retain any agreed commission on book debt realisations or to the extent that book debt realisations exceed or are exceeded by an agreed figure.

The parties to the business sale agreement may also wish to tailor the agreement to their specific requirements which again will depend ultimately on the bargaining strength of the parties and the market for purchasers of the business and its assets. Typically, these modifications might include an arrangement whereby book debt realisations must be paid over to the administrative receiver in the order that they are realised, those payments operating as separate credits against the account of each particular debtor. The purchaser of the company's business should, however, bear in mind the potential cash-flow problems caused by such an arrangement and, wherever possible, should seek to exclude such an arrangement notwithstanding any other provisions relating to the collection of book debts.

### 13.2.8 Subsisting contracts

Certain problems arising with employment and non-employment contracts in relation to the sale of the business are dealt with later in this chapter at para 13.9 and in Chapter 10 at para 10.5 respectively.

## 13.3 Sale of Real Property

The appointment of an administrative receiver is not capable of being entered on the register of any title of which the company is registered proprietor, in the case of registered land. It will therefore be pointless for a purchaser to conduct any search of the register to ascertain whether or not an appointment has been made. Instead, an inquiry should be made directly of the company itself or, alternatively and perhaps more reliably, a search of the company's register will reveal the appointment.

On a sale of real property by an administrative receiver a purchaser will inevitably raise questions as to the covenants for title which are to be given. Whether or not any such covenants for title are actually given remains a matter for the office-holder although it should be noted that, unlike the case of a company in liquidation, the covenants are likely to be of significant practical value. Indeed, a purchaser may well indicate an unwillingness to proceed until such assurances are given.

The onset of liquidation is significant for the statutory power of sale conferred in favour of an administrative receiver by Sched 1 to IA 1986. One effect of winding-up is to terminate the administrative receiver's deemed agency for the company, extinguishing the power to commit the company to new contracts (s44(1)(a)). As a consequence, the administrative receiver will also lose the benefit of his statutory right of indemnity from the company's assets in respect of new contracts (as opposed to existing contracts) entered into by him. The statutory right of indemnity would appear not to be lost, however, where any new contract is entered into by the administrative receiver with the authority of the liquidator or is ratified subsequently by him.

It is a matter of conjecture as to whether the administrative receiver retains any right of action against the company or the liquidator for any benefit which enures subsequently, although such an action might well be founded on the basis of restitution.

Liquidation does not, of course, bring to an end the administrative receivership and, indeed was held that winding-up does not affect the power of a receiver to convey a legal estate in *Barrows v Chief Land Registrar* (1977) *The Times*, 20 October. It should be noted, however, that the *Barrows* case relates strictly to the situation where the administrative receiver conveys a legal estate, by selling in the company's name by virtue of the power conferred on him by the debenture as implied by Sched 1. The *Barrows* decision reflects the contractual rights enjoyed by a receiver under a debenture. Nevertheless, there is no good reason why, following a winding-up, a sale may not be made by a company as mortgagee, acting by its attorneys the debenture-holder at the request of the receiver in exercise of the power of sale conferred on the company by the mortgage (and as conferred by statute on the administrative receiver). Indeed, this was held to be the case in *Sowman v David Samuel Trust Ltd* [1978] 1 All ER 616, where the Chief Land Registrar had originally declined to effect a registration in favour of the purchaser because the receiver did not have power to convey the legal estate following the commencement of the winding-up of the company. It should be noted that an argument that the disposition contravened the Companies Act 1948 s227, as now provided for in IA 1986 s127, was rejected on the grounds that the post-liquidation disposition did not amount to a sale of property which was beneficially owned by the company, on account of the property being subject to the debenture-holder's security. Curiously, this was so notwithstanding the fact that the sale was actually made in the name of the company.

One point which should be made in relation to the *Sowman* case is that it is important to draw a distinction between a power of attorney granted in favour of the debenture-holder by the company and one which is granted in favour of a receiver. This is because, whilst a power of attorney given by the company to a receiver will terminate on liquidation (notwithstanding the contractual rights conferred on the receiver by the debenture-holder as in the *Barrows* case), a power of attorney granted in favour of a debenture-holder, which is less common in practice, will survive liquidation by virtue of the Power of Attorney Act 1971 s4(1). The implications of this are that a purchaser from an administrative receiver will be required to include with the other documents for the registration of the title of the property a statutory declaration that, at the time of the transaction, the declarant was not aware of any revocation of the power or the occurrence of any event, such as the winding-up of the transferor company, which had or would have the effect of revoking the power of attorney (see Land Registration (Power of Attorney) Rules 1986 (SI No 1537).

When a transfer of real property is effected by an administrative receiver it must be executed personally by the office-holder and must also be executed by or on behalf of the company. In practice, there are a number of methods of effecting execution. First, the deed may be sealed by the company and countersigned by duly authorised officers (or the liquidator or joint liquidators if applicable). Alternatively, where the company has elected not to have a common seal, the deed may be executed by a director and the company secretary or by two directors (Companies Act 1985 s130(2)). Secondly, the deed may be executed by the administrative receiver pursuant to a power of attorney as discussed above; alternatively, if conferred on the debenture-holder, the deed may be executed by the debenture-holder as mortgagee of the property. Thirdly, and as is common in practice, a deed may be executed by the administrative receiver pursuant to his contractual powers, acting in the name of and on behalf of the company. The following form of execution will suffice in practice:

> Signed as a deed by
> VENDOR Ltd (in administrative receivership)
> (and in liquidation, if applicable)
> by AB
> (and CD, if applicable)
> by its administrative receiver(s)
> pursuant to powers granted by clause .................. of a
> debenture dated ............................ in favour of
> EF in the presence of:

An alternative to the above form might be:

> The Common Seal of VENDOR Ltd
> (In Administrative Receivership) (and in liquidation, if applicable)
> was affixed to this deed in the
> presence of .........................................
> AB (and CD), administrative receiver(s)

One point should be made in relation to the affixing of the company's seal by the administrative receiver. Some uncertainty remains, albeit of largely academic relevance in view of common practice, as to the administrative receiver's power to use and affix a company's seal. This had been recommended by the Cork Committee as a new power in favour of the administrative receiver (see *Cmnd 8558* at para 824). This arises largely because under the pre-1986 legislation it had been held that a receiver only enjoyed a contractual right to affix the company's seal if this was expressly permitted by the company's articles of association (*Industrial Development Authority v William T Moran* [1978] IR 159). However, as mentioned in Chapter 8 it is submitted that this line of authority will no longer operate, since Sched 1, para 8 contains an express power in favour of the administrative receiver to use the company's seal. The powers conferred on an administrative receiver by the debenture pursuant to which he is appointed are deemed to include (except insofar as they are inconsistent with any of the provisions of the debenture) the power specified in Sched 1 (s42(1)). On this basis it is submitted that an administrative receiver will have a power to use the company's seal notwithstanding the absence of such an express power in the company's articles of association. This is because, whilst the power to affix the company's seal is usually conferred on the directors or those acting on behalf of the directors, that power may be validly delegated to an administrative receiver, albeit on a contingent basis, at the time when the directors execute the debenture into which the Sched 1 powers are implied in favour of the debenture-holder. Taken positively, and in view of the valid delegation by the directors, s42(2)(b) makes it clear that the powers implied by Sched 1 are conferred for the purposes of getting in and realising the property of the company. To this end, it is difficult to see how a power in favour of the administrative receiver to use the company's seal might be denied.

On the completion of a disposal of registered property an administrative receiver will have to provide a transferee with the following documents:

(a)   the transfer document;

(b)   the land certificate;

(c)   a certified copy of his deed of appointment;

(d)   a certified copy of the debenture pursuant to which he was appointed (this will not be necessary where the debenture is already registered or noted against the relevant title);

(e)   a Form of Release in respect of the floating charge pursuant to which the administrative receiver was appointed. A vacating receipt or form of discharge (in Form 53) will also be needed in respect of any fixed charges comprising the debenture-holder's security which relate to the property sold, other than the floating charge which will have crystallised into a fixed equitable charge;

(f)   an office copy of any court order made under s43 where the order refers to the property subject to the transfer. The administrative receiver will have been provided with two sealed copies of the order by the court (IR r3.31(4)).

Following a sale of the real property by an administrative receiver the transferee should lodge the documents listed below to register the transaction. This should be done within 30 working days of the date of the Land Registry search (ie Form 94A) to enjoy the priority period offered by the search. Failure to effect registration within that period runs the risk of taking the property subject to any third party interest registered in the intervening period or, worse still, failure to obtain registered title to the property. The documents which should be lodged are:

(a)  Form A4 (or A5 in the case of a transfer of part). This will indicate the nature of the application as a 'Discharge of Charge' or 'Transfer';

(b)  the transfer document;

(c)  a certified copy of the debenture pursuant to which the receiver was appointed. This will not be necessary where the debenture is already registered or noted against the relevant title;

(d)  Form of Release from the debenture pursuant to which the receiver was appointed;

(e)  a vacating receipt or form of discharge (in Form 53) or a Form of Release (in the case of a fixed equitable charge ie a crystallised floating charge) in respect of each prior-ranking or subordinate charge. These discharges or release will only be required in respect of those charges which actually appear on the register and do not, therefore, appear to be required where a charge is not registered even though it is registered with the Registrar of Companies pursuant to the Companies Act 1985 s395 (as amended);

(f)  a certified copy of the deed of appointment of the administrative receiver. It is usual practice that evidence must also be provided by the debenture-holder to the effect that the power of appointment has arisen under the debenture. Ideally, this should be in the form of a statutory declaration and should be executed by a duly authorised official of the debenture-holder;

(g)  where applicable, a statutory declaration by the applicant transferee for the purposes of the Land Registration (Powers of Attorney) Rules 1986 as discussed above;

(h)  in the event that the company is in liquidation, the name and address of the liquidator;

(i)  the applicable fee.

Where the title to property to which the transfer by the administrative receiver relates is unregistered, it will be necessary to consider a registration of the unregistered title. Since December 1990 the sale of the freehold of any unregistered property triggers the requirement for first registration. The time limit for first registration is two months from the date of completion and it is vital that this is adhered to, since a failure to make an application for first registration within the two-month period will effectively lose legal title in favour of the transferee, which will revert to the vendor. The transferee's interest will therefore be equitable only, as indeed will be the interest of the transferee's mortgagee. The application for first registration is made on Form 1B. The application should be accompanied by the following documents:

(a) the conveyance or rule 72 transfer together with a certified copy;
(b) the transferee's mortgage document together with a certified copy;
(c) all other documents relating to the property such as registration on title and reply thereto;
(d) a list of the documents supporting the application for registration in triplicate;
(e) the applicable fee.

## 13.4 Order of Application of Assets and Realisations

In an LPA receivership, the application of assets and realisations is governed by the Law of Property Act 1925, which is usually extended in practice and which may be varied. The 1925 Act is not applicable to administrative receivership in which, where the company is not also in the course of being wound up, the application of assets and realisations by the administrative receiver will be subject to the priority claims as set out below (*Batten v Wedgwood Coal and Iron Co* (1884) 28 ChD 317; *Re Glyncorrwg Colliery Co* [1926] Ch 951).

First, the claims creditors secured by way of fixed charge are discharged in full. Where the appointing debenture-holder's security in priority ranks subject to the security of another creditor then the letter is entitled to be discharged in full out of the proceeds of sale of the particular secured assets in priority to the appointing debenture-holder, whose interest vests in the equity of redemption. Section 43 now offers an innovative facility for avoiding priority claims of this type by sanctioning their disposal by the administrative receiver subject to a court order.

Claims on fixed-charge assets are not subject to preferential claims (*Re Lewis Merthyr Consolidated Collieries Ltd* [1929] 1 Ch 498). However, a preferential creditor which ranks also as a secured creditor is entitled to appropriate his security at his discretion (*Re William Hall (Contractors) Ltd* [1967] 1 WLR 948).

Secondly, the administrative receiver is entitled to recover the costs of realisation, expenses and remuneration. This claim ranks in priority to preferential debts and secured claims of the debenture-holder by way of floating charge (*Re Glyncorrwg Colliery Co Ltd* [1926] 1 Ch 951). In that case it was held that assets were to be applied in the following order of priority (assuming fixed charge claims were to have been discharged or not subsisting):

(a) costs of realisation;
(b) costs, expenses and remuneration of the receiver;
(c) costs, charges and expenses of the debenture trust deed, including remuneration of the deed trustees;

(d)  the plaintiff's costs in pursuing the action (if any);
(e)  preferential creditors;
(f)  claims of the debenture-holder under the floating charge.

In other words, preferential debts do not necessarily rank immediately prior to principal and interest due under the debenture pursuant to the debenture-holder's claims. These categories warrant some further clarification.

The costs of realisation will cover costs of sale, collection and enforcement but will not extend to the costs of preserving assets with a view to their sale (*Lathorn v Greenwich Ferry Co* (1895) 72 LT 790). The remuneration of the administrative receiver will be subject to the provisions of the debenture and any application to the court by a liquidator to fix the level of remuneration under s36(1) and (2) (see, for example, *Re Potters Oils Ltd (No 2)* [1986] 1 WLR 201). In the event that the administrative receiver is appointed pursuant to a debenture trust stock deed covering an issue of debenture stock, the costs, expenses and remuneration of the trustees of the stock deed will only be payable in priority to the secured loan if this is provided for in the debenture or trust deed itself (*Re Piccadilly Hotel Ltd* [1911] 2 Ch 534). On the other hand, that entitlement will rank after the secured debt in priority if the company has merely undertaken to discharge it as in *Re Accles Ltd* (1902) 18 TLR 786. In practice, the costs of a debenture-holder's action, as in the *Glyncorrwg* case, will not usually arise. Perhaps the most obvious circumstance in which they may do so is where an application is made to court under s45 for an order removing an incumbent administrative receiver where another debenture-holder asserts a priority right of appointment. If no surplus will remain after payment of the secured debt to the debenture-holder, the plaintiff debenture-holder will be entitled to costs on a full indemnity basis since no other party is thereby prejudiced by such an order (*Re A Boynton Ltd* [1910] 1 Ch 519). If a surplus is refundable, the plaintiff debenture-holder will only be entitled to costs on a standard basis (*Re Queen's Hotel Co* [1900] 1 Ch 792). After payment of preferential creditors pursuant to s40, the claim of the debenture-holder under his floating charge will not be prejudiced in terms of any discount being made on the claim by virtue of the fact that the terms of the debenture provide that repayment of the secured debt may only be made on a stipulated date (*Wallace v Universal Automatic Machines Co* [1894] 2 Ch 547). This caters for the practice in most well-drafted standard-form debentures where the secured debt, together with interest, is usually stated to be repayable on the occurrence of any number of stipulated breaches or defaults or on demand.

Thirdly, preferential debts rank in priority as a claim on assets subject to a floating charge, as defined in s251, although the same claim does not extend to fixed-charge assets (*Re Lewis Merthyr Consolidated Collieries Ltd* [1929] 1 Ch 498).

Fourthly, if any surplus remains after discharge of preferential debts, floating charge claims are discharged in order of priority. However, if a surplus remains following the discharge in full of the claim of the debenture-holder under the fixed charge(s), then the surplus cannot be seen to be subject to the floating charge since the floating charge subsists to secure a debt which itself is no longer in existence. As a consequence, the surplus is not payable to preferential creditors, since no floating charge exists in priority to which they may stake a claim. Instead, the surplus is payable to the company or, if in liquidation, the liquidator (*Re G L Saunders Ltd* [1986] 1 WLR 215).

The priority of claims may be affected where the company in administrative receivership goes into liquidation or where an effective subordination or subrogation is in force. However, it appears that only those parties subject to any subordination or subrogation agreement may pursue an action against the administrative receiver for failure to apply assets and realisations in accordance with the agreement, on the basis of the decision in *Yourell v Hibernian Bank* [1918] AC 372.

## 13.5 Litigation

A company in administrative receivership may sue and be sued in the normal course of litigation. The administrative receiver is specifically empowered by Sched 1, para 5 to bring or defend any action or other legal proceedings in the name of and on behalf of the company unless his power is varied or limited by the terms of the debenture itself (although this would be unusual) (s42(1)). This power is in addition to the power implied by Sched 1, para 1 to take such proceedings as may seem expedient to the administrative receiver for taking possession of, collecting and getting in the property of the company (*Wheeler & Co v Warren* [1928] Ch 840). Nevertheless, the administrative receiver has no automatic right to the company's statutory books and records nor to those records and documents of the company which relate solely to its management, nor to take steps to recover assets other than those comprising the debenture-holder's security (*Gomba Holdings UK Ltd v Minories Finance Ltd* [1989] 1 All ER 261; and see s234).

Where the company in administrative receivership is plaintiff in an action, the usual practice is for the proceedings to be initiated in the name of the company (in administrative receivership) and shown as acting by its administrative receiver. It should be noted here that the directors of the company retain certain residual powers which also enable them to initiate actions in the name of the company, as considered in Chapter 8 at para 8.11. In those cases the company plaintiff will be shown as being in administrative receivership but clearly will not be shown as acting by its administrative receiver. It is unusual for an undertaking to be required in respect of both costs and liability incurred by the company where an action is taken by the company at the instigation of the directors pursuant to their residual powers.

Where a company in administrative receivership institutes proceedings, it is usual for the defendant to request that security for costs be given by the company. Invariably this is granted by the court, in that the administrative receiver will usually give grounds for the court to believe that the unsuccessful company would be unable to pay the defendant's costs for the purposes of the Companies Act 1985 s726(1). Until security is given in such cases the same provision requires that the proceedings must be stayed. Security for costs may be given by the company acting by the administrative receiver pursuant to the general and incidental power in Sched 1, para 23 or pursuant to any express power to do so as conferred by the debenture. Alternatively, the security for costs may take the form of a personal undertaking by the administrative receiver, although this is less common in practice and will usually give rise to the office-holder requiring a supporting indemnity in his favour from the appointing debenture-holder. In either case, the office-holder should consider in advance the need for further security for costs being required as any litigation progresses.

Two practical matters arise in regard to litigation when a company in administrative receivership goes into liquidation. First, actions brought by either the administrative receiver or liquidator in the name of the company must include the company as being in both administrative receivership and liquidation. Secondly, any security for costs given and remaining in court at the time of the liquidation is unaffected in respect of the security given by the liquidator (*W A Sherratt Ltd v John Bromley (Church Stretton) Ltd* [1985] QB 1038). The liquidation will, however, clearly prejudice the giving of further security by the administrative receiver from the company's assets.

Where an action is taken against a company in administrative receivership (which in practice may well be of doubtful commercial expediency in view of the company's financial situation) the company is sued in the normal way. Again, the onset of liquidation will not affect this position. One common practical question which arises, however, is whether or not to include the administrative receiver and/or the debenture-holder as a defendant to the action. An administrative receiver is amenable to an action brought against the company in his capacity as agent of the company, and thus may appropriately be pursued as a party to the action. This would appear to be the case even where the appointment arises subsequent to the commencing of an action, although the administrative receiver may not be joined in his personal capacity in such a case. Whilst the office-holder may be included as a defendant in a personal capacity where the cause of the action follows his appointment, care should be taken in doing so and clear grounds established for why the action is being taken against the administrative receiver personally and not as agent of the company. In certain cases, however, it will be appropriate to include the administrative receiver as a defendant both in his personal capacity and as agent of the company. One obvious example of this is where it is alleged that the administrative receiver has failed to return goods to a supplier under an effective retention of title clause.

It is not uncommon for an appointing debenture-holder to be included as a defendant in litigation as a matter of course. The practicalities of this are that good reason should be made out as to exactly why the debenture-holder is included in the first place and what it is the plaintiff hopes to achieve by doing so. Perhaps the most obvious examples of this relate to those matters considered in Chapters 9 and 10 as regards the duties and liabilities of the debenture-holder.

Finally, where an administrative receiver has already been appointed, a *Mareva*-type injunction will be discharged as against the office-holder with immediate effect, since such an order does not confer on the plaintiff any type of security interest (*Capital Cameras Ltd v Harold Lines Ltd* [1991] 3 All ER 389).

## 13.6  Hiving-down

Hiving-down involves the transfer of the company's business and/or property to a subsidiary—usually formed for the purpose—prior to sale or disposal of the subsidiary to a third party. This represents an alternative to a direct sale of the business and/or property, which carries with it for the third party the attendant risks of the transfer of liabilities, potentially including accrued employee liability rights, as well as assets. The administrative receiver enjoys an express power to hive-down, unless removed or vested by the debenture pursuant to which he is appointed, by virtue of Sched 1, paras 15–16, which provides for the power to establish subsidiaries of the company and the power to transfer to its subsidiaries the whole or any part of the business and (which perhaps should read 'or') property of the company.

### 13.6.1  Advantages

Hiving-down is clearly advantageous for the sale of a company's business and/or assets in comparison to a direct sale for seven main reasons:

(1)  The technique allows the office-holder to 'cream off' profitable assets, profitable contracts and key employees to the new undertaking, whilst retaining depreciating assets, losses, unprofitable contracts and surplus employees at the time of the transfer within the company in administrative receivership.

(2) Hiving-down protects those profitable elements of the company from any winding-up petition presented against it, which will clearly not affect the subsidiary.

(3) Similarly, the establishment of the new company and business avoids any right of set-off being exercised by creditors of the company in administrative receivership.

(4) The administrative receiver will not be required to give personal guarantees for the supply of utilities as otherwise required by s233 in respect of the newly-formed company.

(5) The technique potentially enables the newly-formed company, subject to statutory limits, to set off its future trading profits against past trading losses of the company in administrative receivership for corporation tax liability purposes, as provided for in the Income and Corporation Taxes Act 1988 s343 (as amended).

(6) The establishment of a new subsidiary allows it to obtain VAT registration in its own right, thereby enabling it to recoup repayments if generated and avoid the exercise of a right of set-off by Customs and Excise in respect of any pre-administrative receivership VAT liabilities of the company in administrative receivership.

(7) The newly-formed company will not have attached to it the commercial stigma of administrative receivership which should favour its trading prospects and supplier relations.

### 13.6.2 Adoption of contracts

Hiving-down depends on the administrative receiver's ability to avoid the adoption of contracts existing at the time of his appointment. As stated previously, the administrative receiver may cause the company to repudiate or ignore existing contracts provided he acts in good faith (*Lathia v Dronsfield Bros* [1987] BCLC 321). Moreover, the administrative receiver is protected from personal actions by third parties for wrongful interference with contractual relations where he acts as agent of the company (*Airlines Airspaces Ltd v Handley Page Ltd* [1970] Ch 193; *Telemetrix plc v Modern Engineers of Bristol (Holdings) plc* [1985] BCLC 213).

Hiving-down also brings to the fore the question of adoption of employment contracts by the administrative receiver and the techniques employed by him in dealing with those contracts in view of s44(1) and (2) as amended by the 1994 legislation and the provisions of the Transfer of Undertakings (Protection of Employment) Regulations 1981 (SI No 1794). In practice, the hiving-down agreement often provides that the 1981 Regulations are applicable to a specific scheduled list of employees, notwithstanding the fact that some or all of those employees may have been made redundant previously by the administrative receiver. It is also common for the sale agreement of the hived off undertaking to contain provisions whereby its purchaser agrees to indemnify the administrative receiver and the company in administrative receivership for claims against it by employees subject to the hiving-down operation. This requires a closer examination of the 1981 Regulations themselves.

The Regulations were originally introduced in the United Kingdom to implement the European Acquired Rights Directive 77/187. A 'relevant transfer' is defined as a transfer of an undertaking (or part of one) from one person to another and extends to any trade or business. The definition does not depend on whether there is an actual transfer of the business or any of its property, but whether there has been a change in the natural or legal person operating the enterprise (*Berg and Busscher v Besselsen* [1990] ICR 396). A management buy-out or a hive-down operation may therefore amount to a relevant transfer for the purposes of the 1981 Regulations. At a European level, the approach of the European Court of Justice has been to examine the substance of a transaction as opposed to its form in deciding whether or not a transfer has taken place, and technical or sham avoidances of the provisions therefore have little worth or merit (see, for example, *Landsorganisationen i Danmaark v NY Molle Kvo* [1987] IKLK 37). In practice it is common for administrative receivers to seek to avoid liability under the Regulations by including a clause in the business and asset sale agreement which expressly provides that certain employees, usually listed in a schedule to the agreement, are expressly subject to the 1981 Regulations.

The 1981 Regulations provide that the sale of the business which changes its ownership from the vendor to the purchaser will not be deemed to terminate contracts of employment in respect of employees of the business and, furthermore, the contracts of employment of those employees shall take effect after the transfer as though they had originally been made with the purchaser of the business and not the vendor. The effect of this is in practical terms to bring about a statutory novation of employment contracts. Furthermore, reg 8(1) provides that if an employee is dismissed either before or after a relevant transfer, and the principal reason for his dismissal is the transfer or a reason connected with it, then the employee will be deemed automatically to have been unfairly dismissed. The Regulations do, however, go on to provide that dismissal will not be deemed to be unfair if there is an economic, technical or organisational reason for it which justifiedly entails changes in the workforce. If that is the case then there may be deemed to be 'some other substantial reason' justifying the dismissal for the purposes of the Employment Protection (Consolidation) Act 1978 s57, which also requires that the employer has acted reasonably in bringing about the dismissal.

Regulation 5 of the 1981 Regulations makes it clear that they only apply to employees employed 'immediately before the transfer'. The courts have made it clear that they are not prepared to entertain attempts to avoid the effect of the regulations by permitting sham dismissals to be made immediately before the transfer of the business. For example, in *Litster v The Forth Dry Dock Engineering Co (in receivership)* [1989] 2 WLR 634, the House of Lords was not prepared to entertain dismissals made by receivers approximately one hour before the transfer of the business so as to avoid the assumption of employee rights by the purchaser. However, it should be noted that the House of Lords expressed dissatisfaction with reg 5(3) of the 1981 Regulations, which required that employees should have been employed 'immediately before the transfer'. The court considered that the words 'or who would have been so employed if they had not be unfairly dismissed within Regulation 8(1)' should be inserted which would provide that the dismissal of an employee would be justifiable on the grounds of an economic or technical reason or a reorganisation in the work-force. As a consequence, an administrative receiver may dismiss employees justifiably on the economic, technical or organisational grounds provided that these are *bona fide*. In such a case an employee will not obtain rights against the purchaser of a business, assuming that the administrative receiver has acted reasonably for the purposes of the Employment Protection (Consolidation) Act 1978 s57 in dismissing the employee. In any other circumstance an employee who is otherwise dismissed will retain a right of action against the purchaser for unfair dismissal, wrongful dismissal or redundancy or any other liabilities arising on termination of his contract of employment.

The *Litster* decision is heavily relied on in practice, and an administrative receiver is well advised to establish solid grounds for dismissing employees in connection with a transfer of sale of the company's business for the purposes of avoiding liability on contracts of employment. *Litster* also over-rules previous unsatisfactory decisions such as *Secretary of State for Employment v Spence* [1986] IRLR 248 which had permitted a purchaser to avoid the effect of the 1981 Regulations by agreeing with receivers that employees would be dismissed shortly before a relevant transfer so as to avoid the scope of the previously unqualified condition in reg 5 of the 1981 Regulations that an employee need only be employed 'immediately before the transfer'. In the *Spence* case the dismissals had been made three hours before the transfer and were subsequently upheld by the court.

The *Litster* decision has been overtaken and extended recently by the decision of the Employment Appeal Tribunal in *UK Security Services (Midlands) Limited v Gibbons* ([1990] EAT 104). In that case the company went into receivership and the receivers sought to sell the business as a going concern by way of tender. Two tenders were received by the closing date, the employees being dismissed before the tenders were opened at 12.30 pm on that day. Contracts for the sale of the business were exchanged three days later, following which the employees applied to the Secretary of State for redundancy payments from the National Insurance Fund. The Secretary of State refused to make these payments on the basis that the 1981 Regulations applied. The view of the Industrial Tribunal was that the dismissals had been for redundancy purposes, and that the receivers had dismissed the employees in order to make the company more attractive to potential purchasers. As a consequence, reg 8(1) applied and liability for the dismissals was effectively transferred to the purchaser of the company. Before the Employment Appeal Tribunal the purchaser argued that it had not known of the circumstances of the dismissals, or indeed even of the existence of the applicants, and as such the dismissal could not be viewed as being by reason of the transfer. Nevertheless, the Employment Appeal Tribunal agreed with the view of the industrial tribunal that reg 8(1) applied. It should be noted that the Employment Appeal Tribunal rejected on the facts an argument by the purchaser that the reason for the dismissal had been economic, technical or organisational on the basis that the dismissal had been by way of redundancy. Notably, the Employment Appeal Tribunal made it clear that they would in any event have found the dismissal of the employees unfair under the Employment Protection (Consolidation) Act 1978 s57(3), on the grounds that there had been no consultation or explanation for the dismissal. The upshot of this case for purchasers of a business from administrative receivers is that express enquiries should be made, prior to completion of the sale, as to the existence of employees and details of any dismissals which have been made prior to the completion of the sale agreement. Nonetheless, the *UK Security Services* case remains a grave concern for prospective purchasers.

### 13.6.3   The mechanics of hiving-down

In practice it is usual for the mechanics of a hiving-down operation to run on the following lines. Initially, a newly-formed company ('Newco') with a nominal share capital is obtained, its issued shares (usually two in number) being held by the company in administrative receivership or, less commonly, by it and the administrative receiver. The relevant business and assets of the company are then transferred to Newco, the consideration for these being payable on demand. The shares in Newco are then sold to the purchaser of the hived-off business.

The consideration element of the hiving-down operation is usually dealt with in the following way. First, the consideration payable by Newco to the company in administrative receivership is, in effect, a book debt in the form of an inter-company loan which is repayable on demand. Less commonly, this element of the consideration will take the form of fully paid-up shares which reflect the net assets underlying them. The consideration is paid over (on the sale of Newco) by its purchaser to Newco, and the purchaser undertakes to cause Newco to discharge the liability to the company in administrative receivership. The value paid over by the purchaser may not be determined until the time of sale, and therefore it is common practice to insert the value of the purchase price into the agreement—frequently a supplementary agreement—between Newco and the company in administrative receivership. It may also be necessary to tailor the supplementary agreement in such a way as to exclude certain assets which the purchaser of Newco is not prepared to take, but which had originally been subject to the hive-down agreement. In addition, the purchaser will need to pay over a nominal value to Newco in respect of shares taken by it, usually stated as being payable in cash.

### 13.6.4 Tax implications

From the purchaser's point of view one major attraction of hiving-down is that it permits a transfer of trading losses of the company in administrative receivership to be made, for the benefit of the purchaser. The scope of this transfer was substantially undermined by the Finance Act 1986 s42 and Sched 10 to the Income and Corporation Taxes Act 1988 s343(4). This provides that any losses which may be carried forward are limited by imposing an obligatory deduction from the transferor's trading losses of any excess of relevant liabilities over relevant assets (ie to the extent that the company is insolvent in that those liabilities of the transferor exceeds its assets immediately following the transfer of the trade to the new subsidiary). For these purposes a 'relevant liability' is one which is not transferred to the new subsidiary but which subsisted immediately prior to the transfer. Expressly excluded from this definition are share capital, including share premium account, reserves or loan stock other than monies owing to a creditor anyway on the business of moneylending. 'Relevant assets' are those vested in the transferor immediately before the transfer and not transferred with the trade, together with any consideration paid over by the subsidiary in respect of the transfer. Those assets are valued at a reasonable open market value immediately prior to the transfer.

Tax relief is only available under s343 of the 1988 Act if the transfer takes place during the subsistence of a group relationship between the company in administrative receivership and the subsidiary. That relationship will cease on the company in administrative receivership being wound up, since at that time the company will be deemed no longer to be the beneficial owner of its assets (ie the shares in the subsidiary) but will hold them on trust for its creditors (*IRC v Olive Mill Ltd* [1963] 1 WLR 712). For example, in *Ayerst v C & K Construction Ltd* [1976] AC 167 the House of Lords refused to permit a wholly-owned subsidiary to which a business had been hived-down, to carry forward losses and capital allowances following the company in receivership going into liquidation. This was despite the fact that both receiver and liquidator had joined in the hive-down agreement. From a tax perspective, the company in receivership no longer beneficially owned the shares in the subsidiary, which contravened the carry-forward provisions in the former analogous legislation. The price itself will usually be framed realistically so as to avoid any profit or loss arising for tax purposes on the sale of the assets and business to be hived down. Provision is usually made in the agreement for the price to be certified by an independent valuer (or the administrative receiver's firm), although commonly the supplementary agreement executed on completion will dispense with the need for such a certificate, the valuation having been agreed between the parties for the hived-down assets for sale purposes being inserted in its place. Alternatively, the independent valuer's certificate may be incorporated into the agreement itself.

### 13.6.5  Other liabilities

Whilst the establishment of a subsidiary in the way outlined above constitutes a convenient method of separating off the attractive elements of the company for sale purposes in a single 'package', it does not follow that the administrative receiver of the company in administrative receivership is free of any liabilities in respect of the newly-formed company. In particular, the administrative receiver may be deemed to be a shadow director of the subsidiary for fraudulent or wrongful trading purposes and, as such, may also fall liable to disqualification under the Company Directors Disqualification Act 1986 or in misfeasance proceedings under s212. In reality, these liabilities only exist in the period between incorporation and the transfer of the subsidiary's shares to a purchaser, although they nonetheless represent liabilities which should be prompt consideration of the level and scope of any indemnity held by the administrative receiver from his appointor and the commercial motives underlying the hiving-down operation itself.

### 13.6.6  Assets

The assets subject to the hive-down agreement should be clearly identified in any schedules to the agreement, which should be completed fully for identification purposes. The property usually subject to the agreement will comprise fixed assets such as plant, machinery, stock, equipment, stock-in-trade and the like as well as intangible property such as goodwill, work-in-progress, the benefit of existing contracts and intellectual property rights which are likely to be income-generating. In practice, it is common for patents, copyrights, licences, trademarks etc to be retained by the company in administrative receivership, usually until such time as it is ascertained that the subsidiary will be able to trade on the hived-down business successfully. In all cases involving the assignment or transfer of intellectual property rights, a standard check should be made to ensure that the consent of some third party, such as a computer software house, is not required prior to the assignment or transfer. Failure to comply with any consent requirement may render the administrative receiver liable for inducing a breach of contract. The same considerations as regards immediate transfer to the subsidiary are also usually true of cash and book debts and other debts although, depending on the perceived quality of the debts, the agreement may provide for these to be collected by the newly-formed subsidiary, possibly on a commission basis, as agent of the company or, alternatively, for a variation to be made in the overall consideration for the assets transferred.

Since it is only practically necessary to transfer to the newly-formed subsidiary those assets necessary to maintain the ongoing trade, it will not be necessary to transfer immovable property, such as fixed plant, land or business premises, which may be licenced to the subsidiary for a fee. Indeed, there may be a real disadvantage in effecting a transfer since, on the transfer of shares in the subsidiary being transferred to a third party whereupon the group relationship between the company in administrative receivership and the subsidiary is deemed to cease, a disposition of the capital assets is deemed to occur at market value (whereas the transfer by the company in administrative receivership to its subsidiary is deemed to produce neither a chargeable gain nor an allowable loss) (Taxation of Chargeable Gains Act 1992 ss178, 179). The effect of this deemed market value disposition may give rise to corporation tax liability on the deemed capital gain arising, which will clearly affect the valuation of the shares in the subsidiary by their purchaser.

### 13.6.7 Leasehold problems

Particular problems may arise in the transfer of leasehold property where the lease prevents an assignment of the lease without the landlord's consent. In such a case the burden rests on the landlord to show that his refusal to consent is reasonable (Landlord and Tenant Act 1988 s1(6)). In addition, the landlord is required to respond to a written request for consent within a reasonable time and to provide reasons for his refusal, the omission of which may show that consent is withheld unreasonably (*Midland Bank plc v Chart Enterprises Inc* [1990] 2 EGLR 59). Inevitably, all cases will turn on their own facts (see for example, *Beale v Worth* [1993] EGCS 135). Section 1(5) of the 1988 Act also provides that it is reasonable for a landlord to withhold his consent only if the tenant would be in breach of covenant if the landlord were to withhold his consent to the completion of the proposed transaction (*International Drilling Fluids Ltd v Louisville Investments (Uxbridge) Ltd* [1986] 1 All ER 332). In the event that the consent of the landlord may not be obtained in time for the completion of the hive-down agreement, consideration should be given to the granting of a short-term non-exclusive licence to the subsidiary as opposed to an outright transfer, assuming of course that this does not contravene the terms of the lease itself. Alternatively, it may be possible for the company in administrative receivership to run the trade to be transferred at the leased premises for the benefit of the subsidiary, although this would appear not to utilise the tax avoidance provisions in the Income and Corporation Taxes Act 1988 s343 as well as requiring indemnities from the subsidiary, which it may well not be in a position to honour.

### 13.6.8  Implications of a winding-up petition

It appears from the wording of s129(2) that the winding-up of a company commences at the time of a presentation of the winding-up petition in a compulsory liquidation. For tax purposes on a hive-down, however, it is submitted that this cannot be correct, not least as it would enable a tactical petition to be presented which would not in any case upset the substance of the hive-down transaction itself (*Re Christionette International Ltd* [1982] 1 WLR 245). Beneficial ownership for the purposes of s343 of the 1988 Act would also appear to be lost if prior to the hive-down agreement there exists a binding agreement for the sale of shares in the subsidiary (*Wood Preservation Ltd v Prior* (1968) 45 TC 112; and see also Income and Corporation Taxes Act 1988 s768 where there is a significant change in the business of the subsidiary three years prior to or following the transfer of the shares in it to the purchaser).

### 13.6.9  Further tax problems

The hiving-down operation will also require a consideration of potential liability for chargeable gains tax which will arise on the sale of the shares by the company in administrative receivership to a third party, whereupon the subsidiary will cease to be a member of its former group. This is because the subsidiary will be deemed to have disposed of any chargeable assets transferred to it by any group member within the previous six years on ceasing to be a member of the group, by virtue of the Taxation of Chargeable Gains Tax Act 1992 s179. It is not therefore common to transfer assets which carry potentially significant chargeable gains tax liability at the time of the hive-down itself, although there is no reason why these assets should not be transferred after the disposal of the shares in it to the third-party purchaser.

Where a hive-down does not offer a realistic means of preserving trade losses, then the company in administrative receivership may be able to set these off against other income or chargeable gains (assuming that the company continues to trade) or, less commonly, it may seek a repayment of tax credits by setting off any franked investment income, which may be treated as trading profit, against actual trading profit as permitted by the Income and Corporation Taxes Act 1988 s242.

For tax and beneficial ownership purposes, as discussed above, the legal ownership of the assets transferred need not be passed at the time the hive-down agreement is entered into. The relevant time period is, rather, the time at which beneficial ownership of the assets passes, which will be the date of any unconditional agreement for the sale or the date of satisfaction of any condition in a conditional agreement.

### 13.6.10 Further considerations and problems

The transfer of any asset of the company in administrative receivership will continue to require the consent of any charge-holder, other than the appointing debenture-holder, who holds valid security over the assets subject to the transfer. It is common therefore on completion for the company in administrative receivership to have undertaken to obtain the necessary consents or to discharge the prior-ranking chargee. Again, s43 may provide a useful device for the administrative receiver in the face of an unco-operative prior-ranking chargee.

Finally, consideration should be given on a hive-down to ss216 and 217, which stipulate restrictions on the re-use of an insolvent company although the provisions do not apply to administrative receivership *per se*. The rules are of particular relevance to management buy-outs from the administrative receiver and extend by virtue of s216(6) to both the name of the company and any trade name employed by it. As well as the serious criminal sanction for contravention of the provision, by virtue of s216(4), s217 (which closely resembles the Company Directors Disqualification Act 1986 s15) imposes personal liability on a person for contravention of s216 (see, for example, the summary judgment in *Thorne v Silverleaf* [1994] BCC 109). It should be noted that IR rr4.228–4.230 provide three exceptional cases and the procedure by which a former director or shadow director may seek leave of the court to re-use a prohibited 'phoenix' name. The first of these lends itself to the acquisition by a company of the whole or substantially the whole of the business of the insolvent company under agreements with its administrative receiver. It is clear from the decision of Morritt J in *Re Bonus Breaks Ltd* [1991] BCC 546 that this first exception applies to sales, including hive-downs, which involve a sale of assets only and not a sale of both assets and liabilities. Although IR r4.228(1) only makes reference to 'the business of an insolvent company' it is submitted that practice dictates that the view in the *Bonus Breaks* case must apply to hive-downs in which liabilities are most commonly excluded from the acquisition of the business by the newly-formed subsidiary.

The hiving-down agreement may also deal with existing contracts, which at the time of the agreement are in the name of the company in administrative receivership. Usually, the business and asset sale agreement will contain a clause whereby the newly-formed subsidiary undertakes to endeavour to secure the novation of the existing contract in its favour. Separate provisions in the agreement will also usually require the newly-formed subsidiary to undertake and carry out outstanding obligations under the contract albeit that the existing contract remains in the name of the company in administrative receivership. The discharge of these obligations is usually stated as being at the cost of the newly-formed subsidiary. Other provisions will also usually provide that the performance of the outstanding obligations is for the newly-formed subsidiary's benefit, which will be accompanied by a corresponding indemnity from the newly-formed subsidiary in favour of the company in administrative receivership in respect of the obligations.

One particular problem which is commonly encountered in practice with regard to existing contracts involves a provision in the contract which prohibits an assignment of the contract without the express consent of the other party. This frequently arises in the case of construction contracts and enables the other party to avoid the assignment of any right of action against it without its consent (see for example, *St Martin's Property Corp Ltd v Sir Robert McAlpine & Sons Ltd* [1993] 3 WLR 408). In the *St Martin's Property* case a party who had assigned a right of action against a contractor was held to be entitled to pursue that right notwithstanding an ineffective assignment. It would appear that where a right of action is pursued by its assignee without the consent of the other party, then any proceeds of that right of action will be held on constructive trust for the assignor. However, an administrative receiver of an assignor company in such a situation would be well advised to seek an indemnity from the assignee of the right of action, in respect of all costs and liabilities which he or the company in administrative receivership may incur as a result of the assignment of the right of action in contravention of any express term prohibiting assignment in the main contract with the other party itself. Clearly, this problem will not arise in the absence of an express clause prohibiting assignment of the right of action or, indeed, any other benefit under the contract (see, for example, *Darlington Borough Council v Wiltshire Northern Ltd* (1994) *The Times*, 4 July).

## 13.7 Dealing with Contracts of Employment

Liability for contracts of employment was dealt with previously in Chapter 10 at para 10.6. Prior to adoption of contracts of employment after the statutory 14-day period, an administrative receiver as agent of the company may see fit to dismiss all or a substantial part of the company's workforce in order to avoid liability. Those dismissed employees may, however, have claims on the company as a result of the dismissal for redundancy, on the basis that they are unfair or, in the absence of a correct notice period, that they are wrongful. These claims may be pursued against the company by employees following the completion of the administrative receivership; alternatively, the claims may be submitted to any subsequently-appointed liquidator.

Where an administrative receiver considers that the retention of some or all of the company's employees is necessary—usually for the purposes of maintaining it as a saleable concern—consideration should be given to the possibility of contracting out of the consequences of adoption of the contracts of employment to those employees. There appear to be two possible ways of seeking to do this as considered below. First, the administrative receiver may by express agreement amend the terms of the contract of individual employees, thereby limiting the scope of 'qualifying liabilities' which will arise on adoption. Secondly, and alternatively, the administrative receiver may seek to contract out of the personal liability otherwise imposed on him as a result of adoption by virtue of s44 (as amended). In effect, this amounts to an extra-contractual agreement to exclude the liabilities which would otherwise be deemed to arise following adoption of the contract of employment on the expiration of the statutory 14-day period.

### 13.7.1 Contractual variation

In order to renegotiate and conclude a new contract of employment with an employee, the administrative receiver may, within the statutory 14-day period following appointment, seek the written agreement of the employee to the amended terms of the contract. In view of the apparent scope of the term 'qualifying liability' as being applicable to periods when employees are laid off (ie as absence through good cause, for example when no work is available for them) the terms of any new contract should specifically provide that no payment will be made for such periods. The administrative receiver should also seek to exclude and keep to a minimum contractual bonuses, profit-related pay and other similar benefits which would otherwise be assumed by him as a liability under any otherwise operative contract of employment. In the event that an employee is not agreeable to new terms, then the risk run by the administrative receiver in imposing such terms unilaterally—particularly when they are significantly different from those previously operated—is that the employee may be deemed to be constructively dismissed. The administrative receiver should consider carefully whether it may not be more advisable to simply dismiss an employee summarily within the statutory 14-day period, thereby avoiding any liability on his own part as a consequence. The effect of terminating the contract within the 14-day period is likely to be that the employee will not have received any appropriate period of notice, which may give rise to a claim by him in damages for wrongful dismissal (ie for breach of contract) as an unsecured claim against the company.

### 13.7.2 Contracting-out

As an alternative to variation of an employee's contract of employment, a number of comments made in the Court of Appeal in the *Paramount Airways* case also suggested that it may be possible for an administrative receiver to seek the agreement of employees in contracting out of the liabilities otherwise imposed as a consequence of adoption of contracts of employment by him. Although Dillon LJ suggested *obiter* that he would be unwilling to consider the notion that contracting out was possible, the matter was ignored by Leggatt LJ, who considered that the question of contracting out simply did not arise in the case. At first instance Evans-Lombe J had actually stated that there was no public policy or public interest requirement which prevented contracting out in the case of an administration, and the same considerations would apply equally to administrative receivers. This suggests that, whilst the effect of adoption itself may not be avoided by an office-holder, it may well be that the office-holder can seek to contract out of the liability arising as a consequence of that. In effect, it is not the efficacy of contracting-out which appears to be in issue but rather the mechanism by which that end is achieved. This view now appears to be supported by the decision of the House of Lords in *Paramount*. In the House of Lords in *Paramount* Lord Browne-Wilkinson held:

> It is not possible for an administrator or receiver to avoid [the] result of adoption or alter its consequences unilaterally by informing employees that he is not adopting their contract or only doing so on terms.

The crucial point here is that the House of Lords had an ideal opportunity to discount the possibility of contracting-out which was not taken. Neither did the Lords take the opportunity to cast aspersions on comments made at first instance and in the Court of Appeal in *Paramount* which at least hinted at the viability of contracting-out, although Dillon and Leggatt LJJ in the Court of Appeal had both refrained from expounding on the question of contracting-out. Again, the refrain shown in those judgments must add weight to the argument that contracting out is possible post-15 March 1994. On the other hand, Dillon LJ did discount the relevance of the decision in *Guardians of the Poor of Salford Union v Dewhurst* [1926] AC 619, which had been cited by counsel as authority for the general principle that it is not open to persons on whom a statutory requirement is imposed and those persons for whose benefit that requirement exists to contract out of the requirement itself. This was in effect a weak attempt at discounting contracting-out on public policy grounds, although the point was not taken up by the court.

Whilst Dillon LJ was prepared to acknowledge what he conceded were the important principles of statutory construction and applications set out by the case, the point was not advanced. With respect, there is good reason why it should not be. The *Poor of Salford Union* case does not appear on a reading of the decision to be authority for the point referred to by counsel, and it is certainly not referred to in any leading texts in the field as such. The better view, it is submitted, is that expressed by Evans-Lombe J at first instance to, the effect that the provisions of s19(5) (in administration) 'do not prevent an administrator from contracting out of the effect of adoption of contracts of employment'. There is every good reason why exactly the same principle should operate in administrative receivership.

As an afterword on the point, office-holders who are deemed to have adopted contracts of employment prior to 15 March 1994 may seek to argue that effective contracting-out arrangements have in fact been made with employees who have by implication acquiesced in the arrangements set out in any standard-form *Specialised Mouldings*-type letter issued by them. This is an argument which remains to be tested judicially.

### 13.7.3 How might contracting-out be achieved?

In practice, agreement to contracting-out arrangements is clearly best evidenced in writing, preferably with the signature of both the office-holder and the relevant employee. Any contracting-out documentation should set out clearly the contracting-out arrangements, and should certainly go further than the standard *Specialised Mouldings* disclaimer in which both statements merely disclaiming personal liability on the part of the office-holder were commonly used. Indeed, the *Specialised Mouldings* case would suggest that mere notices of disclaimer will simply not be effective and it is anticipated that these would be frowned on in any case by the court. This is also clear from the decision of the House of Lords in *Paramount* and the first instance decision of Lightman J in *Leyland DAF Ltd v Ferranti International plc* [1994] BCC 658, where the judge considered that, for personal liability to be excluded by an office-holder, it is plain that what is required is a contract to that effect between the office-holder, and the employee, but nothing short of that will suffice. It is equally helpful that Lightman J recognised that there is nothing in theory to prevent an administrative receiver from contracting out of personal liability under a new contract of employment, the comments of Evans-Lombe J at first instance in the *Paramount* case being referred to in support together with the absence of any real comment by the Court of Appeal in that case. This concurs with the view of the House of Lords in *Paramount*. Furthermore, Lightman J considered that the court should be slow to infer that employees have entered into such contracting-out arrangements whereby their statutory rights are surrendered unless it is plain to the court that they have given a full and informed consent to the waiver. In practice, it may be envisaged that employees will be prepared to do this on a wholly voluntary basis if there is no other option open to the administrative receiver, say where the company's charged assets are limited and no appropriate indemnities are available in his favour, other than to dismiss the employees summarily.

In the *Leyland DAF* case the letters issued by both companies, which were in substantially similar form to the *Specialised Mouldings* letter, were not such that they could reasonably have been understood by the recipient employees as an offer requiring acceptance or rejection. As such, Lightman J considered that they constituted mere unilateral declarations of non-liability, which were wholly ineffective. In addition, the judge took the view that even in the event that such letters did constitute offers to employees, it would be wholly unrealistic and unfair to treat the continued performance by those employees under their contracts of employment as an implied acceptance of a new contract by way of variation whereby personal liability on the part of the office-holder was excluded. That approach, it is submitted, has much to commend it as an equitable and pragmatic balancing of the interests of the administrative receiver with the protection of employee rights.

How then might contracting-out be brought about? There is certainly no judicial guidance on this point as yet, although what is clear from the *Paramount* decision is that unilateral waivers are no longer of any effect. Both the view of Lightman J at first instance in the *Leyland DAF* case and the view of the House of Lords in *Paramount* suggest that the court will be influenced by what might broadly be described as the relative bargaining powers of the parties to the employment contract and the particular circumstances of the case. Certainly it would appear that any attempt at contracting out would need to be bilateral and evidenced in writing. Ideally, employees should be given notification at the earliest possible time of the specific legislation which the office-holder proposes to contract out of and the practical effects of that proposal. Employees should also be given a reasonable opportunity to seek independent legal advice and perhaps recommended to do so. In practice, those measures may not be effective depending on the size and nature of the workforce involved. Certain employees, for example, may prefer simply to take redundancy. In that event, it is unlikely that any significant harm is done by the office-holder in attempting to continue the contracts of employment, in that those employees who are prepared simply to opt for dismissal may themselves avoid the need for any slimming down exercise of the workforce which may have otherwise been necessary by the office-holder. Each case will of course turn on its own specific facts, although the office-holder may wish to consider individual or group meetings as a follow-up measure to his initial proposal at contracting-out for the purposes of clarifying any anomalies which exist. Certainly it must be assumed that bland statements such as 'the administrative receiver does not accept or contract with personal liability' have no place in the contracting-out process.

### 13.7.4 Notification requirements

Procedurally, an employer is obliged to notify the Secretary of State of impending redundancies, at least 90 days before the first dismissal takes effect where 100 or more employees are to be dismissed over a 90-day period, or at least 30 days before the first dismissal where between 10 and 99 employees are to be dismissed over a 30-day period (Trade Union and Labour Relations (Consolidation) Act 1992 s193(1) and (2)). Notably, no duty to notify arises where less than ten employees are involved. The employer is also under an obligation to consult with a recognised trade union regarding planned dismissals (*GMB v Rankin* [1992] IRLR 514). Although an employer may be exempt from his duty to notify if what s193(7) of the 1992 Act refers to as 'special circumstances' render it not reasonably practicable to comply, provided the employer does his reasonable best, it is clear from the decision in *Secretary of State v Helitron Ltd* [1980] ICR 523 that a lack of awareness of a duty to notify does not amount to a special circumstance. Neither is the duty to consult obviated by the size of the undertaking involved, although the size may effect the nature or formality involved in the consultation process (*De Grasse v Stockwell Tools Ltd* [1992] IRLR 269). The Employment Appeal Tribunal has recently held that where consultation takes place between an employer and a union with regard to the choice of criteria applicable to a potential redundancy situation, the employer is not released from his obligation to consult with the union or the employees about the actual application of those criteria (*Rolls Royce Motor Cars Ltd v Price* [1993] IRLR 203).

Failure to comply with the notification formalities renders the employer liable to a fine under s194(1) of the 1992 Act. Although contravention amounts to a criminal offence carrying a maximum fine of £2,000 which is enforceable by the Secretary of State, it appears that no criminal proceedings have ever been taken under the provision or its earlier equivalent. However, in practice, an administrative receiver should take steps to comply with the notification requirements at the earliest possible time.

The circumstances of a particular administrative receivership may require that the office-holder acts very speedily in making dismissals in connection with the continued operation of the company's business or, as is less likely, the sale or transfer of it (ie by virtue of the 1981 Transfer of Undertaking Regulations (above)). For notification purposes the office-holder's position is assisted by the recent decision of the Employment Appeal Tribunal in *Heron v City Link - Nottingham* [1993] IRLR 372 which held that the obligation to consult may be obviated by the clear need for immediate decisions on the part of the employer, provided that the circumstances of a particular case make it necessary for the employer to dismiss employees when they did and at no later time.

Failure to consult as provided for may result in unfair dismissal. Also a copy of the notice must be sent to any appropriate recognised trade union by virtue of s193(6) of the 1992 Act.

## 13.8  Pension Schemes

Increasingly in recent years companies have established funded pension schemes for the benefit of employees. Employee pension schemes are almost invariably established by way of an irrevocable trust so as to obtain exempt approved tax status from the Inland Revenue for the purposes of the Income and Corporation Taxes Act 1988 s592(1)(a).

### 13.8.1  Trust Assets

It is common in practice for a pension scheme to be established by way of an interim deed, which will usually provide for the execution of a definitive deed and scheme rules within a period of up to 24 months thereafter. The Inland Revenue may, however, be prepared to extend this period where agreement cannot be reached on the final scheme provisions. The definitive deed itself will usually be stated to be subject to scheme announcements. The effect of this is to accommodate periodical variations in liabilities applicable to the scheme and members' eligibility under it.

The major practical implication of pension fund assets being held on trust is that as trust assets they are not assets of the company. This is despite the fact that the company itself, and/or any number of its directors, may be the trustees of the scheme in whom the scheme assets are legally vested. As such, the scheme assets will be held on trust for the scheme members, and will not comprise part of the estate available for creditors (see, for example, *Carreras Rothmans Ltd v Freeman Matthews Treasure Ltd* [1985] 1 All ER 155, and see generally the controversial and questionable decision in *Re Kayford* [1975] 1 WLR 279). It follows that scheme assets will not be caught by a fixed or floating charge which extends to the whole of the company's business and undertaking. On the other hand, a suitably framed floating charge will catch any surplus from the scheme which is subsequently payable to the company on its winding-up as a future asset of the company. The question of dealing with a surplus will, however, only arise on a subsequent liquidation (or alternatively, on the scheme itself being wound-up), as considered further below, but will not be relevant to the administrative receiver who is vested with no power to deal with the scheme assets themselves (but see *Simpson Curtis* (1993) unreported, referred to in Chapter 8 at para 8.2).

It is usual in the constitution of company pension schemes for the company itself to be referred to as the employer under the scheme. Following appointment, the immediate practical matter to be addressed by the administrative receiver in relation to the scheme is whether the company should continue to make any further payment contributions to the scheme. Where a surplus exists on the scheme (ie the scheme is over-funded) the discontinuance of contributions to it will not usually be problematic. However, where the scheme is in deficit (ie the scheme is under-funded), the discontinuance of contributions by the company (as employer) may result in a claim being made on the company by the trustees of the scheme. Clearly, such a claim may not be forthcoming where the company and its directors are themselves the trustees of the scheme or, alternatively, where the trustees perceive that there is little merit in pursuing an action against the company for the outstanding contributions due in view of the company's financial position. Whilst the discontinuance of contributions to a funded scheme by the company at the behest of the administrative receiver may give rise to an action against the company by the scheme trustees, it will not usually give rise to any liability on the part of the appointing debenture-holder, other perhaps than where a debenture-holder expressly instructs the administrative receiver to follow that course of action (*American Express v Hurley* [1985] 3 All ER 564). Certainly the debenture-holder is under no duty or obligation to become involved with the actions of the administrative receiver in this regard (*National Bank of Greece v Pinios* [1990] 1 AC 637).

### 13.8.2 Discontinuance of contributions

The discontinuance of contributions to a funded scheme by the administrative receiver may have two wider implications than simply preserving the company's immediate financial position. First, it now appears that the administrative receiver is under an express duty to give notice to the trustees of the scheme and eligible employees under it of any change in the basis of contributions made to the scheme by the company (*Larsen's Executrix v Henderson* [1990] IRLR 512). Secondly, one of the qualifying liabilities to which an administrative receiver will become personally liable on adopting a contract of employment on or after 15 March 1994 is contributions due to an occupational pension scheme (s44 (as amended) and see Chapter 10 at para 10.6). This second point assumes of course that the relevant contributions to the pension scheme constitutes part of a particular employee's contract of employment. In the event that it does not, or where the administrative receiver does not adopt a contract of employment or otherwise contracts out of the consequences of adoption, any claim by a scheme member against the company for a shortfall in respect of his contributions will rank as an unsecured and non-preferential claim.

The discontinuance of contributions to a so-called contracted-out pension scheme (ie from the state earnings related pension scheme (SERPS)) may be of very little practical benefit if the discontinuance of contributions results in the Inland Revenue revoking the scheme's contracted-out certificate. Indeed in practice this will be usual. The consequence of this is that the company in administrative receivership will fall liable to pay higher National Insurance contributions towards the equivalent additional state pension, which will commonly relate closely to the contributions made to the contracted-out scheme in any case. Equally seriously, in the case of the money purchase scheme where a personal pension is purchased for an individual employee or group of employees and contributed to by the company, discontinuance of the employer's contributions may constitute a breach of contract by the company. The administrative receiver may be liable for this breach personally if he has adopted any particular contract of employment. Where the administrative receiver seriously considers discontinuance in such situations, consideration should be given to the possibility of terminating the pension scheme with prior notice, as may be provided for in the scheme rules. In all cases these matters should be checked as a matter of course.

### 13.8.3   The effect of the appointment

It is uncommon, but not unknown, for the scheme rules of a pension scheme to provide that the scheme terminates and is wound up automatically on the appointment of either an administrator, an administrative receiver or a liquidator, or on a company entering into some compromise or arrangement with its creditors. In most cases, however, the scheme will only wind up automatically on the appointment of a liquidator. Again, specific reference should be made to the scheme rules in each case.

Where the company in administrative receivership is itself a trustee of the pension scheme, then the administrative receiver is capable neither of occupying the company's position as trustee nor of exercising any powers of the company as trustee. The reason for this is that the position of the company as trustee falls beyond the scope of the administrative receiver's appointment. Furthermore, any power of the employer relating to the pension scheme will not constitute an asset caught by a floating charge, even one extending to the whole of the company's business and undertaking (*Re William Makin & Son* [1992] PLR 20). On the other hand, an administrative receiver may exercise the power of the company in making an appointment of the trustee to a pension scheme, where that power may be exercised by the company (*Simpson Curtis Pension Trustees Ltd v Readson Ltd* (1994) unreported). In the latter instance the exercise of the power does not relate to the pension scheme assets and falls within the ambit of the management of the company's business. Even though the power is not expressly provided for in Sched 1 to IA 1986, it probably falls within the scope of para 23 thereof.

### 13.8.4   Claims against the company

The trustees of the pension scheme may maintain a claim against the company in respect of unpaid contributions to it where the company has underfunded its contributions to the scheme. This may also arise as a result of a statutory claim for a non-preferential debt where the scheme is being wound up or, more commonly, where the employer is in liquidation. In the case of unpaid contributions there is a risk that these may rank as preferential and, as such, must be discharged by the administrative receiver from floating-charge assets (s40; and see Pension Schemes Act 1993, Sched 6, para 8, and Sched 4). Other than those preferential debts specifically provided for by these provisions and to the extent that the company is liable to the pension scheme for borrowings, those liabilities will rank as unsecured.

Where the pension scheme is under-funded and the company is in liquidation, the liquidator may pursue an unsecured and non-preferential claim against the company for the amount outstanding under the Occupational Pension Schemes (Deficiency on Winding up etc) Regulations 1994 (SI No 895). The 1994 Regulations provide for statutory claims as from 2 June 1992, although these are not available in respect of money purchase schemes. Whilst the 1994 provisions do not come into operation on an administrative receivership, they will be triggered on a winding-up and will enable the liquidator to make a claim, albeit unsecured, on those company assets over which the administrative receiver will be or is appointed. The quantum of those claims is provided for in guidelines published by the Institute of Actuaries.

### 13.8.5 Pension surpluses

The administrative receiver should consider the possibility of any surplus on the pension scheme which becomes repayable to the company as a future asset, and which will usually therefore be caught by an appropriately framed floating charge. A surplus will only usually be repayable to the company where the scheme is wound up or where the company goes into liquidation, the latter being the most common example of the former. Any surplus will be subject to the discharge of the liabilities of the scheme which, as with the administration of the scheme generally, may be a lengthy process actually extending beyond the period of the administrative receivership. Whether the administrative receivership is suspended or protracted so as to catch any future surplus will necessarily depend on its expected value and the possibility of its arising. In addition, whilst the Inland Revenue requires that a surplus on a pension scheme be capable of being returned to the company, this may not be provided for in the pension scheme rules themselves which may require amendment through an application to the Occupational Pensions Board. Again, this process may be a lengthy one which is difficult to expedite.

The extent of any surplus which may be payable to the company will also be subject to the way in which the trustees of the scheme choose to deal with it prior to accounting to the company. In practice it is most common for the company to be entitled to any surplus on the scheme assets which remains after the exercise of any power or discretion vested in the trustees. Such a power or discretion—the two terms being mutually exclusive—will depend on the legal construction of the relevant scheme rules, and will effectively permit the trustees to enhance entitlements of members eligible under the scheme. The difference between a power and a discretion is that in the case of a power the trustees will be under a fiduciary duty to consider the interests of the members of the scheme whereas, in the case of a discretion, the trustees have no overriding duty to act in the best interests of members and, as a consequence, are less constrained in the way in which they may dispose of the scheme assets. This is not to say that the trustees enjoy an unbridled discretion in disposing of scheme assets where a mere discretion is conferred on them; rather, they must exercise their discretion in view of what Warner J described in *Mettoy Pension Trustees Ltd v Evans* [1991] 2 All ER 513 as 'their duty to the beneficiaries to consider whether and how the discretion ought to be exercised'. (See also *Smith v Somes* [1896] 1 ChD 250 per Chitty J and *Re Courage Group Pension Schemes* [1987], 1 All ER 528 per Millett J).

The distinction between what constitutes a power and what amounts to a discretion is not always a clear one. For instance, in *Icarus (Hertford) Ltd v Driscoll* (1989) unreported, the scheme rules provided that in the event of liquidation the trustee of the scheme '...shall subject to Revenue limitations at their discretion apply the whole or part of such [surplus] as they may determine to augment entitlements of members...'. The fact that the provision included the words 'or part of...at their discretion' implied that the trustees were at liberty to use any part of any surplus (as opposed to simply 'the whole' of it) to enhance the entitlements of members up to Inland Revenue limits. By implication, the trustees must therefore have been able to permit a return of part (or 'the whole') of the surplus to the employer at their discretion in accordance with the scheme's provisions. Such a right amounts to a discretion, in the exercise of which the trustees will not be subject to a general duty to act in the best interests of the scheme members. However, the decision in the *Mettoy* case suggests that the trustees should at least consider (ie as opposed to being required to act in) the members' best interests. The situation will be quite different in a case where the relevant provision is framed in such a way as not to permit the trustees to decide whether or not to enhance members' entitlements but, rather, to stipulate how and to what level to effect that enhancement. In such a case, the power conferred on the trustees, it is submitted, will amount to a power and, as such, will impose a duty on the trustees requiring that they act in the best interests of the scheme members.

## 13.9 Pension Schemes and Independent Trustee Obligations

An office-holder, including an administrative receiver, who is appointed and commences to act in relation to a company which is a participating employer in an occupational pension scheme, must have regard to the appointment of independent trustees. The office-holder must be satisfied that there is an independent trustee of a pension fund relating to the company to which he is appointed and, if not so satisfied, he must appoint such an independent trustee or secure the appointment of one (Pension Schemes Act 1993 s119 (formerly Social Security Pensions Act 1975 s57(c), as inserted by Social Security Act 1990 s14, Sched 1, para 1), and the Occupational Pension Schemes (Independent Trustee) Regulations 1990 (SI No 2075).

### 13.9.1  Scope of the independent trustee rules

The provisions provide that the duty to appoint an independent trustee does not extend to:

(a)  money purchase benefit-only schemes;

(b)  schemes which are not established by a trustee (such as unfunded arrangements);

(c)  schemes where each member (including former employees who continue to participate in the scheme) is also a trustee;

(d)  schemes where the only benefits arising are payable on the death of an employee; and

(e)  insured schemes where all benefits are secured by individual insurance policies in favour of each member.

The independent trustee provisions are designed to deal with the conflict of interests which arises where an office-holder is charged with a power or discretion in dealing with any surplus in the scheme. This was usually vested in the company either as trustee of the scheme or as a potential beneficiary of any surplus on it. The exercise of the power or discretion inevitably required the office-holder to weigh up the interests of the beneficiaries of the scheme with the interests of those staking a claim on the company's assets, which would be enhanced by any surplus paid over to it from the pension scheme. The 1990 Regulations attempt to mitigate that conflict, although they have been the subject of much criticism on account of the anomalies they contain. These criticisms stem from two major practical problems arising from the requirement that the office-holder should ensure and continue to monitor that at least one of the trustees to the pension scheme is and remains independent.

The first of these problems is that the 1990 Regulations and the 1993 Act carry no sanction for failure to comply with their provisions. This ignores the recommendation of the Occupational Pension Board's 1989 Report to the effect that contravention of the independent trustee regulations should be penalised by a fine. It is now apparent that a relatively large number of liquidations and administrative receiverships have taken place over recent years in which no independent trustee has been appointed. Seemingly one common reason for this is that the office-holder involved has perceived that no potential recoverable surplus exists in the scheme, so that he has simply viewed the appointment of an independent trustee as a line not worth pursuing. More cynically, it may that that certain insolvency practitioners have merely been unaware of the existence of the independent trustee provisions.

The second major problem arising from the independent trustee regulations is the meaning of the term 'independent'. Regulation 2 of the 1990 Regulations provides that to be independent, a person must neither (a) be interested in the assets of the scheme or the employer; nor (b) have provided services to the trustees, managers or employer in relation to the scheme. The Regulations go on to provide that a person is also not independent if persons associated or connected with him, as defined in IA 1986, are either (a) interested in the assets of the scheme or the employer; or (b) have provided services to the trustees, managers or employer in relation to the scheme.

### 13.9.2  *Clark v Hicks*

The decision in *Clark v Hicks* [1992] PLR 213 involved an application to court by a solicitor, a partner in a firm of solicitors who had been appointed an independent trustee of a pension scheme. The application sought directions as to whether the trustee had ceased to be independent by virtue of using the services of an assistant solicitor in the firm or by using a partner in the firm to investigate title to a property which constituted one of the pension scheme assets. Alternatively, the application sought to determine whether by using the partner's firm in relation to certain litigation matters undertaken on behalf of the scheme, the trustee's independent status had been lost. Mervyn Davies J held that once advice and services had been provided to the independent trustee, the trustee ceased to be independent. In other words, the independent trustee requirement provided by the 1990 Regulations is of a continuing nature and is not satisfied merely because the trustee is independent at the time of his appointment.

The decision in *Clark v Hicks* may cause problems for all professionals who take appointments as independent trustees, although it is likely to be most acute for solicitors. The decision suggests that, whilst an individual within a firm may freely take an appointment as an independent trustee, his independent status will cease as soon as he calls upon the services of that firm in performing functions or providing advice pursuant to the discharge of his functions as a trustee. Initially, this would suggest that the independent trustee might seek such services from an alternative source, although this gives rise to a very unsatisfactory state of affairs for most independent trustees who will take appointments in the first place on a *bona fide* basis in a paid professional capacity. One alternative is that the independent trustee renders a bill personally, as opposed to raising it through his firm. Again, the problem here is that the independent trustee would need to be able to show that he had not in any way utilised the services of his firm, and had acted absolutely independently, in order to establish the validity of his functioning as an independent trustee on an ongoing basis. One other alternative which has become relatively commonplace in practice is the formation of a private company, which itself acts as an independent trustee, as a vehicle for the expertise and work undertaken by individuals who would otherwise themselves take appointments as independent trustees. Again, the problem here is that the independent trustee company needs to be able to show that it had not utilised the services or advice of the firm in discharging its functions which, in practice, may well be difficult. It is common therefore for such companies to employ the services of a separate firm of solicitors on the basis of reciprocity.

### 13.9.3 Practical problems

The fundamental problem posed by the independent trustee regulations is that no guidance is given as to the dividing line between the provision of services to the trustees and the conduct and discharge of the function of the ordinary duties of the trustees acting as such. In *Clark v Hicks* [1992] PLR 213 the court was of the opinion that the expression 'providing services to the trustees' seems likely to mean services for which a trustee usually pays, such as the services of a solicitor or accountant. The judge also referred to the need for an independent trustee to be able to undertake such work as is 'normally' undertaken by a trustee in a personal capacity. What is not clear from this test and the judgment is which specific tasks an independent trustee would be able to undertake legitimately and those which he will not. It is unclear, for example, to what extent an independent trustee may rely on his own knowledge and expertise in perusing and considering the terms of the pension scheme documentation, or the extent to which the independent trustee is able to enter into correspondence and negotiate with the scheme members and their advisors as to individual entitlements under the pension scheme.

The risk in not acting independently is that a trustee will be unable to recover his costs where he does not act in an independent capacity. Nevertheless, it would appear at least arguable that the trustee would be able to claim and recover his costs on a statutory basis from the date at which his appointment ceased to be independent, on the ground that he constitutes a constructive trustee for himself. This is notwithstanding the fact that an independent trustee ceases to be a trustee by operation of law on losing his independence except where there would otherwise be no trustees remaining (Pension Schemes Act 1993 s121(4)). Furthermore, the trustee is also under an express duty to inform the insolvency practitioner of his loss of independence.

# Index

411

429

433